I0754181

THE

FOUR GOSPELS;

ARRANGED AS

A PRACTICAL FAMILY COMMENTARY,

FOR

EVERY DAY IN THE YEAR.

BY THE AUTHOR OF "THE PEEP OF DAY," ETC.

EDITED, WITH AN INTRODUCTORY PREFACE,

BY STEPHEN H. TYNG, D. D.
RECTOR OF ST. GEORGE'S CHURCH, IN THE CITY OF NEW YORK.

ILLUSTRATED WITH TWELVE HIGHLY FINISHED STEEL ENGRAVINGS.

NEW YORK:
D. APPLETON & COMPANY, 200 BROADWAY.
PHILADELPHIA:
GEO. S. APPLETON, 164 CHESNUT-STREET.
MDCCCL.

INTRODUCTORY ESSAY.

Among all the varied departments of religious usefulness, no effort can be of greater importance than to make the sacred word of God interesting and attractive to youthful minds. This divine book contains within itself instruction which is of infinite value to the soul. It conveys this heavenly instruction by means and methods exceedingly adapted to awaken and gratify the curiosity and delight of the youthful mind, when they are properly illustrated, and brought out to view. It is susceptible of such explanation and comment, by a wise and affectionate teacher, who has himself been taught by the Holy Spirit in the things of God, as shall clothe its expositions with the deepest and most absorbing interest, and enchain the attention of those to whom they are addressed. The amazing variety of forms in which God has been pleased here to reveal his holy will and purpose, and to proclaim his mercy and his truth to men, furnish a subject for study and meditation, compensating the utmost devotion of time and thought, and able to engage and reward the attention and interest of the most youthful student or hearer. The one great purpose of the Holy Scriptures is, to reveal a Saviour for man, in all the fulness, and power, and glory of his work; and to make men wise unto salvation, through faith in him. There is probably no single portion of the Bible which is not intended to be particularly connected, in some way, with this great subject, and, in its proper application, to illustrate, explain, or enforce it. To understand this, to find everywhere a Saviour revealed,—or, as Bernard has said, "Christus in omnibus,"—is the desire and effort of every real believer in Jesus, in his study, and in his expositions of the word of God. When this great light is once truly discovered in the Scriptures, it is seen to shine everywhere. The garden of Eden and the flood of Noah,—the journeys of the patriarchs and the sorrows and deliverance of Israel,—the wilderness and the land of promise,—the tabernacle and the temple, with all their rites and festivals, and divine appointments for the worship of the children of Jacob,—each appears intended to give witness to the grace and glory of a Saviour; and shines most attractively, glowing with the excellence and beauty of his merits and grace. The effort to understand this sacred purpose, to ascertain "the mind of the Spirit" in every passage, imparts a very peculiar interest to the private study of the sacred word, and to its familiar expositions to others. The Bible thus becomes, in every passage, important to every reader, and presents in each, some new and peculiar view of gospel truth to the attentive and spiritual mind. Redemption,—glorious and complete redemption for man, in the incarnation, death, resurrection, and dominion of the Son of God, and in all the wonderful results of this amazing undertaking, in the history and experience of man redeemed by his sacrifice and power,—becomes the special theme of instruction in every history and event recorded in the Scriptures, however local and individual they may at first appear. Now, to interest the minds of the young in this great subject,—to show to them, simply, but clearly and effectually, what God really means to teach in his holy word,—to take off the dull, technical, and barren aspect under which this word habitually appears before them, and to make them feel that it is really attractive, striking, and full of instruction which they will truly love to receive, is an object worthy of the labor and devotion of any human mind; an employment large and important enough to command any exertions, or any study, on the part of those who feel a real desire to be spiritually useful to others.

This is a department of Christian usefulness which was scarcely touched in the Church until the present age, and which even now has been but very partially improved. In our time, some effort has been made to bring the precious truths of the Bible within the reach and comprehension of the young. Much benefit has been thus conferred upon them. Doubtless the eternal salvation of many will be found to have resulted from the various instruments of this most interesting and important class of Christian labor. The excellent author of this present familiar commentary, —a Christian lady, if we are rightly informed,—has accomplished an important measure of this desired work. Her other publications named in the title-page of the present, are most successful efforts to make scriptural truths acceptable and engaging to the young. The present work, published under the rather indefinite title of "Light in the Dwelling," is an undertaking in the same line, equally valuable, and likely to be equally successful. It is a familiar practical commentary upon the Gospels, in language extremely simple, and in the character and matter of its instruction, most valuable and correct. This is a very fair specimen of a work which yet remains to be accomplished, and which, if well done, would be an invaluable gift to the Christian church. We mean an interesting and familiar commentary on the Scriptures, suited in language and sentiment to the minds of the young. Who shall have the blessed and exalted privilege of being thus "a teacher of babes," in the great and gracious truths of the word of God? Where is the faithful spiritual guide whom God will raise up, prepare, and instruct, for this important design, of giving a clear, evangelical, and attractive exposition of his sacred word, illustrated in language and style adapted to families, and especially to the youthful members of families, in the church of Christ? We believe no work could be more important, or would be more likely to be useful, popular, and successful, than such a commentary, wisely designed, and intelligently and truthfully executed. The attention and interest of youthful minds can always be easily drawn to the Bible, when expositions of it are within the reach of their comprehension, and adapted to their habits of thought. There would scarcely be found an exception to this remark, whether children were individually or collectively addressed by such expositions. And while the far greater portion of those who are really taught of God in the revelations of his word, are early interested by the Holy Spirit in these great subjects, and become, while they are yet young, spiritually and truly the members of his kingdom, this precious and important class of minds constitute a field of labor, which all ministers and mature Christians ought to feel it a privilege to cultivate with eagerness and perseverance.

The deep interest which the author of the present work felt in this field of effort, to which she has devoted her powers and pen, may be gathered from the following striking passage from her own preface:

"And what is *success?* No circulation, however extensive,—no approbation, even of the wise and good, could be deemed success, if unattended by the conversion or edification of immortal souls. But if, at the last day, it should be made manifest that, through the means of this humble work, some thoughtless girl, removed from a beloved home, and sojourning among strangers, had been led to cry, 'My Father, thou art the guide of my youth,'—that some ignorant boy, in times past unprofitable to all, had, like Onesimus, become profitable to his employer and to the church of God,—that some self-righteous person, faithful to her *earthly* master, but a rebel against the best of Masters, had been brought, in her declining years, to seek His righteousness, and devote herself to His service,—that some unhappy wanderer, stained with secret crime, and tormented by the pangs of a guilty conscience, had been encouraged to plead for pardon, and to wash in the Saviour's precious blood,—that some little child, sitting at the feet of its father, or of its mother, turning over the leaves of its first Bible, had learned to love the Friend of little children,—this, *this* would indeed be SUCCESS. Will the reader join his prayers to mine that such a boon may be granted me by 'the FATHER OF LIGHTS, from whom cometh down every good and perfect gift?'"

Such success as this, we have no doubt, the author will find, in a very abundant measure,—success which will cheer her soul and enlarge her blessedness in a world, where the works of men are made manifest, and the faithful people of God have praise of him. It is in the full conviction that this present work is eminently adapted to produce this happy result, and to open the precious and imperishable blessings of the Gospel to those who familiarly use it, that we are able to recommend it in a very cordial and unqualified manner. It will be a faithful and attractive guide both in family reading and in the private study of the young. If God shall be pleased to accompany it, and bless it with his own Holy Spirit, it will prove to all who employ it for their instruction, a guide to the knowledge of a Saviour, and a faithful interpreter of his sacred word. It may serve also as a very excellent pattern and guide for the discharge of a similar duty by other Christians, to whom the opportunity may be given. It will encourage them to attempt the plan of similar familiar expositions of the Scriptures in their own families, or in Sunday-schools, or on other occasions, where a way may be opened for a word of exhortation or counsel. And thus the author's labor may be crowned with an enlarging and perpetuating influence, quite beyond the modest and limited expectations she would herself have formed.

CONTENTS.

INTRODUCTION.

CAN there be any account in the world so interesting to us as the history of our Lord and Saviour, while he spent thirty-three years upon earth? There were persons with him who heard his sayings and observed his actions. Four holy men, as you are aware, wrote accounts of his life. It might well be supposed that these histories would not contradict each other, for they were all true. But the writers not only wrote what they knew to be true—the Holy Spirit instructed them *what* to relate. They were inspired of God. When we read their writings, we read the words of God himself. With what reverence should we attend! As some of these four Evangelists related one event, and some related another, it is interesting to place their accounts together, endeavoring to observe, as well as we can, the order of time in which the events occurred. Such an arrangement is called a "Harmony."

We shall begin with the words of John, because he speaks of Jesus *before* he came into the world, even when he was with his Father in heaven. We shall find that the Son of God made the world. He did not appear in it as a man, till four thousand years had rolled away; but long before he came, he was promised by God, and described by the prophets, such as Moses, David, Isaiah, and many others,—of whom Malachi was the last.

At length he appeared, and fulfilled all that had been said of Him.

Let us read of Him, as of one that came into the world to save *us*. Every thing that concerns him is of the greatest importance to us; for if we do not believe on him, and love him above all, we shall perish forever. Let us, therefore, always before we read, lift up our hearts to God in prayer.

"O Lord, grant unto us thy Holy Spirit, that our souls may be saved by the knowledge of thy blessed Son!"

We shall not always meet together to worship God as we do now. A day will come when each of us will unite with the rest in reading and prayer for the *last* time.

But if we believe in Jesus, we shall not part forever. We shall meet again in Heaven. *Then* how delightful it will be to look back upon the time, when as one family, we used to assemble to hear about our beloved Lord. Many hours which we spent below may then be remembered with regret ; but not those precious moments devoted to hearing about Him, whose presence will make us happy through eternity.

THE FOUR GOSPELS;

A PRACTICAL FAMILY COMMENTARY.

JAN. 1.*

JOHN I. 1–5.—*The Word.*

WHO is the Word spoken of in these verses? He is the Son of God. He is called the Word, because he makes God his Father known to us. How is it *our thoughts* are made known to our fellow-creatures? By our *words*. Thus the unseen Father is made known to men by his Son Jesus Christ. No man can know the *Father*, but by the *Son*. The Son and the Father are distinct persons, for it is written in the first verse, "The Word was *with* God;" that is, the Son was *with* the Father. Yet the Son and the Father are *one God*, for it is added, "The Word was God."

But even if we had not found this sentence, "The Word was God," we should have known that he was God, by the things that are said of him in the following verses.

First, it is declared that he was from the beginning with God.

Now God is the *First*, and if the Son of God is from everlasting, then he is *First*, and he must be God. Again it is declared that *all* things were made by him. Thus we know the Son is the Creator of the world. He cannot then be a creature; for no creature can "create." God alone can create.

Then again it is said, He is the "Life." He gives life. All the angels in heaven cannot give life to the smallest insect, or even to the meanest flower: but the Son can give life to the creatures he has made; not only *natural* life, but *spiritual* and *eternal* life. Lastly, it is declared that he is the Light of men: a brighter light than the sun, a light which shines into the heart and enlightens the dark mind.

And what is *man* called? Observe the name that is given to him. He is called "Darkness." In verse the fifth it is written, "The light shineth in darkness, and the darkness comprehendeth it not." Ever since Satan, the prince of darkness, tempted Adam and Eve to eat the forbidden fruit, the minds of men have been dark; they have neither

* Though it cannot be supposed that *families*, in reading these sections, will be able to adhere to the days of the month, yet the date is marked for the advantage of young persons who may read the work in private.

known what is right, nor loved what is good. Christ came into the world to bring light to the dark minds of men. But alas! how few receive him! Most people are so much pleased with the trifles of time, or so much taken up with the cares of the world, that they turn away from the Son of God. This blessed book which we hold in our hands tells us about Him. Does not each of us wish to be happy for ever? Then let us listen attentively, and let us entreat God to give us faith that we may believe and be saved.

Scripture portion for the other part of the day.*
Gen. I. ***The Creation.***

JOHN I. 6–11.—*The Witness.*

BEFORE the Lord Jesus came into the world, God sent a man called John to be a witness to him. He is called the Baptist, and was *not* the same John who wrote the history we are now reading.

John the Baptist was a faithful preacher, a burning and a shining light, but he was not *that light;* he was not the Son of God.

He was only a man; but he loved the Son of God, and he desired that all men through him, that is, "through his preaching," might believe in Jesus. It is the desire of every faithful minister, that *through him* men should believe in Christ. God does make men the instruments of turning the hearts of their fellow-creatures to God. Many of the children of Israel did John turn to the Lord their God. It is not *ministers* only who turn the hearts of sinners; but other Christians also. There is an account of a poor gipsy woman who, by her conversation, converted no less than twelve persons.† What an honor it would be to us if God should cause any one to believe in Jesus through *us*—through what *we* said or did! May our light so shine before men, that they, seeing our good works, may glorify our Father who is in heaven!

In the ninth verse it is said that Jesus lights every man that comes into the world. This means that Jesus is the *only* light—just as there is only *one* sun in the sky to give us light: so there is only *one* Saviour to save us. But Jesus does not light those who never heard of him. The heathen sit in darkness and in the shadow of death. Neither does he light all who have heard of him. He shines around *us:* but if we are *blind*, he does not give *light* even to *us*.

How affecting it is to read that his OWN *world* did not know him when he appeared, that his *own nation* the Jews, his brethren accord-

* As the portion of Scripture in which remarks are made is often very short, another larger portion has been selected for reading at another part of the day.

† See the history of "The Aged Gipsy:" a tract published by Nisbet.

ing to the flesh, did not receive him! "He came unto his *own*, and his own received him not." As if a mother were to appear among her children, and they should deny that she was their mother. How many people are there now who are not ashamed to say, "I do not pretend to be religious," which means, "I do not pretend to love God," as if they had nothing to do with God, as if he had not made them, and did not feed them, and watch over them continually. What should we think of a child who should say of an affectionate parent, "I do not pretend to care for him?" What would a parent feel, who heard a child speak thus? There is no parent who feels so tender an interest in his children as Christ felt for his people the Jews. Remember the tears he shed over Jerusalem, when he uttered those touching words, "How often would I have gathered thy children together, as a hen gathereth her chickens under her wings, and ye would not!"

Are there any here who now refuse to receive the loving Saviour into their hearts? Let me entreat you no longer to grieve him by treating him thus. You are the work of his hands. He longs to make you happy. Open your hearts to him, and receive him as your Lord.

Evening Scripture portion. James V. *Conversion of sinners.*

JOHN I. 12, 13.—*The sons of God.*

WE know that when the Lord Jesus came into the world, the greater part of men despised and rejected him; but there were a few who received him. They believed in him; that is, they received Jesus into their *hearts*. And now observe what a glorious privilege God bestowed upon these believers. He gave them "power to become the sons of God." He adopted them as his sons and heirs. It is written in Romans viii. 15, "Ye have received the Spirit of adoption, whereby we cry, Abba, Father;" and again, "If children, then *heirs*." God will bestow upon his adopted children his riches in glory. "He that overcometh shall inherit all things. I will be his God, and he shall be my son."—Rev. xxi. 7.

But what is the *reason* that *some* believed in Jesus? Were they by nature better than others? Were their hearts softer, so that they *could* not reject their dying Saviour? No: they were by nature like others—but they were born of God. As it is written in the *thirteenth* verse, "Which were born of God;" that is, of the Spirit of God.

We are also told what they were *not* born of. Let us consider each of the expressions:—

"Not of *blood*:" that is, they did not believe because they were of the blood of any good man, such as Abraham. Many who were of the blood of Abraham did not believe in Christ! Neither were they born of *the will of the flesh.* They did not believe, because it was the will of their flesh, or of their nature to believe. They did not choose Christ from their own power. If they had been left to themselves, they would have refused him; for the natural man receiveth not the things of the Spirit of God. 1 Cor. ii. 14. Neither were they born of *the will of man.* They did not believe because it was the will of any *man* that they should believe. Such persons are not converted as a minister most desires to convert, or as he thinks it most likely will be converted. It is the will of *God* that makes a man believe.

If *we* have been born of God, we see that it was *not* because we were of the blood of any pious parents or ancestors; it was *not* because it was the will of our *flesh* to believe, for we were *dead* in sins. It was *not* because it was the will of *man.* No pious minister or friend could have made us believe. But if we have been raised from the death of sin, it was the power of *God* that raised us. Therefore to God be all the glory.

If we have *not* been born again, then let us go to God, who alone can convert us, and entreat him to put forth his *great* power to make us believe that we may become the children of God and heirs of the kingdom of glory. For it is too true that until we believe in Christ, we are the children of Satan, and not the children of God. Who can bear the thought of being the child of the devil, and an heir of wrath! Yet what does the Apostle Paul say to the Ephesians? He says of himself and of them, "We were by nature the children of wrath, even as others."—ii. 3. But we *may* be born again; we *must* be born again. Then we shall belong to the family of God, and be the heirs of heaven.

Evening Scripture portion. Eph. II. ***Regeneration.***

JOHN I. 14—18.—*The testimony of John.*

IN the beginning of this chapter we read of a great wonder, that the Word was with God, and yet was God. We cannot understand how this could be. In this passage we read of another wonder, yet we are so much accustomed to hear it, that we almost forget to consider the greatness of the wonder, "The *Word* was made *flesh.*" God became man; he "dwelt among us."

When we look around us at this great world, and at the heavens spangled with stars, and think that *He* who made all these things became a weak man, who ate, drank, and slept like ourselves, do we not feel amazed? We may well inquire *why* God became a man, and dwelt among us?

It was to save us from everlasting misery. We are told in verse 14, "He was full of grace and truth." He came to bring grace to sinners, to pardon their sins by his free grace. He came to suffer all he had said he would suffer. He had said he would suffer our punishment, and he was full of *truth*, and suffered it *all*, showing that God hated sin, and that he would punish it with death.

Now, John the Evangelist, when he speaks of Jesus, breaks out into an exclamation at the remembrance of his *glory*. He says in verse 14, "*We beheld* his glory, the glory as of the only-begotten of the Father." John had really seen Jesus. As he says in his First Epistle, i. 1, speaking of Jesus, "that which our eyes have seen, which we have looked upon."

"We beheld his glory." *What* glory does he here refer to? Does he refer to the glory which shone on the mount, when "his face did shine as the sun, and his raiment was white as the light?"—Matt. xvii. 2. Perhaps it is to this glory he refers, or perhaps it is to the glory of holiness which always shone in Jesus, and which the world could not see; for they saw "no beauty in him, that they should desire him."—Isaiah liii. 2. But those who believed in him saw this glory. Do *we* see it? Has the Spirit opened our inward eyes, so that we see Christ to be worthy of all our love?

There was a man who saw this glory, and pointed Jesus out to others. His name was John the Baptist.

He spoke of him long before he saw him. At last he saw him, and said to the people, "This is he of whom I spake. He that cometh after me is preferred before me; for he was before me." Jesus was six months younger than John the Baptist, therefore John said he came *after* him. Yet he was *before* him, because he was with his Father *before* he came into the world.

Who is speaking in verse 16? Not John the Baptist, but John the writer of this history. He speaks in the highest terms of love and praise of our great Saviour. How happy are they who can say with John, "Of his fulness have all we received, and grace for grace." In Jesus there is a full store of grace, sufficient for every believer. And do we not need these graces? Do we not often lament our want of patience, meekness, kindness, and charity? Jesus is willing to bestow them *all* upon us. Moses was a great lawgiver; but he could not bestow grace. Moses appointed many forms and ceremonies, to *represent* the way of salvation, but Jesus brought salvation. Therefore it is written, "Truth came by Jesus Christ."

The Father dwelleth in light which no man can approach unto; but he spared his Son from his bosom that we might behold him. Though we have not seen him ourselves, we have heard enough about him to make us love him. If our hearts were not like stones by nature, we should have loved him from the first moment we heard of him; and yet perhaps there may be some here who had lived twenty or thirty years in the world before they *began* to love him; and there may be others who do not love him *yet*. May the Lord soften their hearts.

Evening Scripture portion. 2 Cor. IV. *The glory of Christ.*

LUKE I. 1—4.—*The Preface to St. Luke.*

THE holy Evangelist Luke writes a short preface before his history of the Lord Jesus Christ.

This preface is a kind of letter to Theophilus, for whose use especially he wrote the history. Let us inquire who Luke was, and who Theophilus was. Luke is not mentioned in any of the Gospels; but Saint Paul speaks of him in his epistle to the Colossians, as, "the beloved physician," iv. 14. There is reason also to suppose he was not a Jew, but a converted heathen;* yet he had the honor of writing a part of the holy Word of God. Theophilus was probably a governor; therefore he was called "most excellent," as dukes are now styled "your grace," and kings "your majesty." Theophilus, though a nobleman, had been instructed in religion by some of God's servants; but Luke wished him to know the history of the Lord still more perfectly. He says in the fourth verse, that he had written this account that "thou (Theophilus) mightest know the certainty of those things wherein thou hast been instructed."

It appears that other persons had written histories of Christ. These persons had not been directed by the Holy Spirit, as the Evangelists had; neither had they themselves witnessed the events they had related. They had written from "report," and their accounts contained errors. It is happy for us that these erroneous accounts have not been handed down to us, but only the inspired histories of the four Evangelists.

Saint Luke himself had not been an eye-witness of the events he records; yet we cannot say he wrote from "report:" for he was directed by the Spirit of God. He had enjoyed great opportunities of knowing about Jesus: he declares in v. 3, that he had had perfect understanding of all things from the "very first," or from the very earliest part of our Saviour's life. Still his history would not have been reckoned a part of the holy Bible, if the Holy Spirit had not directed him what to write. This book has always been read in the assemblies of Christians, and called the word of God.

Let us thank God for this part of his word. How many interesting events and parables are related by Luke, which we should never have known had he not written! How we ought to value every thing that concerns the Lord Jesus! When we love a friend, we desire to know every thing about him, and to hear what he did even when he was a child! When we have lost him, we think over his dying words, and lay them up in our hearts! How much more should we delight in knowing all that concerns the best of friends! When we consider

* In Colossians iv. Saint Paul speaks of several persons who were of the circumcision, that is, who were Jews, and then adds, "These *only* are my fellow-workers unto the kingdom of God, which have been a comfort to me." Yet he afterwards mentions Luke. He must have been a comfort to him: therefore it is concluded he was not a Jew

who he was, the Lord of Glory, we can compare no earthly friend to him; all is wonderful that relates to him. It is affecting to hear how the poor heathen, when first converted, value the word of God! Before the missionaries in the South Sea Islands could print the Bible in the language of the people, the poor natives eagerly listened to all that was read aloud on the Sabbath, and many wrote down upon the leaves of trees the texts they had heard, and studied them wherever they went till they knew them by heart. We are without excuse if we remain ignorant of the history of our Lord. Let us not, however, forget for what purpose we read: that we may learn to love Jesus. We are apt to become fond of human creatures whom we know intimately. How much more might it be expected that hearing of Jesus would make us love him; for he is far more excellent than any creature, and far more full of love to us than our dearest friend. Yet our hearts are naturally so much hardened against God, that unless the Holy Spirit soften them, we shall not love him. May that Spirit be with us, while we read day after day the history of our blessed Lord.

Evening Scripture portion.
1 Tim. III. *Inspiration of the Scriptures.*

LUKE I. 5–14.—*The Angel's visit to Zacharias.*

LUKE said in his preface, that he had perfect understanding of all things from the very *first;* so we find that his history begins very early indeed, and describes events that happened before the birth of Jesus.

John the Baptist was born six months before Jesus. In this chapter we have an account of his parents. His father was a priest named Zacharias. His mother Elizabeth also was of the family of the priests, the descendants of Aaron.

Zacharias and Elizabeth "were righteous before God." How could they be righteous? Is it not written, "There is none righteous; no, not one?" God, who knows all hearts, has made this declaration. But when a man believes in Christ, he becomes righteous, for the righteousness of Christ becomes his. Jesus bare *our sins* that we might obtain *his righteousness.* But it may be said, "How could Zacharias and Elizabeth believe in Christ? Did they not live before he came into the world?" They did. But they believed in the *promise* of a Saviour; and thus they became partakers of his righteousness. It was in this way Abraham was righteous. It is written, "He believed in the Lord, and he counted it to him for righteousness."—Gen. xv. 6. Faith is the means by which sinners receive the righteousness of Christ. It has often been compared to the *hand;* and righteousness to a *treasure*. As the hand grasps the treasure, so faith lays hold of Christ's righteousness.

Zacharias and Elizabeth were pardoned sinners. Therefore they were sanctified by the Holy Spirit. Though still subject to sin, they indulged in no sinful *habits*. They were not satisfied (as hypocrites are) with observing those commandments that it was convenient to obey, while they neglected those that were more difficult: but they walked in *all* the commandments of the Lord blameless. We shall soon have a proof that they were still subject to sin; for we shall soon read how Zacharias was overtaken by unbelief.

Zacharias and Elizabeth had no child; and the want of children was considered by the Jews as a heavy affliction. Yet at length they became the parents of one of the greatest prophets that ever appeared in the world. All the circumstances connected with this event were very remarkable.

As Zacharias was a priest, it was his office at certain times to burn incense in the temple. The priests were so numerous, that they could not all live at Jerusalem. They were divided into twenty-four courses; and each course came up to Jerusalem in its turn, to serve for one week in the temple. It was determined by lot every morning who was to enjoy the privilege of burning incense that day at the golden altar. The priest, on whom the lot fell, went alone into the temple both morning and evening, to burn sweet spices as an offering to God, while the people remained in the court repeating public prayers for a blessing upon all nations.

On the day when God purposed to speak to Zacharias, he caused the lot to fall upon him. The most minute circumstances are under his control, and are often the beginnings of very great events.

When Zacharias beheld the angel standing by the altar, he was troubled. We always find that men are troubled at the presence of angels. Yet Zacharias had no reason to fear, for the heavenly messenger came not to destroy him, but to bless. He said, "Thy prayer is heard." What prayer? Was it for a son that Zacharias had prayed? Or was it that the Saviour might soon come into the world? Both these blessings were soon to be bestowed. A son was to be born to Zacharias, to prepare the way for the Saviour that was to be given to men. Well might a father rejoice at the birth of such a son! His very name showed that God would bless him and make him a blessing. The word "John" signifies "the grace or favor of God." When a child has been born, it has very seldom been known whether he would become a curse or a blessing. There has often been joy at the birth of children, who have lived to do great harm, and even to break their parents' hearts. When Cain was born, Eve rejoiced; saying, "I have gotten a man from the Lord:" little thinking how wicked a man he would be. Other children have been born undesired; perhaps the family was already numerous and ill-provided for; yet some of those unwelcome little strangers have lived, not only to rejoice their parents' hearts, but to save souls from eternal death. Did Christians know when a faithful minister was born into the world, how much they would rejoice! We cannot tell, when we look upon a helpless babe, what it will become; but we may offer up our earnest prayers that it may be a blessing and not a curse.

Evening Scripture portion. Rom. III. *Righteousness.*

LUKE I. 15–17.—*The Prophecy concerning John the Baptist.*

How happy was Zacharias to hear such a character of his promised son from the lips of an angel! His son was to be "great in the sight of the *Lord.*" It would not be a blessing to have a son great in the sight of the world. Those who are great in the sight of the Lord are despised by the world. Men said of John the Baptist, "He hath a devil," and they counted the apostles as the offscouring of all things.

The angel said that John was to drink neither wine nor strong drink. He should be filled with the Holy Ghost, and many of the children of Israel should he turn to the Lord their God. Why then was John to drink no wine? Because he was a Nazarite. A Nazarite was a person separated unto the Lord in a very singular manner. Sometimes the Israelites made vows thus to separate themselves for a week, or a month, or a longer space of time. During that time they tasted neither wine nor grapes; and they suffered the locks of hair on their heads to grow long. Some children were made Nazarites from their birth. Samuel was thus devoted to the Lord by his praying mother; and Samson by the appointment of an angel. John the Baptist was also a Nazarite from his birth. Jewish ceremonies have ceased since the Lord Jesus has made known his Gospel. But though we ought not to become Nazarites, we ought, like them, to be devoted to the service of God, and separated from the sinful pleasures of an ungodly world.

The angel also declared that the child soon to be born would go before the Lord in the *spirit* and *power* of Elias. If we read the history of the prophet Elijah, we shall see a great resemblance between him and John the Baptist.

They were like each other in *spirit.* Both were faithful and courageous. Elijah prophesied in the court of the wicked king Ahab, and his more wicked queen; and by his boldness endangered his life. John reproved King Herod so faithfully for his sins, that he was imprisoned, and at length murdered at the request of the cruel Herodias. In *spirit* therefore John resembled Elijah.

He came also in the *power* of that great prophet; and, like him, he had great success. At one time Elijah thought there was not a single pious prophet in all Israel; and he complained to God, saying, "I, even I, only am left:" but such *power* accompanied his instructions, that before he was taken up to heaven, there were numerous young men, called sons of the prophets, all over the land, training up for the ministry. John the Baptist also had great success; and some of his disciples were numbered among the apostles of the Lamb.

But the most delightful part of the angel's message to Zacharias was the promise that the Saviour should soon come. He spoke of the Saviour as the Lord God of Israel; for he said, "And many of the children of Israel shall he turn to the *Lord their God;* and he shall go before *him* in the spirit and power of Elias."

The Son of God was coming into the world to shed his blood to save sinners; yet it was necessary that one should go before him to *turn* the hearts of men towards him. What a proof this is of the wickedness of the human heart! It is turned against God. Satan, in the garden of Eden, turned the heart of Eve against her best friend. Now every one is an enemy of God, until he is converted. God sends his faithful preachers to turn our hearts towards himself. Have not some tried to persuade us to turn to the Lord? Have they succeeded in persuading us? It is an awful thing to hear sermons, and to disregard what we hear. Time is passing swiftly away—Jesus will come again in power and great glory. If, when he comes, he finds us unprepared, we shall be shut out of his presence forever.

Evening Scripture portion. Numbers VI. 1–12. *The Nazarite.*

LUKE I. 18–23.—*The Unbelief of Zacharias.*

ZACHARIAS was so much astonished at the message of the angel, that he wanted to see some sign or miracle to prove that the angel came from God. Why was it wrong in Zacharias to desire a sign? Because he had already had one. The glorious appearance of the angel, which had filled him with fear, was a sufficient sign. God does not wish us to believe things without *any* proof. If he were to send a prophet to speak to us, he would give us some sign to show us that the prophet really came from him. When Moses spoke to the Israelites in Egypt, he gave them two signs; his rod was turned into a serpent, and his hand was made white with the leprosy, (Exod. iv.) God is angry when men will not believe, when he has given them a sign. It was sinful in Zacharias not to believe after he had seen the glorious angel. Thus we find that though he was righteous before God, he was still subject to sin.

Unbelief is a great sin; for it is an insult to the truth of God. The angel rebuked the unbelieving priest, saying, "Thou shalt be dumb." This gentle chastisement would at once remove the doubts of Zacha rias and remind him of his sin. In this way, God deals with his own people, when they forget what a great God He is.

Zacharias at length came out of the temple. It was now expected that he should bless the people in those beautiful words recorded in Numbers vi. 24—27, beginning, "The Lord bless thee and keep thee;" but he could not speak, and he made signs to show the people what he had seen in the temple.

Each division of priests remained to serve in the temple from one Sabbath to the next; in a few days, therefore, at the furthest, Zacharias returned to his own house among the hills. What a history he had to unfold to Elizabeth! For he was able to inform her in writing. What a proof she beheld of the power of God in the dumbness of her husband! We should take notice of God's dealings with others. "Whoso is wise, and will observe these things, even he shall understand the loving-kindness of the Lord."—Psalm cvii. 43.

How humbly and gratefully Elizabeth behaved on this occasion! She acknowledged the goodness of the Lord in having condescended to look upon her affliction; for she had been exposed to much reproach on account of having no child. When troubles are removed, we are apt to overlook the Lord's merciful hand! Perhaps we have been suffering under some trial; the unkindness of a relation, the dread of sickness, or the pressure of poverty: God removes the trial, and we forget how much it weighed us down before, and so we omit to thank the Lord heartily.

A holy minister named Rutherford, in one of his letters, written two hundred years ago, says, that one of the things which most showed him his own wickedness by nature, was his feeling more disposed to call upon the Lord in trouble, than to thank him when delivered. Let us think over the things that troubled us a few years ago, and bless the hand which has lightened our load.

Evening Scripture portion. Ex. IV. 1–17. ***Two Signs wrought by Moses.***

Luke I. 26–33.—*The Angel's visit to Mary.*

God appointed that his Son should be born six months after John. So six months after the angel had spoken to Zacharias, he came to Mary. She was a poor woman, of a low, mean city, called Nazareth. She was indeed descended from King David, who had lived more than a thousand years before, and she was engaged to be married to a man called Joseph, also descended from King David. It had been prophesied that the Son of God should be born among David's family. Isaiah calls the Saviour "A rod out of the stem of Jesse," (Isaiah xi. 1,) for Jesse was the father of David. Jesse was like a tree, of which Jesus was a rod or branch.

It seems probable that the angel visited Mary when she was alone. He said, "Hail," bidding her rejoice because a wonderful favor was about to be conferred on her.

The Roman Catholics pretend that the words "highly favored" mean "full of grace;" and say, that Mary can now impart grace, and that the angel worshipped her. But we know that Mary was but a creature, and even a sinful creature, and that it is idolatry to treat her as the Lord.

Mary was full of humility; and God loves to honor the humble. She was alarmed at the salutation or speech of the angel; but she was soon desired not to fear, and was informed of the wonderful event about to happen.

The Saviour so long expected was to be her son. He was to be called "Jesus," which signifies Saviour, and is the same name as Joshua.* The angel said this Saviour should be a great king. Perhaps you will inquire, Was he not equal with God? was he not King of Kings from everlasting? Yes: but the angel spoke of his greatness in his human nature. As a *man*, he was to be king; therefore it was said that "the Lord would give unto him the throne of his *father* David." He was to be King over the house of Jacob, that is, over the Jews, the descendants of Jacob. The words that were afterwards written over the cross were true, "The King of the *Jews*." But is he not King of the Gentiles also? Yes; he is: and the day shall come when *every* tongue will confess that he is Lord; and when *every* knee will bow to him. (Phil. ii.)

Of his kingdom there shall be no *end*. Other kingdoms have come to an *end*. Nebuchadnezzar saw in a dream an image which represented all the kingdoms of the world: and he saw a little stone overthrow this image, and this stone become a mountain. (Dan. ii.) The stone represented Christ. He will bring all kingdoms to an end; and then he will be King over all the earth. (Zec. xiv. 9.) Then there will be no more war, nor famine, nor misery; men will obey Christ's laws, and live in holiness and peace.

That day is not come yet. Very few persons have submitted to Christ; very few seek to do his will. Christ is a king against whom his subjects have rebelled. But do you not think that a king loves his faithful subjects at such a time? How dear to him is their obedience, when others scorn him! Does our King and Saviour count *us* among his faithful subjects? Then he will acknowledge us when he comes in glory. This song shall soon be sung in heaven by the saints: "We give thee thanks, O Lord God Almighty, which art, and wast, and art to come; because thou hast taken to thee thy great power and hast reigned." (Rev. xi.) Then He will give reward to them that fear his name, small and great.

Evening Scripture portion. Is. XI. *Christ the rod out of Jesse's stem.*

* Joshua is called Jesus in Hebrews iv. 8.

LUKE I. 34–45.—*Mary's visit to Elizabeth.*

THE angel had told Mary of the great power and glory of the Son she should have. He next told her of the *holiness* of his nature. His body was to be miraculously formed by the power of the Holy Ghost; though born of a human mother. Jesus had flesh and blood like ourselves, (Hebrews ii. 14;) and he was subject to all our bodily weaknesses; he needed food and sleep; he suffered pain; he shed tears and sweat drops of blood; but he was without *sin;* (Heb. iv. 15:) he was "holy, harmless, undefiled." (Heb. vii. 26.) Such was the child of whom Mary was to be the mother! Were such wonderful tidings ever delivered to any human creature, as were then spoken to Mary? Yet she believed. Her faith was greater than that of Zacharias; and she received no rebuke from the angel.

What a prospect lay before her! Many would disbelieve her story, and treat her with contempt. Yet Mary was willing to bear the trial. She said, "Be it unto me according to thy word." God often makes those suffer most deeply whom he designs to honor most highly. When God intends that persons should do much good to souls, (and this is one of the highest honors,) he often permits suspicion to be cast upon their characters; but at length he clears their innocence.

Mary had heard from the angel of the mercy shown to Elizabeth; and she went immediately to see her.

How interesting it is to hear what happened when these two holy women met! There was a great difference between their ages. Elizabeth was very old: Mary was not old: it is probable she was very young. Yet she was far more highly honored than her aged relative. The old are often envious of the young; but the pious Elizabeth was ready to do honor to Mary. When she saw her, she spoke by the power of the Holy Ghost, and acknowledged her as the mother of the Lord.

It must have comforted Mary to find that Elizabeth also believed in the things that were coming to pass. How it must have rejoiced her, to hear her say, "Blessed is she that believed."

These words do not apply to Mary alone; but to *every one* that believes. What ought *we* to believe? All the promises of God.

He has promised to cast out none that come to him, but to give them everlasting life. If we believe this promise, we shall come to him. If we *have* come to him, how *many* precious promises belong to us! God has promised to hear our prayers, to make all things work together for our good, to deliver us out of every temptation, and to give us, even in this life, peace which passeth all understanding. Those who trust in these promises find there is a performance of the things that were told them.

It was a good answer that was once given by a poor woman to a minister who asked her, "What is faith?" She replied, "I am ignorant: I cannot answer well: but I think faith is taking God at his word."

Evening Scripture portion. Heb. II. *Christ's human nature.*

Luke I. 46–56.—*The Song of Mary.*

This beautiful song shows us what was Mary's state of mind at this time. We must remember that there was much to try her in her present circumstances, for many people would not believe her account of the angel's visit, and would treat her with scorn. Yet she was filled with joy, because she enjoyed the favor of the Lord. She said, "My soul doth magnify the Lord: and my spirit hath rejoiced in God my Saviour." How great was Mary's faith! Faith enables us to rejoice in the midst of trials. Saint Paul had this faith when he said, "I reckon that the sufferings of this present time are not worthy to be compared with the glory which shall be revealed."

Mary knew that whatever men thought of her *then*, that all generations would "call her blessed," as the mother of the Saviour. Do *we* not think her blessed? Surely we do. Let us not forget that *we* may be blessed also; for Jesus said that "Whosoever shall do the will of my Father, which is in heaven, the same is my brother, and sister, and mother." (Matt. xii. 50.) And at another time, when a woman said how blessed his mother was, Jesus answered, "Rather blessed are they that hear the word of God, and keep it." (Luke xi. 28.)

It is sad to think what a wrong use the Roman Catholics have made of the words of Mary. They not only call her "blessed," (and she *is* blessed,) but they worship her, as if she were equal to him, "who is over all, God blessed for ever." (Rom. ix. 5.) No: Mary was but a creature like ourselves; though she was made, by the grace of God, a holy creature, and was honored in so remarkable a manner.

We see in her song how great a value she set upon the blessings of redemption. She would not have done so, if she had not felt her need of a Saviour. How she delights in praising God! She calls him *mighty*—"He that is mighty." She calls him *holy*—"Holy is his name." She speaks of his *mercy*—"His mercy is on them that fear him."

What does she mean in verse 51, when she says, "He hath shown strength with his arm; he hath scattered the proud in the imagination of their hearts?" Pharaoh and his proud captains once desired to destroy Israel: this was "the imagination of their hearts," but God drowned them in the Red Sea. Thus God at last will destroy *all* the enemies of Christ and his people.

From this song we may learn to *what* people the Lord is merciful;

"He fills the *hungry* with good things." He fed the poor Israelites, when they were hungry, with manna. But it is another sort of hunger which Jesus delights to satisfy. "Blessed are they that hunger and thirst after righteousness." Such hungry souls shall never be sent empty away. If a beggar is sent empty away from *one* house, he can go to another; but if God were to send us empty away, and refuse to give us everlasting life, there is no other being to whom we could go. *Will* he send us empty away? No: he will *not*, if we feel our need of pardon; but if we fancy ourselves *rich* in goodness, He will give us none of His goodness or righteousness. Those only who know they are poor blind miserable sinners, will obtain any thing from the Saviour. Let us go *now* to his throne of grace to ask for mercy, and to obtain help in this our time of need; let us go with lowly hearts, feeling our unworthiness and confessing our sins, and He will not send us "empty away."

Evening Scripture portion. Ex. XIV. *The Red Sea.*

LUKE I. 5–7.—*The Circumcision of John.*

WHEN Elizabeth's son was born, her relations and friends came to rejoice with her. Worldly people, when they are prosperous, are often envied by their friends: but pious people, when they have received any great mercy, generally have friends who *really* rejoice with them.

How richly were Elizabeth's friends rewarded for their sympathy! During their visit they witnessed a wonderful proof of God's power.

It appears that Elizabeth knew what the angel had told Zacharias; for she said that the child was to be called "John," or "the grace of God." The friends, by signs, asked the father what the child should be called. We see by their making signs to him that he was deaf as well as dumb. He asked for a writing table, or tablet. These tablets were often spread with wax, and written upon with a piece of steel. Zacharias wrote, "His name *is* John:" not "he *shall* be called John;" but his name *is* John, for the angel had already given the child that name. As soon as he had written these words, his tongue was loosed; and he made *that* use of it for which it had first been given him: he praised God.

The angel had sentenced him to be dumb until the day that the things he had told him of, should be performed, (verse 20.) That day was now come.

We perceive in this event how God can bring good out of evil: Zacharias by unbelief had become dumb; but his gaining his speech again, must have helped others to believe.

His friends related the things they had seen; so that people all around wondered what sort of a man John would become. Thus many were prepared to pay attention to his preaching when he grew up We shall hear little of the childhood of John; but we know that he was holy from his birth. How acceptable to God is the offering up of our early years! as the poet says—

"A flower, when offered in the bud,
Is no mean sacrifice."

How bitter is the remembrance of a childhood and youth of wickedness! Saint Paul could never remember without grief that he had once persecuted God's people.

Let not those who are young imagine that if they are at *length* converted, it will be of no consequence having long resisted the gracious offers of God. It is delightful to be able to sing with David, "Thou art my trust from my youth." Those who have not turned to God till their youth was past, often think within themselves, "O that I could pass my time over again! Had I loved God sooner, what sins I should have avoided! what sorrows I should have escaped! how much good I might have done! how much glory I might have brought to God!"

Is it not very ungenerous, because we know that God is willing to receive the returning prodigal, to go far from him, not intending to return till all worldly pleasures are exhausted? Yet many who would be ashamed to treat an earthly friend in this manner, act thus towards their best, their heavenly Friend.

Evening Scripture portion. Eccles. XII. *Early piety*

LUKE I. 67 to end.—*The Prophecy of Zacharias.*

WHAT great mercy God showed to Zacharias! Not only He restored his speech, but He enabled him to prophesy. Zacharias in his song does not speak so much about his own son, as about the Saviour whom his son was to serve. This shows that his heart was fixed upon spiritual blessings, and not upon his own earthly comfort, or honor.

In the beginning of his song, he speaks of the Saviour under the name of "A horn of salvation," (verse 69.) Why does he give him that name? With its horn an animal destroys its enemies. Christ came to destroy the devil and his works. Why then is He not called a horn of destruction? Because he *destroys* his enemies in order that he may *save* his people: therefore he is called "a horn of salvation."

In the latter part of his song, Zacharias calls the Saviour by another name, "The dayspring," (verse 78.) The world sat in darkness and the shadow of death till Christ appeared. They were like travellers, who had lost their way among dangerous cliffs and precipices, and were suddenly overtaken by the darkness; so that they durst not stir, lest they should fall into some deep pit. All at once the sun arose "to guide their feet into the way of peace."

Our native land once sat in this darkness, and was filled with idols, till missionaries came and preached the gospel. But even now that Christ's name is known in every town and village, each soul sits in darkness till the "Dayspring from on high" shines into the heart.

In the midst of his song, Zacharias addresses his own infant son, saying, "And thou, child, shalt be called the prophet of the highest." At the time he uttered these words, John was a helpless infant; but his father knew how great he would become. Very little is related of his childhood. In the last verse of this chapter it is declared that he grew like other children; and also that he waxed *strong in spirit.* We know what it is to wax strong in *body.* But what is it to wax strong in *spirit?* It is to have faith in God's word, and to resist in God's strength the temptations of Satan. The apostle John in his first Epistle says, "I have written unto you, young men, because ye are strong, and the Word of God abideth in you, and ye have overcome the wicked one," (ii. 14.) Believers who are strong in spirit are called "young men." How then did John become thus strong in spirit? No doubt it was by secret prayer and meditation in the deserts. It is written that "He was in the deserts until the days of his showing unto Israel;" or till the time when he began to preach publicly, which he did either at twenty-seven or thirty years of age. Those who teach others must be prepared by learning first of God.

And what did John the Baptist teach? His father declares in his song what he taught, (76, 77:) "Thou shalt go before the face of the Lord to prepare his ways; to give knowledge of salvation unto the people by the remission of their sins, through the tender mercy of our God."

It was salvation through Christ that John proclaimed. None of the old prophets showed the way as clearly as the holy Baptist. But we have heard it still more clearly described by Jesus and his apostles. Have we rejoiced in hearing that sins are pardoned through the blood of the Lamb? None ever rejoiced in hearing these tidings, except those who knew that they *needed* pardon.

If a man were to enter this room with a pardon from the governor in his hand, *we* should feel neither joy nor gratitude. We should say, "There must be some mistake; we have never been brought to justice, nor convicted, nor sentenced to death. What is the use of this pardon to us?" The reason that most people hear the Gospel with such indifference is, that they do not know that they are condemned by God's law. They say, "Our sins can easily be forgiven; they are neither many nor great; others have sinned more than we; surely we shall escape punishment." But when a sinner feels that he deserved to die, then he thanks God for his *tender mercy*, in having sent the Saviour into the world.

Evening Scripture portion. 1 John II. *Strong in spirit.*

MATT. I.—*The Angel's visit to Joseph.*

MATTHEW wrote his gospel before any of the other evangelists. He wrote it for the Jews especially; and therefore he very often refers to the Old Testament, (held in such reverence by the Jews,) and shows that Jesus fulfilled what the prophets had said. Luke and Mark, who wrote for the Gentiles especially, often *explain* Jewish customs, but Matthew always alludes to them, as customs well understood. Matthew himself had been a publican, or tax-gatherer, before he was called to be one of the apostles of the Lord. His other name was Levi. Luke speaks of him by that name. Luke v. 27.

St. Matthew begins his history with an account of the forefathers of our Saviour: to show that Jesus was descended from Abraham, and from David, as God had promised the Messiah should be. This account is called a genealogy. It is *Joseph's* descent, and *not* Mary's, which is here recorded. St. Luke in his third chapter gives us another genealogy. That genealogy is a little different from this; it must therefore be the genealogy of Mary. It is true the name of *Joseph* is mentioned there also; but the names of women were never inserted in public registers.

There is one seeming contradiction between the two genealogies. St. Matthew says that *Jacob* was the father of Joseph. St. Luke says that *Heli* was the father of Joseph. We must conclude that Heli was the father-*in-law* of Joseph, and the father of Mary. How easily the difference is explained to a candid mind! And yet it has been taken up by unbelievers and brought forward as an objection against the Christian religion. How much at a loss must those be for an objection, who lay hold of such a one as this!

We will now proceed to the interesting history itself:—

Joseph is not blamed for his suspicions of Mary, for it appears he had no proof that a miracle had been wrought. Still the kindness of his heart made him unwilling to expose her publicly. God in his great mercy sent an angel to tell him the whole truth. Thus our gracious Father will keep us from falling into errors through ignorance, if we desire earnestly to know what is right.

Mary probably suffered much grief from Joseph's suspicions: but God cleared up her innocence. Every person who is falsely suspected may trust in His fulfilling His promise in Psalm xxxvii.; "Commit thy way unto the Lord, trust also in him, and he shall bring it to pass: and he shall bring forth thy righteousness as the light, and thy judgment as the noonday." When falsely accused, we should not make a loud and angry defence; but commit our cause to God, and He will defend us.

The concluding words of the angel are very remarkable. They are written in verse 21, "Thou shalt call his name Jesus, for he shall save his people from their sins."

The name "Jesus" means God the Saviour. Observe, however, the nature of this salvation. It is not a salvation *in* sin, but a salvation *from* sin. "He shall save his people from their sins." If we knew what sin was, we should feel what a great salvation this is. Sin has ruined this world; and it will ruin each of us eternally, unless we are saved from it. There is only one who is able to save us. That is Immanuel, or God with us. Jesus, the Son of God, came down to dwell with us that he might save us from dwelling forever with Satan. How does he save? By shedding his own blood as an atonement for sin, and then by washing all who believe in him in that blood. Therefore his people sing this song of praise to his name: "Unto him that loved us and washed us from our sins in his blood, and hath made us kings and priests unto God and his Father; to him be glory and dominion forever and ever. Amen." Rev. i. 5–8.

Evening Scripture portion. Isa. VII. 10 to end.

Luke II. 1–7.—*The birth of the Lord Jesus Christ.*

It is very interesting to observe the providence of God with regard to the *place* of Christ's birth.

The prophet Isaiah had said that the Saviour should be born in Bethlehem, (v. 2.) Yet Mary lived in Nazareth, about seventy miles distant from Bethlehem. God could easily have commanded Mary to go to Bethlehem: but instead of doing this, he caused circumstances to happen which induced her to go there.

The great emperor of Rome, who possessed all the chief countries in the world, and among the rest, Canaan, the land of the Jews, desired at this time to number his subjects. He sent forth an order to have their names *enrolled*, (as you will find the word is also translated in Bibles with marginal readings.) Joseph being descended from King David, went to the city of Bethlehem, (whence David came,) to have his name enrolled, and Mary his wife accompanied him.

Cæsar Augustus, the Emperor of Rome, little knew that by this decree he was causing a prophecy concerning the Son of God to be fulfilled; for he knew nothing of the true God, or of his word. But we, who read the history, ought to admire the ways of God: how easily he can bring every thing to pass which he has determined to do; for he is "great in counsel" (or in making plans) "and mighty in work," Jer. xxxii. 19, (or in bringing his plans to pass.) It is therefore very unbelieving in us to trouble ourselves about the future, for there is nothing we can desire that God could not easily cause to happen; and if he does not bring it to pass, it is because the thing we desire does not agree with his own wise and gracious designs.

When Mary arrived at Bethlehem, she was obliged to lodge in a stable; for the inn was full, many people having come to have their names enrolled also. Thus it happened, that her holy babe was born in a stable, and laid in a manger.

Are we surprised that the glorious Son of God should thus be received into this world! Let us remember *why* he came. Not to *enjoy* himself, but to *save* us. In order to save us, two things were necessary. That he should obey the law of God, which we had broken, and that he should suffer the punishment due to us for breaking it.

In order that he might do these things, he was always placed in suffering circumstances. Poverty and contempt nursed him in his infancy. The most splendid palace on earth would have been too humble an abode for him whom the heaven of heavens cannot contain. But instead of opening his infant eyes in a palace, he opened them in a stable. It was wonderful condescension in him who was equal with God, to dwell with *men*, but in the stable he was surrounded by *beasts*. What must the angels who had worshipped him in heaven have felt when they saw him thus degraded! Yet this treatment was not to be compared to that which he afterwards endured on Calvary. As he walked through this world at each step his way became rougher; his *first* bed was a *manger*, but his *last* was a *cross*. And it was *men*, whom he came to redeem, who treated him in this manner. And have we not *all* treated him in the same, casting him out of our thoughts, and crucifying him by our sins? Yes, we are all guilty before God, and Jesus alone is righteous. But he is not righteous for himself, but for *us;* neither did he suffer for himself, but for *us*. He was *cast out*, that we might be *brought in*. He was *rejected* of *men*, that we might be *accepted* of *God*.

Evening Scripture portion. Micah V. *Bethlehem*.

LUKE II. 8–14.—*The Angels' appearance to the Shepherds.*

IN the circumstances of our Saviour's birth, there was a great mixture of meanness and glory. Jesus was laid in a manger; yet angels announced his appearance. But to *whom* did angels announce it? not to princes, but to shepherds; thus showing that God had chosen the poor of this world. Through all our Saviour's life, there was the same mixture of meanness and glory: he lived with fishermen, yet was sometimes visited by angels; he had a sorrowful countenance, yet once it shone brighter than the sun; he was meanly clad, yet, on one occasion, his raiment was whiter than any fuller on earth could whiten it; he was so *weak* that he could not bear his cross, yet so *strong* that he could raise the dead from their graves.

Christ's people are like their master; they are often poor and afflicted, yet there is a glory about them that makes them as the sons of God; for their minds are filled with nobler thoughts than those which occupy the kings of the earth. While princes are thinking of their sumptuous feasts, their high titles, and glittering crowns; the children of God are meditating upon the supper of the Lamb, the thrones of light, and the God of glory.

How much astonished the poor shepherds were with the appearance of the angel, who turned the darkness into day! How much his *message* must also have surprised them! He told them that the Son of God was now come into the world, and was in the city of David, (or Bethlehem.) Was not this news hard to believe? But what the angel added made it harder still; for he said that this glorious babe was lying in a manger. Immediately, however, God confirmed his words by causing a multitude of angels to appear in the heavens; not *two* or *three* witnesses, but, perhaps, two or three millions.

These angels were not *silent* witnesses; they sang a song, whose very words are handed down to us. It is the only song sung by angels upon *earth* that we ever heard. In the book of Revelation some of their songs in *heaven* are recorded; such as "Worthy is the Lamb to receive honor, power, and glory;" and "Thou hast created all things, for thy pleasure they are and were created." But here we read of a song to which poor shepherds listened. It is a short song, but contains much; for it explains the *purpose* for which the Saviour was come into the world, and the *reason* he was sent.

The purpose was to bring glory to God and peace on earth. The reason he was sent was because God had good-will towards men. "Glory to God in the highest, and on earth peace, good-will towards men."

Has not Christ's coming brought glory to God? Since Christ came into the world, how many redeemed sinners have glorified God for the gift of his Son! But what are these praises compared to the songs of saints and angels throughout eternity! Never will they cease to praise the God of love for sending his only Son to die for wretched men. But we may ask, "Is there peace on earth?" Not *yet;* but there *will* be. This earth shall be filled with the knowledge of the Lord, and then war shall cease; the swords shall be turned into ploughshares, and the spears into pruning-hooks, (see Isaiah ii.;) because the Prince of Peace shall reign.

And are these God's gracious promises to men? Let us not doubt the Lord's *good-will* towards us. It hurts a tender parent, if he perceives that his children doubt his *good-will* towards them: he tries to convince them of it by numerous acts of kindness; and he is much disappointed if he cannot succeed in winning their confidence. Has not the Lord done enough to convince us of his good-will? Ought we not always to say, "If God spared not his own Son, but gave him up for us all, will he not *with him* freely give us all things."—Rom. viii. 32

Evening Scripture portion. Rev. V. *Angels' songs in heaven.*

LUKE II. 15–20.—*The Shepherds' Visit to Bethlehem.*

WE find that the shepherds believed the news they had heard They did *not* say, "Let us go and see *whether* this thing is come to pass;" but they said, "Let us now go and see this thing which *is* come to pass." They believed *before* they had seen. "Blessed are they who have not seen, and yet have believed." They spoke also as if they felt grateful for having heard the tidings; for they added, "which the Lord hath made known to us." Truly they had reason to be grateful: for God had shown them very great favor. Let us not forget that we also are among those to whom the Lord has made known the birth of his Son. There are millions on this earth who have never heard of the love of God, in sending a Saviour; but we have heard of it from our infant days. Do we, like these shepherds, long to see our blessed Redeemer?

How much Joseph and Mary must have been delighted at the entrance of the shepherds! Though overlooked by the world, the holy child was honored by these poor men. Even now there are only a few who acknowledge him as their Lord and Master, and these few are generally poor, like the shepherds of Bethlehem.

These good men did not keep the things they had heard and seen, a *secret.* The angel had said that he brought glad tidings which should be to *all* people; therefore the shepherds *told* the news to *all.* Like them, if we believe in Christ ourselves, we shall speak of him to those who know him not.

How did the people *receive* the tidings the shepherds brought? They *wondered;* but probably they soon forgot what they had heard: while Mary "kept all these things, and pondered them in her heart." This is the way in which sermons should be heard, and in which the Bible should be read. All who get good from what they hear, keep it, and ponder it in their hearts. But how many cast from their minds what they hear!

There are *two* comparisons used in the Scriptures to show the careless way in which people hear the word of God. One of these comparisons is contained in Ezekiel xxxiii. 31, 32. The Israelites listened to the preaching of Ezekiel as people listen to one who can play well on an instrument, and who can sing a lovely song. It is not necessary to think of the music we have heard; it is enough if it pleases us while we are hearing it: but we should not listen to sermons in this manner, and think it enough, if they amuse us.

The other comparison may be found in the first chapter of St. James's Epistle. It is there said that some listen to God's word as a person looks in a glass, and then goes away and forgets what he has seen. Such listeners soon lose the good impressions they have received, and continue worldly-minded, and ungodly.

There is a beautiful description in the first Psalm, of the right manner of receiving the word. The godly man is represented as meditating in God's law, day and night.

One verse of God's holy word laid up in the heart will do us more good than a whole chapter hastily read, and little considered. Are there any passages of the Scriptures which are dear to our hearts? Has any verse strengthened us in the hour of temptation; or comforted us in the day of trouble? Have we laid up any in store against the day when we shall walk through the valley of the shadow of death, when flesh and heart will fail, and when no mortal arm can sustain our sinking souls?

Evening Scripture portion. Ez. XXXIII. 21 to end.
Ezekiel's words listened to as a lovely song.

Luke II. 21–32.—*The Song of Simeon.*

We read that when the Saviour was eight days old, he was circumcised, and named Jesus. It was not necessary that he should be brought to Jerusalem for that purpose; but at the end of forty days, when he was nearly six weeks old, he was brought to Jerusalem, for two purposes.

His mother was then first permitted, after the birth of her son, to enter the temple. She went there with an offering of thanksgiving. If she could have afforded it, she would have brought a lamb of a year old; but being very poor, she presented two doves, or pigeons. (See Lev. xii.) In the second place, Jesus as a firstborn son was presented to the Lord; for, ever since the slaying of the firstborn of the people of Egypt, and the passing over the firstborn of Israel, God had claimed all the firstborn as his own. (Ex. xiii.) The firstborn of cows, sheep, and goats were offered in sacrifice: the firstborn of other beasts were not offered, but money was presented in their place, and this money was used in buying sacrifices. Neither did God suffer firstborn *children* to be offered in sacrifice; but he permitted them to be redeemed with money.

Mary accordingly came to the temple to present her firstborn son to the Lord. When was so acceptable an offering made to the Father! His only beloved Son was brought to his Father's house, and given into his Father's bosom. The priest supposed that he was redeemed by money; but this holy child could not be redeemed by money; he was a Lamb without blemish, and upon the altar of the cross he was soon to be laid, a willing, a sufficient sacrifice for the sins of the whole world.

When Mary brought her child into the temple, a most interesting event took place. An aged prophet appeared, and owned the infant Saviour as his Lord.

Prophets had almost ceased to prophesy for many years before Jesus came into the world. Malachi, who had prophesied four hundred years before his coming, was the last whose name is recorded. But at the time of his coming, the spirit of prophecy was again shed upon some holy persons. We have read the prophecies of Elizabeth, and Mary, and Zacharias, in the first chapter of St. Luke, and we now read the prophecy of Simeon. God had informed him that he should not die till Christ came; and He had also let him know the precise moment when the parents had brought the divine infant into the temple. Simeon entered and found Joseph and Mary doing for their child after the custom of the law, that is, presenting him to the Lord before God's priest. At this interesting juncture, the aged saint first beheld his Saviour, took him in his arms and blessed him; for his faith was so strong that he was able to believe that the infant of the poor woman he saw, was the Lord of all.

The words that he uttered as he held the child are very beautiful. We perceive that it had been his earnest desire to see his Lord with his bodily eyes before he died. This was a very natural desire; and some people who do not really love Christ might desire the same; they might desire it from *curiosity*, but Simeon desired it from *affection*. And why did Simeon love the Saviour? Because he valued his great salvation; he was waiting for the "consolation of Israel," (the name given to Christ in verse 25.) He was a penitent sinner, and it was a consolation to him to know that God had provided a Saviour. He calls Jesus "his salvation," in verse 30. "Mine eyes have seen thy salvation." He rejoiced also to think that *other* men would be saved through Jesus, both Jews and Gentiles; for he said, (verses 31, 32,) that God had given him to *all* people, a light to lighten the Gentiles, as well as the glory of Israel.

This shows the love to *other* men that dwelt in Simeon's heart. He longed that *all* should know his Saviour. It is recorded of a celebrated minister, named John Howe, that in his latter days he greatly desired to attain such a knowledge of Christ, and feel such a sense of his love, as might be a foretaste of the joys of heaven. After his death, a paper was found in his Bible recording how God had answered his prayer. One morning, (and he noted the day,) he awoke, his eyes swimming with tears, overwhelmed with a sense of God's goodness in shedding down his grace into the hearts of men. He never could forget the joy of these moments: they made him long still more ardently for that heaven, which, from his youth, he had panted to behold. How happy thus to see Jesus by *faith* before we die! *then* we too shall behold him some day with our bodily eyes; for though we die without that sight, we shall be raised again to gaze upon our glorious Redeemer, coming in the clouds of heaven.

All true believers may now say, with Job—"I know that my Redeemer liveth; and that he shall stand at the latter day upon the earth; and though after my skin, worms destroy this body, yet in my flesh shall I see God; whom I shall see for myself, and mine eyes shall behold and not another." Job xix. 25–27.

Evening Scripture portion. Job XIX. *Seeing the Redeemer.*

LUKE II. 33–35.—*The words of Simeon to Mary.*

BOTH Joseph and Mary marvelled at the things spoken of Christ by Simeon. The things that made them marvel were that he should be "a light to lighten the Gentiles," as well as the glory of Israel; for God's goodness to the Gentiles was a mystery long hidden from the Jewish nation. But we happy Gentiles have experienced it, and some among us have found Christ to be a light to lighten our darkness.

Simeon blessed Joseph and Mary: and then he addressed Mary in particular, and prepared her for all the shame and sorrow that her Son should undergo; for what he had said before might have led her to think that joy only was to be his portion, and that all men, Jews and Gentiles, would immediately do him honor. But this was not to be the case. So great would be the agonies of the Son, that a sword would pierce through the mother's heart. And was not the soul of Mary thus pierced, when she beheld her Son expiring on the cross?

Simeon's words concerning the child demand attentive consideration,—"This child is set for the fall and rising again of many in Israel." Let us inquire into their meaning, for all that concerns our Saviour is very important to us. How was he the *fall* of many in Israel? Does Christ make men fall? Simeon here compares Christ to a stone over which many stumble and fall. St. Paul says, in 1 Cor. i. 23, that Christ was to the Jews a stumbling-block, or something over which *they fell. How* was it they fell over him? Through pride. They would not believe that their own righteousness was worthless in God's sight, and that Christ's righteousness alone could be accepted. This is the account St. Paul gives of Christ's rejection by the Jews. His words are, "For they being ignorant of God's righteousness, and going about to establish their *own* righteousness, have not submitted themselves unto the righteousness of God: for Christ is the end of the law for righteousness to every one that believeth." Rom. x. 3, 4. And what is the reason that any still refuse Christ? Is it not because they do not feel their need of his righteousness? Is it not because they feel satisfied with their own performances, and imagine that God is satisfied also? And when they are told that they are sinners, they answer in their *hearts*, if not with their *lips*, "We are not such great sinners as others." People in this state of mind fall over Christ as over a stumbling-stone: they cannot receive him, because they do not desire his salvation. St. Peter, in his Epistle, says that Christ was to such persons, "A stone of stumbling, and a rock of offence, even to them which stumble at the word, being disobedient." 1 Peter ii. 8.

But Simeon said also that the child was set for the *rising again* of many in Israel. Many of those who fell over him *at first*, afterwards believed, and rose from sin and death by Christ. Many of the priests who joined in crucifying the Saviour were *afterwards* obedient to the faith. Acts vi. 7.

The poor penitent sinner rises by Christ; that is, he finds in him a rock on which to set his feet; he finds in Christ one who can forgive his sins, and save his soul; then he can say with David, "He brought me up also out of a horrible pit, out of the miry clay, and set my feet upon a rock, and established my goings." Ps. xl. 2.

Simeon next declared that Christ should be set for "a sign which shall be spoken against," (verse 34.)

We should observe that the words, "Yea, a sword shall pierce through thine own soul, also," are between marks, and the words are called a "*parenthesis;*" they might be left out without hurting the sense. Let us read the sentence without them, that we may better perceive the meaning, (verses 34, 35.)

"A sign which shall be spoken against, that the thoughts of many hearts may be revealed." Had Christ *not* been spoken against, many who despised him would have followed him. The people applauded him till they heard the scribes and Pharisees speak so much against him; then they cried out, "Crucify him, crucify him."

True religion is still spoken against. People must often give up the favor of the world, if they would be faithful to Christ. For a *time,* perhaps, they may profess to be religious, and lose nothing by it: but something soon occurs to try them, and to reveal the real state of their hearts. Is a young person willing to lose an opportunity of a good settlement, or a tradesman the favor of a rich customer, or a gentleman the respect of his acquaintance, sooner than disobey his Lord? Then their *faithful* thoughts are revealed. Christ is now like a king disgraced; only those who *really* love him will be faithful to him. But when he comes in his glory to take possession of his kingdom, he will not fail to remember those who are now cast out for his sake.

Evening Scripture portion. 1 Peter II. ***Christ a stone of stumbling.***

LUKE II. 36–40.—*Anna the Prophetess.*

WE have read of Simeon's blessing the infant Saviour: and we now hear of another witness, even Anna, an aged prophetess.

Anna, it appears, had led a very holy life. We do not know her exact age; but if she had been a widow eighty-four years, and if she had been married for seven years, she must have been at this time above a hundred, even supposing that she had married at a very early period of life. It is said that "she departed not from the temple." By this, we understand that she lived so near the temple, as to enable her to attend all its services. When, at nine in the morning, the lamb was offered on the altar, Anna was there; and again at three, when the evening lamb was sacrificed, Anna was not absent. She delighted in the psalms continually sung in the holy courts; she listened to the daily blessings of the priest. There are now many aged Christians, who, like Anna, dwell near some house of God, and delight in attending the services; and, even when their power of hearing has failed, they yet take pleasure in joining in the prayers of God's assembled saints. How sweet for them to think that they will soon ascend, where

"Congregations ne'er break up,
And sabbaths never end."

We hear also that Anna "*served* God with fastings and prayers." She not only fasted and prayed, but she *served* God when she fasted and prayed. She might have fasted and prayed, and *not* have served God; because she might have done these things in a self-righteous spirit, as some of the Jews did, whom God reproves in Isaiah lviii., because they fasted and prayed, and yet were living in their sins.

It is said that Anna fasted and prayed "*night and day*:" no doubt she was occupied also in many good works, yet she lived in a constant habit of prayer. We are desired to pray without *ceasing*, and to *continue* in prayer, and this is what Anna did.

In one of St. Paul's Epistles we read a description of such a widow as God approves, and we find that such a widow both prays constantly, and does all kinds of good works. It is written in 1 Tim. v. 5, "She that is a widow indeed, and desolate, trusteth in God, and continueth in supplications and prayers *night and day*." It is also written that a widow should be "well reported of for good works: if she have brought up children, if she have lodged strangers, if she have washed the saints' feet, if she have relieved the afflicted, if she have diligently followed every good work." From these we see that a person may at once pray constantly and do good works also.

We are not told whether Anna came in by the Spirit, as Simeon did, or whether she had been called by some person, or whether she came in accidentally; but we are told that when she did come in, she knew the infant Saviour as her Lord. "She gave thanks."

With what fervor Anna must have thanked the Lord! None could sincerely thank God for Christ in an indifferent, cold manner. Could we thank a person for saving our lives in the same manner as we thanked him for doing us any trifling service! Surely, if we thank our deliverer at all, we must thank him warmly. Have we ever given our *warm* thanks to God for sending Jesus into the world? If we have only thanked him *coldly*, we have insulted him by our thanks.

Anna not only thanked God, she also spoke of Jesus to "all them that looked for redemption in Jerusalem." It is evident that there was a little company of persons there who were looking for redemption from *sin* through the promised Saviour.

How much refreshed Joseph and Mary must have been by the prayers and exhortations of Simeon and Anna! It is said by St. Luke, that they returned to their own city Nazareth; but we find from St. Matthew's history, that they did not return *immediately;* they went first to Bethlehem, afterwards into Egypt, and at length settled in Nazareth.

And now we turn from the aged saints to the holy child. There is but little said of him, but that little shows how holy a child he was. He "grew and waxed strong in spirit." Not only his limbs increased in strength, but his affection towards his Father waxed strong. It is a great mystery how this could be, for he was God; but we know that he had not only a human *body*, but also a human SOUL; and it was this *soul* that waxed strong. It is also written that he was "filled with *wisdom:*" his *human* mind received more and more knowledge by degrees, like the mind of another child. "The grace of God was upon him;" that is, the "*favor*" of God was upon him. God looked upon his human nature with favor, for as the *Son of God*, he was always *infinitely* beloved by the Father.

How different was he from other children, who generally grow more wayward and wilful as they grow older! Even if good impressions are made on their minds at six or seven years old, how often do they wear off when they become twelve or fourteen! their hearts seem to grow harder, and to love worldly things more. Was not this the case with some of us! Do we not often look back with sorrow upon the days of our childhood? Have we not reason to say with David, "Remember not the sins of my *youth*, nor my transgressions?" Perhaps some are now removed from us, whom we pierced by our heedless or perverse conduct. What would we give to recall the time and to act differently! but we can only express our penitence to God, and plead for his pardon.

Evening Scripture portion. 1 Tim. V. ***A widow indeed.***

MATT. II. 1–8.—*The wise men's arrival at Jerusalem.*

WE find from St. Matthew's account, that our Saviour returned to Bethlehem after he had been presented to the Lord in the temple. Perhaps his parents intended to bring him up in Bethlehem, as it was the city of David their forefather. But God did not choose that his

Son should be brought up in a renowned city, but in the despised city of Nazareth; and we shall see that he caused events to happen which obliged him to leave Bethlehem.

While the Redeemer was yet an infant, some wise men came to Jerusalem, inquiring for the King of the Jews. Who were these wise men? They were heathen by birth, but it is not known from what land they came. They must have heard of the true God; perhaps some Jews had instructed them. They had seen a star in the east, probably some light which they had never seen before. But how did they know that this star was the sign of the birth of the King of the Jews? We must conclude that God *told* them *why* the star appeared; but whether he told them in a dream, or by what other means, we are not informed. Many nations were at this time expecting some great deliverer to arise; for the Jews knew from the prophets that such a deliverer would come, and as they were scattered over all countries, they had the opportunity to make their expectation generally known.

These wise men, when they came to Jerusalem, *openly* asked for the expected king, supposing that the Jews, who were God's own people, would know more about him than they did, and would be glad to receive him. Had these wise men known of Simeon and Anna, they would surely have inquired of them; but they inquired of the chief men of Jerusalem, and these knew nothing of him.

"When Herod the king heard these things he was troubled, and all Jerusalem with him." (ver. 3.) This Herod was a very wicked man: he was an Edomite; that is, he was descended from Esau, but he had become a Jew in religion; and he had been appointed king over Jerusalem by the Romans, who had conquered the Jews. Herod shed much blood during his reign, and caused his own wife and two of his sons to be slain. He was afraid lest some person should take the crown from him, and therefore he was much alarmed when he heard the wise men inquire for the King of the Jews.

We may ask, "Why were the people in Jerusalem alarmed also, and why were they not rather glad at the thought of having another King?" Perhaps they were afraid of Herod's filling the city with confusion and blood in opposing the new King. Herod was so artful, that, instead of telling the wise men of his fears, he pretended to assist them to find out where the child was. For this purpose he adopted a very wise method: he desired the chief priests and the scribes, who studied the Old Testament a great deal, to tell him where the expected Saviour would be born. They examined the writings of the prophets, and found that it was declared in the prophet Micah, that he should be born in the town of Bethlehem.

Only one thing more remained to be done; to find out how old the child must be. Herod supposed that the star had first appeared at the time the child was born: he inquired of the wise men *when* it had appeared, and discovered that it was more than a year ago. He told the wise men to go to Jerusalem and to seek for a child of that age, promising, when they had found him, to come and worship him also. He completely deceived the wise men by his hypocrisy; but what would all his plans avail against the Lord, who searches the hearts? The Lord, that sitteth in the heavens, laughs at all such attempts to injure him, as it is written in the *second* psalm, verse 2–4.

Herod is an instance that a man may *believe* the word of God, while he *hates* it. Herod *believed* that the prophets had spoken truly, and had known the place where Christ would be born; he *believed* that the Messiah would come; and yet he desired to destroy him, and thought it possible to effect his purpose. What madness this appears! It is the faith of devils: like Herod, they believe, and tremble. James ii. 19. Let us beware of having *such* a faith; a faith that will make us afraid of God, and yet not make us love him, or delight to please him. This faith will only make us miserable. How different was the faith of Simeon and Anna, of the poor shepherds, and of the wise men! They were filled with joy on account of a Saviour's birth. Have we ever rejoiced at the thought that Christ has been born into the world?

Evening Scripture portion. Ps. II.
Matt. II. 9–11. *The opposition of the wicked to Christ.*

MATT. II. 9–11.—*The wise men's journey to Bethlehem.*

HEROD had not been able to give the wise men exact information respecting the place where the King they sought would be found: he had only told them that he was in Bethlehem. But God did not leave them to search in vain. As they were on the way, the star they had seen in their own country appeared again, and stopped over the very house where the Saviour was. This star could not have been like the stars we behold in the height of the heavens, for one of those stars could not point out any particular house: it must have been a light, floating in the air.

No doubt the house in which Mary dwelt was a lowly one, but the wise men were not discouraged by its meanness from worshipping its glorious inhabitant. How often now does Christ dwell with the poor tenants of a cottage! How seldom is he found ruling in the mansions of the great, or the palaces of kings! Yet even among the rich, noble, and wise, there are a few who love their despised Saviour. These men from the East seem to have been rich, as well as wise; for they brought treasures with them from their native land, and laid them at their Redeemer's feet. What must have been their joy at that moment! If the sight of the star caused them to feel exceeding great joy, what transport the sight of the Lord himself must have occasioned! The luxuries, the splendor, the honor they had enjoyed in their native land, can never have given them the satisfaction they felt when gazing on the glorious infant.

These men were very different from the shepherds of Bethlehem in their *circumstances*. The most remarkable difference between them was this; the shepherds were Jews, the wise men were Gentiles. They were the first Gentiles whose coming to Christ is recorded; their coming was a sign that Gentiles as well as Jews would be saved through him. How interesting this fact is to *us* who are Gentiles. Though Christ was born among the Jews, he is our Saviour as well as theirs. And his name is *now* known by millions of the Gentile nations; and it shall be known by every nation under heaven; for *all* nations shall serve him, and all kings shall fall down before him, as it is written in Ps. lxxii.

But let us not read the history of these wise men without seeking to learn something from their example. What *earnestness* they displayed in their search for the Saviour! They travelled far to seek him; they inquired diligently after him; they watched anxiously for the sign, when it had ceased to be visible, and rejoiced exceedingly, when it again appeared. Surely these wise men, by their conduct, condemn those who are living in Christian lands, unmindful of their Saviour. There are some who confess they know but little of him, and who yet seem unwilling to take any trouble to know him better. How would those wise men have valued our advantage! how dearly would they have prized one of our Bibles, one of our faithful ministers, one of our blessed Sabbaths! Some there are now among the poor heathen, who, by their eager desire to obtain a missionary, remind us of these wise men. An African chief sent two hundred oxen to a missionary settlement, hoping with them to purchase a teacher; such was his ignorance, that he thought he might obtain one by such means. Robbers seized upon his herd as it was being driven along. Though his disappointment was great, he did not abandon his project of obtaining an instructor. But while he was contriving some other method of gaining the precious boon, God, in his gracious Providence, directed the steps of some missionaries to his land. These good men were travelling to a more distant spot, but they could not resist the chief's earnest entreaties; they took up their abode in his country, and soon enlightened its darkness with the glorious beams of gospel light.* Did not that African resemble these wise men, and were not his hopes, like theirs, fulfilled? Here is encouragement for all those who desire spiritual blessings. The Lord will give them the desires of their heart.

Evening Scripture portion. Ps. LXXII. *Kings shall worship Christ.*

* See Moffat's Southern Africa, the beginning of the last chapter.

MATT. II. 12–15.—*The heavenly warnings.*

TWICE in a very little space God sent messages to his faithful servants in the dreams of the night. One dream was to warn the wise men not to inform Herod that they had found the infant King; the other was, to warn Joseph not to remain in Bethlehem. We perceive how easily God can defeat the plans of the wicked, as it is written in the fifth chapter of Job: "He disappointeth the devices of the crafty, so that their hands cannot perform their enterprise." There is a beautiful prayer in the liturgy, entreating God to exercise this power in our behalf. "Graciously hear us, that those evils which the craft, or subtlety of the devil or man, worketh against us may be brought to naught, and, by the providence of thy goodness, may be dispersed." We see how God dispersed those evils which Satan and Herod were working against the Son of God. Satan still stirs up wicked men to form plans against the children of God; and still the Lord, by his gracious providence, disperses these evils. Are we distressed at the thought of any malicious plan being formed against us, either by Satan or by our fellow-creatures? Let us pray to the Lord to defend us. No one can harm us, if we are followers of that which is good.

We have all heard of the Gunpowder-plot. What a diabolical scheme it was! The Roman Catholics had contrived a plan for blowing up the king of England, with his family and parliament, because they supported the Protestant religion; but God defeated their malicious design. One of the conspirators wrote a letter to Lord Monteagle, warning him not to go to the house of parliament, when the king next should open it. God gave such discernment to the king, that when Lord Monteagle showed him the letter, he suspected that a gunpowder-plot had been formed. Thus this dreadful evil was dispersed.

We find also many instances in the lives of God's servants, of the same gracious interference. The missionary Williams was saved from falling into the hands of four cruel heathens, who had determined to kill him. It was his custom to go sometimes to a neighboring island on Saturday to perform the Sabbath services. Four young men, who hated the Christian religion, offered to convey him to the island. They appeared as if they wished to show kindness to the missionary; but in reality they had agreed, when he was at a distance from the shore, to throw him into the sea. Williams accepted the offer. God, however, by a very trifling circumstance, rescued him from the snare. He had lately painted his boat with a peculiar kind of paint, that did not dry as quickly as he expected, and fearing to venture out to sea while his boat was in that state, he refused to go with those who desired to be his murderers. Thus was the wicked scheme frustrated. At length, indeed, he fell by the hands of cruel savages; but not till his *work* was done.

If we knew all the plans that Satan formed against *us*, we should be filled with wonder at the deliverances we experience. But perhaps we may remember some instances in our own lives, in which we discovered that the attempts of *men* to hurt us were frustrated. What wonderful proofs of the Lord's watchful care over his people will be revealed in another world! Then shall they know those things that they know not now. Then it will be found that Job was not the *only* saint whom Satan sought to cast down by the weight of his sorrows; nor Peter the *only* disciple that he desired to sift by the force of temptations; nor the blessed Saviour, the *only* child that he sought to cut off by an untimely death. *Then* it will appear how the Lord kept his people in the hollow of his hand from all the blasts of the enemy; and *then* there will ascend a chorus of hallelujahs from the happy redeemed, and from the glorious angels that were their appointed guard during the years of their weakness.

Evening Scripture portion. Job V. *Disappointment of wicked devices.*

MATT. II. 16–18.—*The Slaughter of the Babes.*

EVERY one who reads this passage must shudder at the dreadful cruelty of Herod. There was a singular barbarity in ordering the *babes* to be slaughtered; little creatures who could not have offended him, and were unable to resist him. Who can bear to think of the anguish of the mothers in that terrible day! When the firstborn of Egypt were slain by the destroying angel, the cry was terrible. Can it have been less terrible when the *youngest son* of many a mother was murdered by the pitiless executioner? We know that the mother's heart clings closely to her helpless infant. Tears and entreaties were all in vain: not only the babes of Bethlehem were slaughtered, but the babes in all the coasts or places round about.

We might be disposed to ponder how any human creature could perpetrate so atrocious a deed, did not the history of ungodly men disclose every kind of bloody act. This very Herod, just before his death, knowing how glad people would be when he expired, caused a number of Jews to be shut up, and desired that as soon as he was dead they should be killed; for by this means he hoped that the relations of the slaughtered Jews would be *obliged* to mourn. This command, however, was not obeyed. Such a king as Herod cared not for the lives of infants in comparison to his own security. Though few in a Christian land would dare to commit such *acts* of cruelty as Herod did, yet are not the *feelings* of unconverted men as selfish as his? Are we not *all* by *nature* so selfish, that we care not what calamities come upon others, if we gain any thing by them? For instance, are not people glad of a war, if it will promote their trade, though they know war brings misery upon thousands of their fellow-creatures ?

How interesting was the fate of these infants ! they died in the Saviour's stead. Some have called them martyrs, because they died for Christ, though without their own knowledge. In the service of the Church of England they are spoken of as the *Innocents*. A babe may be called "innocent," because it has not yet committed any acts of sin ; still it has a sinful nature, and would, if it lived, sin as soon as reason dawned. There never was but one truly innocent babe : it was the infant Saviour.

Why is Rachel spoken of in the passage quoted by Jeremiah ? Because Rachel was the mother of Joseph and Benjamin, and many of those babes were descended from her. She is represented in a poetical way, as weeping over her murdered offspring.

This was the scene on *earth*. How different were the scenes then witnessed in heaven ! What a multitude of happy spirits then entered together into glory ! David was comforted when he lost his little one, by the thoughts of beholding it again. He said to those who wondered at his cheerfulness, knowing, as they did, his affection for his child, "I shall go to him ; but he shall not return to me." 2 Sam. xii. 23. If David, who lived *before* the coming of Christ, was supported by this confidence, how much more ought parents who live *after* his coming to be consoled by such thoughts when they lose their darling infants ! Do not *they* know how Christ loved little children, and how he took them in his arms and blessed them, and how he said, "Of such is the kingdom of heaven ?" The believing parent may feel assured that he shall see his child again among the cherub choir. Well may he love that Saviour to whose grace he owes the happiness of his departed little one.

Evening Scripture portion. 2 Sam. XII. 13–23

MATT. II. 19–23.—*Joseph's return.*

WHAT an important charge was committed to Joseph ! The care of the infant Saviour and of his mother. How honorable was the post he occupied ! He was a shield from the darts of the enemy to the blessed child. God did not leave him without assistance in performing his allotted work. Joseph knew not how to protect his little family ; he knew not when dangers awaited them, or when those dangers were removed.

In this chapter, God directs Joseph three times by dreams how to act ; he tells him when to depart into Egypt, when to return to Canaan, and in what city to fix his abode. Does not this kindness shown to

Joseph give us reason to expect that God will direct his people now, when they are perplexed and at a loss how to act? Persons who desire to act right, are often in much perplexity respecting the path of duty. They know not, in some cases, what plan it would be best to pursue; whether to settle in this village or in that town; to form an engagement with this person or with another; to go, or stay, to consent or to refuse, to speak or to be silent. Though they consult the Holy Word for wisdom, they can gain no light upon their path; though they consult pious friends, they can get no certain advice; and though they pray to God, they seem to obtain no answer. What then are they to do? Would the Lord direct them by a dream, how happy would they be! but no such dreams as Joseph had, are vouchsafed to them.

Is not the Lord, by their perplexities, teaching them *patience?* Is he not teaching them to *persevere* in prayer, and to feel more deeply their own weakness and ignorance? If they continue to look up to God, either some circumstance shall occur that shall show them the path of duty; or God will send some messenger (though not an angel) to point it out; or He himself will in some way or other make it clear to their minds. Or if he do not make it clear *before* the period of decision arrives, He will show them *afterwards* that their steps were ordered by Him. But no such guidance shall be granted to those who are not desirous to act uprightly. "The way of the wicked is as darkness; they know not at what they stumble." Prov. iv. 19. This is the *threatening;* but the *promise* is, "In all thy ways acknowledge him; He shall direct thy paths." Prov. iii. 6.

Joseph, as we have already observed, was commanded in a dream to return to his own land. The angel said, "They are dead which sought the young child's life." It seems, therefore, that some one beside Herod sought to destroy Jesus; for the angel said, "*They* are dead." Perhaps this other person was Herod's eldest son Antipater; for he may have desired the destruction of the infant for the same reason as his father. This Antipater died a few months before Herod, but not a natural death. His father had unjustly suspected him of plotting against his life, and had caused him to be executed. Soon afterwards the bloody tyrant himself died in the most horrible torments: his illness began about the time of the slaughter of the innocent babes; in vain he travelled about his kingdom to obtain a cure; no earthly hand could heal him; his disease grew worse and worse, till he became intolerably offensive to all about him, and even to himself. He expired two years after the murder of the infants, eaten by worms.

Thus God often inflicts judgments on those who persecute his people. Several persecutors have died in the manner that Herod did, and others have been cut off suddenly in God's wrath. In this sudden manner a wicked Roman Catholic bishop of England once perished. His name was Gardiner. He had sworn that he would not eat till he had heard that two pious Protestant bishops had been burnt for the truth's sake. He generally dined at twelve. The news did not reach him till four. He then sat down to dinner, and the first mouthful he took, he expired. Surely all men must have said, "This is the finger of God." True believers are dear to God as the apple of his eye, and those who dare to hurt or mock them, are abhorred by him.

Joseph and Mary must have been rejoiced to leave Egypt, the land of idols; for if David sighed after the services of the temple when absent from them, as the hart panteth after the water-brooks, surely these pious persons did so also.

It appears that they intended to live near Jerusalem, probably in Bethlehem, which was only seven miles distant; but when they arrived in Canaan, they heard that the Romans had appointed a cruel son of Herod's, called Archelaus, to be governor instead of his father; therefore they were afraid to remain near him. Joseph was then directed in a dream to go to Nazareth, where they had formerly lived. God chose that his Son should be brought up there, that he might be called a Nazarene. There is no prophet who has said *these very words*, but several have said that Jesus should be despised. The name Nazarene was very disgraceful, because Nazareth was a very mean and wicked city.

And did Jesus bear so despised a name? Ought we to be proud, when our great Lord was so humble? We are disposed to be ashamed of the meanness of our family, or circumstances, or education, and we are anxious to conceal such things from the world. This pride is very sinful, and comes to us from our first parents, who wished to be as gods. But Jesus has set his people an example of suffering contempt.

Evening Scripture portion. Prov. III. *Promise of direction.*

LUKE II. 41 to end.—*Christ among the doctors.*

WE only hear *one* anecdote of our Saviour in his childhood. We should like to hear many particulars concerning him in early life, but the Holy Spirit has caused us to know the things the *most* necessary, and it is more necessary that we should know what Christ said and did when he was a *minister* than when he was a *child.*

We find that his parents were accustomed to attend the passover at Jerusalem every year. The men were *commanded*, the women were *permitted* to attend this feast. At twelve years old it was the custom for boys to begin to accompany their parents, and at that age our Lord accompanied his parents.

The feast of the Passover continued seven days, during which time unleavened bread was eaten. The parents of Jesus fulfilled the days of the feast, that is, they remained *seven* days in Jerusalem, and then began to return homewards. There was a large company of persons

returning to Nazareth, distant about seventy-six miles from Jerusalem. The parents of Jesus at first supposed that the child was with some of their friends, till evening coming on, they sought him, and found him not. They returned with heavy hearts to Jerusalem, and found him in the temple. Altogether they had not seen him for three days; they had gone one day's journey and returned during another day, and they saw him again on the third.

What was Jesus doing in the temple? He was sitting in the midst of the doctors. These doctors were men learned in the scriptures, who explained them to the people: but they were not in general pious men. Was Jesus *teaching* the doctors? Far from it. He was listening to them: for it was the custom for these doctors to instruct the young people, asking them questions, and answering their inquiries.

But we naturally wonder why Jesus did not *inform* his parents of his intention to remain longer in Jerusalem. No doubt he knew that it was his heavenly Father's will that he should *not* tell them, for he would not have caused them any useless sorrow. Probably God wished to remind Mary by this circumstance, that her Son was come into this world to do a great work, and that she must expect to find him continually engaged in it. All parents ought to be ready to give up their children for God's service, and to part with them to a distance, even as missionaries in a foreign land, if it be God's will. When the mother of the famous Wesley was asked, whether she was willing to part with her two sons, to go as missionaries to America, she answered, "Had I ten sons, I should rejoice that they should be so employed."

Mary gently reproached her son with having caused her and Joseph so much anxiety, (verse 48.) Accustomed no doubt to the most affectionate behavior from him, she was surprised at any conduct that *appeared* unkind.

Our Lord answered, "How is it that ye sought me? Wist ye not, (or know ye not,) that I must be about my Father's business?"

This reply was full of the dignity that belonged to him, as the Son of God. In his obedience to his mother on other occasions, he set an example to *all* children, but in his conduct on this occasion, he acted as became the King of kings and Lord of lords.

But what was the business which our Saviour said that his Father had given him to do?

We can discover what it was from other parts of the Scriptures! What did he come down from heaven for? Was it for his own pleasure? No, it was to do his Father's work. This work was the salvation of sinful man. In order to accomplish this salvation, he fulfilled the law that we have broken, and suffered the punishment due to us for breaking it. He began to fulfil the law, as *soon* as he came into this world. While yet a child of twelve years old, he was intent upon his great work. Therefore he said to his parents, "Wist ye not that I must be about my Father's business?"

Has God sent us on any business? Yes! He has appointed to each of us a work to perform. A glorious work it is;—a work in which angels are always engaged, and of which they are never weary. It is *not* to accomplish our own salvation. That work Christ has done for all who believe in him. It is to promote the glory of God our Father. Yet who that looked around him and observed men's actions, would imagine that they had this work to do? What are the things about which men seem most anxious? Does not each seem to say, by his conduct, "How shall I please myself?" or "How shall I enrich myself?" or "How shall I gain credit to myself?" How few behave as if their chief desire was to *please God!* Yet is it not very sinful to be careless about pleasing him, who sent his Son to die for us? When that excellent minister, Dr. Payson, was on his dying bed, he said, "Oh how often have I begun the day thinking, 'How shall I please myself?' instead of 'How shall I please God?'"

Yet Payson had led a very holy life, and God had converted many sinners by him; but when a saint is dying he often sees his actions in a light in which he never saw them before. O that every one of us, now that life is before us, may seek to do our Father's business; for we know not how soon we may be called to render an account of the use we have made of our time upon earth.

Evening Scripture portion. 2 Cor. V. *Serving the Lord.*

MATT. III. 1–6.—*John preaches in the wilderness.*

WE hear nothing of John the Baptist during his youth, excepting that he was pious, and lived much in the deserts. When he was twenty-seven or thirty years of age he began to preach. He did not, however, go to the cities, but remained in the wilderness.

We may wonder how he found a congregation there. Probably his singular habits and his holy life had caused him to be much spoken of. He was clothed in a manner unlike persons of his station; for he wore a sort of cloth made of coarse camel's hair, and a leathern girdle; and he ate locusts, little animals, about an inch long, which, being nourished by leaves, are fit to eat; he fed also on honey, which is abundant in the woods and among the rocks of Judea. Men went into the wilderness to see him, and these bringing back a wonderful report of him, induced others to come, till at length crowds were collected to hear his sermons. God can easily draw people to hear his faithful ministers, if he will. No doubt John was rejoiced to behold such multitudes of persons, for he longed to point them all to the only Saviour.

What was the subject of his first sermons? Repentance! What is repentance? Is it change of conduct *only?* No; people who have never repented, sometimes reform their lives. A person may see it to be his *interest* to lead a better life, and for that reason he may amend. Is it sorrow for sin? Sorrow is *part* of repentance, but there is a sorrow that is not repentance; sorrow for the *consequences* of sin is not repentance. Saul, the king of Israel, was sorry when he heard he had lost his kingdom by disobedience, but he was not sorry for his *sin*, only for his *punishment*. True repentance is a change of mind and *heart*. A man who really repents, feels grieved because he has offended God, and he longs to serve God better in time to come.

Can a person change his *own* heart? It is impossible; therefore we know that repentance must be the gift of God. Yet John told the people to repent, because he knew that God was willing to bestow repentance.

The chief object of John's ministry was to announce the coming of the Lord. This he did when he said, "The kingdom of heaven is at hand." No doubt he explained to the people the meaning of this declaration. We may understand its meaning by comparing it with other parts of Scripture. When Satan tempted our first parents to eat the forbidden fruit, he set up his own kingdom upon the earth; he became the god of this world. But God sent his son to dethrone Satan, and establish his own kingdom. As soon as a sinner believes in Christ, he passes into the kingdom of heaven, or of Christ. St.Paul, in his epistle to the Colossians, speaking of the Father, says, "Who hath delivered us from the power of darkness and hath translated us into the kingdom of his dear Son."—Col. i. 13.

John the Baptist was like a herald who proclaims the approach of a glorious monarch, or like a pioneer who prepares his way through a desert. He knew that unless men repented of their sins, they would not receive the Saviour with gladness. He did not preach in vain. Many felt convinced of their sins, and anxious to be cleansed from their guilt and pollution; then they were baptized in Jordan, confessing their sins.

But could the waters of *Jordan* cleanse their souls? The waters of all the rivers in the world could not wash out one spot from the soul. Why then were they baptized? It had long been the custom for the Jews to baptize *heathens* who had forsaken idols for the worship of the true God. But John baptized the *Jews*, as a testimony that *they* also needed purification. At length he pointed to Jesus and cried, "Behold the Lamb of God which taketh away the sins of the world." It is the blood of that Lamb which cleanses from sin, and that blood alone. The saints in heaven are now clothed in pure and spotless garments. But was it *baptism* that made them white? Hear what the Scripture saith, "These are they which came out of great tribulation, and have washed their robes and made them white in the *blood of the Lamb*." —Rev. vii. 14.

Evening Scripture portion. Isaiah XL. 1–17. *Prophecy concerning John.*

MATT. III. 7–12.—*John warns the Pharisees and Sadducees.*

AMONG the people who came to hear John preach in the wilderness, were many of the Pharisees and the Sadducees. Curiosity drew them to hear that famous preacher. It will be well to stop a moment to inquire into the character of these men. They were called Pharisees and Sadducees, *not* because they belonged to foreign nations, (as we call some persons French and some English,) but because they had particular opinions on religious subjects; they belonged to two *sects* among the Jews.

The Pharisees professed to observe all God's laws concerning sacrifices, tithes, and ceremonies, and also many *other* laws which *men* had made; and they thought that by doing these things they should be worthy of places in heaven. At the same time they did not love God, but loved money and the praise of men. Such was the character of the Pharisees.

Are there any Pharisees in these days? There are none of us who do exactly the same things as the Pharisees did, but there are many who have the same kind of righteousness; they wish to be religious, or at least to *appear* religious, and therefore they read the Bible, go to church, take the sacrament; and they think they are the better for these services, while their hearts are still full of the love of pleasure, or of money, or of praise. There is only one way of salvation—it is by believing in Jesus Christ; when we believe in him, our sins are forgiven on account of his sufferings, and our hearts are made holy by his Spirit. Are there any of us who are endeavoring to deceive God by a little outward service? Let us give up the vain attempt—God will not be mocked; unless we really wish to forsake *all* our sins, we are hypocrites, like the Pharisees.

But who were the Sadducees? They were unbelieving men, proud of their understandings, and who thought themselves much wiser than common people. They said that there were no angels nor spirits, and no rising again of the dead; and they sneered at those people who believed all the wonderful things written in the Bible. They only professed to believe the first five books of the Bible, called the books of Moses. Are there any Sadducees now? Alas! there are too many who resemble them. Such persons are called infidels, or deists. They have written many wicked books for the purpose of turning the Bible into ridicule. Their writings are poison to the mind, and they have destroyed many souls. There are numerous proofs that the Bible is the Word of God. To mention only one or two; behold the desolation of Jerusalem and the scattering of the Jews according to God's prophecy.

When these self-righteous Pharisees and scoffing Sadducees came to hear John preach, was he afraid of them, because they were rich and learned? Did he preach elegant sermons to please them? No;

he spoke plainly and faithfully to them. He said, "O generation of vipers;" he called them the seed of the serpent, or the children of the devil; he said, "Who hath warned you to flee from the wrath to come?" he knew that because they were rich and learned, few would dare to warn them of the wrath to come; therefore out of love to their souls, *he* warned them. He did not tell them there was *no hope* for them, but he told them there was *no time* to lose. He knew that when he called them children of the devil, they would answer in their hearts, "We are the children of the pious Abraham, not of the devil; we have Abraham to our father." When ministers are preaching, people are very apt to be making some excuse in their hearts. John told the Pharisees that they would not be saved because they were the children of Abraham according to the *flesh*, for God could make the stones into Abraham's children; and God soon *did* make the *Gentiles*, whom the Jews despised as though they had been *stones*, into the children of Abraham in the *spirit*. Then John told them of their awful condition, while they were bringing forth bad fruit, or doing evil works. The axe, as it were, was laid ready to hew them down. Could we see death and judgment as near as they really are, we should tremble at the thought of continuing in sin.

St. Luke tells us in his gospel, (iii. 15,) that many people began to think that John was, perhaps, the Saviour so long expected—that is, the Christ, or the anointed one. Did John wish them to think this? No; he wished no glory for himself; he said that *his* baptism was nothing compared to that which Jesus would bestow. John could wash the *body* with water as a *sign* of repentance, but Jesus could wash the *soul* with the Holy Ghost; he could even cleanse it, as by fire. There is nothing cleanses like fire; *water* can not cleanse *gold* from its dross, but *fire* can. The Spirit of Christ can consume our sins, as fire consumes dross.

Then John showed the terrible consequences of not believing in this Saviour. He compared Jesus (v. 12) to a thrasher, who separates the wheat from the chaff. We are accustomed to hear of the *meek and gentle* Saviour, and so he is, for he wipes away the tear of the penitent, and binds up the wound of the broken-hearted; but he is also the *holy* Jesus; he cannot bear *proud* sinners, and at the last day his wrath against them will be so terrible, that they will call upon the rocks and mountains to hide them from the wrath of the Lamb. (Rev. vi.)

Evening Scripture portion. Phil. III. ***The righteousness of Christ.***

Luke III. 10–14.—*John instructs various classes in their duties.*

We have seen that John the Baptist was a very faithful preacher; one who spoke to the *rich* as well as to the *poor* of their sins; but we do not hear that the Pharisees and Sadducees took warning from his sermons; yet there were some persons who did. The people (that is, the common people, as they are called) said, "What shall we do, then?" What did they mean by this question? Did they mean, "What shall we do to be *saved?*" No, that was not the question. We read, in the Acts, of a penitent jailer who said to the apostle Paul and his friend Silas, "Sirs, what must I do to be *saved?*" And they replied, "Believe on the Lord Jesus Christ, and thou shalt be saved." (Acts xvi. 31.) No doubt John would have answered the people in the same manner, if they had asked him the same question; he would have said, "Believe in him who cometh after me."

But the people did *not* ask this question. John had just been exhorting them to bring forth *fruits* worthy of repentance, and had been telling them that every tree that brought forth bad *fruit* was cast into the fire. By fruit, you well know that he meant good works. John wanted the people to show by their conduct that their repentance was sincere. It must have gladdened his heart, when, after his sermons, they came to inquire *what* good works they ought to do. It is a good sign when people ask questions about their duties.

John, by his answer, shows us what was the *chief* sin of the people. He said, "He that hath two coats, let him impart to him that hath none, and he that hath meat let him do likewise." The chief sin of the people was covetousness. These people were not all of them rich. Covetousness was the sin of the *poor*, as well as of the rich. As we read in Jer. viii. 10, "Every one, from the least, even unto the greatest, is given to covetousness."

Is this sin still very common? It is. People's hearts are still wrapped up in their property—their money, their clothes, their houses, their furniture, or their lands, whether they have little or much. People are so fond of their property that they are loath to part with any of it. But the word of God tells us that we should be ready to give—that we should even *labor* that we *may* have something to give. (Eph. iv. 28; Acts xx. 34, 35.)

Perhaps it will be asked, "Is it wrong to have *two* sets of clothes?" No; the expression "two coats," need not be taken *literally*. What then does it signify? That those who have *more* than enough for themselves, ought to give to those who have *less* than enough. The Scriptures do not *forbid* our saving against old age or sickness; but they *command* us to give to those who are in need. God will never suffer any one to languish in distress through following this command; he will raise up friends for them in the time of need. "Blessed is the man that considereth the poor." (Ps. xli. 1.) Cast thy bread upon the waters, for thou shalt find it after many days. (Eccles. xi. 1.)

There was a poor servant who gave all her money to her destitute parents, she was overtaken by sickness early in life; she became unfit for service, and had no means of support; but God put it into the heart of the Rev. Thomas Scott (who wrote the Commentary on the Bible) to take her into his house, and, though not rich himself, with the aid of some of his friends, he gladly supported her all her days, thinking it a blessing to have so pious a person in his family. Where could she have passed her life in greater peace than beneath the roof of a faithful minister?

If people spend their money, when young, in pleasures, in fine dress, or in useless things, there is no promise for *them* to depend upon; but if they delight in giving for God's sake to the poor, they shall never be forsaken.

The *publicans* also asked John what they must do. These publicans were not like the publicans of these days; they did not keep public-houses; they collected the *public* taxes for the Romans. Their chief sin was *dishonesty*. They made people pay more taxes than the government required, and by their impositions they enriched themselves. In most trades and employments there is some temptation to dishonesty, and many people think that they may do whatever it is the *custom* to do. Let each of us inquire, "Is there any thing I do in my station, that I wish to conceal from my master or my customer?" *That* practice is *dishonest*, however *common* it may be. If you really repent, you will leave it off, though others should call you over strict and precise, and even try to injure you, because your conduct is a reproach to them.

Some *soldiers* next inquired what they must do. Does it surprise us to find that even *soldiers* had been moved by John's preaching? War is a terrible calamity. Were all men true Christians, there would be no war; yet John did not tell the soldiers to leave off being soldiers, for the *guilt* of unjust wars lies rather upon those who begin and continue them, even kings and rulers, than upon the men who are hired to fight. John warned the soldiers against the sins most common in their profession. One of these was violence; the soldiers were apt to take things away by force; therefore John said, "Do violence to no man." They were also accustomed to accuse others falsely before the judges, perhaps for the sake of bribes; therefore he said, "Nor accuse any man falsely." They were also disposed to be discontented with their pay; therefore he said, "Be content with your wages."

Should *we* like to inquire of John the Baptist what *we* ought to do? He would not give us all the *same* answer; he would point out *different* duties to us according to our station, as servants or masters, parents or children; or according to our trade or profession. But need we wish that John the Baptist were risen from the dead, that he might instruct us? Let us look into the epistles of Paul and Peter, and we shall find directions to servants and masters, to parents and children. Servants are desired to be meek, honest, and submissive; masters to be just and kind; children to be obedient and respectful. Parents are commanded to bring up their children piously, and not to provoke them to wrath. Young men are instructed to be sober-minded; young women to be keepers at home. Older men and women are warned against the love of wine. (See the epistles to Titus, and to the Colossians, and the first epistle of Peter.) Thus we are all set on our guard against the temptations of our age and station.

No doubt if people had come *separately* to John, he would have given still more particular directions. *Each* of *us* has some *particular* sin into which he is very apt to fall; one is most disposed to anger, another to vanity, another to envy, another to idleness, and another to intemperance.

We shall never *deserve* heaven by leaving off our sins; it is Christ who has purchased heaven by his blood to bestow it on those who believe in his name. But if we do *really* believe we shall bring forth good fruit, and forsake our sins. It is God only that can change our hearts; but we must not *wait* till we *feel* right *feelings*, before we *begin* to *act* right. We must avoid every thing that we know to be wrong, and entreat God to overcome the evil feelings of our hearts, (which *we* cannot subdue,) and to enable us to do that which is pleasing in his sight.

Evening Scripture portion. Titus II. ***Relative duties.***

MATT. III. 13, to the end.—*The baptism of Christ.*

ONE of the most wonderful events ever transacted on this earth is recorded in this passage.

We behold the Son of God in great humility coming to be baptized of John, as though he had been a sinner; and we behold the Everlasting Father and the Spirit, honoring him with unspeakable honor. Well might John be surprised to see the Son of God apply to him for baptism! He objected to baptizing one so much greater than himself, saying, "I have need to be baptized of thee, and comest thou to me?" It appears, therefore, that John knew who he was; yet we read in St. John's gospel (i. 33) that he knew him not; God therefore must have made John know him at the *time* of the baptism. It may appear strange that John should not have known him, as Elizabeth, his mother, was the cousin of Mary, the mother of Jesus; but then we must remember that they had been brought up in distant parts of the land. God had wise reasons for not permitting them to be known to each other till this time. If John had known Jesus before as a relation, it might then have been supposed that he had been deceived by him; but now that he had never seen him, no deception could be suspected.

How full of reverence and humility were John's words—"I have need to be baptized of thee,"—*baptized*, not with *water*, (for Jesus baptized none in this manner,) but with the Holy Ghost and with fire.

The angel had declared that John should be filled with the Holy Ghost, even before his birth ; still John felt his need of the Saviour's baptism. Does not this teach us that we *all* need this baptism continually ? Though we have been baptized with water, though we have even undergone a change of heart, yet still we need fresh supplies of the Holy Spirit. If we *feel* our need, we shall come often to Jesus, that he may baptize us. Blessed Jesus, we have need to be baptized of thee !

What was the Saviour's *reason* for coming to be baptized ? He condescends to explain it—" Thus, it becometh us to fulfil all righteousness." It was God's will that *all men* should be baptized, and therefore it was necessary that Jesus, when he was a man, should be baptized, for he came to do *all* God's commands, that by *his* obedience many might be made righteous. Whom did our Saviour mean by *us*, when he said, " It becometh *us* to fulfil all righteousness ?" Himself and John. It was necessary that John should do the will of God, and baptize him whose shoes he was not worthy to bear. True Christians feel their unworthiness to do any thing for their Master, but this feeling ought not to hinder them from doing God's work ; for they would not be *fit* to do it, unless they *felt* their exceeding sinfulness.

Immediately after the baptism, the Saviour came out of the water. We find in St. Luke's gospel, what he was doing as he came out ; he was *praying*. When sinners were baptized, they confessed their sins ; but he had no sins to confess.

After he had humbled himself by being baptized, his Father exalted him by sending the Holy Spirit down upon him, and by declaring, " This is my beloved Son, in whom I am well pleased."

What must John the Baptist have felt when he beheld this scene ! Here were no terrors like those on Mount Sinai ; here were no thunders nor lightnings ; no blackness, and darkness, and tempest ; all was light, and peace, and love. It is wonderful to think, that a mortal man should have been permitted to witness such a display of the divine glory. But as John was appointed to direct men to the Saviour, it was right that he should receive the strongest proof of his being the Son of God. And could he have received *stronger* proof than he did receive on the banks of Jordan ? Impossible.

What exceeding love is expressed in the words, " This is my beloved Son, in whom I am well pleased !" This declaration must have comforted the heart of the man of sorrows ; though the world hated him, he knew the Father loved him. Would it comfort us to think the Father loved us, and was well pleased with us ? If we believe in Jesus he *does* love us, and *is* well pleased with us for *his sake*. All believers are " accepted in the beloved !" What sweet words are those! They have sustained the children of God in a dying hour. How could any man bear the thought of entering God's presence, were it not for the assurance that the Father will receive him in the name of his own beloved Son!

Evening Scripture portion. Eph. I. "*Accepted in the beloved.*"

MATT. IV. 1–7.—*The temptation of Christ.*

WE have read of the great honor that Christ received at his baptism. Immediately afterwards, he was exposed to terrible sufferings and temptations. It is God's method often to prepare his people for great sufferings, by granting them great consolations beforehand. Jesus was "led up of the spirit into the wilderness to be tempted of the devil." He fasted forty days and forty nights. He was alone amidst the wild beasts of the desert; as it is written in Mark i. 13, " he was with the wild beasts." This wilderness was probably the same as that through which Moses led the Israelites. We are told in Deut. viii. 15, what kind of a place it was; a place " wherein were fiery serpents, scorpions, and drought, where there was no water." The prophet Jeremiah calls " it a land of deserts and pits; of the shadow of death, that no man passed through, and where no man dwelt," (ii. 6.) But what was more terrible than all, when Jesus was there, Satan came to assail him with temptations. He had just heard the Father's voice; he had just been anointed by the Holy Spirit! Behold him now in this horrible place, with his more horrible enemy, Satan.

Now observe, that it is said that he was led up of the *Spirit.* It was his Father's will that he should meet Satan as an enemy in battle. He had come into the world to destroy his works, and to bruise this serpent's head, according to God's threatening to Satan in paradise. "The seed of the woman shall bruise thy head." Satan probably hoped to overcome Jesus, as he had overcome Adam and Eve; but though he could not overcome him, he did give him pain; for it is written, concerning Christ, " He *suffered* being tempted," (Heb. ii. 18.) It will be very interesting for us to consider his temptations, especially as Satan still offers the same temptations to Christ's people that he once offered to Christ himself. These temptations will show us how he tries to draw away those who have escaped from his chains. The world in general are led captive by him according to his will; he finds it easy to keep them in his power; but O! what pains he takes to regain his sway over those who have left his service! Let us consider the first temptation that he offered to our Saviour. He said, " If thou be the Son of God, command these stones that they be made bread." Observe the *time* at which he made the proposal; when Jesus was an *hungered.* Why did Jesus refuse to turn the stones into bread? Because his Father had engaged to provide him with bread; therefore he needed not to use his divine power in supplying his own wants.

Satan often attacks the people of God in times of deep affliction. When they are sorely diseased, or when their children are dying, or when they know not how to provide them with food, or when they are disappointed or unkindly treated; then the malicious fiend insinuates hard thoughts of God into the mind. He would fain make them believe that God has forgotten them, that their troubles will never end, that there is no way of escape, and that they must try to help themselves, even by some *wrong* means. If there seem a way of helping themselves by doing something not quite upright, not quite open, or honest, not quite according to the commands of God, Satan recommends them to take that away, assuring them, that if they are too conscientious, they will never get out of their difficulties. But how did our Saviour overcome this temptation? He referred to the word of God, and answered from Deut. viii., "Man shall not live by bread alone, but by every word that proceedeth out of the mouth of God." What is the meaning of this passage? It declares that the word of God is more than bread; bread cannot keep us alive, when God chooses that we shall die; but God can keep us alive without bread, when He chooses that we shall live. We know also that God can make us happy in the greatest affliction; but nothing can make us happy, if God wills that we shall be unhappy. Have we not seen persons miserable in the midst of abundance, and happy in the midst of pains and losses? Let us never listen to Satan's wicked counsel, when he would induce us to sin that we may escape from suffering. He is deceiving us. When the sin is committed, we shall find ourselves in a far worse case than we were before.

The second temptation was exactly the opposite of the first. Satan took Christ to the pinnacle, or high tower of the temple in the holy city of Jerusalem. He there tried to deceive him by quoting Scripture; he referred to a passage in Ps. xci., "He shall give his angels charge concerning thee;" but he left out the words, "To keep thee in all thy ways." Yet these are very important, and ought not to be left out. God will command his angels to guard the Christian from harm *in all his ways*, that is, in all the ways in which he *ought* to walk. Had Jesus cast himself down from the temple, he would not have been walking in God's ways, but in Satan's ways.

This is the manner in which Satan tries to deceive the Christian, when he sees him full of confidence in God. He then tempts him to presumption: he would persuade him that he need not watch and pray, but that he may go into worldly scenes, and receive no harm. He says to him, "Has not God promised to keep you from falling, and to preserve you to his heavenly kingdom? Has he not said, 'I will never leave thee nor forsake thee?'" Thus he perverts the word of God. This is a very dangerous moment for the Christian. Let him then remember what his Lord replied to Satan; these words from Deuteronomy, "Thou shalt not tempt the Lord thy God." We tempt God to forsake us, when we thus presume upon his promises. The apostle says, in 1 Cor. x., "Let him that thinketh he standeth take heed lest he fall." We have heard of Peter's sin: he ventured to follow Jesus into the palace of the High Priest, and to warm himself among the ungodly servants, thinking that he could never deny his Master; thus he tempted the Lord, and he *did* deny him.

What dangers there are on the right hand and on the left! One moment we sink into distrust; the next, soar into presumption. Let us watch and pray, that we enter not into temptation.

Evening Scripture portion. Deut. VIII. ***The wilderness.***

MATT. IV. 8–11.—*The same continued.*

THOUGH Jesus had resisted *two* temptations, Satan was not dismayed. Here we have an instance of the *perseverance* of our great enemy. Though he may have failed in one attempt to injure us, he will make another, and sometimes he succeeds better the second time than he did the first. Balaam resisted the *first* temptation, and refused to go with Balak's messengers; but he was tempted a *second* time, and then he yielded. The man of God from Judah refused the invitation of Jeroboam, but was enticed by the solicitation of the old prophet. Satan was not discouraged when Job was patient under his first trials: he asked God to permit him to assault him again; but that *second* time he still failed to tempt Job to curse his God. We ought to learn, from these facts, to be very watchful after we have overcome one temptation, and to be ready for another attack.

There is one circumstance in the third temptation which may surprise us. Satan proposed a more glaring sin to our Lord than he had proposed before; for it is a much more glaring sin to fall down and worship Satan than to turn stones into bread, or to run unnecessarily into danger. How could Satan suppose that when Jesus had refused to commit those sins, he would consent to so flagrant a transgression as worshipping the devil? Perhaps he saw that it was vain to try to *deceive* our Saviour; therefore he declared his purpose, and hoped to persuade by the greatness of the *bribe*. He had not offered him such a *reward* before, as the kingdoms of the world: he had ruined the first Adam by promising him a *reward* for disobedience, and he hoped to ruin the second Adam by the same means.

What is that glory of the kingdoms of the world which Satan displayed before our Lord?

It may be divided into three principal points—pleasure, profit, and praise: these tempt men to forsake God's service. It is *not true* that

Satan can give them to whom he will. When Satan offered them to Christ, he offered what it was not in his power to bestow. In saying that he could bestow them, he acted in his own character of a liar and the father of lies. It is, however, true, that God often permits the servants of Satan to enjoy the vain delights of this world: thus we read in the Psalms, that the wicked are often in prosperity.

How did Jesus overcome the last temptation? By the word of God, which is the sword of the Spirit. He spoke *openly* to Satan, and declared that God had commanded that men should worship him *alone*. He did not dispute with the tempter, or tell him that the world was not his to bestow, or that it was a perishing portion, but he simply appealed to the *command* of God. Thus we are taught how to meet Satan's temptations. We ought not to stand questioning; but we should remember the *command* of God, and not take any step in life, or follow any course which will lead us into sin. How many warnings are there in the Scriptures against the love of the world, its pleasures, its profit, and its praise. This is what the Scripture says of worldly *pleasure*, (1 Tim. v. 6,) "She that liveth in *pleasure*, is dead while she liveth." One of our most faithful female missionaries, Mrs. Judson, was first aroused when a vain and worldly girl, by reading this sentence. Afterwards she went to the East, and suffered great persecution for the truth's sake, and now she is with God, drinking rivers of pleasure at his right hand. And what does the Scripture say against the love of profit, or of *money?* 1 Tim. vi. 10. "*Which*, (that is, *money*,) while some have coveted after, they have erred from the faith, and pierced themselves through with many sorrows." Now hear what is said of those who seek human *praise*. We read in John xii. 42, 43, of some who believed in Christ, and yet would not confess him, lest they should be put out of the synagogue; "for they loved the *praise* of men more than the praise of God."

Satan will offer these things to our acceptance, (not *all* of them, but *little portions* of them,) upon condition that we worship him, that is, do his will in some respect; for he cares not for *knee*-worship; he knows that we are really the servants of *him* whom we *obey*, and not of him whom we *call* Master. May the Lord give us grace to resist, through our Captain, who has overcome, and is set down upon his throne.

How soon the blessed Saviour found obedience to be sweet! The angels came, and fed him. Thus God will more than make up to us, even in *this* life, all we give up for his sake. When he has filled our hearts with the peace which passeth all understanding, we shall not regret the loss of any earthly thing!

Evening Scripture portion. Gen. III. ***The fall of man.***

John I. 19–34.—*The record of John concerning Christ in Bethabara.*

During the time of the Lord's temptation, John was preaching in the wilderness. Many supposed he was the promised Saviour; for though he did no miracle, (John x. 41,) he was evidently a very wonderful prophet. There were in Jerusalem seventy chief men, who met together to consult about public matters, and who were ealled the council, or the Sanhedrim. These Jews were proud and unbelieving. They sent a company of priests and Levites to ask John who he was, probably supposing that he would readily answer persons who filled holy offices, especially as he himself was a priest. But he did not wish men to honor him, and he plainly told these priests he was not the Christ. Then they wanted to know whether he was Elias or Elijah; for Malachi the prophet had declared that Elijah should come before Christ came, (iv. 5, 6.) But though John had come in the spirit and power of Elijah, he was not Elijah himself. The priests then asked him whether he was *that* prophet. *What* prophet did they mean? They meant to ask whether John was *any* one of the old prophets risen from the dead. He declared that he was not, and then told them who he was: A voice crying in the wilderness. But these priests were not satisfied with the answer: they wanted to know why he baptized, as if he were some great person, and had great authority. As they were of the sect of the Pharisees—those formal self-righteous persons—they must have been much offended with John for having once called them a generation of vipers. John took this occasion to praise the Lord Jesus, and to speak of his greatness. He even told them that he stood among them, though they knew him not.

The next day John was able to point out the unknown Saviour to the people who surrounded him; but we are not told whether these priests were still near or not. How remarkable is the name by which he called his Lord! "The Lamb of God." Why did he give him this name? Was it because he was meek and gentle? Not chiefly for that reason; but because he was to be sacrificed for the sins of men. A lamb was offered up at the temple every morning and evening; its blood could not take away sin; but there was a Lamb whose blood could take away the sins of the *world!* Consider how immense the sum of the sins of the world must be! The sins that one of us commits in one day are very numerous. If all our proud thoughts could be known, and all our rebellious feelings against God could be exposed, how vast would be the amount! But consider what millions of millions of men have lived on this earth; what treachery, what blasphemy, what murders, what idolatry, have defiled it in every place, at every moment. Yet all these multiplied crimes Jesus can take away; so great is the power of his blood. O that all the world would *come* to the Lamb of God, that they might *all* be cleansed from their innumerable transgressions.

Evening Scripture portion. Numb. XXVIII. 1–25. *The daily burnt-offerings.*

JOHN I. 35–42.—*Andrew leads Simon to Christ.*

IT was with great delight that John the Baptist pointed sinners to the Saviour. He had no greater joy than to see men leave him to follow Christ. On one occasion he saw the Lord, probably at some distance from the place where he stood, and he pointed him out to two of his disciples; for John had disciples, or persons who followed him to learn his doctrine. He was more pleased that they should follow the great Master, than that they should stay with him. Behold in John the spirit of true religion! The faithful minister does not wish to be admired himself, but tries to persuade all to admire Christ.

Who were these two disciples? One of them was called Andrew: but we are not informed of the name of the other. *Perhaps* the other was that John who was afterwards called the disciple whom Jesus loved. One reason for thinking so is, that he wrote this account, and it is usual with him not to mention his own *name*, when he refers to himself.

It signifies little, however, to us, what were the names of these disciples. Let us imitate their blessed examples. See them following Jesus. At first his back was towards them; but he knew well they were following him, and soon gave them kind encouragement. He said, "What seek ye?" They replied, "Master, where dwellest thou?" It was not from curiosity they desired to see his abode, but that they might know him and converse with him. How sweet were the hours which they spent with their Saviour in his lowly dwelling, his cottage in the wilderness!

Would he welcome *us*, as he did those disciples? Yes; he says *to us*, as he did to them, "Come and see." Are we willing to go? Do we desire to know him, and to taste his grace? He will meet us in secret prayer, and make himself known to our hearts. But does he ever find us in prayer? or are we so taken up with the world, that we have no time to seek the Lord?

Let us observe the conduct of one of these disciples after he had found the Saviour. "He first findeth his own brother Simon." How anxious he was to bring his dear brother to the knowledge of his precious friend! He tells him what a treasure he himself has found, and invites his brother to share it. Are we acting thus? Are we trying to persuade our kindred and our friends to come to Christ? What pains some have taken to bring brothers or sisters to Christ! they have sent them letter after letter—they have visited them in sickness;

have persuaded them to hear faithful ministers—have prayed without ceasing to bless their efforts. David Nasmith, the founder of town-missions, sent a letter every week to his ungodly brother, till at length he brought him to Christ.

As soon as Simon approached the Saviour, he received encouragement. Jesus gave him a new name, to describe the new character he should bear. He called him Cephas, or Peter, which the one in Hebrew, and the other Greek, signifies "a stone."

And why was Simon to be called "a stone?"

The Lord intended to build a great temple of living stones, that is, of believers, and he chose Simon to be one of the foundation-stones. He purposed to make him a great preacher, so that many should believe through his word, and thus be built upon him; therefore he compared him to a "stone."

The scriptures declare that the saints "are built upon the foundation of the apostles and prophets, Jesus Christ himself being the chief corner-stone; in whom all the building fitly framed together groweth unto a holy temple in the Lord."—Eph. ii. 20, 21.

Jesus knows each of us as well as he knew Simon. He knows whether we are living stones in this glorious temple, or whether we are like the rubbish lying round the building, to be swept away when it is finished.

Evening Scripture portion. Is. LV. ***Invitation to come to Christ.***

JOHN I. 43 to end.—*Philip leads Nathanael to Christ.*

IT is very interesting to know how holy men were brought to the knowledge of Christ. In this passage we have an account of the means by which Philip and Nathanael were first led to their Saviour. Jesus himself found Philip, and said, "Follow me." Have we heard the voice of Jesus thus speaking to our hearts? He *does* thus call to us from heaven. May we have grace to reply, "Lord, I will follow thee." When David heard the Lord say, "Seek ye my face," he replied, "Thy face, Lord, will I seek." (Ps. xxvii.)

Philip acted as Andrew had done before; he endeavored to persuade his friend to come to Jesus. He behaved openly and frankly to Nathanael; he did not conceal from him that the Lord he had found was called Jesus of Nazareth. Nathanael was prejudiced against Nazareth because of the bad character of its inhabitants, and naturally exclaimed, "Can any good thing come out of Nazareth?" Philip did not stop to argue with him, but said, "Come and see." He was full of hope that the same word which had such power with him would convince Nathanael also. Philip sets us an example how to behave to our relations and friends. It is better to say, "Come and see," than to argue much with them. Let us try and persuade them to read the Bible which has taught us to pray to that God who has had mercy on us. If we can only induce them "to come and see," to apply to the Lord themselves, we may feel sure that they will be brought to the knowledge of the true Saviour.

With what great kindness did the Lord treat Nathanael! He knew that he had doubts, and he removed them. He did this in a very remarkable way. When he saw him coming he described his character. "Behold an Israelite indeed, in whom there is no guile or deceit." By saying this, he showed Nathanael he was acquainted with his secret thoughts. He declared that Nathanael was a *sincere* man: this was great praise. Jesus had seen many hypocrites, but he had seen few *sincere* persons. It is very uncommon to be sincere. Most persons *think* they are sincere. They will say, "Though I do not pretend to be religious, yet I am not a hypocrite—I am sincere." But these people deceive themselves. Let us consider what it is to be sincere. It is to be really anxious to find out our sins, and to forsake them. The sincere man says, with David, "Search me, O God, and know my heart: try me, and know my *thoughts*, and see if there be any wicked way in me, and lead me in the way everlasting." Ps. cxxxix. 23, 24. The sincere man desires that every evil *thought* may be taken away; he longs to have his *heart* cleansed; therefore he is often in prayer to God, confessing his sins. As soon as he *suspects* that any of his practices are wrong, he inquires whether they really are sinful; and if he finds they are contrary to God's word, he forsakes them, however much he may lose by giving them up. Is this a *common* character? Is this *our* character? Do we *thus* walk with God? Does Jesus say of you or me, "Behold an Israelite indeed, in whom there is no guile?"

Nathanael was surprised to find that Jesus knew him, but he was more astonished still when he discovered that he had seen him under the fig-tree. No doubt he had been confessing his sins beneath the shade of a thick fig-tree, where no human eye could see him. God had answered his prayers, by leading him to the Saviour. Nathanael could no longer doubt; he acknowledged Jesus to be the Son of God, the King of Israel.

Then Jesus promised that the day should come when he should see angels ascending and descending upon the Son of man. To what day did he refer? Was it not to the day when he will come again in the glory of his Father with all his holy angels? Both his enemies and his friends will then perceive that he is the Son of God. *Every eye* shall see Him, (Rev. I.) Some shall wail when they see Him whom they despised and neglected, sitting on the throne of judgment; but *some* will *rejoice* when they behold *Him* to whom they often prayed under fig-trees or in closets, sitting on his throne of glory amidst ten thousand times ten thousand angels. Are there any here who often pray to Christ in secret? Is it not a comfort to you to think that he sees you, and that he will acknowledge you as his children at the great day?

Evening Scripture portion. Ps. CXXXIX. *God's all-seeing eye.*

JOHN II. 1–10.—*Jesus turns water into wine.*

THE Lord Jesus began his ministry by a miracle. Several of his disciples beheld this display of his power. It is probable Nathanael was one of them; for though he is not mentioned in the list of the twelve apostles, it is generally supposed that Bartholomew, the apostle, was the same person as Nathanael.

When Jesus had been three days in Galilee he went to a marriage feast. It is plain, therefore, that there are some feasts to which it is not sinful to go. We are sure, however, that Jesus would not have gone to a feast where there was profaneness, drunkenness, or rioting; nor would the newly-married have invited such a holy guest, if they had intended to give an unholy feast. Wine was the common drink of the land of Canaan, and was not so strong as the wine used in this country, which is mixed with brandy. As grapes grew in the fields of Canaan, wine was so cheap that even poor people could afford to drink it. It is probable that the newly-married were poor persons, because Jesus himself, as well as his disciples, was poor, and he had not yet become celebrated as a prophet. Poverty may have prevented them from providing sufficient wine for the company. When the store was exhausted, the mother of Jesus spoke to him as if she expected her son to provide more by a miracle; she said, "They have no wine." The Lord's answer may *appear* disrespectful, but it was not so. In the Eastern countries "woman" is as respectful a title as "madam" would be here; and even princesses are thus addressed. When Jesus said, "Woman, what have I to do with thee, mine hour is not yet come;" he meant to show his mother, that though he had obeyed her commands in common things, he could not be directed by her in his *heavenly* Father's business. He had told her this when he was a child, and was found by her in the temple. The Roman Catholics, therefore, much mistake when they entreat Mary to *command* her Son to bestow blessings on them.

And do not *we* also mistake when we venture to dictate to Jesus?—when we think he *ought* to give us any blessing, or remove any affliction? When we thus think in our hearts, let us hear Jesus addressing us in these words: "What have I to do with thee; mine hour is not yet come." Perhaps He may intend to do what we desire; but we must not hasten him, his *own* time is the best.

The mother of our Lord still expected that her Son would do some wonderful deed, and she said to the servants, "Whatsoever *he* saith unto you, do it." This was a safe command to give. We may say this to each other at all times. "Whatsoever *he* saith unto you, do it."

You know that the Jews had many customs about purifying or washing themselves: some of these customs were commanded by God, and some were invented by men. They always kept large jars for water in their houses. These jars Jesus desired the servants to fill; they obeyed without questioning, and even drew out the water to hand to the ruler of the feast, without knowing what they presented. The jars were filled to the *brim*, so that it was certain that no wine could be added secretly to the water.

The ruler of the feast was a man who had the management of it intrusted to him by the bridegroom. He was surprised to taste such excellent wine, and calling the bridegroom, expressed his surprise that he should have kept the good wine until the *last*, when men usually give the *best* wine *first*, as the flavor is most relished at the beginning of a feast. In this speech the ruler bore witness, without intending it, to the excellence of Christ's works, and gave his testimony to the perfection of the miracle.

How benevolent a miracle this was! It showed forth Christ's tender concern for our comfort even in the smallest matters; though he would not turn the stones into bread to satisfy his own hunger, he turned water into wine to supply the guests at the marriage feast. But his chief purpose in working this miracle was to show forth his glory as the Son of God, that his people might believe in him to everlasting life. He can bestow upon us that *wine* which will make our hearts glad throughout eternity. All who come to him will find reason to say, "Thou hast kept the good wine until now." It is his method to keep the best things to the *last:* but it is Satan's method to do the reverse. The children of this world have their best things *first*. They find life grow darker and darker as they advance; their youthful days are their happiest, (they confess this themselves;) cares soon overcloud them, disappointments depress them, infirmities overtake them; the gloom continually increases, till it ends in the darkness of the grave. Such is the worldling's portion. Satan gives the *good* wine first, and *then* that which is *worse*. What a miserable portion is the world!

Christ deals just in a contrary manner: "The path of the just is as the shining light, which shineth *more* and *more* unto the perfect day." Every truly religious person finds his happiness increase with his age; so that he would not be as he was once, no, not for the sake of again possessing youth, and health, and relations, and comforts, which he may now have lost. The *more* religious he becomes, the *more* happy he finds himself. Even upon *earth* he begins to say, "Thou hast kept the good wine until now." What then will he say in *heaven*, when he drinks of the fruit of the vine with his Saviour; that is, when he partakes of the sweetness of redeeming love in all its perfection! This happiness is offered to us. Shall we reject it, and prefer looking for our happiness from a world which is withering in our grasp?

Evening Scripture portion. Prov. IV. *The path of the just.*

JOHN II. 11–17.—*Christ purifies the temple.*

AFTER working his first miracle, the Lord Jesus went to Capernaum, a city in Galilee, but he did not take up his abode there at present. Highly favored city, to be so early and so often visited by the Son of God! Truly she was exalted unto heaven, so great were her privileges. Do not we also enjoy very great privileges—*we*, who hold the word of God in our hands? May we profit more from our privileges than Capernaum did from hers!

Shortly after visiting this city, the Lord travelled up to Jerusalem, to keep the passover. In the gospel of St. John, all the passovers from this time till the Lord's death are recorded. It is by counting them, that it has been discovered how long Jesus exercised his ministry, and at what age he died. He became a minister at thirty, his ministry lasted three years and a half; and he died at the age of thirty-three years and a half.

When he was at Jerusalem at the passover, he made a public display of his power and holiness. The *courts* of the temple (not the very temple itself) were crowded by those who brought beasts and birds for sacrifices, and also by those who changed Roman money for Jewish coins, to be cast into the treasury. No doubt these traders in animals and money excused themselves for making God's house a place of trade by the thought of the holy use for which the animals and money were designed. But this excuse was not sufficient in God's sight. His temple was called a house of *prayer*, and it was made into a house of *merchandise*. He was displeased by the disturbance given to his worship, and by the disrespect shown to himself. And may there not be customs common among Christians which are displeasing to God? We may have excuses ready to offer for our conduct; but are they *such* as will be received at the day of judgment?

It was wonderful that the people selling animals and changing money submitted to the authority of a poor and almost unknown man, armed only with a whip, and unsupported by the rulers. But such divine power accompanied his words and his actions, and such terror from the Lord spread among the multitude, that the traders fled before him. At the same time, Jesus openly declared that he was the Son of God, for he called the temple his "*Father's* house." The disciples were much struck by their Lord's conduct; they were no doubt astonished to see one usually so meek and gentle, acting with so much boldness and courage. Then they remembered a sentence in the Psalms, describing the character of the expected Messiah: "The zeal of thine house hath eaten me up." (Ps. lxix. 9.) What is the meaning of this verse? *Zeal* signifies an ardent desire. Jesus was full of zeal, but on what account? For God's house. By "house" we understand not only the temple, but God's service, his people, his commandments, and all that belongs to him. A zeal for God's house means an ardent desire for his glory. Jesus had so strong a zeal that it ate him up, or consumed him. It is common to say, "Such a one is swallowed up of grief." It might be said of Jesus that he was swallowed up with a desire for God's honor. This was his chief desire, his ruling passion.

How different from this zeal is the desire that fills us by nature. By nature, we are eaten up with a zeal, not for God's house, but for our *own* pleasure, and honor, and interest. This is the reason that we take up so warmly any insult offered to *ourselves*, but are so indifferent respecting insults offered to God. If any person reproach us, or injure us, we turn in our minds how we can prevent his continuing to annoy us. We are uneasy and restless till we can defend ourselves. But how do we feel when we hear of God's commands being broken? Are we anxious to find out some way of stopping the evil? Do we feel as David did, when he said, "My zeal hath consumed me, because mine enemies keep not thy law;" or when he said, "Rivers of waters run down mine eyes, because they keep not thy law?" O that such a spirit dwelt in us! If we love God, we do feel *something* of this grief already. There are some among our magistrates and rulers who openly speak for God, and are ready to bear scorn and hatred for His sake; for all must be prepared for such treatment who endeavor to prevent the commission of sin. Faithful ministers, who oppose plays, fairs, and wakes, and other popular amusements, and who speak in the pulpit against sabbath-breaking, intemperance, and all ungodliness, are generally hated on that account. Even Jesus was hated, because he testified of the world that its works were evil. The reproaches of those that reproached God fell upon him. (Ps. lxix. 9.) May we hate evil as he did, though men should hate *us* also. If we sincerely hate sin, we shall hate it *most* in our *own* hearts, and ask God to cleanse them, and to render us vessels meet for the Master's use.

Evening Scripture portion. Ps. LXIX. ***Zeal for God's house.***

JOHN II. 18 to end. *Christ speaks of the temple of his body.*

How could the Jews desire a *sign* of Christ's right to clear the temple of the traders? What could have enabled him to send out these profane men but the power of God? Was not that a sign of his authority? Yet still the Jews, or the chief men of Jerusalem, desired a sign; but Christ refused to give them any, except that great sign of his own resurrection from the dead. This is God's constant way of dealing: he gives no sign to those who *wish* not to believe in him, and who only ask for a sign as an excuse for their unbelief.

What a remarkable name Jesus gave to his body!—He called it a temple. What is a temple?—the habitation of God. Christ's body was indeed a temple, for the Godhead dwelt in him. It is true, all real Christians form one great temple; for St. Paul says to them, "Ye are the temple of the living God; as God hath said, I will dwell in them, and walk in them." (2 Cor. vi. 16.) But Christ was a temple in a still higher sense, for he and his Father were one.

When he said, "Destroy this temple, and in three days I will raise it up," neither his *friends* nor his *enemies* understood him. Yet these words were not forgotten; they were brought forward against him by his *enemies* when he was judged, and they were remembered by his *friends* after his rising again. No doubt there are many things in scripture which we do not yet understand. Let us look to Christ to teach us what we find to be dark and difficult. In the day of sorrow God often reveals the secret meaning of his words to his children. Some texts, in which we *now* see little beauty, may be our rod and staff when passing through the valley of the shadow of death.

There were some persons at Jerusalem, who, seeing the miracles that Jesus did, felt convinced that he was a true prophet, but they did not love him, nor desire his love. Now observe how Jesus behaved towards these persons. "He did not commit himself unto them;" (ver. 24;) that is, he did not place any confidence in them, but was on his guard when before them; he did not open to them his secrets, and tell them all the things that the Father had told him, as he did to his beloved disciples. (John xv. 15.) He treated his true disciples as "friends;" but these persons he knew still to be his *enemies*, for their hearts were not made new, and the natural heart of man is *enmity* against God. (Rom. viii. 7.)

It is a solemn thought that Jesus knows the hearts of all men. Men often deceive each other by false professions of piety, but they never can deceive him; he knows what is *in* them. It is said in the book of Revelation, that his eyes are like a flame of fire. When he writes to the Seven Churches by the hand of his disciple John, (Rev. ii. iii.,) he begins each letter with these words, "I know thy works." There is a beautiful history contained in a tract called Jejana, in which we are told of a little Hottentot maid, who, entering a church for the first time, heard the minister preach from these words, "I know thy works." In her ignorance, she thought the preacher himself was God, and tried to hide herself from his sight behind a pillar in the aisle where she was standing; for all the lies she had uttered and the thefts she had committed, rushed to her remembrance as the sentence was uttered, "I know thy works." But how light was the guilt of this heathen child, compared to that of a well-instructed person who is yet unconverted! It is not only for having committed *such* sins as she had committed, that persons in a Christian land will be condemned at last, but for having refused to believe in the Son of God, with the *heart.* Christ knows the heart of every one of us; he knows what is *in* us; ke knows whether we truly *love* him or not. If we do not *love* him, we do not believe in him in the *right manner*, and our faith can only be a *dead* faith, and such as will not save us.

Let each of us ask himself, "Do I *so* believe in Christ, that he might commit himself unto me, that he might consider me as a *friend* if he were upon earth?" Can we say like the apostle Peter, "Lord, thou knowest *all* things; thou knowest that I love thee?"

Evening Scripture portion. Rev. II. 1–17. *Christ knows our works.*

JOHN III. 1–8.—*Christ's conversation with Nicodemus.*

WHAT can be so interesting as to hear how the Saviour instructed a person who desired to know the way of salvation! What a privilege Nicodemus enjoyed when he talked alone with the Son of God! What a privilege *we* enjoy when we read the account of this conversation!

Jesus could suit his conversation exactly to the case of Nicodemus, for he knew the state of his heart, and could tell with certainty what it would be the most profitable to say.

Nicodemus was a Pharisee; one of that sect who placed their trust in the outward observance of the law, and who neglected to purify the *heart.* He was a *chief* person, a ruler and teacher. It was not surprising, therefore, that he was ashamed to come to Jesus openly. He came by night for *fear* of the Jews, as we are afterwards told in John xix. 39. Jesus did not refuse to receive him on that account, so compassionate is he to the infirmities of men; but if Nicodemus had not conquered this base fear of man, he could not have become the disciple of Him who has said, "Whosoever shall deny me before men, him will I also deny before my Father which is in heaven," (Matt. x. 33.) Nicodemus afterwards grew so bold, that when the name of Jesus was held in the greatest contempt he came forward with Joseph of Arimathea, and begged his body, that he might give it an honorable burial. But at the time we are reading of, he was still unconverted, and ignorant of his need of conversion; he was, however, desirous of instruction, and did not shrink from a private interview with the Lord. He came to the light, even the light of the world, the Son of God.

He began the conversation by telling the Lord that he believed he was a teacher come from God, because of the miracles he did; but it does not seem that he knew him to be the Lord of glory. Jesus immediately spoke to him of the concerns of his soul. The words "Verily, verily," show that the truth he was going to disclose was very important: "Except a man be born again he cannot see the kingdom of God." How necessary it is for us well to consider the meaning of this declaration! Do we desire to see the kingdom of God? We must then desire to be born again.

What is it to be born again? Nicodemus did not understand the expression; he thought it related to the *body*, but it related to the soul. Our *souls* must be born again; that is, they must undergo a great change. As, when an infant is born, it undergoes a change, enters into a new world, has new desires, and joys, and sorrows; so when our hearts are born again, they have new desires, and joys, and sorrows. This doctrine has offended many persons, who, knowing that they themselves were not born again *in this manner*, have attempted to deny the true meaning of the words. Some have declared that all who have been baptized are born again; but this cannot be true, for we read in Acts viii., of a man called Simon, who was baptized by the apostles, but who yet was *not* born again; for Peter said to him, "Thou hast neither part nor lot in this matter; thy heart is not right in the sight of God."

Water is the *sign* of the cleansing effects of the Spirit. God has appointed the use of water in baptism, to remind us of the necessity of being purified by his Spirit. No *man* can bestow saving grace upon another; it is the work of God alone; the apostles could not change the *hearts* of men; Peter could not change the heart of the wicked Simon, to whom we have just referred.

"That which is born of the flesh is flesh; and that which is born of the Spirit is spirit." What is meant by the term "flesh?" Does it mean the body? It means not only the *body*, but also the soul. The soul as well as the body is called "flesh," in Scripture, because the unconverted *soul* loves *fleshly* things; it only delights in the earth—all its desires are after the things of the world, its pleasures, profits, and honors. But when the Spirit changes a man's fleshly heart, then he has a spiritual nature; then he has desires after spiritual things, after holiness and heaven. By this sign we must examine ourselves. Do we love the things of earth most, or the things of the Spirit? For it is declared in Rom. viii. 5, "They that are after the flesh, do mind the things of the flesh; but they that are after the Spirit, the things of the Spirit."

But perhaps you may ask, "*How* is this change effected?" How does the Holy Spirit enter into the soul? Can a person see him enter in? No; the change is wrought silently and secretly; for this reason the Spirit is compared to the wind which bloweth where it listeth; that is, which *seems* to blow where it likes, for man cannot control it, or even tell whence it comes. Thus, God sends his Spirit where *He will*, and we cannot tell how this holy Spirit changes the wicked heart of man. We cannot see the wind, or understand its course; yet we perceive the *effects* of the wind; we can also behold the *effects* of the Spirit. Is it our great happiness to *feel* these effects in our own soul? Those who have felt the refreshing breeze spring up in the evening of a sultry day, need no argument to convince them that the wind blows. How refreshing to the soul are the *effects* of the new birth! Before a soul is born again, it pants for happiness, but pants in vain; but when it knows that its sins are blotted out by the Saviour's blood, then it feels satisfied, and like a long-lost child just restored to a parent's arms, cries out, "Abba, Father."

Evening Scripture portion. Rom. VIII. 1–17. *The earthly and the spiritual mind.*

JOHN III. 9–21.—*The conversation concluded.*

NICODEMUS was very ignorant of the *meaning* of the Scriptures; he knew the *words* familiarly, but not the *things* spoken of. He had no idea that a change of heart was necessary. He *ought* to have known it, because he had often read the words of the prophet Ezekiel, "A *new* heart also will I give you, and a *new* spirit will I put within you; and I will take away the stony heart out of your flesh, and I will give you a heart of flesh," (that is, a soft, tender, feeling heart,) Ezek. xxxvi. 26. Now this promise of a new heart, refers to the blessing of the new birth.

Nicodemus was a master, or a *teacher* in Israel, yet he knew not these things. Are there not many things which *we* ought to know, and which yet we know not? We ought to seek to know the meaning of the Scriptures, inquiring of our minister or pious friends, reading books they recommend, and, above all, comparing one part with another, while we entreat the Lord to open the eyes of our understandings, to behold the wondrous things in his law.

Jesus did not explain the new birth to Nicodemus; it could not be explained—it must be experienced to be understood; but he told him that he ought to *believe* in it; for he said, "We speak that we do know." By "*we*," He meant himself and the prophets, who all spoke of this new birth. How wrong it is in men not to believe heavenly messengers, especially the Son of God! "Ye receive not *our witness*." May it never be said of us, that we do not receive the witness of the Lord and his apostles! Nicodemus, however, was willing to be instructed, so Jesus continued to teach him, in spite of his ignorance and unbelief, for He is a *patient* teacher; he will instruct the foolish and the slow of heart, if they will but listen to his words.

He began next to unfold the wonders of redeeming lóve. Nicodemus had often heard of the serpent of brass that Moses lifted up on a pole in the wilderness, in order that the Israelites that had been bitten by fiery serpents, might look, and live. This brazen serpent he declared to be a type of himself. He then spoke to Nicodemus of his Father's love to man. O that these words might sink deep into *our* hearts. " God so loved the world, that he gave his only-begotten Son, that whosoever believeth in him should not perish but have everlasting life." What a gracious declaration ! What a free salvation ! " *Whosoever.*" No sinner is shut out, however horrible his sins ; *every one* who believes shall receive pardon and everlasting life. What can be the reason that *all* men do not believe ? This is the reason, " They love darkness," and why ? " Because their deeds are evil." Every sinner's conscience bears witness to this truth. There are many who say they desire to be religious, who profess to lament that they cannot pray—that they cannot love God. Were they sincere in *what they said*, they would use the means of becoming religious ; they would try to pray ; they would read God's word, and seek the company of religious people. If one of you were to lose your precious sight, through an accident, you would not be satisfied by saying, " I wish my eyesight were restored ; but I have no skill to restore it myself, and I cannot find my way to an oculist ; I must therefore remain as I am." O no ; you would prevail on some person to lead you to one who had already cured blind people, and then you would follow his directions, however irksome they might be.

Now if you desired to become truly religious, you would act in the same manner—you would use the means of grace—you would ask your pious friends to help you to find the way of life, and you would cry earnestly to God. What excuse shall we give to God at the last day, if we refuse to come to the light ? Great will be our condemnation. Has God given us his only Son, and shall we refuse to come to him ? Shall we remain unconcerned about him, and occupied with worldly trifles and cares, and then think to escape the just judgment of God ? Whatever excuses we may make to ourselves now for such conduct, they will not be accepted at the day of account. The sin and folly of neglecting the way of salvation will then be openly seen, and all those who are condemned will have nothing to say in their own defence.

Evening Scripture portion. Numbers XXII. 1–9. *The brazen serpent.*

JOHN III. 22 to the end.—*John's testimony to Christ at Enon.*

How little did the Jews understand the character of John the Baptist ! Some of them thought that he would be jealous of the Lord Jesus. How was that possible, when he came into the world to bear witness to Him, and to persuade men to believe in Him? Some people came to John, complaining that Jesus baptized, and that all men came to him. John earnestly desired that all men should come to Christ; not come to him only to be baptized with *water*, but to be washed from their sins, and baptized with the Holy Ghost.

John's answer shows in the most beautiful manner the humility of his heart and the sincerity of his love to Christ. Though he had been much admired as a preacher, he was not lifted up with pride. He knew and declared that "a man can receive nothing, unless it be given him from above." O that we could always keep this truth in our minds! Then we should perceive the *folly* of pride, as well as its wretchedness. What have we that we have not received? Yet how apt we are to be puffed up, as though we had not received, and even to boast to others of our abilities, our possessions, our connections; of our numerous friends, and amiable qualities! We ought only to feel thankful to God for his gifts, and to humble ourselves in his sight, because we are unworthy of his notice; this is what the angels do who excel in strength, in wisdom, and in beauty. How awful it is when we feel proud of God's *spiritual* blessings! If he has put grace in our hearts, or enabled us to convert others, how unspeakably thankful we should be! To be proud of such mercies is, indeed, the blackest ingratitude.

John the Baptist was full of love to the Saviour; he compared him to a bridegroom, and himself to the bridegroom's friend. The bride is the church, Christ's believing people. It was John's desire to lead all men to love Christ. He had succeeded in persuading some to love him, and now he knew that Jesus was rejoicing over these believers. To hear the bridegroom's voice was his chief joy; he delighted in praising the bridegroom! he called himself *earthly*, but he declared Jesus to be *heavenly*, for he came from above. He himself had only received a *measure* of the Spirit; but Jesus had received the Spirit without measure, that is, in an infinite degree.

He then described the exceeding happiness of believers in Christ, and the miserable condition of unbelievers. These are John's words: "He that believeth on the Son hath everlasting life, and he that believeth not shall not see life, but the wrath of God abideth on him." It is *not* said, that he that believeth *shall* have everlasting life, but that he *hath* even *now* everlasting life. It is *not* said that he that believeth not, *shall* taste the wrath of God, but that *now* the wrath of God abideth on him. Every person is at this moment in one of these conditions; he either has everlasting life, or he is under the wrath of God. How *very happy*, or how *very miserable* every creature ought to be! Ought not that person to be miserable, who knows that at any moment he may be snatched away from the scene of his enjoyments? If we were to see a man living in splendor, in a magnificent house, surrounded by luxuries, and were told that he had immense debts, and that numerous creditors might at any moment thrust him into prison, should we count him happy? He could not be happy, if he reflected upon his circumstances. Perhaps he would *not* reflect; perhaps he would run from one diversion to another, and thus endeavor to keep up his spirits. Now all unbelievers owe an immense debt to the justice of God, and they are in danger at any moment of being thrust into prison, even that prison of hell whence none ever escape. They would not enjoy a moment's peace if they reflected on their condition.

How different is the state of the believer! If you were to see a poor man, coarsely clothed and scantily fed, and if you were to be assured he was the heir of a large estate, you would expect him to bear his present hardships without murmuring. If *we* believe in the Son of God, we are the heirs of God; we *were* his debtors, but Christ paid our debt by his blood, and when we believed, we were free from it; and not only so, but we were made the heirs of a heavenly kingdom. Ought we not to rejoice exceedingly, and to reckon nothing of our present losses and disappointments, because of the great inherit ance promised to us?

Evening Scripture portion.
Ps. LXXIII. *The wicked and the righteous.*

Luke III. 19, 20.—*John's imprisonment.*

The beautiful discourse that we lately read was the last discourse of John the Baptist that we find in the Scriptures. Soon after delivering it, he was cast into prison. It was Herod who imprisoned him. This Herod was the son of that Herod who slew the babes of Bethlehem, and he resembled his father in wickedness. As he was the governor of a fourth part of the land of Canaan, he is called a tetrarch, (which means the governor of the fourth part of a kingdom.) The Romans had made him governor of Judea. He had heard John preach. We are not informed whether he had gone into the wilderness to hear him, or whether he had sent for John into his palace; but we are told what *effect* John's preaching produced upon him. If we refer to St. Mark's gospel, we shall find an account of the sort of impression it made upon him. (Mark vi. 20.) "Herod feared John, knowing that he was a just man and a holy." Herod had a reverence for the character of John; though a wicked man, he respected John. This affords us a lesson. Perhaps we feel a respect for some holy men, yet this is not a proof that we are holy ourselves.

Herod did more than this: "He observed John." He took notice of what he said; he remembered it. Unconverted persons are often struck with the sermons they hear. But Herod did more still: "He did many things." He reformed many parts of his conduct. Perhaps he showed more kindness to the poor, more attention to public worship, or more justice to his subjects. We are not informed *what* were the things which he altered; but we know that he altered not a *few*, but *many* things. Have *we* altered many things in our conduct, since we heard the gospel? It is well if we have: it is well if we read the Bible more; if we give away more; if we have left off openly breaking the Sabbath; or using profane language; or partaking of worldly amusements; but none of these things prove that we are converted.

But Herod did more still; "Herod heard John *gladly*." He took delight in his instructions. Was not that a good sign? It is a good sign if we take pleasure in listening to a faithful preacher, or to a pious friend, or in reading good books; but it is possible to do so, and yet to love sin; for though Herod heard sermons gladly, when John told him that it was not lawful for him to have his brother's wife, he was angry. Herod had committed a great crime: he had divorced his own wife, that he might marry Herodias, his brother Philip's wife; he could not bear to part from her. This was the sin he would not give up.

What a faithful preacher John was! though he knew that Herod had power to kill him, he feared not to tell him the truth. How difficult it is to act like John! A minister knows that he shall give offence to sinners, if he speaks to them plainly of their sins. As long as he speaks in *general* terms, he does not offend them; but as soon as he points out the peculiar sins of each class of persons, then he makes them enemies. When he reproves tradesmen for selling on the Sabbath, young people for frequenting places of worldly amusement, the poor for committing secret acts of dishonesty, the rich for living in pride and luxury, then he is hated for his interference. But how wicked it is to be angry with a faithful minister for pointing out our sins! If we do *not* turn from our favorite sins we shall perish. Herod would not pluck out his right eye, which was Herodias; he would not go with one eye to heaven, he preferred going with two to hell; he preferred his pleasure upon earth to everlasting joy.

See how one sin leads to another. Herod added this above all, that he shut up John in prison. Great as was the crime of marrying his brother's wife, the sin of shutting up John in prison was greater in God's eyes. And why was it greater? Because it was an insult committed directly against God; for God considers his *children* as himself. Whoever injures one of *them*, injures Him; for they are as dear to him as the apple of his eye. Besides, by shutting up John in prison, Herod hindered the preaching of the gospel; and thus he murdered men's souls. It is a dreadful sin to hinder the spread of the gospel. How much those will have to answer for, who have discouraged persons from *hearing* the gospel!

Herodias was more bitter against John than Herod himself, and would gladly have prevailed upon the monarch to kill him. But there were two reasons which prevented his committing this crime; the fear of man, and his own conscience. We find in St. Matthew's gospel, xiv. 5, the following words: "And when he would have put him to death, he feared the multitude, because they counted him as a prophet." The fear of man often prevents people following the commands of God, but it sometimes for a season hinders the wicked from doing bad actions. Herod's own conscience also made him unwilling to kill John, for the conscience of sinners restrains them as well as the fear of man. May we be kept from sin by better motives than those of Herod! The *love* of God in our hearts would make us *hate every* sin. Let us inquire whether there is any sin we refuse to part with. If we are not seeking to please God in *all* things, we cannot have confidence towards him: our own hearts condemn us, and "God is greater than our heart, and knoweth all things." 1 John iii. 20.

Evening Scripture portion.
Ezek. XIV. *The stumbling-block of iniquity.*

JOHN IV. 1–15.—*Christ's conversation with the woman of Samaria.*

EVERY one must desire to know what our Saviour thought fit to say to a poor ignorant woman, whom he met beside a well. He was always watching for opportunities of doing good to the souls and bodies of men. Though He was weary, and doubtless hungry and thirsty also, he was intent upon his Father's business; while we are continually making excuses for not speaking to persons about their souls!

Observe how he begins the conversation: he asks the woman to give him some water to drink. She returns an uncivil, unfeeling reply: "How is it that thou, being a Jew, askest drink of me, which am a woman of Samaria?" It was true that the Samaritans and Jews did live at enmity with each other; but this was very wicked, and our Saviour would not follow such wicked customs. However, he did not enter into a dispute on this subject, but passed on to one more important. In talking to people upon religion, we should keep the *chief* object in view, and not be induced to dispute on less important points.

How soft an answer did our Saviour return to the uncourteous woman! He saw her ignorance, and pitied her: he saw she was ruining her own soul by her refusal to have any dealings with him. How majestic and how touching is his reply! (v. 10.) "If thou knewest the gift of God, and who it is that saith unto thee, 'Give me to drink,' thou wouldest have asked of him, and he would have given thee living water."

The woman did not understand this answer; she did not know what the stranger meant by the "gift of God." She did not know that He himself was the gift of God, the Father, to a lost world; neither did she know what he meant by "living water;" she thought he meant running water; she did not know that he spoke of the Holy Spirit. She began, indeed, to suspect that he was some great person, though he appeared a poor man; but she could not believe that he was greater than Jacob who had digged the well in old time. Neither could she imagine that any water could be better than the water of that well, and *that* water she was sure the stranger could not give to *her*, as he could not procure it for *himself*. But though she could allow the blessed Lord to remain parched with thirst, He was willing to supply her with the water of everlasting life.

He continued the conversation by pointing out a defect in the water of Jacob's well. "Whosoever drinketh of this water shall thirst again." There is the same defect in *all* earthly pleasures and comforts; they seem to satisfy us for a little time, but soon the tormenting thirst returns. Have we not often experienced the truth of this? We have partaken of some pleasure, and have felt satisfied; but O how short was our satisfaction? We soon become restless and uneasy again. Thus we continue to thirst till we are made partakers of the Holy Ghost; then we feel satisfied. Then we find within ourselves a source of happiness. What is this source of never-failing delight? It is the sense of pardoned sin, of God's love in Christ, the hope of heaven, and of meeting our Redeemer there. Have you not heard of persons racked with pain, who yet enjoyed a peace that passeth all understanding? Perhaps you have seen such persons, and have wondered at their case. Behold the mystery explained; they drank, indeed, of no stream of earthly comforts, but there was in them a well of water springing up that never could be exhausted, and therefore they thirsted not after the muddy waters of this world.

The Samaritan woman did not understand the Saviour's meaning, yet she made the right request, for she said, "Give me of this water." O that we might all make this prayer, understanding for what it is we ask! God would certainly grant it. What! did God give his own Son to die for us, and shall He think any thing too *great* to give us? Who could have *thought* of such a gift? much less who could have dared to *ask* for it! that the Judge should give his only Son to die for the criminal! But as God has done this, and slain his beloved Son for us, is it not extreme ingratitude in us not to come to Him for the gifts the Saviour purchased with his blood! Jesus laid down his life to procure for us the Holy Spirit, the living water; and shall we neglect to ask for this precious gift? God forbid! Let each of us cry earnestly—constantly to God, "Give me this living water, O thou who hast so loved the world as to give thy only-begotten Son!"

Evening Scripture portion. Rev. XXII. *The water of life.*

JOHN IV. 16–24.—*The conversation continued.*

WHEN the Lord said, "Go call thy husband and come hither," the woman may have thought that he knew nothing about her circumstances; but his next words showed that he was acquainted with her whole history. Why then did he desire her to call her husband? He wished to bring her sins to her remembrance. It is probable that she had been divorced from these husbands, or had left them in a wicked manner. It was painful to her to be reminded of the sins of past years, and to be detected in pursuing even at that time an immoral course. But why did Jesus inflict this pain and this shame? That he might afterwards confer on this unhappy sinful woman everlasting glory and felicity. Let us not turn away from the remembrance of our sins. Every one must be brought low before he can be lifted up. We naturally shrink from being exposed even to ourselves; this is our folly and our sin.

The Samaritan woman (though now convinced that the stranger was a true prophet) did not like to dwell upon the circumstances of her history. She attempted to turn the conversation, and instead of inquiring how she might obtain forgiveness, referred to the chief points in dispute between the Jews and the Samaritans. The Jews said that Jerusalem was the place where men ought to worship God, and the Samaritans professed to worship him on a mountain in Samaria. Now Jerusalem was the place where God had commanded men to offer sacrifices; but he permitted them to pray to him everywhere. The Samaritans had done very wrong in building a temple on Mount Gerizim; their excuse was, that the Israelites in ancient times had pronounced blessings from this mountain, (as recorded in Deut. xxvi.) It was to this the woman referred when she said, "Our fathers worshipped in this mountain."

The Samaritans boasted of being descended from the Israelites, though they were chiefly of Assyrian origin. For when the king of Assyria took captive the last king of Israel and his people, he filled the land with Assyrians. At first these Assyrians worshipped idols, but afterwards they left off idolatry. Yet though they did not worship idols, they did not worship God. Jesus said to the woman, "Ye worship ye know not *what.*" There are many in Christian countries who, like these Samaritans, do not worship the true God, though they think they do. God is a spirit. Do those believe that He is a spirit, who while they feel no love, nor reverence for his name, yet bend the knee and move the lip in seeming adoration? If we knew that an earthly sovereign could see into our hearts, and if we felt no love, no reverence for him, should we not be afraid of entering into his presence? Till we love God, we cannot worship him. What then is a sinner to do who is conscious that he does not love God? Let him confess his sins; let him ask for a new heart; let him think of God's love in giving his Son to die for a guilty world.

Though God is surrounded by millions of angels who worship him in spirit and in truth, yet He seeks for other worshippers. He is so condescending, that he delights in the praises of penitent sinners: He even seeketh such to worship him. Perhaps last night or this morning He saw you worshipping him alone in your chamber; perhaps your voice was heard by no human creature, but your heart was full of sorrow for past sins, and of gratitude to God for having spared you so long. The Father of your spirit heard that prayer. He will answer it.

Evening Scripture portion. 2 Kings XVII. 24 to end. *Samaria.*

JOHN IV. 25–38.—*The spiritual harvest.*

THE ignorant Samaritan woman was much struck with the conversation of the stranger sitting by the well. It put her in mind of the promise she had heard of a Messias, who should come into the world and instruct men. She seems at length to have desired instruction. She said, "When he is come, he will tell us all things." He *has* come already, and *has* told us all things. Are there not some here who love his words, and desire to keep them?

What a joyful moment that was when the Lord revealed himself unto the woman, and said, "I that talk unto thee am he." In her joy, it is probable, she did not remember that she had refused him a cup of cold water. She was now anxious that others should hear the heavenly stranger, and she ran with haste into the city. She told her countrymen *how* she had been convinced that Jesus was the Christ. She said, "Come see a man that told me all the things that ever I did. Is not this the Christ?" Now one great proof that the Bible is the word of God, is, that it tells us all things that ever we did: not that it can tell *each* person his own life in particular, but it describes *such* men as we are, shows us the secrets of our hearts, and makes us feel that He who wrote it knew every thing concerning us. For this reason some hate the word; they will not believe that their hearts are deceitful above all things, and desperately wicked. This woman did not turn away from the Saviour's word because it exposed the sins of her life. Had she turned away, what infinite blessings she would have lost!

The disciples were astonished when they returned from the town with food, to find their Master talking in a friendly manner to a Samaritan woman. They thought that he was as prejudiced as themselves; but He who has made of one blood all the nations upon earth, is no respecter of persons. There are white people in some countries at the present day, who treat the poor blacks with as much contempt as if they had not souls to be saved; but these persons have not the mind of Christ: "He that despiseth his neighbor sinneth." When we look down upon another on account of the circumstances of his birth, we sin against God.

The disciples showed both respect and affection for their Master in their conduct on this occasion. They had too much *respect* to ask him *why* he talked with the woman; and they had so much *affection*, that they could not bear to see him refuse the food they brought him. But Jesus was too intent upon the souls he was now going to save, to be able to eat. When we are going to enjoy a great delight, our appetite is taken away, and so it was with Jesus; his meat was to do his Father's will, and to finish his work. What was that will? What was that work? To seek and to save those which were lost; to glorify his Father by the salvation of sinners. John xvii. 4. O what love Christ had, to take delight in saving us, his enemies! Did *He* thus spend his life in willing labors for us, seeking no other pleasure than that of doing good; and shall we spend ours in doing *our own* will, and seeking *our own* glory?

Jesus directed his disciples' attention to the people who were thronging to hear him from the town. He compared their conversion to a harvest he was going to reap. Then he explained to his disciples that God often appointed one person to sow and another to reap. A minister who enters a place where the gospel has never been heard, may be compared to one who sows the good seed. Sometimes he is removed without seeing any fruit of his labor. Another follows him, and meets with great success in converting souls; and this last minister may be compared to a reaper. Thus it was in Greenland. When Hans Egede first visited that land of ice and snow, he met with neglect and scorn; and though he remained there fifteen years, he could not make an impression upon a single creature. Other missionaries from Germany followed in his steps, and they reaped an abundant harvest of souls; and Greenland is now a Christian country. Shall not Hans Egede who sowed the seed rejoice in heaven with the blessed men who reaped the sheaves? Jesus promised his apostles that they should reap many souls when they preached; his prophets had sown good seed long before, and had not reaped. Would God forget those poor persecuted prophets?

It is a great delight to be permitted to reap; but it is a great comfort to think, that if we only *sow*, and even shed tears because we meet with no success, yet that our labor is not in vain in the Lord; and that at the last day we shall doubtless come again, bringing our sheaves with us. There have been parents who have died fearing that their instructions had made no impression on the hearts of their children, and yet after their death some friend or minister has reaped those children's souls. Will not the parent rejoice with that friend when they all appear before God? He that soweth and he that reapeth shall rejoice together.

Evening Scripture portion. 1 Cor. III. ***Ministers compared to husbandmen.***

JOHN IV. 39 to end.—*The conversion of the Samaritans, and the healing of the nobleman's son.*

SOME of the Samaritans were longer in believing than others. Some believed on account of the woman's testimony, others—not until they had heard him themselves. We know it is best to believe without hesitation, for Jesus once said, " Blessed are those who have not seen, and yet have believed." You remember how readily Mary believed the angel's message ; and Elizabeth said to her, " Blessed is she that believeth, for there shall be a performance of the things told her of the Lord." But though some of the Samaritans were *slow* in believing ;—after they believed, they were *bold* in confessing their faith. They said, " We know that this is indeed the Christ, the Saviour of the *world*." O what a title that is ! The Saviour of the " *world* ;" not of *Jews* only, but of SAMARITANS also, of some of every kindred and of every nation. May we all know him as *our* Saviour. We shall never truly love him till we know him, not only from report, but from experience. How different is the state of that person who only knows Jesus from what others have said of him, from *his* state who has received answers to his *own* prayers, and felt that his *own* sins are forgiven !

Jesus could not stay more than *two days* with these Samaritans ! We perhaps have heard a thousand sermons, and have read the Bible through many times. Is it possible that any one among us does not love the Saviour ? Would not these Samaritans rise up in judgment against one so much favored and yet so unfeeling !

Jesus did not return to Nazareth, which was his own country. There he was more despised than in any other place, because the people were accustomed to him. Though they had heard his blessed conversation year after year, and beheld his lovely example, they esteemed him not. It often happens that the gospel is most neglected where it has been longest preached. The excellent Baxter said, " I wish to be the minister of a place, either where the people have *heartily* embraced the gospel, or where they have *never* heard it ; but I dread being the minister of a place where the people have heard in vain." Those who have heard without profit become hardened, and are more rarely converted than others.

We find in this chapter an instance of a nobleman coming to Jesus. Not *many* noble are called, yet *some* are called. This man was brought to Jesus by his afflictions. In his sorrowful circumstances this nobleman found himself as dependent upon God as a beggar. There was none but Jesus who could relieve his sorrow. The Lord did not favor him more than others, but treated him with the greatest plainness. Had this nobleman been proud, like Naaman, the Syrian, he might have gone away in anger ; but he stood the trial of his faith. It was to try him, Jesus said, "Except ye see signs and wonders, ye will not believe." The nobleman showed by his answer he believed already, for he replied, "Sir, come down ere my child die." Yet he had not *such* faith as the Centurion had, of whom we afterwards read; for this nobleman did not believe that Jesus could save his child unless he came down to the spot where he lay. But the Lord is compassionate to *weak faith*, when it is *real*. Jesus gave a greater proof of his power than the afflicted father had ever thought of: for he is able to do exceeding abundantly *above* all that we *ask* or THINK," (Eph. iii. 20.) "Go thy way," said the Lord, "thy son liveth." The nobleman's faith was grown so strong, that he believed the declaration. Nor was that faith disappointed: for, while returning home, he learned that his child had recovered at the very hour that Jesus spake the word. He now acquaints his family with this great display of the power and love of Jesus. What is the result? The whole family, wife, children, servants, believe. What a happy family they must have become! The master's journey was blessed to his whole household. It is the fervent wish of every master who loves God, to bring his whole house hold to the knowledge of him. May *this* family and *this* household be joined to the household of faith, and to the family in heaven and earth who are named after Jesus the Lord!

Evening Scripture portion. 1 Thess. II. *Converts to the Gospel.*

LUKE IV. 14–32.—*Christ preaches at Nazareth.*

THE people of Nazareth were much offended with the Lord for not visiting them *immediately* after his return from Jerusalem. They thought they had the best *right* to his presence. What a temper of mind was this! Had they any *right* to Jesus, because he had condescended to be brought up among them? What pride there was in the thought!

And what was their reason for desiring to have him among them? Were they thirsting for *spiritual* blessings, the forgiveness of sins, the renewal of the heart? No; the Nazarenes were only anxious to partake of *temporal* benefits; they wished Jesus to heal *their* sick, as he had healed the sick of other cities. When, at length, He came to Nazareth, he was invited to read. It was usual for seven persons in succession to read a portion of the Scriptures; one of them was a priest, another a Levite, but the other five might belong to any tribe. There was a minister of the synagogue, but his office was not like the office of ministers in our churches. It was his part to appoint which of the readers he pleased to read the lessons for the day. One of the lessons was taken from the law, and one from the prophets. The various books of the Scriptures were written on rolls of parchment. The roll containing the prophecy of Isaiah was presented to Jesus. The words he read were probably the lesson for the day, and they applied most forcibly to himself. Did the Nazarenes understand the meaning of the sublime passage which the Saviour read on that day? Perhaps some thought that Isaiah spoke of himself when he said, "The Spirit of the Lord is upon me, because he hath anointed me to preach the gospel to the poor." But it was Jesus who really came to preach glad tidings, or "the gospel," to the poor in *spirit*. In that passage poor lost man is compared to a miserable prisoner, whose eyes had been put out, and who had been thrust into a dark dungeon. One of our Christian poets describes our condition by nature in the following stanza :—

> "Plunged in a gulf of deep despair,
> We wretched sinners lay,
> Without one beam of cheerful hope,
> Or spark of glimmering day."

Jesus came to deliver the poor blind captive, bruised, or galled by the chains of sin. He came to preach the "*acceptable year of the Lord.*" There was a year of deliverance among the Jews : it occurred every fiftieth year, and was called the year of Jubilee. That year was a figure of Christ's great salvation from death and hell. Let each of us ask himself, "What do I know of this deliverance? Am I still tied and bound with the chain of my sins; or have I been set free from the power of Satan?"

The readers in the synagogue were permitted to explain the lesson they had read. Our Lord availed himself of this permission, and said, "This day is this scripture fulfilled in your ears." For a moment the people were astonished at his words; but the next their *pride* rose. They remembered that he was considered to be the son of a carpenter, and they made this an excuse for despising him. It is *pride* which causes numbers to reject the word of salvation; they think to themselves, "Who is that man that I should listen to *him?* Why should he know more than I do?" Thus the Nazarenes reasoned. Jesus knew well that rage was working in their hearts : he knew that they were angry with him for having healed the sick of other cities before he had healed theirs; and he answered their thoughts by showing them that God had *always* chosen whom he *would.* Elijah in time of famine had sustained with oil and meal a widow of a *heathen* city; and Elisha had cured a leper of a *heathen* country, and not of his own. Jesus would not encourage those earthly-minded people to expect *any* benefits from him : while they rejected the *greatest*, he would not give them the *least.*

We see how hateful a worldly mind is to Jesus. If we are more anxious to possess an earthly portion than a heavenly inheritance, we are none of His. Yet you know well that the desire of the heart by nature is only for health, riches, pleasures, for worldly honor, or domestic comforts. If Christ would bestow these on all who asked, what constant fervent prayers would be offered at his throne! The heathen imagine that their idols will bestow earthly blessings upon them, and that is one reason they pray to them so earnestly.

Behold with wonder the madness of the Nazarenes! They cast out the Saviour of the world, and forfeit their part in all his blessings! His Father preserved his life, for his hour was not yet come, and it has been well observed, "His children are all immortal till their work is done."

Can we behold without dismay such treatment of the Lord of heaven and earth? If *He* who was so lovely and so gracious was thus treated, ought not *we* to be prepared for similar usage? Had he been less *faithful*, the gentle Saviour might have avoided persecution; but he sought not to please *men*, but *God;* he desired not to get *honor*, but to save *souls*. We may often escape persecution by acting insincerely and unfaithfully. But what, if we should also lose our peace of mind, and the approbation of God!

Evening Scripture portion. Is. LXI. ***The acceptable year.***

MATT. IV. 12–17.—*Christ takes up his abode at Capernaum.*

THE Lord Jesus chose to reside principally in the most *ignorant* part of Canaan; he selected the part at the *greatest* distance from Jerusalem, and which bordered on the wicked cities of Tyre and Sidon. And what led him to do this? Was it not pity for the ignorant and neglected? There are some who are now employed in visiting the courts and alleys of great cities, and some who are going into desolate villages, and some who are leaving their country to dwell among the heathen. Are they not walking in the steps of their Master?

Jesus fulfilled a prophecy of Isaiah, by preaching in Zebulon and Naphtali. The words in the prophecy are difficult to understand, but learned men have offered a satisfactory explanation. Let us first read the prophecy in Isaiah ix. 1. Now let us read it with this alteration. Instead of reading "more grievously afflict," let us read, "made glorious." What is the sense of the passage? It is this: *Once* the tribes of Zebulon and Naphtali were *afflicted*, (because, being situated on the borders of Canaan, they were exposed to the invasions of the enemy,) but afterwards they were "made glorious." How? By the preaching of the Gospel. Yes, the Saviour by his presence and preaching bestowed glory on those sequestered spots. How great a blessing is the Gospel! it may well be compared to a great light, for it sheds peace and joy around it. How melancholy is the condition of those who do not hear the Gospel! Well may they be said "to sit in darkness and the shadow of death." They do sit on the very brink of hell. We sometimes see a smiling village, seated on the side of a verdant hill, full of neat cottages and blooming gardens. We feel disposed to exclaim, "O! what a lovely spot!" But if the Gospel is not known there, it is, in the sight of God and of angels, a *dismal* place; while on the gloomiest, darkest alley, where Christ's word is heard, they look with joy.

In vain, however, the great light shone upon the people of Zebulon and Naphtali; for the light did not shine into their *hearts*. Christ afterwards pronounced a wo upon some of their cities, Capernaum, Chorazin, and Bethsaida, because they repented not.

Let us take warning from this. If God do not shine into our *hearts*, in vain for us are the splendors of the noonday sun; in vain the clearest, most affecting preaching; even the preaching of Christ himself.

And about what did Jesus preach? Repentance. And why did he preach "repentance?" Because sorrow for sin and turning from it is the *beginning* of religion; but though it is the beginning, it must never cease upon earth. As Philip Henry said, "Repentance shall follow me to the gates of heaven." Rowland Hill also observed, that if he could regret any thing when he entered heaven, it would be that he should no more shed the penitential tear. There is no religion without repentance. "A broken and a contrite heart, O God, thou wilt not despise." May God bestow it upon each of us!

Evening Scripture portion. Is. IX. *The light that shone in Zebulon and Naphtali.*

MATT. IV. 18–22.—*Christ calls Peter, Andrew, James, and John.*

WAS it not a high honor to follow the Lord Jesus from place to place, to hear his word both in private and public, and to behold his works of power and love? *Whom* did he call to enjoy this honor? Poor ignorant fishermen; these became his intimate companions, his bosom friends, and his holy apostles. Thus, our glorious Lord stained the pride of all human glory; as he had done before, by lying in a manger, and as he did afterwards, by dying on a cross between two thieves. How ill pride befits *us*, when the Lord of glory was so lowly! Ought we to look down upon any one as beneath *our* notice, when the Son of God was so condescending? It is true that there are different stations in society, and some stations are counted high, and others low. It is well that this difference should exist; it is God's own wise appointment. But it is *not* his will that the rich should *despise* the poor;

no, he has made us all of one blood, and he has commanded us to love each other as brethren.

Jesus might have chosen *princes* for his companions, or even *angels*, and sent them out as ministers of his Gospel; but he preferred to prepare poor fishermen for the glorious work. Before he sent them out, he taught them for three years, and afterwards the Spirit caused them to know in a moment various languages. Education is *now* an important preparation for the work of the ministry, as the wonderful gifts the apostles enjoyed are no longer bestowed.

These men were employed in an industrious manner when Jesus called them. When God called Moses, he was keeping sheep; Gideon, he was thrashing; Elisha, he was guiding the plough. Industry in our common callings is pleasing in God's sight; a Christian should not be slothful in business. Yet these men were not so fond of their trade, or of their gains, as to prefer them to the service of Jesus. When he called, they left all and followed him. He did not bribe or entice them to come by promising them temporal rewards; he told them plainly that his design in calling them was to make them fishers of men. The net they would hereafter use would be the Word of God; the fish they would catch, the souls of men; and the reward they would obtain, a heavenly crown. They had often toiled in fish ing, but they would toil more arduously in preaching; they would find men more hard to catch than fish, and the hatred of the world more terrible to bear than the winds and the waves. Christ has now many faithful fishermen, who, for his name's sake, are laboring to convert souls. Has their labor for *us* been in vain? Have we yet been caught in the Gospel net—willing captives? The poor fish, indeed, finds *death* in the net, but we find *life* in it. Well may the fish struggle and strive to escape; but it would be in us the height of folly; for the day in which a perishing sinner is caught in the heavenly net, is the *first* happy day of his existence; even the tears of the penitent are sweeter than the laughter of the world.

Evening Scripture portion. Judges VI. ***The calling of Gideon.***

LUKE V. 1–11.—*The miraculous draught of fishes.*

As these disciples had toiled all night and had taken nothing, it is probable they were in distress for food when Jesus bid them launch into the deep. Was it only to supply their *temporal* wants that He caused them to enclose so large a multitude of fishes? No; for though he delighted in relieving their bodies, he delighted more in helping their *souls*. By this wonderful draught he taught them many great truths: he taught them something of the greatness of his power;

he taught them something of the blessedness of obedience. Peter had said, "At thy word I will let down the net." How richly was his *obedience* rewarded! The apostles were to become fishers of men. Who could enable them to catch men, that is, to convert souls? None but Jesus. Though ministers preach—till God pour down his Spirit, no souls are converted; yet ministers, like Peter, should be obedient, and continue patiently to let down the net of the Gospel. And should *ministers* only act thus? All Christians ought to exhort each other daily, and their common conversation should minister grace to the hearers. We ought to distribute tracts and Bibles, to teach children, to contribute our property to the support of missionaries, and to do whatever we can to benefit the souls of our fellow-creatures; yet our exertions will be vain, unless God add his blessing. Let us then entreat God to put forth his great power and to prosper the feeble efforts which we make in obedience to his command.

The remembrance of this miracle should encourage us; and still more the remembrance of the sermon Peter afterwards preached, recorded in Acts ii., when three thousand were converted. Probably there were not three thousand fishes in the net. Lately God has done wonders in America, and in India, and in the islands of the South Seas; thousands have been converted. We must pray for the outpouring of the Spirit, and then sinners will be awakened, and will cry out earnestly, "What shall we do to be saved?"

What do you think of Peter's prayer after the miracle? "Depart from me, for I am a sinful man, O Lord." It was a good prayer, and yet it was a mistaken prayer. It was a good prayer, because it contained confession of sin. Peter was overwhelmed with a sense of his unworthiness; (that is the right spirit in which to make a prayer;) his heart was broken and contrite.

Perhaps he had indulged unbelieving, murmuring thoughts when toiling all night without success, and now he was overcome by the mercies of the Lord. This is true repentance—when we are grieved the more for our sins, on account of the Lord's goodness to us. Would not a person feel cut to the heart who had been suspecting another, and speaking against him; if suddenly he discovered that the man whom he counted an enemy had labored to serve him, and contrived schemes for his good. The discovery would fill him with compunction; he never could forgive himself for his ungenerous suspicions. Thus, "The goodness of God leadeth us to repentance." It leads us to feel our unworthiness and ingratitude.

But why did Peter desire so gracious a Lord to depart from him? *Jesus* knew the *spirit* in which he made this prayer, and he would not take him at his *word*. Though Peter said, "Depart from me," Jesus knew he sincerely loved him.

When the *wicked* say to God, "Depart from me, for I desire not the knowledge of thy ways," He often takes them at their word; but He does not deal thus with the trembling penitent, but receives him in his arms, and bids him abide with him forever. "Fear not," answers the blessed Saviour, "from henceforth thou shalt catch men." Instead of departing from Peter, the Lord never suffered Peter to depart from him.

Evening Scripture portion.
Acts II. 32d to the end. *Conversion of three thousand souls.*

MARK I. 21–28.—*Christ casts out a devil in the synagogue.*

THOUGH the Lord was continually working miracles, yet the miracle here related seems to have caused *unusual* wonder. And it might well do so, for in it Christ's power over the devil was displayed. One of the most mysterious subjects in the Bible is the manner in which devils possessed men in former times. It is *so* mysterious, that some have chosen not to believe it; but if we were to believe nothing that we could not clearly understand, how *little* we should believe! We should not believe in our own existence, for we cannot tell *how* we live, or what life is; yet we know that we do live. It is very reasonable to suppose, that when Jesus came to destroy the works of the devil, that wicked spirit should make great efforts to resist him. Some have thought that the persons possessed with devils were in a state of madness; but we find that the mad or lunatic are mentioned by St. Matthew, separately from those possessed with devils; therefore madness is a different calamity from being possessed of devils. (Matt. iv. 24.)

It is true that Satan even *now* enters into men's hearts, to fill them with wickedness; but it was not in this way that he had entered into the man in the synagogue; for had this man been filled with Satan, as Judas afterwards was, Jesus would have spoken to him as to a wicked man; but He did not rebuke the *man*, He only rebuked the *devil.*

The evil spirit had permitted the man to go to the synagogue. Had he known whom he would meet there, surely he would not have suffered him to go; for he seemed full of fear when he saw Christ. He cried out, "Let us alone; what have we to do with thee, thou Jesus of Nazareth? Art thou come to destroy us?" We know that devils believe and *tremble.* They cannot feel *hope*, but they can feel *fear.* They have no *hope* of growing happy, but they have a *fear* of becoming more miserable. Nor do they fear without cause; for their continual wickedness must render them more and more miserable throughout the ages of eternity, and must bring down upon them larger measures of God's wrath.

Even the praises of devils are abominable to Christ. When the evil spirit said, "I know thee who thou art, the Holy One of God,"

Jesus replied, "Hold thy peace." He cannot bear the praises of those who hate him.

Let none think that while engaged in the service of Satan, the Lord accepts their praises. Though they may join in the responses at church, and say, "Thou art the king of glory, O Christ;" or repeat daily upon their knees, "Hallowed be thy name," yet while they are living in sin, their services are displeasing to God. He is ready to silence their tongues with "Hold thy peace." To the wicked, God saith, "What hast thou to do to declare my statutes, or that thou shouldest take my covenant in thy mouth, seeing thou hatest instruction and castest my words behind thee?" (Ps. l. 16, 17.) Such is the awful condition of the children of the devil—of the unconverted, even *now*. What will it be hereafter? Judge what it will be from the malice the devils displayed towards this poor man. When commanded to come out of him, the devil first tore him, and (as St. Luke informs us) "threw him in the midst." Though obliged to obey the Lord of all, with what reluctance he quitted his victim! He made him feel his malice before he left him.

It is to the malice of such devils that the wicked are to be forever given up. These are to be their companions through eternity; no Saviour's voice will penetrate the gates of hell to bid the raging fiends cease from tormenting. Let us consider the horrors of the future, and remember that these spirits *now* fill the air, and that Satan is called, "the prince of the power of the air." (Eph. ii. 2.) This prince seeks now to *deceive* the soul, in order that it may be cast into hell hereafter. There will be no escape for us, if not washed in the blood of Christ, and sanctified by his Spirit. What do we know of pardon and holiness? Have we obtained these precious gifts from Christ? He died that we might obtain them. Are there any of us, of whom it may be said, that "they are taken captive by the devil at his will?" Jesus can command the devil to let us go, and he *will* do so, if we implore his help. But the devil will not let go his captives, unless he is compelled; he diligently watches over them, lest they should believe and be saved, accompanies them to church and follows them home. Yes, he follows them *close*, for he has a numerous train of servants at his command. But there is a place where he cannot come; the shadow of the Almighty's wings. O enter into the secret place of the Most High, and there you shall be safe; for He shall cover thee with his feathers, and under his wings shalt thou trust; the young lion and the dragon shalt thou trample under foot. (Ps. xci.)

Evening Scripture portion.
Ps. L. *God's rejection of the services of the wicked.*

MARK I. 29–39.—*The scene at sunset and sunrise*

IT is our privilege to possess an account of the chief events of one whole day that our Saviour passed upon earth. It was a Sabbath-day. In what labors of love was that Sabbath spent! In the morning Jesus was at the synagogue, where he cast out a devil. After the service he returned to Simon Peter's house, which was in the city of Capernaum. There he healed Peter's wife's mother of a fever. How much tenderness there was in the manner in which the miracle was per formed: "He took her by the hand and lifted her up." At his touch the fever fled, and strength returned. After a fever, a person is always exceedingly weak; but this woman arose, and waited upon her de liverer. How gladly must she have waited on him by whom she had been restored! Has Jesus done nothing for us? Has he never healed us when we were sick? Are we anxious to serve him?

When the sun was set, the Sabbath was ended; for the Jewish Sabbath began on Friday evening, and ended on Saturday evening. Then numbers flocked to Jesus, and he healed them all. This was a painful and laborious service. Could Jesus behold unmoved the diseased creatures that were brought to him? Could he hear the ravings of those possessed with devils, and the cries of those in pain, without anguish of spirit? Impossible; for his heart was full of compassion. Some persons turn away from the view of misery, because it gives them uneasiness; but such conduct is selfish. Our blessed Saviour felt far more at the sight of suffering than we can feel; yet he was willing to bear the pangs of sympathy. In this self-denying compassionate behavior, he fulfilled Isaiah's prophecy. "Surely he hath borne our griefs and carried our sorrows," (Is. lvi. 3;) or as St. Matthew expresses it, "Himself took our infirmities, and bare our sicknesses."—(Matt. viii. 17.) He did this, not only by *partaking* of them, but by *relieving* them. He left us an example that we should follow his steps. We are not to give ourselves up to selfish enjoyment, while our fellow-creatures are groaning. No; we are to lay ourselves out for their good; to visit the sick, to give them food and medicine, and kind words of sympathy, and to be ready, if needful, to nurse them. Thus shall we follow Christ, who bare our sicknesses.

The Lord Jesus rested when his day of labor was over, but he rose a long while before the dawn to pray. He thirsted for communion with his Father. We always find time to do those things in which we much delight. Those who say they have no time to pray, show that they do not love to pray. A Christian finds prayer as necessary for his soul, as food for his body.

The Saviour's retirement was interrupted by his disciples, (and by the people of the city, as St. Luke tells us,) who said, "All men seek thee." Was this addressed to him who was despised and rejected of men? But how few of those who sought him truly loved him! Thus it is now. Multitudes will flock to hear an earnest, interesting preacher; but only a few receive into their hearts the blessed Gospel he proclaims.

Jesus, however, could not stay in Capernaum; and he said, "Let us go into the next towns, that I may preach there also; for therefore came I forth." He ever remembered the *purpose* for which he came into the world: not his own pleasure, but the glory of God in the salvation of sinners. For what purpose were *we* sent into the world? Our own amusement? O no; yet many live as if they were born merely to live in pleasure, and then to die like the beasts. We were born that God might be glorified by us and in us. A young lady was once converted by meditating on the first answer in the Assembly's Catechism. The first question is, "What is the chief end of man?" The answer, "To glorify God, and enjoy him forever." She felt that she was not fulfilling this end while spending her time in vain and worldly pleasures. By the grace of God she gave them up, and became an eminent Christian.

Evening Scripture portion. Job XXIX. *Deeds of mercy.*

MATT. IV. 23–25. MARK I. 40–45.—*The cure of the leper and of multitudes with divers diseases and torments.*

How full of labors of love was our Saviour's life below! His *principal* object was to preach the Gospel, but he confirmed his word by various cures. These *bodily* cures represented the *spiritual* blessings he came to bestow. As he healed *all manner* of *diseases* without any exception, so he could forgive *all manner* of *sins;* for his blood cleanseth from all sin. No disease was too bad for him to cure, no devil too strong for him to cast out; neither was any sin, if repented of, too great for him to forgive. He declared, "All manner of sin and blasphemy shall be forgiven unto men."

We cannot wonder that crowds followed Him, when He bestowed such abundant *temporal* benefits. We know how men value the health of the body. But Jesus was far more anxious to save the *souls* than to heal the *bodies* of men, and therefore he sought for opportunities to preach his holy word. Probably one reason for his charging the leper not to mention the means of his recovery was, that he foresaw that if the miracle were made known, a still greater throng of diseased persons would be collected, and that by this means his preaching would be interrupted. Disease of body must have appeared to him very light, compared to that disease of the soul which leads to destruction. We judge of diseases by their *end,* and not by their *beginning.* If we have seen a man die in torments from any disease, when we see the *be-*

ginning of that disease in another we are filled with horror. Jesus had seen souls tormented in burning flames, and he knew that *sin* was the beginning of hell.

Of all diseases none represents sin in a more striking manner than the leprosy. In the first place the leprosy was a *polluting* disease. It rendered a man unfit to enter the temple, or even to associate with his fellows; as by God's law any one who touched him became unclean. Thus sin unfits man from entering heaven, and for the society of spotless saints and angels.

The leprosy was also a *spreading* disorder. It covered a man with white scales from the crown of the head to the sole of the foot. Thus sin has defiled *all* our powers. It has disordered our affections, blinded our understandings, hardened our consciences, and perverted our wills.

The leprosy was a *painful* disease. The hands and feet of the poor leper are often eaten away, and in this crippled state he drags out a miserable existence. But what disease is as painful as sin—the swellings of pride, the tumults of passion, the anxieties of covetousness, the gnawings of envy, the gloom of unbelief? Some have been induced to pray for a new heart, *not* from fear of the wrath to come, but on account of the *present* misery of their unconverted state.

The leprosy also was *incurable.* When the king of Syria in former times asked the king of Israel to cure Naaman his captain, the terrified monarch rent his clothes, saying, "Am I God, to kill and make alive, that this man doth send unto me to cure a man of his leprosy?" (2 Kings v. 7.) Sin also is incurable by MAN. None can *forgive* sins but God alone; none can *overcome* sins but God alone. Tears cannot wash out our past sins, nor can good resolutions keep us from committing them in time to come.

Having then a leprosy in our souls, let us imitate the poor leper of whom we read. Behold him falling at the feet of Jesus, beseeching his help. Are our prayers earnest like his? or do we ask for eternal blessings with less earnestness than a beggar asks for an alms?

The leper's prayer is remarkable: "If thou *wilt* thou *canst* make me clean." He doubted, *not* the *power* of Jesus, but his *mercy.* Yet his mercy is as great as his power. It is true that by his *power* he stretched out the heavens, and laid the foundation of the earth. But it is also true that, "High as the heaven is above the earth, so great is his *mercy* towards them that fear him." Had this leper known the compassion of the Saviour's heart, he would not have said, "*If* thou wilt!"

Observe how tenderly Jesus felt for him: "Moved with *compassion,* he put forth his hand and touched him." He showed his condescension by touching the loathsome leper, from whom all others fled. Thus he encourages polluted sinners to approach him. He will not repel them, and say, "Stand by thyself, for I am holier than thou;" He invites them to come near, and he offers by his holy touch to heal them. Fear not, penitent sinner; stay not till you are better; believe that Jesus will welcome you as you are. His blood is a fountain for sin and uncleanness; he himself stands by to wash you in it. Come to him to be healed; your cure shall be *perfect; all* your sins shall be forgiven and cast into the depths of the sea, and you shall be restored to the favor of God, and admitted into the heavenly Jerusalem.

Evening Scripture portion. II. Kings V. *Naaman.*

LUKE V. 16–26.—*The paralytic let down through the house-top.*

THE Lord Jesus, being prevented for a time from entering the towns by the immense crowds that collected wherever he came, retired into the wilderness. How blessed was the use which he made of his retirement! He gave himself unto prayer. And shall *we* venture to live without prayer—without much prayer—without fervent prayer! How can we hope for any peace of mind without prayer to the God of peace?

Soon, however, our Saviour came into the towns again. It was in Capernaum that he healed the man sick of the palsy. He was then preaching in a house, and many of the wise and great were present, watching maliciously his words and actions.

It was on this occasion that four men, bearing a poor paralytic, unable to get in at the door, ascended to the top of the house, (probably by some stairs outside,) and let down their sick friend through the roof. Great surprise must have been felt by the crowd below when the bed descended in the midst. Our Saviour was not annoyed by the interruption; he was always ready to help the afflicted, and rejoiced at beholding any proof of faith in his power. In this instance he seems to have perceived some *spiritual* desire in the man; for, instead of healing him immediately, he said, "Thy sins be forgiven thee;" and, as St. Matthew relates, he said also, "*Son,* be of good cheer;" as if he regarded him with especial tenderness, as a *son,* who mourned more for his sins than for his sufferings. This man was surely one of the broken-hearted ones that Jesus came to bind up.

But what do you think of the conduct of the friends of the paralytic? If they had not been very anxious about the recovery of the sufferer, they would have retired when they saw the crowd around the door; but they had set their hearts upon bringing him to Jesus, and they were ingenious in finding out a way. If we are as anxious to obtain spiritual blessings, as they were to benefit the sick man, we shall be ingenious too. We shall find time in almost any circumstances for prayer, and for reading the Scriptures. Some pious prisoners were once confined in a dark dungeon, and only had light allowed for a few minutes at meal-time. How could they read the Bible? They used the light to read it, and they ate in the dark. What holy ingenuity they displayed! There are others who have used a like ingenuity in contriving means to bring sinners to Jesus. The last day will reveal how abundantly their pious plans have been blessed.

Jesus knew that his power to forgive sins was doubted by the enemies who surrounded him; therefore he inquired which was easier, to forgive sins, or to heal the man. He knew which they *thought* the easier—to forgive sins. Mistaken idea! It was *so* hard, that Jesus shed his blood, that he might procure this forgiveness. Little did his enemies know what it would cost him to be able to say, "Thy sins be forgiven thee."

The pardon He bestows is valued only by those who groan beneath the burden of sin. The great reformer, Martin Luther, soon after he had become a monk, fell dangerously ill. Though he had long sought for pardon, he was filled with terror at the prospect of eternity. It was then that an aged monk visited his cell, and reminded him of those words in the creed, "I believe in the forgiveness of sins."—"Believe," said the old man, "not only that the sins of David or Peter are forgiven, but that your *own* are pardoned." These words were a balm to Luther's wounded heart. He thought no more of gaining heaven by his own righteousness, but looked with confidence to the mercy of God in Christ.

Evening Scripture portion. Ps. XXXII. ***Forgiveness of sins.***

JOHN V. 1-9.—*The miracle at the pool of Bethesda.*

CAN we hear of this pool without being reminded of that fountain for sin which Jesus has provided in his Gospel? This pool was called Bethesda, which signifies "House of mercy." And has not Jesus opened a house of mercy in his Word? The poor sick people who sat near the water's side represent diseased souls, such as we all have by nature; only our souls are far *more* diseased than their bodies were: for some of them were blind, and others halt, and others withered, but our souls are diseased in all their powers. Neither had they all been afflicted *many* years. Even the man who had been thirty-eight years sick had not been sick from his *birth:* but our souls have been diseased by sin ever since we were *born.*

The pool of Bethesda is not an exact image of salvation: for only the *first* that stepped in it was cured. But what would become of sinners, if Christ's salvation were thus straitened? Blessed be God, the fountain of Christ's blood is opened to *all* sinners unto the end of the world. How much selfishness must have been displayed at the borders of this pool! how each man must have viewed his neighbor with an evil eye, fearing lest by another stepping in before him he should himself be deprived of a cure! How differently ought we to view our fellow-sinners! *Their* salvation will not hinder *ours*.

Yet in one respect we ought to imitate the sick people around the pool,—in their *earnestness*. As they knew the *first* only would be cured, how patiently they watched around the pool, how eagerly they rushed in after the troubling of the water! We ought to seek God as *earnestly* as IF only *one* could obtain salvation; then *not* one should fail to obtain it.

It appears that Jesus was not known by these sick people. Had they known the great Physician was so near, what a cry would have been raised from a multitude of suffering lips! Jesus approached one of these pitiable objects. It was one who had been very long afflicted, who had been anxiously seeking a cure, and who had no friend to help him into the pool. Some person indeed had brought him to the edge of the pool; but not one had watched by him to plunge him in at the critical moment.

Jesus knew his desolate condition, and the bitter disappointments he had suffered. He selected him as a fit object on whom to display his power and mercy. The poor paralytic was not accustomed to the voice of kindness. It must have refreshed his weary spirit to hear Jesus inquire, "Wilt thou be made whole?" Immediately he began to pour out his complaints into the ear of the compassionate stranger, hoping perhaps that he should obtain his help the next time the water was troubled. But there was richer mercy in store for him, than any man or angel could bestow; for by a *word*, Jesus restored him suddenly, and perfectly.

That Saviour knows the circumstances of all his creatures now scattered over the world; and we know that he pities those who have no friends to teach them the way of salvation, especially when they themselves are concerned about their own souls. He may let them remain for a time in distress and perplexity; but He will not let them perish in their ignorance.

Evening Scripture portion. Lev. XIII. *Fountain of sin.*

JOHN V. 10–16.—*Christ's interview with the restored paralytic.*

WE have in this history an instance of the bitter hatred of men to the truth. *Why* did the Jews accuse Jesus of having broken the Sabbath? Was it because they reverenced that day? By no means. We may judge of their respect for the Sabbath by their regard for the *temple;* and we know that they made it a den of thieves, and filled it with sheep, and oxen, and money-changers. They did not care in their hearts for the service of God. And had Jesus caused the paralytic to break the Sabbath? No; for though God had forbidden men to bear burdens on the Sabbath-days, He never intended that a sick man suddenly healed should not carry home his bed.

The reason the Jews objected to the action was, that they suspected *who* had cured the paralytic; and they were offended with the rebukes that Jesus had often given them in his sermons, and in his conversation. Holy men are generally watched in this way. Why have faithful preachers in later days been insulted? Because they interfere with the vices of men.

The restored cripple was unable to gratify the malice of the Jews, by informing them of the *name* of his deliverer. He knew it not. Must he not have longed to discover it? Soon Jesus afforded him the opportunity. He found him in the temple. We are glad to hear that the poor man went there. For thirty-eight years he had been *unable* to tread God's courts, and perhaps before that period he may have been *unwilling;* for, from the words of the Lord addressed to him, we have reason to fear he had been an ungodly youth.

This was the warning he received. "Behold thou art made whole; sin no more, lest a worse thing come upon thee." It appears that his affliction had been sent as a punishment for early sins. *All* afflictions are *not* sent as punishments. Those of Job were trials of his faith. But they are often sent to those who know not God, that they may remember their sins and turn from them.

It was a heavy chastening that the paralytic had endured—an illness of thirty-eight years. At length he was delivered. What, if he should return to sin! how many have acted thus!—After vows and tears they have risen from their sick beds, to requite their God with black ingratitude. What must be the consequence of such conduct?—a *worse* thing will come upon them. Is there *any thing worse* than a palsy of thirty-eight years' continuance? Let the lost spirits speak, who have spent but *one hour* in the flames of hell. How gladly would they exchange their place for the most suffering bed to be found on earth!

He who gave this warning was soon to taste the punishment of sin himself, and to know by experience that *worse* thing of which he spoke. In two or three short years Jesus would be extended on a cross, and nailed there for our sins, and would bear the weight of God's infinite wrath. By the blood he then shed, he is able to save us from eternal wo. But those who go on in sin shall taste something *worse* than any thing they have known on earth.

Are there any here who still love sin? Remember these words: "Sin no more, lest a worse thing come upon thee." It is *Jesus* who utters them; *He* who has delivered sinners by his own *death;* HE, even He, entreats them not to continue in sin.

Evening Scripture portion. Amos IV. *Warnings against sin.*

JOHN V. 17–30.—*Christ's defence of himself before the Sanhedrim.*

THIS is part of our Lord's defence of himself against the Jews. We know not in what *place* he made this defence. Some think he made it before the great council of seventy persons, called the Sanhedrim; and others think He made it in the temple. But all must allow that he made it *publicly* to the great and learned Jews, who were his deadly enemies, and who even then sought to kill him. They wanted to find an accusation against him, and the accusation they now made was that of Sabbath-breaking. The first sentence our Saviour uttered in his defence is difficult to understand.

Ver. 17. "My Father worketh hitherto, and I work."

What works did his Father work? He had made the world in six days, and had then rested. He had rested from *creating*, but not from *preserving*. God preserveth man and beast continually. He is working in this manner on every side continually. Were he to cease from this work on the *Sabbath-day*, or on any other day, all creatures would sink into death; for it is God that preserves even the angels of heaven from death every moment. It is in Him we *live*, and move, and have our being. Jesus, in curing the paralytic, had done a work of this kind: he had renewed his life by imparting new strength to him. Thus the Jews were accusing him of *sin* for doing works which the Father was always doing, and which *he* also was always doing; for his Father and he were joined together in *every* work. Jesus, as well as the Father, had created the world, and he, as well as the Father, upheld all things by the word of his power; therefore he said, "My Father worketh hitherto, and I work." And why are the Father and the Son always thus united in their works? Because they are one God: Father, Son, and Holy Ghost are one God.

The defence Jesus made of his work only brought fresh matter of accusation against him; because he had called God his Father, and thus had made himself equal with God. Now they not only accused him of breaking the Sabbath, but of the greater crime of blasphemy. And how did Jesus defend himself from the charge? Not by denying that He had said that He was equal with God, but by speaking of those great works which He would do, and which would show who He was. Those great works are to give life, and to execute judgment. Who could do such works but God himself! Even at the moment Jesus was speaking, He was able to give spiritual life to dead souls; for he said, (verse 25,) "The hour is coming, and *now is*, when the dead shall hear the voice of the Son of God, and they that hear shall live." He has been doing this work ever since that hour. *We* do not see the dead souls arise, but Jesus does. He knows when he quickens a sinner who was dead in trespasses and sins. A time is approaching when his power will be publicly displayed as the Life, and as the Judge of the world, (verse 28.) "The hour is coming, in the which all that are in the graves shall hear his voice, and shall come forth: they that have done good unto the resurrection of life, and they that have done evil unto the resurrection of damnation."

This is an awful declaration. It once awakened an aged sinner from the sleep of death. He went to the church where the Rev. Joseph Milner preached, and heard this passage given out as the text. He heard no more, for the words took possession of his mind, and filled him with anguish. He sought the Lord, obtained forgiveness, and became as eminent for holiness as he had before been for iniquity. God alone knows all the conquests of his own word. Verses of Scripture which are heard by many with indifference, have, through the power of the Holy Spirit, given life to souls now rejoicing in the presence of God.

Evening Scripture portion. Acts XII. 16 to end. *The Judgment day.*

JOHN V. 31–39.—*The defence continued.*

IT is supposed that Jesus at this time was standing in the presence of the great council of the Jews, called the Sanhedrim. He had been accused of having healed the paralytic on the Sabbath-day; and then of having made himself equal with God. Did he *deny* either charge? By no means; but he more fully declared his own glory as the Son of God. He brought forth his witnesses. His first, a great witness, was his Father who *sent* him. (See ver. 32.) "There is *another* that beareth witness of me."

Yet He condescended to appeal to a *human* witness also, even to John the Baptist. He said, "Ye sent unto John, and he bare witness unto the truth." You have not forgotten what is recorded in John i. 19–23. "The *Jews* (that is, the chief men) sent priests and Levites from Jerusalem to ask John, Who art thou?" They came to him in the wilderness where he was preaching; and he took that opportunity of bearing witness to Jesus. He said, "There standeth one among you whom ye know not; he it is who coming after me is preferred before me, whose shoe's latchet I am not worthy to unloose." (Ver. 26, 27.)

How could the Jews resist this testimony? For a season they had rejoiced in his light; that is, for a time they had admired his preaching; yet they would not believe. John had now ceased to preach, for he was shut up in prison.

Jesus next described the different ways in which his Father witnessed to him. There were *three* ways: *First,* By enabling him to do miracles, such as healing the poor paralytic: those were "the works which his Father had given him to finish," mentioned in verse 42.

Secondly, (see verse 37.) His Father *himself* had borne witness of him, by speaking from heaven at his baptism, saying, "This is my beloved Son, in whom I am well pleased." Such a voice had never been heard at ANY TIME before, witnessing for the old prophets, nor had *such* a display of glory been seen. It was the *excellent* glory, as St. Peter calls the brightness of the Father. (2 Peter i. 17.)

Thirdly, The Father had borne witness to his Son, in the Scriptures, that is, in the prophecies. Jesus bade the Jews search the Scriptures; saying, "They are they which testify of me." (See ver. 39.)

Had not the Jews of old sufficient proofs that Jesus was the Son of God? And we also have abundant evidence of this important truth.

We have not heard John the Baptist preach, *that* burning and shining light, but we have heard other preachers speak of Christ with devoted affection.

We have seen no miracles wrought, no blind eyes nor lame feet restored; but we have seen greater works than these. We have seen miracles done upon the SOUL. Have we never known a person, who lived a wicked life, changed by the power of the Gospel into a holy creature? Is it not far more wonderful to see a man's *mind* changed than his *body?* None can make such a change but God. "Can the Ethiopian change his skin, or the leopard his spots? then can they who are accustomed to do evil learn to do good." Had we seen a black man changed into a white man, we should not have seen so great a wonder as if we had seen a child of the devil changed into a child of God.

We have another witness—the Old Testament Scripture. It is filled with prophecies concerning Christ. Have you read them? See how Isaiah declares, that he shall be brought like a lamb to the slaughter: how Zechariah says he shall ride on an ass, and be sold for thirty pieces of silver: how Micah foretells, he shall be born in Bethlehem; and how David in the Psalms predicts, that vinegar shall be given to him in his thirst, that his garments shall be parted, and his hands and feet pierced. The Jews, though they will not believe in Jesus, regard these prophecies as the word of God, and have kept them sacred for many ages. How can we disbelieve such proofs? And if Jesus be the Son of God indeed, and in truth, let us consider whether we are prepared to stand before his judgment-seat? Have we believed in him with our hearts?

Evening Scripture portion. Heb. I. ***The Divinity of Christ.***

JOHN V. 40 to end.—*The defence concluded.*

THUS ended the Saviour's defence of himself before the chief Jews. These last verses we may call the *application* of the sermon. How forcibly could *He* speak to the conscience, who is himself like a two-edged sword, piercing to the dividing asunder of the soul and spirit, and of the joints and marrow! (Heb. iv.) He knew that those to whom he spoke *would* not come unto Him. "Ye will not come unto me, that ye might have life." And He knew *why* they would not. It was because they had not the *love of God* in their hearts. He said, (ver. 42,) "I know you that ye have not the *love of God* in you." As Jesus was one with the Father, if men did not love God, they could not love *Him.* He was not such a Saviour as they liked; he cared not for the pomps and vanities of the world, and he did not promise them as rewards to his followers: therefore men did not desire him for their Saviour.

It is very important for us to consider this subject, because the same reasons cause men *now* to despise Christ. Why are they so careless about religion? Why do they treat the Bible as if it were not true? Is it because there is not proof enough? No; but because Jesus is too holy to suit the taste of sinners.

If we were to visit heathen countries we should find the people devoted to their idols: as the Scripture says, "*mad* upon their idols." (Jer. l. 38.) You have heard of the car of Juggernaut, in India. When it came forth, with what transports of joy it was viewed! Thousands travelled over sultry plains to attend it on its way; hundreds pressed forward to drag it along; some even threw themselves beneath its wheels, ready to be crushed in honor of the frightful idol that sat enthroned upon the ponderous machine. Why are people so fervent in the worship of idols? Because they imagine that these idols will indulge them in sin. The Roman Catholics show the same zeal in their religion of forms and ceremonies. They are ready to spend their money in decking images with flowers, and in illuminating the pictures of saints with candles. Men are willing to do any thing to please God, but to give up their sins.

And why is it that they have no taste for a holy and spiritual Saviour? Because they have a taste for the world. Why is it they do not love God? Because they love the world. Jesus pointed out this reason to his enemies. He said, "How can ye believe, which receive honor one of another?" They cared for the opinion of their fellow-men; therefore they would not come to a despised Saviour.

But, O how *foolish* were they to prefer the honor that *mortal man* could give, above the honor that the *everlasting God* could bestow! What shame will overwhelm them at the last day, when even Moses, the prophet in whom they professed to trust, will disown them! Had they believed his writings they would have believed the Saviour's words; for Moses had plainly declared, in Deuteronomy xviii., that God would raise up a prophet like himself to be the teacher of the Jews; and such a prophet was Christ. When they shall see the Lord appear in all his glory surrounded by his saints, and among them Moses and all the prophets, they will feel ashamed of their treatment of that blessed Saviour. Would *we* enjoy true honor hereafter, we must now faithfully cleave to His despised name, and to His despised people. We must not inquire, "What will the world think of me, if I follow this command of the Lord Jesus?" but we must only ask, "Will God approve my conduct?"

Evening Scripture portion. Deut. XVIII. ***The prophet like unto Moses.***

MATT. XII. 1–8.—*Christ defends his disciples when falsely charged with the breach of the Sabbath.*

THE Pharisees were so much inflamed against Christ, that now he was in Jerusalem they sought eagerly to find some accusation against him, or his disciples. They particularly watched them on the Sabbath day; and now they thought they had caught them in a fault, because they observed them plucking ears of corn, and rubbing them in their hands, (as St. Luke informs us,) and eating, as they passed through some fields on their way to the synagogue.

It was particularly mentioned in the law of Moses, that men might pluck either corn or grapes as they went through fields or vineyards, and eat them while they were passing along, though they might not carry any away. Surely the Pharisees could not really have thought it was wrong in the disciples to satisfy their hunger; but there is nothing so foolish that malice will not say against the object of its hatred. What trifling and absurd accusations have been brought at all times against the people of God! It is a great trial to the followers of Christ to know that they are the subjects of criticism, and the butt of slander. Some are deterred from professing to be religious, by the fear that their conduct will then be canvassed, and that they shall be blamed even when innocent. But why should this prospect alarm them? The reproaches aimed at them are intended for their Master. Is it not an honor to share in His shame? O that our enemies could never find greater *cause* to blame *us* than the Pharisees had on this occasion to blame Christ's disciples! Then indeed should we shine forth as the sons of God, harmless and without rebuke. With what meekness the Lord Jesus defended his disciples! he returned no railing accusation, but he mildly argued with his enemies. His example ought to lead us, when unjustly attacked, neither to give an angry retort, nor to preserve a sullen silence, but to endeavor, in a gentle spirit, to convince our opponents by forcible arguments.

These were the arguments Jesus offered. He said, "Have you not read what David did?" (1 Sam. xxi.) Have *we* not read what David did? He once was fleeing from Saul, and was overtaken with hunger at Nob, where the tabernacle was then placed. In the tabernacle there was a table, on which twelve loaves, called shewbread, were placed every Sabbath, and when removed, were eaten by the priests. Yet the priests gave David that *holy* bread, because they had no other to give him; and they were right in doing so; and even the Pharisees, when they had heard the history, had never blamed David for eating it. This was one of the Lord's arguments: if David might eat *holy bread* when he was hungry, might not the disciples pluck corn on a *holy day*, when they were hungry?

Another argument was this: the priests did much work on the Sabbath-day in the temple; they killed animals, and kindled fires, though the people in general were forbidden to do these works on the Sabbath-day; but the priests might do them when serving God in the temple. Jesus then declared himself to be greater than the *temple;* for not only God dwelt in his *body* as in a *temple*, but he *was God:* therefore his disciples might perform any works while waiting upon him. How this declaration must have exasperated and maddened the Pharisees! It teaches us, that on the Sabbath all works are lawful which are done in the service of Christ. We may use animals in *his* service, and to advance his kingdom. We may collect money for holy uses, or bestow it. We may write upon holy subjects, or distribute holy books. All these acts are like the services of the priests in the temple; they are done in honor of One greater than the temple.

But Jesus added one argument more: he quoted a verse from the prophet Hosea, well known to the Pharisees in the *letter*, but not in the *spirit*—"I will have *mercy*, and not sacrifice." God gave the Sabbath as a *mercy*, and *mercy* must never be forgotten on that day, in order to pay *sacrifice* or outward service. The hungry must be fed and the sick nursed. God does not wish any creature to *suffer* on that day. Whatever is necessary for *our* health, or for the health of others, may be done on that day. St. Mark relates, that Jesus added, "The Sabbath was made for man, and not man for the Sabbath." The Sabbath was given by God to man for the benefit of his *soul* and *body*. Of course the soul is to be the *most* considered, because it is of the *most* worth. If any way of spending the Sabbath does good to our *bodies*, but hurts our *souls*, it is a *cruel* and not a *merciful* way. On the Monday morning we ought to observe whether we are more inclined to pray than before, for thus we may discover whether we have spent the Sabbath as its Lord would desire.

"The Son of man is Lord of the Sabbath-day." Jesus showed that he was *Lord* of the Sabbath, by afterwards changing the day from Saturday the seventh day, to Sunday the first day, because then he rose from the dead. We ought therefore upon that day to think much of our risen Lord. How many tears were dried, when angels first declared, "He is risen!" The joy *then* felt shall never pass away. Every returning Sabbath bids us rejoice again. It was on the Lord's day that the apostle John once heard a voice saying, "I am he that liveth and was dead."

Evening Scripture portion. Hosea VI. ***Mercy and not sacrifice.***

MATT. XII. 9–13.—*Christ heals the man with the withered hand.*

IT was upon the way to the *synagogue* that the disciples had plucked the ears of corn; for our Saviour did honor to the ordinances of public worship by attending them himself. He *taught* at the synagogue, (as St. Mark relates;) he sat among the readers, and expounded. His enemies were present; for they observed the *forms* of religion, though they knew not its *power*.

Jesus noticed among the congregation a man with a withered hand. He would not be restrained by the malice of his enemies from dis playing his mercy. The Pharisees observed what he was going to do, and asked him whether it was lawful to heal on the Sabbath-day. Jesus answered their question by another; for, in St. Mark's gospel, we find that He replied, "Is it lawful to do *good* on the Sabbath-days, or to do *evil?* To *save* life or to *kill?*" Thus he showed that he read the wicked hearts of his enemies, and perceived their design of killing him. It was impossible for them to resist this appeal to their consciences; they held their peace, as all the wicked shall do at the judgment-seat of Christ. "The mouths of them that speak lies shall be stopped;" (Ps. lxiii. 11.) "The wicked shall be *silent* in darkness." (1 Sam. ii. 9.) Jesus regarded this poor man as a sheep fallen into a pit of affliction. He had looked upon all mankind as such a sheep, and had come down to redeem their precious souls from death. With what compassion he viewed his poor sheep, "plunged in a gulf of dark despair," whence it never could extricate itself?

St. Mark describes our Saviour's *feelings* towards his enemies on this occasion. "He looked round about him with anger, being *grieved* for the hardness of their hearts." Well might it grieve him to behold sinners endeavoring to hinder the healing of a poor sufferer, only because the Saviour's glory would shine forth the more brightly on that account? What an awful instance of hardness of heart! But are there not some in these days who commit similar sins, by opposing the preaching of the Gospel, which can alone restore a withered *soul?* Does not Jesus view such persons *now* with anger and with grief?

The *manner* in which he healed the poor man is very remarkable. He *could* have cured him by a *word;* but he desired him to stretch forth his hand. Was not this a strange command? It was the man's disease, that he could not stretch forth his hand. The man might have replied, "I have often endeavored to stretch forth my hand, and have not been able. Why should I try again?" But he made no such unbelieving answer; he confided in the power of Jesus, and his attempt was successful. The Lord in his Gospel commands us to do things that seem to be *impossible.* He says, "Repent and believe." We are sinners, and *cannot* repent and believe, except by a miracle of grace. Our hearts are hard—how can they *repent* and feel *grieved* because we have sinned against God? Our minds are *blind,* how can we *believe* and see the glorious salvation of Christ? Let us beware of saying, "We cannot repent and believe: we have often tried, and we have not been able." There is an awful history of one who reasoned thus. It was Dr. Priestly. In his youth he discovered that he was not born again: at first he was greatly distressed at finding he *could not* repent and believe; but instead of looking to the power of Christ to enable him, he listened to the devil, who suggested that there was no such thing as repentance, faith, or regeneration. He believed the lie; he preached it; and how did he *die?* Comforting himself with the thought that there was no eternal punishment;—another lie suggested by Satan. He said to a friend, "Reach down that *book*—(he did not mean the Bible—he did not desire to hear its precious promises)—that book has greatly consoled me; it has convinced me that we shall *all* come to heaven *at last,* whatever sufferings we may endure first." Thus he died, expecting to be cast into hell for a *time,* and then to be translated to heaven. But who could bear the thoughts of passing *one day* in the lake of fire, or even *one hour!* Let us beware of the *first* unbelieving thought, lest it should increase to more ungodliness. Jesus commands, "Stretch forth thy hand: Repent—believe." If we have not repented or believed, let us make the effort now, confiding in his strength who gave the command.

Evening Scripture portion. 2 Thess. II. ***Believing a lie.***

MATT. XII. 14–21.—*Isaiah's description of the gentle and compassionate Saviour.*

THOUGH Jesus had *silenced* his enemies in the synagogue, he had not overcome the enmity of their hearts. Though they could not *an-*

swer him, they could *hate* him. So great was their hatred, that when they left the synagogue, "they held a council against him how they might destroy him." Without the grace of God, public worship cannot benefit the soul. From the church where the Saviour has been present to bless many of the congregation, we may retire only "to do evil with both hands, earnestly."

Jesus retreated from his enemies to do good in another scene. He permits his followers to flee from persecution; but he enjoins them, wherever they go, still to seek to serve God.

Great multitudes followed Him into his retreat by the side of the lake, desiring to be healed of their diseases. Many people have wondered *why* he desired those whom he healed not to make him known. It appears that one reason was, that he did not wish, by the report of his miracles, to increase the rage of his enemies, and thus to provoke them to acts of violence before his work was done, and his hour was come. Another reason was, that he did not desire to add to the throng who followed him, and who pressed upon him to a painful degree. Already the concourse was so immense, that he was obliged to escape from the crowd into a ship. People flocked from the most distant parts of the land, and even from heathen cities. We find it recorded in Mark iii. 8, that they came from Idumea, or Edom, and from Tyre and Sidon, the habitations of idolatrous nations. Jesus did not desire the praise of multitudes; it gave him no pleasure to hear their shouts as he passed; he delighted in the petitions of the poor trembling sinner, and in the love of those whose sins he had forgiven. Was not his gentle, retiring, compassionate character truly described by the prophet Isaiah in the passage beginning, "Behold my Servant, whom I uphold!"

Now in this prophecy there are several deeply interesting points. A glimpse is here afforded of the everlasting covenant, that covenant which the Father made with the Son respecting our salvation. It was made before the world began; for God foresaw our ruin, and knew that none but his only-begotten Son could save us; therefore he appointed his Son to do this mighty work. The Son consented, and replied, "Lo, I come—I delight to do thy will, O God; yea, thy law is within my heart," (Ps. xl.) And lo, he *came*. Thus Christ became the *servant* of God his Father. He finished the work that his Father had given him to do, and then ascended to sit at his right hand as our Intercessor. He now pleads the merits of his service, and asks for his reward, the salvation of sinners. His Father has promised that he shall prevail. That is the meaning of the words, (v. 20,) "He shall send forth judgment unto *victory*." Yes—all the ends of the world shall remember themselves, and turn unto the Lord, (Ps. xxii.) That glorious day has not yet arrived. Meanwhile, let us trust in him. See what a gentle Saviour he is. "He will not break the *bruised* reed," or the broken heart. "He will not quench the smoking flax." The first desires of a soul after Christ may be compared to the smoke of flax, after it has received a spark, and before it is kindled into a flame. Will he quench these feeble desires? No—he will fan them into a flame. How can we refuse to trust in so compassionate a Saviour! Ought we not to come to him with confidence, knowing that what he *was* on *earth*, he *is* now in *heaven!*

Evening Scripture portion. Isaiah XL. 11. *The gentleness of Christ.*

LUKE VI. 12–16.—*Christ chooses his twelve apostles.*

WE must remember, that though Jesus was God, yet that he was clothed in a body like our own, and was subject to all our feelings of fatigue. What ardor of love must have filled his bosom to have driven sleep from his eyelids, and to have sustained him in prayer for a *whole* night! How long do *we* pass in prayer? Half an hour? perhaps not five minutes morning and evening; perhaps the greater part even of that time our thoughts are wandering to the ends of the earth. Or do we *never* pray in spirit, with hearty desires after God? Do we feel our prayers a burdensome task; and do we *never* pour out our souls, as a child pours out his feelings into his father's bosom? If this be the case, how awful is our condition!

But even if we *do* know what it is to pray to God, yet we must feel that we do not pray as much, or as earnestly as we ought.

What blessings we should receive if we prayed to God more fervently, and entreated him and implored him to fulfil his promises! Why are we so apt to make excuses, and to think that we are too busy, or too much fatigued to pray! Is it because we do not believe that God hears us? or is it because we think that He will give us blessings without our asking for them? Let us beware lest we provoke God, by our negligence, to withdraw the blessings he has already bestowed.

We may conclude what was the subject of our Saviour's prayer that night, when we observe what was his employment the next morning. Then he chose twelve from among his disciples to be *apostles*. Was he not praying in the night for them, and for the success of their ministry? What blessings have been poured down upon thousands in answer to those midnight prayers!

But even *we*, unworthy as we are, might assist our Redeemer's cause by joining in his petitions; for he once said, "The harvest is plenteous, but the laborers are few; *pray* ye therefore the Lord of the harvest, that he will send forth laborers into his harvest."

Yes, even *we* may entreat God to choose holy men, and to make them his ministers. Human creatures may build churches, but they cannot place in them holy ministers, unless God prepare men for the ministry. And what is a church without a man of God in it! False teachers ruin men's souls; *they* are not the ministers of Christ. Let us pray that God may send us pastors after his own heart to feed us with good knowledge, and understanding, and that he may send his shepherds forth to the ends of the earth to bring in his lost sheep into his fold.

These twelve apostles were not to become ministers *immediately* If you refer to St. Mark iii. 14, you will find that Jesus ordained them that they should *first* be with him, and *then* go forth and preach. All who teach others must be *with* Jesus to be taught by him.

Who were the men whom Jesus chose to be his apostles or messengers? (for apostle means "person sent forth.")

Some were fishermen; Matthew was a publican; and probably none were great in this world.

James and John, the sons of Zebedee, were called Boanerges, or sons of thunder; and it is supposed that they afterwards preached with great power, for though John is famous for writing about love, he wrote *terrible* warnings to sinners, and no doubt uttered them also, even as Jesus his gentle master did.

There was *another* James, who had a brother called Judas or Jude. They were relations of the Lord Jesus, and they wrote the two epistles called by their names.

The last mentioned is Judas Iscariot, or the man of Carioth, the traitor! And why did Jesus choose such a man, when from the beginning he knew he would betray him, and once said, "Have I not chosen you twelve, and one of you is a devil?" *Why* then did he choose him? No doubt one reason was to fulfil the prophecy in Ps. xli.: "Mine own familiar friend in whom I trusted, which did eat of my bread, hath lifted up his heel against me." Might he not also have intended to teach us a solemn lesson by the example of Judas? It is possible to be with Jesus, to hear him night and day; it is possible to *appear* religious and to preach holy doctrines, and yet to perish everlastingly. There are too many instances of persons who have *appeared* to have been born of God, who have died in sin. Baxter relates that in his youthful days he had a friend who *seemed* more earnest than himself, who prayed with him and exhorted him, and who finally fell away, and made shipwreck of his faith. Can we hear of such instances without lifting up our hearts to God to keep us from falling?

Evening Scripture portion.
Jer. III. 12th to end. *Promise of good pastors.*

LUKE VI. 17–19.—*A multitude of persons healed by touching Christ.*

WE have lately read how Jesus spent a whole night in prayer, and in the morning chose his twelve apostles. After choosing them he came down from the mountain, and found a vast multitude collected together in a plain beneath.

What a scene of *suffering* must have been witnessed upon this occasion, and what a scene of *joy* must have succeeded when the tongue of the dumb sang, and the lame man leaped as the hart, when mothers again beheld their drooping infants restored to all the freshness of health, when fathers rejoiced over children once tormented with devils, suddenly become gentle, reasonable, and happy? Yet these changes are but faint emblems of the glorious works which are now wrought where the gospel is preached in power: for virtue (that is, a *divine power*) still goes out of Jesus, and where his name is proclaimed, tongues that were dumb in his praise are loosed; feet that could not walk in his ways are strengthened; parents behold their wandering children returning to their forsaken God; and even angels in heaven survey the scene and look forward with joy to the time when redeemed sinners shall be their companions in heaven. O blessed gospel, which can effect such wonders! May it be preached all over the world, and rescue every sinner from the power of Satan!

There were probably some *spiritual* cures wrought by Jesus on that plain; for the multitude came not only to be healed, but also to *hear* him. This seemed a favorable opportunity for preaching a public discourse. This sermon is recorded by Saint Luke. It is doubtful whether that recorded by St. Matthew is the same as this, or whether it was delivered on a different occasion. But the two sermons are so much alike, that it will be best to select *one* only, and as St. Matthew gives the *fullest* account, we will consider the sermon recorded in his gospel.

Never could a congregation have had such motives to listen to a preacher as the audience that surrounded our Lord at this time. With what feelings of grateful love the newly-restored sufferers must have regarded their compassionate Saviour! And with what emotions of reverence and awe those who had witnessed the miracles must have gazed upon the Almighty Lord!

But much as we must admire the *power* displayed in his miracles, we must be chiefly touched by that *love* which induced him to welcome and relieve the suffering throng. The selfish heart of a fallen man would soon be wearied and disgusted with such a crowd of miserable objects. But the Son of God shrunk not from the leper's touch, nor the maniac's shriek.

The love of Jesus flowed out to meet the misery of man. It is thus even now. His love is still shown in listening to the cries of the most degraded outcasts. Those whom proud men would trample under foot, need only cry to the condescending Saviour, and they shall be heard, received, and welcomed. The beggar in his hovel is visited, even the felon in his cell, when, in the hour of trouble, he calls upon the name of Jesus. Could we track the steps of the Saviour through the world, we should find that while he passed by many a gay mansion and many a grand palace, he often cheered by his presence the hut of the African slave, and softened by his love the hard bed of the dying pauper. How blessed are they who tread in the steps of the Saviour, and who delight more in relieving the sufferer than in shining in elegant society, and partaking of splendid entertainments! Every one has heard of Howard, the prisoner's friend; and of Wilberforce, the negro's friend; and of Ashley, the friend of the factory child: but there are many whose names the world has never heard, who have imitated Christ as nearly as they in labors of love. An aged outcast one night wandered to the door of a poor Christian. The wanderer was a beggar, and almost an idiot, but for Christ's sake she was received. Her new-found friend never grew weary of her charge, but year after year sustained her by the labor of her hands, dressing her wounds with a sister's tenderness, and praying with many tears for the salvation of her soul. When asked why she did so much for a stranger, she replied, "The love of Christ constraineth me. Has He not said, Bring the poor that are cast out to thy house?" (Is. lviii. 7.)

Evening Scripture portion. **Ps. CVII. 1–22.** *The mercy of God to the miserable.*

MATT. V. 1–10.—*Christ begins his sermon on the Mount by pronouncing the beatitudes.*

THE blessed Saviour had been just engaged in healing the *bodies* of men, when he ascended the mountain to preach words that might save their *souls*. He opened his mouth to speak with a loud voice to the vast multitude. What heavenly words proceeded from those gracious lips! He began with pronouncing blessings; for he came to bless and to save. These eight blessings are called the beatitudes. They are very instructive, because they teach us whom Christ counts happy or blessed.

We all naturally desire happiness, but we fall into this great mistake: we think that we must have earthly good in order to be happy. Do not the world show by their conduct, that if they were to speak the language of their hearts, they would say, "Blessed are those who have houses and lands: Blessed are those who enjoy health and long life: Blessed are those who are held in honor and reputation among men?" But God speaks very differently. He assures us that happiness is only to be found in his *presence*, and in *likeness* to himself. The Psalmist declares, "In thy presence is fulness of joy;" and again, "I shall behold thy face in righteousness; I shall be satisfied when I awake in thy likeness." In order to become happy we must become holy like Him.

God will bestow upon us, in answer to our prayers, all the graces mentioned in these beatitudes—humility, penitence, meekness, spiritual desires, mercy, purity, love of peace-making, and joy in persecution. None but real Christians possess these dispositions. Unconverted persons may sometimes *appear* to be meek. It is no doubt true that there are some people more meek by nature than others. But how different is natural meekness from that of the true Christian! He is meek, *not* because he does not *feel* an insult, *not* because he is *afraid* of showing resentment, *not* because he sees it is most to his *interest* to endure in silence; but—because he traces the hand of God in every injury man is permitted to inflict, because he knows that he *deserves* worse treatment than he receives, and because his Saviour suffered far more for his sake. These are *some* of the motives which lie at the root of the Christian's meekness. When David was cursed by Shimei, he meekly replied, "Let him curse," because the Lord hath said unto him, "Curse David." He felt that the Lord had appointed the chastisement, and he did not desire to resist it. This was the meekness, not of nature, but of grace.

Some persons are more merciful or kind-hearted by nature than others; but none exercise true mercy except those who have themselves received it from God. These are the only persons who show mercy to the *souls* of men.

There are some also who naturally delight more than others in making peace; but the right motive must ever be wanting, where true religion is absent. How beautiful is the character of a Christian peacemaker! We might all do something in preventing quarrels, and in healing them. The children of Satan delight in seeing people divided, and often by their malicious tales create differences between friends: but the children of God delight in seeing hearts fondly attached to each other; and often by their kind efforts reunite the cord of love when it has been broken. Two celebrated ministers, Robert Hall and Charles Simeon, had quarrelled; they refused to speak to each other; when John Owen, another eminent minister, adopted the following plan to reconcile them, after several others had been tried in vain. He wrote and left at the house of each these lines:

How rare that task a prosperous issue finds,
Which seeks to reconcile discordant minds!
How many scruples rise at passion's touch!
This yields too little, and *that* asks too much;
Each wishes each with others' eyes to see:
And *many* sinners can't make *two* agree.
What mediation then, the Saviour show'd,
Who *singly* reconciled us *all* to God!

It is said that upon receiving the lines, each minister left his residence to seek the other, and that they met in the street, where a perfect reconciliation took place.

This is an instance of the manner in which the true Christian makes peace between his brethren, and of the success with which God blesses his efforts.

Let us now turn to another of the beatitudes. "Blessed are the pure in heart: for they shall see God." All who know any thing of their own hearts, must acknowledge that they are not by nature pure. We learn from the scriptures that the heart is purified by *faith.* (Acts xv. 9.) When a man believes in Christ, his heart no longer delights in sin, but desires to be holy like God. Lest, however, any penitent sinner should be cast down by reading this verse, let me mention a little circumstance for his comfort:—

When the Esquimaux, in North America, first obtained the Gospel of St. Matthew in their own language, they perused the sacred treasure with the greatest attention. One day the missionary found a poor lad weeping bitterly. He inquired the cause of his grief. The youth replied by pointing to the passage in the eighth verse of this chapter. "Look there," said he, "it is only the pure in heart who shall see God; and I am not pure, so I can never see him." "But stop," said the missionary, (placing his finger on the fourth verse,) "read again, Blessed are they that mourn, for they shall be comforted."

Evening Scripture portion.
2 Sam. XVI. 1–14. ***David's meekness towards Shimei.***

MATT. V. 11–16.—*Christ prepares his disciples for persecution.*

THE sermon which the Lord Jesus preached on the Mount astonished those that heard it. Who would have thought that the persecuted could rejoice? Yet Jesus said, "Blessed are ye when men shall revile you." There are a great many different kinds of persecution; but only one of them is mentioned in this place. It is a kind that some might think not very difficult to bear—the persecution of the *tongue.* "Blessed are ye when men shall revile you, and persecute you, and say all manner of evil against you falsely for my sake." But those who have endured this kind of persecution, know that it is very painful to the natural feelings. Yet all who follow Jesus must suffer it; for "if they have called the master of the house Beelzebub, how much more shall they call them of his household?" (Matt. x. 25.)

Slander is a part of the martyr's portion. No man was ever yet put to death *as* a *good* man. His enemies take away his good name before they venture to murder him. Thus they did to Jesus. They said that he was a rebel and a blasphemer, before they crucified him. The most dreadful calumnies were spread abroad respecting the early Christians. The first persecution was set on foot by the emperor Nero, on the ground that the Christians had set fire to the city of Rome, though it is supposed he himself had committed the crime. When warriors expire on the field of battle, they know that their names will be honored by their countrymen; but martyrs often die amidst the curses and insults of the multitude.

Many Christians have tried to escape persecution by concealing their religion. But the Lord Jesus does not approve such conduct. He has compared his people to two things, salt and light. Why has he compared them to salt? Because if salt has lost its savor, it is *utterly useless.* Thus, a Christian who hides his religion, or who disgraces it by his conduct, is useless. Light also is a great blessing; but if it be concealed, it is no blessing at all. There have been Christians, in countries where persecution was violent, who have concealed their sentiments even from their own children. In Bohemia, some fathers, when going to die, acknowledged that all their lives they had been Protestants in heart, but had not had courage to avow it. While they lived, they often retired into a shed to read the Bible, which they buried in the earth. But did these men give *light* unto all that were in the house? Were their children brought up in the nurture and admonition of the Lord?

The prophet Daniel acted in a very different manner, when, in spite of the king's decree, his windows being open in his chamber toward Jerusalem, he kneeled upon his knees three times a day, and prayed, and gave thanks before his God, as he did aforetime.

There are two things which Christians must do if they would glorify God; they must lead holy lives, and openly acknowledge the Saviour, in whom they believe. If they do not openly acknowledge him, how can they do him honor by their *lives?* And if they do not lead holy lives, they disgrace the cause by making an open profession of his name.

"Let your light so shine before men, that they may see your good works, and glorify your Father which is in heaven." We must expect that they will *now* speak evil of us; but afterwards, when they are in *affliction,* they may be led to turn to our God; according to the words of the apostle Peter, "Having your conversation honest among the Gentiles, that whereas they speak against you as evil-doers, they may by your good works which they shall behold, glorify God in the *day of visitation.*" (1 Peter ii. 12.)

Evening Scripture portion. Dan. VI. ***Den of Lions.***

MATT. V. 17–32.—*Christ explains the spiritual nature of the law.*

IT is a very common idea, that Christ came to set aside the law; but it is a mistaken one. He said himself, "I came not to destroy the law, but to fulfil." He knew that man had broken it; and he came to fulfil it in his stead, and to bear the punishment due to man for breaking it. But he came to do still more; he came to take out of man's heart, his hatred of God's law. For ever since the fall, men have hated that law. As it is written, "The carnal mind is enmity against God: for it is not subject to the law of God: neither indeed can be." (Rom. viii. 7.) The Pharisees professed to keep the law: but in their hearts they hated it.

No doubt it astonished the people exceedingly to hear Jesus declare, "Except your righteousness shall exceed the righteousness of the Scribes and Pharisees, ye shall in no case enter the kingdom of heaven." But what sort of righteousness can those men have had, who in their hearts hated righteousness! But this was the case with the Pharisees, and it is the case with every unconverted man. The law is too holy to please such sinful creatures as we are by nature. It may appear, at first sight, an easy thing to keep the sixth commandment, "Thou shalt not kill." But if we think it easy to keep it, it is because we do not understand its spiritual meaning. It forbids not only the *act* of murder, but the *thought*. Hatred is the beginning of murder. This may be proved. When we hate a person, we do not like the *presence* of that person; we feel uncomfortable when he is near, and wish he were at a distance. This must have been Cain's first feeling against Abel. It was fostered in his bosom, till it led to murder. Before he murdered Abel with his *hand*, he murdered him in *thought*. And what is the beginning of hatred? It is anger There is a righteous anger. God is angry with the wicked; but if they would turn from their wickedness, his anger would cease; for he says, "Let the wicked man forsake his way, and the unrighteous man his thoughts, and let him return unto the Lord, and he will have mercy upon him." But sinful anger is very different from the anger of God; it is anger without a cause, or without a *sufficient* cause. Perhaps some one has slighted us and wounded our self-love; or, perhaps, he has gained some advantage that we should like to possess, and has excited our *envy*. Perhaps he has faithfully reproved us, or set us an example which makes us feel ashamed of our own conduct. This was the reason that Cain was angry with Abel, and it was the reason that the Pharisees were angry with Jesus. Worldly people are still angry with real Christians on the same account. How sinful is such anger! It is usually vented in abusive words. Raca and fool were terms of reproach used by the Jews. Raca signified "vain worthless fellow," and fool, "wicked and abandoned wretch." And have none of us in our anger been led to use very improper expressions? Even little children sometimes utter very violent words in their fits of passion. And does not God notice these words? He does notice them, and though *we* may forget them, *He* will not. He is an adversary to the wicked, and will shut them up in a prison whence they can never escape. We are now going to pray to God

Do any of us cherish malice in our hearts? Malice is the worst kind of hatred. God will not accept the prayers or the praises of any person who hates his brother. It is a difficult thing to part with our sins. Many people would rather part with a foot, or an eye, than with their sins. But we *must* part with them, or we shall be cast into hell. Blessed be God, He will give new hearts to those who ask for them; He will make them righteous, and He will pardon all their sins for his dear Son's sake.

Evening Scripture portion.—Gen. IV. 1–16. *Cain and Abel.*

MATT. V. 33–37.—*Christ forbids irreverent swearing.*

THE Lord Jesus observes the expressions we use in our common conversation; he notices every reproachful word we utter to each other; he notices also every irreverent word we speak of God. He heard with displeasure the Jews of old calling their brethren raca and fool, and swearing by heaven, by the earth, by Jerusalem, and by their own heads. Let us never forget that he still listens to our discourse, and is displeased with every profane expression, such as, "God bless us," "The Lord knows," "Upon my soul." Ungodly people are so much in the habit of uttering these exclamations, that they scarcely know when they use them. But they could not have acquired the habit, if they had felt reverence for the majesty of the Almighty God. But when men became sinners, they began to despise Him. If they were to hear his terrible voice, they would be filled, as Adam was, with fear; but when they do not see him, they feel no dread, and care not how they insult his name.

But with what solemn awe the Son of God speaks of his Father! Even the heavens and earth are not common things in his sight. When we look up at the blue vault above our heads, we are gazing upon the throne of its Creator; and when we look around upon this green and smiling earth, we are gazing upon the footstool of its glorious Monarch: even our own heads are His, and not ours; for He made them, while we cannot make one hair, white or black. If men were not sinners, they would be satisfied with saying "yes" and "no," without using oaths to confirm their words. For Jesus said, "But let your communication be yea, yea; nay, nay; for whatever is more than these, cometh of *evil;*" "that is, from the evil *one,* or the evil *heart.*"

There is one difficulty that may be urged respecting the rule Christ laid down. How is it that St. Paul in his epistles often appeals to God, saying, "God is my witness, I speak the truth in

Christ; I lie not. I call God for a record upon my soul." Did Paul speak profanely? That is impossible, for he spake by the Holy Ghost. It is therefore lawful to appeal to God on solemn important occasions; as in a court of *justice*, when our words may affect the life of a fellow-creature. It is even mentioned in Isaiah as a proof of piety in future days, that men instead of swearing by false gods, will swear by the true God. "He that sweareth in the earth, shall swear by the God of truth." (Is. lxv. 16.) In Deuteronomy also, God said, "Thou shalt fear the Lord thy God, and serve him, and swear by his name." (vi. 13.) It must therefore be lawful on some occasions to use solemn oaths.

How condescending God has been to us in having used an oath to confirm his promise to us! Because he could swear by no greater, he sware by himself, and he said, "As I *live*." This he did to quiet the unbelieving fears of his own people. He says to each of those who have fled to Christ for pardon, "Surely blessing I will bless thee." He adds his oath to his word, and says, "As *I live*." Thus by *two* immutable or unchangeable things, his word and his oath, he gives strong consolation to the poor penitent trembling at his footstool. He uses the same oath when He threatens to destroy His enemies. "I lift up my hand to heaven, and say, 'I live forever.' If I whet my glittering sword, and mine hand take hold in judgment, I will render vengeance to mine enemies, and will reward them that hate me." (Deut. xxxii. 40, 41.) Well, then, may we fear this glorious and fearful name, "The LORD THY GOD."

Evening Scripture portion.—Heb. VI. *The oath of God.*

MATT. V. 38–42.—*Christ enjoins long-suffering.*

THESE directions have excited a great deal of surprise. It seems to proud man impossible that God should expect him to bear injuries without complaint, or desire of revenge. Let us inquire in what manner these directions are to be understood. The words, "An eye for an eye, a tooth for a tooth," are the words of God, and Jesus did not *contradict* his Father's words, which were his own also, but he *explained* them. The Pharisees had misunderstood them, and represented them falsely to the people. Those words, "eye for eye," were a direction given to the magistrates. See Ex. xxi. It was to be their rule of punishment. If a man put out another man's eye, the magistrate might not take away his *life* on that account, but might assign a punishment equal to the injury he had inflicted. But this command was never intended to encourage revenge. The magistrate executes justice for the *public* good, and men may bring others to justice on the same account; but they may not practise *private* revenge from feelings of hatred and anger. The Pharisees had explained this law very ill, and had deceived the people. Jesus told them that far from revenge being allowable, we ought to suffer injuries without complaint, or resistance. He did not forbid us to remonstrate with our enemies, when we had the opportunity; for it is right to do all we can to deter others from committing sin. He himself expostulated with the man who dared to smite his cheek, as he stood before the high priest, saying, "If I have spoken *evil*, bear witness of the evil; but if *well*, why smitest thou me?" (John xviii. 23.) When our Christian brethren trespass against us, we are bound to rebuke them, (though with mildness,) for it is written, "Thou shalt not hate thy brother in thine heart; thou shalt in any wise rebuke him, and not suffer sin upon him." (Lev. xix. 17.)

Are we not then to turn the left cheek to him that has smitten us on the right? The command is to be obeyed in the *spirit*, rather than in the *letter*. And what is the *spirit* of the command? It is a willingness to yield up our rights. We owe duties to others, and others owe duties to us. Now by nature we are apt to think *little* of the duties which we owe to others, and *much* of the duties they owe to us; that is, we think little of our *duties*, and much of our *rights*. We are inclined to watch the conduct of others towards us, and to feel angry when they do not behave as we think they ought. This is a ruinous course of thought; it not only makes us unhappy in THIS world, by leading us to feel dissatisfied and revengeful, but it endangers our happiness in the next, by taking off our thoughts from Christ, our atonement, and our example.

It is *useless* to think of the duties of others to us; they ought not perhaps to expect so much from us, or to behave to us with such disrespect, or with such harshness; but by dwelling on these subjects, we do not improve *their* conduct, but lose our *own* peace. On the contrary, it is most *useful* to think of the duties we owe to others, because we shall have to account for all our conduct at the last day. *Then* to have been ill-treated will be nothing, but to have ill-treated others will be dreadful. If we are engaged upon this profitable subject, we shall often not *observe* when our fellow-creatures behave ill to us, and thus we shall miss many occasions of uneasiness, and also of sin. But if we *do* observe any ingratitude, or unkindness, there is one great use we may make of the trial; we may examine whether there is no person to whom we have behaved in a similar manner. It is almost certain that we shall remember having done something *like* the offence we have received, to some of our fellow-creatures; but at all events, we shall find that there is *One* to whom we have behaved *far, far* more ungratefully than any have behaved to us. All that our fellow-creatures can do to us is but a faint shadow of the manner in which we have insulted God. What has He not a right to expect from us! If a man had expended all his property in ransoming a poor prisoner, would he not expect some grateful return for his generosity? But God has given up his only Son for our sakes. O sacrifice surpassing human thought! And how have we behaved towards him? How coldly! How unfaithfully! What reluctant obedience have we rendered! More frequently still, what open *disobedience!*

This consideration should make us very meek when we receive injuries. If it really sinks into our *hearts*, we shall become less ready to complain of others, and more earnest in our endeavors to behave well to them.

Evening Scripture portion. Deut. XIX. *Eye for eye.*

MATT. V. 43 to end.—*Christ enjoins the forgiveness of enemies.*

IT is written in Lev. xix., "Thou shalt love thy neighbor as thyself." The Pharisees for many ages past had given a very imperfect explanation of this law. They had not explained the term "neighbor" aright. They had declared that it applied to those who loved us, and did not include those who hated us. But this was not true. Every human creature is, in one sense, our neighbor. We are therefore commanded to love all. God had never said, "Thou shalt hate thine enemy;" for, though he had desired the Jews to form no friendships with heathen nations, he had never commanded them to hate or injure them from feelings of revenge. It was man who had added, "Thou shalt hate thine enemy." How easy it was to obey such a law! By nature we love our friends, and hate our enemies. As Christ said, "Even the *publicans* love those that love them." The publicans were people of very bad character, who generally defrauded in collecting the taxes, and who were therefore much despised: yet even *they* behaved with kindness and respect to their particular friends. The Pharisees had no reason to be proud of such righteousness as this. Well might our Saviour say to his disciples, "Except your righteousness shall *exceed* the righteousness of the Scribes and Pharisees, ye shall in no case enter into the kingdom of heaven." Yet this is the sort of righteousness which men are still inclined to think sufficient to entitle them to everlasting happiness. How often people say, "Have I not been a good mother to my children, a faithful friend, a kind brother—what harm have I done?" They claim a reward from God for such goodness as this! But our Saviour expects far more from his disciples; he expects them to love those who hate them; to speak kindly to them, in spite of their abusive words, and to pray for them, notwithstanding repeated injuries. And yet even this conduct deserves no reward, because it is no more than our duty.

Do we say, how is it possible for us to do this? It *is* impossible, without a new heart. We are too *sinful* to do it. Those who have been renewed by grace are enabled to love their enemies. The missionaries who went to Greenland to dwell amidst plains of snow and mountains of ice, were treated in the most unfeeling manner by the natives. Once the ship that was to have brought them provisions did not arrive at the expected time, and they were reduced to the brink of famine; for they could not procure food by hunting seals, as the natives did. The cruel Greenlanders mocked at their sufferings, and refused to relieve them. At length the ship containing provisions arrived. The missionaries might have gone back in it to their native country, but they remained in Greenland. Soon afterwards, many of the people were in want of food, as through their improvidence their summer stores were exhausted. Did the missionaries refuse to feed them? They shared their little stock with them. The people were attacked with the smallpox; the missionaries nursed them with the greatest tenderness. This conduct had a great effect in softening the minds of the heathen towards their teachers, and in preparing them to receive their message. It is by such behavior we may show that we are the children of God.

How does God behave towards ungrateful man? Our Saviour reminded his disciples that God sent rain, and the light of day, to all, even to those who hated him. But he did not *then* speak of a still *greater* proof of love—the gift of his Son. For a *righteous* man some might even dare to die; but God commendeth his love towards us, in that while we were yet *enemies*, we were reconciled to him by the death of his Son. This shows us what *kind* of love we ought to feel for our enemies. The *same kind* that God feels for us. *Not* the love of *approbation*, (*that* we can only feel for the righteous,) but the love of *compassion*. It is *this* love that God felt for the world when he gave his Son to die for it. To love an enemy is to be *perfect;* for it is to have charity, the bond of perfectness. If we have this charity, this love to all, we are like God, though our love can never be so great as His.

If we earnestly desire the salvation of our enemies, then we may know that we are the children of God. Let us endeavor to melt their hearts by acts of kindness. Such efforts are often blessed to the conversion of sinners. A holy man was once, for the truth's sake, shut up in a prison, and obliged to share the cell of a murderer. The conduct of his wicked companion was so intolerable, that his fellow-prisoner complained of him to those who overlooked the prison. An order was issued that the murderer should be removed to another dungeon. When the unhappy man heard to what place he was to be committed, his dismay was great, for he knew that the damp and closeness of that dungeon would cut short his life in a few days. He implored his fellow-prisoner, with many tears, to ask that the sentence might be reversed. The holy man felt that it was his duty to yield to these entreaties. He requested that the murderer might be permitted to remain with him. His petition was granted, but with this condition, that he should complain no more of the conduct of his companion. The murderer was melted by the generosity of the man he had once hated and annoyed. He fell at his feet, and with tears of gratitude implored his pardon. Henceforth he listened to his instructions, and through the grace of God, repented, and believed the Gospel.—(Related by the Rev. Cesar Malan.)

Evening Scripture portion. Lev. XIX. 1–18. *Love of our neighbor.*

MATT. VI. 1–4.—*Christ forbids ostentation in almsgiving.*

THE Lord Jesus now began to show the emptiness of the *good works* in which the Pharisees gloried. He had declared what false views they entertained of the *law of God*, and now he shows that their best actions were nothing worth, because they were done from wrong *motives.*

Let us remember that he said, in the early part of the sermon, that except our righteousness shall exceed the righteousness of the Scribes and Pharisees, we shall in no wise enter into the kingdom of heaven. Here is an instance of what their righteousness was. They sometimes bestowed large sums of money on the poor, or on the service of the temple; but their desire was to be seen *of men.* They did not care so much for God's favor, as for men's admiration. Therefore they took care to have their charities *known.* They did not *literally* sound a trumpet before them; but they endeavored as much to attract notice, as if they had sounded a trumpet. They *did* gain much praise from men, and this was their reward, and their *only* reward.

We all by nature care for the praise of men more than for the praise of God. The reason is, that we have no faith. We see men, we hear their praise; but we do not see God, nor hear his voice. But when a person has faith, he begins to value God's favor more than the praise of men. To hear every human tongue united in applauding him, would not give him as much delight as the hope of hearing God say, " Well done, good and faithful servant."

Now the point we should examine is this: Which are *we* most anxious to obtain, the praise of men or the favor of God?

It may sometimes be best that our charities should be *known.* David, for instance, gave the gold and silver he had saved for the temple in a *public* manner. But *why?* Not to gain praise, but to encourage others to give also. Should we even *hide* our charities, and at the same time *desire* that they should be discovered, God would not be pleased with us. He looks at the heart. He wants us to act to him alone. We ought not to think that our charities *deserve* to have a reward from God. If we do them with this idea they will not be acceptable. What can *we* give to God? Nothing worthy of his acceptance. All we can bestow are but like the flowers that the cottager may gather from his garden, and present to the monarch as a slender token of his gratitude for the gift of his cottage, and for his garden, and for all that he possesses. A gracious sovereign would not refuse the gift, if *humbly* offered, though the flowers were common, and though his own garden contained the rarest and the finest; but if the cottager presented them to gain the praise of his neighbors, or thinking he conferred a great favor upon his king, both the offering and the offerer would deserve to be rejected. And shall those who give money for God's service in such a spirit, be accepted? Cornelius gave alms from the overflowings of a grateful heart, therefore the angel said to him, "Thy prayers and thine alms are come up as a memorial before God," (Acts x. 4.) The poor widow gave her two mites with a single eye to God's glory. She gave her *heart* with them, or it would not have been said of her, "She gave more than they all." Mary poured the ointment on the head of Jesus, under a deep sense of her own unworthiness, and of the preciousness of her Saviour; therefore Jesus accepted the service, and has caused it to be remembered through all ages. All we do from a feeling of grateful love to *Him*, who laid down his life for us, shall be remembered by God, when the costly gifts of ostentation shall be buried in eternal forgetfulness.

Evening Scripture portion. 1 Chron. XXIX. 1–19. *David's gift to the Temple.*

MATT. VI. 5–8.—*Christ forbids ostentation in prayer.*

OUR Saviour continued to expose the emptiness of the works in which the Pharisees prided themselves. One of these was *almsgiving*. This has been *already* considered. Another was *prayer*. Let us now direct our attention to this subject. The customs of Judea were very different from ours. The synagogues were always open, and persons resorted to them, as well as to the temple, in order to pray. There was no harm in the custom, and many persons no doubt went to the synagogues to pray in sincerity, as we know one poor publican went to the temple, and sincerely said, "God be merciful to me, a sinner." But others went only to be *seen of men*. There were also certain hours of the day at which the Pharisees said certain prayers; and if at these hours they found themselves in the streets, they stopped to repeat their task; and for this purpose preferred the corner of a street to a more private place. Jesus bade his disciples avoid such ostentatious conduct, and advised them to retire to their closets to pray, and to conceal from the world their communion with their heavenly Father.

If we really love God, we shall pray to him in *secret*. It is clear, that if we pray in church and in the family, but neglect *secret* prayer, we are only seeking human approbation.

It is a great proof, both of *faith* and *love*, to be frequent in secret prayer. If we were told that a departed friend was hovering near us, though unseen, and that he could hear us, though he could not answer us aloud, should we feel inclined to speak to him? This would depend upon two circumstances: *first*, upon our *faith* in the statement, that is, upon our really believing that the friend was near; and secondly, upon our *love* for this friend. If we both believed he was near, and loved him, we should find great delight in talking to him. "He that cometh to God, must believe that he *is*." If we doubt whether God hears us, no wonder we find prayer a burdensome task. If, also, we do not *love* God, how can we find it pleasant to speak to him? But if we believe that he is very near us, and if we love him with fond attachment, O how delightful to shut our closet door, and to pour out our hearts before him! And will he give us a *reward* for doing so? What! A reward to his needy creatures, for calling upon him for help! The reward will be, He will answer our petitions as He has promised, and at the last acknowledge us as His children.

Jesus also tells us in what *manner* we should pray. It is not words alone that move God. The heathen think they shall be heard for *much speaking*, and say, Baal, hear us, Baal, hear us. The Roman Catholics repeat the Lord's prayer many hundreds of times, and count the numbers upon their string of beads. But of what use are such prayers; for what are *words* without *desires!* We should *use words*, because in using them our desires grow stronger; but words without *desires* are but unmeaning noise. A Christian poet beautifully describes the nature of prayer in the following lines:

Prayer is the soul's sincere desire,
Utter'd, or unexpress'd;
The hidden motion of a fire
That trembles in the breast.

Prayer is the burden of a sigh,
The falling of a tear;
The upward glancing of an eye,
When none but God is near.

Sometimes the *mouth* cannot express what the *heart* feels. But sometimes the soul feels dead, and we cannot pray in spirit and in truth. An unconverted heart is always dead; but even the renewed heart has seasons of barrenness. How are desires to be stirred up? Take the Scriptures—consider the things revealed in them—Heaven, Hell, God, the Judge of all—the crucified Saviour—a precious soul—a fleeting life. Is there nothing you desire to escape? Nothing you desire to possess? Have you nothing to say to Him who can do every thing for you, and who has done so much already? What would many a lost soul give for such an opportunity as you now possess? God, who sees your efforts, will send his Holy Spirit to teach you how to pray. Let us remember that prayer is our safety; without prayer we must be lost. When a person can receive no nourishment, we give him up; we know he must die if he can take nothing. If we cannot *pray*, we must perish.

Evening Scripture portion.
Gen. XXXII. 13 to end. *Jacob wrestling with the Angel.*

MATT. VI. 9–13.—*The Lord's Prayer.*

THIS prayer is so familiar to us, that we are in great danger of not considering its weighty meaning. A prayer taught by our blessed Saviour himself ought to engage our deepest attention. Had we been told that such a prayer had been given, and had never heard the words, how we should have desired to hear them!

We ought not to suppose that we are bound to use this prayer every time we pray. Jesus said, "After this *manner* pray ye." We find in this prayer a pattern for our prayers. We see in what way we should address God, and what kind of petitions we may present. The title we are allowed to give to Him is the tenderest that can be conceived—Our *Father*. He is our Father, because he made us in his own image; but by *sin*, we became children of the devil. How then are we restored to our Father? By Jesus Christ. He became our brother in the *flesh*, that we might become *his* brethren in the *spirit*. He makes us the children of God by faith in him. Thus he said to Mary Magdalene, after he rose from the dead, "Go to my brethren, and say to them, I ascend to my Father, and to *your* Father, and to my God, and to *your* God."

Our Father is a *king* also; but a dethroned king. His subjects have risen up in rebellion against him. Therefore his children entreat him to return. His return is the darling wish of their hearts. It is a great sign of faithfulness in subjects, when they maintain allegiance to a sovereign who is in banishment. At such a time it is dangerous to be faithful; for if discovered in sending letters to their monarch, inviting him to take possession of his throne, they would be regarded as enemies by their rebellious countrymen. Yet faithful subjects would be continually forming plans for the restoration of their lawful sovereign, and would run all risks rather than desert him. The children of God feel and act in this manner while they live in the world. Their desire is, that their Father's name should be hallowed, praised, and adored; that his kingdom should come, and that his will should be done on earth, as it is in heaven. In their prayers they express this desire *first*, and they endeavor to promote its fulfilment by persuading men to submit to their king. Nor shall their desires and efforts be disappointed, for God shall one day be king over all the earth. We see, therefore, that only converted persons can offer this prayer in sincerity, for none who are not converted long for God to be acknowledged as king.

The next requests relate to such things as we desire for *ourselves*. In the first place we ask for bread; not for a *great* supply, but *daily* bread. Then we ask for the forgiveness of sins, declaring at the same time that we have forgiven others their sins against us. Thus we see that this prayer suits none whose hearts cherish hatred and revenge; for if we do *not* forgive those who offend us, every time we use this prayer we are pronouncing our own condemnation, and asking God *not* to forgive us.

We have before remarked, that this prayer is only fit for those who love *God*, because they ask that his kingdom may come and his will be done. We now see that it is only fit for those who love *man* also; and we know that those who do love God, love their fellow-creatures also. These are the two great commandments—Love God and love thy neighbor. When people believe in Christ they have new hearts, and they begin to love God and man. Then this prayer suits them. They still have sins to be forgiven, and it is the sense of God's grace in forgiving them, that makes them so ready to forgive others. When God has forgiven them a debt of thousands of pounds, how can they exact a debt of a few pence from their fellows! They feel that no one has acted towards them as ungratefully as they have towards God, and so their mouths are stopped from uttering reproaches against their fellow-creatures.

A penitent sinner hates sin. He can say from the heart, "Lead us not into temptation, but deliver us from evil, (or the evil one.") By nature we delight in temptation and in evil. All our pleasures are temptations; we are always running into it and longing for it. But the Christian dreads temptation; therefore he does not desire to be rich, nor to see much company, nor to obtain high praise, because he knows he might be tempted to be proud, and foolish, and to forget God.

The prayer is ended as it was begun—with the praise of God. Thine is the kingdom, the power, and the glory. This is the consolation of the child of God; though none may acknowledge his Father, yet he knows his Father is glorious, and that some day his glory will be displayed before an assembled universe.

Christ would not have given his people such a prayer, if he had not determined to *grant* it. He knows what he will do, and he delights to hear us asking him to perform his gracious designs. Then let every devout soul say, "Come, Lord Jesus, come quickly, for thine is the kingdom, the power, and the glory."

Evening Scripture portion. Rev. XI. *The kingdom of God.*

MATT. VI. 14, 15.—*Christ declares whom God will forgive.*

JESUS here gives some instructions concerning the frame of mind in which prayer must be made. In the Lord's prayer we are directed to say, "Forgive us our debts, or trespasses, as we forgive our debtors, or those who have sinned against us." This petition seems like asking God *not* to forgive us if we do *not* forgive others. Some people might have been induced to wish that some part of the sentence was omitted, and that they were instructed simply to ask God to forgive them, whether they forgave others or not. But it would be of no use to make such a prayer; for God is determined not to forgive us unless we do forgive others.

It is therefore necessary that we should inquire whether we do really forgive them; for our hearts are so deceitful that we are apt to imagine we forgive, when we still harbor a grudge against an offending brother. What then are the signs of having really forgiven an offender? When we have heartily forgiven him, we cease to indulge the *thought* of his offence, and we take no pleasure in *speaking* of it. When we have heartily forgiven him, we neither wish evil to befall him, nor feel glad if it do befall him; but, on the contrary, wish all manner of good to happen to him. When we have heartily forgiven him, we neither speak bitterly of him *ourselves*, nor do we feel gratified if we hear *others* speak harshly of him. This last, perhaps, is the best test of our state of feeling; for some who would not dare to speak harshly of an enemy themselves, would be glad to hear others do so. These should be our feelings even towards one who has *not* asked our forgiveness; but if our offending brother ask us to forgive him, we ought to restore him to friendship and endearment, and our heart ought to be towards him as before: and thus we ought to continue to act, in spite of *repeated* offences.

Is it an *easy thing* thus to forgive? No; it is *impossible* to nature, and can only be done through the Holy Spirit working in our hearts a sense of our own unworthiness, filling us with love to God for his mercy towards us, and then with love to our fellow-creatures.

Though thousands offer this prayer of our Lord every day, it is only accepted from those whose hearts are renewed by grace. Before our *prayers* are accepted, we *ourselves* must be accepted. Cain's *sacrifice* was not accepted by God, because he *himself* was not accepted. Abel's sacrifice was accepted, because he himself was accepted. Would we, therefore, offer acceptable prayers, we must first give our own selves to the Lord; we must come in the name of Jesus, and on account of his sacrifice that he offered on the cross, God will accept *us*, renew our hearts by his grace, and answer our prayers. God will not be mocked. Man would fain put God off with formal, heartless prayers; but He will not receive them. He spurns the offering, and says, "Who hath required this at *your* hands—to tread my courts? When you spread forth your hands I will hide mine eyes from you. Yea, when you make many prayers I will not hear." (Is. i. 12–15.)

But let no penitent sinner be discouraged by these declarations. We may come with our sins to Christ, if they are a grief and a burden to us, for it is He alone who can *forgive* them, and it is He alone who can *subdue* them. His Holy Spirit will make us *hate* our sins, help us to strive against them, and enable us to overcome them.

Evening Scripture portion.—Is. I. 1–20. *The prayers of the wicked*

MATT. V. 16–18.—*Christ forbids ostentation in fasting.*

THERE was another duty upon the performance of which the Pharisees prided themselves—fasting. Some of them fasted twice a week. On those days they neglected the care of their persons, and went abroad that men might see they fasted, and admire them for their religion. In the day of a *public* fast for the sins of the *nation*, men should not conceal that they fast; but, like the king of Nineveh, who repented at the preaching of Jonah, they should set an example of penitence and self-denial. But when men fast for their *own* sins, then they ought to conceal the deed, and not seek to obtain human praise.

The scriptures teach us that fasting is a duty. It brings down the spirits, and sobers the mind; and, by the blessing of the Holy Spirit, disposes the soul for prayer and meditation. But there are some persons so delicate, that their health would be injured by long fasting. It surely cannot be a duty for them to fast, for they would thus be less fit to pray.

But *all* should beware of excess in food, which drowns the soul, and renders it sensual and stupid. It is written concerning one of the most wicked cities of old, "Pride, FULNESS OF BREAD, and abundance of idleness was in her and her daughters," (or inhabitants.) This fulness made them haughty, and brought on their destruction. (Ez. xvi. 48, 50.) Let none think that they are too pious to stand in need of such a warning. Christ warns his *own* disciples against surfeiting and drunkenness: "Take heed lest at any time your *hearts* be overcharged with surfeiting and drunkenness." (Luke xxi. 34.) Constant moderation in meat and drink is as important to the soul as to the body.

But when we fast let us beware of *pride;* for as dead flies spoil the most fragrant ointment, so pride mars the most self-denying actions.

We should perform religious duties secretly, when we are among those who will think highly of us for observing them. This rule applies to fastings, prayer, reading the scripture, and doing good. But when we are among those who would ridicule us for religion, then is the time boldly to confess our Master, and to show that we are not ashamed of him. How *easy* it is to speak against vain amusements, to quote the scriptures, and to make pious remarks in the presence of religious people: but how difficult, when surrounded by scoffers, to be faithful to Christ! We need a lively sense of the presence of God, that we may always act as in his sight, neither courting the smiles of our fellow-creatures, nor fearing their frowns; neither seeking their *applause*, nor shrinking from their *ridicule*. Let us labor to be accepted of *Him*, to whom we must each give an account. In that solemn hour how worthless will the *praises* of our fellow-creatures appear, their *censures* how harmless!

Evening Scripture portion. Jonah III. IV. *Fasting.*

MATT. VI. 19–23.—*Christ forbids covetousness and double-mindedness.*

OUR Saviour had exposed the apparently *good* actions of the Pharisees, as their prayers, fastings, almsgivings. He now reproves their *wicked* practices. The first thing he attacks is their *covetousness*,—their delight in laying up earthly treasures. In those days riches consisted partly in valuable *clothes*, and therefore He speaks of moth and rust corrupting.

The Lord shows, in the first place, the *folly* of covetousness. Riches make themselves wings, and fly away. How *foolish*, then, to set the heart upon them! But if we do not *lose* them, we must *leave* them. We brought nothing into this world, and we can carry nothing out; it is therefore evident to *reason*, that if there is another world in which we shall *eternally* dwell, we ought to be extremely anxious to lay up treasures there.

But *how* are we to lay up treasures in heaven? By good works. St. Paul, in his epistle to Timothy, says, "Charge them that are rich in this world that they do good, that they be *rich* in *good works*, ready to distribute; willing to communicate, laying up in store for themselves a good foundation against the time to come, that they may lay hold on eternal life." But some may inquire, "Can we gain heaven by good works?" O no. Jesus Christ has gained heaven by *his* righteousness, and he freely *bestows* this heaven on all who believe in him. We cannot lay up treasures there, till we have believed in Him.

We lay up treasures there, when we do things that please God. Good works are the fruits of faith. It is written, "Blessed are the dead which die in the Lord." It is added, "Their works do follow them." (Rev. xiv. 13.) These blessed dead had believed in Christ; therefore their works were accepted. The Pharisees could not please God; they could not lay up treasures in heaven. And why not? Because the eyes of their minds were shut; and they saw not the glory of God in the face of Christ Jesus.

How great is the darkness of the unawakened mind! God alone, by his Holy Spirit, can enlighten this darkness. Jesus came to give sight to the blind. Has he given it to us? Our actions show whether he has or not. When we see a blind person, we are not always aware at first that he is blind; but if we watch him closely we soon discover his condition. If a mad dog pass near him, he does not try to avoid it; and if the most splendid illuminations be displayed, he does not stop to admire. The *actions* of men show clearly whether they are blind or not. Unawakened souls evince no dread of hell, no desire after heaven, no contempt for earth, no love for Christ. God frowns, but they are not alarmed; He stretches out his arms, but they perceive it not; He opens the gate of heaven, they do not strive to enter it; He points to the abyss of hell, they do not shrink back; He lifts up his crucified Son, they are not softened, or subdued.

There is an eye to the mind: if that eye be shut, we can do nothing right. This is what our Lord meant when he declared, "The light of the body is the eye; if therefore thine eye be single, (or clear,) thy whole body shall be full of light; but if thine eye be evil, (or blind,) thy whole body shall be full of darkness." When the eye of the mind is made clear, then we begin to *act* aright, and not till then. Do we wish to know where *our* treasure is? Let us inquire where our heart is. They are in the same place. If our *affections* are set on things above, then we may know that we have *treasures* there; but if our *heart* is in our possessions, whether they be few or many, small or great, there our *treasure* is. Some unhappy creatures have shown in their last hours that their hearts were fixed upon some earthly trifles. A vain and foolish girl has been haunted in her expiring moments by the thoughts of her new dresses. A miser has been known eagerly to clench paper in his trembling hands, thinking it was his bank-notes. Had these dying persons possessed treasures in heaven, they would not have clung so closely to their perishing property on earth.

Evening Scripture portion. Prov. XXIII. *Riches have wings.*

MATT. VI. 24 to end.—*Christ forbids worldly carefulness.*

OUR Saviour had charged his disciples not to lay up treasures upon earth. In this passage He gives them another command that appears much more difficult to obey, that is, He forbids them to be anxious about needful food and raiment. We are naturally inclined to think it impossible *not* to be anxious about the means of our support; but God graciously offers many arguments to prevent our indulging in such cares.

Do we doubt God's *power* to provide for us? Who was it gave us *life*, and made our bodies? Is it not much easier to clothe, and to feed, than to create us? Do we doubt the *kindness* of the Lord? Does He not condescend to feed the ravens and clothe the lilies? and are *we* not much *better* than they, that is, much more precious in his sight than birds or flowers? Therefore we see that we dishonor God by doubting whether He will provide for our need.

It is also *useless* to be anxious about the future. By taking thought we cannot add one cubit to our height, nor one moment to our lives. We know from other parts of scripture, that God does not desire us to be idle or improvident: he only forbids useless tormenting fears about the future.

And why does He forbid such thoughts? Because there is a nobler object set before us, which requires *all* our thoughts—"The kingdom of God and his righteousness." This kingdom we must seek *earnestly*, or we shall not obtain it. If our thoughts are occupied about earthly things, we shall lose this earthly inheritance. Christ said, "Ye cannot serve God and mammon," (or the world.) Neither can we be intent upon what we shall eat, and drink, and wear, and at the same time be seeking God. Christ said, that the Gentiles thought of these things. The Gentiles at that time were ignorant heathens, they knew not God, therefore they were occupied with earthly cares; but we ought not to be like them.

If we wish to discover our state before God, let us examine with what subjects our thoughts are generally occupied. Of course, while we are engaged upon any business, our minds must be on that business; but after it is done, our thoughts fly to the objects we most delight in. If we are God's children, our thoughts will often fly to heaven, our Father's house; but if we are not born again they will grovel upon the earth. This is God's own rule, "They that are after the flesh do mind the things of the flesh; but they that are after the Spirit the things of the Spirit."

It may appear to us a trifling sin to be engrossed with earthly thoughts; but it is a sign that we are in the flesh, not born again of the Spirit. Now it is written, "They that are in the flesh cannot please God." (Rom. viii. 8.) How dreadful it would be to die in this state!

How kindly God undertakes to keep us from want, while we are seeking spiritual blessings with all our hearts! "Seek ye *first* the kingdom of God and his righteousness, and all these things shall be added unto you."

How happy should we be even in this world, if we would obey this command! "Sufficient unto the day is the evil thereof." It is much *pleasanter* to be thinking of heaven and Christ, than to be dwelling upon the evils of life; and O! how much *safer* is it! For though it is *useless* to take thought about *earthly* things, it is of the greatest *use* to take thought about *spiritual* things. By thinking of hell we shall be led to flee from it; by thinking of sin, to dread it; by thinking of righteousness, to implore God to bestow it upon us, even Christ's righteousness upon us His guilty creatures.

Evening Scripture portion.
Ps. CXLV. *The goodness of God to his creatures.*

MATT. VII. 1–6.—*Christ forbids hypocritical judgment.*

THE Lord Jesus had been warning his disciples against many of the evil practices of the Pharisees. There was no sin to which they were more addicted than to "judging." They did not judge righteous judgment, according to the word of God; but they judged according to their own wicked passions. Because they hated Christ, they endeavored to find faults in his conduct, and accused him of breaking the Sabbath, of encouraging sinners, and of being a gluttonous man and a wine-bibber. The men of the world still walk in the steps of the Pharisees: they are continually looking with a malicious eye for faults in the children of God, and attributing wrong motives to all their actions.

We may be sure that such judgment is sinful, because it is passed in a spirit of *hatred.* In how different a spirit the Christian judges! He cannot but know that the world lieth in wickedness; he sees it with grief, and exerts all his powers to persuade sinners to flee from the wrath to come. By this rule we may know whether we are judging righteously or unrighteously. Do we *rejoice* over the faults of others, or do we *lament* over them! If we are seeking for their faults, and watching for their halting, then we have the spirit of the Pharisees, who maliciously watched the conduct of Christ and his disciples; then we may be sure that we are offending God, that we shall be judged by him, and that with the same measure we mete it will be measured to us; for "*he* shall have judgment without mercy that hath showed no mercy." (James ii. 13.) It is in this spirit that irreligious people judge those whom they call "evangelicals and saints." They accuse them of hypocrisy and of pride; they watch their conduct with an eagle's eye, and triumph over their infirmities with a demon's joy. Such persons have a beam in their own eye. This beam prevents them from seeing their *own* sins. We may be assured, that if we do not see *ourselves* to be very great and miserable sinners, there is a beam of unbelief in our eyes which prevents our seeing it. While we cannot see our *own* sins, we cannot see the sins of *others* aright. What *we* call sins in them, perhaps are *not* sins. We do not know how to reprove till we have discovered what sinners we *ourselves* are.

But when God, by his converting grace, takes the beam out of our eyes, then we may help our brother to overcome *his* sins. Then we shall warn him in a spirit of humility and love, feeling our own unworthiness, and anxious for his good.

But there are some characters, in dealing with whom great caution must be used. Hypocrites may be compared to dogs and swine. As these animals feed on carrion and the vilest refuse, so hypocrites delight in sin. It would be wrong to give holy food, such as the priests ate, to dogs; and it would be foolish to cast pearls, such as queens wear, to swine.

But is it wrong or foolish to declare the holy and precious word of God to wicked men? O no—for Jesus said to his apostles, "Preach the gospel to every creature." But when men, having heard the truth, trample it under foot by their blasphemies, and turn and rend by their revilings those who speak it, then they must be left to themselves. In this manner the apostle Paul dealt with the wicked Jews of Corinth. "And when they opposed themselves and blasphemed, he shook his raiment." "Your blood be upon your own heads: I am clean: from henceforth I will go unto the Gentiles!" (Acts xviii. 6.) Thus the apostle left the dogs and swine, that he might feed the sheep committed to his charge.

Evening Scripture portion. Acts XVIII. ***Enemies of the truth.***

MATT. VII. 7–11.—*Christ promises that prayer shall be answered.*

THIS is one of the most encouraging passages in the whole Scriptures. How many have been led by this invitation to approach the throne of grace! Here is not only an *invitation* which assures you of a welcome, but also a *promise* of success—your petition shall be granted, "for *every one* that asketh receiveth."

Christ knew how apt we are to doubt the love of our Heavenly Father. Therefore he appealed to all the parents present, and said, "What man is there of you, whom if his son ask bread will he give him a stone?" Every parent who heard this question must have felt that he could not treat his child in so unfeeling a manner: much less would he give his child a serpent instead of a fish, or a scorpion instead of an egg. There are in the East white scorpions, about the size of an egg; but no parent would deceive and mock his child by giving him that venomous animal instead of wholesome food.

There are few who cannot recollect the kindness their parents showed to them in their helpless days. There are few who have no recollection of a father's or a mother's love. In childhood we knew not its value, but in later years it melts our hearts to think of it. How readily our dear parents listened to our requests! They were not always able to grant them, and sometimes they saw it would not be well to give us what we desired. But they never denied us food when we needed it. They would rather have gone without it themselves, than have seen us suffering from hunger. How carefully they guarded us from every thing that would injure us! They warned us not to approach too near the fire, or the water, and not to touch poisonous berries or venomous reptiles. Far from giving us a scorpion, they would have been terrified, if they had seen it in our hands. And does God feel the same tenderness for his children? Hear what Jesus says who came forth from the bosom of the Father: "If ye then, being evil, know how to give good gifts unto your children, how *much more* shall your Father which is in heaven give good things to them that ask him?"

But if any trembling soul should reply, "How can I be sure that He is *my* Father? He is not the Father of the wicked," let him know that none but the children of God ask him for *good* things. The little lamb is shown to belong to its own mother by running to her to be fed. The children of Satan do not desire to have those things which God has promised. They seek for an earthly portion. They never *really* pray. When they are miserable, they often complain, but these complaints are not prayers. God said of Israel, "They have not cried unto me with their hearts, when they howled upon their beds," (Hos. vii. 14.) Sometimes in distress they make vows, as well as complaints. But are their vows prayers? God calls them flatteries, and lies. "Nevertheless they did but flatter him with their mouth, and they lied unto him with their tongues, for their heart was not right with him," (Ps. lxxviii. 36.) How different from these were the prayers of David! He could say to God, "I entreated thy favor with my whole heart." And he could also say, "Blessed be the Lord because He hath heard the voice of my supplications." Every one who is now earnestly seeking God shall sooner or later say the same. Therefore, "let the heart of them rejoice that seek the Lord," (Ps. cv. 3.)

Evening Scripture portion. Prov. II. ***Earnestness in seeking the Lord.***

MATT. VII. 12–14.—*Christ describes the wrong and the right way.*

WHO can hear our Saviour's golden rule without approving it! And who can hear it without condemning himself! "Whatsoever things ye would that men should do unto you, do ye even so to them." He who has kept the same is a perfect man, and has done all the law and prophets taught. We must confess with sorrow that we have broken it a thousand times, and that we need pardon through the Saviour's blood for these manifold transgressions. But though we have transgressed, yet if we desire to please God, we shall find this rule an admirable guide. God knows our ignorance, and has graciously furnished us with a rule that will apply to all circumstances in which we can be placed. On every occasion we should imagine ourselves to be in the place of our neighbor, and say, (for instance,) "If I were a parent, how should I expect my child to behave towards me; if I were a child, my parent; if I were a master, how should I require my servant to conduct himself; if I were a servant, how should I wish my master to deal with me; if I were suffering pain, what should I desire the healthy to do to alleviate my misery; if I were sunk in poverty, what should I think the rich ought to do, when they beheld my destitution?" We may go further still, and say, "If I were a perishing heathen, now standing before the bar of God, what should I then think Christians ought to have done for me?" We must, however, ask these questions with *this* condition—"What would it be *reasonable* for me to expect another to do for me, if I were in his circumstances?"

How ill can we bear to be examined by this rule! And yet we have behaved *far, far better* to our *fellow-creatures* than we have to *God.*

Our Saviour, by his next declaration, has often excited astonishment and anxiety. He declared that the gate of life was strait, and that the way was narrow; by which he meant that men find it difficult to be truly religious. The narrow way is not broader *now* than it was when these words were first spoken, and *still* there are but few who find it. And if there are but *few* who find it, let us never conclude that any practice is right, because *many* indulge in it. The way in which *many* walk must be wrong. If we would please God and save our souls, we must be singular.

In the broad way there are many *travellers*, and there are many *paths* in which those travellers walk. People of all sorts of character walk in it; the intemperate, and the miser; the pleasure-lover, and the self-righteous; and each different kind of character condemns the other. Yet they are all alike in this respect, they do not love God, nor do his will; and they are *all* hastening (however little they may think it) to the *same* destruction.

Christians, on the contrary, all walk in the same path. They are all alike in spirit, though some are more excellent than others. They enter in at the same strait gate, that is, they believe in the same Saviour. Though they come from the opposite ends of the world, yet they know each other's minds, and sympathize with each other's feelings. The greatest king and the meanest beggar have a sympathy with each other, if they both love Christ.

Yet this narrow way is little sought. The reason is, men cannot bear the sacrifices which they must make before they can enter in: they do not like to give up their pleasure and their pride. If they would walk in this narrow way, they would find it pleasant. In some places it is steep, and in others it is rough; but the *prospect* makes it pleasant. It is a prospect that would make any path pleasant. It is a prospect that grows brighter as the traveller proceeds; it is the prospect of the everlasting hills, crowned with the golden city and the pearly gates. And the *Companion* makes it pleasant. He is at once the guard, the guide, the friend of all who walk in the narrow way.

And though but *few* walk in it *now*, yet in the home to which it leads a multitude shall be found, yes, a multitude without number; for in *every* age, there have been *some* who travelled in this path, and in the ages yet to come there shall be many more. The broad road shall not be always thronged. When Satan, who now deceives the world, shall be shut up in prison, then the broad way shall be forsaken, the people shall be *all* righteous, and none shall say any more to his neighbor, "Know the Lord," for *all* shall "know Him from the greatest to the least." Our journey may be lonely, but our Father's house shall not be *empty*. There are *many* mansions in it, and not one of them shall want a blessed inhabitant. Then will our divine Lord be satisfied, when he beholds gathered around Him his innumerable family.

And shall the straitness of the gate deter us from seeking to enter in? Or shall the narrowness of the way induce us to turn back? It would be well to go through fire and water to attain such an inheritance. But the *sufferings* of this way are far less than its *consolations*, and these cannot be *compared* with its *end*. "I reckon," said the apostle Paul, "that the sufferings of this life are not worthy to be compared with the glory which shall be revealed in us," (Rom. viii. 18.)

Evening Scripture portion. Isa. LX. *Multitudes of believers in the last days.*

MATT. VII. 15–20.—*Christ warns against false prophets.*

OUR Saviour had been showing his disciples the necessity of walking in the narrow way to heaven. He knew that many false teachers would arise, who would point out an easier way; and the Pharisees at that very time encouraged people, by their instructions and example, to walk in the broad road which leadeth to destruction.

There have been false teachers in all ages. There were some among the Jews of old. Jeremiah and Ezekiel warned the people against prophets, who said, "Peace, peace, when there was no peace," and "healed the wound of the daughter of God's people slightly," and "daubed the wall with untempered mortar." (Ez. xiii.) By these comparisons we are taught that the false prophets encouraged people to remain in sin. False ministers do so now; they do not teach the necessity of a living faith, and of an entire change of heart; therefore their hearers are not led to wash in the fountain of Christ's blood, or to pray that they may be truly converted.

It is quite necessary to warn people against such teachers; for many listen to their words, and follow their pernicious ways. These ministers are compared to wolves, because they destroy the souls of God's people. They are described as wearing sheep's clothing, because they often speak in a religious tone, and use Scripture language. When Lord Cobham was tried in London, in the year 1413, these hypocritical sentences were written by the Papists in his bills of condemnation: "Following Christ's example in all that we might, who willeth not the death of a sinner, but rather that he be converted and live, we took upon us to correct him. . . . . Pitying him of fatherly compassion, and entirely desiring the health of his soul, we appointed him a competent time of deliberation. Christ we take unto witness, that nothing else we seek in this our whole enterprise but his glory."

This language was sheep's clothing. Those who used it were inwardly ravening wolves. They sought to kill a pious nobleman, because he would not believe the errors which they taught. At last they obtained their heart's desire; for Lord Cobham was sentenced by the English parliament to be hung in chains and roasted over a slow fire.

Christ has told us *how* we are to detect false teachers when disguised in a fleece—by their fruits. The fruits of the Spirit are love, joy, peace, long-suffering, gentleness, goodness, faith, meekness, temperance. These heavenly qualities adorn every faithful minister, though in some they flourish more than in others. Love reigns in the heart of every true Christian, and shines forth in his actions. He may be known by his kindness to *all* the saints, by his patient behavior to his enemies, and by his unwearied efforts to save the souls of men. None but a converted person brings forth such fruits as these. There are many unconverted persons who lead moral, respectable, and even benevolent lives, but their hearts do not overflow with this *love* that we have described; and as their apparently good actions do not proceed from the right motive, they are worthless in the sight of Him who searches the hearts. None but a good tree can bring forth good fruit.

We are all bad trees by nature ; but God can make us good trees by his Spirit.

How awful is the declaration—" Every tree that bringeth not forth good fruit, is hewn down and cast into the fire." Should not this terrible sentence lead us all anxiously to inquire, " Have I received a new nature ? Have I become a good tree ? Has the heavenly Husbandman found good fruit growing upon my branches ?" The loving, the tender Saviour would not have alarmed us, had there been no cause for alarm.

Evening Scripture portion. Ezek. XIII. *False prophets.*

MATT. VII. 21–23.—*He predicts the rejection of the false professor.*

IN this passage, Jesus gave a solemn warning to his own disciples, to those who professed to believe in him, and to those who called him " Lord, Lord." At the beginning of this sermon, he had declared, that except their righteousness should exceed the righteousness of the Scribes and Pharisees, they could not be saved. He had shown that the righteousness of the Pharisees was a mere outward form of religion, and he had warned his own followers against being satisfied with a mere form also. He declared that *many* would be lost through this sad mistake. " Many will say unto *me* in that day, Lord, Lord, have we not prophesied in thy name ?" and I will profess unto them, " I never knew you." In these words Jesus revealed *himself* as the *Judge* of men—even as the Son of God.

Now let us hear what our Judge says. He declares that none shall enter heaven, but those who do the will of his Father. Does this make us tremble ? Surely we must feel (if we know ourselves at all) that we often sin. But, " doing the Father's will," does not mean *never* being overtaken by a fault ; for Christ declared to his Father in his last prayer for his disciples before his crucifixion, (John xvii.,) that *they* " *had kept his word.*" Yet we know that they had often fallen into sin, such as disputing which should be the greatest, desiring to resent injuries, and sending away poor suppliants. But what is it to do the will of God ? It is sincerely to seek to please him from LOVE to his name. None do this but those who have received the *Spirit of God*, those who are born again. Jesus did not explain this subject *fully* in *this* sermon ; but he said enough to show that we must seek for grace from God in order to be saved. Did he not say, " Seek first the kingdom of God and *his righteousness ?*" and also, " *Ask*, and ye shall receive ; seek, and ye shall find ; knock, and it shall be opened unto you?" If we would do the will of God, we must seek for new hearts.

There is a passage in the epistles, which shows clearly that nothing short of the power of God working in our hearts can enable us to perform any action acceptable in his sight. (Heb. xiii. 20, 21.) "Now the God of peace which brought again from the dead our Lord Jesus, (that great Shepherd of the sheep,) through the blood of the everlasting covenant, make you perfect in every good work *to do his will, working in you* that which is pleasing in his sight, through Jesus Christ, to whom be glory forever. Amen." These verses show us that the power of that God who raised Christ from the dead, must work in our hearts to enable us to do his will. Neither can we do it, but through faith in Christ's *blood*, which was shed for us according to his everlasting promise or covenant.

Do we dread the idea of meeting with a repulse at the last day? Now is the time to examine whether we have been born again; whether the blood of Christ has washed away our sins; whether the Spirit has been shed abroad in our hearts; and whether we are doing the will of God. It is possible to depart out of this world, imagining we are going to heaven, and after all be disappointed. Many will suffer the severest of all disappointments. Will any of the lost spirits weep as bitterly as those who thought, till the very last, that they were going to be admitted into the mansions of bliss? Jesus would save us from receiving this agonizing refusal. He warns us beforehand not to be satisfied with a form of religion, but to seek for a new heart and a right spirit.

Evening Scripture portion. Heb. XIII. *Doing the will of God.*

MATT. VII. 24 to end.—*The parable of the house on the rock and the house on the sand.*

CHRIST ended his sermon on the mount by warnings against the danger of an empty profession of religion. He first gave the warning in *plain* language, saying, "Not every one that saith unto me, Lord, Lord, shall enter into the kingdom of heaven." Then he related a parable on the subject. It is the *first* of his parables recorded. It resembles his *last* parable in this point: both of them convey an awful warning to false professors of religion. In the parable of the talents an unprofitable servant is described, who is cast into outer darkness. (Matt. xxv. 30.) And in *this* parable a foolish builder is spoken of, who, we have reason to believe, was crushed beneath the ruins of his own house. Why did Jesus thus begin and end his series of parables with warnings against the same sin? Was it not that he knew the great danger in which we stand, of being satisfied with a mere form of godliness?

Nothing is said about the sort of house the wise man built upon the rock. It may have been a large, or a small one; a splendid house, or a mean one, we know not; but it was a *safe* one. The foundation was good. The foundation is the unseen part of a house, and yet the most important. So it is in religion. The unseen part is the most important. What is the state of the heart? that is the most important question. Has it been humbled before God? Has it believed in Christ, and been sprinkled with his blood? Has it been sanctified by the Holy Ghost? These are the important points; yet these are the invisible points. None do the sayings of Christ but those who are truly converted; they alone love him; and there is no obedience where there is no love.

The foolish man may have built a better house, in some respects, than the wise man did. The passers-by may have admired it more. He himself may have been much pleased with it. But it had one capital fault, the foundation was bad. Instead of digging deep down in the solid rock, as the wise man did, he had been satisfied with a foundation in the sand. His house was *unsafe;* the higher it was, the greater would be its fall in the stormy day. As long as the weather continued fair, the house remained standing. As it was situated by the seaside, it was exposed to the fury of the waves as well as that of the winds. The tempest at length arose, and the house fell. How awful was the crash! how total the ruin! The waves would carry its beams and its planks to distant shores.

There is a day coming when the floods of great waters will try every building, and prove its strength. How strange it is that any should imagine themselves safe because they have *heard* the gospel! This is one of Satan's devices. If he cannot keep us from hearing the truth, he tries to persuade us to be satisfied with hearing; whereas, hearing should always be followed up by praying, and praying by doing. Yet, after all, it is not our own obedience that will save us, but the obedience of Him who bore the punishment of our sins upon the cross. If we believe in Jesus, we are built upon the rock of ages, and shall be able to endure the storm that will destroy the world, and all that is therein.

Evening Scripture portion. James I. *Hearers of the word.*

LUKE VII. 1–10.—*The believing Centurion.*

How interesting every character must be whom the Saviour approved! He, who will be the Judge of each of us, has shown us beforehand what sort of persons he approves. This centurion was highly commended by the heart-searching Redeemer. Yet we should not have expected to find pity in a *centurion*. For, in the first place, he was a *soldier*, and a warlike life is a great hinderance to the soul. In the second place, he was a man of *rank:* and rank, we know, is a temptation to be proud. He was placed over a hundred soldiers, who were themselves men of some consideration; so that this centurion was perhaps equal in importance to a general in our armies. Thirdly, he was a *Gentile*, and therefore a heathen by birth. He had been sent by the Romans, who had conquered the Jews, to reside in Canaan. There he must have heard the Old Testament, and become acquainted with the true God, and believed the promise of a Saviour. The report of our Lord's miracles had reached him, and had convinced him that Jesus was the Son of God. Thus, though a soldier, a man of rank, and a Gentile, he was a true believer.

Now let us examine the character of him who was commended so highly by the Lord.

Observe his *compassion*. He was deeply interested in his poor servant's illness, for this servant was *dear* unto him. True religion binds the hearts of masters and servants together, and makes them brethren, beloved in the Lord. (See Epistle to Philemon, v. 16.)

Observe also *his love to the people of God*. He loved the *Jews*, because they were the peculiar people of God; and he did not love them in *word* only, but in *deed* and in truth, for he had built them a synagogue. Thus he had shown his love by his liberal actions.

Observe also his *humility*. Far from being puffed up with a conceit of his own merit, in having built a synagogue, he thought himself unworthy to come to the Saviour, or to receive him beneath his roof. St Matthew in his Gospel says the *centurion* came to Jesus; but, it is com mon to say people do things *themselves* when they cause *others* to do them. St. Luke gives a *longer* account of the circumstance, and mentions that some elders of the Jews were *sent* by the centurion. His respectful conduct was the more remarkable, because Jesus was poor and despised, but in the eyes of this honorable soldier, the lowly Nazarene was greater than the greatest of the sons of men. Being a *Gentile*, he thought he was less acceptable to Christ than the Jews, who were descended from the beloved Abraham, the friend of God. But in this he was mistaken, for Christ is no respecter of persons, and ever loved the children of Abraham in *spirit* above his children in the *flesh*. This Gentile *resembled* the Father of the Faithful, and was his son in *spirit*.

Lastly, let us consider his *faith*. It was in faith that he resembled Abraham. He had such faith, that he believed that if Jesus did but speak the word, all creatures must obey, even as his *own* soldiers and servants obeyed *him*. He thought that Christ's power was equal to that of God, who said, "Let there be light, and there was light." Nor was he mistaken; for all things were created by Jesus Christ, and are

upheld by the word of his power. This faith was exceedingly pleasing to the Saviour. Jesus loves faith. He plants it in the heart as the root of every other grace. Behold how he rewarded the centurion's faith! he healed his servant.

What peace we should enjoy, if in all our difficulties we felt that Jesus was able to deliver us! When our dear friends are sick, let us believe that He need only speak the word, and they would be well. Whatever anxiety presses on our hearts, let us bring it all to him, spread it before him, and trust him to do what will be best for us. If we act thus, we shall experience such mercies as will overwhelm us with gratitude.

Jesus declared that he had never met with such great faith in *Israel*, as he had found in this *Gentile.* He then took occasion to declare a very delightful and a very awful truth. It is recorded by St. Matthew, (viii. 11, 12,) "*Many* shall come from the east and west, and shall sit down with Abraham, Isaac, and Jacob, in the kingdom of heaven; but the children of the kingdom shall be cast out into outer darkness; there shall be weeping and gnashing."

By the "children of the kingdom," Jesus meant the Jews. They *heard* the sayings of Christ, and *did* them not; but many in distant lands would hear them and do them.

In our days the gospel has been preached in the North and South, the East and West; and already some in every part have believed. The Esquimaux, known among his nation as "the man the Saviour took to himself," shall he not come from the *north* to sit down with Abraham, Isaac, and Jacob? Africanus, once a ferocious chief, afterwards the missionary's faithful friend, shall he not come from the *south?* Abdool, the proud Mohammedan, grown as humble as a little child, shall he not come from the *East?* and though poor and despised like her Lord, shall not Sarah, the Indian widow*—the patient, the forgiving Sarah, come from the West to join the blessed company of patriarchs and prophets? God grant that none of us may be thrust with unbelieving Jews into outer darkness.

Evening Scripture portion. Heb. XI. 1–19. *Faith.*

Luke VII. 11–17.—*The raising of the widow's son.*

There are only *three* instances recorded of the Lord Jesus raising the dead, and in each instance was a case of aggravated sorrow.

The dead man of Nain was the *only* son of a widow; he was the

* See a tract published by the Religious Tract Society, entitled "Poor Sarah, the Indian Widow."

earthly *all* of his mother, the object of her fondest affections, and perhaps the support of her declining years.

If any of us have ever seen a widow who has sustained such a loss, what anguish of heart we have witnessed! How has she dwelt on the attractive qualities of the lost one; how has she lamented her own desolation, and said, in the bitterness of her soul, Is there any sorrow like unto my sorrow? No doubt we felt compassion for the bereaved parent, but not *such* as Jesus felt at the sight of the widow of Nain; for no heart was ever tender as the heart of the Redeemer.

What tenderness he showed in his manner of performing the miracle! He first addressed the sorrowful mother, saying, "Weep not." *We* should but mock the afflicted, if we were to say, "Weep not." We can only weep *with* those that weep. But Jesus could remove the cause of grief. Though himself a man of sorrows, he tasted the pure joy of comforting mourners. If the mother looked up, she beheld him through her tears approach the bier. What a moment of expectation that was! We do not know whether the bearers had faith to believe that Jesus could raise the dead, but they stood still in his presence. Then the majestic command was heard, "I say unto thee, Arise."

On what a scene that young man opened his eyes! There was his fond mother—but who was this wonderful person standing close beside him? He began to speak. By speaking he proved that he was really alive. What were his first words? We are not informed. Did he inquire who had restored him to life? He soon must have known, for he who had snatched him from the grasp of death, now delivered him into the arms of his mother. This sweet office the Lord would perform himself. It must have been a solace to his loving heart to behold the joyful meeting of the parent and the child.

But his chief reason for performing miracles was to confirm his word. By raising the widow's son, he showed that he could bestow life. He had declared, "All that are in the graves shall hear my voice, and shall come forth." Yet there will be a great difference between *that* resurrection, and *this* of the young man, because the dead will then be *changed;* whereas, this young man wore again his corruptible body. Jesus was the *first* who rose from the dead with a glorified body, no more to die.

Would we be partakers in the resurrection from the grave, we must *now* experience *another*—a resurrection from the death of trespasses and sins. This is the most wonderful of all; but Jesus can bestow it by his word. "The hour is coming, and *now is*," said the Lord of life, "when the dead shall hear the voice of the Son of God, and *live*." Yes, the hour *now is* when the dead hear the voice of the Son of God and live. The dead in trespasses and sins hear the voice of the Christ in his holy word; they believe, and *live*. As the apostle Paul said to the Ephesians, "You hath he quickened, (or made alive,) who were dead in trespasses and sins." (Eph. ii. 1.) These very words that

Jesus spake to the widow's son, "Young man, I say unto thee, Arise," have aroused some dead in *sins*, and caused them to live to God.

Evening Scripture portion.
1 Cor. XV. 35 to end. *The resurrection of the dead.*

LUKE VII. 18–23.—*The visit of John the Baptist's disciples.*

WE know that John at this time was shut up in prison. While there he was visited by his disciples. Though they had often been directed to look to Jesus as the Saviour of the world, it appears they now doubted whether he was the true Messias so long expected. They did well to come to their teacher to express their doubts. It is always well to confide such thoughts to those who are able to help us, for by hiding them in our own bosoms, we may often occasion ourselves much uneasiness, and expose ourselves to great danger. It would, indeed, be very wrong to express our doubts to ignorant, or unbelieving persons, but it is wise to open our minds to experienced Christians.

The disciples of John must have heard reports of the miracles which Jesus did, but they did not believe these reports. Probably they were prejudiced against the Lord on account of his manner of life, which was very unlike that of John; for Jesus freely mixed with sinners, and ate and drank with them, while John had always led a solitary life, and had lived upon the coarsest fare. John took an excellent method to convince his unbelieving disciples. He sent them to Jesus.

We often find that the Lord refused to perform miracles to convince unbelievers. When the Pharisees asked him for a sign, he said they should have none but that of the prophet Jonas, (the sign of the resurrection.) But he did *not* refuse to perform miracles to convince these inquirers. What was the reason of this difference? No doubt he knew that they were *desirous* to believe, and he always treats those with great compassion who are *anxious* to know the truth.

If any doubt whether the Gospel is from heaven, let them go and witness its effects. Behold John Newton, the slave-dealer, transformed into a tender-hearted man, who delights in freeing the slaves of Satan. Behold thousands of blind idolaters throwing away their idols and abandoning their vicious practices. But time would fail us even to glance at the wonders the Gospel has wrought among all nations, from the days of Paul until now.

Yet still it is necessary to hearken to our Saviour's warning: "Blessed is he, whosoever shall not be offended in me." Blessed is he whosoever shall believe in me in spite of all he sees in me to hinder his believing. By these words Jesus taught John's disciples, that notwithstanding his miracles, many would refuse to believe in him.

There are still many temptations not to believe in Jesus. The world does not believe in him—this is one temptation; there are so many hypocrites and inconsistent Christians—this is another temptation; the people of God are generally poor, mean, and unlearned—this is another stumbling-block; and the doctrine of salvation by faith is unpleasant to proud and earthly hearts—this is the greatest stumbling-block of all. But those who believe, notwithstanding all these hinderances, shall receive this blessing. "Blessed is he, whosoever shall not be offended in me."

We have reason to hope that John's disciples did believe in Jesus, because they appear to have been men of a right spirit. When they returned, according to the Saviour's command, to their imprisoned master, and related the wonders they had seen, how great must have been the joy of that faithful man! His gloomy prison must have been enlightened by the tidings of his Saviour's glory. Nothing cheers the servants of God so much as to hear of the triumphs of their Lord. They rejoice when they read of the success of missionaries in far distant lands, and they look forward to the day when every knee shall bow to the eternal Son of God. Are *our* hearts interested in these great and glorious subjects? are they wrapped up in the insignificant occurrences of the passing hour? We all have selfish hearts by nature; but God can enlarge them by his grace, and make them delight in those events which are the joy of saints and angels.

Evening Scripture portion. Isa. XXXV. *The triumphs of the Gospel.*

MATT. XI. 7–17.—*Jesus commends John the Baptist.*

GOD has said, "Them that honor me I will honor."—(1 Sam. ii. 30.) John the Baptist honored Christ much in his preaching, and now we hear how greatly Christ honored him. The Lord, who knows all men, declared that no prophet greater than John had ever appeared. Elijah, who raised the widow's son, was not greater; for though John had performed no miracle, he knew more of Christ than any who had come before him.

Jesus reminded the people of the time when John preached in the wilderness, and asked them why they had gone there. Was it to see one of the *reeds*, shaken by the wind? No; they had not gone to see a *common* sight, but to see an *extraordinary* sight. Was it a magnificent *worldly* sight that they had gone into the wilderness to see? No; if they had desired to behold splendor and magnificence they would not have gone into the *wilderness* to search for it. It is kings in their palaces who are arrayed in gorgeous dazzling garments; whereas John the Baptist was only clothed in skins, and a leathern girdle; there was nothing to please the eye in his appearance. Why then had they gone into the wilderness? To hear a *prophet*. Jesus reminded the people of this, to show them how much spiritual good they *ought* to have gained from their visits to the wilderness. But many had derived no benefit from these visits; if they had, they would have received Christ as the Son of God, for John had preached concerning him.

Jesus then declared that the least in the kingdom of heaven was greater even than John. The Lord had come to establish the kingdom of heaven upon earth. He had come to shed his blood for the sins of men. Those who believe in the crucified Saviour are greater in knowledge than John the Baptist; for they know the way of salvation more fully than he did. We live in the latter days, and God has spoken to us by his Son, and by his apostles, the least of whom was a greater prophet than John. How shall *we* escape if we neglect so *great* salvation?

What did Jesus mean by the expression, "The kingdom of heaven suffereth violence, and the violent take it by force?" By the *violent*, we believe, He meant those worldly persons who persecute his servants. As John had suffered imprisonment, and would also suffer death, for preaching the truth, so from his days would all the faithful servants of the Lord be subjected to much suffering for their Master's sake. Violent men would endeavor to *rob* and destroy by force the kingdom of heaven.

Then the Lord made a declaration that must have surprised many of those who heard him. He said that John was the Elias (or Elijah) spoken of by Malachi in the last chapter of his prophecy. (Mal. iv. 5.) "Behold, I will send you Elijah the prophet before the great and dreadful day of the Lord." John was not Elijah himself, but he had come in the *spirit* and *power* of Elijah, being fervent in spirit and great in power, turning sinners to the Lord. Yet Jesus knew that many would not believe what he was now declaring, for he said, "*If* ye will receive it, this is Elias that was for to come. He that hath ears to hear let him hear."

We see from this passage, that Jesus knows what advantages we have enjoyed, and what use we have made of them. Have we heard faithful and impressive preachers? What effect have their sermons had upon our hearts? Have we been persuaded to strive earnestly to enter the kingdom of heaven? If we merely float down the stream, we shall at length be plunged into an abyss of misery. The tide is against us, and the wind is contrary. We must be anxious and earnest. The prayer of Jacob suits every perishing sinner, "I will not let thee go, except thou bless me."

Evening Scripture portion. Mal. IV. *Elijah*

Luke VII. 29–35.—*Jesus reproves the Jews for their perverseness.*

We now refer to St. Luke's account of our Saviour's discourse about John the Baptist, because it contains some particulars omitted by St. Matthew.

The Lord Jesus declared that the people, and even the publicans, believed John the Baptist's preaching, while the Pharisees despised it. The publicans were gross sinners, most of them being notoriously dishonest in the collection of taxes. When John declared to them that their sins were great, and deserved punishment, they justified God, that is, they acknowledged that God's sentence was *just*, and they gladly received baptism as a sign of their need of being cleansed from their iniquities. But when John delivered the same truths to the Pharisees, telling them they were the children of the devil, and a generation of vipers, they were offended; they rejected the counsel of God *against* themselves, and did not desire to be baptized, because they thought they were already clean in heart and in life. Thus it often is *now*. Some who have committed open gross sins are brought to repentance; while others, who have led regular, and apparently religious lives, will not believe that on account of the *secret* sins of their *hearts*, they ought to humble themselves before God.

The Pharisees treated the Lord Jesus in the same way that they had treated John—with contempt. They had found fault with John, because he led so solitary and so strict a life, being clad in skins, feeding on locusts and honey, and refusing to taste wine or strong drink, therefore they had said that he was possessed with the devil. But they could not find the same fault with Jesus; for he led quite an opposite life, eating and drinking like men in general, and mingling with the vilest sinners, that he might win their souls to God. Yet the Pharisees were not better pleased with him than with John, and profanely called him a glutton, and a winebibber, and a friend of sinners. But what was the reason that both John and the Lord Jesus were assaulted by the Pharisees' reproaches, when they were so different from each other in their manner of life? The reason was, that they both had declared the same unwelcome truths; they both had preached the necessity of repentance and faith.

Jesus related a short parable to describe the Pharisees' conduct. It was common for children in the market-place to play at rejoicing and at mourning. One party of children imitated the glad songs of the Jews at their marriages, and on other joyful occasions, (such as the return of a long-lost son,) while another party were expected to dance to the sound of their music. But sometimes sullen and wayward children would not join in the amusement. Then the other party would good-naturedly change the play and imitate the mournful music of funerals, (such as that made by the minstrels when Jairus' daughter lay dead,) expecting their companions to use sorrowful gestures and to appear to weep; but the same froward children would object to this play also. Thus the Pharisees liked neither the strict manners of John the Baptist, nor the condescending behavior of the Lord. This was a proof that they hated their words of wisdom, for Jesus declared, "Wisdom is justified of all her children;" or rather, "Wisdom is justified *by* all her children." The children of wisdom, (or of God,) acknowledge his heavenly wisdom by whomsoever declared. If the Pharisees had been the children of God, they would have justified God both when John preached, and when the Lord himself preached.

People who hate the Gospel continue to excuse themselves for not attending to it, by accusing those who preach it of faults in their manner, or of errors in their life. These accusations proceed from enmity to the Gospel, and will not be received by God as excuses for neglecting it. If men could find fault with the Saviour's conduct, how impossible it is for a true Christian to escape censure, especially as he is liable to commit *real* errors! But O how great is the guilt of those who thus oppose the servants of God! They are enemies to their own souls.

God tries *every* means to turn sinners to himself; in his holy word, sometimes using tender entreaties, and sometimes denouncing awful warnings;—in his providence sometimes heaping mercies on our heads, and sometimes executing judgment. Should every means fail to melt, or to subdue our hearts, well may his wrath wax hot against us! Let us pray for an obedient and docile spirit, ready to listen to the word of the Lord, whether He speak in thunder, or in a small still voice.

Evening Scripture portion. Jer. VI. *Refusing to hearken.*

MATT. XI. 20–24.—*Christ upbraids three cities for their impenitence.*

WE find from this passage that the preaching of the Lord Jesus produced very little effect upon men's hearts. In order that people be converted, it is necessary, not only that the *preaching* be faithful, but that the *hearts* of the hearers be prepared: for otherwise the tongues of holy men, or of angels, or even of the Son of God, may speak in vain.

The cities in which our Saviour most frequently preached were Chorazin, Bethsaida, and especially Capernaum. We are inclined to exclaim, "Blessed cities!" But Jesus says, "*Wo* unto thee, Chorazin!" The preaching of the Son of God was not a blessing to that city, but a curse. And now the very place where it stood cannot be ascertained. Travellers may still visit Bethlehem and Nazareth, Jericho and Sychar, and many other ancient cities; but if they inquire for Capernaum, and Chorazin, and Bethsaida, they will get no certain answer.

There is a very wonderful truth contained in the words of Christ, just read by us. Jesus declared that Tyre and Sidon, two heathen cities, would have repented, if they had seen the miracles he had performed in Israel; and that Sodom, that most wicked city, would also have repented, and been spared the "vengeance of eternal fire." We see therefore that Jesus not only knows all that *does* happen, and all that *will* happen; but that he also knows all that *would* have happened, in every possible case. He knows how each heathen city would have received his word, had she heard it. He does not explain to us his reasons for not giving that light to Tyre and Sidon which he bestowed on the cities of Israel. He giveth an account of none of his matters. The Judge of all the earth will do right, and none may dare to say, or even to *think*, "What doest thou?" At the last day his justice in his dealings with men will be seen and acknowledged by the assembled universe. The degree of every person's punishment will be exactly proportioned to his guilt; and that guilt will be measured by his advantages, and by the use he made of them. And can we hear this without reflecting upon our own case? How great are the privileges we enjoy! There have been heathens, who, as soon as they were told of the love of Jesus in dying for their sins, began to repent. A Hindoo set out on a pilgrimage to Juggernaut, carrying with him a few tracts which he had not read. Being detained on the way by the illness of his wife, he had the opportunity of reading them attentively. Did he proceed to Juggernaut? No; he set out on a better pilgrimage. Desiring to persuade his countrymen to turn to the Lord, he often read aloud to little assemblies in the open air. While thus engaged, a poor native passed by, stopped to listen, was struck by what he heard, asked a few important questions, and immediately determined to give himself to Him who had bought him with his blood.*

Are not those Hindoos a reproach to any who, having heard many sermons, and read many chapters, and received much instruction, have not repented yet? Surely if *we* repent not, we shall be thrust down to the *lowest* hell; far, far below the wickedest of the heathens.

But Jesus will himself bestow repentance on all who seek this precious grace. "Him hath God exalted with his right hand to be a Prince and a Saviour, for to give *repentance* to Israel and forgiveness of sins," (Acts. v. 31.)

Evening Scripture portion. Jer. XVIII. ***Judgment on impenitent nations.***

*** Report of the Religious Tract Society for 1845, p. 58.**

MATT. XI. 25 to end.—*Christ offers a thanksgiving to his Father, and invites the heavy laden to come to Him.*

WE have now read the end of our Saviour's discourse to the people, after John the Baptist's messengers had departed. The *beginning* of the discourse contains warnings and reproofs, but the *end* is filled with thanksgivings, invitations, and entreaties. Jesus intermingled prayer to his Father with his addresses to the people. What a privilege we enjoy in being permitted to know what he said to his Father! He spoke aloud that men might be edified; for on one occasion he declared, when engaged in prayer, "because of the people which stand by, I said it," (John xi. 42.)

Often our blessed Lord offered up prayer accompanied by tears, (Heb. v. 7;) but on this occasion heavenly joy must have enlightened his countenance, for St. Luke informs us that "he rejoiced in spirit," (Luke x. 21.) And what was the cause of his joy? It was, that God had revealed these things to babes, *though* he had hid them from the wise and prudent. *What* things? Things respecting himself; the things about which John the Baptist's disciples had inquired: "Art thou he that shall come, or look we for another?" (ver. 3.) These things many babes knew. By *babes* ignorant people are meant, those who *feel* their ignorance, and desire to be taught of God. To such babes (whether learned or not in *worldly* things) God reveals his Son, while he leaves the wise and prudent in *their own sight* to blindness and darkness. Such were the Pharisees. Though really blind and dark, they thought they knew the way of salvation; for *Satan* had blinded their minds, as it is written in 2 Cor. iv. 3, 4: "The god of this world hath blinded the minds of them which believe not, lest the light of the glorious gospel of Christ (who is the image of God) should shine into them."

Let us pray to God to give us the spirit of a *babe*, a humble, teachable spirit, and then Christ will reveal to us that heavenly knowledge which can save our souls. It seemed good in the Father's sight that babes should be instructed. We need not, therefore, fear a repulse from our heavenly Father, if we come confessing our ignorance and desiring to be taught. And who is the Teacher that He has appointed? It is the meek and lowly Jesus. Hear him say, "Learn of me, for I am meek and lowly in heart." Who would not delight in receiving instruction from such gracious lips? How sweetly he encourages sinners to approach!—"Come unto me, all ye that are weary and heavy laden, and I will give you rest." And does not his invitation include every child of man? Every sinner is weary and heavy laden. Penitent sinners mourn for the *guilt* of sin; but those who are not penitent feel the misery of its *bondage*. They may not know what it is that interrupts their happiness; they may think it is the circumstances in which they are placed; but it is the sin that dwells in them, and holds them in captivity. Jesus alone can free the soul from the chain of its sins; he alone can bestow rest. They that believe in him do enter into rest; they can say of their Shepherd, "He maketh me to lie down in green pastures; he leadeth me beside the still waters."

How happy are they who early choose the Lord for their friend and master! They will find his yoke easy, and his burden light; they will find that, instead of binding burdens upon them, he himself bears their burdens. Ask those who have been *long* engaged in this service, whether they have not found his yoke easy and his burden light. They will tell you that in the brightest days of heedless youth, they never tasted that peace which they have found in the darkest nights of pious old age.

Evening Scripture portion. Ps. CXVI. *The rest of the soul.*

LUKE VII. 36 to end.—*The penitent weeping at the feet of Jesus.*

Two opposite characters are described in this interesting history; Simon the Pharisee and the weeping sinner!

Simon was probably respected by his neighbors, and accounted a religious man, but he was *not* accepted in the sight of Jesus. The woman had been a gross and open sinner, yet she was accepted by her Saviour. Now what was the reason of this difference? Does Jesus love sin? God forbid!

The reason of the difference was, that Simon did *not* love Jesus, and the poor woman did love Him. The Pharisee showed his want of love by neglecting to pay him the attention usually shown in that country to guests. He neither gave him water to wash his feet, nor ointment to anoint his person, nor did he bestow the customary salutation. The woman showed her love to Jesus by coming into the house where he was, notwithstanding the scoffs and frowns of the master and his friends; by standing at his feet washing them with her tears, kissing them with respectful affection, and anointing them with precious ointment. The customs of that country rendered it easy for the poor penitent to enter the house. Jesus was reposing, according to the eastern fashion, upon a sofa, and his feet were in such a position that the woman, while she stood behind him, could weep over them and anoint them.

Let us now ask *why* the woman loved Jesus so *much*, and the Pharisee loved him so *little*, or rather not at all? Jesus himself explained the reason in his parable. He had forgiven the woman a mighty debt. She knew that he had forgiven it, and *therefore* she loved him; for this is the meaning of the 47th verse. Her sins, which are many, are forgiven, (not *because* she loved much, but) *therefore* she loved much. Jesus *first* forgave her, and *then* she loved Him.

Jesus does not say that the Pharisee's debt was *really* small. He related this parable to show his host that if he *thought* his debt small, he could not love him much, even *if* he forgave him his debt. Do we wish to know whether *we* love Jesus much? Let us ask ourselves what we think of our *debt*. Do we think it *small* or large? Do we think that our sins are many or few? By nature we *all* think that our debt is small. Yes, even murderers think that their sins are not so great as they appear, and that they are excusable on account of their many temptations.

Thus we all excuse ourselves in our own sight, and think it an easy thing for God to forgive us such little debts. While we remain in this state of mind, we cannot love Jesus much. In fact, we cannot love him *at all*, and we cannot be accepted in his sight. But if Jesus, by his Spirit, touch our hearts, then we perceive that our sins are very great, and we cry to Him, "Pardon mine iniquity, for it is *great*." It is not the *acts* of sin that we chiefly lament, but the *secret* sins of our hearts. These, we feel, are set in the light of God's countenance, and cannot be forgiven without the shedding of the Saviour's blood. People often remain a long while in great distress on account of their sins; but when they can believe that there is forgiveness with God, and that he has washed them from their sins, they are filled with gratitude; then they love much, because Jesus has forgiven much.

Never do we lament our sins so much, as when we think of our Saviour's infinite love. When is it we regret most our offences against an *earthly* friend? Is it not when we find that while we have been *neglecting* him, he has been *laboring* for our good; that when we have been *suspecting* him, he has been *pleading* for us? This is the grief that the true penitent feels. This was the grief that caused the woman to shed such abundant tears upon the feet of Jesus.

Evening Scripture portion. 1 Peter I. *Love to Christ.*

LUKE VIII. 1–3.—*The women who followed Jesus.*

IN these verses we have a description of our Saviour's diligence, of his poverty, and of his humility.

His *diligence* was unwearied. He went as an itinerant (or a wandering preacher) from place to place. He knew the value of the souls of men, and the danger in which they lay; and being full of love, he delighted in declaring the glad tidings of salvation.

Though all are not called to *preach*, as he was, all are called to promote the salvation of their fellow-sinners. Yet how many, far from endeavoring to convert others, are themselves content to remain unconverted! They are too *slothful* to inquire earnestly, "What shall we do to be saved?" though they are often eagerly asking, "What shall we eat, and what shall we drink, and wherewithal shall we be clothed?" How strange it seems to spend so much anxiety upon a *dying* body, and so little upon a *never*-dying soul!

While Jesus was upon earth, there were some women who accompanied him from place to place to hear his word. They were bound to him by ties of gratitude, having been healed by him of various infirmities.

Mary Magdalene, or Mary of Magdala, (the town from which she came, as it is supposed,) had once been possessed by seven devils. We should not conclude from this circumstance that she had been peculiarly wicked. The possession of devils seems to have been an *affliction* rather than a sin; for we never find that Jesus rebuked the *persons* who were possessed, but only the *devils*. Many have supposed that Mary Magdalene was the woman who washed the Redeemer's feet with her tears; but there is no evidence to prove this opinion to be true. Yet Mary loved Jesus with the same devoted affection as that poor weeping sinner did; she followed him to his cross, and shed tears at his grave, and had the honor of being the *first* to behold him after his resurrection.

Another woman, who followed him, was the wife of Herod's steward. The bad examples of Herod, and of Herodias, had not hindered her from embracing that Gospel which her superiors despised. She also continued faithful to Jesus at his death, and at his grave.

Such was the *poverty* of Jesus, that he permitted these holy women and many others to contribute to his support. "They ministered unto him of their substance." Surely we think it *was* an honor to be allowed to give to him, who gave them all things. It is an honor that *we* may share with them. Though we may have little to give, yet, if we bestow that little in a spirit of love upon the least of the saints, we give unto Jesus himself.

Observe the *humility* of Jesus in accepting alms. That independent spirit, which the world so much commends, proceeds from pride of heart. It is right to desire to work for our own subsistence, rather than to receive charity; but when reduced to poverty, it is wrong to feel pain in accepting gifts from those who are richer than ourselves. Jesus *could* have turned *stones* into bread, but he chose rather to *receive* bread from his creatures. Thus he set us an example of humility.

It is supposed that it was about this time that a circumstance recorded by Mark took place. "They went into an house, and the multitude cometh together again, so that they could not so much as eat bread. And when his friends heard of it, they went out to lay hold on him, for they said, He is beside himself." (See Mark iii. 19–21.) It seems probable that Jesus went into this house that he might rest his wearied frame and refresh himself with bread; but the multitude, anxious for his presence, induced him to resume his fatiguing labors. His friends, perhaps his unbelieving relations, (for some of them did not believe on him,) thought that he was mad, because he complied with the people's desire. They knew not his *motives*, and *therefore* they thought he was beside himself. When a person acts in a manner for which we can see no *motive*, we think that person must have lost his reason. If a person were to rush into this room, uttering loud cries, we should conclude he was mad; but if we found that the house was on fire, we should no longer wonder at his behavior, for we should think a house being on fire a sufficient *motive* to justify his earnestness.

The world are astonished at the earnestness of devoted Christians, because they cannot understand their *motives*. The believer beholds by faith a glorious heaven, and a dreadful hell; a gracious Saviour, and a malicious tempter; immortal souls, and approaching judgment. He must therefore be earnest in attempting to save his fellow-sinners from perdition. The world beholds none of these things, and naturally wonders at the conduct of the Christian. Does the earnestness of devoted Christians astonish *us?* Do we say, "What is the need of all these exertions? Why cannot people be religious without pressing their opinions upon others?" If we think thus, is there not reason to fear that we know not the value of souls, and that we believe not in the wrath to come?

Evening Scripture portion. Acts XXVI. *Paul accused of madness.*

MATT. XII. 22–30.—*Christ disproves the Pharisees' blasphemous accusation.*

How dreadful was the accusation which the Pharisees ventured to make against the Saviour! They were not able to deny that he had performed an astonishing miracle; therefore they accused him of casting out devils through the power of Beelzebub, (or Satan,) the prince of the devils. We see from this instance, that wicked men will always find some excuse for not believing in God. Sometimes they say that there is not sufficient proof that the Bible is true; but if their objections are answered, still they refuse to believe, and find some other excuse, however absurd, rather than give up their sins, and come to Christ for pardon. But we ought not to be impatient with those that oppose themselves to the truth. We should imitate Christ, who calmly answered the Pharisees. Jesus sometimes spoke severely to them, but never in answer to their reproaches against himself. He always behaved meekly when reviled by his enemies; thus setting us an ex ample, that we should follow his steps.

He gave *two* reasons to prove that he did not cast out Satan by Satan's help. In the *first* place, he said that Satan would not assist him to injure his *own* kingdom; and in the *second* place, he asked the Pharisees by whom their children cast out devils; for there were certain persons among the Jews, called exorcists, who *professed* to be able to cast out devils, though it is not certain whether they could *really* do so or not. Sceva, mentioned in Acts xix., was one of those "exorcists." Jesus knew that the Pharisees would never acknowledge that their own children, or friends, cast out devils by Satan, and therefore he declared that it was unreasonable to say that *he* was assisted by that evil spirit.

Then He related a very short parable to describe the work he was doing in the world. He compared himself to a man come to take possession of a house, and of the things in it. This house was the world, and the goods in the house were the souls of men. Jesus came to rescue these precious souls from Satan's power. He compared Satan to a strong man, who was in the house, and who tried to prevent him from coming in. Jesus came down to earth, and became a man that he might first bind Satan, and then spoil his goods; that is, redeem the souls that had been taken captive by the wicked one.

Jesus is still engaged in releasing captives. He calls upon all whom he has rescued to join in the mighty work. Can there be any so base and ungrateful as to hesitate to obey the summons? Those who hold back are counted by Jesus as his enemies. What an awful declaration there is in verse 30! "He that is not with me is against me; and he that gathereth not with me, scattereth abroad." None can remain neuter; all must be on one side or the other.

Great injury has been done to the Redeemer's cause by *not* speaking in its favor. When missionaries first proclaimed the gospel in Tahiti, they received this answer from some of the heathens! "Were these things true, would not Captain Cook have told us of them long ago? But neither he nor his sailors spoke about the religion that you teach?" Thus we see that ungodly mariners, by *not* gathering with Christ, scatter abroad.

Some people imagine that if they do no harm *themselves*, they may go to those places where *others* speak and act wickedly. But there is a promise to him who shuts his eyes from *seeing* of evil. (Is. xxxiii. 16.) Those who love their crucified Saviour cannot stand by and hear his name profaned, and see his laws broken. Instead of being amused, they feel as Moses did when, coming down from the Holy Mount, he found Israel engaged in the worship of the golden calf.

Evening Scripture portion. Acts XIX. *Sceva the exorcist.*

MATT. XII. 31, 32.—*He warns against the unpardonable sin.*

THIS is a very awful part of our Saviour's discourse to the Pharisees. There *is* a sin which cannot be forgiven, and it is a sin of the tongue. Certain *words* which may be spoken against the Holy Ghost, are called, "Blasphemy against the Holy Ghost." There is a mystery in this subject which we would not presume to attempt to remove. Yet we may form some idea of the nature of blasphemy against the Holy Ghost, by examining the conduct of those whom Jesus now addressed. The Pharisees seem to have been convinced by the miracles of the Saviour, that he was a true prophet; but though convinced, they were determined to reject him, and to set the people against him also. In this awful state of mind they accused him of working miracles by the power of Satan, and not by the Spirit of God. Had they *really* supposed he was assisted by Satan, their sin would not have been so enormous; *then* they would have sinned, as Saul of Tarsus did, "ignorantly, in unbelief;" but now they sinned against the convictions of their conscience, and with deliberate malice.

That man has reached the highest pitch of wickedness, who, though himself convinced of the truth of the gospel, endeavors to persuade *others* to disbelieve it. We hope there are not many who act so daring a part. It is probable that infidels are generally deceived themselves, before they attempt to deceive others. Such a state of unbelief, dangerous as it is, is far better than conviction of the truth, accompanied by determined hatred against God. Such is the condition of devils, and of all the lost spirits. They cannot doubt the power of God; but while they believe and tremble, they vent blasphemies against his holy name. Is any soul distressed with the fear lest he should ever have committed the unpardonable sin? let him take comfort. His fears prove that he is not sealed up in final impenitence. At the same time, let us all beware of the deceitfulness of sin. Though every sin is not *unpardonable*, every sin is *dangerous*. Many who have never been guilty of the unpardonable sin, will nevertheless die unpardoned. Who can conceive how dreadful it is to feel you are dying, and that you are not pardoned. Some impenitent sinners die resting on *false* hopes; but others die in despair. Those who have stood by their death-beds, have declared that the sight of their agonies was too horrible to be endured.

Pardon, so little sought for by sinners while they live, is not always obtained when they are dying. The Hon. Francis Newport, an infidel, who died in 1692, in his last illness was heard to say, as he looked upon the fire, "O that I was to lie upon that fire for a hundred thousand years to purchase the favor of God, and be reconciled to him again! But it is a fruitless, vain wish; millions of millions of years will bring me no nearer the end of my tortures than one poor hour." This miserable man had not faith to come to the blood of Christ to wash away his sins. The understanding may be convinced, while the enmity of the heart against God is not removed.

Evening Scripture portion. 1 John V. *Sin unto death.*

MATT. XII. 33–37.—*Jesus warns against idle words.*

BEHOLD an instance of the severe terms in which the meek and gentle Jesus sometimes rebuked sinners. He called the Pharisees a "generation of vipers." Thus he declared them to be the seed of the old serpent, and the children of Satan. They had accused him of casting out devils through the power of Satan, while they themselves belonged to the family of the wicked one. It is to be expected that the children of the devil should utter blasphemies, even as a bad *tree* brings forth bad *fruit.*

Though all have not reached the same height of wickedness as these Pharisees, yet all have by nature wicked hearts, that cannot bring forth really good fruit. If our hearts were in a right state, our *words* would be good. The tongue was given to man to bless God. David for this reason calls it his *glory.* "Awake, my glory." The tongue would indeed be the glory of man if his heart were right with God. What a noble use the angels make of their tongues! they unite in a never-ceasing song of praise to God. Adam, when first created, doubtless used his tongue for the same glorious purpose. But since the fall, the tongue has become the outlet of the abominations of man's heart: the evil treasure of his heart—his pride, his malice, his envy, his deceit—flow forth from his tongue. His heart is the black *fountain* of sin; his words are only the *streams.* We must be born again before we can utter words acceptable to God.

At the last day our words will be produced as the *evidence* of our state before God. It is true that many have *said,* "Lord, Lord," who have not loved God; but will *their* words be considered proofs of love? By no means; words *insincerely* spoken will be regarded as crimes. Those who *said* what they did not *feel,* whether to God or man, will be pronounced liars, and we know that *liars* shall have their part in the lake that burneth with fire and brimstone. It is only good words that have proceeded from our *hearts* that will then justify us, or show that we were born again and washed in Christ's blood. If, then, we feel that we are not fit to stand this test, let us entreat God to bestow new *hearts* upon us. Then our common discourse will be tinctured with the love of God. Just as an affectionate parent is often *speaking* of his children, because he is always *thinking* of them; so, when we love *God,* we shall be disposed to be often speaking of his power, and wisdom, and goodness, because we shall be often *think-*

ing of them. The daily duties of life will not interfere with our thoughts of God, any more than they prevent a loving mother thinking of her children. Every thing will remind us of our God. The beauties of creation, and the events of Providence, will lead us to think and to speak of Him; for in every thing we shall see his hand. What the world calls "good luck," we shall call "great mercy;" and what the world speaks of as unfortunate accidents, we shall own to be "loving corrections." But most of all shall we differ from the world in our expressions concerning the Son of God and his believing people. That Saviour we shall call "precious," his people "happy." It is true, those living in a Christian land seldom dare speak openly against Christ, but they show their real feelings by the contemptuous names they bestow on his most devoted servants. Their contemptuous words are *noticed* and *noted* down by God in his book, and shall be produced against them another day to their everlasting shame. "By their words they shall be condemned."

Evening Scripture portion. James III. ***Sinful words.***

MATT. XII. 38–42.—*He refuses to give a sign to the Pharisees.*

IT was *not* with a *sincere* desire to be convinced of the truth that the Pharisees wished for a *sign*. They had already witnessed so many miracles that they could not avoid knowing that Jesus was the Son of God. This was their great sin, that when they *knew* the truth they would not *confess* it. As our Saviour afterwards said, (in John xv. 24,) "If I had not done among them the works that none other man did, they had not had *sin:* but *now* they have both seen and hated both *me* and my Father."

The Pharisees were *determined* not to believe in Jesus. Whatever miracles he might perform, whatever signs he might show, they had made up their minds already; they would not believe on him themselves, nor let *others* believe on him. It is evident that this was their state of mind from their conversation when together. (See John xi. 47, 48.) "Then gathered the chief priests and the Pharisees a council, and said, What do we? for this man doeth many miracles. If we let him thus alone, all men will believe on him, and the Romans shall come and take away both our place and nation." Did not these words betray an awful state of mind? It was worse than *unbelieving;* it was *malicious.* It is in this spirit that Satan himself opposes the kingdom of God.

And *what* was this *sign* from heaven for which the Pharisees asked? Probably it was one of those displays of glory that God once made on Mount Sinai, when He spoke from the midst of the fire, surrounded by clouds and darkness, thunderings and lightnings. Christ could easily have manifested his glory in the same manner, and he will do so when he comes again to judge the world. But he refused to grant the Pharisees' arrogant demand, and told them that they should have no other sign than the *sign* of the prophet *Jonas*. And what was that sign? It was his own resurrection; for Jonah's burial in the midst of the whale was a type of his burial in the heart of the earth; and Jonah's escape through the mouth of the fish, was a type of his bursting the barriers of the tomb.

It may surprise us to know that Jesus would be *three* days and *three nights* in his grave, seeing he only lay there from Friday evening to Sunday morning. But the Jews had a peculiar way of reckoning time: they considered a day and night as *one* period, and they counted a *part* of this period, as if it were the *whole*. Therefore, as Jesus was *part* of three days in the grave, he was there three days and three nights, according to the Jewish mode of speaking.

The Saviour well knew that the Pharisees would not acknowledge him to be the Son of God, even when he rose from the dead; and so it proved; for when he did rise, and when the history of his resurrection was repeated to the chief priests and elders, how did they act? They bribed the soldiers who had guarded the tomb to deny the fact, and to say that the disciples had stolen his body away while they slept.

Well, therefore, might Jesus contrast the men of Nineveh with the Pharisees. The Ninevites repented when Jonah declared that in *forty days* their city should be destroyed. It is remarkable that in *forty years* from the time of our Saviour's resurrection, Jerusalem was destroyed, because the Jews repented not. The Pharisees despised the Ninevites on account of their being Gentiles, yet these Gentiles were far better than themselves.

The Lord then brought forward an instance of another *Gentile* who acted in an opposite manner from the Pharisees: it was the queen of Sheba, who came from a distant country to receive instruction from Solomon. There have been heathens in later days who have resembled this ancient sovereign in her desire to obtain heavenly wisdom. Some years ago, two natives of Ceylon left their spicy isle, and came to dwell for awhile in our cold climate, that they might learn the gospel of the blessed God. When they were about to return home, a friend presented to them a magnificent mirror, but they refused to accept it. They said to their venerable teacher, Dr. Adam Clarke, "Tell our friend we cannot accept the mirror. We will take nothing home with us but the Bible you gave us and the gospel of the Lord Jesus Christ. To learn that gospel we crossed the ocean, and with it alone will we cross it again."

How unlike these disinterested Cingalese are those who for worldly reasons forsake the preaching of the truth! Whatever may be the advantages for which they give up that joyful sound, they make a poor exchange. Happy are those who can say with David, "One thing have I desired of the Lord, that will I seek after, that I may dwell in the house of the Lord all the days of my life to behold the beauty of the Lord, and to inquire in his temple." (Ps. xxvii. 4.)

Evening Scripture portion. 1 Kings X. *The Queen of Sheba.*

MATT. XII. 43–45.—*The parable of the unclean spirit.*

IT was in this alarming manner that our Saviour concluded his rebukes to the wicked Pharisees. We can scarcely call this short history a *parable*, because it appears to be a literal account of an event that has taken place. Still it is a parable, because it is partly figurative; the heart of a man is *likened* to a house. And is it really true that unclean spirits make the hearts of men their habitation? How can we doubt what our Saviour has so plainly declared?

Sometimes an evil spirit *forsakes* his habitation. This devil having left his house, travelled far through dry, or desert places, but found no rest. It seems probable that in the course of his wanderings he found no opportunity of injuring souls. Our enemy, we know, walks about seeking whom he may devour. Sometimes there is a restraint laid upon him, and he *cannot* perpetrate the evil that he desires; for he can do nothing without the permission of God. Perhaps this devil had left the man, hoping to make new conquests, and to increase the number of his victims; but when disappointed, he thinks of returning to his old abode. He says, "I will return unto my house, whence I came out." He claims the heart as his own property; he says, "*My* house." He returns and finds no obstacle to regaining possession of the soul he once inhabited. The house is not the less acceptable to him, because it is swept and garnished, or adorned. Nothing pleases Satan more than a show of piety in a wicked heart. The unclean spirit is not satisfied to dwell *alone*, but finds seven of his fellows to share his spoil. He selects some *more* wicked than himself, as his associates. There are *degrees* of wickedness even among *devils*, and no doubt pre-eminence in wickedness is their glory. It had been better for this miserable man, if the first inmate of his heart had never quitted it. But O! how infinitely better would it have been for him, if, when the devil had left him, he had opened his heart to the gracious Saviour! Jesus is willing to come whenever he is invited; often he stands and knocks, and no man opens the door, and at length he withdraws, no more to return. Then the wretched soul must become the prey of demons. Even as a house forsaken by man soon becomes the habitation of beasts and birds, so does the heart, when Jesus is absent, become the habitation of the spirits of hell.

The greater part of the Pharisees did not profit from the warning

Jesus gave them; they grew more and more wicked; they crucified the Lord of glory, and persecuted his apostles. But let *us* profit from it, and never count ourselves safe, except Jesus reign in our hearts. Saul, the King of Israel, appears to have been such a man as our Saviour described in this parable. The evil spirit that once tormented him, departed for a *season*, but soon returned and rendered him more wicked than before. All the evening of his days was spent in malicious persecutions of the innocent David, till he filled up the measure of his iniquity by consulting the witch of Endor.

Real conversion of the heart is the only preservative from Satan's malice. True believers alone are secure. There are evil days, days of peculiar temptation that come upon them, but neither seven wicked spirits, nor seventy times seven, can harm the heart fortified by the towers and bulwarks of *faith*. It is written, "He that is begotten of God keepeth himself, and that wicked one toucheth him not," (1 John v. 18.) And how does he keep himself? He remembers his Lord's command, "Watch and pray, that ye enter not into temptation."

Evening Scripture portion. 1 Sam. XXVIII. *The witch of Endor.*

MATT. XII. 46 to end.—*He describes who are his mother and his brethren.*

SUCH were the gentle words which our Saviour added to a discourse containing many severe reproofs and awful warnings. The former discourse, recorded in Matthew xi., also ended with sweet encouragement: "Come unto me, all ye that are weary and heavy laden." But the passage we have just read is still more condescending! Who can value enough the honor of being mother, brother, and sister of the Lord of heaven and earth! How wonderful it is that sinners like ourselves should be raised to the enjoyment of such a privilege!

What was the occasion on which the Saviour uttered the blessing to which we have just alluded? His mother and brethren desired to speak with him, but were unable to approach on account of the crowd that surrounded him. By the term "brethren," we must understand not only those whom we call brethren, but also more distant relations. It is probable that they wished from motives of affection to interrupt his labors, which appeared too severe for his strength. Why would not Jesus comply with their request? Because he saw multitudes of precious souls thronging around him, eager to hear the words of eternal life. Instead of admitting his relations immediately to his presence, he pronounced a blessing on his own disciples; saying, "Behold my mother and my brethren."

We must not suppose that he felt no regard for his mother, or for any of his relations, for we know that he bore to his mother such affection, that when hanging on the cross, he commended her with his expiring breath to the care of his beloved disciple. But by this expression, "Who is my mother? and who are my brethren?" he taught us, that those united to him in *spirit* are nearer to him than those related to him in the *flesh*. His mother, indeed, was *spiritually* connected with him, for she was a true believer. Before the birth of her divine Son, she said, "My spirit hath rejoiced in God my Saviour;" therefore he loved her both as his mother, and as his own redeemed. But he did not love *her alone;* he loved all those who did the will of his Father in heaven.

It was to do his Father's will that he came down from heaven; as he said, "I came down from heaven, not to do mine own will, but the will of him that sent me;" (John vi. 38;) and he always did it *perfectly*. On one occasion he declared, "I have kept my Father's commandments, and abide in his love." How different is the state of the world! Every one by nature does his *own* will. Children soon betray their evil nature by striving to do their own, and not their parents' will. When they grow older, and hear the commandments of God, naturally they show no inclination to obey.

As soon as a person is converted, he begins to desire to do God's will. The 119th Psalm shows us how earnestly David sought to please his heavenly Father: "O that my ways were directed to keep thy statutes," (verse 5.) "Behold I have longed after thy precepts; quicken me in thy righteousness," (verse 40.) But why did David utter these prayers? Because he felt that he could not of himself do God's will; therefore he prayed for grace from on high.

The holy apostle Paul could say, "I delight in the law of God after the inward man." Yet the sin of his nature troubled him. He said, "I see a law in my members, warring against the law of my mind." All the children of God endure the same inward struggles that Paul and David endured. Each of them can say,

"Though I fail, I weep;
Though I halt in pace,
Yet I creep
To the throne of grace."

But though they do not keep the Father's commandments *perfectly*, as Jesus did, they are comforted by knowing that He loves them.

It must have been delightful to hear him say on *earth*, "Behold my mother and my brethren!" How endearing was his attitude when he stretched forth his hands, to point out the objects of his love! The day will come when he will enclose his redeemed family in his everlasting arms, and declare, "Behold my mother and my brethren."

Evening Scripture portion.
PS. CXIX. 1–32. *Prayers for grace to do the will of God.*

MATT. XIII. 1–18.—*Christ relates the parable of the sower, and explains why he spake in parables.*

WE have much reason to rejoice that our blessed Saviour explained the parable of the Sower; for had he not done so, many different opinions respecting its meaning would have been held, but now the signification is fixed and certain. We will, however, defer the consideration of it until we read our Lord's explanation.

After Jesus had finished his *public* discourse, he conversed privately with his disciples. In this conversation he declared some truths which have been much objected to by the world. His disciples inquired *why* he spoke in parables. In his reply, their Master unfolded some of the secrets of his Father's government. Can any thing be so interesting as the ways of God towards man! In this passage some light is shed upon them.

Jesus said to his disciples, "Unto *you* it is *given* to know the mysteries of the kingdom of heaven, but to them it is not *given*." We learn from this declaration that heavenly knowledge is the *gift* of God. All men by nature are without the knowledge of their Maker, as it is written, "There is none that understandeth; there is none that seeketh after God." When Adam sinned, he lost the knowledge of his God, and all his children are born in this state of ignorance. They are not only ignorant of God: they have no *desire* to know him. There are many things of which we may be ignorant, yet which we should much like to learn. If a man well skilled in some useful art were to offer to teach gratuitously all who wished to learn, many would flock around him and become his scholars: for we naturally desire to learn useful arts. But though God offers to teach all who are willing to be instructed, very few come to him and say, "Teach me to do thy will." Nor would *any* come and make this prayer, unless God first, by his Holy Spirit, put the desire into the heart. When this desire is *felt*, then the prayer is made, and the longing soul is taught. This is what Jesus meant when he said, "Whosoever *hath*, to him shall be given, and he shall have more abundance." There is an interesting account contained in a tract called "Jejana," of a little Hottentot girl who earnestly desired to know God. A black man, who knew but little himself, directed her to make this prayer, "Lord, help me; Lord, teach me." This prayer she often uttered when she knelt alone in some thicket. Such was her simplicity, that she added, "For David says thou wilt." The pious black man's name was David. And did God fulfil his promise to this poor child? Assuredly he did. She became known to a faithful missionary, who took her into his service, and fully instructed her in the gospel of Christ.

Such is God's goodness towards those who desire to know him. The Pharisees, far from having this desire, were determined to reject the warnings of the Saviour; therefore God gave them up to the blindness and deafness that they loved. Every warning they rejected closed their eyes in deeper night.

How awful was their condition! But all are in danger of falling into it, who are not obeying the gospel call. Those who hear the Bible read from day to day—who listen to the preacher's earnest en treaties from Sabbath to Sabbath,—and who yet make no effort to go to Christ, are becoming more hardened and more difficult to be converted. How blessed might our eyes be, for round us the true light shines! Yet how doubly cursed will these eyes be, if we wilfully close them against that light.

Evening Scripture portion. Ps. XXV. *The secret of the Lord.*

MATT. XIII. 18–21.—*The explanation of the former part of the parable of the sower.*

THERE is one circumstance which renders this parable peculiarly interesting. It describes the characters of *all* persons who hear the gospel; therefore it must describe *ours*. Let us endeavor to discover by the help of God to which class we belong.

First: there are the way-side hearers: these seem to be careless persons, whose minds are so trifling that though they *hear* the words of the preacher, they do not *reflect* upon their meaning. We know that the seed represents the word of God, whether spoken by faithful ministers and parents, or instructors or friends, or in whatever way conveyed to the mind. But though the seed is good, it does not spring up in every heart. Why does it not? Because every heart is not *prepared* to receive it. As a beaten path is a soil not prepared to receive seed, so a heart full of trifling thoughts is not prepared to receive the gospel. Such a heart finds religious instruction a weariness, and rejoices when the sermon is over, and the chapter is finished.

It is to be feared that every congregation contains many of these careless hearers, who hear the sermons with little interest; but even on the way-side, a seed might occasionally spring up, were it not for the passers by who tread it down, and for the birds who pick it up.

How can we calculate upon the amount of good that is prevented by those spirits that throng the air! They are all marshalled under one experienced commander, even that old serpent who tempted our first parents. Satan knows how to choose the most favorable opportunities for exerting his power. It is after faithful sermons have been preached that his hosts are on the alert to efface any impression that may have been made. The persons who lie most exposed to his attacks are the inconsiderate, who have offered up no prayers for a blessing on the instructions they have received. What havoc is made every

Sabbath night and every Monday morning in the paths where the faithful preacher was seen sowing just before! If Satan found people endeavoring to fix the sermon in their hearts by prayer and meditation, he would not have such great success. But is it surprising that he succeeds, when he finds so many who neglect secret prayer!

The next class of hearers appear at first sight more hopeful than the wayside hearers. The seed sometimes falls on stony ground, where there is a little light, though dry earth; it soon springs up, but is soon withered by the heat of the sun.

The stony ground hearers receive the word with joy. When they hear the gospel, they attend, they remember, they are delighted, they determine to be Christians; they begin to do many things that are right, but when they find difficulties in their way they change their minds, and become as worldly as before. What is the reason of this? It is that their hearts were never softened by the Holy Spirit. They never were convinced of sin, they never *repented.* Repentance is the beginning of religion. Our Saviour's first sermon was, "Repent." If we think we can be Christians without repentance we are mistaken. We *must* be brought to see what ungrateful creatures we have been to our best Friend. We must be led to mourn over such ingratitude, and to entreat for pardon and grace. Paul sat three days after his conversion fasting, before Ananias came and said, "Arise and be baptized, and wash away thy sins." Christians may feel different *degrees* of grief; but they all *grieve.* Those who have felt no godly sorrow will easily be induced to return to the world; they will never consent to make any great sacrifice for Christ's sake. They *cannot* resolve to give up a brilliant prospect, or to lose an advantageous situation, or to forfeit the favor of honorable persons. No; they will sooner give up their religious profession, lose their hopes of heaven, and forfeit the favor of the glorious God.

Evening Scripture portion. 2 Tim. IV. *Demas.*

MATT. XIII. 22, 23.—*The explanation of the latter part of the parable of the sower.*

LET us now consider the two latter kind of hearers which our Saviour has described.

One is the thorny ground hearer: the soil of his heart is not so dry and barren as that of the stony ground hearer. The word sinks into it, and springs up, and blossoms, and buds, and produces fruit; but, alas! not good fruit. What is the reason of this failure? Thorns have grown up with the good seed, and have injured the heavenly plants. The thorns may have appeared very small and insignificant when first the seed was sown, but they increased in strength, and at length destroyed the hopes of the husbandman.

We cannot be at a loss to discover what the thorns represent; for our Lord distinctly declared them to be cares, riches, pleasures, and the lusts of other things. There are some people, who, when they hear the word, are arrested, touched, convinced, persuaded. They acknowledge they are sinners, they see Christ is the only Saviour; they feel the value of their souls, and they desire to lead a religious life. But their affections are drawn off from God by worldly things. The *stony* ground hearers were induced to abandon their profession through fear of persecution; the *thorny* ground hearers, while they continue to make a profession of religion, are enslaved by the love of the world. They attempt to serve God and mammon. What must be the result of such an attempt? Destruction. "For if any man love the world, the love of the Father is not in him."

The world wears many different forms, and tries to win us under various disguises. According to our age, our dispositions, and our circumstances will be our temptations. Pleasure allures the young, and care entangles the old: reputation is the desire of one, ease is preferred by another; but each of these is a thorn, and will prevent the good seed flourishing in the heart. What then can we do to avoid making a fruitless profession? We must apply to God to take the thorns out of our hearts; we cannot do it ourselves, but God is willing to do it for us. He can quench every inordinate desire, he can overthrow every earthly idol; he can come with sovereign power, and reign in our hearts.

No heart by *nature* is an honest and good heart. "There is none that understandeth and that seeketh after God." Every heart of nature is like the way-side, the stony ground or the thorny ground. God alone can prepare sinners to receive his word. He can plough up the way-side, can take away the stones, and can pluck out the thorns.

There is a gracious promise in the Scriptures that He desires us to remember: "I will take away the stony heart out of your flesh, and I will give you a heart of flesh." Let us plead this promise in prayer. There is abundance of good seed scattered all over this land—thousands of Bibles, and millions of tracts. Why are not more souls converted? The hearts of men are unprepared.

Has God graciously prepared *our* hearts? Have we received the word, and brought forth fruit? If it be so with regard to any of us, to Him be all the praise who softened our hard hearts. Perhaps we can remember the time when sermons made no impression upon us, when holy counsels were disregarded, and even a mother's entreaties despised. And how did God prepare our hearts? Did He make us eat the bitter fruits of our works, till, like the prodigal, we said, "I will arise and go unto my Father?" Or did He subdue us in a sudden manner, as He did Paul, when He stopped him in the midst of his wicked career, ploughing up his heart by the Spirit, as the seed was cast in, "Saul, Saul, why persecutest thou me?" Or did He lead us by gentle and gradual methods to seek his face, watering the ridges of our hearts, settling the furrows, making it soft with showers, and then blessing the springing of His word? (Ps. lxv.)

Evening Scripture portion. Ez. XXXVI. 22 to end. ***The heart of flesh.***

MATT. XIII. 24–30.—*The parable of the wheat and tares, with the explanation contained in ver.* 36–43.

THE parable of the wheat and tares in some respects resembles that of the Sower of the seed, but it differs from it in this respect. In the parable of the Sower we heard only of *good* seed; here we read also of *bad* seed. While Christ, by his faithful ministers, sows good seed, or the pure gospel, the devil by his servants sows *bad* seed, or false doctrines.

The good seed, where it takes root and prospers, produces the children of the kingdom, or true believers, while bad seed produces hypocrites, formalists, heretics, and other wicked characters, who are the children of the devil. We here behold the great danger to which we lie exposed, of having *bad* seed sown in our hearts. If we receive not the gospel, we shall receive some false doctrine. We all must have *some* kind of religion, and if we do not receive the *truth* in the love of it, we shall cling to our own foolish imaginations, or to some errors that we have heard; and shall flatter ourselves with the hope of reaching heaven by some other way than the Scriptures have revealed.

The bad seed is sown *cunningly* by the great enemy. Often he employs persons who *appear* religious to sow it; so that the hearers are deceived, and fancy that they are receiving *good* seed. But no seed is good but the doctrine of Scripture. How carefully we ought to study the Scriptures! reading them daily, endeavoring to understand their meaning, asking the help of pious people; above all, upon our knees entreating to be taught of God. We ought to believe no doctrine that cannot be clearly proved from the Scriptures; for, if it cannot be found there, it must be bad seed.

We see also from this parable, that the wheat and tares often resemble each other so much, that it is difficult to distinguish between them. For *why* did the lord of the field forbid his servants to pull up the tares? It was for fear lest they should mistake, and pull up wheat instead of tares. The servants represent ministers; they cannot always distinguish between true and false believers. It is God alone who knows the heart; he knows them that are his, and he alone knows it with *certainty*. The disciples did not know that Judas was a devil; but Jesus knew it from the beginning. When Saul of Tarsus was first converted, the disciples at Jerusalem did not know that he was sincere, and were for some time afraid to receive him. We should not therefore be too much delighted with the approbation of our fellow-Christians, nor too much disquieted by their suspicions. We should come to God, and entreat him to examine our hearts. Like David, each should say, "Search me, and try me, and see if there be any wicked way in me, and lead me in the way everlasting."

But though true and false believers may appear so much alike in this world, the hour will arrive when their true characters will be made known. There is really the greatest difference between the character of the *weakest* child of God and the most *plausible* hypocrite. The hypocrite may appear even *better* than the child of God; but there is a difference in their *hearts*, which will cause them to be separated from each other to all eternity. God will give his angels wisdom to discern between the righteous and the wicked: they will separate many who have partaken of the same ordinances and lived in the same family.

The wicked shall be bound in bundles. Perhaps this expression is intended to show how they will add to each other's misery by mutual reproaches. The righteous will shine forth as the sun without one spot of sin to darken their brightness. It has been well said that three things will surprise us, if we enter heaven: first, to see so many there whom we did *not* expect to see; secondly, to miss so many whom we *did* expect to see; and thirdly, to find ourselves there; yes, ourselves, we who are so unworthy—lifted up from the dust, and exalted to a throne. O! may this surprise be ours! for there is another surprise that awaits many seeming Christians, who will confidently cry out, "Lord, Lord, open to us." Now, therefore, let us judge ourselves, that we may not be condemned with the world.

Evening Scripture portion. 2 Tim. II. *False doctrines.*

MARK IV. 21–29.—*Jesus encourages his disciples to communicate the word.*

THIS is part of a *private* conversation between our Lord and his apostles. If our minds were in a right state, how much more deeply should we be interested in such scenes than in the worldly trifles that surround us.

What did our Saviour say in these confidential moments? He

compared his disciples to a candle which he had lighted by his instructions, and was going to make burn still brighter by his explanation of the parables he had related in public. For what purpose did he give them light? that they might *conceal* it? No; but that they might set it upon a candlestick, and in *public* proclaim their Lord's *secret* communications. Jesus said, "There is nothing hid which shall not be manifested." He hid many holy truths under parables, but these truths were to be made manifest by the apostles' preaching. This command was fulfilled after his ascension. *Then* the apostles could say, that their sound had gone forth to the ends of the world. *Then* was fulfilled the prophecy, "How beautiful upon the mountains are the feet of him that bringeth good tidings." *We* hear these glorious secrets: they are contained in the epistles, where the secret counsel of God is revealed. Do we attend to these things? Do we look into them, as the angels do? or are we indifferent? Have we need of the rousing command of our Saviour? "If any man have ears to hear, let him hear."

The Lord encouraged his disciples to preach the truth, saying, "With what measure ye mete, it shall be measured to you again." If they meted out, or gave the truth which they had received, abundantly to others, they should themselves receive abundantly from Christ, spiritual blessings. And so it is now: "He that watereth others, shall be watered also himself." In trying to do good to others, we gain a blessing on our own souls.

Our Saviour then related a short parable to encourage his disciples still more to sow the seed of the word. He spoke of a man who sowed seed, and who slept and rose night and day; that is, who, after sowing the seed, went about his usual business, sleeping at night and rising in the day; and who, after some time, found the seed had sprung up, but not by his *own* power, for he could not even tell *how* it had sprung up. God, who had made it spring up, made it grow also without his assistance, till it was ripe and fit to be cut down.

Thus a minister, after sowing the seed of the word, is obliged to leave the success with God; for he cannot make it spring up in the heart, neither can he even understand *how* souls are converted; for the manner in which men are born of the Spirit is even a greater mystery than the way in which the seed is quickened in the earth. Yet the hearts of ministers are often rejoiced by seeing the effects of the words they have spoken. Sometimes, however, the seed they sowed does not spring up till after their death; nevertheless, at the harvest of the last day, souls who heard their words shall be their crown and rejoicing. Now is the time to sow, though in tears, knowing we shall reap in joy.

Let all who *know* the word seek to *sow* it also, though it be only in the heart of a little child; for sowers on earth shall certainly be reapers in heaven. But let us remember that the seed sown does not come to perfection *immediately:* first, the blade appears, then the ear, at last the full corn in the ear. We must, therefore, be patient with young converts. If we ourselves know any thing of Christ *now*, do we not feel that we have been grown very slowly?

It is refreshing to behold a Christian who is like full corn in the ear. Perhaps we have had the privilege of seeing such a person. It may be some poor destitute creature, lodging in a garret, has breathed a spirit that we longed to imbibe, and we have felt, while listening to her heavenly words, "It is good to be here." Do we *desire* to grow in grace? It is a good desire. The Lord will answer prayer, and give us more faith and love, and every heavenly grace, and then treasure us up in his eternal garner.

Evening Scripture portion. Eccl. XI. *Sowing seed.*

MATT. XIII. 31–35.—*Parables of the mustard-seed and of the leaven.*

WE will now consider several short parables that our Saviour related, but of which he gave no interpretation; still we may endeavor from other parts of Scripture to discover their meaning. The seed of the mustard-tree is smaller *in proportion* to the size of the tree it produces, than any other seed. In eastern countries the mustard-tree has immense spreading branches, which afford a fit shelter for the birds.

The religion of Christ was very small in its beginning. Behold the stable in Bethlehem, and that weak babe sleeping in the manger. From him shall spring a multitude that no man can number, of glorious saints, who throughout eternity shall surround the throne of God. These his spiritual children shall exceed the stars in multitude. Already how wonderfully has the Christian religion spread! though preached at first by twelve poor unlearned men—the kings of many nations profess to believe in it. It shall spread yet further, till men shall not merely *profess* the name of Christ, but till all shall praise him with unfeigned lips—till all shall know the Lord from the greatest unto the least.

The next parable, of the leaven that leavened by degrees a large quantity of meal, much resembles the parable of the mustard-tree, and it has been generally supposed to have nearly the same meaning. There is one great difference between the parables; the growth of the mustard-tree is *open;* the effects of the leaven in the meal are *secret.* Some persons have thought that while the growth of the mustard-tree represents the progress of the gospel in the *world*, the leavening of the meal shows its influence in the *heart.* The leaven is generally considered to signify the word of God, which works gradually and silently in the heart, as leaven works in meal.

But a learned writer* has lately suggested, that as leaven is used in

* Rev. Alfred Jenour.

other places to represent *wickedness*, it may represent it here also. St. Paul says, in his epistle to the Corinthians, "Purge out therefore the old leaven, that ye may be a new lump." (1 Cor. v. 7.) And Christ once said to his disciples, "Beware of the leaven of the Pharisees and of the Sadducees;" by which he meant their false *doctrine*. (Matt. xvi 12.) If leaven represents wickedness in this parable, then we learn from it how artfully Satan corrupts the pure religion of Christ; just as he sows tares among the wheat, so he mixes falsehood with truth.

By relating parables, our Lord fulfilled the prophecy of the seventy-eighth Psalm: "I will open my mouth in a *parable;* I will utter dark sayings of old." If we refer to that psalm, we shall find that it contains a history of the deliverance of the Israelites from Egypt, and of their passing through the wilderness. Was this history a parable? Yes, it was a parable, or dark saying, for all that happened to Israel had a hidden meaning. The apostle Paul, speaking of the afflictions of Israel, declares—"All these things happened unto them for ensamples; and they are written for our admonition upon whom the ends of the world are come." (1 Cor. x. 11.) There is one event especially that took place in the wilderness, which is full of the richest instruction. That event is the lifting up of the brazen serpent. Few, perhaps, understood at the time what it signified. But we see in that serpent the image of Jesus in the likeness of sinful flesh, crucified for our iniquities.

The Bible is full of dark sayings like this. Men naturally love mysteries and wonders. Why do they not love the Bible? Why does it lie neglected, while many foolish and hurtful books are eagerly devoured? Because men love sin, and the Bible speaks against it. Therefore St. Paul exhorts us to lay aside all malice, and guile, and hypocrisies, and envies, and evil speakings, that as new-born babes we may desire the sincere milk of the word. We cannot relish the Bible while we delight in sin.

Evening Scripture portion.
Ps. LXXVIII. 1–33. *God's dealings with Israel.*

MATT. XIII. 44–46.—*The parables of the hidden treasure and of the pearls.*

WE should be much astonished if a man were to show such eagerness to possess a common field, that he was willing to give *any* price for it. But if we afterwards found that he had discovered in it a mine of precious ore, we should not be surprised at his anxiety to obtain the field, even at a very high price.

Now it is in like manner that the world wonders at the eagerness of the believer to secure heavenly blessings. They see no such attraction in religion as to account for his earnestness, and they are ready to consider him a fool and a madman. But they have not discovered the *treasure* which he has discovered. Not that he *hides* it from them, (as the man in the parable did,) but he cannot persuade them to believe his testimony. In vain he assures them that true joy is to be found in Christ alone; they reply that religion is full of gloom and restraint, and that it is only fit for the sick, or the sorrowful. The believer knows well that the favor of God is of infinite value; he buys the field, he secures the treasure, and rejoices in his possession. Now is the time when the field may be bought. That time will soon be past. Awful and endless will be the regrets of those who neglected the opportunity of laying hold on eternal life.

In the next parable, a man is represented *seeking* goodly pearls. By nature we all seek for happiness; but we can never find it, except in the knowledge of Christ; nor can we find it there, unless we are willing to renounce all sinful pleasures for his sake. Augustine, the African bishop, (who lived four hundred years after Christ,) endured many sharp struggles before he would consent to part with his sins. But at length the grace of God subdued his stubborn heart. He cast himself down before the Lord under a fig-tree, and prayed, saying, "How long, Lord, wilt thou be angry? Forever? Remember not my old iniquities. How long shall I say 'To-morrow?' Why should not *this hour* put an end to my slavery?" God, by whose Spirit this prayer was suggested, answered it and revealed Christ to Augustine's soul. Then this man, once so miserable, could say, "How sweet was it in a moment to be free from those delightful vanities, to love which *had been* my dread—to part with which—was *now* my joy! Thou didst cast them out, O my true and highest delight;—and then, O sweeter than all pleasure, enteredst in their room. How was my mind set free from the gnawing cares of sinful passions, and I conversed intimately with Thee, my Light, my Riches, my Saviour, and my God." Surely this penitent sinner had now found the Pearl of great price. Can we say that Jesus is precious to our hearts? Upon a dying bed we should feel that none but He could comfort or save us —what should we do, if we had not found him then?

Evening Scripture portion. Job XXVIII. *The preciousness of wisdom.*

MATT. XIII. 47 to 52.—*The parable of the fishing-net.*

THE parable of the net cast into the sea was calculated particularly to interest the disciples, many of whom were fishermen. They were accustomed, after the toils of the day, to sort the fishes they had taken. This employment affords a lively image of the distinctions that will be made at the last day. The net represents the word of the Gospel, which is preached to *many*, and which *many* profess to believe. The disciples were shortly to begin the work of preaching it. Great success would accompany their endeavors; but yet that success would be attended by much disappointment. Many to whom they preached would prove hypocrites. *Some* of these would be detected in their lifetime, but *others* not till the judgment-day.

Unbelievers have urged, as an objection against the Christian religion, that hypocrites are found among professed believers! But this is rather a *proof* of its truth, than an objection. If no hypocrites existed, how could we account for our Saviour's declaring that they would arise in the church?

A striking instance was afforded of the truth of our Lord's words in the history of seven missionaries who labored many years ago in Tahiti. Would you not have concluded that men who had sacrificed country and friends in order to instruct savages, must have been true Christians? But out of these seven *two* proved reprobates. The force of temptation brought their real character to light. Had they remained in their own country, it is possible that no temptation might have arisen strong enough to entice them into open sin; but surrounded by savages, they became immoral in their lives, and, it is to be feared, continued impenitent till death. What a lesson does this fact afford! Should it not lead us to examine ourselves, and to call upon God to search us and try us, lest we should deceive ourselves by a mere *form* of godliness? Such a deception can last but a short time. The great sorting day approaches; then angels will divide the good from the bad, the true believer from the empty professor.

When our Saviour had concluded his parables, he asked his disciples whether they understood them; for he had not interpreted them ALL. They replied, Yes, Lord. Then he reminded them of the *use* they should make of the things they had learned; they should store them up in their minds, that they might have them ready upon every occasion; even as a master of a family provides all things necessary for different circumstances, and produces them when wanted. The teachers among the Jews were called Scribes. The disciples were to become teachers, and would need a great store of truths for the instruction of others. Some of these truths might be called "*new*" truths, because not known to them before, and some might be called "*old*" truths, because already familiar to their minds.

We ought to be storing up in our minds the things we have heard, gaining fresh knowledge of the Scriptures and deeper insight into their meaning. We cannot tell how soon we may need them for our own support in trial, or how useful we may find them in enlightening the ignorant, in strengthening the tempted, and in comforting the afflicted. It is very distressing when we see those we love sinking under trouble, to feel that we are not able to give them solid comfort. An affectionate child has sometimes beheld a parent groaning under a burden of wo, and has felt, "I know there are consolations that might assuage her grief, but I cannot impart them ; for I have neglected the word of God." Then let us for the sake of *others*, as well as for ourselves, store our minds with the holy truths of God, that we may produce them when most needed.

Evening Scripture portion.
Acts XX. 17 to end. *The apostle Paul's parting discourse to the elders at Miletus.*

MARK IV. 33 to end.—*Christ sleeps in the storm and awakes to still it.*

IT was in this manner that the Lord Jesus ended a day of great labor. His friends in the midst of it had desired him to desist, but seeing multitudes assembled to hear the word, he continued to teach. In order to be seen and heard more conveniently, he removed into a ship. The parable of the sower, and many others, were spoken by Jesus while he sat in a ship on the lake of Gennesareth. (See Mark iv. 1.) Afterwards, he had a private conversation in the house with his disciples, when he explained his parables. In the evening he crossed the lake in a ship.

Doubtless he knew of the approaching storm, though it appears that there were no signs of it observed by others, for *many* little ships accompanied him on his voyage. But he was not deterred by his knowledge of the coming storm from setting out, for he intended by it to teach his disciples an important lesson.

They knew little of their Master's *power*, and still less of his *love*. The storm ought not to have alarmed them, because they were with *Him*. God *intended* to alarm Jonah by the storm that arose on the way to Tarsus, for the prophet was fleeing from his presence. We must not suppose, because difficulties and troubles arise, that we are doing wrong. Before we take any important step in life, we should examine the word of God with prayer, and ask pious persons to help us to discover from the Scriptures, whether it is a *right* step ; and if we feel assured that it *is*, no difficulties in the way ought to alarm us. Christians have observed that they have met with most hinderances in setting about those works which in the end have been most richly blessed. A vessel laden with missionaries has been captured by the enemy. Was that calamity a sign that God disapproved the holy purpose of his servants ? Assuredly not. Those who are walking in the commandments of the Lord, may walk without fear, and say in the midst of troubles, "None of these things move me."

Our Saviour was displeased with the disciples' behavior in this storm.

He was displeased by their want of *faith*. They doubted his love, and said, "Carest thou not that we perish?" Because He slept, they thought he was indifferent to their distress. These are the thoughts that too often arise in our minds. Conscious that we are apt to forget the Lord, we fear that He has forgotten us; for we naturally attribute to others the feelings that we ourselves experience. Now his delivering mercies are intended to remove these unbelieving thoughts, and to convince us of his exceeding power and love. For this purpose, he brings his children into straits, and to the very edge of destruction, that he may appear to their rescue in the last moment, and thus force them to believe in his fatherly tenderness.

This is the meaning of the apostle in Rom. v. 3–5: He says that he glories in tribulations. *Why?* Because they work patience, and patience, experience. Experience of *what?* Of God's power and love. And experience worketh hope. God's deliverances are intended to strengthen our hopes of his mercy, and to convince us that he *never* will forsake us. And shall this hope be disappointed? No; *this* hope maketh not ashamed; it shall never prove vain.

The stilling of the storm on the lake of Gennesaret is calculated to lead our thoughts to another scene, and to remind us of that storm of God's wrath against our sins which Jesus stilled, not by his *word*, but by the *sacrifice* of himself. If we are enabled to trust in him, as our Saviour from *hell*, we need not fear any storm that can arise. Let us never say, or even think, "Carest thou not that we perish?" It is a sin to entertain such a thought of *Him* who endured the cross that we might not perish forever and ever. He cares for us more than we care for ourselves; he numbers the hairs of our heads, and watches over us with unceasing, unwearied love.

Evening Scripture portion. Romans V. *God's love to man.*

MARK V. 1–20.—*Christ delivers the demoniac who dwelt among the tombs.*

THE history of the poor demoniac affords a striking instance of the malice of devils, of the power of Christ, and of the wickedness of man.

How great was the malice of the devils that assaulted this poor man! They led him to dwell in solitary places among the tombs; for in those days tombs were generally made in lonely spots, among barren hills and rocks. Cut off from the company of his fellows, he spent his miserable days in crying, and cutting his own flesh; and when his friends mercifully bound his hands in chains, and his feet in fetters, he burst through these restraints and again escaped to his desolate abode. Thus he became a terror to the neighborhood, and a torment to himself.

This is the state to which devils would reduce *all* men, if they were permitted to vent their malice. They do reduce numbers to a *spiritual* state which resembles that of the demoniac, tempting them to flee from God and his saints, to dwell among the wicked, and urging them to resist all attempts to do them good, and make them happy.

Nor is the malice of devils confined to *men.* They love to torment even the brutes. These devils earnestly desired to enter into the swine, and then hurried them over the precipice, and plunged them in a watery grave. By this act they showed what they *would* have done to the *man*, had they not been restrained; they would fain have hurled him into the pit of eternal destruction. There is not one single soul that could escape perdition, if it were not for the *power of Christ.* Even the devils were obliged to acknowledge his power. They believed and trembled. They could do nothing without his permission. They saw in him their future judge, who would at last condemn them to imprisonment in the lake of fire. In the mean while they had great wrath, knowing that they had but a *short* time in which to vent their malice, (as we read in Rev. xii. 12.) That *short* time is shorter now, and Satan continues to be diligent in using this short space in making efforts to enlarge his kingdom.

We see in the conduct of the owners of the swine an instance of the wickedness of man. Untouched by the sight of him, who, lately a spectacle of terror, was now become gentle and peaceful, they only thought of the loss of their property.

Does not the same disposition prevail now? People will often show zeal for religion, as long as it does not interfere with their gains; but as soon as they are in danger of suffering the slightest loss, through the spread of the gospel, they complain, and would sooner let souls perish than become poorer.

Jesus was not *astonished* at this awful instance of human depravity; for he knew what was in man. So great was his compassion for these wicked men, that he bade the poor creature he had delivered, endeavor to reclaim his unfeeling countrymen. With the same compassion ought we to view every proof of man's fallen nature. Have we not ourselves in times that are *past* desired Jesus to depart from us, fearing lest he should interfere with our worldly schemes? How patiently has he borne our insults! If now we feel the value of our souls, we are dismayed at the remembrance of those days when we preferred a prosperous earthly lot to heavenly knowledge. And if we now love the merciful Saviour, we cannot bear to think of the time when we cared not for his presence,—for *that* presence which we now esteem our supreme happiness.

Evening Scripture portion. Acts XIX. 21 to end. *Demetrius the silversmith.*

MATT. IX. 9–13.—*The calling of Matthew and the publican's feast.*

WE have great reason to be interested in the calling of Matthew, for it was he who wrote the history of our Lord which we are now reading. It is supposed that his calling took place some time before the events we have lately considered; but we have deferred noticing it, because the feast to publicans and sinners was given at *this* period of the history; and it seemed most convenient to consider the calling and the feast at the same time.

The other name of Matthew was Levi, and *that* name is used by two of the evangelists. He was a publican, or tax-gatherer. Persons of this class were detested by the Jews; because, as the taxes were paid to the Romans, by whom the Jews had been conquered, none but the worst kind of people would undertake the odious office of collecting them; and these people rendered themselves still more hateful by their dishonest practices. To this despised order of men, Matthew belonged at the time Jesus called him. He was found sitting by the sea-shore, receiving the duties upon the goods that were landed or embarked. Jesus saw him at the table, which was covered with moneys, and inclined his heart to obey his call, to leave all and follow him.

And why did he choose a *publican* to be one of his apostles? Did he not, by exalting those whom the world despised, intend to stain the pride of all human glory?

Matthew made a feast to his old companions in office, (and who were probably his companions in *iniquity* also,) that they might partake in the high privilege of hearing the Lord converse. Nor did that gracious Lord turn away from these guests, polluted as they were by long habits of unrighteousness. The proud and envious Pharisees scoffed at him for keeping such company. But he answered their taunts by a divine lesson and reproof. He taught them in a short parable his *object* in associating with men; it was *not* to please *himself*, but to save *them*.

How does he save them? By healing their spiritual diseases; therefore he is called the Physician of souls. Would we obtain his notice, we must come and spread our *sins* before him. A good physician will not waste his time in visiting the healthy, however honorable, but flies to the relief of the poorest creature that is dangerously ill. Neither will the Lord grant his presence to the self-righteous, however high in man's esteem; but he will come and bless the humble and contrite soul, however deeply stained by crime, and degraded in the eyes of his fellow-creatures.

Do *we* understand what *that* meaneth? "I desired mercy and not sacrifice," (vi. 6.) It is a verse in the prophet Hosea. The Pharisees knew the words well, but they understood not their meaning. Their *behavior* showed they understood it not. They blamed Jesus for showing *mercy* to perishing sinners; and instead of showing any themselves, they only gave God *sacrifice*, or outward service. And why did they act thus? Because they *thought* they were righteous. If they had *really* been righteous, they would have felt compassion for sinners. The *angels*, those spotless beings, take a deep interest in our fallen race, and rejoice over each sinner who repents. Though they have never felt the working of evil in their own hearts, yet they do not turn away from us with contempt and disgust. But *men* never feel compassion for their fellow-sinners, till they discover the wickedness of their own hearts. When David was deeply humbled by his transgressions, he felt anxious to save perishing souls. This was his prayer, "Restore unto me the joy of thy salvation, and uphold me with thy free spirit. Then will I teach transgressors thy way, and sinners shall be converted unto thee."

The missionary Vanderkemp gave a beautiful example of the same spirit. Not only did he go out as a missionary to the heathen, but he desired to make the voyage to Africa in a convict-ship. His wish was granted. He went with a depraved troop; but many of their hearts were melted during their voyage: some who had secretly filed off their chains, confessed what they had done, and quietly submitted to have them again riveted upon their hands and feet. Thirty-five died of putrid fever on the passage. Vanderkemp attended them in their last hours, and saw not a few, before they departed, full of joy and peace through believing in a crucified Saviour.

Evening Scripture portion. Micah VI. *Mercy better than sacrifice.*

LUKE V. 33 to end.—*Christ explains by parables why his disciples did not fast.*

THIS is a difficult passage, and it has been explained in different ways; so that we can scarcely forbear wishing that our Saviour himself had given an explanation of these parables. Yet surely he would not have left them unexplained, if it were not possible by attentive consideration to unravel their meaning.

It was the disciples of that imprisoned saint, John the Baptist, who inquired why the disciples of Jesus never fasted. The Pharisees fasted often. As one of them boasted in his prayer, "I fast twice a week." These fastings were part of that righteousness by which they excited the admiration of the people, and by which they hoped to purchase heaven. John the Baptist had not taught his disciples to fast with such views. It was in grief for their sins that they fasted; and it was with the same holy feelings John himself fasted. Jesus, however, did not fast *openly*: how much he may have fasted in *secret* we know not; but he was seen to eat and drink in the usual manner, and on that account was called a gluttonous man and a wine-bibber. We know this accusation was false, and that the holy Jesus set an example of temperance, as well as of every other virtue. Once, when very weary, he refused to eat, saying, "My meat is to do the will of him that sent me, and to finish his work." And at other seasons he "had no leisure so much as to eat," (Mark vi. 31.)

The Lord related several little parables to explain his *reasons* for not teaching his disciples to fast. In the first parable he compared himself to a bridegroom. This was a title that John himself had given him, saying, "He that hath the bride is the bridegroom." The Church was the bride: Christ was the bridegroom. The disciples, the ministers, were compared by Jesus to the children of the bridechamber, or to the friends of the bridegroom, who could not mourn at the wedding. The disciples were too full of joy to fast when they were following their Master from place to place, witnessing his miracles, and listening to his discourses. But the days would come when they would no longer enjoy the presence of the bridegroom, and when they would be called to endure heavy trials, to suffer hunger and thirst, and to be in fastings often.

Jesus prepared his disciples, just before he left them, for the afflictions that awaited them. He said, "The time cometh that whosoever killeth you will think that he doeth God service," (John xvi. 2–4.) And he added, "These things I said *not* unto you at the *beginning*, because I was with you." In the same manner he often now protects a *new* convert from heavy trials. It is very common to find the *entrance* upon a religious course fraught only with delight: the new convert is sometimes inclined to think that he shall weep no more, but pass his days in a course of uninterrupted usefulness and joy. But trial comes at last.

The homely employment of mending garments was the subject of one of the Lord's parables. Every one who has ever repaired woollen garments, knows that it would be unwise to mend them with stiff unprepared cloth. Another parable was taken from the eastern custom of putting wine into bottles of *skins*. These skins, when they were old, were unfit for *new* wine, because they were then too weak to bear its fermentation. These two parables seem to have a similar meaning. Did they not allude to the present weakness of the disciples? They were new converts, and not able yet to suffer great trials. For though garments and skin-bottles are strong at *first* and weak *afterwards*, it is just the contrary with believers; they are weak at first and strong afterwards. Peter was so weak at first, that he was induced by a few scornful speeches to deny his Master; but he was so strong afterwards, that he was able to bear crucifixion for his sake.

The Lord concluded his discourse with another parable: "No man also having drunk old wine, straightway desireth new: for he saith, The old is better." The gospel is like the best wine. Jesus gave

this wine to the weeping penitent, when he said, ' Thy sins are forgiven thee." He gave it to his beloved disciples when he said, " In my Father's house are many mansions : I go to prepare a place for you." He gave it to the dying thief, when he said, " To-day shalt thou be with me in Paradise." Has he given it to us ? He has *offered* it to us. These are his words : " Look unto me and be ye saved, all the ends of the earth," (Is. xlv. 22.) If we have obeyed this call, and believed in Jesus with our hearts, then we have tasted the best wine ; then we enjoy true happiness, and shall enjoy it forever ; for " Blessed are they whose iniquities are forgiven, and whose sins are covered. Blessed is the man to whom the Lord will not impute sin." To whom does this blessedness belong ? Not to those who are striving by their good works to gain God's favor, but to those who " believe on Him that raised up Jesus our Lord from the dead ; who was delivered for our offences, and was raised again for our *justification*."

Evening Scripture portion. Rom. IV. *Justification by faith.*

LUKE VIII. 40–48.—*Christ heals the woman who touched him in the throng.*

THOUGH the Gadarenes desired the Lord Jesus to depart out of their coasts, there were others who gladly received him. So it is now: while some find religious privileges a burden, there are others who are longing to possess them. While some occupy seats in the house of God, and count the service a weariness ; there are others, confined at home by various causes, envying, as David did, the happiness of the swallow, who builds his nest on God's altars.

The people on the opposite coast of the lake soon found the advantage of having the presence of Jesus. A ruler bows before his feet, laid low by sore distress respecting his only child.

On his way to the ruler's house, people thronged around the blessed Saviour. How patient was the love that led him to submit to every inconvenience ! Each step he took was encumbered by an oppressive crowd ; yet he complained not of the heat and the noise of the throng. As he went, very *many* touched him, but only *one* did so in faith and with *intention*. Even so it is now ; thousands offer prayers, yet few offer them with *intention* and with *expectation* of relief. Yet no other worshippers are noticed by Jesus. No other *touch* was noticed by him but that of the poor woman who said to herself, " If I may but touch his clothes, I shall be whole." Is it in this spirit we come to Jesus ? Do we *expect* an answer to our prayers ?

Our case by nature is desperate, like that of the woman. She had applied to many physicians, and had reduced herself to poverty, yet had obtained no relief; and having now spent all her money, her hope of human assistance must have failed her. Thus some persons who have been convinced of their sinful state, have tried to obtain relief by multiplied services, and good works, but have never found peace till they came to Jesus.

Let us observe the Lord's condescending approbation of *true* faith, however *weak*. There was much ignorance mixed up in the faith of this woman. She thought that she might touch Jesus *unperceived*. She knew not that he saw her thought afar off, and that her inward groaning was not hid from him. But Jesus does not despise *weak* faith, or quench the smoking flax.

Though he healed the woman upon her *secret* application to him, he desired her to make a *public* acknowledgment of her cure. He desires every sinner to do the same. "With the *heart* man believeth unto righteousness, and with the *mouth* confession is made unto salvation." The woman willingly made this confession, when she found it was required by her benefactor. Gratitude to Jesus should overcome every other feeling in our hearts, and make us willing to acknowledge what he has done for our souls, and from what a *depth* of misery he has delivered us. The saints above are not ashamed to acknowledge their obligations to the Saviour. They are willing that their past sins should be known, in order that his power and love may be exalted. The song of the blessed is, "Thou wast slain, and hast redeemed us to God by thy *blood*." They own that blood was required to atone for their guilt. If we join that happy throng, we shall appear among them as *sinners* saved by grace. We shall not desire to conceal from our heavenly companions that we were once polluted. We shall only desire that the wonderful power of our Redeemer may be made known among the assembled multitude. The thief who repented on the cross will extol the grace of his crucified Lord, who atoned for his flagrant crimes. And though we may not have committed the *same kind* of sins as that thief, we have all committed sins which, but for faith in the blood of Christ, must sink our souls into everlasting wo.

Evening Scripture portion. Ps. LI. *Confession of sin.*

MATT. V. 35 to end.—*He raises Jairus' daughter.*

WITH what eagerness the ruler must have watched the Saviour's progress towards his house! It must have been a trial to him to see the steps of his deliverer retarded by the surrounding crowd. But what a blow it was to hear his child was actually dead! Those who brought the message thought that Jesus *could* not *now* relieve the poor father. They said, "Why troublest thou the Master any further?"

Yet why did they speak thus? Is there any thing too hard for the Lord? If he could *heal* by his power, could he not also restore *life* by the same power?

Probably the ruler partook of the doubts of the messengers; for Jesus immediately encouraged him, saying, "Be not afraid, only believe." How apt we are, though we know that Jesus is almighty, to think, that while he can relieve us in a *small* trouble, he cannot help us in a *great* one! How apt we are to imagine that there are some cases too *hard* for him. Does not this show that our faith is very weak? The truth is, that God delights in showing the greatness of his power by delivering us out of the most overwhelming distresses. If we *believed* in him more, we should see more of his wonderful works. And though he does not now raise the dead, it is not because the work is too great for his power, but because the *time* is not yet come.

When Jesus came to the ruler's house, he shut out of the room the scoffing attendants, and only permitted the parents of the child and three of his apostles to witness the miracle. There are wonders of his love and power, which Christ displays to his believing people *alone*. The parents would not have been admitted into their daughter's chamber, had they been disposed to scoff at the Saviour's words. Their sorrowful hearts must have been looking and longing for deliverance.

How many who have expected deliverance in trial, have received it! A way has been opened in a manner least expected. Thus Abraham, when he had lifted up the knife to slay his son, believed that God could raise him; and his faith was rewarded. He called the mount Jehovah Jireh; or, "in the mount of the Lord it shall be seen;" that is, "the Lord will see, or provide;" thus leading all believers to look for similar deliverances in the hour of extreme distress.

Can the parents who beheld the glorious deed have regretted the sufferings they had endured? If they had suffered less, they had seen less of the power of the Lord. When Christians come out of their afflictions, they have wonderful histories to relate concerning God's faithfulness, which they would never have known had they remained at ease. But there are proper *seasons* in which to relate these histories. The time was not yet come for publishing abroad the miracles that Jesus had wrought. When he himself had risen from the dead, then it was the duty of his followers to declare all they had seen. His wonderful works have been recorded, and handed down to us. Do we believe that Jesus will raise the dead at the last day? Then we can lay our beloved ones in the tomb without that distracting, hopeless sorrow, which the unbelieving world experience.

Evening Scripture portion. Gen. XXII. *The offering up of Isaac.*

MATT. IX. 27–34.—*Christ gives sight to two blind men, and speech to a dumb man.*

IT appears that the Lord Jesus put the faith of the two blind men to a short trial; for he did not cure them as soon as they asked him; he waited till he was come into the house before he granted their petition. But how well they were rewarded for waiting, by their conversation with their Lord in the retirement of the house! The blind men spoke but little: "Yea, Lord." Those were their words; but these simple words pleased Jesus, for they were sincere words. What could we reply, if the Lord were to ask us whether we believed that he was able to do every thing? Could we reply, "Yea, Lord." Let us in times of trouble remember that Jesus can do every thing.

After the Lord had left the house, he cured a dumb man. This miracle he performed publicly, in the presence of his enemies. The poor man was an object of great compassion, for *he* could not (like the blind man) plead for himself: others brought him to Jesus. Should not this teach us that we should pray for those who, through the power of Satan, are dumb unto God, and cannot pray for themselves? This cure excited much astonishment, and caused men to exclaim, "It was never so seen in Israel." There had been other prophets, such as Elijah and Elisha, who had done miracles, but not such great, or numerous miracles as Christ performed.

Jesus now performs wonders on men's souls, which cause many to exclaim, "It was never so seen before." The gospel produces effects, which nothing *but* the gospel can produce. What has it not wrought in the South Sea Islands! It has changed thousands of blind idolaters and murderers into sons of truth and peace. In England, the preaching of the gospel has oftentimes transformed the most abandoned characters into holy men. Yet these wonders do not silence the enemies of Christ. The Pharisees were so wicked as to exclaim, "He casteth out devils through the prince of the devils." They knew that they spoke falsely, but they hated Jesus so much, that they used *any* means to hinder the people from believing on him. There are still persons to be found who will slander the servants of God even when they know them to be innocent. There lived in the last century a pious curate named Maddock, who converted many souls by the preaching of the gospel. Those who hated his doctrine invented slanders concerning him, and so shook his spirits, as to cause him to fall ill and to resign his curacy. But some time afterwards two of his bitter enemies relented, and acknowledged that the reason of their wicked conduct was, that they could not endure the doctrine he had preached to them; and that they had never believed the reports they had spread. And what were the feelings of this holy man upon the occasion? He wrote in his journal, "Now my enemies have confessed their enmity against God, and his word, and against me for preaching it. O Lord, by this 'onfession thou hast greatly eased my mind. Thou hast made mine enemies confess that they have persecuted thy servant out of malice. Remember, I beseech thee, their blindness and ignorance, and pardon them freely for thy dear Son's sake." Like his blessed Master, this pious minister pursued his work in other towns and villages, and continued to the end of his days to heal sin-sick souls.

Evening Scripture portion. Is. XXXII. *The blessed effects of the gospel.*

MARK VI. 1–6.—*Christ's second visit to Nazareth.*

THIS is the *second* visit that we read of Jesus making to Nazareth after he had begun his ministry.

In his *first* visit there he had been shamefully treated, for his countrymen had attempted to hurl him headlong from the hill; yet he was so forgiving that he made a *second* visit to the ungrateful city. Jesus does not hastily give up any sinners whom he once has favored. Even when the first offer of mercy has been rejected, he vouchsafes another, and perhaps another still; for He is the God of patience. While he was preaching, very contemptuous thoughts arose in the people's hearts. None could deny that he had done mighty works, and that he spoke with extraordinary wisdom; but yet, because the people remembered him as *the carpenter*, and because they knew his relations to be poor persons, with whom they were familiar, they would not listen to his words. What an instance their conduct affords of the greatness of human folly!

As it was *then*, even so it is *now;* people are apt to consider, *not* so much *what* is spoken, as by *whom* it is said. The servants of God are still despised when they are poor and unlearned, and their message is often rejected on these accounts; but those who despise them sin against their own souls. How foolish we should consider that person, who, though dying of thirst, refused a draught of water, because it was contained in a common earthen cup! No thirsty person ever acted in so absurd a manner; but many ignorant souls have displayed still greater folly. When faithfully warned by a true believer, they have taken no heed to his words, because he did not possess the learning, or honors of this world. They have said, "How should this man be able to teach me?" Yet perhaps that man had been taught of God. Such persons would surely have despised their Saviour when he was upon earth.

Great was the loss that the men of Nazareth brought upon themselves by their conduct. They would not even come to Christ to be healed; that was the reason that Jesus *could* do no mighty work there.

He *marvelled* at their *unbelief;* as he had once marvelled at the *faith* of the centurion.

The Nazarenes abused *singular* privileges. They had beheld for a long period the spotless example of the Son of God. They had witnessed the lovely qualities that adorned his childhood, and which grew brighter and brighter during the years of his youth and early manhood. Could they refrain from loving a being of such perfect excellence, and whose excellence they knew so well? Yes. His faithfulness in reproving sin caused them to hate him. Hatred produced contempt, and contempt confirmed them in unbelief.

We never can expect to meet with a human creature faultless like the Lord Jesus; but all Christians in a degree resemble their Master; and some resemble him more than others. It may have been our privilege to know some eminent saints. They may now be in their graves; but the very remembrance of them is blessed. We shall meet them again at the judgment-seat of Christ. If we rejected their counsel while living, let us attend to them now they are departed, that we may not incur the guilt and misery of the men of Nazareth.

Evening Scripture portion. Jer. XI. *The persecutions of Jeremiah.*

MATT. IX. 35 to end.—*His compassion for the multitude.*

THE Lord Jesus was permitted to teach in the synagogues, but he did not confine himself to them; nor did He preach only on the Sabbath. He taught in all *places* and at all *times*. There have been faithful men, who have closely copied his example, and have proclaimed their Master's name with an untiring zeal. They have been much despised, but they have turned many sinners unto the Lord; for the *preaching* of the gospel is the most effectual means of converting souls.

Great multitudes followed Jesus from place to place. When he beheld them he was moved with compassion. What constant proofs we find of the tenderness of his heart! He could not see the multitude fainting from hunger and weariness without feeling for their *bodies;* neither could he consider their destitute spiritual condition without feeling still deeper compassion for their *souls*. They seemed to him like sheep without a shepherd. There were indeed appointed teachers in every city and village; but these teachers were unfaithful, and did not feed the sheep with the knowledge of God, but misled their minds by false explanations of the Scriptures. Such teachers Jesus would not acknowledge to be true shepherds; for they only poisoned the flock.

He then made another comparison. He likened the people to a field of corn ready to be reaped, and he declared there were few reapers prepared to reap it. There were *many* persons ready to come into the kingdom of God, and but *few* able to lead them into it; therefore he desired his disciples to entreat the Lord of the harvest to send forth laborers into the field. The world is still in the same case: there are but few laborers compared with the number of persons willing to be taught. In some countries, the people have cast away their idols, and are longing and praying for teachers.

When Christ ascended on high, he gave *gifts* unto men. And what were those gifts? Apostles, teachers, pastors. It is not only blind idolaters who need their instructions. Israel of old needed teachers to stir up their hearts to love God. All of us require the exhortations of faithful ministers, lest we be hardened by the deceitfulness of sin. Those who try to live without the blessing of a good minister, (when they can obtain one,) suffer greatly from the attempt; their souls grow cold, their steps turn aside, and, even in old age, they often slide into error.

What gifts to perishing sinners can be so great as the gift of faithful pastors? To patients in a hospital, no boon could be so great as able physicians. Do we ever pray to God that he will raise up faithful ministers to feed his church? If we felt the compassion that Jesus felt for immortal souls, we should pray earnestly and constantly that ministers might be sent to show them the way of salvation. It is God alone who can send forth faithful laborers; He alone can make men able to teach others.

Evening Scripture portion. Zec. XIII. *Fountain for sin.*

MATT. X. 1–7.—*He sends out his twelve apostles.*

THE Lord Jesus had exhorted his disciples to pray that God would send laborers into his harvest. He had scarcely given the command before he answered the prayer by appointing these twelve disciples to preach the word. He sent them forth by two and two, that they might have a counsellor, a companion, and a friend upon the journey. It is well not to enter upon difficult undertakings *alone*. We are creatures that need sympathy. Fellow-laborers in Christ's vineyard have often found great comfort in each other, and become mutually endeared. None but Christians know the love that binds those together who work, with a single heart, in the same spot for the same Master.

It must have been a time of great anxiety to the twelve when they were called to leave their gracious Master's side, and enter without him upon the labors of the ministry. Hitherto they had been sheltered beneath his wing; but now they were to encounter the enemy alone; yet not *alone*, for though invisible, they would still be watched over by their ever-present Lord. Jesus endowed them with a measure of the same powers that he possessed himself; for having a *new* message to deliver, it was necessary that they should confirm it by wonderful works. Yet sometimes they could not exercise these powers from want of faith. We do not know whether they ever raised the dead till after Jesus was ascended on high.

Before they set out, their Master gave them some counsels. How deeply these counsels ought to interest us! they are full of the wisdom of God, and show us his mind and will.

Jesus first told the disciples to *whom* to go—to the *Jews* only, not to the Gentiles, or to the Samaritans, (who were a mixed people, descended from Jews and Gentiles,) but to the Jews. What was his reason for this command? Did He not *afterwards* desire his apostles to preach the gospel to *every* creature? It appears that he chose to give the *first* call to the Jews; because they were beloved for the fathers' sakes. Abraham, Isaac, and Jacob, had been the sheep of his fold. Their sinful children had wandered from that fold; therefore the Saviour viewed them as *lost* sheep. Our God is very slow to give up those whom he has once favored. It is not till after repeated provocations, and the most obstinate negligence, that he forsakes them. Has he granted us, as He once did the Jews, many spiritual privileges? Then he will not lightly leave us. He will dig about the fig-tree before he cuts it down; he will trim the lamp again and again before he puts it out in obscure darkness. But O! terrible will be his wrath when once it is aroused; for he will then execute strict justice upon those who have rejected abundant mercy.

Jesus directed his disciples, not only to *whom* to preach, but *also* WHAT to preach. They were to say, as *he* had said, and as John the Baptist had said, "The kingdom of heaven is at hand." These words contained a solemn warning; they signified that the opportunity of entering the kingdom was afforded, and might soon be over. A door was opened, the promise of pardon and of grace was offered, and all might enter in by this door to escape the judgment due to their sins; but it would at length be closed, and then, wo to those who had lost the precious opportunity. It is *still* true, that the kingdom of heaven is at hand; an opportunity of obtaining life is afforded to us: "Now is the accepted time; *now* is the day of salvation." Ministers proclaim with uplifted voice, and sometimes with tears which they cannot restrain, the unbounded mercy of our God. They entreat us to accept his offers of pardon through the blood of Christ. Some listen to their entreaties, fall down before the Son of God, and call upon him to save them. Have we thus humbled ourselves, and pleaded for mercy? Here is a gracious promise for our encouragement. God has said, "To this man will I look, even to him that is poor and of a contrite spirit, and *trembleth* at my word." (Is. lxvi. 2.)

Evening Scripture portion. Acts XXVIII. *The gospel rejected by the Jews.*

MATT. X. 7–15.—*He directs them with whom to abide during their journey.*

BEFORE the twelve disciples set out on their journey, their Master gave them many directions respecting their conduct. He desired them to make no provision for their wants, to take no money in their purses or girdles, no food in their scrips or bags, and no new clothes to supply the place of the old when worn out. How then were they to be supported during their travels? Jesus appointed that the people to whom they preached should supply their wants; for "The workman," he said, "is worthy of his meat." Pious persons would consider it a privilege to supply the wants of their teachers. The apostles, by accepting their gifts, would imitate the humility of their Master, who, though he *could* have turned stones into bread, and *did* turn water into wine, chose rather to accept the gifts of his pious followers. How many of God's most devoted servants in all ages have been placed in circumstances of dependence! But God has never forgotten his children when reduced to deep poverty. He has always put it into the hearts of some charitable persons to help them in their need, or by some other means He has supplied their necessities.

It is recorded of an excellent minister, who lived nearly two hundred years ago, that once when obliged by persecution to leave his family, he set out without any money in his pocket, and not knowing where to go. He suffered his horse to take its own course, and towards evening he found himself at the door of a small farm-house. He requested the mistress to allow him to take shelter beneath her roof, but frankly told her he had no money with which to reward her hospitality. Both she and her husband kindly entertained him. In the course of conversation they inquired after a minister, named Oliver Heywood, whom, they had heard, was persecuted with great bitterness. After some time, the traveller acknowledged that he was the very person they spoke of. Great was the joy of his pious hosts. They called their neighbors in, requested their honored guest to speak to them from the word of God, and afterwards made a small collection to help him on his way.

In this manner God has often unexpectedly relieved his suffering servants. No doubt the apostles, during the course of their journey, experienced the same providential care.

But though the Lord promised to provide for their wants, he warned them against indulging a covetous disposition: "*Freely* ye have received, *freely* give." He forbade their making a gain of their power to heal. They might easily have amassed large fortunes by their cures; but riches so acquired by ministers of his word would have been a curse.

Jesus directs his apostles to *whom* to go in each city—"To the most worthy." They were to make inquiries respecting the character of the inhabitants of each place they visited. Probably the neighbors would speak most highly of the most upright and benevolent inhabitants of the village. In general, it would be found that the person who bore the best character was also the most godly. What a blessing *he* would enjoy who would obtain the company of the apostles, and have the opportunity of hearing their instructions! It is considered an honor to entertain princes; but it is a far higher honor to receive the servants of God. When they have departed, the remembrance of their words, and of their spirit, leaves a holy fragrance on the mind. But sometimes the apostles would enter the door of an *unworthy* host, perhaps of some hypocritical Pharisee, who had succeeded in establishing a good reputation among men. Still they were to pronounce the blessing of peace upon the house. But that blessing would not descend upon an unworthy head. No; it would return into the bosom of those who uttered it. Thus we perceive, that if we are deceived in the characters of others, and bless those whom God has determined not to bless, yet still the blessing shall not be lost.

The Lord prepared his apostles to find some who would refuse to hear their message. It would be their duty solemnly to warn these despisers of the awful guilt they incurred. The sin of rejecting the gospel is far greater than any sin that the heathens *can* commit. *Men* may think that the idolater who leaves his aged parents to starve, or who cruelly slaughters the innocent children of his enemies, is the most wicked of the human race. But the Bible declares that the man who refuses to accept the merciful offers of the Son of God, is far worse than any of the heathen, and that he shall suffer the hottest wrath of his insulted Redeemer. Shall God speak, and man refuse to listen? Shall God stretch out his hands in merciful entreaty, and shall man turn away and despise the gracious invitation? How awful is the threatening denounced against such scorners. "I will also laugh at your calamity; I will mock when your fear cometh." (Prov. i. 26.)

Evening Scripture portion. Prov. I. ***The doom of those who reject God's mercy.***

MATT. X. 16–26.—*He prepares them for persecution.*

OUR Saviour fully prepared his disciples for the treatment they would receive from the world. He compared ungodly men to wolves, and his apostles to sheep. He described the manner in which these wolves would treat his sheep—in *thought*, *word*, and *deed*. The *thoughts* of ungodly men towards the apostles would be thoughts of hatred. Jesus said, "Ye shall be *hated* of all men." (verse 22.)

The world has ever hated the children of God. There is nothing more painful to our feelings than the ill-will of our fellow-creatures. No abundance of possessions can make amends for hatred; while love can console in the midst of trials. Jesus therefore warned his disciples against being turned back from him by the hatred of the world, saying, "He that endures to the end (in spite of these trials) shall be saved."

The hatred men felt in their hearts would lead them to utter hateful *words* against the disciples of Jesus. They had called the Lord Jesus himself Beelzebub. Ought his disciples to expect better treatment? Was it not enough if the servant was not *worse* treated than his Lord?

Christians have always been slandered; they have been accused of hypocrisy, as well as of secret crimes. Jesus comforts his disciples under their accusations by this assurance in verse 26: "There is nothing covered that shall not be revealed; nor hid, that shall not be known." Would it not comfort those who are falsely accused, to know that the day is coming when the truth would be made known? Such comfort all Christians possess, when slandered by their enemies.

Men would not only speak *words* against the disciples, but would commit cruel *actions* against them. They would imprison them and scourge them, and even cause them to be put to *death*. Yea, parents would turn against their own children, and persecute them in the most unnatural manner.

All these trials did not come upon the disciples during their *first* journey; but as Jesus knew they would come upon them after his ascension, he directed them how to behave under these trials. They were to do every thing to avoid persecution, *except* concealing the truth. In their characters they were to resemble serpents and doves; *serpents* in caution and prudence, *doves* in gentleness and inoffensiveness: they were not to be *malicious* as serpents, or *silly* as doves, but *wise* as serpents, and *harmless* as doves. Yet notwithstanding all their endeavors, they would be persecuted for preaching the gospel.

One great advantage would arise from their being brought before kings and judges; they would have an opportunity of declaring the truth to those high personages; as Paul did to Felix, who trembled on his judgment-seat. Jesus bade his disciples *take no thought what* they should speak when examined by their judges. Though they could not foresee what perplexing questions would be put to them, they were not to be disquieted with the fear lest they should not be able to answer well; for God would assist them with his Spirit.

Peter and John were the first among the apostles who were brought before rulers for their Master's sake. It is written, that when Peter was called upon to defend his conduct in healing the lame man, he "was filled with the Holy Ghost." He spoke with such power, that his judges could make no reply. "When they saw the boldness of Peter and John, and perceived they were unlearned and ignorant* men, they marvelled." (Acts iv. 13.)

In later days many poor uneducated men have been questioned by learned judges, and have been able to give answers which have quite confounded their enemies. In Foxe's Book of Martyrs, there are accounts of many such men who suffered death in this country, because they would not worship the Virgin Mary and the saints, or profess to believe Roman Catholic errors. And it has been remarked, that some of the *least* learned of the martyrs spoke with the *greatest* power; because they relied most simply upon the help of God, and appealed only to his Word.

Though we may never be called upon to stand before an earthly judgment-seat, yet we must be willing to confess our faith whenever an opportunity occurs. It is written in the first Epistle of Peter, "Be ready always to give an answer to every man that asketh you a reason of the hope that is in you, with meekness and fear." We may trust in God to teach us on such occasions how to reply. Let us lift up our hearts to Him before we speak, and our answer may be made the means of converting the unbelieving inquirer.

Evening Scripture portion. Acts XXIV. *Paul before Felix.*

MATT. X. 27–39.—*Jesus encourages them to be faithful.*

THE Lord Jesus had declared that his disciples would be exposed to great sufferings through preaching the gospel—that they would be scourged, imprisoned, and even put to death. Would not this prospect be a great temptation to conceal the truth? Yes, it would; therefore Jesus taught them by commands, warnings, and promises, to preach the gospel *openly*.

First, he gave them a *command*. He said, "What I tell you in darkness, that speak ye in light; what ye hear in the ear, that preach ye in the housetops." He had told his disciples many doctrines *privately*, that they were to preach *publicly*. How anxious Paul afterwards was that he might open his mouth *boldly*, and speak the

(* *Private*, not official persons.)

gospel as he ought to speak it, concealing no *part* of the truth, however men might dislike to hear it!

Jesus not only gave a command, he added *warnings*, reminding his disciples that God was able to kill both their bodies and souls in hell; declaring that he would deny them before his Father, if they denied him before men; and asserting that "he that findeth his life shall lose it;" that is, that he that saves his life by forsaking Christ, shall perish. But perhaps some may ask, "Did not Peter deny Christ? Will Christ deny him before his Father?" Assuredly not; for Peter repented of his sin, and obtained mercy, and no sin repented of and forgiven, shall be punished at the last day.

Christ also gave *promises* to his disciples to encourage them to preach his gospel. He told them that their hairs were all numbered, and that they themselves were of more value in God's sight than many sparrows. He did *not* promise that his disciples should be preserved from sufferings or from death by their heavenly Father; but he assured them that their trials were all appointed by a loving parent. The ungodly will sometimes say in trouble, "It is all for the best;" but it is *not* all for the best with those who do not desire to please God; sufferings only add to the guilt of those who do not repent of their sins. The children of God *alone* may feel assured that all that befalls them is for the best; sickness and health, riches and poverty, life and death, are all made to promote their everlasting welfare. "We know," says the apostle Paul, "that all things work together for good to *them that love God*." (Romans viii. 28.)

Jesus prepared his disciples for occasioning a great deal of confusion by the preaching of the gospel. He said, "Think not that I am come to send *peace* on earth." It was natural that the disciples should suppose that he came to send peace. Isaiah had called him the Prince of Peace. At his birth angels had sung, "Glory to God in the highest, on earth *peace*." He did, indeed, come to bring peace in the *end*, but persecution and confusion *first*. It would be wicked men who would create this confusion by their hatred of the Saviour. How many families have been divided by the gospel! one member has become religious, has turned to God in earnest, and the rest have turned against him. But should these trials prevent any from coming to Christ? O no; we ought to love the Saviour better than our dearest relations—better than father or mother, son or daughter. Nor must we in any thing disobey him, in order to please a dear friend, or connection. There are many children who are unkindly treated by their parents on account of their religion, and there are many parents who are despised by their children for the same reason. It is a great temptation to an affectionate parent to indulge children by allowing them to taste pleasures which are forbidden in the holy Scriptures. But to do this is to be unfaithful to God. We should always remember that Jesus is nearer to us than parent or child can be. He is our *God*. The Lord said to Abraham in ancient days, "I will be a GOD unto thee." This is more than if He had said, ' I will be a *Father* unto thee." David said unto the Lord, "Thou art my God!" (Ps. cxl. 6.) When any who are near and dear to us would entice us to forsake Him, let us remember that He is our *God.*

Evening Scripture portion. Deut. XIII. *Fidelity to God.*

MATT. X. 40 to end; XI. 1.—*He pronounces blessings on those who show kindness to his disciples.*

THE Lord Jesus had forbidden his apostles to take any thing with them in their journey, either scrip, (that is, bag of provisions,) or money in their purses; and He had desired them to go to the house of the most worthy person in each town, though that person might also be the poorest. It must have been a great comfort to the apostles to know that a rich blessing would rest upon those who received them into their houses, and that their kindness would be repaid at the resurrection of the just.

St. Paul felt this comfort when the Philippians sent gifts to him in prison. *He* could not repay them, but he said, "My *God* will supply all your need according to his riches in glory in Christ Jesus." (Phil. iv. 19.)

But is it not possible that a *wicked* man might receive a servant of Christ and treat him kindly? Yes, doubtless it is possible. Would *he* receive a heavenly reward? We must consider the *motive* of every action, before we can pronounce it to be good or bad. It is only those who receive a prophet in the *name* of a prophet, (that is, *because* he is a prophet,) who shall receive a prophet's reward. He who receives a prophet *because* he is an admired preacher, or an amiable man, or an old acquaintance, he will not receive a prophet's reward for his hospitality. The *motive* in receiving him must be, *because* he is a servant of Christ. If *that* is the motive, *all* faithful prophets will be treated with kindness, and not only some favorite prophet. The blessing, we perceive, is pronounced not only on those who receive *prophets,* but also on those who receive *righteous men* who are *not* prophets; and also on those who are kind to Christ's little ones, or to the weakest believers.

In these days it is often difficult to discover whether any kindness we show to God's people proceeds from the right motive. It is now so easy a duty, that many practise it, who would not incur any danger, or make any sacrifice for the sake of Christ and his people. In former days the case was different. Then it was often dangerous to show kindness to true Christians. Those who visited them in prison, or who harbored them in their houses, drew upon themselves persecution.

Even in this country, at the time people were beginning to turn from popery, both men and women were often put to the rack to induce them to confess the names of those who had been kind to them. If a person were known to have sent money to a poor prisoner, or if he were seen giving him a loaf through the prison bars, the enemies of the truth would send to apprehend him. It was not an easy duty in those days to befriend the people of God. Few, if any, would do it who did not love Christ sincerely.

But even in these happier days, *some* of the saints are held in general contempt. If we countenance and encourage *all* those who serve our Master, *we* also shall be despised. But if we would be faithful to Christ, we must not consider to what sect or party men belong, but only, "Do they serve our Lord?" and if they do, we ought to receive them, and help them; we ought to defend their characters when aspersed, to bear with their infirmities, and to forgive their offences. This will be a sign that we should not have despised the Lord Jesus, if we had lived when he was upon earth. The feelings of the true believer are well expressed by a Christian poet, in the following lines:

Thy people by the world abhorr'd,
I for my people take,
And serve the servants of my Lord,
For their dear Master's sake.

Evening Scripture portion. 1 Kings XVIII. 1–20. *Obadiah.*

MARK VI. 12–29.—*The death of John the Baptist.*

VERY little is related concerning the events that happened while the apostles were absent from their Lord. This however we know;—Jesus continued to preach, and to perform miracles. His fame was so great that it reached the ears of Herod, the governor. It may appear surprising that Herod had not heard before of his miracles; but the great are often ignorant of the things passing around them among the poor; and sometimes they do not even know the names of the most eminent of God's servants.

When Herod heard of the miracles of the Lord, he supposed that John the Baptist was risen from the dead; and though John in his *life*-time had performed no miracles, he imagined that if risen from the dead, he could do mighty works. Amid all his splendor and his power the wicked monarch could not forget his faithful reprover. He had silenced the *prophet* long ago by committing him to prison; but he could not silence his own *conscience,* which upbraided him with the murder of the holy man. If *before* sin was perpetrated, it could be known what would be the state of mind *afterwards*, many would tremble to do the deed.

Herod was a miserable man ; for he had a guilty conscience and an impenitent heart. His crimes were so flagrant, and so presumptuous, that they haunted him in his palace. But they were not followed by repentance. If Herod had really lamented his wickedness, he would have desired to acknowledge it to *him*, whom he supposed to be the murdered prophet. He would have found in him the only being who could take away his guilt, and give peace to his conscience. But when at last he did see Jesus, it was to insult him, and to array him, just before his crucifixion, with a gorgeous robe, that ill-became his wounded, bleeding form.

And by what steps did Herod sink into this depth of depravity? Once he had heard John the Baptist gladly, and had attended to his words, and had reformed many parts of his conduct. But he had indulged one darling sin ; he had refused to part with Herodias, his brother Philip's wife ; and had imprisoned the man who rebuked his wickedness. This act hardened his heart, and prepared him for greater crimes. While the prophet languished in a gloomy prison, the unfeeling tyrant revelled in his palace. The elegant dancing of Salome enticed him to make an imprudent promise. He *intended* not to murder the prophet ; perhaps he intended some day to release him from prison ; at all events, he was reluctant to shed his blood. But having made an oath, he feared lest his guests should despise him if he broke it. He dreaded their scornful *smile* more than the angry *frown* of an offended God. But he soon experienced that it is an awful thing to provoke the Almighty We learn from history, that Herod, with his idolized Herodias, was at length expelled his kingdom, and that he died in banishment and disgrace.

For a moment it seemed as if the devices of a malicious woman had prevailed against God's faithful servant. But was not early death a welcome boon to the holy Baptist? Was not the executioner an acceptable visitant in his prison? The messenger who fetched Joseph from his dungeon to the presence of Pharaoh, was not so welcome as the executioner who removed John from his prison to the presence of his God. He had done the work which was appointed for him to do ; he had announced the coming Saviour to rebellious men. The servants of God have various posts assigned to them. Each has some commission to perform, and when it is executed, he is recalled It may *appear* that he has died in the midst of his work; but this cannot really be the case. God will raise up others to carry on his labors ; even as He appointed the apostles to continue to preach that gospel, which John the Baptist had begun to proclaim.

The disciples of the martyred prophet were permitted to enjoy the melancholy satisfaction of burying his headless corpse ; for Herod, who would gladly have spared his *life*, did not withhold his *body* from them. They must have viewed the early, sudden, and cruel death of their revered Master, as a mysterious event. To lose a friend by the hand of violence is far more bitter than to lose him through disease or accident; for it is more difficult to see God's hand in the loss when man's cruelty has had a share in it. With bursting hearts, these bereaved disciples went and told Jesus of their trouble, (Matt. vi. 12.)

He could have explained the dark perplexing event. He knew that John was taken away from the evil to come, and was spared the sight of his own ignominious death. But we do not know what He said to comfort these mourners. None can sympathize with the sorrowful as the Son of God can. He came "to comfort all that mourn." His sympathy is not only tender; it is *powerful.* He is not only *touched* with the feeling of our infirmities, he can *succor* us when tempted. He can pour consolation into the heart. No wound was ever really healed, except by His touch. He declares, "I wound and I heal." Though the death of John the Baptist was his appointment, yet He alone could comfort the bereaved disciples. Israel in her distress applied to a foreign king. But did she obtain relief? God said, "Yet could he not heal you, or cure you of your wounds." (Hos. v. 13.) But the saints can say, "He healeth the broken in heart, and bindeth up their wounds." (Psalm cxlvii. 3.)

Evening Scripture portion. Phil. I. *Paul's desire to depart.*

MARK VI. 30–44.—*Christ feeds five thousand with five loaves and two fishes.*

BEHOLD another instance of the compassion of our Lord. See how ready he was to sacrifice his own ease and comfort that he might promote ours.

It appears that he longed to rest awhile with his disciples, and to hear them relate the things that had befallen them during their travels; and that for this purpose he crossed the lake, intending to land at some desert place; but the multitude, who saw him embark, ran round the lake, and were waiting to receive him at the place where he landed. Was he provoked by this interruption? No; he was moved with compassion for the destitute state of their *souls.* He regarded them as sheep without a shepherd, because their public teachers were ignorant of God. There is no outward deprivation which he pities so much as the want of a faithful ministry, and there is none which *we* should lament so much. A famine of the word of the Lord, is far worse than a famine of bread.

When evening came, the apostles wished to send the people away; but the people were willing to remain without food rather than to leave Jesus. They were rewarded for their anxiety to be with him by obtaining nourishment both for their bodies and souls.

Before Jesus brake the bread, he looked up to heaven. He knew whence every good gift came. Have we not often eaten our food without thinking of the Giver, and without considering his kindness in supplying our daily need?

Christ did not distribute the food *himself*, but employed the apostles in that service. This bread was an emblem of his own flesh, which he gave for the life of the world. The apostles were appointed to proclaim the crucified Saviour to perishing sinners. It was necessary that they should believe that He could save by his death the souls of all believers. They now saw with their own eyes that He could make a *little* bread sustain a *vast* multitude. They would remember this in future days, when preaching his name to assembled thousands. This simple truth, that Jesus gave his flesh for the life of the world, has fed innumerable souls, and will feed innumerable more till the multitude without number are gathered around the throne; and then the Lamb *himself* will feed them through eternity with food which we know not of.

After the simple meal was ended, Jesus bade the apostles gather up the remains. By doing this, it was made evident that the hunger of the multitude had been fully satisfied, and the greatness of the miracle was thus proved. But Jesus gave another reason for the command; he said, "Gather up the fragments that remain, that nothing be lost." (John vi. 12.) By this command He showed us how precious he esteemed even the least of the works of God, that we might not dare to waste the food that our heavenly Father has provided.

But if earthly bread is too precious to be wantonly trampled under foot, how inestimably precious must heavenly bread be! Every word that cometh out of the mouth of God is bread for the soul. Yet how much is suffered to fall to the ground! How carelessly we sometimes read the Scriptures! How many heart-stirring sermons have we heard, and then immediately forgotten! It is not that our *memories* are too weak to retain them, (for we can recollect the news of the town, or the village,) but it is that our *hearts* are too indifferent. It would be a blessed custom, after reading or hearing, to gather up the fragments; that is, to recall to our minds what we have heard, and to apply them to our consciences, "that nothing be lost."

It appears that the twelve baskets contained *more* bread than there was at first, and that the store had been *increased by distribution*. In the same way, by feeding the hungry we shall often enrich ourselves; for God will bless our earthly substance, as He did in the case of the widow who fed Elijah. But how much more will he bless those who feed souls with the word of God! Those teachers who in a humble spirit search the Scriptures, that they may scatter the crumbs among poor little ignorant children, find rich nourishment for their own souls.

Evening Scripture portion.
Amos VIII. *A famine of hearing the words of the Lord.*

MATT. XIV. 22 to end.—*He walks upon the sea.*

THIS history contains a beautiful instance of the care of our Saviour over his people. On another occasion the disciples were alarmed, because Jesus was *asleep* when a storm arose. How much more alarm they probably felt now he was *absent!* Yet it ought to have comforted them to remember that he himself had *constrained* them to enter into the ship. They were evidently in the path of duty. How then should any evil befall them! It is a great comfort to *us* when we can feel sure that we are doing the will of God; for whatever trouble may threaten us, we can trust Jesus to bring relief in the storm. On the contrary, when we are acting wilfully, we have reason to be alarmed at every difficulty that occurs, and to be apprehensive that God will punish us for our waywardness.

Yet the faith of the disciples was so weak, that, though they knew they were in the path of duty, they were alarmed by the storm; and when they beheld Jesus walking on the sea, they were still more terrified, thinking that he was a spirit. They knew not that while he was praying on the mountain, he had seen them, "toiling in rowing," and was come in the most wonderful manner to their rescue.

Peter, who possessed a warm, eager disposition, said, "Lord, if it be thou, bid me come to thee on the water."

Why did Peter make this request? *Love* suggested it? Did he not affectionately desire to be with his Lord? *Faith* enabled him to comply with the command, "Come." Yet this love, and this faith, were mixed with self-ignorance and self-confidence. He knew not the weakness of his own heart; he fondly imagined that he loved the Lord more than his brethren loved him, and that his faith was stronger than theirs. Upon the waves he learned a humiliating lesson. His mind was not resting solely upon Christ; he partly gloried in himself, and soon the tumult of the winds and waves shook his faith, and he began to sink. But his faith, weak as it was, did not fail, for he called on the Lord to save him.

If Peter had taken a lesson from this event, he might have been spared the sharp sorrow, as well as awful sin, of denying his Lord. Had he learned upon the *waves*, to distrust his own heart, he had not in the *hall* experienced its deceitfulness. If we reflect upon the events of Providence, we shall find that God often causes those events to occur in *miniature*, which happen afterwards upon a *larger scale.* An act of wilfulness in youth is permitted to produce evil results; but the same wilfulness at a later period is again displayed, and is followed by worse consequences. The deceit that David practised at the court of Achish entangled him in many difficulties; but the Lord extricated him from them all. He was guilty of a deeper and fouler deceit in the matter of Uriah, and was entangled in a net from which he was never extricated in this life. It is very profitable to review our past conduct, that we may learn the lessons the Lord would teach us, and avoid the evils we have already experienced.

Are we, like Peter, disposed presumptuously to venture into scenes of temptation, and to desire trials of our faith? Does not past experience show us how weak and foolish we are? It is those who *dread* temptation, who are supported when exposed to it? It is those who feel their unfitness to occupy important stations, who are strengthened when exalted to them. Let us not rashly ask Jesus to bid us come unto him on the *water;* but ask him rather to come unto *us* in the *ship.* Yet the Lord does not forsake his servants, even when their own temerity and want of faith have brought them into difficulty. No; even *then* he hears them when they call. He who stretched out his hand to sinking Peter, will extend his mercy to each of us in *every* trouble. The cry, "Save me or I perish," touches the Saviour's heart, even as the infant's cry awakens the mother's tenderness. Never then let us be discouraged from looking to Christ for help. No past folly of ours can harden his heart against us, when by faith we come to him in our distress.

Evening Scripture portion. Job. IX. *God treads upon the waves of the sea.*

JOHN VI. 22.–29.—*The multitude seek Jesus from interested motives.*

IT must be remembered that when Jesus walked on the sea to his disciples, he left a great multitude on the other side of the lake. These people had been fed by him in the evening; but afterwards many of them had remained near the mountain, to which he had retired to pray. They had seen with pleasure the disciples embark *without* their Master, in the *only* ship then upon the sea; and had felt certain of finding him near them in the morning. But what was their consternation, when morning came, at *not* being able to find him! They were at a loss to imagine *how* he could have departed.

While they were in this state of perplexity, some boats arrived. In these they joyfully embarked, and crossing the lake, soon reached the city of Capernaum. They sought there for Jesus, and found him teaching in the synagogue, (v. 59.) They expressed their surprise at the meeting, saying, "Rabbi, when camest thou hither?" Jesus, however, did not satisfy their curiosity, by answering their inquiry, but proceeded to unveil their hearts, and to expose the selfish, earthly motives that led them to seek him so earnestly. Could we have supposed that a meal of bread and fish was more valued by them than the precious words of the Saviour! Yet this was the case. Though Jesus was the Son of God, and had the most valuable gifts to bestow, the earthly refreshment he had afforded was more prized by the grovelling multitude than heaven and all its blessings.

The Saviour reproved their earthly-mindedness by saying, "Labor not for the meat which perisheth, but for that which endureth unto everlasting life." Did he mean to forbid honest labor for our living? By no means. It is commanded that if any will not work, neither should he eat. The expression signifies, "Labor not *so much* for the meat which perisheth, as for that which endureth unto everlasting life. Labor *not at all* for it in COMPARISON with the earnestness with which you labor for heavenly blessings." Do we obey this direction? Are we indeed *much more* eager and anxious about eternal things than about earthly pleasures, or comforts? What we are most anxious about will be uppermost in our thoughts. What *is* uppermost in *our* thoughts? Perhaps we are not as poor as these people were, and are not therefore as anxious as they were about one meal. But if it be wrong to be so much engrossed about *necessary* food, surely it is much *more* wrong to be engrossed by *unnecessary* earthly things—such as pleasures, even *harmless* pleasures—the favor of men—the increase of our property—or the success of our studies! There is *one thing* needful: the meat which endureth unto everlasting life.

Yet we, helpless, sinful creatures, never could obtain *this* by our most earnest strivings, were it not intrusted to the Son of God to bestow upon us. God the Father hath given eternal life to the Son for us, and *sealed* the Son. A king places his own seal upon his written commands, that men may know they are *his;* so God the Father sealed his Son, by enabling him to do miracles, and thus showed men that He had sent him. Our duty is to believe upon this Son, who can give us eternal life.

The people asked, in a self-righteous spirit, "What shall we do that we might work the works of God?" They seemed to think that they could *do* something to entitle themselves to eternal life. This was impossible. Guilty, polluted creatures can do nothing really good. But there is a Saviour to whom they may apply for pardon and grace. Jesus directed them to Himself when he said, "This is the work of God, that ye believe on him whom he hath sent." He calls believing a *work*. Yet it is not a work of *merit;* for it is the beggar coming to the king for alms; it is the criminal suing to the judge for mercy. This is the first work that each of us must perform. There is *one* who is able to save and to destroy: He is the Son of God. All power is committed unto him. Do we earnestly apply to him for salvation? How foolish only to ask Him for fading flowers, when he could bestow a crown of life! How foolish only to fear the pricking of the thorns and thistles, when the sword of eternal wrath is in his hand! Let us not insult this Saviour by seeking his *lesser* gifts, while we neglect to implore *that* gift which he bought for us with his blood!

Evening Scripture portion. Ps. XIX. *The preciousness of God's word*

JOHN VI. 30–34.—*They ask him to give them bread.*

OUR Lord frequently took occasion from *circumstances* to explain spiritual truths. Once, when sitting by a well, he instructed a woman who came to draw water, and exhorted her to seek for living water. Now Jesus was speaking to persons who had shown a great anxiety for bread, and he took the opportunity to direct their attention to the bread that came down from heaven.

There was much unbelief and ignorance displayed by the Jews in this conversation. They pretended that they had not received sufficient proof of his authority, and said, "What *sign* showest thou then, that we may see and believe thee?" He had already given them a most wonderful sign in the miracle of the loaves, yet they required more evidence; but this was not granted to them. They even ventured to dictate to the Saviour what he *ought* to do, and referred in an insolent way to the miracle of the manna, as if they wished Him to understand that Moses, in giving bread from heaven, had wrought a greater miracle than himself. Jesus took no notice of the bad spirit they displayed, but showed them they were *mistaken* when they said that Moses had given them bread from *heaven*. The manna had not come from the heaven of heavens, where God's glory is manifested, but from the *lower* regions of the skies; besides, *Moses* did not give that bread; *he* did not create it: nor was it *living* bread; it would not give life to the dead, or even preserve the life of the living. But there was a bread that could both give life to the dead, and preserve life for evermore: this bread was the Son of God.

The people understood not what Jesus meant, when he spoke of the "Bread of God;" but ignorantly cried, "Lord, evermore give us this bread." How many have made prayers as ignorant as this, and have received answers that they little expected! The woman of Samaria knew not what she asked when she said, "Give me of this water, that I thirst not, neither come hither to draw." But her petition, so blindly offered, was graciously granted, for she soon received the water of the Holy Spirit into her heart. We may also believe that those who ignorantly asked for heavenly bread, were satisfied beyond their expectations. If God did not deal thus graciously with sinners, who could be saved! For we are all found by Him in a state of ignorance and enmity: our first prayers resemble the cry of this people: "Lord, evermore give us this bread." Some of us perhaps can remember our feelings just before we turned to God. We felt the misery of our state; we longed to find something better than we had found; but we knew not what we needed. We had heard that there was help in God; we cried to him, but in such a manner that any Being less gracious than Himself would have disregarded us. But his ways are not as our ways, nor his thoughts as our thoughts. He pitied us in our low estate, and led us by ways that we knew not, to a knowledge of his Son.

Evening Scripture portion. Ex. XVI. 1–21. *Manna given.*

JOHN VI. 35–40.—*Christ declares himself to be the bread of life.*

AMONG the crowd who surrounded the Lord while he taught in the synagogue, there were *some* who believed *not*, (v. 64.) But there were *some* who would come to him, and be his crown forever. *This* he knew: *this* was his consolation among all the taunts and jeers of the multitude while in the synagogue, and even afterwards when he was on the Cross.

It was to those people, who did, or would believe on him, that Jesus referred when he said, "All that the Father giveth me shall come unto me." They had not all *yet* come unto him, but he knew they *would* come unto him, for his Father had given them to him. O what a gift it was! Polluted, guilty, helpless sinners were the gift the Father bestowed upon the Son as the reward of all his sufferings. It was the compassion of his heart that made the Saviour value such a gift.

A family of poor children was once bequeathed by a dying parent to a rich man. The legacy was accepted. Many were astonished at the kindness and condescension of the rich man. What trouble, and care, and expense such a gift involved! The children must be fed, and clothed, and educated, and provided for: the rich man was willing to do it all; and he *did* it all. And what will not the Saviour do for those whom the Father has given to him! He will receive them, even as he said, "Him that cometh unto me, I will in no wise cast out." When they come to him, however helpless and diseased and destitute they may be, he will graciously welcome them into his house of mercy, and place them at his children's table.

Nor is this all; he will *raise* them up at the last day. It is appointed unto *all* men once to die, (whether they believe in Jesus, or not;) but it is also appointed that *some* shall rise to everlasting life. Jesus promises to be with his children as they pass through the valley of the shadow of death, to receive their souls into paradise, to watch over their sleeping dust, and then at the sound of the last trump to raise them from their graves, to clothe them with glorious bodies like his own, and to welcome them into mansions of everlasting bliss. All this will Jesus do for every one that comes to him.

And *why* will he do all this? He himself tells us why. Because it is the will of the Father that sent him. "This is the will of him that sent me, that every one that seeth the Son and believeth on him, may have everlasting life; and I will raise him up at the last day." The Son delights in doing his Father's will, even more than he does in showing mercy to sinners. It was the Father who *appointed* him to be the Saviour of the world; and the Father knew how much the Son delighted in the work. When a person we love exceedingly gives us a command, we are ready to obey that command, however *painful* it may be; but when the work he appoints is that in which our soul delights, there is a double joy in obedience.

Ought we not to be astonished to think that the Father and the Son, who fill heaven and earth, should have interested themselves in our wretched race,—should have cared for *you* and *me!* How guilty we must be, if we reject such wonderful mercy! We can have no excuse for not coming to Jesus, when we are so fully assured of a gracious reception. We shall not be repulsed, we shall not be upbraided, we shall not even be coldly received. Why then need we fear to come?

Evening Scripture portion. Ex. XVI. 22 to end. *Manna laid up.*

JOHN VI. 41–58.—*He promises to give his flesh and blood for the world.*

To what unbelieving earthly hearts Christ addressed this heavenly discourse! The Jews murmured, because they could not understand the truths he declared. They said that Jesus did *not* come from heaven, and the reason they alleged for thinking so was, that Joseph was his father. Had they inquired into his history, or meditated upon the prophecies, they could not have urged this objection.

They said also that Jesus *could* not give them his *flesh* to eat. The Lord did not attempt to answer their objections, because he knew they were not in a fit state of mind to receive his words. He replied to his enemies in a very different manner from that which might have been expected. (See v. 44.) "No man can come unto me, except the Father which hath sent me draw him." He quoted also this verse from the prophet Isaiah: "And they shall be all taught of God." *Who* shall be taught of God? His children. Whom does a father teach? His own children. God also teaches *His* children. *What* does he teach them? He teaches them their *need* of a Saviour. None will come to Christ till they have been taught that they cannot do without him. It may appear strange that men do not find out this by themselves. But they do not. Starving people know that they are starving; but starving SOULS do not know that they are perishing, till God teaches them. They feel uneasy; but they do not know the cause of the aching void in their own hearts; and even when the bread of life is presented to them, they refuse it. But when God by his Holy Spirit has convinced them that they are in a perishing state, and that none but Christ can save them, then they thankfully accept the living bread. Has God taught any of *us* to feel our need of the Saviour? Then may we say in the words of the poet:

Why was I made to hear thy voice,
And enter while there's room;
When thousands make a wretched choice,
And rather starve than come?

But Jesus spoke not only of *bread*, he spoke also of *flesh* and *blood*. He said, "Except ye eat the *flesh* of the Son of man, and drink his *blood*, ye have no life in you," (v. 53.) The Jews were forbidden to taste blood, because it was the life of the animal. What did Jesus mean by eating his flesh and drinking his blood? He spoke of his own *death*. By his *death* sinners have *life*. Man has long been accustomed to kill beasts to preserve his own life. It seems fit that such creatures should die, in order that we may live. But how wonderful it is that the *Son of God* should die, that *worms* of the *earth*, such as we are, should live eternally. It would not be right that a *man* should die in order that *beasts* should live. Yet the Son of God laid down his life for *us*.

But his death will not save us, unless we *believe* in him. Believing in him is compared to eating and drinking. His flesh has been broken on the cross; his blood has been shed on Calvary; but has each of us believed in him? Have *I* believed in him? Have *you* believed in him? Eating bread and drinking wine at the Lord's supper will not save us. The sacraments are only *signs* of something greater than themselves. It was not till long after Jesus had spoken these words, that he ordained the holy communion of bread and wine, saying, "Do this in remembrance of me." He did not speak of that communion, when he said, "Except ye eat the flesh of the Son of man, and drink his blood, ye have no life in you." No; he spoke of *faith* in his *death*. There is a supper to which he invites you: it is not administered in a church; it is not bestowed by human hands; it is not received into the mouth. This supper is spoken of in this passage of the Revelation: "Behold I stand at the door and knock: if any man hear my voice, and open the door, I will come in to him and will *sup* with him, and he with me." (Rev. iii. 20.)

Evening Scripture portion. Rev. III. *Supping with Christ.*

JOHN VI. 59–65.—*He explains the spiritual meaning of this declaration.*

WE find that many of the disciples of Jesus were offended by his discourse concerning his own flesh and blood. We must remember that *all* the followers of Christ were called *disciples*, whereas only *twelve* were called "*apostles*." The twelve *apostles* are *not* meant by the word *disciple* in this passage. Why did these disciples murmur? Because they could not understand how Jesus could give them his flesh to eat. They thought he meant that his flesh must literally be eaten; whereas he spoke of a *spiritual* thing;—of obtaining life through faith in his death.

He told them that they would be still more astonished when he ascended up where he was before, even into heaven; for then it would be clearly seen that he did not speak of his *real* flesh and blood, as they would be changed, and return to heaven. "What and if ye shall see the Son of man ascend up where he was before!" What would you say *then?* Jesus proceeded to explain his words, as far as they *could* be explained.

He said, "The *Spirit* quickeneth, or gives life." Bread and wine cannot give life. No, the Spirit alone gives life. "The *flesh* profiteth nothing." By "*flesh*" forms and ceremonies are meant. They cannot profit the soul by any power in them. It is right to keep the ordinances of Christ, and to partake of the Supper he has ordained in remembrance of his death. Believers account it an unspeakable privilege to approach their Lord's table; but no ordinances, not even those of *divine* appointment, can impart *spiritual* life. Jesus directs us to his Father as the only source of life.

When he saw men did not believe, he told them, "No man can come unto me, except it be given unto him of my Father." Why did he declare this doctrine? Has it not often furnished unbelievers with an *excuse* for not coming to him? His reason for declaring it was that he might convince man of his danger and helplessness. Many have been alarmed from hearing it, and have been led to call out, "What shall we do to be saved?" A reasonable creature is often led to think, "Am I indeed in a state of death! And can I not raise *myself* from it? What will become of me, if the Father do not lead me to believe in Christ!" These are profitable thoughts, and often induce the sinner to call with earnestness upon God. A few years ago, the son of pious parents entered into a church. He had lately lost a praying mother, and his heart was softened by the event: but he had not turned to his mother's God. The preacher set before his audience the declaration of the Lord Jesus, "No man can come unto me, except the Father which has sent me, draw him." The youth was alarmed, "What, is my mother dead," thought he; "is her voice silent, and am I still unconverted? And *what* if God should never bestow upon me his converting grace?" He offered up earnest prayers. The Lord heard him, blessed him, and chose him to be one of his faithful ministers.

What ought to be the feelings of believers when they reflect that they never could have come to Christ, if it had not been given unto them of the Father. Have *we* believed? Then what thanks can we render for our escape from perdition, and for our hope of glory! We would ever be "Giving thanks unto the Father, who hath made us meet to be partakers of the inheritance of the saints in light, who hath delivered us from the power of darkness, and translated us into the kingdom of his dear Son."

Evening Scripture portion. Col. I. *Thankfulness for conversion.*

JOHN VI. 66 to end.—*He asks the apostles whether they will go away.*

No minister ought to be surprised when people are offended by his sermons, seeing that some were so much displeased with this discourse of the blessed Jesus, as to walk no more with him. What was the doctrine that gave offence? It was this, "No man can come unto me except it be given him of my Father." This truth wounds the pride of man. It shows him that he cannot repent when he chooses, or turn to God at his own time. Proud sinners do not like to find that they are so utterly dependent upon God's mercy. Yet are we not dependent upon God for *every thing?* For life, for food, for raiment, for health, for earthly happiness? Surely, then, upon God we *must* be dependent for eternal life and heavenly bliss. Happy dependence! for has not God promised to give these blessings to *all* who ask him?

Great was the folly of the disciples who forsook the instructions of infinite wisdom! Could the compassionate Jesus behold their conduct without feeling grief on their account! He looked at the little flock that still remained faithful, and addressed to them this tender appeal: "Will *ye* also go away?" We may well conceive that it was in a tone of fatherly affection these words were uttered. They went to the heart of the frank and generous Peter, and drew from him (on behalf of the rest as well as himself) this earnest declaration: "Lord, to whom shall we go? Thou hast the words of eternal life, and we believe and are sure that thou art that Christ, the Son of the living God." Peter's warm expressions of love and fidelity were acceptable to his Divine Master. Though the world may deride *professions* of attachment to Christ, they were never reproved by the Lord himself.

There was no insincerity in Peter's assurances, but there was more weakness in his heart than he was aware of. No temptation had yet occurred to induce him to forsake his Saviour; but Jesus well knew that the day would come when *all* that little band would leave him in the hands of his enemies. The *doctrines* that He had declared had not offended them, but the *sufferings* that he must undergo,—*these* would prove their stumbling-block. Peter, who was loudest in his professions of attachment, would not only *forsake*, but also *deny* his Master. Could he at that moment have foreseen his base conduct in the judgment-hall, he would have added *petitions* to his *professions*. In the Epistles he wrote many years afterwards, he speaks of the saints as "kept by the *power of God* through faith unto salvation." He found to his cost that he could not stand by *his own power*. In the same epistle he warns believers against the *enemy* who had nearly destroyed him, and says, "Be sober, be vigilant; for your adversary the devil walketh about, as a roaring lion, seeking whom he may devour."

Do *our* hearts at this moment glow with grateful affection to our Saviour? Are we ready to exclaim, "To whom shall we go, if we forsake him? No other teacher can show us the way of life; no other friend can comfort us in the hour of sorrow; no other advocate can plead for us in the day of judgment!" Yet let us remember that this love, we think so strong, will be *tried.* In what *manner* it will be tried, we cannot foresee. The devices of Satan are innumerable. He knows our characters, and understands how to assail us to the greatest advantage. He has succeeded in causing eminent saints to forsake their God for *a while.* Jerome of Prague, and our Cranmer, as well as the apostle Peter, were tempted to deny the Master they loved; yet at last all three laid down their lives in his cause; for the children of God are brought back by their loving Shepherd's rod into the fold whence they have wandered.

Jesus knew that all his beloved apostles would be restored, excepting one, who was "*a devil.*" Judas was distinguished from his brethren by this dark token, "indifference to his Lord." It was *he* who so strongly objected to Mary's memorable act of love, the pouring the precious ointment on her Saviour's head. Yet he so far succeeded in deceiving his fellow apostles, as to be intrusted with the bag containing their little all. The love and esteem of professed Christians for each other, are often very much misplaced. We ought not to solace ourselves with the thought that the best of men approve us, if our hearts are conscious that we do not *love* the Saviour. Jesus is loved by all the saints in earth, even by the *weakest:* he is still *more* loved by the saints in *heaven;* he has been *ever* loved by the innumerable hosts of glorious angels. By whom then is he not beloved? By devils in hell; and by some ungrateful men, who, though they know he died for them, yet refuse to love him.

Evening Scripture portion. 1 Cor. XVI. *Love to Christ.*

MATT. XV. 1–20.—*Jesus eats with unwashen hands.*

IT has often been observed, that in the character of Jesus, opposite qualities were united. We seldom (or perhaps never) see a man *remarkable* at once for meekness, and for boldness. Yet our Lord was remarkable for both. The incident we have just read, affords an instance of his boldness in dealing faithfully with his powerful and malicious enemies.

He would not countenance the custom of washing the hands before taking food. Yet was not this a harmless custom? Why did he not comply with it? Because, though harmless in itself, it was enforced on the people as a *religious duty.* The Jewish teachers taught the people that food defiled them unless eaten with washen hands. Now this was not a doctrine of God's word. These elders (or teachers) ought to have taught the truths contained in God's holy word. It was their office to explain the Scriptures to the people; but instead of doing this, they added commandments of their own. Jesus expressed his disapprobation of their conduct by not observing these human commandments. The custom of washing the hands before eating was innocent in itself; but there were other commandments taught by the elders that were very pernicious. Jesus gave an instance of one of these. God had commanded children to honor their parents. A child who honors his parents will provide for them in old age. But the Jewish teachers taught the people, that if they gave some money to the priests for the service of the temple, that then they might be excused from supporting their aged parents. They instructed children to say to their decrepit parents, "It is a gift; what I should have given *you* has been bestowed upon the temple; so that I can do nothing for you." Such conduct was exceedingly wicked; yet the Jewish teachers said it was right.

We see from this instance that it is very dangerous to follow the opinions of men concerning what is wrong, or what is right. What God commands is good—what he forbids is evil; and the word of God is the only rule of good and evil.

Of course the Pharisees were extremely enraged against Christ for exposing their false instructions. But Jesus had so much compassion for the poor ignorant people, that he chose to undeceive them; though by this line of conduct he increased the hatred of his enemies. Had we more compassion for the ignorant, we should have less fear of man. A father would not stand by and see his child poisoned, whomever he might offend by his opposition.

Jesus explained clearly to the people in the presence of their teachers, in what respect they were deceived. He called them, and said, "Not that which goeth *into* the mouth defileth a man; but that which cometh *out* of the mouth, that defileth a man." Yet even the *disciples* could not understand this simple truth, and Peter called it a "*parable*," and asked Jesus to explain it. It is very hard to get rid of prejudices which have long darkened the mind. The heathen, even when converted, are apt to retain many superstitious ideas imbibed in their infancy. We are all naturally disposed to think that ceremonies can profit our soul; whereas none can sanctify us but the Spirit of God, and nothing can *defile* us but *sin*. Neither is it the sinful *action* only that pollutes: the sinful *thought* (which gives rise to the action) pollutes far more. It is not the *act* of stealing only, but the *desire* to possess our neighbor's property, that defiles; it is not the *words* of the lie merely, but the WISH to deceive, that stains the man; it is not so much the blasphemous expressions, as the irreverent *feeling* towards God, that constitutes the essence of profaneness. We perceive, therefore, that even if we have not committed gross and open transgressions, we are, notwithstanding, deeply polluted. Such defilement, no ceremonies can remove. Water cannot wash the heart. The blood of Christ alone can cleanse the inner man. It is a *spiritual* washing that we need; Jesus himself must wash us or we perish. He is gracious, and will pardon the vilest sinner that implores his mercy; he will not only pardon him but *sanctify* him, and give him a new heart full of holy desires.

Evening Scripture portion. Is. XXIX. 1–19. *Hypocrisy.*

MATT. XV. 21–28.—*The woman of Tyre.*

IT is very interesting to observe the various ways in which Jesus behaved to afflicted persons. Some, he *offered* to relieve; saying to one at the pool of Bethesda, "Wilt thou be made whole?" and to another with a withered hand at the synagogue, "Stretch forth thy hand." Others he restored on their FIRST application to him;—while he suffered the woman of Canaan to plead long and earnestly before he showed her mercy. Yet even this delay was the cause of her obtaining greater favor in the end; for it gave her the opportunity of proving the strength of her faith. Before he exposed her to this test, he knew that she could endure it. The compassionate Saviour proportions our trials to our strength, and will bring upon us no temptation greater than we are able to bear. A sharp trial is often a sign that he confides in our fidelity. Had a weak saint been tried as Job was, he would have been overwhelmed; but God knew that his servant would prove faithful.

When we consider who this woman was, we have reason to be astonished at the attainments she had made. She was a Canaanite, a daughter of the cursed race. She was not descended from Abraham, the friend of God;—she was not one of the nation of Israel. No; she was descended from ignorant heathen. She resided in the wicked city of Tyre; and she had been brought up in the Greek or heathen religion; yet it appears evident that she had obtained some knowledge of the true God, and that she possessed a hearty faith in his name. How could she have called Jesus the Son of David, had she not heard of the prophecy made unto David concerning One who should sit upon his throne? She was evidently a child of God, born again of the Holy Spirit, and bringing forth the fruits of the Spirit,—faith, patience, and humility. She had such *faith*, that she believed that Jesus would have mercy on her, in spite of his apparent unkindness; she had such *patience* that she continued, notwithstanding repeated denials, to press her suit; and she had such *humility*, that she could bear to be called a dog.

Let us now observe Christ's conduct towards this woman. The disciples in a spirit of selfishness, and not of compassion, entreated their Master to send away the poor suppliant. Jesus is never weary of the cry of distress; above all, the voice of faith, though choked with tears and sighs, ever sounds sweet in his ears. The mother is glad to hear those cries which prove that her babe lives; and the Saviour rejoices to hear those petitions which are the tokens of spiritual life.

Have we ever prayed as this woman did? Have not we as great requests to make as she had? She implored a *temporal* blessing, and received an answer. Had she never prayed for *spiritual* blessings? Her faith, her patience, her humility, prove that she must have prayed for them—whether beneath some fig-tree, as Nathanael did, or in some chamber of her heathen home,—we know not. She was a true believer, and therefore must have been a secret worshipper. She had learned to trust in her God from his dealings with her in times past, and therefore she was not dismayed by her Saviour's seeming sternness. *We* also must have secret transactions with our God. When we have experienced his pardoning mercy, we shall be able to trust him with *all* our concerns. It is indeed a comfort to a mother, when a child is sick, to have a God in whom to confide. Sometimes he may see good to take her child away; but He will in the end reward believing prayer by imparting unspeakable consolation.

Evening Scripture portion. Job I. *Trials.*

MARK VII. 31 to end.—*The deaf and dumb man.*

WE here find the Lord Jesus again visiting Decapolis on the borders of the lake. On a former occasion he had healed two poor demoniacs, who dwelt among the tombs. The treatment which he had received from the owners of the swine, did not prevent him from again visiting their shores. There were many sufferers there whom he designed to relieve and to bless. It is probable that his way had been prepared by that poor man who had desired to accompany him, but who had remained behind that he might tell "what great things the Lord had done for him." With what warmth that man must have spoken to his countrymen of the compassion of his Lord! Those who have lately experienced the loving-kindness of the Saviour cannot speak of him with coldness. The testimony of one such person often produces a great effect upon the minds of many.

We know not by what means the friends of the deaf and dumb man were induced to apply to Jesus. Though deprived of two valuable faculties, the afflicted man possessed the blessing of affectionate friends, who *besought* the Lord to heal him. We read of a paralytic at the pool of Bethesda, who had no friend to help him in his weakness.

The Lord did not relieve the deaf and dumb man *immediately;* he first took him to a retired place, where he might perform the miracle unseen by the multitude. He healed him in a remarkable manner. Before he uttered the words, "Be opened," he put his fingers in the man's ears, spit, touched his tongue, looked up to heaven, and sighed. These actions were, no doubt, designed to instruct the deaf and dumb man. Though this man could not *hear,* he could feel the sacred touch, he could see the eyes uplifted, and perceive the deep-drawn sigh. The touch taught him that it was through the power of *Jesus* he was healed; the upward look that it was by the will of his Father in *heaven,* and the sigh, that the Saviour felt compassion for his infirmities.

Had this man been cured by *natural* means, he would have had to learn the use of language *gradually;* but those whom Jesus healed were endowed with the power of using their restored faculties *immediately.* The dumb man spake plain. Thus the prophecy of Isaiah was in one instance fulfilled, "The ears of the deaf shall be unstopped, and the tongue of the stammerers shall be ready to speak plainly."

We have seen, in this miracle, that Jesus adapted the *mode* of cure to the *circumstances* of the afflicted man. By what *various* means he now cures the *spiritual* infirmities of men! He knows how to treat each case in the most *suitable* manner. There are many different states of mind to be found among the unconverted, and all seem to us cases very hard to cure. The wisdom of Jesus enables him to meet the difficulties of each case that he undertakes to relieve. He knows how to solemnize the light mind of one, and how to abase the proud spirit of another; how to tame the violent temper, and to enlarge the selfish heart. It is very interesting to consider the peculiar circumstances attending the conversion of each sinner to God.

"By *what* way has the Lord brought *you* to listen to his voice?" Have you indeed been brought to listen to it? Or are you still deaf to his gracious invitations?

Evening Scripture portion. Jòb XXXIII. *God's dealings with men.*

MATT. XV. 29–31.—*Christ heals the multitude on the mountain-top.*

THE miracle wrought upon the deaf and dumb man brought a host of suppliants to the feet of Jesus. The mountain-top was his throne of mercy, and thence he rebuked the diseases of the imploring multitude. Could any occupation have more gratified his loving heart! Yes; there was one which would have been still more delightful to him. Had penitents implored his pardon as earnestly as these sufferers besought his healing mercy, he would have felt a deeper joy. The day shall come when *all* men shall apply to Him for the forgiveness of their sins; with weeping and with supplication shall they come, each one mourning for his iniquity.

It is to be remarked, that the poor sufferers were brought by their friends, who cast them down at the feet of Jesus. The afflicted creatures were not able to come alone. How could the lame have climbed the hill? How could the blind have found the way, and how could the dumb have sued for mercy? But by the kindness of their friends they reached the blessed spot, and made known their wretched state. It may be we ourselves owe to the kindness of our friends, under God, in times past, the salvation of our souls. Was there no affectionate relative who expostulated with us in the days of our folly, who persuaded us to accompany him to hear some faithful preacher, and who encouraged us to forsake the world, and to serve the Lord? In some instances it was a mother's prayers, long offered to God in secret, with many tears, that drew down upon the soul eternal blessings. How much do we owe to such friends for all their love to us, and all their exertions for our good! *We* ought to show the same kindness to others, that *they* once showed to us. Have we no unconverted relatives to cast at the feet of Jesus by secret supplications? Have we none to whom we might send a letter of entreaty, or a book adapted to their case? Are there none whom we might draw to the house of God, to hear the gospel preached with fervor and with power? These services of love bind the hearts of the children of God to each other.

You may conceive how much the sufferers who had been cast at the Saviour's feet must afterwards have loved those who had laid them there. When restored, did they not go to seek for others, afflicted as they once had been? There was no room here for strife and contention; there was enough virtue in Jesus to heal *all* who came. When *men* bestow gifts, there must be a limit to their extent, and this circumstance gives rise to competition and jealousy; but Jesus is like the sun in the heavens, who has shed his beams for ages upon benighted worlds, and is still as full of glorious light as when he first began to shine. There is no rivalry among penitent sinners. There is a fountain in which *all* may wash, and be clean; there is a heaven to which *all* may go, and be happy. In that abode of bliss, benefits received from our fellow-creatures upon earth will not be forgotten. There will exist in those worlds stronger ties than the nearest known in this. The converts who form the joy and crown of the blessed apostle Paul, are nearer and dearer to him than children are to any father upon earth.

But if saints entertain a grateful love towards *each other*, what must they feel for the Saviour who died for them! Surely the dumb, the blind, the maimed, whom Jesus healed, must have loved their gracious benefactor. It is recorded of a poor blind boy, that such was his affection for the physician who had couched his eyes, and restored his sight, that he never saw him without shedding tears of joy; and that when disappointed of an expected visit, he could not forbear weeping. The saints on earth *begin* to feel this love for their Saviour; but now they love imperfectly. In heaven this love will be the spring of all their thoughts. It is written upon the tomb of one of God's servants,* this saying, which he had expressed in his life-time: "To love is heaven; to love a little less imperfectly is the fore-taste of heaven."

Evening Scripture portion.—Ps. CIII. *The Lord's mercy.*

MATT. XV. 32 to end.—*Christ feeds five thousand with seven loaves.*

FOR three days seated upon a mountain, surrounded by the afflicted and the ignorant, our blessed Lord had manifested his compassion for our fallen race. At the end of that period, he displayed his beneficence by feeding the multitude. He had refused to feed them when they came *because* of the loaves; but now that they had been gathered together from *other* motives, he provided for their wants. It is so now. The Lord does not promise to provide for the *temporal* wants of those who attempt to serve him from *interested* views, but only for those who seek *first* the kingdom of God and his righteousness.

Is it not surprising that the disciples should say the *second* time, "Whence should we have so much bread in the wilderness, as to fill so great a multitude?" How soon they had forgotten the five loaves and the five thousand! But can *we* remember no similar instance of forgetfulness in our own history? Has not the Lord on many occasions in times past gone beyond our highest expectations? And yet are we not prone in every fresh difficulty to doubt his power and his faithfulness? David remembered that God had delivered him out of the paw of the lion and the bear, and therefore he believed that He would deliver him out of the hand of the mighty giant. Whenever we find ourselves placed in difficulties, we should remember the "years of the right-hand of the Most High;" that is, we should remember the events of past years, and the deliverances we have received. How many fears have we entertained! Have they been realized? Has not the Lord been better to us than our *fears?* and better than our *hopes* too? The Lord, who fed the multitude, can supply the largest family with bread. The pious parent may trust Him to send provision for all his little ones. The affectionate daughter may feel assured that the Lord will help her to sustain her

* See the Life of Gonthier, the Swiss Pastor.

widowed mother. The weak in health, and declining in years, may confide in the Lord not to leave them to pine neglected and forlorn; for the eyes of the Lord are over the righteous, and his ears are open unto their prayers.

The Lord is able to supply his perishing creatures with more enduring food than *bread.* The disciples ought to have known that the bread they distributed signified that flesh which Jesus would give for the life of the world; for they had lately heard their Master discourse upon this subject. The Lord has already raised up many faithful ministers who proclaim to his people the crucified Saviour. This was his promise in days of old: "I will give you pastors according to mine heart, which shall feed you with knowledge, and with understanding," (Jer. iii. 15.) If all congregations had the same appetite for the bread of *life* that this multitude had for *common* bread, how joyfully would pastors exercise their ministry! But of what congregation can it be said, "They did *all* eat and were filled?" Too many persons have no appetite for the heavenly feast; they sit as God's people sit, but they partake not of the sacred fare: they go away to feed again upon ashes, and at length die without having tasted of *that* bread, which if a man eat, he shall live forever. But there is a congregation above, in number far exceeding *four* thousand, or one hundred and forty-four thousand—a multitude that no man can number, who are fed by the Lord himself with heavenly manna. They hunger no more, because the Lamb which is in the midst of the throne *feeds* them.

Evening Scripture portion. Ps. XXXIV. *The blessedness of trusting in God.*

MATT. XVI. 1–4.—*Christ refuses to grant a sign to the Pharisees and Sadducees.*

IT is not certain *what* the sign from heaven was that the Pharisees and Sadducees desired to see; probably it was some display of Christ's glory, such as he afterwards gave to his most favored disciples upon the mount. But whatever the sign required might be, the *motive* that led these men to ask for it was a very evil one—it was the *desire* not to believe. And why did they entertain this desire? Because they hated Jesus. It is our *desires* and our *feelings* that mark our characters in God's sight.

And what were the feelings of the Saviour on this occasion? St. Mark records a circumstance which shows us what they were. In Mark viii. 12, we read, "And he sighed deeply in his spirit." The hardness of men's hearts grieved the Saviour more than all the sufferings of his life. It is a sign of grace in the heart when a man is deeply grieved by hearing of sin committed against *others;* but it is a still better sign when he is *grieved,* rather than *angry,* at sins committed against *himself.* There are some to be found among the followers of Jesus, who have imbibed this feeling from their Master. The most cutting reproaches have excited no other emotion than this regret: "Alas, he who hates me is blind, and knows not what he does."

The Lord condescended patiently to argue with these unbelievers. He proved that their doubts respecting his being the Son of God did not arise from want of *understanding;* for they showed their understanding by knowing the signs of the weather. Their *understandings* were good enough to enable them to know that he was the Son of God, because all the signs the prophets had described, had come to pass. We cannot now consider *what* these signs were. The miracles Jesus performed were among them; for Isaiah had prophesied that the tongue of the dumb should sing when the Saviour came, that the ears of the deaf should be unstopped, and that the lame man should leap as an hart, (Is. xxxv.)

Jesus declared that *one* sign only should be given to these unbelievers,—the sign that God once gave to the Ninevites.

Jonas was cast into the sea, and was swallowed by a whale. Thus Jesus would be cast into the grave, and lie hid in the tomb. As Jonas was delivered from the whale, so Jesus was raised from the tomb. As Jonas warned the people of Nineveh that their city would be destroyed in forty *days,* so Jesus warned the people of Jerusalem that their city would be destroyed in forty *years;* that is, before that generation would pass away. But whereas the Ninevites repented at the preaching of Jonas, the Jews did *not* repent at the preaching of the Lord and his apostles.

The words which are recorded in the conclusion of this passage (verse 4) are awful: "Jesus left them and departed,"—left them in mingled sorrow and displeasure. To be left by Jesus is *almost* the greatest calamity that can befall a human creature! There is *one* calamity greater, which is this—to hear Jesus say, "Depart from me." If left by Jesus, we may implore his return; but when he says "Depart," we never can be admitted any more into His presence. Some, who have despised religious privileges while they possessed them, have learned their value after they have lost them; and *sometimes* God has graciously *restored* the blessings they had forfeited. But it too often happens that when Jesus leaves a people, he leaves them to their impenitence and hardness of heart, and that when they see Him again, it is to hear Him say, "Depart from me, ye cursed, into everlasting fire."

Evening Scripture portion. Jonah I II. ***The whale.***

MATT. XVI. 5–12.—*He warns his disciples against the leaven of the Pharisees and Sadducees.*

WE often find that people did not understand our Saviour when he spoke of spiritual things under the image of earthly ones. Thus, when he spoke of living water to the woman of Samaria, the woman did not understand him. Neither did his disciples now understand him when he spoke of leaven. He did not *reprove* the woman of Samaria for not comprehending his meaning, because *she* had never enjoyed opportunities of instruction; but he expected better things from his own disciples, and he rebuked them, saying, "How is it that ye do not understand that I spake it *not* to you concerning *bread?*" And *how* was it that they did not understand? Had they not lived long enough with their Master to know his way of discourse?

It was unbelief which clouded their minds. Because they had taken no bread with them in the ship, they feared that they should suffer from hunger; though their Lord was in the ship, and though He had promised to supply all their need.

They did not express these unbelieving thoughts aloud; but their Master knew they cherished them in their hearts. Who ventures to go to God to express in words his secret unbelief? Who could say in prayer, "We cannot trust thee in time to come? We think it likely that thou wilt forsake us, that thou wilt not care for our tears, or heed our cries." We dare not *speak* thus to our heavenly Father. Why then should we *think* what we dare not *speak?*

Jesus was displeased with his disciples on *two* accounts: for their want of *faith*, and for their want of *spiritual understanding*. How could they suppose that the earthly leaven of the Pharisees was worse than any other leaven? Leaven could not be the worse for belonging to wicked men. Jesus had lately shown his disciples that nothing but *sin* could pollute; yet their minds were so much darkened by early prejudices that they could not receive this simple truth.

And what was the leaven of which the Saviour bids his disciples beware? It was the false doctrine, or teaching, of the Pharisees and Sadducees. Both these sects taught errors; but *opposite* errors. The Pharisees *added* to the word of God;—the Sadducees *took* from it. The Pharisees added to it commandments of their own invention; the Sadducees took from it *all* but the five books of Moses, and even these they did not fully believe, for they would receive nothing that they did not *understand.* The Pharisees were superstitious,—the Sadducees were skeptical. The world is now full of persons, who, though bearing different names, preach doctrines like those of the Pharisees and Sadducees. Papists resemble the Pharisees, and infidels the Sadducees.

Were even the *disciples* in danger of being tainted by bad doctrine? Ought *we* not to fear its evil influence? Bad doctrine, like infected air, finds entrance through the smallest aperture, and unseen spreads a pestilence all around. As leaven will change the nature of a whole lump of flour, so bad doctrine will injure *all* the powers of the mind, and all the feelings of the heart. The venerable Howells used to say, "Error in *principle* is the parent of vice in *practice*." If it be so, how carefully we ought to shun bad doctrine! Though we may be well instructed in the truth, yet we are liable to be corrupted by false teachers. There are some melancholy instances of persons who had instructed thousands by their pious writings, receiving in their advanced years false principles into their minds, and attempting to pervert those whom once they had edified. Our constant prayer ought to be, "Hold thou me up, that my footsteps slip not."

By what mark may we distinguish good doctrine from false? By this mark; the true doctrine exalts Christ, and humbles man; it is summed up in these words: "O Israel, thou hast destroyed thyself; but in *me* is thy help," (Hosea xiii. 9.)

Evening Scripture portion. 1 John IV. ***The truth.***

MARK VIII. 22–26.—*He cures a blind man by touching him twice.*

THERE is one circumstance in this miracle which we do not meet with in any other—it is the *gradual* manner in which the cure was effected; the blind man was not *suddenly* restored to sight, but by *degrees*.

There are several other interesting circumstances connected with this miracle, though they are not *peculiar* to it. It is evident that this man did not belong to the town of Bethsaida, for after he was cured, Jesus desired him to return to his *house*, but *not* to enter the town. Bethsaida was one of those cities most highly favored, and most deeply guilty, for it repented not at the preaching of Jesus. On this account a wo was pronounced against it. "Wo unto thee, Bethsaida." The friends of the blind man heard that the Lord was arrived at Bethsaida, and they went thither, and besought mercy for the afflicted creature.

It often happens when the gospel is preached in a town, that while it is despised by the inhabitants of the place, it is valued by those who live in distant villages. The Lord showed his displeasure against the people of Bethsaida, by leading the blind man out of the town before he cured him, and by forbidding him to return there afterwards. Those who hate the gospel often take great pains to avoid hearing it, and God sometimes meets their wicked desires by taking measures to prevent their being troubled by the unwelcome sound.

How touching is the account of the kind manner in which Jesus conducted the blind man out of the town! "He led him by the hand." Behold the Son of God leading the blind by a way that he knew not, to the retired spot in which he intended to restore him to sight. Perhaps this blind man was but little acquainted with his benefactor, and was not fully aware of his power to cure his blindness. Thus many are led by Jesus to the place where they are converted. They know not whither the events of Providence are guiding them; they know not why they are removed from one place to another; why one path is blocked up, and another opened before them, till at length they find that all was arranged to bring about this blessed end, the opening of their blind eyes.

Jesus cured this blind man by the use of outward means, and not by his word alone; He spat on his eyes, and touched them. Perhaps he did so that he might more fully convince him that *He* alone was the author of his cure; there was a virtue in his touch, a power in the simplest means when applied by Him, that could remove blindness. Thus it is now. The most trifling circumstances are made by the power of Christ effectual to open the eyes of unbelievers.

A few years ago, an infidel saw a child reading the Bible, and said to him, in a scornful manner, "You cannot comprehend that book, why do you read it?" The child replied, "I delight in it, and therefore I try to understand it." This simple answer struck the infidel so powerfully, that he was led to reflect seriously on the cause of his unbelief, and to apply to God for his Holy Spirit.

This blind man, it appears, had not been *born* blind, for he knew the names of surrounding objects. His sight was so imperfectly restored at first, that it was only by their movements that he could distinguish men from trees; he knew that those were men that he beheld, because they walked. Jesus would not suffer him to *remain* in this state, but soon completely restored his sight. He laid his hand upon him the *second* time. Are not we reminded by this account of our own case? Has spiritual light been bestowed upon us? Is that sight *perfect?* Can we understand spiritual things distinctly and fully? We must reply, "No, we see through a glass darkly." Not through such a glass as in *these* days admits light into our rooms; but we see spiritual truths in the same confused manner that objects are seen reflected upon *ancient* mirrors, which were only made of polished brass. This is the state of the most enlightened Christian; he sees eternal things "*darkly*." How much more is it the state of *new* converts! They can just discern (though faintly) what it is most necessary to know; they see that sin is hateful, that God is holy, and that Christ is precious; but there are many important truths they cannot distinguish; and when they meditate on them they are perplexed and distressed.

What is the only remedy for the darkness of our minds? The touch of Jesus. Let him touch us by his Spirit the *second* time, and the *third* time. Let him continue to touch our eyes with his divine eye salve, till we can see him as he is, that we also may be like him. When the apostle Paul wrote to the Ephesians, though he knew they were converted, yet he told them that he constantly prayed that the eyes of their understanding might be enlightened, that they might know the hope of their calling, and the riches of their glorious inheritance. (Eph. i. 18.) These are the things that we so dimly discern. We do not behold the excellency of heaven with sufficient clearness. But the day shall come when those who now see *imperfectly* shall see face to face, shall know even as they are known.

"O glorious hour, O blest abode,
I shall be near and like my God,
And flesh and sin no more control
The sacred pleasures of the soul."

Those are indeed miserable who say, "We see," though they see not. Let us continually cry, "Anoint our eyes, that we may see more and more of thy divine glory, O blessed Lord!"

Evening Scripture portion. Ex. XXXIII. *The request of Moses.*

MATT. XVI. 13–20.—*He pronounces a blessing upon Peter.*

IN this passage we are permitted to behold Jesus and his disciples in sacred retirement. The towns of Cæsarea Philippi were situated at the northern part of the land, where the Lord was in some degree relieved from the pressure of the multitude. Such seasons he devoted to the instruction of his beloved apostles. With them he joined in holy exercises. We never hear of his praying with the multitude; but we know that he often prayed alone with his chosen flock. After his prayer, he conversed with them upon sacred subjects. He asked them, "Whom do men say that I the Son of man am?" It appears from their answer, that the multitude did not believe him to be the Son of God. But when he asked his disciples who he was, Simon Peter answered for the rest: "Thou art the Christ, the Son of the living God."

The Lord was pleased with this bold confession of faith, and he said, "Blessed art thou, Simon Barjona." When Peter first came to Jesus, Simon was his name, but Christ gave him the name of Peter which means a stone. Who was it had taught Peter that Jesus was the Son of God? Flesh and blood had not taught him; that is, no *man* had taught him; but the *Father* himself. Men can never make us believe in Christ; they cannot give us *faith*. It comes from God alone. Those who have not been taught by God, may *appear* to be religious; but they will forsake Christ in times of persecution. But

Peter would in the end (though not at first) prove firm as a stone. Christ knew this when he said, "Thou art Peter."

But was *Peter* the rock on which Christ would build his church? No. There is only one rock, that is Christ himself. Peter had just declared, "Thou art the Christ." By believing this truth, sinners are saved. Peter, after his Lord's ascension, often proclaimed this truth. On one occasion, he said before the enemies of his crucified Master, "This is the stone which was set at naught of you builders, which is become the head of the corner; neither is there salvation in any other, for there is none other name given under heaven among men whereby we must be saved." (Acts iv. 11, 12.) Have we believed in this name? Unless we do believe, we must perish.

True believers are called the church. It was of this church that Christ spoke when he said, "The gates of hell shall not prevail against it." By the gates of hell he meant the powers of darkness, or Satan and his angels, who are now trying to destroy the church of Christ; but they never can succeed, because it is built upon the eternal rock.

Christ showed great favor to Peter, when he said, "I give unto thee the keys of the kingdom of heaven." Power belongs to God alone. He shuts, and no man opens, and opens and no man shuts; but Christ communicated some of his own power to his apostles. Before he ascended to heaven, he breathed on them and said, "Receive ye the Holy Ghost. Whosesoever sins ye remit, they are remitted to them, and whosesoever sins ye retain, they are retained." The apostles proved their authority by the miracles they wrought.

It was not to Peter *alone* that power was given, but to *all* the apostles. We find from reading the book of Acts, that Peter possessed no authority over his brethren. Why then did Jesus on this occasion say to *him* especially, "I give unto thee the keys of the kingdom of heaven." The reason seems to be, that as it was Peter who had made the declaration, "Thou art the Christ," it was to him that Jesus replied. After the Lord had ascended, Paul became an apostle, and though he called himself the least of the apostles, he was in nothing behind the very chiefest of them; and he proved his apostleship by the signs and wonders which he wrought.

The apostles were stewards of the mysteries of God. They had the keys in their hands, and they unlocked their Lord's treasury, and distributed among men his unsearchable riches. While many trample these pearls under their feet, may we count all things but dross for the excellency of the knowledge of Christ Jesus our Lord.

Evening Scripture portion. Acts III. *The apostles heal a lame man.*

MATT. XVI. 21 to end.—*Christ reproves Peter.*

IN our last reading, Peter was called "blessed," and was promised many privileges; now he is rebuked as "*Satan.*" Yes, the meek and gentle Jesus uttered this severe rebuke, "Get thee behind me, Satan." Thus we see that a true believer is liable to displease the Lord.

Peter was a true believer; yet on this occasion he acted the part of *Satan* towards his Master, by advising him not to endure suffering. No doubt he was partly actuated by affection, but his Master did not overlook the fault on *that* account. Peter ought to have had the glory of God more at heart than to have wished the Son of God *not* to fulfil his glorious work, even unto death. Christ therefore calls him an *offence*, or a stumbling-block. Those are not our best friends, who endeavor to persuade us to please ourselves, rather than to please God. We should be afraid to listen to them, and we should prefer the friendship of those who counsel us to endure hardness, as good soldiers of Jesus Christ.

Probably there lurked at the bottom of Peter's heart a desire himself to escape suffering *with* a suffering master; therefore Jesus told him plainly that he must deny himself, and take up his cross. Nor did he speak to *him* alone, but to each of *us*. "If *any* man will come after me, let him deny himself," that is, his earthly desires, for ease, pleasure, riches, esteem,—"and let him take up his cross," that is, let him prepare even to die for my sake. The spirit of a Christian is the *spirit* of a martyr; he is *ready* to give up all things, even life itself, for Christ.

Many souls have been converted by this solemn appeal, "What is a man profited if he shall gain the whole world and lose his own soul?" It was a sermon preached upon this text that first led the missionary John Williams to care for his soul. He was an ungodly youth at the time he heard it; but afterwards he gave up the world, took up his cross, and followed Christ. At length he lost his life in his service. Having landed upon the island of Erromango, in the New Hebrides, hoping to preach the gospel there, he was pursued by the natives. He had just reached the sea, when he fell down, was overtaken, and bruised to death by the clubs of the savages. His blood was mingled with the waves, his flesh was devoured by cannibals, and his bones made into fish-barbs. But will he regret the choice he made, in the day when the Son of man shall come in his glory? When we consider what the Son of God gave up for our sakes, how little every sacrifice appears that we can make for him! Our *great* motive ought to be "*gratitude*" to him who shed his blood for sinners; and *it is* the great motive of all true Christians.

What did Jesus mean when he said, "There be some standing here which shall not taste of death, till they see the Son of man coming in his kingdom." He could not mean that some of his apostles would live till he came to judge the world; for he has not come yet, and they have long been dead. Did he mean that some of them should soon see him in his glory? In the next chapter there is an account of his glorious appearance upon a mountain, in the presence of three of the apostles. Could men now see Jesus as he will appear when he comes in clouds as King of kings, and Lord of lords, how mean and worthless all earthly glory would appear!

Evening Scripture portion. 2 Cor. XI. *Sufferings for Christ's sake.*

MATT. XVII. 1–4.—*The Transfiguration.*

WE lately read of Jesus conversing with his disciples respecting his *sufferings*. Now we read of his unveiling to them his *glory*. The prophet Isaiah foretold that his face should be more marred (or disfigured) than the face of any man. (Is. lii. 14.) No doubt, therefore, he wore usually an aspect of care and sorrow; but on this occasion he permitted the glories of his divine nature to shine forth through his frail earthly tabernacle. Thus he gave us a glimpse of the glory which awaits *all* the saints; for when they shall see Him as he is, they shall be like Him, and their vile bodies shall be changed into the likeness of his glorious body.

The mountain upon which this change in the appearance of the Lord took place, is supposed to be Mount Tabor, in Galilee. This mountain stands alone, and its top is not pointed like that of most mountains, but broad and flat, and therefore well-suited for a resting place. Its height is not great. In one hour it may be ascended. In this retired and lovely spot our Saviour was *praying* (as St. Luke informs us) with three of his disciples, when his form underwent a most glorious alteration. Have not many of his servants in all ages experienced a like glorious change in their *feelings* when engaged in prayer? Has not the gloom that oppressed them when they began to pour out their souls before God, been succeeded by the light of heavenly day?

The Saviour was attended on the mount by two heavenly visitants, Moses and Elias. Like their Lord, both these holy men, when on earth, had fasted for forty days in the wilderness. But all *their* sufferings were over, while the bitterest sufferings of Jesus were yet to come. These prophets were well prepared, by what they had themselves endured, to comfort their Lord in the prospect of his agonizing death. That death was the subject of their discourse. The Saviour could obtain no *consolation* from his apostles; their minds were still dazzled by hopes of earthly glory; but he could obtain the most tender sympathy from the discourse of his glorified servants.

The appearance of those departed saints on the mount, is calculated to comfort *us* also in the prospect of death. Are we not led from this fact, (as from many others,) to believe, that the spirits of the saints do *immediately* pass into glory, and that they do *not* wait for the general resurrection to be introduced into the presence of Christ?

How was it that Peter knew that the glorious persons he beheld were Moses and Elias? We are not informed by what *means* the discovery was made. But does not this circumstance give us reason to believe that we shall *know* the saints in glory,—not only our *own* friends, whom we loved upon earth, but *all* the saints? How delightful is the prospect! What will be the raptures of fellowship with such a company! And yet this will be one of the *lesser* delights of heaven, for the presence of Jesus will be the *chief*.

Peter was delighted with the scene, and desired that it should never be interrupted. In the warmth of his feelings, he made an unwise request; he asked permission to prepare three tents, for the abode of Christ and his prophets. It was *unwise*, because Peter himself was not fit to continue in such a scene; flesh and blood cannot inherit the kingdom of God; we must therefore all be *changed*, and this mortal must put on immortality. Besides this, Peter forgot the unwelcome truths that his Master had lately revealed; he forgot that Christ must be offered as a sacrifice for sin before he could enter into his glory, and that his disciples must *partake* of his *sufferings*, before they could partake of his *glory*. But though the request betrayed an ignorant mind, it showed an affectionate heart. Had not Peter's heart been full of love to his Lord, he would not have thought it such exceeding joy to behold Christ and his saints, and to hear their conversation. No ungodly man would feel satisfied in such company; he would feel anxious to escape to his earthly delights, and his congenial society. He would not say, "It is good for me to be here." It is a sign we have made one step in religion, if we really prefer the society of the godly to any other pleasure. Yet there may still be much that is weak and wavering in *our* hearts, as there was in Peter's. It is hard to attain to the feelings of Paul when he said, "I reckon that the *sufferings* of this present time are not worthy to be compared with the glory which shall be revealed in us." (Rom. viii. 18.)

Evening Scripture portion. Ps. XVI. XVII. *Heavenly desires.*

MATT. XVII. 5–9.—*The voice of God on the Mount.*

IN the Old Testament, we read of God speaking to Israel from the top of Mount Sinai. On that occasion there was blackness, and darkness, and tempest, and the sound of a trumpet, and the voice of words;

so terrible was the *sight*, that even Moses said, "I exceedingly fear and quake;" and so terrible was the *sound*, that Israel entreated that they might hear the voice of God no more. (Deut. v. 25.)

In how different a manner God spoke to the three favored apostles on the summit of Mount Tabor! And what was the *reason* of this difference?

The words that the Father spoke tell us *why* he laid aside his terrors, and arrayed himself in the mildest beams of celestial glory. He was well pleased in his beloved Son. His *wrath* against a *guilty world* was displayed upon Mount Sinai; his *delight* in his *righteous Son* was manifested upon Mount Tabor. Neither was his favor shown to his Son *alone*, but to those three trembling apostles who loved that Son; for they also entered into the bright cloud. Why then were they so sore afraid? Why did they fall on their faces? Because, since man became a sinner, he has never been able to bear the manifestation of the glory of Jehovah. The smoke and the torments of hell are not the only sights that would overwhelm a mortal man; the brightness and the joys of heaven would be more than he could bear to behold. Now Peter perceived how unwisely he had spoken when he had requested always to abide on that mountain top. But God, who knew the weakness of his dying creatures, did not prolong the glorious scene. In a little while the apostles were left alone with Jesus. Though they felt his familiar hand, and heard his well-known voice, yet at first they could hardly believe that the heavenly vision was past. St. Mark records that they "looked round about, and saw no man any more, save Jesus, with themselves."

Who can conceive the feelings with which those three apostles descended the mount! They had seen heaven come down to earth; how could they return to earth again! They had beheld glorified saints; they had heard the voice of the eternal Father; they had witnessed the glories of their beloved, yet despised Master. Who can doubt that their hearts were burning with the desire to describe the wonderful scene to their brethren at the foot of the mount, and perhaps even to declare it to the proud enemies that continually assailed them with taunts and reproaches. But Jesus imposed silence upon them. He said, "Tell the vision to no man, till the Son of Man be risen again from the dead." He knew that at this time they would have been disbelieved, if they had related what they had seen. It was enough for these blessed disciples that they themselves had enjoyed a glimpse of celestial glory. The recollection would help to sustain their faith when they should behold their Lord agonizing and bleeding in the garden; for it is remarkable that Jesus chose the *same* men to be witnesses of his glory and of his agony.

And why did he distinguish these three above their brethren? Was it not because they were appointed to endure *peculiar* trials? The Lord foretold that James and John would drink of his cup of bitterness, and be baptized with his baptism of suffering; and he prepared

Peter for the painful and ignominious death of the cross. Jesus knows beforehand what sufferings each of his servants will be called to endure, and he knows who most needs bright displays of his present glory, and near views of his past agonies. In acute suffering of any kind, the thoughts that most sustain the mind are the remembrance of Christ crucified, and the anticipation of beholding Christ glorified. How many have said, when in great pain, "What are *my* sufferings compared to the sufferings of Jesus for my sins!" How many when pressed down with sorrow have felt, "How soon will the sight of my glorious Redeemer make my present grief appear light as air!"

Evening Scripture portion. Ex. XIX. ***Mount Sinai.***

MATT. XVII. 10–13.—*Christ converses with his disciples respecting Elijah.*

As the disciples descended the Mount of Transfiguration, they ventured to enter into conversation with their Lord. They knew so well the condescension of their Master, that they even proposed a difficult question on a subject that perplexed them. It was this: "Why say the Scribes that Elias must *first* come?" (that is, *before* the Messiah.) Their thoughts naturally dwelt upon the wonderful scene they had just beheld. They had seen the prophet Elijah. They remembered having heard their Scribes, or teachers, declare that God would send Elijah before his great and dreadful day. Nor had the Scribes been mistaken in this declaration, for it is contained in the last chapter of the Old Testament, in Malachi iv. Yet the appearance of Elijah on the Mount was not the real fulfilment of that prophecy. Our Lord himself explained this difficult subject, and declared that John the Baptist had been prophesied of under the name of Elijah. It is evident that this explanation surprised the disciples. Perhaps they had never heard that the angel had told Zacharias, (the father of John the Baptist,) that his expected son should come in the *spirit* and *power* of Elias. There was a great resemblance between these two prophets; their characters, their offices, their habits, their afflictions, were similar. But in *one* point the difference between them was striking—their manner of departing out of this world; Elijah ascended, like a conqueror, in a chariot of fire; John was executed, like a criminal, in a prison. In this *one* point wherein John the Baptist *differed* from Elijah, he enjoyed the far greater honor of *resembling* his divine Lord.

The Saviour, after alluding to the treatment John had received, added, "Likewise also shall the Son of Man suffer of them." The disciples were unwilling indeed to believe that their Master should suffer. Though *John*, who was a *mortal man*, might fall a victim to the malice of his enemies, they thought it impossible that the Son of God should thus end his glorious career. But the Jews always persecuted the *living* prophets. They venerated those who were no longer on earth; but they hated those who lived in their own day. The name of Elijah was much set by; but the name of the Baptist was despised. The Jews little imagined that the preacher in the wilderness, clad in rough garments, and followed by the poor among the people, was the representative of the illustrious, the glorified Elijah. Jesus truly said of John the Baptist, "They *knew* him not." Even so it is now. The world knows not the servants of God. They speak with reverence of some holy men who are dead, such as the apostles, the martyrs, the reformers; while they often treat with contempt many of the *living* who most resemble those departed saints.

In their own day, how were the apostles regarded? One of themselves declares that they were counted as "the filth of the earth," and as "the offscouring of all things." (1 Cor. iv. 13.) And how were the martyrs esteemed in *their* day? When that undaunted sufferer, Bennet, was burning at the stake near Exeter, in the reign of our eighth Henry, the men and women who stood around, ran with the alacrity of demons, to gather either a stick, or a bundle of furze; that each might have some share in the death of one whom they esteemed a "vile heretic."* Truly "they knew him not."

Evening Scripture portion. 2 Kings II. *Elijah's translation.*

MARK IX. 14–27.—*The afflicted father.*

WHEN the Lord reached the foot of the Mount, he beheld a scene of sin, and sorrow, and suffering. There were the scornful scribes, the weak and wavering disciples, the poor demoniac, and the afflicted father, with the wondering multitude gathered around them. How unlike was this scene from that which the three apostles had just witnessed on the top of the mountain! There all was light and love, perfect bliss, and ineffable joy. Angels behold the same painful contrast, for as they gaze upon the glory of God, they also watch over the sorrows of men.

It seems as if our Lord must have retained a measure of brightness upon his countenance; for it is said that the people were greatly amazed when they saw him, and it is difficult to conjecture any other cause for their amazement. At that moment might be seen on one

* See English Martyrology, by Charlotte Elizabeth, vol. i. p. 86.

spot the effects of *heavenly* influence, and *hellish* power. The Son of God still shone with some lingering beams of the Father's glory; while the afflicted youth was reduced by *Satan* to the most degraded condition. How affecting was the sight! A human being, made in the image of God, lay on the ground, and wallowed foaming. Each of us stands now between two opposite states. Shall we ascend to a fairer world, where Christ and his glorified saints enjoy unspeakable bliss? or shall we sink into that place where the slaves of Satan suffer every sort of degradation and misery? Now is the time to apply to Jesus, as the sorrowful father did, that we may obtain deliverance from our great enemy. The same power that released this youth from Satan's chain, can free every other captive.

The case was a very inveterate one. It was one of long standing, and great malignity; therefore it was the better suited to display the Almighty power of Jesus. He loves to save where it is *most* evident that no *other* hand but *His* can afford help.

The prayers of the father showed a *weak*, though a *true* faith. "If thou *canst* do any thing, have compassion on us and help us." A severe master would have rejected such a prayer as this. But Jesus cherishes the tenderest bud of living faith. He answered, "If thou canst *believe*, all things are possible to him that believeth." The poor man was encouraged by this assurance to offer up a still more earnest prayer than before. He cried out with tears, "Lord, I believe; help thou mine unbelief." Did not the Holy Spirit dictate this prayer? "We know not what we should pray for as we ought; but the Spirit itself maketh intercession for us with groanings which cannot be uttered." (Rom. viii. 26.) Have our hearts ever been so full of good desires that we could only speak a few words? And were these words half choked with tears and sobs? God has heard those prayers. He never despises the broken and contrite heart. He attended to the prayer of this poor man.

Satan showed his malice against the youth who was going to be delivered from his power. The evil spirit rent the youth sore, before he came out of him, and he left him as one dead. Many have found that Satan has pursued them with the most painful temptations, just as they were escaping from his bondage. The tenderness of Jesus is as striking as the *malice* of Satan. The Lord took the poor youth by the hand and lifted him up.

It was the *father's* faith that had obtained the restoration of his son. Here is an encouragement for parents. If Jesus showed so much compassion to one who prayed for a *bodily* cure for his son, how much more must he feel for those who implore *spiritual* blessings for their children!

Evening Scripture portion.
Rom. VIII. 18 to end. ***The Spirit's intercession.***

MATT. XVII. 19–21.—*Christ speaks to his disciples on the power of faith.*

IT was very right in the disciples to inquire *why* they could not cast out the evil spirit. Whenever we have been foiled in an attempt to overcome sin, we ought to inquire what is the *reason* of the failure, and we shall find that the cause was the unbelief of our hearts. Perhaps before the Lord came and showed his power in casting out the spirit, the disciples thought that the obstacle to success was in the *father*. But it had been clearly proved that the father was in a fit state of mind to receive the mercy he implored. The hinderance was in the disciples' hearts: they had not *faith* enough in the power of God to enable them to exercise the miraculous gifts that had been bestowed upon them.

The Lord, after having told them of their unbelief, added these remarkable words: "If ye have faith, as a grain of mustard-seed, ye shall say to this mountain, Remove hence to yonder place, and it shall remove; and *nothing* shall be impossible unto you." It is supposed that our Saviour in this declaration made use of the words of a proverb, well understood among the Jews. A mustard-seed was a term used to represent a very small quantity; because a mustard-seed is the smallest of all seeds, in *proportion* to the size of the tree it produces. A mountain was a term used to represent a very great difficulty; because a mountain cannot be removed by the power of man. The meaning of our Saviour's words appears therefore to be this: "If you have even a small degree of real faith concerning the gifts that I have bestowed upon you, you will be able to perform astonishing miracles." It was the duty of the disciples to believe that God would help them to work miracles. And why was it their duty? Because Christ had *promised* to enable them to perform them. Faith is the belief of God's *promises*. It is *not our* duty to believe that God will help *us* to work miracles. And why not? Because God has *not* promised to give *us* that power. But he has given us *other* promises, exceedingly great and precious; and if we possess *true* faith, which, like a mustard-seed, will *grow* continually, we shall at length be able to overcome every difficulty that stands in the way of our salvation.

What difficulties has God promised to enable us to overcome? He has promised to enable us to overcome the *world*. "Who is he that overcometh the world, but he that believeth that Jesus is the Son of God?" (1 John v. 4.) He has promised to enable us to overcome *the body of death*, that is sin. St. Paul said, "O wretched man that I am, who shall deliver me from the body of this death? I thank God through Jesus Christ our Lord." (Rom. vii. 24, 25.) He has promised to enable us to overcome the devil: "Resist the devil, and he will flee from you." God will fulfil *all* his promises to us, if we have faith And how is faith to be obtained, and increased? By prayer, and, in some cases, by fasting also. It appears the disciples had neglected to pray and fast. The evil spirit that possessed the youth was of a peculiarly malicious and violent kind, but still even *that* kind might be cast out by prayer and fasting. Let us therefore never complain that we cannot overcome *any* sin; for if we prayed earnestly we should obtain help according to our need. There is nothing too hard for God to do, and there is nothing too hard for *believers* to do, when called and assisted by the Lord. St. Paul declared, "I can do *all* things through Christ which strengtheneth me."

Evening Scripture portion. Heb. XI. 23 to end. *The power of faith.*

LUKE IX. 43–46.—*Christ foretells his sufferings.*

THE Lord Jesus took every opportunity to prepare his disciples for his approaching death. He knew what a fearful trial it would prove to their weak faith. When men succeeded in apprehending him, and in crucifying him, it would appear to human eyes as if he could not be the Son of God. How could he preserve his disciples' faith from failing at that very time? By showing them that he knew beforehand all he should suffer.

It is in the same way that the Lord now seeks to preserve the minds of his followers from discouragement. Does it perplex a young convert to find that true religion is despised by the great and the learned? Is it not written, "Not many wise men after the flesh, not many mighty, not many noble are called?"—Is he staggered when he detects hypocrites among the professed followers of Christ? Is it not written, "Not every one that saith unto me, 'Lord, Lord,' shall enter the kingdom of heaven?"—Is he dismayed by meeting with numerous temptations and difficulties in his own path? Is it not written, "In the world ye shall have tribulation?" Thus the Lord has mercifully prepared his people for every trial of faith that can come upon them.

Yet there is need to say continually to them, "Let these sayings sink down into your ears." We are disposed to pass over lightly those things which we do not like to hear. The disciples could not bear to hear of their Lord's painful and ignominious death. Each display of his power and glory filled them with fresh hope that nothing but success and triumph awaited their beloved Master. Therefore, after every such display he reverted to the unwelcome, but profitable subject. When descending from the Mount of Transfiguration, he spoke of his sufferings; when he had wrought one of his most splendid miracles, (the deliverance of the furious demoniac,) he dwelt upon the mournful topic of his death. Yet the disciples could not receive this truth into their hearts. They believed it in a degree, for St. Matthew says,

"They were exceeding sorry," but they believed it in a very faint degree. Whence arose this dulness of understanding? The Lord needed not to impress *all* truths upon them so repeatedly. They understood that he was the Son of God, and that he was able to conquer all his enemies. They understood these *joyful* truths, because they *loved* them; but they understood not those *mournful* truths, because they did *not* love them. Their hearts were still full of worldly desires. Instead of being humbled by the want of faith which they had lately betrayed, they disputed, as they followed their Master, which should be the greatest.

If our understandings are dull in spiritual things, it is because our hearts are sinful. Every wrong feeling is like a film over the eye of the mind. Till we are converted we can see *nothing* of the glory of God; but even after conversion we see indistinctly; because much sin remains in our hearts. If we would grow in the *knowledge* of Christ, we must grow in *grace.* St. Peter concludes his second epistle with these words: "Grow in *grace,* and in the *knowledge* of our Lord and Saviour Jesus Christ. To whom be glory both now and forever. Amen."

When God would teach his servants, he often first sends them afflictions to subdue their sins, and then he instructs them in his heavenly truths.

Evening Scripture portion. 1 Thess. III. *The afflictions of believers.*

MATT. XVII. 24 to end.—*Christ pays tribute.*

WE now find our blessed Lord returned to his own city, Capernaum, and to the house where he generally lodged. The collectors of tribute-money called at that lowly abode, and seeing Peter near it, asked him whether his Master would pay the sum required of him. This tribute was *not* to be paid to Cæsar, the emperor, but to the *priests,* for the sacrifices of the temple. Every person above twenty years of age was required to pay yearly half a shekel, or about one shilling and threepence of our money. The Lord Jesus, as the *Son* of *God,* might have excused himself from paying this tribute for the service of his own Father, because *kings* do not demand taxes from their *own* children: yet he would not use this privilege, because he knew that it would be made a matter of accusation against him. The world would have misunderstood his motives. They would have suspected him of indifference to the service of the temple. He knew this was an occasion on which to exercise his miraculous powers. His divine attributes now shone forth in a most glorious manner. He displayed his *Omniscience,* for he described the circumstances of a certain fish then swimming in the lake of Gennesareth. He showed his *Omnipotence*, for he caused that very fish to come to Peter's hook. He showed also his *love* for his disciple; as the piece of money found in the fish was a *whole* shekel, (in value about half-a-crown,) and would suffice to pay Peter's tribute as well as his Master's.

This miracle was calculated to strengthen the apostle's weak faith under approaching trials. It was evident that He, who knew all about an insignificant fish, must foresee the manner of his own death; it was evident that He, who could direct the movements of that little animal in the depths of the sea, *could* escape from his own enemies, if he pleased to exert his Almighty power.

And surely this miracle must be a comfort to all God's people. The most minute circumstances concerning ourselves are seen by that eye which discerned the little fish in the water: the smallest incidents in our lives are ordered by that hand which brought the fish to Peter's hook. Why then should we fear? What evil can betide us, if we belong to Christ, and trust in him? *We* know not what a day may bring forth; but *He* does. We may (like him) be reduced to our last piece of money, but he can supply us with more at the needful moment. How can any be so unwise, as not to seek the favor of the Governor of the whole universe? What a privilege it is to belong to his family! What a comfort to be under his fatherly care!

Evening Scripture portion. 1 Kings XVII. ***Elijah miraculously fed.***

MARK IX. 33–37.—*Christ teaches humility by the example of a child.*

IT is interesting to hear what the Lord Jesus said to the *multitude* in his *public* discourses; but it is still *more* interesting to hear what he said to his *disciples* in his *private* conversations. In these retired scenes we behold, and admire, not only his wisdom, but also his *patience.*

How displeasing it must have been to the Lord, while he was talking of his sufferings, to know that his disciples, who were accompanying him on the road, were disputing who should be the greatest! Yet he *patiently* waited for a seasonable opportunity of reproving them.

When he was come into the house he asked them, "What was it that you disputed among yourselves by the way?" Their own consciences told them that they had acted wrong, and they were ashamed to acknowledge their fault to their Master. What a dignity the Lord preserved among his most familiar friends! Though gentle and condescending, he made them feel ashamed of sin.

Seated among his disciples, as a father among his children, he began to explain to them their error. What was it he disapproved? It was the *feeling* whence the dispute arose. It was the *desire* to be first. Eve ate the fruit with a desire to be as God. We, her children, inherit this wicked desire. The grace of God alone can root it out of our hearts.

In order to make a stronger impression upon the disciples' minds, the Lord took a little child, and set him in the midst of them, as an example of humility. A very little child has not understanding enough to desire to be first; the thought never enters into its mind. It follows its mother from place to place, caring not whether she be a queen or a peasant. It never looks for admiration, and shrinks from the notice of all, but its beloved parents and nurses. The Christian, also, ought to be indifferent to earthly distinctions. He is, in fact, a pardoned criminal, and should be too deeply penitent for his transgressions against his Lord, to wish for honor among his fellows.

Observe what affection Christ showed to the young child. He took him in his arms, and while he still held the little creature in his embrace, thus spoke to his disciples: "Whosoever shall receive one of such children in my name, receiveth me." The humble, the contrite, and the penitent, are *such* children. If we wish to please our Lord, we shall show great tenderness to his *humble* disciples. Whatever crimes they may have committed in past times, we shall forget them, because the blood of Christ has blotted them out. It is *not* those who have committed the fewest open sins that God loves best; but those who are the least in their own eyes; these are his dearest children. It is our honor to be allowed to comfort them.

Evening Scripture portion.
Numbers XVI. 1–35. *The rebellion of Korah, Dathan, and Abiram.*

MARK IX. 38–42.—*Christ directs his disciples not to forbid the man who cast out devils in his name.*

WHEN our Saviour was instructing his disciples, he permitted them to ask him questions, and to express their doubts. While he was teaching them the duty of humility, a doubt occurred to John's mind respecting his own conduct on a late occasion.

It was frank and ingenuous in the apostle to *express* this doubt to his Master. He suspected that he had acted wrong, but he did not on that account conceal his conduct. How apt we are to conceal from the friends we most revere, those actions which we fear have been faulty! while, if we were frankly to acknowledge them, we might obtain valuable counsel.

Though it was *John* only who *mentioned* the circumstance, yet it appears that *all* the disciples had united in forbidding the man to cast out devils. Nine of them had very lately, from unbelief, failed in working a miracle; and yet they ventured to forbid a man whose faith was evidently greater than their own. Did not this conduct betray much presumption? How dreadful, too, was the calamity from which this man released his fellow-creatures, even from Satan's bondage! Could the disciples see the poor demoniac just before writhing and foaming, now peaceful and thoughtful, and forbid a brother to attempt to deliver *others* from their sufferings? Yes, they were so blinded by one false notion, that they overlooked all other considerations. They imagined their Master would set up a temporal kingdom, and that it would consist of those only who were called (as they had been) to follow him from place to place. But our Lord had servants who were not required, or even permitted to follow him, as the apostles did; yet *they* also were dear to him. They were dear to him, because they would not lightly speak evil of him. The world spoke evil of Christ, of his words, of his works, of his people. Those who did *not* speak evil of him, spoke *well* of him; for there is no such thing as being *neuter* in the cause of Christ.

What did Jesus mean by these words: "He that is not against us, is on our part?" He meant, that there is no such thing as being *neuter* in religion. All men are on one side, or the other. There are many who *wish* to keep neuter. They are afraid of being on the side of Satan, but they have not resolved to be on the side of Jesus. The devil reckons these among his most trusty servants; such cowardly spirits are *less* likely to escape from him than those who *openly* do his work.

But the man who cast out devils in the name of Jesus was not one of those undecided characters. At a time when all the rich and great were joined together against the Son of God, he was not ashamed to acknowledge him. Such are the men respecting whom our Saviour declared, that those who give them a cup of cold water shall be blessed. How careful we ought to be never to discourage the least of God's servants! They may not belong to *our* party, but they may belong to Christ. They *do* belong to Christ, if, instead of speaking lightly of him, they take delight in praising him before an ungodly world; and especially, if by the power of his word, they release sinners from the bondage of Satan. We must wish those to prosper, who convert sinners from the error of their ways, save souls from death, and hide a multitude of sins.

Evening Scripture portion.
Numbers XI. 16 to end. *Moses will not forbid the prophets.*

MARK IX. 43 to end.—*Christ warns his disciples against the unquenchable fire, and never-dying worm.*

THE Lord ended his private conversation with his own disciples in this awful manner. He knew that ambition was not cast out of their hearts. It was *ambition* that led them to dispute who should be the greatest, and that caused them to forbid the man who followed them not. They were full of self-importance, and of worldly desires. Though they did possess some living faith and some sincere love; yet how weak was that faith, how cold was that love!

Their Master knew that if they continued to cherish a worldly and proud spirit, they could not obtain a place in his kingdom; therefore he earnestly warned them to mortify the sinful desires of their hearts. He compared those desires to hands, feet, and eyes; because it is as painful for a person to mortify a darling passion of the heart, as to cut off a precious limb from the body.

Are there any desires in our hearts that must be subdued in order that we may escape eternal fire? Though we may have tasted of God's grace, yet we may need these warnings. Do we desire to be much praised, and highly thought of? Do we desire to rise to a higher station than that we now fill? Do we impatiently desire to possess some earthly good which God has seen fit to withhold? Are our affections engrossed by some creature, so that we are more anxious to please that creature than to please God? Let us carefully examine our own hearts, and then implore God to give us strength to strive against these earthly passions. We need not (as Papists often do) *reject* the gifts of God, because we are prone to *abuse* them. We need not dress in sackcloth, live upon the coarsest fare, or withdraw from human society, in order to become humble. The evil lies not in the *objects* that surround us, but in our own *hearts*. The struggle against sin will be severe and painful, but the danger is so terrific that every effort should be made. An unquenchable fire, an undying worm, must be the eternal portion of those who *continue* wilfully to harbor sinful passions in their hearts. Had the disciples persisted in their sins, they would have perished. One of them did persist in sin; he still indulged in the love of money, and he perished. He was the son of perdition.

Our Saviour, in concluding his admonition, uttered these remarkable words: "Every one shall be salted with salt." What did these words mean? The sacrifices, offered in the temple, were salted with salt. (Lev. ii. 13.) Thus the condemned in hell will be kept from being consumed, even as things are preserved from corruption by salt. God's *wrath* will be as *salt*, to render them capable of enduring eternal sufferings. But God's grace is also like *salt*,—it preserves the soul; therefore Jesus said, "Have salt in yourselves." It was grace the apostles needed to keep them from destruction.

Then our Saviour concluded with these words: "Have peace one with another." No longer dispute which shall be the greatest, but love and serve each other. If we have the salt of *grace* in our hearts, we shall have the fruit of *peace* in our lives. "Only by pride cometh contention." (Prov. xiii. 10.) Let us crucify at the *cross* of our dying Lord all those evil passions that disturb our peace now, and which would, if cherished, destroy our souls.

Evening Scripture portion. James IV. *Resistance of evil.*

MATT. XVIII. 10–14.—*Christ declares how precious the little ones are in the Father's sight.*

THESE verses form part of a most interesting conversation that our Lord held with his own disciple in his house at Capernaum. Some passages in that conversation are calculated to alarm the stoutest heart; but others are of the most soothing and endearing nature. How delightful it is to know that God regards with the tenderest love even the little ones of his family!

These *little ones* are true believers, however weak in faith, and imperfect in knowledge. They have angels for their servants. "Their angels do always behold the face of my Father which is in heaven." We understand what is meant by this verse, from the declaration of St. Paul concerning angels: "Are they not all ministering spirits, sent forth to minister to them who shall be heirs of salvation?" The angels are ministering spirits, or servants: they serve the heirs of salvation,—believers upon earth. They may be compared to the nurses of infant princes; for they wait upon those who shall hereafter be greater than themselves. Believers shall, in some respects, rise above angels in the world of glory; they shall stand nearer the throne, and sing that song which none can learn, but those who are redeemed from the earth, even the song of redeeming love.

Do we believe that each saint has angels for his servants? Can we then despise *any* saint? An unconverted *monarch* may have lords and ladies to attend on him; but a converted *beggar* has angels to wait on him. How much higher is his state! These angels shall shortly convey his soul into the assembly of the saints, and at the last day shall separate him from the wicked forever and ever.

But there is a still higher light in which we may view the saints;—as those whom Christ came to seek and to save. Each saint is the purchase of Christ's blood. As the shepherd with anxious care seeks for his wandering sheep; so the Son of God, by his Spirit, has sought for each believer when wandering among the dark mountains of sin and death, and has brought him into the fold of grace, and has bidden angels rejoice over him. If we ourselves are among the children of God, we have been the objects of all this care. There is none of us that has not gone astray; the holy angels alone have never wandered. We never should have *desired* to return, had not God sent his Spirit into our hearts. We never should have been *able* to return, had he not borne us home in his own loving arms. Having taken all this care for us, will he suffer us to perish? No; it is not the will of our Father in heaven that his little ones should perish.

But for what *purpose* did Jesus speak of his love to his little ones on this occasion? To remind the disciples of the love *they* ought to bear to *all* the saints. The ambition still cherished in their hearts, led them to despise many other believers, especially those who followed not with them; therefore their Master set forth in their hearing the tender love his Father bears to *all* true believers. Could *they* despise those whom the Father honored? Whenever we see a believer, however weak and mean, we should consider, "Here is one whom angels serve, whom Jesus came down from heaven to save, whom the Father will not suffer to perish, but whom He guards with his all-seeing eye."

Evening Scripture portion. Gen. XXVIII. *Jacob's dream.*

MATT. XVIII. 15–17.—*Christ directs his disciples how to treat an offending brother.*

WHAT a privilege we possess in having these directions how to behave towards a fellow-Christian who has done us wrong! But how seldom are any of these rules observed! How much more apt we are, either to indulge in sullen spleen, or to break out in angry invec tives, than mildly to remonstrate with an offending brother! We ought to go, in the first place, and tell him of his fault *alone.* That would be the most probable way to win him. Perhaps we might discover that we had suspected him unjustly; or, if *not,* that he was ready to change his conduct, when he found that it displeased us.

Directions like these are given in Lev. xix. 17, 18; "Thou shalt not hate thy brother in thine heart; thou shalt in anywise rebuke thy brother, and not suffer sin before him. Thou shalt not avenge, nor bear any grudge against the children of thy people."

But if the offender should persist in his evil conduct, we are directed to take two or three persons with us; and if he should still persevere, to tell his fault to the Church, that is, to the public congregation of believers; and then the persons we had taken with us would be witnesses of the truth of our report; so that, through them, our words would be established. If the offender should refuse to obey the church, then he must be cast out of the society of believers, and not permitted to partake of the Lord's Supper.

We find, from the epistles, that the apostles and the early Christians pronounced this sentence of exclusion, when great offences were committed by professed Christians. We read of a man in 1 Cor. v., with regard to whom St. Paul gives these directions: "In the name of our Lord Jesus Christ, when ye are gathered together, and *my spirit*, with the power of the Lord Jesus Christ, to deliver such an one unto *Satan*, for the destruction of the *flesh*, that the *spirit* may be saved in the day of the Lord Jesus."

Some, on hearing these directions, may reply, "How can we follow these commands?" But do we follow them *as far* as we can? When a professing Christian behaves ill to us, do we in the first place tell him his fault *alone?* There are many called Christians who take delight in exposing the faults of their brethren. Sometimes they will even tell them to the *world.* The *Church* weeps over iniquity, and prays for the sinner; the *world* rejoices, and blasphemes the name of Christ.

When we have used all the means in our power to reclaim an offending brother, and all the means have failed, then it is our duty to show by our conduct that we disapprove the course he is pursuing. Whether the offence is committed against ourselves, or against another, or against God alone, we must not encourage sin. It is better that the world should know of the sin, than that they should think that Christians approve of it. The first missionaries in Tahiti acted on this principle. They refused to hold intercourse with one of their number, named Lewis, because he had married a heathen woman. The backslider speedily came to an awful end: he was cut off suddenly by an unknown hand.

When an offender repents of his sin, then we ought "to forgive him, and to comfort him, lest perhaps such a one should be swallowed up with overmuch sorrow." (2 Cor. ii. 7.)

Evening Scripture portion. 2 Thess. III. *Brotherly admonition.*

MATT. XVIII. 19, 20.—*Christ promises to hear the united prayers of his disciples.*

Do the Scriptures contain a more encouraging promise than this? "Where two or three are gathered together in my name, there am I in the midst of them."

There are some promises which are addressed to the *apostles* in particular. It was to *them* that Christ said, "Whatsoever ye shall bind on earth, shall be bound in heaven; and whatsoever ye shall loose on earth, shall be loosed in heaven." That promise has been fulfilled; the apostles' words have the same authority as those of Christ himself. Their writings form part of the Holy Scriptures. But did Christ speak to the *apostles* alone, when he said, "If two of you shall agree on earth as touching any thing that they shall ask, it shall be done for them of my Father which is in heaven?" This promise is ours as much as theirs: for it is added, "Where two or three are gathered together in my name, there am I in the midst of them." It is *not* said where two or three *of you* are gathered together, but where two or three. It may be two or three apostles, or it may be two or three peasants, or two or three women, or two or three children; yet, if they are gathered together in the name of Christ, he will be in the midst of them to bless them, and answer them. Praying together greatly helps Christians to love each other. If those who live beneath one roof would meet together, not only in the regular family worship, but also by two or three, they would often find their mutual love increase, and they would live in greater harmony, and enjoy more happiness, and obtain richer blessings.

There are some petitions which are especially suited to be presented to God by several of his children in united prayer. If one has committed a fault, then he may confess it to his brethren, and ask them to accompany him to the throne of grace to plead for mercy. St. James, in his epistle, says, "Confess your faults one to another, and pray *one for another*, that ye may be healed." It is when we wander from God, and *most need* his mercy, that we are the *least able* to implore it. Then how comforting it is to have a Christian brother to lead us back to God!

Sometimes a particular favor is desired by the members of one family. It may be the safe return of an absent brother, or the conversion of an unbelieving relation. Six youthful sisters have met together every morning to implore a blessing upon an aged parent. They have prayed that the light of truth might shine into his benighted soul.

When God answers the prayers of several believers, his name is more glorified than when he answers the prayer of one alone; for then there are *several* witnesses of his truth and faithfulness.

Towards the end of the last century, six or seven pious ministers of the Church of England, (Mr. Romaine being one,) agreed to meet together at a certain hour to entreat God to raise up more faithful preachers of the gospel in their own church. They could not all meet in one *place*, for many of them were separated from each other by great distances, but they all met at one time at the throne of grace. Before their course was finished, they beheld the answer to their prayers. Instead of six or seven, there were six or seven *hundred* clergymen of the Church of England, of like spirit with themselves.

Evening Scripture portion.
Acts XII. ***The prayers of the Church for Peter.***

MATT. XVIII. 21 to end.—*The parable of the unforgiving servant.*

How odious that servant appears, who after having received such exceeding benefits from his Lord, went out, and acted with such rigor towards his fellow-servant! Yet that unfeeling servant affords but a faint picture of the unforgiving sinner. For what was the obligation that he had received, compared to that under which we lie to God! His Lord had forgiven him a debt of ten thousand talents; but we are not informed, that in order to do this, his Lord had made any painful sacrifice. But before our Lord *could* forgive us, He was constrained by his own holiness to find an atonement for our sins, and that atonement was the blood of his Son. Now if after having received this gift, we should go forth, and willingly retain any unkind feeling against those who have done us wrong, how great would be our guilt!

We should also remember how infinitely greater the debt is that we owe to God, than any debt our fellow-creatures can owe to us. In the parable the disproportion is immense; *two millions* of pounds in the one case, and *three* pounds in the other; (according to the calculations of some;) but there is a still greater disparity between our debt to God, and man's to us.

Consider these *two* circumstances, which most aggravate offences. The *repeating* of them *often*, and after having received great *benefits*. Have not our offences against God these two aggravations in an eminent degree? Who can have provoked *us* so OFTEN as we have provoked God? from our birth until this moment, we have not ceased to sin against him in thought, word, and deed; and yet he is still willing to be reconciled to us. Who can have received such *benefits* from *us*, as we have received from God;—not only *temporal* blessings, but the offer of everlasting life, and the gift of his Son!

If we had a more just idea of the nature and extent of our transgressions against him, we should be *ashamed* of thinking of the sins of men against us. Indeed, perhaps, in *our* quarrels, we may be *most* in fault, and may really owe more than is owed to us; or though we may have been ungratefully treated by *one*, we ourselves may have ungratefully treated some *other* person, so that on the whole *nothing* may be owing to us. How it would quiet the tumult of our passions, if, when disposed to think of the *injuries* we have received from our fellows, we were to turn our attention to the *insults* we have offered to God!

But perhaps we do not feel that God has *forgiven* these insults. Perhaps we are still troubled by the dread of his anger for our past transgressions. Nothing would soften our hearts so much, as a sense of his forgiving love. Let us pray for this blessed assurance. Then we shall feel the force of the apostle's command, "Forbearing one another and forgiving one another, if any man have a quarrel against any: even as Christ forgave you, so also do ye."

Evening Scripture portion. Col. III. *Forgiveness of injuries.*

LUKE X. 1-16.—*Christ sends out seventy disciples.*

THIS charge to the seventy disciples very much resembles the charge to the twelve apostles, that we read some time ago. As it was necessary that the twelve apostles should be generally with their Master, Jesus appointed seventy other persons to preach the gospel in various parts of the land.

He sent them to every place whither he himself would come. Still he sends his faithful servants before his face. When they appear, we may expect to see their Master coming soon afterwards in the power of the Spirit. But as seventy men were too few to instruct all those who were perishing through ignorance, Jesus commanded them to pray that God would send forth laborers into his harvest. Is there not cause still to offer this prayer? There is too small a number of ministers and missionaries scattered over the world. When the Sabbath dawns, how few rejoice to see its beams!

Before the seventy went forth, Jesus informed them *what to expect* in their journeys. They were to expect sufferings, (v. 3,) "I send you forth as lambs in the midst of wolves." They were to expect their message to be sometimes rejected, (v. 10,) "Into whatsoever city ye enter, and they receive you *not*." Those men who resembled wolves, would ill-treat the lambs of Christ. They were to expect that God would incline some to receive them, and to be kind to them. Were *all* to frown upon them, their spirits would be utterly cast down. But the Lord is too tender a Father to suffer his children to remain without any encouragement. At the needful moment a friendly voice cheers, and a friendly hand sustains.

The Lord Jesus also instructed his disciples *what to do* in their journeys. They were to carry no provision nor clothes with them, but to trust to God's promise to provide for them, (v. 4,) "Carry neither purse, nor scrip, (that is, bag,) nor shoes." Missionaries who lived after Christ's ascension, thankfully received gifts from their converts before they set out to teach heathen nations. (See St. John's third epistle, 5, 6.) It is the duty of Christians to provide for the wants of missionaries; but these seventy disciples were placed in *peculiar* circumstances, and received peculiar aid. They were to use haste in delivering their message, and to lose no time in showing useless civilities. "Salute no man by the way." They were to pronounce blessings on every one who received them, saying, "Peace be unto thee." They were to accept the food offered to them; but they were not to seek better fare by going from house to house. They were to confirm the truth of their message by healing the sick. They were to warn their enemies by shaking off the dust from their feet in departing from their city.

The Lord concluded his instructions by denouncing woes upon the favored cities of Chorazin, Bethsaida, and Capernaum. The traveller can witness how the Lord's predictions have been fulfilled in the temporal destruction of those cities, for their very names have perished. Why did he speak to the seventy concerning the guilt of those cities? To remind them how he himself, the Son of God, had been rejected by the cities in which he most frequently preached, and thus to prepare them for similar treatment. Our proud hearts are ready to rebel when we find that our instructions produce no effect upon the hearts of men. But can *we* repine at want of success, when we remember how our *Lord* seemed to toil in vain? Yet, there were a *few* who received him; the woman of Tyre, the weeping sinner, and the sorrowful father who cried, "Help my unbelief." How delightful to be permitted to strengthen *one* trembling believer, or to reclaim *one* wretched wanderer!

And this we should remember for our comfort, that if *we* do not behold the fruit of our own labors, those who come after us will reap the benefit; for the word of the Lord shall not return unto him void.

Evening Scripture portion. 3 Epistle of John. *Kindness to ministers.*

JOHN VII. 1–13.—*The brethren of Christ reproach him.*

SUCH was the conduct of sinners to the Lord of glory when he was upon earth. His brethren (that is, his relatives) refused to believe in him, and treated him with scorn. They ventured to dictate to *him* who possessed all wisdom, saying, "Depart hence, and go into Judea, that thy disciples also may see the works that thou doest." And they insolently hinted, that if he were really a great prophet, he would not remain in retirement; for they said, "There is no man doeth any thing in secret, and he himself seeketh to be known openly." How trying such conduct in relatives must have been! We know that it is easier to bear unkindness from strangers, than from near and dear kindred. But if the Lord suffered in this manner, his people ought to be patient under the same trials.

And how did the *world* feel towards Jesus? How did the rich, the great, the learned esteem him? They hated him; they hated the express image of the Father; they hated the brightness of his glory. And *why* did they hate so lovely a being? Because he testified that their works were evil. The wicked cannot bear to be reproved. The most amiable behavior cannot secure a faithful Christian from the world's hatred. But is it not an honor to share the reproach of the Son of God?

And what did the *people* think of Jesus? They were divided in their opinions. Some said, "He is a good man." What faint praise to bestow on him, who was *goodness* itself! Was this *all* that *they* would say for him who was the fairest among ten thousand, and altogether lovely? Yes, they were ashamed to say more than "He is a good man;" while others dared to accuse him of deceiving the people. Thus have the servants of God been faintly praised, and falsely accused in all ages. How little worth must popular esteem be, when it is so often given to the worst of men, and withheld from the best!

How bright do the perfections of the Lord shine forth when viewed in contrast with the base qualities of human creatures! The Son of God remained unmoved in the midst of all the conflicting storms of human passions. His eyes were directed to his Father, whose will was his only guide, whose favor was his greatest joy. He met his brethren's insinuations by the calm and dignified reply, "My time is not yet come." He knew the *times* that the Father had appointed for all his actions. The time for him to go forth to meet his enemies, was not yet come. It came at last, and then he set his face as a flint, and boldly said, "I am he." But till that time arrived, he avoided danger. Jesus knew all things that were coming upon him. We, like Paul, must always confess that wherever we go, we know not the things that shall befall us there; but, like him, we may also say, "We know that all things work together for good to them that love God."

The Christian *waits* the Lord's time, while unknown, and *welcomes* it, when known. The holy martyr Bradford languished long in prison, not knowing the day appointed for his execution, but patiently waiting the Lord's time. When he knew it, how joyfully he welcomed it! One afternoon the keeper's wife suddenly came up to him, troubled, and almost breathless, saying, "O Master Bradford, I come to bring you heavy news."—"What is it?" said he. "To-morrow you must be burned, and your chain is now a buying." The martyr put off his cap, and lifting up his eyes to heaven, said, "I thank God for it. I have looked for the same a long time, and therefore it cometh not to me suddenly, but as a thing waited for every day and hour. The Lord make me worthy thereof."

Evening Scripture portion. Jer. XI. ***Jeremiah's treacherous brethren***

JOHN VII. 14–29.—*Christ defends himself for healing on the Sabbath day.*

In these verses we have a fresh instance of the insulting manner in which Jesus was treated upon earth.

He was despised for his want of a learned education. "How knoweth this man letters?" exclaimed the Jews scornfully, "having never learned!" Soon afterwards their insolence increased, and they cried, "Thou hast a devil." This treatment gave Jesus an opportunity of displaying his meekness. Every circumstance that befalls us affords the *opportunity* of cultivating some grace. Disappointment affords the opportunity of exercising resignation; enjoyment of showing gratitude; when we are praised, then is the time for humility; when we are insulted, then is the time for meekness; every temptation to sin furnishes an occasion of manifesting faithfulness to God.

Jesus showed not only great *meekness*, but also great *wisdom*, in his dealings with perverse sinners. He knew what accusation they had against him, namely, that on the *Sabbath-day* he had healed the impotent man who lay by the pool. With wonderful skill he unveiled their inconsistency in accusing him of breaking the Sabbath by performing a work of *mercy;* for he said that even they themselves performed the ceremonies of Moses' law on the Sabbath-day. How easy it is for Jesus to show men the deceitfulness of their pretences! At the last day those who profess to have the *best* motives for doing the *worst* things, will be confounded and speechless in the presence of their Judge.

What ignorance those people betrayed who said that Jesus could not be the promised Christ, because they knew whence he was. They *imagined* they knew whence he was; but they were mistaken; they did not know he came from God. So Jesus answered them by a *question;* for the words in verse 28 should be regarded as a question, "Do ye both know me and do ye know whence I am?" By this he meant to say, "You *think* you know whence I am, but you do *not* know."

Then Jesus added these words respecting his Father, "I know him!" How happy are they who can truly say of the Father, "I know him;" for the world does not know him, and no man *can* know him, except Jesus reveal Himself to his soul. But the meek and lowly Saviour is willing to teach all those who desire to know his Father. He came into the world "to bring us to God."

Do we desire to know God? Is this our *chief* desire? It may *appear* that we can pass away our time, and enjoy ourselves without knowing God; but what should we do at the last day if God should say, "I never *knew* you, O ye that work iniquity!"

Evening Scripture portion. Job XXII. ***Acquaintance with God.***

JOHN VII. 30–36.—*Christ speaks of going where his enemies could not come.*

THE discourse our Saviour publicly delivered in the temple, offended his enemies so much, that they sent men to take him. These men found him preaching. Jesus knew for what purpose they were come, and he uttered an awful warning in their presence, telling them that he should be with them only a little while, and that then they should seek him, and should not find him, adding, "Where I am, thither ye cannot come." The Jews experienced the truth of these words when the city of Jerusalem was taken, and they looked in vain for the promised Messiah to deliver them,—but found no deliverer

It will also be fulfilled in the experience of *every* unbeliever, unless he repent. A time will come to all the ungodly, who die impenitent, when they will seek Christ and not find him, and when they will desire in vain to reach the place where he is. Such a day came to the rich man, when he lifted up his eyes, being in torments, and saw Lazarus *afar off*, and heard that there was a great gulf between them, which none could pass. How awful it will be to see Christ *afar off*, and to find the compassionate Saviour deaf to our entreaties! Such a day is spoken of in Prov. I., "Then shall they call upon me, but I will not answer; they shall seek me early, but they shall not find me, for that they hated knowledge, and did not choose the fear of the Lord."

But Christ's enemies did not even understand the warning He had given. They only expressed to each other their wonder. "Can he be going to teach the dispersed Jews who live in Gentile countries," or can he be going to teach the Gentiles themselves?

They thought it a thing impossible that Gentiles should be taught; they imagined that they were unworthy of the least notice from God, and that they would be left to perish in heathen ignorance. But God thought not so; *his* thoughts were not as their thoughts; even *then* he had purposes of mercy towards *our* savage forefathers. He saw them wandering with painted skins among their forests of oak, and offering up their children to horrible idols. He saw them, He pitied, and He sent (if not an *apostle*) the *convert* of an apostle, to proclaim in their untutored ears his glorious gospel. Our fathers sought him, and they found him, and many of them are now with God. Where they are, and where Jesus is, we desire to come.

Jesus has not *yet* said to us, "Where I am thither ye *cannot* come." Shall he ever say it? He never will, if it is our heart's warm desire to be where he is. Has he not said, "Where I am, there shall my servant be?"

This was the sweet verse that an aged minister often repeated in his dying hours:

And when I'm to die,
  "Receive me," I'll cry;
For Jesus hath loved me,
  I cannot tell *why;*
But this I can find,
  We too are so join'd,
He'll not be in glory
  And leave me behind.

Evening Scripture portion. Rom. XV. *The Gospel preached to the Gentiles.*

JOHN VII. 37–39.—*Christ invites the thirsty to come to him.*

THE Saviour delights more in promises than in threatenings. In the presence of his enemies he often uttered most sweet and encouraging invitations.

On the last day of the feast of tabernacles, (even on the eighth,) it was the custom to pour large quantities of water upon the ground, as a type of God's promise of pouring the Spirit upon man in the latter days. It seems probable that it was in the midst of this ceremony, that Jesus stood and cried, "If any man thirst, let him come unto me and drink." And what is the meaning of this invitation? Coming to Christ is believing in Christ; "drinking" is receiving the Holy Spirit into the heart.

Since Jesus uttered these gracious words, the Holy Spirit has been given in large measure; for when he was glorified and seated at his Father's right hand, he sent down the Holy Spirit. Till He had presented an atonement for sin, this great gift could not be bestowed upon guilty man. Those, indeed, who believed in Christ from the *beginning*, received a *measure* of the Spirit; but not so *abundant* a measure as those who have believed in him *since* he was offered up.

This is the substance of the preaching of every faithful minister, "If any man thirst, let him go to Jesus and drink." The whole world is suffering the torments of parching thirst. It is evident that they feel uneasy by their anxiety to obtain wealth, pleasure, and honors; but they know not the only fountain that can quench their thirst. They little imagine that the Holy Spirit would make them more happy than all the enjoyments earth can afford.

Not only would they be happy *themselves*, but they would obtain the power of making others happy. For out of them should flow rivers of living water to quench the thirst of their fellow-creatures. It is an inexpressible delight to make the wretched happy. None but true believers can do this. Kind-hearted, worldly people often try to make their friends and neighbors happy, but they never can succeed. The Christian has discovered the secret by which he can assuage human grief, and quiet the restless heart. None can conceive what will be the delight of God's faithful servants when they look around in the abodes of bliss, and behold those who once thirsted upon earth, but who now thirst no more, and when they remember that it was their privilege to persuade them *first* to taste of the fountain of living waters. But happiness will be as nothing compared to the joy of the Son of God. This joy cheered his heart when he endured the cross. He knew that millions of souls would be made blessed for ever through his blood. It is a pleasure to remember having saved the life of a fellow-creature. Have you ever seen a young person's eyes sparkle with delight at the thought of having extinguished the flames that were raging around her companion? Or have you heard an old man relate how in former days he snatched a poor child out of the water? The satisfaction that they showed may remind us of the infinite joy the Lord of glory will feel when he looks around upon the souls that he has blessed forever. "He shall see of the travail of his soul, and shall be satisfied." (Is. liii. 11.)

Evening Scripture portion. Is. XLIV. *The promise of the Holy Spirit.*

JOHN VII. 40 to end.—*The enemies of Christ dispute concerning him.*

WE here read of the effect of the discourse Jesus delivered in the presence of the officers that came to take him. Many people were there, and they expressed different opinions concerning him. Some thought he was *the prophet*, or the messenger that was to be sent before Christ, to prepare his way. (Mal. iii. 1.) These people did not know that John the Baptist was *that* prophet. Others thought that Jesus was *the Messiah.* There was another party that made objections to this belief. They imagined that Jesus had been *born* in Galilee, though he had only been *brought up* there; and they did not know that he was of the family of David. They remembered that the Scriptures had prophesied that the Messiah should be born in Bethlehem, of the family of David; therefore they thought that Jesus could not be the true Messiah. But had they made diligent inquiries, they would have found that the reports concerning him were false, and that he had been born in Bethlehem, and was of the family of David. These people were much to blame for their negligence. How many persons are now in error, because they have not made diligent inquiries! They believe the reports they hear against the ministers of Christ;—they believe the objections that infidels make against the Bible, and they never examine into the truth of these reports and objections. They do not consider the importance of the subject, or they would not be able to rest till they had discovered the truth.

We find that the officers returned to their masters without having taken Jesus. The reason they gave for their conduct was, "Never man spake like this man." They had been awed by the power of his words. When God pleases, he can make the words of his servants strike awe into their enemies, so that they dare not lift up their hands against them. Scoffers have sometimes entered into the assemblies of God's people with an intention to hurt them, and have been constrained to give up their designs. A daring sinner once prepared a weapon with which he intended to murder a holy man who came to seek the lost among the haunts of vice. He heard him read Isaiah liv. Struck by the words, "No weapon that is formed against thee shall prosper," he renounced his purpose, and even confessed his guilt.

In the conclusion of the chapter, we find an instance of the power of divine grace. Nicodemus, who was once so timid as to go to Jesus by night for fear of the Jews, was grown so bold as to acknowledge him openly in the midst of the council. He was himself one of that council, called the Sanhedrim, composed of seventy chief persons among the Jews. There have always been *some* among the honorable of the earth who have done homage to the Lord of glory. Such persons are exposed to sharper trials than those in humbler stations, and they require a very large measure of grace to enable them to remain firm amidst the derision of their equals in power and grandeur. But God is with them when they stand up in the midst of their enemies, and he will defend his defamed servants. What would a Father feel who should overhear one of his children pleading his cause with rebellious brothers! Does not our God listen with delight to all who take his part when men rise up against him?

Evening Scripture portion.
Jeremiah XXVI. *Jeremiah's apprehension and acquittal.*

John VIII. 1–11.—*Christ refuses to condemn a sinful woman.*

How much wisdom the Lord Jesus showed in the manner in which he withstood the artful designs of the Jews! The Pharisees had in vain endeavored to seize him by *force*,—and now they sought to entrap him by *fraud*. Nicodemus, in the council, had inquired, "Doth our law judge any man before it hear him, and know what he doeth?" The Pharisees seem to have taken these words as a hint to find some accusation against the Lord. They thought that by bringing this woman before him they placed him in a difficulty from which he could not escape; because, if he *condemned* her, they might accuse him to the Romans of interfering in the government, and if he *acquitted* her, they might say he contradicted the law of Moses, by which she was sentenced to die.

But how completely all their expectations were confounded! They desired to hear the Lord pass sentence against the *woman*, but they were compelled to hear him pass sentence on *themselves*. For when he replied, "He that is without sin among you, let him first cast a stone;" the conscience of each accuser was troubled, and one by one the whole band of enemies retreated ashamed from his presence!

Conscience may slumber long, but it often suddenly awakes. God can arouse it when he pleases. Sometimes in this life, it stings a sinner and forces him to confess his iniquities. But its power will be better known at the day of judgment, when all the wicked will be made to feel the justice of their own condemnation.

While the guilty Jews were escaping from the temple, the Lord was stooping down to write upon the ground. It appears that he had not looked up to observe their confusion. But after they were gone, he lifted himself up to speak to the sinful woman. There she was standing in the midst! How awful was her situation at that moment! She was in the presence of one who might have condemned her to everlasting destruction. Instead of condemning, he began to converse with her, "Woman, where are those thine accusers? Hath no man condemned thee?" Her answer was full of reverence and awe. "No man, Lord." With what feelings must she have awaited the Lord's next words! They were full of mercy, and also of holiness: "Neither do I condemn thee; go, and sin no more."

Jesus did not come into the world to act as an earthly judge; but hereafter he will condemn the wicked, as well as save the righteous. This woman will stand before him at the day of judgment; she will then hear either that she is pardoned or condemned. We know nothing of her history after this interview. Was her heart drawn to the Lord by his merciful treatment, or did she go from his presence to plunge into new crimes? It is an awful thing to abuse mercy. Can we remember any period in our lives when we seemed to be on the point of receiving the punishment due to our sins, and when the Lord, instead of dealing with us as we deserved, spared us? Ought not such forbearance to win our love? There was a dying girl who first learned to love the Saviour from reading the account of his treatment of this sinful woman. Though she had never committed open transgressions, she knew she was a sinner, and needed pardon. When she read this history, she felt that Jesus was infinitely gracious, and she believed that he would not cast *her* out.

Evening Scripture portion. Ez. XVIII. 19 to end. "*Why will ye die?*"

JOHN VIII. 12–20.—*Christ declares that the Father is his witness*

WE behold our blessed Saviour again surrounded by those enemies who had so lately retreated *ashamed* from his presence. The *officers* had refused to take him, after hearing him invite the thirsty to come and drink. But the *Pharisees* persisted in their wicked designs, though they heard him say, "I am the light of the world: he that followeth me shall not walk in darkness, but shall have the light of life." Instead of following the light, they accused him of speaking falsehood, and insolently said, "Thou bearest record of thyself: thy record is not *true*." They referred to words Jesus had once uttered, "If I bear witness of myself, my witness is not true," (John v. 31,) but by this he meant, "If I *only* bear witness of myself, and have no *other* witness, *then* my record is not true." But He had another witness, even the Father, who had declared by a voice from heaven that Jesus was his beloved Son, and who had enabled him to do astonishing miracles.

The Pharisees scornfully inquired, "Where is thy Father?" How different from the request which an apostle afterwards made, "Show us the Father, and it sufficeth us!" These unbelieving Jews did not desire to know the Father; yet they thought they knew him already. Jesus told them plainly, "Ye neither know me, nor my Father." Would He say this to any of us, if He were now to speak to us? No reasonable creature can be happy, who does not know his Creator.

If we were not sinful creatures, the first desire of our hearts would be to know God. A child desires to see his parent. If a mother were to tell her little son that his father, who had long been absent in a distant country, would soon return, would not the child be glad? But if the child were wilful and wayward, and had heard that his father would restrain him from fulfilling his sinful inclinations, in that case he would not desire to see him return. Men have heard that God hates evil, and therefore they do not desire to know Him.

If they were not sinful, they would learn to know him from the works of *creation*. It is written, "That which may be known of God is manifest in them, for God hath showed it unto them." (Rom. i. 19.) How hath he showed it unto them? "By the things that are made." By the earth, and sea, the sun, moon, and stars; by the animals—from the enormous whale that agitates the ocean, down to the tiny insect that floats in the breeze. But men did *not* gain the knowledge of God by the works of creation. "They glorified him not as God."

The works of *Providence* are even greater than those of creation. It is of those works that David speaks in the Psalms, when he says, "How great are thy works!" (Ps. xcii. 5.) If men were not sinful, they would learn to know God from the works of Providence. St. Paul said to the Athenians, God "hath made of one blood all nations of men for to dwell on all the face of the earth, and hath determined the times before appointed, and the bounds of their habitation; that they should seek the Lord, if haply they might feel after him, and find him." (Acts xvii. 26, 27.) But did men feel after him? No: they wandered farther and farther from him.

But in the fulness of time God sent forth his Son.

And why did He send Him? That He might teach us to know God. And all who believe in Jesus Christ know the Father. They know Him to be the God of holiness, and yet of mercy; so holy, that he will not clear the guilty; and yet so merciful, that he will pardon the vilest sinner who trusts in the blood of his Son. But they never could have known Him, if Jesus had not come in the likeness of sinful flesh, and died upon the cross for their sins.

Do we know God? Do we *desire* to know him? How awful it

would be to hear the Lord Jesus at the judgment-day declare, "If ye had known me, ye should have known my Father also." No one will be able to reply, "I desired to know God, but could not find him." O no, all who seek to know Him, shall find Him.

Evening Scripture portion. **Rom. I. 1–23.** *The knowledge of God.*

JOHN VIII. 21–27.—*Christ warns his enemies against dying in their sins.*

THE Lord Jesus plainly told his *disciples* in their retired conversations, that he should be crucified; but he did not speak so plainly to his *enemies:* he only gave them hints concerning his approaching death. When he said, "I go my way," they understood him not. At last they formed a conjecture concerning his meaning, and said, "Will he kill himself?" They did not venture to put the question to the Lord himself, but consulted with each other on the subject. He knew their thoughts, and by his reply showed that he had alluded to his death. He would not indeed kill *himself.* Those who with wicked *tongues* now insulted him, with wicked *hands* would slay him. He would die upon the cross, but far worse would be the manner of *their* death: they would die,—perhaps, in a bed, surrounded by weeping friends, but—*in their sins.*

When the Lord said to his enemies, "Ye are from beneath," he did not mean to say that they had ever lived with Satan in hell; but he meant that they partook of the nature of Satan, and were like him in pride, and hatred, and unbelief. All the inhabitants of this world are divided into two classes: of one it may be said, they are from *beneath;* of the other it may be declared, they are from *above,* having been born again by the Holy Spirit. An old writer observes, that though the children of different families are mingled in the day, when night comes on they return home to their fathers' houses. When the night of death comes, the children of Satan will go to their father's dark and horrible abode, and the children of God will go to their Father's light and glorious abode. And whither shall *we* go? Remember the words of Jesus, "If ye believe not that I am he, ye shall die in your sins."

There is only one way of becoming the child of God: it is by believing in Jesus. The Jews scornfully inquired, "Who art thou?" Let us *humbly* ask the same question. Let us say as Saul did when Jesus spoke to him from heaven, "Who art thou, Lord?" He will reveal himself to all who desire to know him. He left his Father's house to seek us who were wandering about this world. He desires to bring us to his home. There is room for us, as well as for Him, in the palace of the great King. He said to his beloved apostles, "In my Father's house are many mansions." When night comes on it will be delightful to go to such a home. But what would it be to feel in dying that we were not going to God! A woman who had lived a careless life, expressed no fears on her dying bed, till—the last day and night of her life arrived. Then she was heard to cry out repeatedly, "I am going, I am going—but *not* to God."

Evening Scripture portion. Rev. XIV. *Judgment and salvation.*

JOHN VIII. 28–42.—*He instructs the new believers.*

WE have followed the Saviour through scenes of contempt and insult; but at length we hear, that while he rebuked his enemies, many *believed* on him. The Lord did not overlook these new believers. As the mother bestows unceasing care, and peculiar tenderness on her infant, especially when so weakly that its life seems doubtful; so the Saviour turned towards those who had just embraced the truth, and addressed to them words of counsel and encouragement. Are there any of us who need such instruction? Let us consider the counsels of the all-wise Saviour to his weak followers.

"If ye continue in my word, then are ye my disciples indeed; and ye shall know the truth, and the truth shall make you free." *Continuance* is the difficulty. To believe for a little while will not save the soul. There are many stony-ground hearers, who receive the word with joy. There are many thorny-ground hearers, who bring forth fruit, but not to perfection. These do not *continue* in the word.

What blessings are promised to those who, in spite of enemies, and temptations, and afflictions, *continue* in the word! Christ said to them, "The truth shall make you free." Are we not free by nature? Men think they are free—that they can *do* what they will, and *be* what they please. But they are deceived. The Jews misunderstood the nature of the freedom of which Jesus spoke: they thought that he spoke of national freedom. But they did not even possess *that* freedom; for though they *said*, "We were never in bondage to any man," the assertion was not true: at that very time they were in bondage to the Romans, and paid taxes to the Roman emperor.

But it was not of *national* freedom that Jesus spoke; he meant the freedom of the *spirit*. All sinners are slaves. "Whosoever committeth sin is the servant (or slave) of sin." Satan has power over the spirits of sinners. He stirs up the evil passions of their hearts, and urges them to commit sinful actions. God *restrains* him in the exercise of his power; but He has not yet *deprived* him of it. How then can sinners be made free? By believing in the Son of God. Then their chains fall off, their cruel master flees, and their gracious deliverer adopts them into his family.

A little parable seems to be contained in our Lord's discourse. In one large house there dwell together a numerous family. God is the master of this house, and knows the character of each member. This house contains all those who profess to believe in Christ. But some of its inmates are really the slaves of Satan, while some are the children of God. Shall Satan's slaves *always* remain in the house? No; they shall be cast out. But the children of God shall *never* quit their father's roof. "The servant abideth not in the house forever; but the son abideth ever." And when the servants of Satan are cast out, then the children of God shall ascend to the upper room, where their Father unveils his glorious countenance, and invites his elder sons and daughters to partake of the heavenly feast.

Evening Scripture portion. Rom. VI. *The slavery of sin.*

JOHN VIII. 43–50.—*Christ accuses his enemies of being the children of Satan.*

IT may well excite dismay in the bosom of a human creature to hear these words; "Ye are of your father the devil." A faithful minister once preached from these words in a village church, to a numerous congregation of very poor people. Great was the consternation with which some of them heard, for the first time, that those who lived in sin were the children of the devil. Poor neighbors met one another, and lamented with tears over the awful truth. Nor did they lament or weep in vain; for some who were then the children of wrath, became by faith the children of God. One of these blessed converts, in extreme old age, would often lift up her withered hands, and thank God for having shown her the danger she was in.

And what are the marks by which the children of Satan may be known? The marks are the features of their father. He was a murderer and a liar from the beginning,—even from that awful and mysterious hour when he departed from the truth; for he was created in the truth. God, who created all things, can create nothing evil; therefore Satan and all the wicked angels were originally good. *How* evil sprang up in them, no human creature knows; it is a deep mystery, not revealed to us. It is sufficient for us to know that Satan was good—that he became evil, and will continue so forever. After his fall, he was a murderer, and sought to murder the souls of Adam and Eve, by tempting them to sin, and to murder *in them* the whole human race—for in Adam all die. So dreadful a crime was never again perpetrated upon earth, till—Satan's own children, at the instigation of their father, murdered the Son of God, who came down from heaven to save sinners.

Satan is not a *murderer* only; he is also a *liar*. He commits his murders by *means* of lies: he used a lie to murder Eve, when he said, "Thou shalt not surely die." And still he murders by lies; for he tempts men by *deceiving* them. He persuades them that sin will make them happy, and that it is not dangerous. Above all, he speaks lies of God. He endeavored to set Adam and Eve against their best Friend, by slanders; for he said that God had forbidden them to eat of the fruit of the tree, because He feared they should become wise.

Satan still speaks lies of God, representing him as a God whose service is bondage, whose promises are unfaithful, and whose threatenings are uncertain. Thus men are induced to keep at a distance from God. As long as men believe Satan's lies, they cannot hear God's words, or understand the Bible. But Jesus came to undeceive us, and to defend his Father's character. Why will not men *believe* his report? Shall we still be deceived by the lies of Satan, when Jesus tells us the truth! Satan has deceived *all* who have trusted in him; the Son of God has never deceived one. Who ever heard of a dying believer exclaiming, "I have been deceived: I trusted in the Saviour, and I have found his promises vain?" No true believer, however afflicted, has spoken thus. All dying Christians have said by their *looks*, and many by their *words*, "He is a faithful God."

Evening Scripture portion. Jude. *The fall of Satan.*

JOHN VIII. 51 to end.—*Christ speaks of Abraham.*

ONE of the most precious promises ever made, was received with the most insulting contempt. The Lord declared, "If a man keep my saying, he shall never see death." The Jews replied, "Now we know thou hast a devil." If they had not been themselves the children of Satan, they would not have uttered such language. They did not choose to understand the meaning of the promise. They said, "The prophets are dead." But to what did our Lord refer when he said, "If a man keep my saying, he shall never see death?" He did not speak of the separation of soul and body. That is not death to the righteous, for the soul rests with God, while the body sleeps in the grave. He spoke of another death, called the second death. It is the separation of soul and body *from God* forever and ever. That is death. None shall taste it who keep Christ's saying. What saying? His saying concerning himself, that He is the Son of God and the Saviour of men. For on another occasion he declared, "God so loved the world, that he gave his only-begotten Son, that whosoever *believeth in him* should not perish, but should have *everlasting life.*"

When the Jews insolently inquired, "Whom makest thou thyself?" the Lord did not choose to tell them plainly who *He* was; but he told them who *they* were NOT. They professed to be the children of God. But Jesus told them that because they said "He is our God," they were "*liars.*" How awful is the situation of that man who cannot say, "My God," without uttering a falsehood! We pity the child who cannot say to any living person, "*My* father," or "*My* mother;" but how much more ought we to pity the soul who cannot look up to heaven and say, "My God!"

What a testimony Jesus bore to his faithful servant Abraham! He said, "Your father Abraham rejoiced to see my day, and he saw it and was glad." The great joy of Abraham's life was not his beloved Isaac, but his more beloved Saviour. It was that promised Son who was the chief object of his faith. When God said, "In thy seed shall all the families of the earth be blessed," then he looked forward to the coming of the Saviour of the world. Then "he believed God, and it was accounted unto him for righteousness." Even *Abraham* was saved, not by his *own* righteousness, but by the righteousness of *another.* Like us, he was by *nature* a child of wrath, and it was by *grace* he became the friend of God, and the father of believers.

The Jews continued to distort the words of Jesus. Because he said, that Abraham had seen his day, they said, "Hast thou seen Abraham?" who had lived two thousand years before. And what was the Saviour's reply? He did not say, "I have seen Abraham;" he said much *more* than that. He did not say, "Before Abraham I *was.*" He said more than that. "Before Abraham I *am.*" The expression "I am," gives the idea of an existence that had no beginning, and will have no end. Such is God—the first and the last. No human understanding can grasp the idea of existence without beginning and without ending. But let us rejoice in the thought that before *we* were God existed. He ever lived. No plans could be formed against us, *before* He had arranged every thing concerning us! "Known unto God are all his works from the beginning of the world." (Acts xv. 18.)

Evening Scripture portion. Gal. III. ***The faith of Abraham.***

LUKE X. 17–20.—*The return of the seventy disciples.*

IN the first verse of this chapter it is recorded that the Lord sent out seventy disciples to preach. Now we hear of their return.

While they had been visiting the towns and villages, their Lord had been engaged in teaching at Jerusalem. We have heard to what trials he was exposed in that wicked city from the scoffs of his enemies. How great must have been the relief to his sorrowful spirit, when he found himself again in the midst of his attached followers! The messengers returned with *joy*. They rejoiced because the devils had been subject unto them through Christ's name. The Saviour seems to have partaken of their joy when he uttered these mysterious words: "I beheld Satan like lightning fall from heaven." Could any sight be more suited to occasion joy to Satan's great enemy and conqueror? When a cruel tyrant is slain, the captives in his dungeons are set free. An interesting account has been written of the destruction of the Inquisition at Madrid in 1809. The wicked men who ruled over that dreadful prison were slaughtered by the French soldiers. At the same time the dungeons were visited, and were found full of miserable captives. Those who had been for many years pining under the fear of death, were suddenly restored to the light of day, and to all the enjoyments of life. Great was the joy felt by the soldiers who wrought this great deliverance!

But who can conceive the joy that our Saviour felt when he looked forward to the consequences of Satan's downfall! Already the people of God are delivered from his power. The day shall come when the old serpent will deceive the nations no more. At the end of the world he will be cast into the lake of fire and brimstone, and "shall be tormented day and night forever." (Rev. xx. 10.) This deliverance Jesus obtained for us by his own death.

Christ gave his disciples power to tread on serpents and scorpions, and over all the power of the enemy. Did He mean *literal* serpents or *spiritual* serpents? Did He not mean *both?* The disciples were shielded from the attacks of all venomous creatures. In our Lord's parting charge he said to them: "These signs shall follow them that believe: they shall take up serpents." (Mark xvi. 18.) In the same charge he said also, "In my name they shall cast out devils." Christ must have alluded to Satan and his angels when he spoke of "all the power of the enemy."

Well might the disciples rejoice in the wonderful gifts they possessed. Yet they had a greater cause for joy. Their names were written in heaven. The Lamb has a book of life, in which he has written the names of all who shall never taste the second death. It contains not only the names of the *apostles*, but of *all* who love Jesus. As a father writes down in his great Family Bible the names of all his children, so God writes down in the book of his remembrance the names of all *His* children. A father may some day have to read, with a sigh and with a tear, the list of his family; but Jesus shall never lose one of the members of *His* family; *they* shall live forever who are written in the book of life. Is it our chief desire to have our names written there? If this be our *supreme* desire, we must be saved. Those who perish, perish because they *will* not come and ask for life.

O that this awful sentence might awaken those who are now unconcerned about their precious souls! "Whosoever was not found written in the book of life, was cast into the lake of fire." (Rev. xx. 15.)

Evening Scripture portion. Rev. XX. *The book of life.*

LUKE X. 21–24.—*The Saviour's joy.*

A MAN's character is shown by the causes of his grief and of his joy! We might learn to know ourselves better than we do, if each would inquire, "What are the things that please, and grieve me most?" We shall find that we are by nature selfish,—that we are too much concerned about the events that befall *ourselves*, and too little about those that befall our fellow-creatures. Above all, we are naturally indifferent to the glory of God. None, except those who are converted, care in the least degree whether God is honored or despised.

The object that lay nearest the Saviour's heart was the glory of his Father. He rejoiced in spirit, because his Father had revealed to babes the things concerning Himself, for by this means the glory of God is increased. If the wise and learned alone were saved, it would seem as if they had saved themselves by their own wisdom and learning; but when it is babes chiefly who are saved, then it is clear that God saved them by *His* great power. Those are compared to babes whom the world esteems foolish and ignorant. Most of the disciples were chosen from among such people. The world called Peter and John *unlearned.* (Acts iv. 13.) The apostle Paul was *not* unlearned; but he did not *trust* to his own wisdom, but came like a babe to learn of Jesus. None can explain the *manner* in which God teaches the soul. We do know the *subject* of his teaching—it is Himself. We are by nature unacquainted with God. To know Him is the great object of life. To die without knowing Him is to perish. The Saviour, in his prayer just before he was crucified, said to his Father, "This is eternal life, to *know* thee, the only true God, and Jesus Christ whom thou hast sent."

No man comes to Jesus till he has heard and learned of the Father. Then he goes as a penitent sinner to the Saviour. How does Jesus receive him? He has declared, "Him that cometh unto me I will in nowise cast out." He teaches the sinner to know the Father; He shows him the Father's love in sending his Son to be the Saviour of the world; he shows it to the *heart*, as well as to the *understanding*. It is with the *heart* we know our friends; it is with the heart we must know God. How different is the feeling that we have when we have become intimate with a person, from that which we experience when we have only heard him described, and have not known him *ourselves!*

We may hear a great deal about God, but till we listen to his voice speaking to our hearts we cannot know Him. It is sweet to hear him say, "Seek ye my face," but sweeter still to hear him declare, "Thou art mine." Then the heart, moved by the Spirit, answers as David did, "Lord, thy face will I seek," and "Thou art my God."

Jesus has observed every desire that has ever entered into the heart of his creatures, and he remembers those of his servants of old. The ancient prophets desired to know him; there were even kings who esteemed the knowledge of God far above their earthly treasures. Such were the feelings of the great Melchisedec, and of the victorious David. But while they were on earth they never knew as much of God as the apostles did while they lived; nor did they ever hear as much as *we* have heard. *Is it our desire to know Him* better than we do? He observes the desires of *our* hearts: and he would be pleased to see in us the same feeling that Moses had, when he said, "I beseech thee, show me thy glory."

Evening Scripture portion. 2 Samuel XXIII. 1–23. ***David's chief desire.***

LUKE X. 25–37.—*The good Samaritan.*

THIS lawyer, who came to Jesus, was a man whose office it was to study the law of God, and to explain it to others. It was therefore to be supposed that he understood it well himself. And he *did* understand the *letter* of it, but *not* the *spirit*. He knew the words of the law, but he was ignorant of their spiritual application.

He came with the wicked intention of insnaring Jesus, by asking him questions that should lead him to give some answer contrary to what Moses had written. But how completely was he foiled in his design! Instead of *answering* his question, "What shall I do to inherit eternal life?" the Lord asked him another question, "How readest thou?" thus showing that he approved what was written by Moses.

The lawyer gave a correct answer. He said that the duty of man consisted in the love of God and the love of his neighbor. But what is this love? It far surpasses man's ideas. Let the angels tell us from their high abodes in glory, what it is to love God. It is to delight in him perpetually, to show forth his praise, and to do his will without weariness and without fault. What is the love of the neighbor? Jesus explained it in the beautiful history of the good Samaritan. *On whom* had the Samaritan mercy? On a *Jew*—a man of a nation whom he had been brought up to detest. Neither did he act from a sense of *duty* alone; he had *compassion* on the poor traveller: he paid him *immediate* attention: he treated him with *tenderness*, binding up his wounds: he *expended* his property upon him, "pouring in oil and wine:" he incurred *fatigue*, and perhaps loss of rest, for he took care of him at night. He made provision for his *future* comfort, by leaving twopence (or two days' wages of a laborer) with the innkeeper, and promised to pay whatever greater sum might be spent, putting no limits on the amount, though he could not know how long the sufferer might languish. And all this he did for a *stranger!* What must that man be to his friend and his brother, who treats a stranger with such generous kindness!

But if we are inclined to think the Samaritan overstepped his duty, let us remember the words of Jesus, "Go thou and do likewise." And when we have done it, we shall still be unprofitable servants, and have only done what it was our duty to do. Remember, remember what HE did for us, who gives the command. The Samaritan showed mercy to a *stranger*, but he showed mercy to his *enemies*. And what mercy! He bore the wrath and curse of God to save us from destruction. None of us *could* bear what he did. But if we have the Spirit of Christ dwelling in us, we shall walk in his steps.

There are at this moment in South Africa, two Moravian missionaries, who have gone to spend their days in a hospital for lepers—among pitiable objects, whose hands and feet are falling off. No one who ever enters that hospital is permitted to leave it. The missionaries saw the door close upon them, and felt content to be banished from human society for the sake of the poor sufferers within.

Let us not be satisfied with admiring the devoted conduct of these men; but let us seek for objects on whom to show mercy. Do we know of none to whom we can be kind? Is there no fatherless child who needs our help? No widow, no stranger, no sufferer, whom we could comfort? Perhaps to-day we may meet with one that we never heard of before. May God put into our hearts the love that dwells in his own, that we may act kindly to every afflicted person we see this day.

Evening Scripture portion. Exodus XXIII. *Kindness to the stranger.*

LUKE X. 28 to end.—*Martha and Mary.*

WHEN a monarch enters into the house of one of his subjects, his looks are observed in order to discover what objects pleased him, his words are treasured up, his minutest actions are noticed and remembered. If the Son of God were to enter into the family of a true believer, with what anxiety would his looks, his words, his actions, be watched! Every sincere disciple would seek with trembling eagerness to ascertain whether the Lord approved his conduct.

And did not those who loved Jesus when he was on earth, experience these feelings? When they saw him approach their dwellings, they must have longed to obtain his company, and when he was seated beneath their roofs, they must have used their utmost endeavors to do him honor. The Lord's visits were, no doubt, hailed with delight by the beloved family of Bethany. Both Martha and Mary desired to please their heavenly guest, but they acted in a very different manner. Martha was so little acquainted with his mind, that she endeavored to provide a sumptuous entertainment; while Mary sat at his feet and heard his word. In the east it is the custom to sit upon the ground or on low couches; therefore there was nothing unusual in Mary's posture. While one sister was listening with devout attention to the words of Jesus, the other was offended because she was left alone to prepare the feast. So confident did she feel of the acceptableness of her services, that she believed the Lord would reprove her sister for not helping her. She said to the Lord, "Dost thou not care that my sister hath left me to serve alone?" If she had been of a more loving spirit, she would have gladly served alone, that her sister at least might enjoy the Saviour's instructions

How many Christians fall into Martha's error! They imagine that much pomp and parade and splendor in religious worship are honorable to God, and they expend strength, and time, and money, in promoting these objects, while they lose many precious opportunities of growing in the knowledge of Christ: and, not content with acting in this manner *themselves*, they often blame those who devote their chief attention to the word of God.

How beautiful an example does Mary afford to those who are unjustly accused by their fellow-Christians! She remained silent, and left it to her Lord to answer for her. Perhaps Martha was surprised at receiving reproof instead of commendation. The sister she blamed was praised, and the conduct she thought so admirable was censured. The Lord will pronounce many sentences at the last day that will surprise even his sincere followers. Though Martha was careful, and troubled about many things, we know that she was a real believer, but she had not so enlightened a mind or so devoted a heart as her meek and lowly sister.

Mary cared as much as Martha for the comfort and honor of her Lord. On another occasion she showed her love by expending her choicest treasures upon his precious body, for she poured the ointment on his head just before his death and burial. But she knew that the day-spring from on high had visited us, "to give light to them that sit in darkness and in the shadow of death," and she opened her heart to receive those living beams.

Do we desire to enjoy the light of life? Let us get alone with Jesus, and speak to him in prayer, and hear what he will say to us in his word.

Evening Scripture portion. Ps. CXIX. 97 to 182. *Love to God's law.*

LUKE XI. 1–13.—*Christ encourages his disciples to pray.*

How blessed must have been those seasons in which the Saviour engaged in prayer with his beloved disciples! Once we find him praying with them on the mount of transfiguration;—at another time in the garden of Gethsemane. On this occasion the name of the place is not recorded. Surely *that* was *hallowed* ground, where the Son of God offered up on the spotless altar of his heart the pure incense of prayer and praise.

After hearing his prayers, the disciples felt conscious of their own inability to pray. They were, like us, compassed with infirmities, and knew not what to pray for as they ought. In the spirit of little children they said to their Master, "Teach us to pray." This petition was pleasing to their Lord: it was immediately granted. The prayer he now taught them he had uttered in their presence when he delivered his sermon on the mount; but the disciples needed *repeated* instructions. It is a prayer for all that can make a human soul happy; nay more—it is a prayer for all that can make the *universe* happy.

The first three petitions may be called *prayers for God*, as it is written in the Psalms: "Prayer also shall be made *for Him* continually." (Psalm lxxii. 15.) The happiness of the universe depends upon God being established upon his throne. All creation would be filled with joy, if the name of the great and holy God were hallowed; if his kingdom were come; if his will were done; as it is written: "Let the floods clap their hands; let the hills be joyful together before the Lord, for He cometh to judge the earth." Were any *other* being raised to this exalted state, he would neither be happy himself, nor would he make his fellow-creatures happy. No Being but God is fit to be adored, to reign over all worlds, and to do what He will. Satan once aspired to sit in the seat of God,—and what was the consequence? He became eternally wretched, and he plunged a host of his angelic companions in the same misery.

There are some petitions in this prayer suitable for *fallen* man alone, in all his weakness and his wo. We are made of clay, and we need *bread;* therefore we say, "Give us our daily bread." We have sinned, and we need *pardon;* therefore we say, "Forgive us our trespasses." We are liable to be conquered by sin and Satan, and we need *deliverance* from their power, and we cry, "Deliver us from evil."

If our hearts are in tune with this prayer, they are right in the sight of God. The unconverted *never* feel desirous for the things mentioned in this prayer, *except* for their daily bread. And are they *satisfied* with daily bread? O no; they are not content with *necessary* things, with food, raiment, and a shelter from the storm; they entertain a thousand exorbitant wishes; they desire pleasure, or praise, or wealth, or some other worldly gift which God has not promised to bestow. Instead of cherishing these unreasonable wishes, the Christian longs for the pardon of his sins, and for his deliverance from the evil one. Will these desires be granted? Will an *ungracious* friend arise to grant a request that is urged in an earnest manner? And shall a *gracious* God refuse to hear fervent prayer? Will a *sinful* father give bread, and *not* a stone to a hungry child; a fish, and *not* a serpent; an egg, and *not* a scorpion? And shall our Holy Father give *hell* to those who ask for *heaven?* Since the beginning of the world He has never treated one of his children in this manner, and He never will.

Evening Scripture portion. Ps. LXV. *The power and goodness of God.*

LUKE IX. 37–44.—*Christ exposes the hypocrisy of the Scribes and Pharisees.*

WE never hear of the Saviour refusing to visit those who besought his company. Yet no scene could have been more trying to his feelings than a Pharisee's house. The society of publicans and sinners was less revolting to Him than that of proud self-righteous Pharisees.

One of his first actions gave offence to his host. Knowing that the Pharisees imagined that washing their hands before dinner rendered them holy, He purposely neglected to observe this custom. The ruling desire of the Pharisees was the *praise of men.* No person can desire *earnestly* both the praise of men and the praise of God; for no man can serve *two* masters. Just in proportion as we seek honor from *men,* we shall be indifferent to honor from *God.* The reward the Pharisees sought was, a high place in the world's esteem. They loved the uppermost seats in the synagogue; (for the most learned and re spected among the Jews were permitted to read the law on the Sabbath-days in their sacred assemblies.) When they entered the market-place, the Pharisees were gratified at receiving tokens of veneration from the multitude; they were constantly seeking the gratification of their pride; and whether in the house of God, or in the public throng, they were thirsting for human honor.

What were the means they pursued in order to obtain it? They diligently observed all the forms of religion: they fasted and made long prayers, and even insisted on giving a tenth of the *smallest* herbs to the priests. But they neglected all *secret* duties. They were so much occupied in pleasing men, that they never thought about pleasing God. *Secret* prayers, *secret* charities, *secret* acts of justice, *secret* feelings of love to God—of all these they knew nothing.

To what did the Lord compare these vain-glorious men? To cups and covered dishes, that looked bright outside, but were full of corruption within: and to graves that were grown over with grass, but that contained dead men's bones.

Are not each of us conscious that we have, *by nature*, a strong desire for the praise of men, and no desire for the praise of God? This is one of the effects of the Fall. Angels are not coveting the admiration of their companions in bliss; their eyes are fixed upon their Father's face, and in *His* smile they live and rejoice.

What confusion it would introduce into heaven were a creature to enter there who wishes to be admired! He would find, that though all the blessed inhabitants *love* one another, that they *admire* God alone, and are perpetually engaged in singing, "Blessing, and glory, and honor, and power be unto Him that sitteth upon the throne, and unto the Lamb, forever and ever." (Rev. v. 13.) How dejected a Pharisee would feel in such a scene!

Does our happiness depend upon our being noticed and honored? If it do, we are not fit for heaven. Job said, "Behold, I am vile." Isaiah said, "I am a man of unclean lips." Abraham said, he was but dust and ashes; David, that he was shapen in iniquity; and Paul, that he was the chief of sinners. Yet these were some of the brightest saints who ever lived upon earth. Do we feel, as they did, unworthy of favor and honor? The wicked boast, "I am not polluted; I am innocent." (Jer. ii. 23, 35.) Some even dare to say to their fellow-sinners, "Stand by thyself, for I am holier than thou." (Is. lxv. 5.) What does God say of such proud sinners? "They are a smoke in my nose." But of a penitent, washed in the blood of Christ, and clothed in his righteousness, He speaks thus: "His beauty shall be as the olive-tree, and his smell as Lebanon." (Hos. xiv. 6.)

Evening Scripture portion. Job XV. ***The insignificance of man.***

LUKE XI. 45 to end.—*Christ exposes the wickedness of the lawyers.*

THE meek and lowly Jesus took no pleasure in denouncing woes upon sinners, but he was too faithful to conceal from them his abhorrence of their crimes.

Among the guests at the Pharisee's house there were some lawyers. They were Scribes of the highest order, whose office it was to explain the law of God to the people. One of them having heard Jesus say, "Wo unto you *Scribes* and Pharisees, hypocrites," (verse 44,) replied, "Master, thus saying, thou reproachest us also." *Reproof* was by him considered as *reproach.* Instead of confessing his sin, and seeking pardon, he only desired to justify himself.

The Lord did not leave these Scribes in ignorance of what particular parts of their conduct he condemned. He mentioned three glaring sins which they committed.

(Verse 46.) "Ye lade men with burdens grievous to be borne, and ye yourselves touch not the burdens with one of your fingers." This was the *first* sin reproved. These lawyers taught the people that they must do many difficult things to please God, such as fasting, washing often, making long prayers; but they did not trouble *themselves* to do the same.

The *second* sin reproved was "building the sepulchres of the prophets." But how was this a sin? It was one branch of the hypocrisy of the Scribes. They did not build the sepulchres of prophets, because they loved their holy characters, but because they thought, that by doing honor to the pious dead, they should appear pious *themselves.* It was evident they really approved of their fathers' persecutions of the prophets. And how was it evident? Because they persecuted the *living* prophets. They *added* to their guilt, when, while their hearts were burning with anger against John the Baptist, or against the Lord Jesus, they desired that a monument should be raised to Elijah, or to some other old prophet. It is easy to praise the *dead;* they cannot offend us by their faithful reproofs, nor shame us by their holy examples. Many praise the reformers and martyrs of ancient days, who hate the piety of a brother, or of a companion.

The *third* sin of the lawyers was, taking away the key of knowledge. This was worse than binding heavy burdens on the people. The burdens might *oppress*, yet they would not *destroy*; but without *knowledge*, the people would perish. If a man took away the key of a place where the fire-engines were kept, and if the whole city were burned through this conduct, how much ashamed he would be to appear among the poor houseless citizens! And how much ashamed will those be at the last day, who have taken away the key of knowledge! Those are guilty of this sin, who keep the Bible out of the hands of the people; and those also are guilty of it who pervert the *doc-*

trines of the Bible, and hide from sinners the only remedy for their guilt,—the blood of the Lord Jesus Christ.

A *faithful* minister takes the key committed to him, and by unlocking the mysteries of God, saves souls from destruction. It is a blessed thing to go into the kingdom of God *ourselves*, and it is a more blessed thing to help *others* to come in with us. The Lord Jesus has declared, "Whosoever, therefore, shall *break* one of these least commandments, and shall *teach* men so, he shall be called the least in the kingdom of heaven: but whosoever shall *do* and *teach* them, the same shall be called great in the kingdom of heaven."

Evening Scripture portion. 2 Chron. XXIV. *Zechariah the prophet.*

LUKE XII. 1–12.—*Christ warns his disciples against hypocrisy.*

WE have lately read the Saviour's warnings to the Scribes and Pharisees; now we find him addressing his own disciples. An immense multitude had been collected by his fame, and were eagerly listening to his wonderful words. Before them all, He plainly said to his disciples, "Beware ye of the leaven of the Pharisees, which is hypocrisy." This was not the first time he had uttered this warning. On one occasion his disciples had not understood what he meant by the leaven of the Pharisees; but now all understood, for he explained the metaphor, and declared that *hypocrisy* was the leaven to which he alluded.

And are the *sincere* disciples of Christ in danger of being infected by hypocrisy? Yes, even they may be *tainted* by this sin, though they cannot be given up to its power; for God will preserve them through faith in his name. Peter, and Barnabas, and several other Christians, were once guilty of an act that bordered on hypocrisy: it is called in Scripture "dissimulation." They dissembled with regard to eating with the Gentiles, and were publicly rebuked by the apostle Paul. (See Gal. ii.)

The Lord suggested a powerful motive to guard the heart against hypocrisy,—the discoveries and exposures of the judgment-day. *Then* all that has been hid will be known. Not only will the mask be torn from the deliberate hypocrite, but the veil which has been cast over any part of the conduct of true believers will be lifted up.

The Lord foresaw all the temptations that would assail his beloved disciples, and he endeavored to strengthen them to meet their trials. One of their most powerful temptations would be (NOT to put on, as the Pharisees did, the *appearance* of religion, but) to *conceal* the love they really felt for their Lord. He knew that bloody crosses and burning flames would be used by their enemies to induce them to deny his name. How tenderly he addresses those who would be called to suffer for his sake! "I say unto you, *my friends*, Be not afraid of them that kill the body." He does not promise his disciples to preserve them from *death:* but he does promise to keep them from *hell.* He does not promise to prevent their being brought before rulers and magistrates; but he does promise to be *with* them in the painful hour, and to teach them by the Holy Ghost what to answer.

How little Peter thought that he should ever be tempted to deny the Son of man! How little he knew that there was comfort for *him* in these words: "Whosoever shall speak a word against the Son of man, it shall be forgiven him!" He spoke against the Son of man when he said in the judgment-hall, "I know not the man;" and when he confirmed his words by oaths and curses. Our Lord knows not only what *trials* we shall suffer, but what *sins* we shall commit. It is most comforting to think that though *all sin* will be followed by *sorrow*, yet that there is only *one* sin that cannot be FORGIVEN. It is the blasphemy against the Holy Ghost, and consists (as we believe) in continuing to oppose the Gospel from deliberate malice, while, at the same time, the Holy Ghost has convinced the mind of its truth. This was the sin of the Pharisees. Though they were fully convinced that Christ was the Son of God, they were determined to hinder the people from believing in him.

Some of Christ's true disciples have been overcome by fear when placed before the bar of cruel judges, and have been tempted to deny their Lord. But how bitterly did Jerome of Prague, and our own Cranmer, bewail their sin; and how fully did the Lord testify his forgiveness by the support he afforded them when bound to the stake! No human heart can conceive the Lord's tenderness for his persecuted people. Could a father forsake a child who had fallen into trouble on *his* account? Can Jesus forsake his people when suffering for *his* sake?

Evening Scripture portion. Gal. II. ***Dissimulation.***

LUKE XII. 13–21.—*The rich fool who was suddenly cut off.*

WHILE Jesus was instructing his disciples in the presence of the multitude, he was interrupted by a man applying to him with this request: "Speak to my brother, that he divide the inheritance with me." This man's thoughts were engrossed by a *perishing* inheritance, while Jesus was pointing to that which fadeth not away.

Had the Lord come into the world to be a judge of temporal affairs, he would have attended to the administration of justice: but he had come for a different purpose, and he spent all his strength and all his time in finishing the work that his Father had given him to do.

He made the request of this man the occasion of warning his disciples against the sin of *covetousness.* He had warned them against *hypocrisy,* one of the chief sins of the Pharisees; and now he bade them beware of *covetousness,* another of their sins. He pointed out the *folly* of covetousness by describing the case of a rich man who was suddenly called away when he had been making plans for future enjoyment. We often hear of these sudden removals, but we do not know the *secret thoughts* of those who are thus unexpectedly cut off. He, who knows all the thoughts of all the men that have ever lived upon earth, has revealed to us what passed in the mind of a certain man just before his death. This man had grown rich through the fertility of his fields; his barns were completely filled with corn, wine, and oil; and he determined to pull down these storehouses, and to build larger. He never thought of distributing among the poor the overflowings of his granary, and it is too probable that much of his property had been acquired by the oppression of his laborers. He made plans for his *own* happiness, but had no desire to make *others* happy. He was so *foolish* as to believe that his *soul* would be satisfied by the abundance of the things he possessed. A beast indeed may be satisfied with a plentiful provision for its body; but a human creature has a *soul* that thirsts for some higher enjoyment than this world can afford. Sumptuous feasts cannot make him happy; nor lovely gardens and splendid houses, nor scientific knowledge and elegant accomplishments;—no, not even affectionate friends and dutiful children. Nothing but communion with God can fill the aching void of the human soul. Adam was happy when he walked with God, but when by sin he lost that privilege, he became wretched. When man returns to God, he feels the first emotions of real bliss. David knew this, therefore he said, "Return unto thy rest, O my soul." How different was David's command to his soul from that of the rich man, who said, "Soul, take thine ease; eat, drink, and be merry!"

But even if the things of this world *could* satisfy an immortal spirit, there is *one* circumstance in our present lot that would embitter every moment. It is the *uncertainty* of life. Many a rich man remembers with uneasiness that he must one day (and he knows not how soon) leave all his possessions. This conviction is like a thorn in many a downy pillow, and in many a glittering crown. But he, whose history the Lord related, had contrived to smother this unpleasant recollection. He was deceived by the fond hope of many years' enjoyment of his riches. Well did he merit the name by which God called him, "Thou *fool!*"

How many lost spirits are now execrating their own *folly* during the short season granted them on earth! What an opportunity we are now enjoying of securing real and eternal happiness! We might *now*, during this life, become rich towards God. Those are truly rich who have *faith* in the Lord Jesus. God has declared that some of the *poor* in this world are *rich* in *faith.* (James ii. 5.) *Faith* is the gold that Christ offers to bestow on all that *ask* it: "I counsel thee to buy of me *gold* tried in the fire, that thou mayest be *rich.*" (Rev. iii. 18.) If faith is in our *hearts*, we shall never hear the summons, "Thou fool, this night thy soul shall be required of thee." But rather, we shall hear in God's appointed time a voice saying to our spirits, "Come up hither." (Rev. iv. 1.

Evening Scripture portion. Eccl. II. ***Search after happiness.***

LUKE XII. 22–34.—*Christ warns his disciples against worldly carefulness.*

DOES the history of the rich man, whose soul was so suddenly required, concern the rich *only?* or does it concern the *poor* also?

It was to the *poor* disciples that Jesus turned after he had related the striking history, and it was to them these words were addressed: "*Therefore* I say unto you, Take no thought for your life, what ye shall eat; neither for the body, what ye shall put on." Covetousness led the *rich* man to say to his soul, "Take thine ease, eat, drink, and be merry;" and covetousness might lead the *poor* disciples to ask, "What shall we eat, what shall we drink, and wherewithal shall we be clothed?"

All sinners are inclined to *over*-value the *creature*, and to *under*-value the *Creator*. The rich man betrayed this disposition by delighting in his well-stored barns, and forgetting his all-sufficient God. The disciples were in danger of repining when their scrips were empty, and of forgetting their all-sufficient God. If you heard a person lamenting greatly because there was no water in his cup, you would suppose that he lived in a dry and thirsty land, where water could not be found; but if you knew that a fountain was playing at his door, then you would be astonished at his lamentations. Is not God a fountain of good? and is He not always near, and able to supply all our need? He does not even limit his goodness to those who acknowledge his benefits: millions of thoughtless beings are fed every day at his table,—men who *will* not thank him, birds and beasts that *cannot.* How many He *remembers* who continually *forget* Him! And can He *forget* those who *remember* Him?

Has he not afforded us abundant proofs of his remembrance of *all* his creatures? Every little bird that sings among the branches, every painted flower that blooms among the grass, is a witness of the Lord's loving-kindness. Each seems to reproach the child of

God with his unbelieving fears, and to say, "Be not of doubtful mind."

The Lord has so formed his living creatures that they need continual supplies of food to preserve their existence. *Why* has he formed us thus? Was it not to teach us dependence upon Himself? As we behold the throngs of people that pass along the street, the thought may naturally arise, "How have all these people obtained their bread this day?" The reply is, "Through the kind providence of God." *Some* of them, indeed, (unwilling to trust to this kind Providence,) have resorted to wicked means to gain their living; they have acted dishonestly and deceitfully. But had they all sought his kingdom and righteousness, would not their heavenly Father have fed them from *His* own hand? Undoubtedly he would. It is awful to think what sins people are led to commit through want of trust in God; they steal, they tell lies, they break the Sabbath, they sell pernicious liquors, and corrupting books; because they believe, that if they did not use these wicked means of gaining a livelihood, they would be left to starve.

It is not surprising that those who do not *know* God should not trust him. The surprising thing is, that any who *do* know him should doubt his watchful care! Has he promised to give a *kingdom* to his little flock, and will he deny them daily *bread?* Has God had mercy on your *soul,* and will he neglect your *body?* Do you believe that He is *love,* and do you think that He will treat you as if He *hated* you?

In the land of Canada there once lived a mother, who in her eagerness to obtain intoxicating drink from a newly-arrived ship, left her babe upon the landing-place, and *forgot* to take it up again. It lay all night neglected and forlorn, and perished before morning. That mother was counted a *monster.* The Lord says to his children, "Can a woman forget her sucking child? Yea, they may forget, yet will I not forget thee." (Is. xlix. 15.) Yet where is the Christian who places as much confidence in his Heavenly Father, as a little child places in his earthly parents?

Evening Scripture portion. Phil. IV. *The Lord's care of his people.*

LUKE XII. 35–48.—*Christ exhorts his disciples to watch for his second coming.*

THERE are three short parables contained in the passage we have just read. In the first of them Christ compares himself to a *master,* and his disciples to *servants.*

He is a master who is expected to return from his wedding to a feast prepared at his own house. It is the duty of the servants to be ready to *receive* their lord; therefore they must have their lights burning. They must also *wait* upon him, and therefore they must be girded, as men in the East are, when about to engage in active employment.

What a joyful view this parable gives of the coming of Christ! There is a marriage supper prepared for the Lamb who once was slain. The servants who are found watching shall be the guests at that feast, and their Lord shall condescend to serve them: they shall hunger no more, neither thirst any more, for the Lamb himself shall feed them.

The next parable compares the coming of Christ to the coming of a *thief*, who always endeavors to attack the house at an unexpected moment. What a *dreadful* view this parable gives of the coming of Christ! How unlike it is to the *first* parable! Will the coming of the Lord be to *some* like the breaking in of a thief? The apostle Paul declares that just when the ungodly are saying, "Peace and safety," then sudden destruction cometh upon them; and they shall not escape. "But ye, brethren, are not in darkness, that that day should overtake *you* as a thief." We see, therefore, why two such *different* parables were used by our Lord to represent the *same* event. He intended to teach us that while some have reason to *rejoice* at the expectation of his coming, others have reason to *tremble* at the thought.

It appears that Peter was alarmed by the latter parable: for he asked this question, "Lord, speakest thou this parable unto *us*, or even to *all*?" His Lord answered the question by relating another parable on the same subject as the former. In this parable he spoke of one servant who was set over the rest, and whom he called a *steward*, and who would be *most* guilty if he betrayed the trust reposed in him. The apostles were stewards, and all ministers are stewards. The word of God is the food, which they are to dispense to the rest of the household. Now, if a steward in his Lord's absence were to begin to ill-treat the servants, and to waste his master's property in rioting and drunkenness, how very much displeased his lord would be with him when he returned! The Scribes had reason to tremble as they listened to this parable; for though it was not *spoken* to them, it *applied* to them.

What idea would lead a steward to conduct himself in a disorderly and oppressive manner? The idea that his lord would not return *soon*. He would say, "My lord *delayeth* his coming." He might not go so far as to believe he would *never* return at all, and say with the scoffers, "Where is the promise of his coming?" but he would not be less guilty than those scoffers; he would be *more* guilty, because he is *intrusted* with more. To abuse *confidence* is to commit the worst sort of injury. In human laws the crime is always considered great in proportion to the trust that had been reposed in the criminal. A servant who betrays his master is counted more guilty than if he had been a stranger. There will be *degrees* in the misery of the lost; and the *deepest* degree of misery will be endured by him who abused the *highest* privileges.

Now let us, like Peter, ask this question: "Speakest thou this parable unto *us?*" Surely the Lord speaks to *us* in *all* these parables: for though we may not be stewards in the same sense that ministers are, we all have *some* charge committed to us. Are we acting *now* as we should wish we had done, if to-morrow we were to find ourselves on the brink of eternity? Is there any sin we are practising, which we should renounce if we thought this day was our last! Who can say that it may *not* be our last! With some persons this *is* the last *day*,—with many more it is the last *week*,—with thousands it is the last *month*,—with millions the last year. Are we prepared to meet the Lord? If *not*, why do we not prepare immediately? There is a fountain opened for sin, in which we may *immediately* wash. Yet how many have never washed in it! If Christ were to come now, he would find them in their sins. Say not, "He will not come *yet;*" for remember it is very dangerous even to think, "My lord *delayeth* his coming."

Evening Scripture portion. 1 Thess. V. *The Lord's second coming.*

LUKE XII. 49–53.—*Christ foretells that the Gospel will occasion divisions.*

THE Lord Jesus is called the Prince of *peace;* yet he did not come to bring *peace* upon the earth, but rather *division.*

Is not this surprising? How can we understand the song of the angels, who joined in chorus at his birth, saying, "*Peace* on earth, good-will to men?" The difficulty, however, may be explained.

Jesus came to bring *divisions first*, and *afterwards peace.* And why did he bring *divisions* first? Why not *peace* from beginning to end? It was because the *wickedness of man* opposes the peaceful doctrines of the holy Gospel.

Can any thing show in a stronger light the depravity of the human heart than the manner in which the Gospel has been received by the world? If any doubt whether man is *very* wicked, and very *far* gone from original righteousness, let them reflect on this fact. If pardon were now offered to the evil spirits in darkness, could they reject the boon with more contempt than the *world* in general has rejected the offer of pardon in the Gospel? But the world has not been satisfied with *rejecting* it—they have persecuted those few happy persons who have accepted it. Even now there is scarcely a large family to be found, *all* of whom have embraced the gracious offer. In many families there are *none;* in others, there is *one* or *two* who have believed, while the rest despise both the message and those who believe it. Sometimes it is a pious parent, who is despised by his thoughtless children: sometimes it is a pious child, who is opposed by his worldly parent. *Nations* are divided in the same manner as *families*. No *wars* have been so bitter as *religious* wars; no persecution so bloody as *religious* persecutions, or, rather, the persecutions of the religious. Shall we think ill of religion because it produces these effects? As well might we deem the medicines of the physician hurtful, because at first they often increase the sufferings of the patient. The Lord Jesus, who foresaw all events, *rejoiced* that his Gospel would be preached in every land.

He said, "I am come to send *fire* on the earth, and what will I if it be already kindled?" What is the meaning of these words?

"What will I?" Do I wish it to be otherwise?

"If it be already kindled," if even *now* the Gospel has begun to create confusion.

The Prince of peace was willing that for a while confusion should prevail, in order that happiness at length might fill the earth, and endure forever. He was willing himself to encounter the most bitter sufferings, in order that afterwards he might be exalted to God's right hand. The baptism he desired was a baptism of blood. Bathed in his *own* blood, he suffered for our sins in Gethsemane and Calvary. He was straitened till this baptism was accomplished. He longed to finish his work, and to receive his reward; and now he longs for the period when the earth will be no more steeped in blood, but covered by the waters of righteousness. He has commanded us to pray for that glorious time, and to say, "Thy kingdom come." In those days shall "the righteous flourish, and *abundance* of *peace* as long as the moon endureth." (Ps. lxxii. 7.) When Jesus comes the second time, he will put an end to all divisions, whether in families or between nations. "Violence shall no more be heard in thy land, wasting nor destruction within thy borders." For this delightful day the saints earnestly hope, and "with patience *wait*." (Rom. viii. 25.)

Evening Scripture portion. Micah VII. *Family divisions.*

LUKE XII. 54 to end.—*Christ reproves the people for not discerning the signs of the time.*

THE long discourse contained in this chapter was addressed to the *disciples*, excepting these few words at the conclusion. They were addressed to the *people*—to the immense multitude who surrounded the Saviour, and who were pressed so closely together that they trod upon each other.

The Lord had spoken to his own disciples with *tenderness*. He had called them his "*friends*," (see ver. 4.) "My friends, be not afraid of them that kill the body." But he spoke to the people with *displeasure*. He called them "*hypocrites*." This was the name he had given to the Scribes and Pharisees. The people were like the teachers they admired. Blind leaders have blind followers. *Hypocritical* teachers have hypocritical disciples. The Scribes would not discern the signs of the time, and the people who reverenced them would not discern them either. "Like people, like priest." (Hos. iv. 9.)

As there are certain appearances by which close observers are able to foretell the kind of *weather* that may be expected, so there are certain signs by which reflecting minds might discover the kind of *time* that is approaching. When the time for the deliverance of Israel from Egypt drew nigh, the parents of Moses knew it was near, and Moses knew it also; but the Israelites understood not the signs of that time. When the captivity of Babylon drew nigh, the people of God knew the time; but the world knew it not. When the time for Israel's release approached, Daniel knew it; but many of the captives knew it not. When, in the fulness of time, God sent forth his Son, some were prepared to receive him. Simeon and Anna knew the signs of *the time*, and spoke of Jesus to those who *looked for redemption* in Jerusalem; but the world knew not the signs of the time.

Thus it shall be in the *last* time. It is prophesied in Daniel, that the wise shall understand, but none of the wicked shall understand. (See Dan. xii. 10.) The wicked shall go on doing wickedly, just as the people did before the flood.

Had the Jews of old understood the *time*, they would have repented before it was too late. They knew not that their opportunity would be so short. The Saviour would remain with them but a little while, the apostles would preach only for a few years, and then their city would be destroyed, their temple burnt, and their country laid desolate.

Their compassionate Lord knew that their day of grace was fast hastening to a close, and he related a little parable (which he had before related in his sermon on the mount) to warn them of their danger. He compared the nation to a criminal on his way to the judge. While on his way, the criminal had the opportunity to entreat his enemy to be reconciled; but if he neglected this short opportunity, he would be tried, condemned, and cast into a prison, whence he would never escape.

The Lord knows for how long a period we shall enjoy the privileges we now possess: He has numbered our Sabbaths, our meetings together as a family to read and pray, our interviews with pious friends, our opportunities of secret prayer. In mercy He often gives signs before He removes these sacred privileges. Sometimes the signs are terrible judgments inflicted upon others, and gracious deliverances granted to ourselves. Thus the Lord said to Israel, "I have overthrown some of you, as God overthrew Sodom and Gomorrah: and ye were as a firebrand plucked out of the burning; yet have ye not returned unto me, saith the Lord." (Amos iv. 11.) "Prepare to meet thy God, O Israel." The Lord Jesus is now easy to be entreated, and ready to forgive; but when He is on his throne of judgment, he will hearken to no entreaties, and grant no forgiveness.

In the lone land of deep despair,
  No Sabbath's heavenly light shall rise:
No God regard your bitter prayer,
  No Saviour call you to the skies.

Now God invites, how bless'd the day!
  How sweet the gospel's heavenly sound!
Come, sinners, haste, O haste away,
  While yet a pardoning God is found.

Evening Scripture portion. Dan. XII. *The time of the end.*

LUKE XIII. 1–5.—*Christ speaks of two awful events that had lately happened at Jerusalem.*

IT is most interesting to us to know what passes in heaven respecting ourselves. In this passage, some of the light of the other world is let into our dark prison.

The discourses of the Lord were often interrupted by the questions and remarks of his hearers. On this occasion some of those present spoke of an awful event that had lately happened in Jerusalem. Perhaps they thought that this event was unknown to the Lord till they told him of it. But all things that ever had occurred, or ever would occur, were *known* to him, for they were *appointed* by him. He knew of this appalling transaction, and he knew its secret causes.

Some of the men of Galilee had lately rebelled against the Roman power. Pontius Pilate, the governor, had sent officers to apprehend the rebels. In what place were they found? In the temple. How were they engaged? Offering sacrifices. Though rebels, they continued to approach God; but their services were odious in his sight. The Roman officers respected neither the place nor the employment, but slew the rebels, and mingled their blood with the blood of the beasts that were ready to be sacrificed. Many persons who heard of the event concluded that because these men perished in so dreadful a manner, they were sinners of the *deepest* dye. But is this the rule of God's government? Does he mark out the *most* signal transgressors for the *most* signal judgments? In human courts of justice it is the *ringleader* who is condemned, when his accomplices often escape punishment. No doubt God also would act in this manner, were this *earth* the *place* of *judgment*. But there is *another* place of judgment: *there* sinners are punished in exact proportion to their guilt. He that knew his Lord's will, and did it not, shall be beaten with many stripes. But in this world some of the most daring offenders live at ease, and die in apparent peace. The rich man in the parable, who lifted up his eyes in torments, had lived in luxury and been buried with honor; while the faithful Lazarus, covered with sores, had languished at his gate. Jonathan, the generous friend of David, fell in battle, and his body, as well as the wicked Saul's, was exposed by the Philistines. When we hear of shipwrecks, and of fires, we often find the wicked and the just have shared the same fate. Sometimes one out of a great number escapes alone. Is he the best, the most approved by God? Perhaps he is the most guilty. When Saul slew the priests of the Lord, one alone escaped. It was Abiathar. Was he a faithful priest? No; he became a rebel and a traitor. Then what are we to learn from the judgments of the Lord? To fear THAT God who CAN destroy *all* his enemies. It is love that arrests his arm, and causes him to suspend the blow that is ready to descend.

Though the righteous are slain with the wicked, they are not involved in their *destruction*. To them sudden death is sudden glory. Those who have witnessed their behavior in the midst of storms, and in the approach of death, have testified to their calmness and their joy. When the Pegasus was wrecked, there was a pious minister on board, named Mackenzie, whose voice was raised in intercessions for his companions in danger, till the billows overwhelmed them all. It was beautiful to behold him, surrounded by the shrieking crew, composed, and peaceful in the midst of the tumult of the waves. Was *sudden* death a *judgment* to this holy man? But it *was* an awful judgment to those who had despised the gospel, and neglected their own souls. Whenever we hear of these calamities, God is speaking to us in a voice of thunder, and saying, "Except ye repent, ye shall *perish*."

Evening Scripture portion. 1 Sam. XXII. *Abiathar the priest.*

LUKE XIII. 6–9.—*The parable of the fig-tree.*

WITH this awful parable the Lord concluded his discourse to the innumerable multitude who were pressed together around him.

It seems to have been uttered as a warning to the whole Jewish nation. That people had long enjoyed distinguished privileges, but their greatest had been the ministry of the Lord Jesus. It had now lasted about three years. How had they profited from it? They were still "*hypocrites*," (xii. 56.) But the Lord was unwilling to give them up. During the course of the coming year further efforts would be made for their salvation. In a few months the great sacrifice for sin would be offered, the great triumph of the Son of God by rising from the dead would take place, and the Holy Ghost would descend in flaming fire upon the disciples, and the gospel would be preached in power at *Jerusalem.* Would the nation repent when they saw and heard these things? No, they would not. The sentence would then go forth, "Cut it down." The sentence has been executed. That fig-tree, the Jewish nation, has been cut down, but the ROOTS are yet left in the earth. The words of Job may be applied to that afflicted people: "There is hope of a tree, if it be cut down, that it will sprout again, and that the tender branches thereof will not cease. Though the root thereof wax old in the earth, and the stock thereof die in the ground; yet through the scent of *water* it will bud, and bring forth boughs like a plant." (Job xiv. 7–9.)

The water from heaven shall at length descend upon the chosen nation, and the dry stump shall send forth green shoots; Israel shall bud, and blossom, and fill the face of the world with fruit; the Jews shall return to their own land, and worship their crucified Redeemer.

But does this parable apply to that *nation* alone, and does it not apply to *individuals?* There is not one *single* plant in God's vineyard that is not watched over by the great husbandman. The Lord exercises great patience towards each; but at the same time he will not allow unfruitful trees *always* to encumber the ground. He had great patience with Saul, the king of Israel, but after giving him repeated trials, and repeated warnings, He *took away his mercy from him.* (2 Sam. vii. 15.) We are not permitted to hear the counsels of heaven respecting ourselves, but we know that our state of heart and our conduct are observed by Him who seeth all things.

The gardener is slow in determining to cut down a tree that he has nurtured with care. How much more unwilling is the compassionate Saviour to cast off those whom he has blessed with great privileges! Many who pray not for themselves, are prayed for by others; their time for repentance is lengthened out,—but not for *ever.* A *sudden* stroke often cuts off those who have long refused to hear the gentle invitations of the gospel: "He that being often reproved, hardeneth his heart, shall *suddenly* be destroyed, and *that without remedy.*"

But there are no sinners more provoking to the Lord than those, who when they hear His threatenings, say in their hearts, "I shall have peace, though I walk in the imagination of my heart." These presumptuous transgressors are likened to roots that bear, instead of fruit, gall and wormwood. And how will God deal with them? His anger, and his jealousy, will smoke against them, and he will blot out their names from under heaven. (Deut. xxix. 18–20.)

Evening Scripture portion. Zeph. III. ***The punishment and pardon of Israel.***

LUKE XIII. 10–17.—*Christ restores a woman who was bowed together.*

THE objects that attracted the Saviour's eye were those that the world overlooks or even derides. A poor creature bowed down, and in nowise able to lift herself up, would incur many a contemptuous glance from the thoughtless and unfeeling. Some poor cripples are afraid of venturing out of their houses, lest they should meet with scornful looks or hear unfeeling remarks. But this afflicted woman was not restrained by such fears from entering the public congregation. With pain and difficulty she must have reached the place of worship. There are pious persons who love the house of God so well, that they drag their decrepit frames along the toilsome way, resting now upon a bank, and now upon a stone, rejoicing when they reach the threshold, as a voyager when he lands upon a distant shore. Souls that thirst after God, spare no pains to get a refreshing draught from the wells of salvation.

How must this poor woman have felt when she heard the Lord Jesus desire her to approach! She did not apply to him for relief; perhaps she did not know that he would be at the synagogue; and as she could not lift herself up, she may never have seen his gracious countenance. But when she heard his voice, she refused not to come near. The Saviour laid his hands upon her and healed her. Her first act was "to glorify God." There were some present who, instead of being touched by the sight of her joy, were filled with indignation. The ruler of the synagogue was one of these. He had not dared to prevent the Lord from teaching in the synagogue, because he knew the admiration in which he was held by the people. But now he could no longer restrain his rage, and he angrily addressed the congregation, saying, "There are six days in which men ought to work; in them therefore, come and be healed, and not on the Sabbath days." The people had *not* come to the synagogue *in order* to be healed; they had come to worship God. The ruler knew this, but he only sought for some *pretence* to hinder the glorious triumphs of the Redeemer.

It was foolish ever to attempt to argue against the Lord of all wisdom. By one word he could confound his most subtle adversaries. He exposed the hollowness of the ruler's heart, by showing that the compassion exercised towards a *beast* on the Sabbath-day must surely not be withheld from a *child of Abraham.* How many arguments are now brought forward against various plans of doing good to souls, that the Saviour would overturn by such an appeal as this!

The same reply that stung the ruler to the quick, must have poured consolation into the poor woman's heart. The Lord called her a *daughter* of Abraham; and he acknowledged none to be the children of Abraham except those who did "the *works* of Abraham." Could the straightness of her body afford her as much joy as the assurance of the safety of her soul?

She discovered also the *cause* of her affliction. It was the power of an evil spirit that had bound her for eighteen years. If her faith was now like that of Abraham, we see it had been exercised by long and heavy trials. But those trials had not been longer nor heavier than was necessary for the perfecting of her faith. From the beginning of her affliction the day of release had been known to the Lord, though unknown to her. The glories of that day must have made her forget the long period of her sorrow. Was not *that* day glorious in which she was called, and touched, and commended by her Saviour? It seems an emblem of that more glorious day when the people of God will be made free forever from the bondage of corruption, and will receive from their Lord the assurance of his everlasting favor. How light all the afflictions of this life will then appear! how *short* their period! Whether they lasted eighteen or *eighty* years, the time will then appear as a *moment*.

Evening Scripture portion. Ps. CXLVI. CXLVII. *The poor afflicted.*

JOHN IX. 1–5.—*The man who was born blind.*

THE disciples asked a very singular question, when they said, "Who did sin, this man or his parents, that he was *born* blind?" How could they suppose that any sin of the man could cause him to be *born* blind? It appears that they must have entertained a superstitious notion common among the Jews with regard to the soul. Some of them imagined that souls passed from one body to another, and that when they had acted wickedly in one body, the next time they were born into the world, they received some punishment. This was an idea taken from the heathen, and was very false and absurd. How dangerous it is for men to follow their own imaginations respecting things unseen! The Scriptures give us a true account of all things; if we would follow them alone, we should be spared many tormenting ideas. How *painful* it must have been for men born blind to think that their blindness was the punishment of sins they could not remember, and which, in fact, they had not committed! How it must have added to the weight of their calamity, to find themselves regarded by their fellow-creatures as objects of God's especial *displeasure!*

But the Lord Jesus viewed this blind man with *especial tenderness.* Those most afflicted in their bodies are sometimes the most honored, and the most beloved of God. There are many persons who could testify that it was through the loss of a limb, or of sight, or of hearing, they were brought to know the Saviour's power and grace.

And why did the Lord take a deep interest in this blind beggar? Was it because he felt compassion for one who had never beheld the light of day? No doubt he did feel this compassion; but there was another feeling, stronger even than *compassion*, that filled his heart. It was the desire for his Father's glory. He knew that in this blind man his Father's power and grace would be shown forth. Therefore, when the disciples asked the reason of the poor beggar's blindness, he told them the reason was, "that the works of God should be made manifest *in him*." When affliction is sent, let each of us reflect, "Perhaps this trial has been appointed that God's power may be shown in sustaining me under it, or in delivering me from it." If we love God fervently, we shall be willing *to suffer* in order to promote his glory.

One mode of promoting it is by *suffering* his will; but there is another mode,—*doing* his will. When we are not pressed down by the weight of some affliction, we should be seeking for opportunities of doing good to our fellow-creatures. How impressive are the Saviour's words: "I must work the works of him that sent me, while it is day: the night cometh, when no man can work." The Lord Jesus knew the exact period when the night of death would put an end to his labors of love upon earth. But we know not *at what moment* that night will overtake us, and deprive us of the opportunity of serving God any more here below. Have we begun to do the works of God? The first work is to believe in the Lord Jesus Christ. Are we spending our days in *pleasing* ourselves, or in *pleasing* God? How many are now wrapped in the shades of night who mispent the short day in which they might have served the Lord!

Sometimes, when night comes on, we remember some business that we have omitted, and that we ought to have done during the day. We think to ourselves, "We will do it to-morrow." But when the night of death is at hand, we shall not be able to make that resolution. What has been left undone, can never be done at all by us. If the *great business* has been left undone,—if the *one thing needful* has been forgotten, how miserable will be our condition! But if we have obtained pardon *ourselves*, this will not satisfy us. We shall wish that we had helped our fellow-creatures out of their misery by directing them to the Saviour. How blessed were the last hours of Count Zinzendorf! They were spent in praising God for having converted so many of the heathen. "I only hoped," said the Count, "to do a little good, to see a *few* poor heathen turn to the Lord, and behold *thousands* have believed." It filled him with joy to think he was going to meet some of them in heaven,—Indians, and Negroes, and Greenlanders, whom he had never seen upon earth, but to save whom he had sent missionaries to distant lands. Many who saw him die were heard to say, "May my last end be like his."

If we wish to die as he did, let us now remember the command, "Whatsoever thy hand findeth to do, do it with thy might." (Eccles. ix. 10.)

Evening Scripture portion. Eccl. IX. *Diligence.*

JOHN IX. 6-23.—*Christ directs the blind man to wash in Siloam.*

THERE were many reasons that might have deterred the Saviour from curing the blind man. It was the Sabbath-day: enemies were watching his actions, in the hope of renewing their accusations against him: the blind man did not *ask* to be healed, neither did the disciples plead for him. Jesus might have passed on without noticing the poor beggar, but He would not lose the opportunity of glorifying his Father. He knew that the restoration of the blind man would be a miracle that would attract public attention; because it was generally known in Jerusalem that the man had been blind from his birth. The *means* He used were peculiar to this occasion. The Lord made clay, and put it over the man's eyes, and then bade him wash in a pool. Who could have thought that clay could be used as a means of restoring sight? But God shows forth his power by employing the most unlikely means for performing his greatest wonders. His greatest wonder of all, the redemption of the world, was effected by the most unlikely means—the crucifixion of the Son of Man; and the *preaching* of the cross, though by some counted foolishness, is to them that are saved the power of God. But the man was not restored by the clay alone—he was commanded to wash in a pool called Siloam, which signifies Sent. If he had not obeyed the command he would not have obtained the blessing. Neither can sinners obtain pardon unless they obey the command to wash in the fountain of Christ's blood.

When this poor man had received his sight, he did not enjoy the privilege of beholding his benefactor. He did not know where to find him, and if he had met him, he would not have known him.

He soon found himself surrounded by enemies, and standing before the Pharisees to be judged. For what? Because he was a witness of the power of Jesus, whom they hated.

What could this poor man do? There was no one to answer for him; his benefactor was not near to defend him, and his parents refused to say a word in his behalf. How did he behave in these difficult circumstances? With more courage than the apostles showed when first placed in similar peril.

When the Jews inquired, "What sayest thou of him?" he boldly replied, "He is a prophet." Thus he was faithful to the truth as far as he knew it. God has promised "to him that hath shall be given."

Those who follow the convictions of their consciences shall receive more grace.

How ungenerous was the conduct of the beggar's parents! They showed no gratitude for the benefit conferred upon their son, nor were they willing to run any risk in order to shield their own offspring from disgrace, but left him to stand alone against the host of his enemies. When asked how he had obtained his sight, they replied, "He is of age: ask him." How little they thought those words would be recorded to their everlasting shame! They sought to escape disgrace; but they have incurred the deepest. They feared lest they should be put out of the synagogue; but they considered not the danger of being shut out of heaven. How the heart of the poor blind man must have sunk within him when he heard his own parents refusing to take his part! It is a heavy trial to pious children when their parents hang back, and say nothing in their defence; much more when they join with an ungodly world in reproaching them. At such a moment they have need to think of the words of the psalmist; "When my father and my mother forsake me, then the Lord will take me up." (Prov. xxvii. 10.)

Many Christians can remember a time in their lives when they were desolate—when they "looked on their right hand, and beheld, and there was no man that would know them." Then it was, they looked to the Lord, and said, "Thou art my refuge, and my portion in the land of the living."

Evening Scripture portion. Ps. CXLII. CXLIII. *The prayers of the desolate.*

JOHN IX. 24–34.—*The Pharisees cast out the man who was born blind.*

THE conduct of the Pharisees was exactly opposite to that of the man who was born blind. The Pharisees betrayed their *hypocrisy* in every word they uttered, while the poor beggar evinced in all his replies *sincerity.* They endeavored to cover their hatred against the Saviour by an appearance of religion. They said, "Give God the praise: this man is a sinner." But the single and straight-forward character with whom they argued was not to be deceived by their affectation of piety. He reasoned well; he kept to *facts.* He said, "Whereas I was blind, now I see." This was a *fact*, a *convincing* fact. There are many who can meet all the arguments used against true religion by this declaration: "Whereas I was a dark, ignorant creature, a stranger to God and myself; now I know that he is gracious, and that I am a sinner. I rejoice in the light that his gospel has poured into my mind, and I am persuaded that His word is *truth.*"

Experience strengthens the mind against the attacks of infidels, more than all the philosophy in the world.

The Pharisees became enraged when they found they could make no impression on the poor man's mind. The inquiry, "Will ye also be his disciples?" offended their pride, and provoked them to use insulting language. But the beggar betrayed neither anger nor fear. He boldly yet calmly answered, "God heareth not sinners." This was a scriptural sentiment: "The prayer of the wicked is an abomination to the Lord." The prayers of *penitent* sinners are heard, but not the prayers of those sinners who are pursuing a course of iniquity. If Jesus had been an impostor, God would not have heard him, or enabled him to do miracles. The poor man did not know that Jesus was the Son of God, but he felt assured that he was a true prophet. He believed, as Nicodemus once did, that he was a teacher sent from God. But how much more courageous he was than Nicodemus! The ruler came to Jesus by night for fear of the Jews, his *equals* in power and authority: the beggar in open day acknowledged Him before his *superiors* in rank and station. Nicodemus had much learning; he was a master or teacher in Israel; the beggar having been born blind, could not even have learned to read. Yet Nicodemus knew less of the truth than the blind beggar.

God delights in showing his power by exalting those whom the world despises. A simple peasant has often a clearer view of the gospel than a learned, though sincere, inquirer. It is the Holy Spirit who opens the eyes of the understanding, and sometimes he enlightens with his brightest beams the most ignorant. If we would be truly wise, we must pray for *His* light.

The poor man was not suffered to go unpunished. The Pharisees, after first reproaching him in an unfeeling manner, saying, "Thou wast altogether born in sins," proceeded to cast him out. Though they still permitted him to enter the synagogue, they forbade him to approach any of the congregation. Did no fears oppress his mind respecting his *temporal* provision? Unaccustomed to work, how could he *earn* his daily bread? or how could an excommunicated man hope to obtain alms from the passers-by? Thus he suffered the loss of all things for his Saviour's sake. He is the *first* whose name is recorded as openly disgraced for confessing Christ. He is the *first* of a glorious train, some of whom suffered reproach, others imprisonment, and others death, because they would not deny Jesus. His case was singular, because he knew not the glory of the Being on whose account he was cast out. He knew not that he was the Son of God.

If we, who *do* know who Jesus is, should be ashamed of him before the world, how would the conduct of this poor beggar condemn us! May the Lord give us grace not to be afraid of a man that shall die, or of the son of man that shall be made as grass; but to fear him who stretched forth the heavens, and laid the foundations of the earth, even Him who raised the Lord Jesus from the dead, and will raise *us* also, if we believe in Him.

For what is man, and what—his smile?
The terror of his anger—what?
Like grass he flourishes awhile,
And then his place shall know him not.
For fear of such an one shall I
The Lord of Heaven and earth deny?

Evening Scripture portion. Is. LI. *Encouragement for the persecuted.*

JOHN IX. 35–38.—*Christ finds the outcast.*

EVEN a human creature, though of an *evil* nature, is interested in one who suffers for his sake. If we knew of a person, who was plunged into trouble for defending us, would not every generous and compassionate feeling lead us to fly to his consolation!

How *much more* must the Son of God, who is infinitely good, have felt for one who was suffering for his sake! Did he not show that he cared for the blind man, by seeking him when cast out by his persecutors? It was easy for the all-seeing Shepherd to find the sheep that had been driven away. He had followed him with his eye, and had strengthened him with his grace, even when he appeared to have forsaken him, and to have left him to suffer alone. He who saw Nathaniel under the fig-tree, saw the once blind beggar when insulted by the Pharisees, and when cast out of the synagogue.

We are not told on what *spot* he found him, but we are told in what *manner* he spoke to him. Did the poor man recognise his benefactor? Though he had never seen his countenance, surely that voice could never be forgotten, which had pronounced the words, "Go, wash in the pool of Siloam." It must have filled his heart with delight when he heard that beloved voice again. After all the bitter revilings that had been heaped upon him, how those kind accents must have soothed his feelings! Jesus had sought him, and found him, and he was come to bestow richer blessings upon him than at the first. He was come to manifest Himself to him. He asked, "Dost thou believe on the Son of God?" The poor man answered, "Who is he, Lord, that I might believe on him?" There was nothing but *ignorance* that hindered this man from believing. The Lord speedily removed it by saying, "Thou hast both seen him, and it is He that talketh with thee." Then the poor man exclaimed, "Lord, I believe." Not satisfied with declaring his belief, he offered his homage: he worshipped the Son of God.

There are none of us who are in his state of ignorance. We cannot say, "Who is the Son of God, that we might believe on him?" We heard from our early childhood that *Jesus* was the Son of God. Though we have not seen him, and though he has not talked with us, yet we know that he died for us, and that he is now living to intercede for us, if we come to God in his name. The beggar did not know so much as *this*, when he said, "Lord, I believe." Yet how hard-hearted and ungrateful we should think him, if he had not believed in the Being who had done so much for him! He knew that every word his benefactor uttered must be truth. Before he had seen him he had loved him, and had suffered for his sake; and when he did see him, and when he knew who he was, he adored him. Do *we* believe in the Son of God? Do we love him? Are we willing to suffer contempt for his sake? Then our first meeting with him will be joyful. God has promised that we shall behold our Saviour, that we shall see him face to face, that we shall hear him speak. What will be our feelings when we actually look upon the glorious Being who died for us! What will be our joy, if he receive us with the same kindness which he showed to the poor beggar! In one moment, that man must have forgotten the reproaches and revilings of the Pharisees. It was worth enduring all their sneers, to obtain one gracious smile from the Lord of glory.

If ever we are exposed to the contempt of our fellow-creatures, on account of our fidelity to Christ, let us reflect on the time when we shall behold *His* countenance. Had the poor man treacherously betrayed his benefactor in the presence of the Pharisees, how would he have felt when he saw him, and knew that he was the Son of God! He would have desired, as Adam did, to hide himself, that he might not encounter his upbraiding glance.

Jesus will come again, with clouds, and every eye shall see him. And shall every eye beam with gladness when it beholds him? O no; all kindreds of the earth shall wail because of him. But *some* among all kindreds will rejoice. "They shall lift up their voice, they shall sing for the majesty of the Lord, they shall cry aloud from the sea." (Is. xxiv. 14.) May we act so faithfully during his absence, that we may be glad when He returns!

Evening Scripture portion. Acts V. 17 to end. *Persecution.*

JOHN IX. 39 to end.—*Christ accuses the Pharisees of wilful blindness.*

WE know not in what circumstances the interview between Jesus and the poor outcast took place, whether it occurred when they were alone, or surrounded by Pharisees.

Soon afterwards, however, we find Jesus again addressing his enemies in these words: "For judgment am I come into this world." But did not he come into the world for *salvation?* Yes, salvation with judgment; that is, with *distinction* of character. He did not save *all*, but those only who *received* him. He came in such a form, and in such a way, that the world would not receive him. Had he come in splendor and glory, then *all* would have received him; but he came adorned with the beauty of *holiness*, and not with the pomp of kings. By coming in this manner he tried men's hearts. The aged Simeon, when he blessed the infant Saviour, declared, "He shall be a sign that shall be spoken against, that the thoughts of many hearts may be revealed."

The proud and worldly-minded rejected the lowly Saviour; the humble and contrite loved and followed him. The man who had just been cast out of the synagogue was one of those whom Jesus came to save. He knew he was a sinner, and that he needed a Saviour. The Pharisees who cast him out, thought they were holy, and needed no Saviour. The Lord drew the characters of the outcast and of his persecutors in these words: "For judgment am I come into this world; that they which see *not* might see, and that they which *see* might be made blind." The Pharisees rightly supposed that the Lord alluded to them in the latter part of this declaration, and they insolently inquired, "Are we blind also?" Jesus returned a mysterious answer: "If ye were blind, ye should have no sin; but now ye say, 'We see;' therefore your sin remaineth." In one sense the Pharisees were blind,—in another sense they were *not* blind. They saw not the glory of God: but why? because they *wilfully shut their eyes.*

God will condemn none of his creatures for ignorance which they cannot avoid. "If ye were blind," said the Saviour, "ye should have no sin." But it is an aggravated case when a sinner shuts his eyes against the light, and at the same time declares that he sees. In such conduct, rebellion, and pride, and falsehood are combined. Yet this was the way in which the Pharisees acted. They were determined not to acknowledge Jesus to be the Son of God. Whether he cast out devils, or raised the dead;—whether his lips poured forth divine wisdom, or his countenance beamed with celestial goodness, they had made up their minds they would not believe in him, and they would hinder the people also from believing. They would never renounce the high character they had obtained among men; they would still persist in saying, "We see." What would be the punishment of such wickedness? It would be this: the eyes they wilfully shut would be sealed up in sevenfold darkness.

Those are in a dangerous state who refuse to think of religion; but those are in a much *more* dangerous state who have a *form* of religion, and *call* it *true* religion. They are the most bitter enemies to the truth. Careless sinners often have a kind of respect for devoted Christians, and express a wish that they resembled them; but those who put their trust in an outward show of piety, despise and hate real believers. While they wilfully close their eyes against the spiritual doctrines of Christ, they confidently assert that they *see*, and *they alone*. What will be the astonishment of Pharisees and hypocrites when their eyes are opened, and they behold in another world the believers whom they despised seated with Abraham, Isaac, and Jacob, around the throne of God! Devils believe, and, in hell, wicked men believe that Jesus is the Son of God. Truths they *would* not understand in the land of gospel light, shall be clearly seen in the land of outer darkness, amid the fire that never shall be quenched.

Evening Scripture portion. Acts XIII. 1–13. *Elymas the sorcerer.*

JOHN X. 1–6.—*The parable of the good Shepherd.*

THE Pharisees had understood the meaning of the Lord when he spoke of *blindness*, but they did not understand the parable of the *good shepherd*. Had they known that *they* were represented under the figure of thieves and robbers, how great would have been their indignation! Yet such indeed they were, because they robbed God, for they destroyed the souls of his people by their false instructions. They loved to feed on the flesh, and to clothe themselves in the fleece of the sheep, but they cared not for the flock. They sought their own gain, and their own reputation, but not the glory of God.

What is meant by their climbing over the wall into the sheepfold, instead of entering by the door? The door represents Christ. The Pharisees did not come in by the door, for they did not believe in the Saviour. But who is the shepherd of the sheep? How many little children could answer, "Jesus is the good Shepherd!" Some could say, "He is *my* shepherd." They know He is *their* shepherd, because they love him.

How did Jesus show he was the true shepherd? By his manner of *coming in* to the fold, and by his manner of *going out*. He did not climb over the wall, as thieves and robbers do, but entered by the door, *openly* declaring that he was the Son of God. "To him the porter openeth." Does not the porter represent the prophets? Christ was the Shiloh of whom Jacob had spoken nearly two thousand years before, and the Lamb of God to whom John the Baptist had lately pointed.

He showed he was the Shepherd of the sheep by his manner of *going out*. He *led* his flock. He called them by their names, according to the custom of shepherds in the East; when he called them, he went *before* them. None but the true shepherd *could lead* the sheep; strangers would have been forced to *drive* them. It is very interesting to behold an eastern shepherd going before his sheep and leading them to their pastures. His flock know the voice of their own shepherd, and would not obey the call of any other.

Nathanael was one of the sheep of Christ. When Jesus saw him, he said, "Behold an Israelite indeed, in whom there is no guile." Thus he showed he knew him. He was like a shepherd calling his sheep by its name. Did Nathanael hear the shepherd's voice? Yes, he replied; "Thou art the Son of God; thou art the King of Israel." The man born blind was another of Christ's sheep. When the shepherd said to him, "Dost thou believe on the Son of God?" he soon replied, "Lord, I believe." Have *we* heard the voice of the shepherd, calling us to follow him to the green pastures? None but his sheep hear that voice. They hear it sounding in the depths of their hearts, saying, "Come unto me, all ye that labor and are heavy laden, and I will give you rest." They listen to the voice, and say to their own souls, "Return unto thy rest, O my soul." They feel safe while they follow their Shepherd. Each says to Him, "Cause me to know the way wherein I should walk." (Ps. cxliii. 8.) The poor helpless sheep cannot tell which is the path that leads to glory, but his shepherd can. After passing through some dark valley, the sheep says, "When my spirit was overwhelmed within thee, thou knewest my path." (Ps. cxlii. 8.) The further the sheep goes in the way, the more trust he feels in his shepherd; and when he comes to the edge of the last valley he is able to say, "Though I pass through the valley of the shadow of death, I will fear no evil, for thou art with me; thy rod and thy staff, they comfort me." We know what lies beyond that valley—Mount Zion. It is to that fair mountain the shepherd conducts his flock.

But while other shepherds are of a different *nature* from the sheep they tend, the good shepherd has taken on him the nature of his flock. "The Lamb which is in the midst of the throne shall feed them, and shall lead them unto living fountains of waters." (Rev. vii. 17.) Having fed, and led them upon *earth,* he will feed and lead them in *heaven.* We shall never cease to require a shepherd's care. It is a delight to those who love Jesus to think that He will *always* be their shepherd and they his sheep.

Evening Scripture portion. Ps. XXIII. XXIV. *The good shepherd.*

JOHN X. 7–13.—*Christ explains the parable of the good shepherd.*

WE are thankful to the Lord for having explained the parable of the good shepherd. Most parts of it can be interpreted with certainty, because they have been explained by the great Teacher.

Nothing can be plainer than the words, "*I* am the door of the sheep." Jesus is the gate of the fold. No man can come to the Father but by him. He is the way to God. He offered himself as an atonement for our sins, and by faith in that sacrifice we can be saved. There are *other shepherds* besides Christ, (for his ministers are his under-shepherds,) but there is no *door* but him.

What do these words signify: "All that ever came before me are thieves and robbers?" Were the prophets thieves and robbers? No; the true prophets bore witness to Jesus; they were his *under*-shepherds; they entered by the *door* and fed the flock. This is the promise made to a faithful minister and to every true believer. "By me, if any man enter in, he shall be saved, and shall go in and out, and find pasture."

But though there are other shepherds *besides* Christ, there are none *like* him. None but Jesus could say, "I am come that they might have life, and that they might have it more abundantly." God only can bestow *natural* life, and He only can bestow spiritual life. How wonderful are the *means* by which he bestows it! by laying down his own life.

In order to describe what he came to do for his sheep, He enlarged his parable, and related a circumstance which often occurs in pastoral countries.

"He that is an hireling, and not the shepherd, whose own the sheep are not, seeth the wolf coming, and leaveth the sheep and fleeth; and the wolf catcheth them, and scattereth the sheep."

The Pharisees are called by another name in this part of the parable. They had been compared to *thieves*, and to *strangers*, but now they are compared to *hirelings*. In what did they resemble hirelings? In their want of love to the sheep. How did they betray their want of love? By fleeing at the approach of danger. It is true they could not by dying save the sheep. Why then did they not seek the protection of Him who *could?* This was their crime: they drove the sheep away from their only Saviour, their true shepherd. The Pharisees had tried to drive the blind man away from him, but they had not been able: they had only driven him closer to his shepherd.

Jesus cares for the sheep, and for every lamb in the flock. He found that poor blind man, and gathered him in his arms, and carried him in his bosom. For those who are just beginning to believe in Christ are weak like lambs, although they may have lived many years in the world. We have a shepherd who cares for his sheep. He knows that many of them have been *scattered*. There are persons at this moment who feel that they are sinners, and long for pardon, but no one has taught them to look to Jesus. The good shepherd knows where they are, and he says, "I will seek out my sheep, and I will deliver them out of all places where they have been scattered in the cloudy and dark day." (Ez. xxxiv. 12.) Has this Shepherd sought us, and found us? Can any of us say,

Jesus sought me when a stranger,
Wandering from the fold of God;
He, to rescue me from danger,
Interposed his precious blood?

Evening Scripture portion. Jer. XXIII. 1–32. *Careless pastors.*

JOHN X. 14–21.—*Christ concludes his discourse concerning the good shepherd.*

IN the conclusion of our Lord's interpretation of his parable there is no allusion made to the Pharisees. The *only* subject dwelt upon is the Good Shepherd's love for his sheep. Those who love their Shepherd must take particular delight in dwelling on this part of the Lord's discourse.

When Jesus said, " I know my sheep," he meant to teach us that he knew them to be *his* sheep, and loved them with parental affection —yes, with more than a mother's tenderness. A woman *may* forget her babe, but Jesus says to his church, " I will not forget thee." And have the sheep any affection for their shepherd? Yes, they return his love. If *he* knows their *names, they* know his *voice;* if he *leads* them out, they *follow* him : " I know my sheep, and am known of mine."

The Saviour makes use of a wonderful comparison to give us some idea of the intimate union that subsists between the good shepherd and his sheep. The sentence would be better understood if read thus : " I know my sheep, and am known of mine, *even* as the Father knoweth me, and as I know the Father," (ver. 14, 15.) What proof has the shepherd given of his love for his sheep? The greatest that could be given : " I lay down my life for the sheep."

When the Saviour spoke of his own death, what painful scenes must have risen before his view! The agony in the garden, the insults in the judgment-hall, the ignominy on the cross. But with these painful thoughts there was associated an overwhelming joy—the thought of the numbers he should save by his sufferings. When he uttered these words, " *Other* sheep I have, which are not of this fold," what an innumerable multitude of beloved children must have been present to his mind! for even at that moment he knew them all by name. Those *other* sheep were the Gentiles : they were then heathens. Thousands were bowing down to idols, slaughtering their enemies, and revelling in sin;—and millions were yet unborn; yet the Saviour called them *his* sheep. He knew they would believe when they heard of his love. Did He think of *us* when he said, " Other sheep I have?" for we are *Gentiles.* If *we* are now in his fold, if *he* is now our shepherd,—then we may be assured that he thought of *us* also, when he said, " Other sheep I have; them also I must bring."

After declaring his *own* love for his sheep, He revealed the *Father's* love also. How much the Father must love the flock, if He loves the Son, because he died for them! This is not the *only* reason of his love for his Son, but it is *one* reason. He does indeed love the flock; He has proved it by a wonderful act. "The Father *sent* the Son to be the Saviour of the world." "Herein is love, not that we loved God, but that He loved us, and *sent* his Son to be the propitiation of our sins." (1 John iv.)

The Son also loved us, and was willing to come: for it is written, "Christ also hath loved us, and hath given himself for us an offering, and a sacrifice to God." (Eph. v. 2.)

Yet this Saviour, so full of love, was spoken of by his creatures in this awful manner. Some said, "He hath a devil, and is mad." How great was the patience of God, to suffer those to live a moment longer who had uttered such an expression! It has been recorded in the Holy Scriptures, and will never be forgotten.

But how many since this discourse was written have felt as they read it, "Truly this was the Son of God! How precious are his words! How sweet are his promises! May the heavenly shepherd own me as his sheep at the last day!"

Evening Scripture portion. Acts XXII. ***Paul sent to the Gentiles.***

JOHN X. 22–30.—*Christ declares that he and his Father are one.*

THE feast of the dedication was not one of the three feasts ordained by *God*, but a feast instituted by *man*, to commemorate the purification of the temple after Antiochus Epiphanes, a heathen king, had defiled it by idols. This feast, however, was observed by Jesus; hence we may conclude that he does not *disapprove* setting apart days for the remembrance of special mercies.

As it was winter, the Lord taught in a part of the court of the temple that was covered in and sheltered from the weather. His enemies came to him, *pretending* to desire to know the truth: "If thou be the Christ, tell us plainly." Jesus, however, knew their malicious design. He knew they sought to accuse him of blasphemy before the Sanhedrim. The answer that he made was not that which they expected, for he told them *first*, not who *he* was, but what *they* were. He said, "Ye are not of my sheep." He did not tell them plainly that they were the thieves, the strangers, and the hirelings, described in the parable; but he did tell them plainly, that they were not *the sheep*.

Christ knows his own sheep; the world cannot distinguish them from wolves in sheep's clothing, but it is enough, if their shepherd knows they belong to Him. However the flock may be scattered, not one of them shall ever be lost. Jesus knew that great efforts would be made to steal, and kill, and destroy them, but that all these efforts would be vain. He promised, "They shall never perish, neither shall any man pluck them out of my hand." The Pharisees had sought to pluck the poor man, born blind, out of his shepherd's hand: to arguments and threatenings they had added insults and injuries; but he had refused to hear their voice, or to follow them.

Do we belong to the little flock? then Satan will seek to pluck *us* out of the Saviour's hand. We know not in what *manner* he will seek to separate us from our shepherd, for Satan has *many* devices. In the histories of the saints recorded in the word of God, we find instances of his temptations. Satan attempted to induce Job to forsake his shepherd by severe afflictions: he endeavored to drive away Peter by the fear of man, and to allure Moses by the riches of Egypt; but he never succeeded in plucking one sheep out of the shepherd's hands,—and he never will. In the last prayer Jesus offered up in the presence of his disciples, He said of them, "These that thou gavest me I have kept, and none of them is lost, but the son of perdition." Judas was not one of Christ's sheep; if he had been one of them, he could not have been destroyed by Satan's power.

And why can neither man nor angel destroy one of the sheep? Because their shepherd is God. Jesus is the shepherd, and the Father is the shepherd, and yet there is *one* shepherd; for Jesus said, "I and my Father are one." The shepherd who gave his life for the sheep is He whom Israel worshipped in days of old, saying, "It is *He* that hath made us, and not we ourselves; we are his people, and the sheep of his pasture."

The glorious Creator is that tender shepherd who carries the lambs in his arms, and gathers them in his bosom.

Evening Scripture portion. Ps. LXXX. ***The Shepherd of Israel.***

JOHN X. 31 to end.—*The Jews attempt to stone Christ for saying he was the Son of God.*

WHAT meekness our Saviour showed when the wicked Jews took up stones to stone him! How touching was his appeal: "Many good works have I shown you from my Father; for which of these works do ye stone me?" He might make the same appeal to us now. When we neglect, forsake, and disobey Him, he might say to us, "I have bestowed on you many gifts,—I have made you many promises;—I have passed over many transgressions: for which of these acts of kindness do you thus treat me?" What could we reply? Should we not be obliged to own that we were ungrateful, hard-hearted creatures?

But Jesus, by his affecting speech, did not soften his enemies, and He next used powerful arguments. He alluded to a passage in the 82d Psalm, in which God speaks to the kings and rulers of the earth under the name of *gods*. "I have said, Ye are gods." And why did he give them this name? Because both kings and priests were anointed, and thus made types of *Christ*, who is *the Anointed*. The word Christ means "anointed." These earthly princes were placed in authority, and thus also made types of the Son of God, to whom all power is committed. Therefore God spoke to them in these words: "I have said, Ye are gods, and all of you are children of the Most High;" but because they abused their authority by oppressing the poor, these words were added, "Ye shall die like men, and fall like one of the princes."

These kings, rulers, and priests, were only *types* and *shadows* of the Son of God, who is alone *worthy* to possess all rule, authority, and power. Now the argument Jesus used with the Jews was this: "If those who only *shadowed* forth my greatness, were called gods, how much more must *I* be the Son of God?" Christ called himself one whom the Father had sanctified, and sent into the world. By "*sanctified*," he meant "set apart" for the office of priest and king. The Father appointed him to be our priest and king before the foundation of the world, and in the fulness of time he sent him forth. "Thanks be unto God for his unspeakable gift!"

But no arguments could convince the Jews that Jesus was the true Messiah, because their hearts were set against him; therefore he went into a retired place beyond the river Jordan, where John had baptized long before his imprisonment.

This spot must have been very interesting to some of the disciples; for it was there that two of them had first beheld the Lamb of God, and had followed him to his own abode. (See John i. 28.) The children of God love the place where first their hearts were opened to receive the truth.

How refreshing the season passed in this retreat must have been to the Saviour's wearied frame and harassed spirit! He had the joy of bringing some souls into his fold; for it is written, "Many believed in him there." The preaching of John had prepared the way for the reception of Christ. After ministers are dead, their past labors are often blessed; and they are joined in the world above by souls born again through their word *after* their own decease.

Evening Scripture portion.
Ps. LXXXI. LXXXII. ***Great men addressed as gods.***

LUKE XIII. 23–30.—*Christ describes the misery of those who shall be shut out of His kingdom.*

THOSE who lived when the Lord was upon earth enjoyed the great privilege of asking him questions. Who would not wish to share it! It was one, however, that might easily be abused. Many asked the Lord unprofitable and curious questions. This inquiry, "Are there few that shall be saved?" seems to have been made by one who was not earnest in seeking to be saved *himself*. For the Lord, instead of replying to the question, addresses an exhortation to his hearers: "Strive to enter in at the strait (or narrow) gate; for many, I say unto you, will seek to enter in, and shall not be able." But did not the Lord once say, "Every one that seeketh findeth?" This promise applies only to the *present time;* there is a period when none who seek will find. The Lord described that period in a parable: "When once the master of the house is risen up, and hath shut to the door, and ye begin to stand without and to knock, saying, 'Lord, Lord, open to us.'"

That period has not *yet* arrived: the door stands open, the master invites, entreats, implores us to enter, and to partake of his glorious feast. But if we disregard his entreaties, he will suddenly shut to the door, and shut us out forever. Those outside will use arguments to induce the Lord to open the door. Some, who have been his companions upon earth, will say, "We have eaten and drunk in thy presence;" and some, who have listened to his discourses in their own cities, will say, "Thou hast taught in our streets." If *we* die in our sins, it will be of no use for us to say at the last day, "We have lived with holy people; we have been instructed by holy ministers."

There are two circumstances that will increase the anguish of those *Jews* who will be shut out of the kingdom of God. They will see their own forefathers, Abraham, Isaac, and Jacob, and their own prophets, sitting down at the heavenly feast. It will seem hard to them not to be admitted into the presence of their own kindred. And will it not seem hard to many other ungodly persons, when they behold a father, or mother, a brother, or sister, sitting down at the supper of the Lamb, and they themselves thrust out! On earth they were ever welcome at their father's table, but even a pious father will have no power to gain admission for an unconverted child into Christ's presence.

Another circumstance that will aggravate the disappointment of the unbelieving Jews, will be this,—they will see Gentiles whom they despised, flocking from the east and west, the north and south, into the new Jerusalem, while they are forbidden to enter. And will it not increase the disappointment of those who live in this *Christian* land, if they should see those who were brought up in *heathen* countries, saved, when they are lost?

When we were little we were taught to pray to God; we heard of heaven and hell; we lisped the name of Jesus, as soon as we could speak. There are many in distant lands who were taught in *their* childhood to bow to frightful idols, and to delight in deeds of cruelty; yet some of these have turned to God, and will go to heaven; and what if *we* should not go there! Then, the last would be the first, and the first last. May God of his infinite mercy save us from the great guilt of rejecting his gospel!

Evening Scripture portion. **Rev. XXI.** ***Everlasting joy and misery.***

LUKE XIII. 31 to end.—*Christ replies to Herod's threatening.*

THE Saviour showed his abhorrence of Herod's character by the name which he gave him, "a fox." The manner in which Herod had treated John the Baptist, rendered him deserving of the name of fox. He had once listened to his preaching, and shown him respect; but had afterwards imprisoned and basely murdered him. The different natures that God has bestowed upon the animals are intended to represent the various characters of men. The children of Satan resemble wolves, bears, and foxes, and all manner of voracious birds and loathsome reptiles; while the children of God are like the gentle sheep and the harmless dove.

But the threats of Herod did not alarm the Lord. Though the Pharisees said, "Herod will kill thee," yet He who knew all things, knew the tyrant *would* not kill him. And why not? Because *that* hour was not the *time*, nor *that* spot the *place* of his death. The Saviour knew *when* He should die. He prophesied that He should live a few days, that is, a short time longer, and on the third day be *perfected*, or rendered complete. In this mysterious language, He alluded to his death: by death He was perfected, or rendered complete as an atoning priest. In *death* He offered that sacrifice which atoned for the sins of his people, and with that sacrifice He appeared in the presence of God for us. Jesus knew *where* He would die. He said, "It cannot be that a prophet perish out of Jerusalem." He did not mean to say, that *no* prophet had perished elsewhere, but that *most* prophets had been slain in that wicked city. Did the prospect of his death, with all its attendant horrors, excite angry feelings in his breast? Instead of expressing anger, He burst forth into the most tender lamentations over the city of his murderers. How touching are the words: "How often would I have gathered thy children together, as a hen doth gather her brood under her wings, and ye would not!"

In the Old Testament the Lord compared himself to an *eagle*, bearing her eaglets *on* her wings to a place of safety. But in this place

He compares himself to a *hen* seeking to guard her little ones *beneath* her wings, from the birds of prey hovering in the air. How suitable are both these comparisons! When Israel was in Egypt, God delivered him from his enemies with the strength of an eagle, by carrying him into Canaan. But when Israel was in the promised land, He promised to guard him with the fond care of a hen, from the enemies that threatened to devour him. When we are in trouble, God is like an eagle in delivering us; and when we have been delivered, He is like a hen in keeping us from evil. How many blessings we possess at the present moment! But there are many dangers on every side. If we take shelter beneath the wings of our God, no evil shall overtake us. But if we refuse to come to Him who calls us, then we shall fall a prey to our enemies. Satan and all his angels are like birds of prey hovering in the air, longing to devour us. But Jesus will preserve his people from their malice. We live in a world full of trouble and temptation, but there is a refuge for us. Here is a prayer for a soul that feels its own helplessness, and dreads the power of its enemies: "Be merciful unto me, O God, be merciful unto me; for my soul trusteth in thee; yea, in the shadow of thy wings will I make my refuge, until these calamities be overpast." (Ps. lvii. 1.)

Evening Scripture portion. Deut. XXXII. 1–29. *The song of Moses near Mount Nebo.*

Luke XIV. 1–11.—*Jesus Christ reproves the ambitious guests.*

The account of the healing of the man with the dropsy reminds us of the healing of the man with the withered hand. It was on the *Sabbath-day* that Jesus performed both these miracles: but the *places* in which He wrought them were *not* the same. The withered hand was healed in a synagogue; the dropsy was cured in a Pharisee's house. On both occasions many of the Lord's bitter enemies were present. But no circumstances could restrain the compassionate Saviour from showing mercy to his suffering creatures. Neither did the displeasure He excited by healing the man with the dropsy prevent Him from reproving the proud behavior of the company.

In the East, it is still the custom for guests to occupy seats that mark their degree of rank. Each person, as he enters, seats himself in the place that he thinks he is entitled to fill, and often he takes a higher place than the company consider to be his due. But the master of the feast has the power to desire him to move either to a higher or lower place. The Pharisees showed a great anxiety to occupy the most honorable seats. Our Lord openly censured their conduct, and alluded to one of Solomon's proverbs, (xxv. 6,) an authority that they professed to revere. There it is written, "Put not forth thyself in the presence of the king, and stand not in the place of great men; for better is it that it should be said unto thee, Come up hither, than that thou shouldest be put lower in the presence of the prince whom thine eyes have seen."

Jesus exposed the folly of the Pharisees' conduct. It is *foolish*, as well as sinful to exalt ourselves. Some worldly people put on the *appearance* of humility, in order to attract notice and admiration. But the true Christian desires not only to *appear*, but to *be* humble. After having lain low at the foot of the cross, can he go forth desiring to be admired in society?

What are *our* feelings in company? Are we highly elated when noticed, and deeply mortified when overlooked? Do we love to be first? Do we envy those who are more regarded than ourselves? This was the spirit of the Pharisees. It is not the spirit of Christ. There are many persons who do not openly contend for places of honor, who are secretly thirsting for admiration. The children of God do not indulge this feeling, but strive and pray against it. The rule of their conduct is, "Be kindly affectioned one to another, with brotherly love, in honor preferring one another." (Rom. xii. 10.)

Evening Scripture portion. Prov. XXV. ***Counsel respecting behavior in society.***

LUKE XIV. 12–14.—*Christ advises his host to invite the poor.*

WITH what faithfulness the Lord acted towards the Pharisee who had invited him to his house! It appears that the entertainment was splendid, and the guests rich and honorable. But it was not such a feast as the Lord approved. He knew the motives which led the rich Pharisees to invite their neighbors: it was the hope that they should be invited again. This was a selfish and sordid motive. In the East, when an animal was killed, it was necessary to eat it *immediately*. The covetous invited none to partake of their dinner who would not be able to return the favor; but the charitable often called in the poor and afflicted, or sent portions to their dwellings. Job appealed to God, saying, "If I have eaten my morsel myself alone, and the fatherless hath not eaten thereof." And Nehemiah on a day of rejoicing said to the people of Israel, "Go your way, eat the fat and drink the sweet, and send portions unto them for whom nothing is prepared." In this country, many benevolent persons, instead of giving feasts to the poor, contrive other means of giving them relief and pleasure. It is the *spirit* and not the very letter of the counsel that ought to be followed.

But some may inquire, Is it wrong to invite our friends and kindred o a feast? We know that in every part of Scripture the joyful meet-ngs of brethren and neighbors are spoken of without censure.

But no feasts impart so much happiness as those given to the poor. Rich guests often come with reluctance, and depart without thankfulness. But the poor assemble with delight around the well-spread board, and go away blessing the bountiful hand that spread it. They enjoy but few pleasures, and they meet with but little kindness. It is in the power of the rich to cast a beam of light across their dark path, and to make them for a short season to forget their sorrows. To invite the poor is pleasing to the Lord. Among those gathered from streets, and lanes, and highways, and hedges, there may be a Lazarus whom we shall meet again at the heavenly banquet. It will be pleasant when we meet to feel that we honored him upon earth as the saint of the Lord. There are no doubt wicked persons to be found among the poor: but the kindness of the rich often opens their hearts to receive instruction. There are pious rich persons who devise means to render the feasts they give profitable to the *souls* of their poor guests, as well as refreshing to their bodies. That venerable reformer and martyr, Hooper, while he was bishop of Gloucester, entertained a certain number of the poor every day with a dinner of whole and wholesome meats in his great hall; but first he examined them in the creed, the Lord's prayer, and the ten commandments; nor would he himself sit down to table till his poor guests had been served.

How rejoiced we ought to be at every discovery of the will of God! If the world in general valued his approbation, there would not be so many entertainments as there now are given to the *rich*, and there would be many more given to the *poor*. Those words, "Thou shalt be blessed," sound very sweetly in the ear of a true disciple of Christ. This is what he desires: "to be blessed." Because the poor cannot recompense him for the kindness he shows them, the Lord will remember it: even as a father takes upon himself to reward every service rendered to his *infant* children.

Let us beware of thinking that any thing we can do *deserves* a re ward. No, that is impossible. When we have done all, we have done only what it was our duty to do. The excellent bishop, of whom we have just spoken, though he had given his goods to feed the poor, and though at length he gave his body to be burned, was so far from trusting in his good deeds for salvation, that, when brought to the stake, he was heard to pray thus: "Lord, I am hell, but thou art heaven; I am a sink of sin, but thou art a gracious God, and a merciful Redeemer."

It will be easy for God to recompense his children for all they have done for him upon earth. One glimpse of his countenance will more than compensate for the martyr's acutest pangs. But how shall his saints recompense *Him* for what He has done for *them?* He found them poor, and blind, and miserable, and fed them with heavenly bread, even with that living bread which came down from heaven. It is this thought that makes them so anxious to please Him.

Evening Scripture portion. Deut. XXVI. *Kindness to the poor.*

LUKE XIV. 15-24.—*The parable of the great supper.*

OUR Lord concluded his conversation at the Pharisee's house by a parable. He had said that those who invited the poor to their houses should be recompensed at the resurrection of the just. This declaration induced one of the guests to exclaim, "Blessed is he that shall eat bread in the kingdom of God." Then Jesus related a parable to show how unwilling the rich men were to come to the heavenly feast. This parable was exactly suited to the company present, and was intended as a warning to the Pharisees, and to all worldly-minded persons, whether rich or poor.

The man in the parable invited his rich neighbors to a feast. It is the custom in the East to send an invitation some weeks before the time appointed, and when the day arrives, to desire the servants to remind the guests of their engagement. Nothing can be more insulting than to refuse to come after the feast has been prepared, excepting there be some real hinderance. The excuses made by these rich men were of a frivolous nature. Neither sickness nor the death of friends detained them at home. They could not have *foreseen* those events; but it showed great contempt to purchase land or oxen, or to contract a marriage at the time they had agreed to come to the feast. It would have been far better to have refused at *first*, than to accept the invitation, and then to make excuses, when the feast was prepared and the master was waiting.

Like the rich men in the parable, the Pharisees *professed* to be willing to come to God; but when the blessings of the Gospel were offered to their acceptance, they began to make excuses. They were hypocrites, because they pretended to be religious, while their hearts were set upon this world. Would the insulted master of the feast permit his plenteous provisions to be wasted, or his table to remain unoccupied? By no means. He sent his servants into the streets and lanes of the city, and directed them to summon the poor, the maimed, the lame, and the blind. Thus, when the self-righteous Pharisees refused to listen to the Gospel, the Lord encouraged publicans to accept its blessings.

Afterwards the master of the feast sent his servants into the highways and hedges, to gather more guests for the feast. Who are the wanderers in the streets and lanes of the city, and who are those in the highways and hedges? Do not the former represent the Jews, and the latter the Gentiles? For the Gospel was first preached at Jerusalem, but afterwards among the Gentile nations, even among us who live in these northern isles. What were our forefathers doing when Jesus uttered his parable? They were worshipping frightful idols among their forests of oak. But even then the Lord had purposes of mercy towards those poor savages.

But why did the master declare that none of those men who *first* were bidden should taste of his supper? Had they not refused to come? What need was there to affirm that they should not come? Do not the words seem to indicate, that a time would arrive when those who had made excuses would repent of their folly, and seek to be admitted to the feast? When they saw the poor wanderers from the city and the country, clothed in white robes, surrounding a sumptuous table,—when they descried the splendid lights, and heard the joyful sound of music and singing, they would change their minds, and desire to join the glorious company. But they would find the door shut against them. When they knocked, they would hear a voice within, saying, "I know you not." They would not be permitted even to *taste* the supper, of which they had once been invited to partake.

And is there any despiser of Christ and his Gospel who will not change his mind when he beholds, afar off, the glories of the blessed, in the kingdom of God? Yes, when all his earthly delights are perished, he will wish for a place at the heavenly banquet. But he will find that no place is reserved for him among the happy guests. O what will then be the bitterness of his disappointment, and the agony of his regrets! Let us now obey the Saviour's gracious call, "Come, eat of my bread and drink of my wine, which I have mingled. Forsake the foolish, and live, and go in the way of understanding."

Evening Scripture portion. Prov. IX. *Wisdom's Invitation.*

LUKE XIV. 25 to end.—*Christ declares to the multitude that his disciples must encounter great difficulties.*

As the Lord Jesus knew all hearts, he could perfectly adapt his discourse to the state of mind of his hearers. We have lately listened to his conversation at a Pharisee's table, and heard his alarming warnings to those who *despised* his Gospel. Now we behold him surrounded by a different class of hearers.

The multitudes did not openly despise the Saviour, they admired him, and many of them wished to become his disciples; but they were not prepared to encounter difficulties, or to make sacrifices for his sake. Therefore the Saviour, turning towards them, set before their eyes the great trials which his disciples must expect to suffer. Parents and kindred would persecute them, and rulers would condemn them to death. How ought they to act when placed in these distressing circumstances? None can suppose that Jesus disapproves of natural affection; the meaning of his declaration is, "Those who would follow me must not yield to the persuasions of their dearest friends, or to the threatenings of the most cruel tyrants, but must be ready to forsake all, and to cleave to me alone." In our days, converted Jews and converted Brahmins have resisted the tenderest entreaties of affectionate mothers and devoted wives, who would have turned them from the faith. And even in our Christian land, there are many instances of children who have endured much unkindness from their own parents, rather than comply with the vain customs of the world.

The Lord Jesus related two short parables to show the folly of setting out in the Christian course, without being prepared to surmount difficulties.

If a man would build a tower, he must first consider whether he has money sufficient to complete the building; and if a captain would meet an enemy, he must first consider whether he has soldiers enough to resist him. It would be better not to *begin* the tower, than to leave it unfinished,—and not to *undertake* the war, than to suffer a defeat.

It would also be better not to *profess* to follow Christ, than to turn back after having set out. It would be *better*,—if we can talk of *better* in such a case. For he who does not set out at SOME TIME OR OTHER in the Christian course, must endure EVERLASTING misery. It will be a poor consolation for him to think that his case would have been still worse, had he turned back after having known the way of righteousness.

Christ never discouraged a sincere soul from following him. But he has given a true description of the nature of his service, so that none can say in the end, "My Lord deceived me, and represented his service to be easier than I have found it." A poor Madagascar woman, who had undergone great persecutions, was once asked whether she was surprised when afflictions overtook her. She replied, "No; from the first we knew it was written, that through much tribulation we must enter the kingdom of God; and when our troubles came, we said, 'This is what we expected.'" This poor woman was once shut up, for five months, in an iron case that prevented her moving a single limb; yet, having counted the cost, she proved more than conqueror through Him who loved her.*

Evening Scripture portion. 1 Thess. III. *Afflictions must be expected.*

LUKE XV. 1–10.—*Parables of the lost sheep, and of the lost piece of silver.*

THERE is a tenderness in these parables which is not to be found in the discourses we have lately read. When the Saviour was at the Pharisee's house, he faithfully reproved both the guests and the host;

* See "Madagascar and its Martyrs," a book for the young.

when he was surrounded by the multitude, he solemnly warned them; but when he sat in the midst of publicans and sinners, he uttered the most touching and encouraging words. The Pharisees showed the pride of their hearts, by murmuring because Jesus received sinners into his intimate society. The Lord answered their murmurings by relating several parables. He knew their *covetous* disposition, and that they would understand the joy of finding a lost sheep, or a lost piece of money, though their hearts were too hard to enable them to understand the joy felt by angels at the salvation of a sinner.

Even penitent sinners themselves can hardly believe that angels should care for them. How many penitents have read with astonishment that there is joy among the angels of God over *one* sinner that repenteth! Could we have conceived that the recovery of *one* of our fallen race should interest those glorious beings? *Why* do they care so much for us? The Son of God, whom they adore, loved us and died for us. They know that *He* cares for each wanderer, and that *He* rejoices over each soul that he brings back to his fold. The angels share in the joy of their beloved Lord. They felt with him in his *sorrows*, and one of them strengthened him in the garden of Gethsemane. They partake also in his *joys;* they delight to see the fruit of the travail of his soul. But *their* joy cannot be compared with *His*. He is an infinite being, therefore his love and joy are infinite.

And if the repentance of *one* sinner causes so much joy, what will be felt on account of the salvation of *all the Church of God!* The mind is overwhelmed at the thought of the boundless raptures of that day. Many joyful emotions have been felt since first the foundation of the earth was laid; the birds have rejoiced at every return of spring; children have smiled each opening morn; the saints have tasted higher delights in their sacred assemblies; and angels have made the heavens ring with their rapturous songs; but all these joys are as a drop compared to the ocean of delight that the glorious company of heaven shall feel, when all the redeemed are gathered together into the celestial city

Are we prepared to taste these joys? Do we *now* feel any satisfaction when we hear that a sinner has repented? We might discover our own state in the sight of God by this token: what are the events that occasion us most joy? If we are saved hereafter, we shall be the *companions* of angels. But if our hearts are not interested in the salvation of sinners, shall we be fit company for them? What a contrast there is between a selfish human creature and a benevolent angel!

How delightful it will be, in ages to come, if we are numbered among the saints, to see the angels who rejoiced over *our* conversion! They will not forget the happiness they experienced on such occasions, and they will feel their joy complete when they see the pardoned sinner, saved from all his enemies, comforted after all his sorrows, and enclosed in the everlasting arms of his Almighty Saviour.

Evening Scripture portion. Rev. VII. *Songs of saints and angels.*

LUKE XV. 11–16.—*The departure of the prodigal son.*

THOUGH the Pharisees were hard-hearted men, yet they possessed the feelings of parents. The parable of the prodigal son was suited to touch every father's heart. But even if the proud *Pharisees* listened unmoved to the Saviour's representation of the father's generous compassion, the poor *publicans* must have heard the wonderful history with grateful astonishment. When the Lord described the conduct of the younger son, they were reminded of their own base departure from God. The Pharisees also had wandered far from their Father's house; but they knew it not. They *imagined* that, like the elder son in the parable, they had always been faithful and obedient. Many persons entertain the same false notion of their own goodness, and forget that it is written, "*All* we like sheep have gone astray."

Every penitent sinner sees his own likeness in the prodigal son. The most striking feature in his character is his *ingratitude*. Instead of being thankful for his daily bread, and his shelter beneath his father's roof, and for all the comforts and privileges he enjoyed, he claims fortune as his *right*, saying, "Give me the portion of goods that falleth to me." This is our spirit by nature. Instead of being overwhelmed with a sense of God's wonderful goodness, we conceive ourselves entitled to further gifts.

When the prodigal had obtained his desire, he showed his ingratitude by going into a country a great way off, and there wasting his father's gifts in riotous living. And have we not acted like this prodigal? We need not move from the spot where we were born in order to do this: it is sufficient that shutting up our hearts from God, and banishing him from our thoughts, we seek our gratification in earthly things.

But behold the *consequence* of this conduct; the prodigal comes to poverty. He has at last spent *all*. It is well when we discover *before* death that we have spent *all*—that we have wasted our hopes and affections upon the world, and have obtained no lasting satisfaction in return. But what will be the despair of those who never discover their poverty, until they are removed to the place where the uttermost farthing is *required*, but not even a drop of water *granted!*

Perhaps the prodigal in his days of revelry may have looked forward to the time when he should have spent all, and he may have intended *then* to enter some service that would preserve him from want. But God defeated his design, and caused a mighty famine to arise at the *very moment* when he was destitute. *Now* there were few masters who could afford to hire, and many servants to be hired, so that the prodigal was forced to engage in the meanest service at the lowest wages; he became a swineherd for a less reward than would provide him with a meal of husks, such as the pigs fed upon.

How easily God can disappoint the sinner, and blast all his devices!

Many think, "When *this* enjoyment is passed, I will betake myself to another," forgetting how God can in a moment take away *every* idol, shut up *every* way of escape, and dry up *every* stream of happiness.

The thoughtless companions of his mirth remembered not the prodigal in his distress. "No one gave unto him." Those who had gladly partaken of his riotous feasts, forsook him in his poverty and hunger. Accomplices in guilt are not comforters in sorrow. For what unfeeling creatures the prodigal had forsaken his loving father, and his happy home! O the folly and the madness that sinners show in preferring the society of the wicked to the favor of the ever-blessed God! Can the world console them in sickness? Will the world be faithful to them in old age? Can the world receive them into glory after death? Happy are they who have made this blessed choice, "I had rather be a door-keeper in the house of my God, than to dwell in the tents of wickedness."

Evening Scripture portion.
Psalm LXXXIV. *The happiness of dwelling in God's house.*

Luke XV. 17–19.—*The repentance of the prodigal.*

God greatly blessed the prodigal's afflictions to his soul. While he was employed as a swineherd a great change took place in his mind—"He came to himself." This expression implies, that before he was *not* himself. A state of sin is a state of *madness.* When a person is converted he is in his *right* mind. How could any one indulge in sin, if he reflected on its awful consequences! "for the wages of sin is *death!*" But sinners are like the brutes that perish, and do not consider their latter end.

It is very interesting to hear the reflections of the prodigal when he was come to himself. He saw every thing now in a new light. He understood the happiness of his father's house. Once he had abhorred its restraints and longed for liberty, but now he esteemed each servant happy who dwelt beneath that peaceful roof. Unconverted persons think religion gloomy, and endeavor to escape from its influence; but when the Holy Spirit visits their hearts, they account the servants of God blessed, and long to be numbered among the saints.

The prodigal now felt convinced of his guilt. He not only lamented his miserable condition, but he traced it to his *own sin;* he blamed no one but himself. Thus the Spirit convinces of sin, and makes us feel that we have sinned against God, more than against any other being, because He is the greatest and best of beings, and our chief benefactor.

The prodigal felt confidence in his father's mercy. Though he felt unworthy to be called a son, yet he resolved to say "Father." Had he not felt this confidence, he might have been devoured by remorse, and have deemed it useless to return. Doubtless his memory furnished him with numerous instances of his father's love, of his readiness to forgive his early waywardness, and of his patient endurance of the provocations of his youth. He had enjoyed opportunities of knowing his father's character, and it now appeared to him in all its loveliness. Happy is it when the convinced sinner can hope in God's mercy. No child ever had such reason to believe that his father would receive him, as the chief of sinners has that God will in nowise cast him out; for God has so loved us, as to give his only Son a sacrifice for us; and He that spared not his own *Son*, will he not with him also freely give us all things?

The prodigal made a resolution to return, and openly to confess his sins, to entreat forgiveness, and to implore permission to become a servant, though not a son, in his father's house.

Have we ever made the resolution to return to God? Can we recall the time when we felt we had wandered from the best of fathers, and that we deserved to be rejected? Every true believer has repented of his sins, and has sought forgiveness with weeping and supplications. Nor does he ever cease to seek it while he lives upon earth. The sense of his own sinfulness increases, as he experiences more of his Father's goodness. Daily he says, "Forgive me my trespasses," and daily he feels that he is not *worthy* to be called a son.

Evening Scripture portion. Jer. XXXI. 1–21. *Repentance.*

LUKE XV. 20–24.—*The reception of the prodigal son.*

THE prodigal had conceived a high idea of his father's compassion before he set out to return home; but his thoughts had not reached the heights of his father's mercy. He could not have anticipated such a reception, at once so affectionate and so honorable. Had he returned as the deliverer of his country from some powerful foe, he could not have been welcomed with more honor. Had he left his home to plead for his father's life, he could not, when he was come back, have been received with more tenderness.

What is the reason that the sinner is treated with so much honor and so much love, when he falls at the footstool of divine mercy? Is he not received in his Saviour's name, with all the honor *that* Saviour won by trampling upon Satan, and with all the love that Saviour deserved for dying upon the cross?

Great must have been the humiliation of the prodigal, as he approached the parental roof. How it must have wounded the natural pride of his heart to return in tatters, with an emaciated countenance and a haggard eye! But when true penitence is felt, natural pride is in great measure subdued. Those who only feel a *slight* regret for past transgressions, are often prevented by pride from asking forgiveness. No doubt the prodigal had *wished* to return as soon as he became a swineherd; but it was not till "he came to himself," that his penitence was deep enough to enable him to face all the humiliation connected with the step. Then he felt he could bear the taunts of unfeeling spectators better than the reproaches of his own conscience—better than the remembrance of his despised home, and of his injured father. But he was spared the most painful part of the expected trial by the tender affection of that father, who "saw him when he was a great way off, and had compassion, and ran and fell on his neck, and kissed him." Did the prodigal repress his humble confession because he saw he was already forgiven? No, he said all that he had purposed to say, excepting, "Make me as one of thy hired servants." When he saw that he was received as a *son*, he could not ask to become a *servant*. The best robe was then put on him, a ring on his hand, and shoes on his feet; a feast was made, and rejoicing was heard on every side.

Could the prodigal doubt his father's full and free forgiveness? All his past transgressions seemed to be forgotten; his father's love was not abated in the least degree; a prospect of happiness was opened to his view beyond his highest expectations.

This is the way in which the Lord deals with the returning sinner. He clothes his guilty soul in the spotless robe of his Redeemer's righteousness, and satisfies his hungry soul with the heavenly food of his gracious promises. Why then do sinners refuse to return to God? They do not believe that He will receive them so affectionately, and render them so happy. The father of the prodigal is *our* God and *our* Saviour. Those who have sought his mercy can witness how He received them, and how happy He has made them.

It is sad to think that any should remain miserable, because they will not arise and return to Him, who offers them full and free forgiveness. The way may appear long; but it would be shortened, for their Father would meet them while they were yet a "*great way off*," and conduct them himself to his own glorious abode.

Evening Scripture portion. Gen. XLV. *Joseph makes himself known to his brethren.*

LUKE XV. 25 to end.—*The envy of the prodigal's brother.*

AMIDST the burst of joy at the prodigal's return *one* complaining voice was heard; among the glad countenances one lowering brow was seen; and that voice and that brow were a brother's. But the father showed as much forbearance towards his envious eldest son, as he had manifested compassion towards his prodigal younger son. He went out, and entreated this unfeeling brother to unite in the festal scene. These entreaties drew forth the pride that reigned in his son's heart. Pride is the root of a whole host of sins, especially of envy, anger, and discontent: all these evil passions gave their coloring to the answers of the eldest son. What a description he gives of his blameless conduct! He reproaches his father with his services, as if he had laid his own parent under obligations: "Lo, these many years have I served thee!" He declares those services were *perfect*, as well as persevering. "Neither transgressed I at any time thy commandment."

While he thus boasts of his *own* goodness, he places his *brother's* conduct in the worst point of view. The father might have turned away in wrath from his ungenerous son, but he condescended to argue with the proud objector. In a few words he describes the rich privileges of his first-born. "Son, thou art ever with me." Surely the continual presence of such a father was happiness in itself. But, knowing the covetous heart of his son, the father added, "All that I have is thine." There was no *argument* required to *prove* that a lost son should be received with joy. The father thought it sufficient to say, "It was meet that we should make merry and be glad."

Could the Pharisees avoid perceiving in the envious brother their own likeness? Now that the Saviour was receiving penitent publicans, and that angels were rejoicing over them in heaven, the Pharisees were boasting of their own goodness, and reproaching the Lord with partiality. They *imagined* that they had served God all their lives, and had never transgressed his commandment. The Lord did not show them (as He might have done) how false was this notion: but He proved, that even if they were as good as they supposed, the spirit they evinced towards penitent sinners was ungrateful and ungenerous. Had the Pharisees really been holy men, they would have rejoiced with angels over pardoned penitents. True believers remember the season when they were received into their father's favor, and they rejoice with each wanderer who returns as they did. There is not a son in the house of our heavenly Father who has not had his festival; except the angels who have been ever with Him, and have never transgressed his commandments. Yet there are some of the children of God, who were sanctified at so early a period, that they cannot remember the *first* feelings of penitence; they have not experienced the bitterness of an unconverted state, and cannot tell by contrast how great is their present happiness. These have enjoyed the best portion, in having been *ever with their Father*. How many days of childhood have been gilded with more than childish joy through the early knowledge of their Father in heaven! How sweet the remembrance of a youth spent in his service, unpolluted by worldly vanities! Yet even *they*—even those sanctified in infancy and devoted to God unto old age, have wandered into some forbidden paths, and have committed innumerable transgressions. They have experienced the forgiving love of God, when returning from their backslidings. They can say with David, "He restoreth my soul; He leadeth me in the paths of righteousness for his name's sake."

Evening Scripture portion. Hosea XIV. *The pardoned backslider.*

LUKE XVI. 1–8.—*The parable of the unjust steward.*

THIS parable has perplexed many persons. They have said, "What a dishonest man this steward was! Did his lord commend him for his wickedness?" No, not for his *wickedness*, but for his *wisdom*—for his *worldly* wisdom. His plan to secure himself from want was very cunning and ingenious. It is supposed that the oil and the wheat that the creditors owed were their rent. It was the office of the steward to make agreements with the tenants concerning the amount of produce that ought to be paid to their lord. This steward, before he was dismissed from his post, made *new* agreements with the tenants, and ingratiated himself by lowering the rents. When he was gone, the lord became acquainted with these proceedings, and expressed his wonder at the wicked policy of his unfaithful steward.

But some may still inquire, "Why did our Lord select a *dishonest* action as an instance of worldly wisdom? Does not the selection seem to countenance dishonesty?" But, if we consider, we shall perceive that the *badness* of the action renders it a suitable instance of the wisdom displayed by *bad* men. This was the point that the Lord wished to prove;—*bad* men take more pains to accomplish their *bad* ends, than *good* men to accomplish their *good* ends.

Perhaps a blush arose in the face of many a Pharisee, as this instance of knavery was related. That very steward may have been present. Many of the hypocritical Pharisees had committed actions equally dishonest. Their own consciences must have convicted them. But it was chiefly for the instruction of the *disciples* that the parable was related. It was addressed to them, and this was the lesson taught: "The children of this world are wiser in their generation than the children of light." By this sentence the Lord turns into a volume of rich instruction the actions of this wicked world among whom we live.

Wicked men are intent on accomplishing *different* wicked ends. One is bent upon accumulating immense riches. How does he set about his design? With the lukewarmness that Christians so often betray in pursuing their designs? Does he not rise early, and sit up late? Are not his thoughts always intent upon devising new schemes for amassing wealth? Is not the crowded city the place where he delights to be, whatever pleasures may allure, or weariness oppress? Were Christians to be as diligent in prayer, as this man in counting his gains, how rich would they grow in faith, and love, and every grace!

Another is bent upon destroying the reputation of his neighbors, in order that he alone may be praised and admired! How dexterously he performs his work! How cleverly he *insinuates* that some evil is practised by his companion! Perhaps he says nothing directly against him, (as this might awaken suspicion,) but he contrives to place him in a disagreeable light. Do we thus watch opportunities to say a word in behalf of our Lord and Master, insinuating something in his praise, when we cannot speak more openly? When we reflect on the *greatness* of the *end* that Christians have in view, we feel that they ought to be most earnestly intent on gaining it. Could heaven be *purchased*, the world would be a bauble to offer for it: it has been bought with more precious blood. Shall we grieve our dying Lord by our indifference to a gift so *dearly* bought, and so infinitely glorious?

Evening Scripture portion. 1 Cor. IX. *Earnest endeavors after salvation.*

LUKE XVI. 9–13.—*Christ exhorts his disciples to be faithful in the use of riches.*

THE Lord Jesus had shown, by the history of the unjust steward, that the children of this world are wiser in their generation than the children of light. He next explained in what particular point they are wiser: in the use they make of riches. The steward made use of the property consigned to his care in gaining friends, who would receive him into their habitations when he lost his stewardship. Therefore Jesus said to his disciples, "Make to yourselves friends of the mammon of unrighteousness, that when ye fail they may receive you into *everlasting* habitations." The name given to riches is very remarkable—"the mammon of unrighteousness." Money is often made an occasion of sin, and the love of money is the root of all evil. Yet even of this unrighteous mammon, a righteous use may be made. Our Lord's precept would be more clear, if rendered thus: "Make to yourselves friends WITH the mammon of unrighteousness." How can friends be made with this mammon? By spending it in the relief of the saints and in the service of God. The widows whom Dorcas clothed, the prophets whom Obadiah fed, the apostle whom Onesiphorus visited, and Phebe succored, with all those brethren and strangers whom Gaius brought forward on their missionary journeys, will be witnesses of their charity and piety before the great white throne.

It is true the disciples were poor; but the poor, by the gift of two mites, show more love to God than the rich by large contributions out of their abundance. The Lord knows that he who is faithful in the *least* would be faithful in *much.* That poor widow who cast her mites into the treasury will be intrusted with true riches in the world to come.

Riches are only *lent* to the possessor, not *given.* This is the meaning of the verse: "If ye have not been faithful in that which is *another man's*, who shall give you that which is your *own?*" Every possession is now, as *if* it were another man's: it is only *lent.* Hereafter a possession will be *bestowed* upon the righteous, even an inheritance that *fadeth not away.* As riches are only lent, an account of the use to which they have been applied will be required. What account will those render who wilfully devote any part of their property to the service of Mammon, the god of this world? Whatever is spent in the encouragement of sin is spent in the service of Mammon. There are some persons who employ *part* of their money in doing good and *part* in promoting evil. They attempt to serve God and Mammon. They support Sunday-schools and Bible societies with part of their property, and with another part they encourage those worldly amusements, and that proud display, which are condemned in the word of God. But those who really love their crucified Saviour cannot act thus. The apostle Paul declares, "God forbid that I should glory save in the cross of our Lord Jesus Christ, by whom the world is crucified unto me and I unto the world."

Evening Scripture portion.
Gal. VI. *Sowing to the flesh, and to the Spirit.*

LUKE XVI. 14–18.—*Christ rebukes the Pharisees who derided him.*

THE Pharisees hated reproof. When they found the Lord's discourses applied to their own case they were angry. Conscious that they were covetous, they could not bear to hear covetousness spoken against. It is natural to the human heart to shrink from the touch of truth. How often ministers find that their hearers have been offended by the most searching parts of their sermons! Let us inquire whether we hate to hear our faults reproved. No doubt it is painful to be told of our sins. But is it not better to be made acquainted with them *now*, than to wait till we stand before the face of God? The kindest friends we have are those who take us apart to say, "Are you acting right in this point, or in that particular?" The most faithful ministers are those who will not let sinners slumber on in their sins, till the fire of eternal wrath devour them.

But none are so angry at reproof as those who make a false profession of religion. The Pharisees were only anxious that *men* should think highly of their characters. As they knew that men could not see into their hearts, they did not care in what state *they* remained. If a monarch were going to pass through a town, the inhabitants would probably cleanse and adorn the *outside* of their houses: but as they would know he could not see through the walls, they would not think it necessary to make the inside beautiful. But if the monarch were to announce that he should enter the house of one of the citizens, then what care would be used to render it fit for his reception! The King of kings searches every heart. A fair outside is not sufficient: God knoweth our *hearts*. A heart, unwashed in the blood of Christ, and unrenewed by his Holy Spirit, is an abomination in his sight. It may be highly esteemed by men, and called a tender heart, a kind, warm, and good heart: but it is pronounced by God to be a deceitful and desperately wicked heart. With such a heart none can enter his kingdom. The Pharisees had unconverted hearts. They professed to love God: but in reality they hated Him. How did they show they hated Him? By hating his law. They did not keep his holy commandments. Christ reminded them of one great sin, which they frequently committed. They broke the seventh commandment by putting away their wives in order to marry others. This sin had been rebuked by the prophet Malachi four hundred years before. He had said, "The Lord hath been witness between thee and the wife of thy youth, against whom thou hast dealt treacherously; and yet she is thy companion and the wife of thy covenant." Yet these Jews in Malachi's time had made a great profession of religion. At the very time they were treating their wives with cruelty, they were offering sacrifices to God at his altar. But did he accept these sacrifices? No, he abhorred them. The injured wives had poured out their tears before the altar, where their treacherous husbands presented their offerings—God saw those tears with compassion, and rejected those offerings with indignation. Let us never imagine that God will accept any of our services, while we are ill-treating any of his creatures. If, when we go and kneel before God to say our prayers, any person is pouring out tears before his footstool on account of our ill-treatment, can we expect our prayers to be heard? God has declared in his word that He will hear the cry of the oppressed, and that He will punish the oppressors: "Ye shall not afflict any widow, or fatherless child. If thou afflict them in any wise, and they cry at all unto me, I will surely hear their cry: and my wrath shall wax hot, and I will kill you with the sword; and your wives shall be widows, and your children fatherless." Ex. xxii. 22–24.

Evening Scripture portion. Mal. II. ***Conjugal treachery.***

MARK X. 13–16.—*Christ blesses little children.*

How many young and tender hearts have been encouraged to come to their Saviour by the sweet declaration, " Suffer the little children to come unto me !" How many dying children have lisped these words in their last moments ! When Jesus uttered them, he knew what comfort they would afford to the lambs of his flock for many ages to come.

It was, however, in *displeasure* that he gave the command, " Let the little children come unto me." It was not with the *children* that he was displeased, nor with their *mothers*, but with his own *disciples*. He was not often *much displeased* with *them*. There must have been some *great* offence to excite this *great* displeasure. It was a *great* offence to attempt to drive away these infants from their Saviour ! How could the disciples take so much upon them, as to forbid the mothers to bring their babes ! Pride lurked in their hearts, and suggested many harsh and ungracious measures. Before Jesus left this world he charged Peter to feed his lambs ;—those lambs whom He carries in his own bosom. Faithful ministers love little children, and are ready to instruct them.

The babes brought to Jesus were too young to receive instruction ; therefore the Lord only took them in his arms and blessed them. He knew even then what should befall each—he knew which fair blossom would be nipped in the bud, and which would bloom in the church on earth. He knew which smiling infant would become a minister, and which would prove a martyr. May we not hope that none of the infants that Jesus blessed were lost forever ? Was not His blessing the pledge of their salvation ?

The parents did well in bringing them to Christ. Many parents had brought sick children to him to be healed : but these parents sought no temporal benefits : they desired that the Saviour should put his hands upon their little ones, and *pray*. Surely Jesus must have been as much *pleased* with these parents, as he was *displeased* with his disciples. He still is pleased when mothers care more for the immortal *souls* of their children than for their perishing *bodies*. How grateful these little children ought to have been to their kind parents, when they were old enough to know what those parents had done for them in their infancy ! Many are indebted to the secret prayers of a mother to her Saviour for the richest blessings they enjoy ! We never can repay our parents for the prayers they have offered up on our behalf. The kindest parents often make mistakes in their manner of bringing up their children : but no mistakes will prove fatal, if they are fervent in their prayers for them, and consistent in their example.

What reason did Jesus give for receiving these little ones so kindly ? He did not say it was because he loved their parents, or because he knew the children would be holy when they grew up; but he said, "For of such is the kingdom of heaven." The disciples had only tc observe the ways of the little creatures, then folded in their mothers' arms, in order to know what they themselves ought to be. Those babes cared not for strangers, but only for the hand that fed them, for the arm that upheld them, for the face that smiled on them. Such ought to be the devoted affection of all believers for their everlasting Friend. How interesting it is to observe a little child, while we think of the words, "Of such is the kingdom of heaven!" Does not this sentence give us ground to believe that there are many little children now in glory?

Why do babes ever taste death? This epitaph was once written upon an infant's tomb:

It died, for Adam sinned.
It lives, for Jesus died.

Every action of our Saviour silently assures us that he loves children. He listens to their songs in the temple,—he rebukes their enemies,—he folds them in his arms,—he lays his hands upon them and blesses them. Will he shut *those* out from his presence in glory whom he would not allow to be sent from his presence upon *earth?* If he prayed for them when he lived here below, does he refuse to intercede for them now he reigns on yonder throne above? Surely he would be *much displeased* with *us*, if we were to harbor any doubts of his tender love for the little creatures that his hands first formed, and that he has never ceased to defend and bless.

Evening Scripture portion. 1 Sam. III. *The calling of Samuel.*

LUKE XVI. 19–24.—*The rich man's petition for his own relief.*

IN this parable the curtain that conceals the eternal world is lifted up;—and by whom? By Him who every moment beholds the sons of men sinking into hell, or soaring up to heaven. He described these solemn scenes that we might be filled with holy awe. They were ever before his eyes, and he wondered at the indifference of sinners to their approaching doom.

No doubt this rich man and this beggar were *real* persons. HE had no need to employ *fiction* who knew all *facts.*

It may appear strange to short-sighted mortals that God should permit one of his own beloved to languish, covered with sores, before a lordly gate. But the eye of faith beholds the happy spirit of the beggar, conveyed by glorious angels along the path of life into the presence of God. Then the mystery is explained. The Holy Spirit had sanctified the sorrowful heart of Lazarus, and Jesus had pardoned all his sins. When we see a poor diseased object, let us remember Lazarus, and say, "This may be one of God's elect." But we know that there are many who suffer afflictions in vain; many who are not softened by poverty or sickness; many who curse God and die.

The rich man does not appear to have committed any flagrant crime; he seems to have been a respectable worldly man. His body was buried with pomp, but his soul was not conducted with honor through the regions of the air to eternal glory. "In hell he lifts up his eyes, being in torments!" What a change was this! instead of a bed of down,—burning coals; instead of purple raiment,—a flaming robe; instead of sumptuous fare,—the want of all things, even of a drop of water. But what a glorious sight he beheld! heaven with its inhabitants. Do we envy him this privilege? How the sight must have added to his misery! *We* should like to behold the saints' abode, for we hope to reach it: but in hell, "Hope that comes to all, comes never." The flame must have seemed to burn with redoubled fury, when the lost spirit saw the stream which makes glad the city of our God. Among the guests at the supper of the Lamb, he descried Abraham and Lazarus. He had been brought up to revere Abraham as his great ancestor, and as the father of the faithful. Though he had never seen him before, yet he knew him. It is probable he had been accustomed to despise Lazarus as a loathsome object; now he saw this despised beggar seated next to the honorable patriarch. God had exalted Abraham when upon earth, and had abased Lazarus, but he had bestowed like precious faith upon them both. When we behold the company of the redeemed, we may expect to know them again, whether we were before acquainted with their *persons*, or only with their *names*. God grant that we may not behold them *afar off*, as the rich man did, but that we may be mingled in their society. We may expect to see among the eminent servants of God, among ministers, missionaries, and reformers, among prophets, apostles, and martyrs, others—who have lived and died in meanness and obscurity, —blind beggars, hospital patients, and workhouse inmates. Some of these will doubtless occupy places next to such revered men as Luther or as Latimer,—as Daniel, Job, or Noah.

The rich man must have been surprised to see the beggar in so honorable a place. Did he recognise none of his kindred, nor acquaintance, nor servants, that he fixed all his hopes of receiving relief upon Lazarus? Where were his father and mother? Where were his friends and neighbors? Had none of them reached the place of rest? It is to be feared that there are ungodly families whose names are unknown among the blessed. They have encouraged each other in forgetfulness of God, and have sunk down together into the pit. Why did the rich man think that Lazarus would be ready to come to his aid? No doubt the crumbs from his table had often been given to the beggar who lay at his gate, and therefore he may have thought he had some claim upon his services now. But surely if this rich man had loved God, he would have bestowed more than *crumbs* upon the poor sufferer dying before his eyes. Now his condition was far worse than that of Lazarus had ever been. The least moisture upon his tongue was the only boon he asked, and it was denied him. The misery of hell is COMPLETE. *Here* in our deepest sorrows there is some alleviation, some comforting circumstance, some ray of hope; but in hell there is none; *all* is darkness, desolation, destitution, and despair.

Evening Scripture portion. Ps. XLIX. *Vanity of earthly glory.*

LUKE XVI. 25–28.—*The rich man's petition for his brethren.*

IF prayers were heard in hell, how many would be offered up! But the abode of despair is not the place for prayer. All the rich man's requests were refused. The first was a very small petition. It was not a petition for release. Lost spirits know that release is impossible. The gates have closed upon them FOREVER. The Redeemer's blood cannot be sprinkled upon their conscience, the Holy Spirit cannot be shed abroad in their hearts; therefore salvation cannot be obtained. But the rich man hoped that the slightest possible relief might be granted. He did not ask that Lazarus might bring him a *draught*, nor even a *drop* of water: he did not ask that he might dip his *hand* or his *finger* in water,—but he asked that he might dip the *tip* of his finger in water, and apply it to his burning tongue. Yet the request was refused. Abraham reminded the tormented spirit that on earth he had received good things, and Lazarus evil things. By the manner in which Abraham reasoned, it is evident that the rich man had desired, when on earth, no *better* portion than he now received; and that Lazarus had been content with the bitter portion allotted to him. It was, therefore, just that each should now abide by his own choice. Lazarus must not feel even for a *moment* the scorching flames of hell, nor must the rich man taste one *drop* of the cooling streams of heaven. God now gives *us our* choice. Do we prefer *heaven*, with any amount of previous *sufferings*, to *earth*, with any amount of passing *delights?* Which would we rather encounter,—the *trials* of the saints, or the *temptations* of the world?

We perceive that if there had been *no* impassable gulf between heaven and hell, yet that Lazarus would not have been permitted to sooth the sufferings of the lost. But there *is* such a gulf. It fills heaven with REPOSE, and hell with DESPAIR. The inhabitants of each world know that there can be no change of state. Hell knows that no celestial comforter will ever enter her gates, and Heaven that no malicious enemy will ever break through hers.

But though the rich man found there was no path from heaven to *hell*, he knew there was a path from heaven to *earth*. He requested that Lazarus might be sent to warn his five brethren of the danger of their condition. It seems that he had left no children upon earth Perhaps he had been cut off in his youth. We cannot tell what his *motives* were for desiring that his brethren should not partake his misery. Can natural affection subsist in *hell?* or was the rich man afraid lest the reproaches of brothers, whom he had corrupted by his example, should add to his own torment? Let us be reminded by his prayer of the privileges we now enjoy. Have we any unconverted relations? We may pray for them, not to *Abraham*, but—to *God*. We will not pray that a departed spirit may be sent to warn them, but we will entreat that God's Holy Spirit may convince and convert them. The saints can witness that God does hear their prayers, and has mercy on others for their sake. It makes a Christian's heart sad to think of those who have shared with him a mother's care, not sharing with him a Saviour's glory. It would add to the joy of a believer, even in heaven, to see every one of his kindred sitting around their heavenly Father's table.

If pious *brothers* feel solicitude for their *brothers'* salvation, what must *parents* feel for the souls of their beloved *children?* They bear them incessantly on their hearts before God, and with tears implore the Lord to preserve them from sinking into the place of torment. They can hardly imagine that it would be possible that they themselves should be happy in heaven, if any one of their dear children were missing. Yet some who have brought down their parents' gray hairs with sorrow to the grave, have repented *afterwards*. Then they have lamented (O how bitterly!) that they did not gladden their parents while they were yet alive. It is their comfort to think that their parents will see them enter into glory. One of these penitents was heard to say, "How much surprised my father will be to see *me* enter heaven!"*

Evening Scripture portion. Rom. IX. *St. Paul's love for his brethren.*

LUKE XVI. 29 to end.—*Abraham's reply to the rich man.*

IT is natural to suppose that the sight of a departed spirit would awaken a thoughtless soul. The rich man imagined that his brethren would turn from sin if Lazarus were to appear to them in the midst of their luxury and their gayety, and to say, "I am the beggar that once languished at the gate: I am now an inhabitant of heaven: I partake of the immortal feast: I sit with the saints, and behold the

* The son of the celebrated Grimshaw, rector of Haworth, Yorkshire.

face of God: I have seen your brother—he is not with us: I heard a doleful cry: it was his voice: he was burning in the flames of hell: he entreated that I might moisten his tongue with the tip of my finger, but the request could not be granted. He has remembered you. He once lived (as you do now) a worldly, thoughtless life; he knows how your course will end: he dreads lest you should join him in the place of torment." The rich man supposed that such a warning voice would alarm his brethren, stop them in their sinful career, and turn them to God. But the Lord has *not* appointed this mode of dealing with men. He *might* have made the departed the ministers of the living. Every dead relative *might* have appeared again; the happy to tell of their happiness, the miserable to tell of their misery. But God devised another method. He spoke to holy men of old, and taught them to write the words he dictated. He appointed living men to speak of those holy words to their fellow-creatures. This is God's method. Thousands and tens of thousands have been saved by these means. They have believed the written message, and the living preacher, and have fled from the threatened wrath. God continues to pursue this plan of dealing with men. He requires us to believe what we do not see, only because HE says it. The Lord Jesus well knew that if he had appeared to his enemies when he rose again from the dead, he would not have overcome their enmity; therefore he did *not* appear to *them*. He appeared to his *friends* for their *comfort*, but not to his *enemies* for their *conversion*.

The Lord's method must be the most excellent way. If we would save the souls of men, we must let them hear the word of God, which he spoke by Moses, by the prophets, by his own Son, and by his apostles. That word has awakened whole families, who were as thoughtless as the rich man's brothers, and has saved them from the place of torment. Every soul that reaches the abode of bliss, will trace his coming there to his having heard the word of God. Some will speak of *one* part of that blessed word, and some will speak of *another*, and all will bless the Holy Spirit who opened their hearts to receive the truth. We shall not need the Bible in heaven, because we shall be with Him who wrote it; but surely it will not be *forgotten* there. Neither will it be forgotten in *hell*. It will add to the fierceness of the flames to remember the slighted warnings, the despised promises, the rejected invitations of the word of God.

Evening Scripture portion. Hebrews IV. *Danger of unbelief.*

LUKE XVII. 1–4.—*Christ teaches the forgiveness of injuries.*

WHEN Jesus was alone with his disciples, he dwelt upon those topics that were the most necessary for them to understand. All who believe in the Saviour must listen with particular interest to these conversations.

Believers *now*, like the first disciples, are "compassed with infirmity." The instructions that suited the little flock who surrounded the Lord when he was on earth, will suit the larger flock that wait at his feet now he is enthroned in the heavens.

On this occasion the Saviour warned his disciples against two things—committing offences, and indulging an unforgiving spirit.

The "offences" spoken of are stumbling-blocks laid in the way of weak believers. Those who are *strong* in faith must be careful not to injure the *weak* in faith, even as the *elder* children in a family must carefully avoid hurting the tender frames of the younger children. A considerate youth would refrain from performing some feats that *he* could with *safety* perform, if he thought that his little brothers might be tempted to imitate his example, and to endanger their limbs or their lives. Believers *strong* in faith ought to act in the same way, and to refrain even from enjoying *lawful* privileges, sooner than endanger their weak brethren. In Rom. xiv. the apostle Paul points out very clearly this duty.

But if it be a grievous sin to wound a weak believer through *carelessness*, how dreadful a crime it must be to injure him *wilfully!* No true believer would commit this sin. It would be better to be cast into the sea, (as criminals often are in the East,) than to be guilty of it. To persuade a child of God to act against his conscience, and to break his Father's law, is to commit a worse sin than *murder*. If you were to induce a person to leap from a high window, you might be the occasion of the destruction of his *body*, but if you were to tempt him to break the Sabbath, to tell a lie, to join in profane discourse, you would endanger his *soul*. God indeed *could* preserve the body from being dashed to pieces, and the soul from being lost, but the person who deceived would be as guilty as if the worst consequences had followed. How watchful we ought to be over our behavior to the children of God, lest we injure those whom God guards with such tender care!

There is another sin that we must strive against, if we desire to please God. It is an unforgiving spirit. The family of God upon earth are so full of defects, that they often annoy each other. If we were surrounded by angels, we should have no temptations to anger. But is there one of us who can say, "I act like an angel to those around me?" Is it not true that we are constantly exercising the patience of our companions? Does it become us to be slow to forgive? When we are conscious that we have wounded another, each of us should say, "I repent;" and when another says to us, "I repent," each of us should reply, "I forgive." But if our brother forget his duty, and omit to acknowledge his fault, we ought not to be rigorous in demanding the confession. Were he to make it, we should find it more *easy* to forgive; but if he withhold it, we have the opportunity of showing a higher degree of grace by forgiving, *notwithstanding* his omission. In most differences, however, *both* parties have something to confess and something to forgive. Mutual concessions and mutual forgiveness are generally needed. He who *first* says, "I repent," acts the most Christian part; for he shows that he has *already* forgiven the trespasses of his brother. Had not Jesus forgiven us *before* any of us said, "I repent," we never should have felt even the *desire* to obtain his forgiveness. It was the thought that He loved us *before* we loved him that melted our hearts, and made us feel truly penitent for our sins.

Evening Scripture portion. Rom. XIV. *Regard for weak brethren.*

Luke XVII. 5-10.—*The disciples pray for more faith.*

Why did the disciples offer up the prayer, "Increase our faith?" Had their Lord just revealed some *mystery* that it was difficult to *believe?* No: but he had just enjoined a *duty* that it was difficult to *practise.* That duty was, "Forgiving oft-repeated trespasses." Whoever has been deeply or often injured, and has endeavored freely to forgive, knows that the wicked heart rises up against the righteous deed—and that the struggle is sharp between the sense of injury and of duty. In vain the person offended reasons with himself, and urges himself to the performance of the command; his unwilling soul hangs back, and refuses to obey. What is the only remedy against this inward repugnance? *Faith.* Had we more faith, we should *run,* where now we cannot *walk.* The disciples felt their need of faith, and they applied to him who alone can bestow it. Jesus is the *author* of faith. Though some *prophets* have been enabled to bestow *temporal* benefits, none have ever had the power to confer *spiritual* good. No mere man was ever known to give repentance, or to strengthen faith. But the Son of God can do all things. If any man lack *wisdom,* let him ask of him and it shall be given him: if any man lack *faith,* let him ask and it also shall be given. Have we any excuse for saying, "I cannot do what my Lord commands?" Do we find it difficult to forgive *repeated* injuries, or *great* injuries, or (which is harder still) to forgive trespasses still *unconfessed,* there is power in Christ to enable us to overcome these mountains.

And when we have succeeded in conquering the deep-rooted sins of our hearts, what ought to be our feeling then? Our Saviour teaches us what it ought to be. When we have done all that was commanded, we must say, "We are unprofitable servants: we have done that which was our *duty* to do." But WE have never done *all,* or *half,* or a *hundredth part* of the things that were commanded us. We are not only unprofitable, but we are provoking and guilty servants. Had we not the God of all patience for our master, we should have been dis missed long ago from his service. But instead of dismissing us, he treats us in the most generous manner. His *yoke* is *easy* and his *burden* is *light*, while his *reward* is a *weight* of glory. He is so infinitely gracious, that after having borne with our imperfect services, he has promised to say to each who sincerely loves him, "Well done, good and faithful servant: enter thou into the joy of thy Lord."

The thought of receiving such commendation ought to humble us more than the severest reproof. It *will* humble those who shall receive it. Every one of them will cast his crown of life at the feet of Him who bestowed it, and say, "Thou art worthy, O Lord, to receive glory, and honor, and power." (Rev. iv. 11.)

Evening Scripture portion. Gen. L. *Joseph confirms his brethren's pardon.*

LUKE IX. 51–56.—*James and John betray a revengeful spirit.*

AND was it the *gentle* apostle John who proposed to consume the Samaritans with fire? Yes, it was even that apostle whom Jesus loved; that apostle who leaned on his breast at supper, who stood by his cross, and who became a son to the Messiah's bereaved mother. Yes, even John once indulged a proud, passionate, and revengeful spirit. When the Samaritan villagers refused to receive the Lord, the apostles James and John thought that they showed a holy zeal in desiring to revenge the insult. How easy it is to deceive ourselves respecting the motives of our actions! Party spirit often appears like holy zeal; but it is of an opposite nature, and comes from a different place.

The Lord felt compassion for these ignorant Samaritans. They refused to receive him into their houses; but had they known who he was, and what he could bestow, they would have asked of him, and he would have received them into *everlasting* habitations. But they knew him not; they looked upon him as their enemy, because he belonged to the Jewish nation.

The sin of the well-instructed apostles James and John was much greater than the sin of the ignorant Samaritans. When Moses and Aaron once said to the Israelites, "Must we fetch water for you rebels!" the Lord was so much displeased with the passionate speech, that he permitted neither of these eminent saints to enter the promised land. Yet was not the spirit of the brothers James and John like the spirit of Moses and Aaron on that occasion? The two leaders of Israel would have suffered the thirsty host to languish for want of *water;* the two apostles were anxious to consume the Samaritan villagers with *fire.*

There was once another prophet who indulged the same wrong

spirit. Jonah desired the destruction of Nineveh. God expostulated with the prophet upon his cruelty in wishing so large a city, containing so many little children, to be destroyed.

God loves better to hear his people intercede for perishing sinners, (as Abraham did for Sodom,) than to hear them plead for their destruction. It better becomes a creature, who deserves himself to be consumed, and who has been snatched by the arm of divine mercy as a brand from the burning—it better becomes such a one to ask *mercy* for his fellow-sinners, than to invoke *vengeance.* When Elijah called down fire from heaven to consume the captains that the king had sent to take him, he spoke in the power of God's Spirit, and not after his *own will.* When Elisha turned and cursed the children of Bethel, he acted by the direction of God. When David in his psalms denounces awful curses upon the wicked, he speaks in the person of *Christ,* and foretells the sentence which the Lord will pronounce upon *His own* enemies at the last day. There is not a word in the Bible, from the beginning to the end, to sanction a revengeful spirit. But nothing can show the hatefulness of such a spirit so clearly as the example of Christ. Even when nailed upon the cross, he prayed for his murderers, saying, "Father, forgive them; for they know not what they do." Do not we feel ashamed of the harshness and heat of our own spirits? Are we not too soon provoked, and too slowly pacified? All who know their own hearts lament that they have not yet attained to that charity which beareth all things, believeth all things, hopeth all things, endureth all things. But let us not be discouraged. Let us pray that the Holy Spirit may sanctify our hearts, and subdue those proud tempers and angry feelings that disturb our peace, dishonor our profession, and displease our Saviour.

Evening Scripture portion. 2 Kings I. *Elijah brings down fire from heaven.*

LUKE IX. 57 to end.—*Christ replies to three persons.*

WOULD not each of us like to know what the Saviour would have said to us had *we* lived upon earth at the time that he honored it with his bodily presence? We have just read of three persons who had interviews with him, each of whom received an answer suited to his real character. The first and the last of these three *offered* to follow Jesus; the second was *called* to follow him. It is natural for us to suppose that those who *offered* to become his disciples were more attached to him than the man who did *not* offer himself, but who only received a call. Yet it is evident from the Lord's replies to each that *he* was *most* approved whom we might deem *least* earnest.

The *first* of the three appears to have mistaken the nature of the Lord's service. He said, "I will follow thee whithersoever thou goest." But was he prepared to follow him to prison and to death? It appears from the Lord's answer that he was not. Jesus replied: "Foxes have holes, and birds of the air have nests: but the Son of man hath not where to lay his head." By this answer the Saviour seemed to say, "If you desire a life of ease, you must not follow me; for I have no retreat from the malice of my foes." Had the man truly loved him, he would not have been deterred by any dangers from following his steps. As no further mention is made of this man, it is most probable that he was discouraged by the reply he received.

Those who cannot read the heart might have thought that the man who said, "Suffer me first to go and bury my father," was *unwilling* to follow Jesus. But the Lord judged differently. He saw in the man the spirit that he approved. It was not *unwillingness* to obey his call, but a sense of duty to an aged, and perhaps a deceased parent, that prompted the request. The Lord replied, "Let the dead bury their dead." It is probable that this man had relations who were *dead* in sins. The Lord appointed that they should bury the dead father, and that the *living* son should preach the kingdom of God. He was not *dead:* he was made *alive* by the Spirit of God. Christ does not say to *every* one, "Preach thou the kingdom of God;" but when he does call a man by his Spirit to the holy ministry, every hinderance to his obedience to the call must be laid aside. Many who have gone forth as missionaries to heathen lands, have broken the dearest ties in order to pursue their sacred work! Some have left widowed mothers, others have sacrificed their brightest earthly hopes, rather than disobey the command, "Preach thou the kingdom of God."

The *last* of the three resembled the *first* in *one* respect. Like him he *offered* to follow Jesus. He resembled the *second* in another respect. Like him he asked permission to delay his coming for a little while; but the reason he gave was different. He wished to bid fare well to those at home in his house. Was this request wrong? Did not Elisha once make a similar request when called by Elijah? It is evident that in this case the *motive* was wrong. The Lord's answer showed that *this* man, like the *first*, was not prepared for the service he offered to engage in. His heart still clung to his earthly interests, and was not devoted to Christ. Therefore the Lord compared him to one, who, holding the handle of the plough, instead of fixing his eye upon the furrow before him that he may make it straight, turns his head round, and gazes on the scenes behind. Such a man, he declared, was not fit for the kingdom of God.

The *first* and *last* of the three appear to have been unsound at *heart*. The first was *eager* to set out, because he knew not the nature of the service; the last was *unwilling* to set out immediately, because he loved too well his earthly portion.

Let us examine our own hearts, to see whether we resemble any one of these three men! Perhaps we are eager, like the first, to undertake some Christian work. But are we prepared for sufferings, and persecution, and poverty? Or our case may resemble that of the last. We may intend some day to become devoted Christians, while we feel so much engrossed by our earthly enjoyments that we are continually putting off the time for beginning to lead a new life. The Lord Jesus knows our most secret feelings. It is useless to attempt to deceive him: if we do not really love him, and think it a privilege to serve him, he will not accept our services. If, like the second character, we really long to do something for his cause, but are hindered by other pressing duties, the way shall be made clear; a door shall be opened, difficulties shall be removed, and the desire of our hearts shall be granted.

Evening Scripture portion. 1 Kings XIX. *Elijah calls Elisha.*

LUKE XVII. 11–19. *The ten Lepers.*

How touching are the words, "Where are the nine?" The Lord keeps an account of the number that he blesses, and he expects to see them at his feet, giving him thanks. He knows how many he has lifted up from the gates of death since the last setting sun. Some called on him *yesterday* out of the depths of distress; he heard them, and *to-day* disease is subdued, and danger is averted. Parents who feared *yesterday* that their absent children had met with some fatal accident, have heard *to-day* that they are safe. Persons plunged in deep poverty, who feared that they should soon perish with famine, or pine in a prison, have received gifts *to-day* that have extricated them from all their troubles. Are those persons to-day pouring forth their thanks at their Redeemer's feet? It is to be feared that the Lord still says, "Where are the nine; the nine *hundred*, the nine *thousand*, the nine *million*, that I have delivered from distress?"

We are astonished at the ingratitude of the lepers; but no doubt they had some plausible excuses to make for their conduct. The Lord had said unto them, "Go, show yourselves unto the priests." As they were going they were cleansed. They still followed the direction that had been given them, and pursued their way. But gratitude ought to have turned their steps back again. If they delayed to go to Jesus, they might never enjoy another opportunity of thanking him; for he was on his way, and would soon be gone. *One*, however, followed not the example of his companions. When he felt the glow of health in his veins, and saw the hue of health upon his hands, he did not hesitate how to act: he returned *alone*, and with a loud voice and in an humble attitude, glorified God. And this man was a *Sa maritan!* He belonged to an ignorant nation, to a nation whom the Jews despised, and whose religion the Lord disapproved. This instance shows that among the most ignorant there are some whose hearts God has prepared to love him. Those who visit the abodes of misery in crowded cities find some of the poor outcasts ready to receive the truth. Missionaries find some in heathen lands who, as soon as they hear the Gospel, embrace it. But there are only a *few* in this state. The mass of mankind in all countries care for the gifts, and not at all for the giver. The human heart is naturally ungrateful. Men are disposed to be ungrateful to their fellow-creatures. They feel humbled under the weight of great obligations, and seek an *excuse* for not being thankful. But they are far more ungrateful to God than they are to any other being. His mercies are considered matters of course. People like to imagine that all things happen by chance, and that God does not trouble himself with their little concerns. By these ideas, they relieve themselves from the burden of gratitude.

There is a charge that will be brought against sinners hereafter, which will involve them in the deepest guilt. It is this: they knew that the Father had given his only Son to die for them, and they were not *thankful*. Even devils will not have *this* black crime to answer for. Are there as many as *one* in *ten* in this Christian land who have *heartily* thanked God for the gift of his Son? who have thanked him *as* heartily for it, as they would thank a fellow-creature who had saved their lives at the risk of his own? or even as heartily as they would a friend for showing them common kindness and hospitality?

Evening Scripture portion. Gen. XL. *The butler's ingratitude to Joseph.*

LUKE XVII. 20–24.—*Christ prepares his disciples for his absence.*

WHEN the Pharisees asked questions the Lord disappointed them by his replies. They made inquiries in the hope of entangling him, but they themselves were confounded by the answers they received. They asked when the kingdom of God should come. The Lord, instead of acquainting them with that great secret, taught a more important truth. Jesus will one day be declared "King over all the earth;" but even now he reigns in the hearts of true believers; therefore he said to the Pharisees, "The kingdom of God is *within* you." It was useless for them to be looking for the appearance of the Lord in his glory, while they had not received him into their hearts.

The Lord would not converse on this subject with his *enemies;* but he turned to his *disciples*, and gave them much instruction concerning his second coming. He said, "The days come when ye shall desire to see one of the days of the Son of man, and ye shall not see it."

What did he mean by *one* of the days of the Son of man? Was not the day in which he was speaking *one* of the days, and is not the day in which he will come again *another* of the days? The Lord prepared his disciples for his approaching departure, and foretold that when he was gone away they should long to see him again—that is, they should desire to see *one* of his days. Were not these words fulfilled? How earnestly John, when banished to the Isle of Patmos, desired to see the glorious day of the Son of man! Almost the last words he wrote were these: "Come, Lord Jesus." And do not all the disciples of the Lord long to see his day of glory? This is one of the marks by which they are distinguished—they "love his appearing." (1 Tim. iv. 8.) They pray for it constantly in the words, "Thy kingdom come."

But though they do not know *when* it will come, they do know *how:* for Jesus has told them that "as the lightning, that lighteneth out of one part under heaven, shineth unto the other part under heaven; so shall also the Son of man be in *his day*." This promise is a great comfort to all his disciples. It would have disquieted their minds, if they had thought it possible that their Lord might return to the earth without their knowing it. They would have been interrupted in their holy pursuits by the idea, "He may now be at Jerusalem, or in the desert, or in some hidden chamber, or in some retired spot." But they now feel sure that when he comes, they shall see him, wherever they may be, or whatever they may be doing. Only a *few* disciples saw him ascend in the clouds from the Mount of Olives: but *every eye* shall behold him when he comes again. How exceedingly great will be the brightness of that day! When the Lord Jesus appeared to the persecuting Saul, the light was beyond the brightness of the sun at noonday, and its dazzling splendor blinded the eyes of the astonished man. (Acts xxvi. 13.) But when he comes again, the light will spread over the whole world; saints will be strengthened to gaze upon the scene, and will be changed into the image of their Lord; while impenitent sinners will find the day of *brightness* a day of *darkness* to them. How striking are the words of the prophet Amos on this subject! Amos v. 18–20: "Wo unto you that desire the day of the Lord: to what end is it for you? the day of the Lord is darkness, and not light. As if a man did flee from a lion, and a bear met him, or went into the house, and leaned his hand on the wall, and a serpent bit him. Shall not the day of the Lord be darkness, and not light? even very dark, and no brightness in it?"

Evening Scripture portion. Amos V. ***The day of the Lord.***

LUKE XVII. 25 to end.—*Christ prepares his disciples for his sudden return.*

THOUGH the Lord did not inform his disciples *when* his kingdom should come, he told them of one event that must happen before that glorious day arrived: that event was his own death. "But *first* he must suffer many things, and be rejected of this generation." His disciples also would suffer many things, and be rejected by generation after generation. The history of their sufferings to the end of time is to be found in the Revelation. That book is a book of *warnings* (as well as promises) to the church of God. It prepares them for enduring much tribulation before their Saviour appears to their comfort, and to the joy of their enemies.

But the Lord has concealed both the *time* and the *place* of his second appearing. When the disciples inquired, "Where, Lord?" he replied by a proverb, "Where the *body* is, thither will the eagles be gathered together." We need not seek to know the *place*, for we shall be gathered to that place, whenever the time arrives.

There is another most important circumstance which the Lord has *not* concealed. In what state will the world be when Jesus comes again? In the same state as it was before the flood. The book of Genesis, as well as the book of Revelation, is a book of warnings; for though it reveals events long *past*, they are types of events yet to *come*. The flood, and the burning of Sodom and Gomorrah, are types of the destruction of the wicked when Jesus comes again. *One family* only was saved when the flood came, and *one family* only was saved when the cities were burnt; and *one family* only will be saved when Jesus comes again. It is his *own* family, the people that he has chosen, and called to be his children. But in that one family, who were saved when Sodom was destroyed, there was a person who is held up as a warning to all who profess to belong to Christ. "Remember Lot's wife." She was *almost* saved: but yet—she was *lost.* And why? Because her heart still clung to the possessions she had left in Sodom. The Lord bids us beware of hankering after worldly goods. "In that day he which shall be upon the housetop, and his stuff in the house, let him not come down to take it away." This direction was *literally* observed by the disciples when Jerusalem was besieged by the Romans, but it is to be *spiritually* observed to the end of time. Occasions will arise when the people of God must sacrifice all they possess rather than be false to their Master's cause. "Whosoever shall lose his life shall preserve it."

It was painful to Lot to leave his wife a pillar of salt upon the plain of Sodom. Such separations as Lot then endured will take place when Christ comes again. Some who are living in the closest intimacy will be forever separated. The believer will be taken away from the side of his unbelieving brother, and transported into the presence of his Lord. None can imagine the despair of those who shall be left, or the horrors that will await them. Who is there who has not a believing relation? How could we bear the idea of seeing that holy person soaring away, and leaving us behind? *Now* he often invites us to walk with him in the ways of God—sometimes he prays *with* us, and more frequently still FOR us. It may seem impossible that an affectionate father, or a tender mother, should leave a child behind to be consumed by the ungodly; but when the righteous are borne by angels into the presence of God, none will be able to mount their fiery chariots, but those for whom they are sent. God is willing to save *all* of us. The way is open, and the invitation is free. "Whosoever will, let him take of the water of life freely." (Rev. xxii. 17.)

Evening Scripture portion. Gen. VI. *The flood.*

LUKE XVIII. 1–8.—*The parable of the unjust judge.*

THIS parable has been a great comfort to Christians while waiting for the second coming of the Son of man. The Lord had told his disciples that he would soon be absent from them. Eighteen hundred years have rolled away, and still the church is as a widow, and still Satan, her great adversary, is permitted to harass her. But has God been like an *unjust* judge? No, but he has *appeared* as *if* he did not hear his people's prayers for deliverance from their enemies. His widowed church has cried day and night to him, saying, "Avenge me of mine adversary," but God has not yet answered this prayer. He has not *yet* bound Satan with a great chain, and shut him up in the bottomless pit. Still our adversary goes about seeking whom he may devour; still he endeavors by various wiles and devices to destroy the people of God. And shall he always be permitted to do this? No; the day appointed for deliverance shall come. God will *not* say, like this unjust judge, "My church troubleth me; I will avenge her, lest by her continual coming she weary me." The Lord is never wearied by the supplications of his people, for he has said, "The prayer of the upright is his delight." He will say, "I will now avenge mine own elect, which cry day and night unto me, though I have borne long with them." Then He will send his Son from heaven to deliver his people, and to consume their enemies.

"Nevertheless, when the Son of Man cometh, shall he find faith on the earth?" Shall he find that his people have believed that he was coming? Will it not be as it was in the day of the resurrection, that even those who loved the Lord remembered *not* his promise? The angels said to the woman, "He is risen, as he *said*." *Then*, and not till then, those women remembered his words. Before Christ comes again many will be inclined to say, (like the two disciples going to Emmaus,) "We *trusted* it had been he which should have redeemed Israel."

While waiting for that day, we may go to our God in *every* hour of distress. He can bring to naught (as it is expressed in the Liturgy) all the devices which the craft or subtlety of the devil or man worketh against us. We always shall find that in the end He will say, "Shall I not hear my afflicted child who cries day and night unto me?" This is one of the comforts of his children, that they have a God to whom they can go in time of trouble. He is on their side; He takes their part. Whether it is disease or death that threatens them, or whether it is the persecutions of wicked men, or the temptations of Satan that harass them, the Lord is greater than their enemies, and is able to subdue them. He would hear his children at *first*, only he knows that waiting will exercise their faith. Therefore he bears long with them. Why did he return answers that appeared severe to the woman of Canaan? Why did he not heed the *first* summons of the sisters of Lazarus? Why did he suffer Job to pine with long sickness and sorrow? Was it not that he designed to teach his beloved this hard lesson, even that he hears them when he *seems* to disregard?

This is a lesson that is not understood by the little ones in Christ's school; they cannot bear delays, and think they are denials; but as their love increases, they can bear *apparent neglect*, and even *repulses*, without suspecting the loving-kindness of their heavenly Father. They know that God is love, and they can reason upon his love, and say, "He that spared not his own Son, but gave him up for us all, will he not with him also freely give us all things?"

Evening Scripture portion.
Lamentations III. 1–36. ***Prayer of the Church in trouble.***

LUKE XVIII. 9–14.—*The Prayers of the Pharisee and of the Publican.*

THERE are thousands of prayers offered up to God every day; there have been thousands offered up this day. Have they all been accepted? No; there are prayers which are not accepted. Are we anxious to know whether the prayer *we* offered up alone this morning was accepted or not?—or did we offer none?

What was it rendered the Pharisee's prayer so hateful to God? It was the pride of his heart. His prayer was in truth no *prayer* at all. He *boasted*, instead of praying; but he deceived his own heart by putting his boast in the form of a thanksgiving. He did not *feel* thankful when he said, "God, I *thank* thee I am not as other men." Had he felt thankful, he would not have despised the poor publican. How different were the feelings of St. Paul, when he said, "By the grace of God I am what I am!" When we are thankful, we are filled with *compassion* (not with *contempt*) for those who are less blessed than ourselves.

How many offer prayers like the Pharisee's, while they use the *words* of the publican! It is possible with all the pride of a Pharisee to smite upon the heart and to *say*, "Lord, be merciful to me a sinner!" But the publican *felt* what he said. He *thought* himself unworthy to lift up so much as his eyes unto heaven. He stood afar off from the Holy of holies, as unfit to enter the presence of God. He knew not that *we* know of a Saviour's love; but he must have trusted in the *promises* of pardon to penitent sinners through an atonement, or he could not have offered up this humble prayer. With what joy penitent sinners like this publican receive the tidings of a Saviour! There were such publicans in the Saviour's days, and they came to Jesus, and heard his word with thankfulness.

In what different states the Pharisee and the publican returned from the temple to their own houses! The publican went down a pardoned sinner, accepted for the sake of Christ. The Pharisee returned with the guilt of his sins upon his head, and that of the proud prayer he had offered, added to his former guilt. Pride is the most flagrant sin in God's sight. It has ruined multitudes of our fallen race, and it has even sunk angels into the bottomless abyss. In what state did we come down from our chambers this morning? Did we come down justified, or not? Have we ever made such humble, fervent supplications to God as the publican did? Are we ashamed of ourselves and of our sins? Have we earnestly implored the infinite mercy of God in Christ? It is an awful thing to be unjustified or unpardoned. To rise up unjustified,—to lie down unjustified,—to go out,—to come in—unjustified! To be exposed to death every moment, and yet—to be unjustified! But this is the state of every one who has not repented of his sins, and obtained pardon through the merits of his Saviour.

Evening Scripture portion. Titus III. *Justification by grace.*

MARK X. 17–22.—*The rich young ruler.*

IT is impossible not to feel interested in this young inquirer. The *respect* he paid to the Lord was rare in a man of rank and property. "He kneeled to him, and said, Good master." It is pleasing to see a *young* person anxious to learn the way of salvation. This youth came *running* to inquire what he should do to inherit eternal life. Though multitudes applied to the Saviour for the cure of their diseases, few inquired how they should obtain *salvation* for their *souls*. This young man's course of life appears to have been correct, and his disposition amiable. We are already disposed to love him, when we read, "The Lord beholding him, *loved* him." Though no doubt Jesus loved all his disciples, and though we know that he loves even sinners, yet this expression is scarcely used on any other occasion. There was a disciple of whom it is said that Jesus loved him, and there was a family at Bethany concerning whom the same is recorded. But they were his devoted followers, while this youth was not even a believer. Yet as the Lord was *man*, as well as *God*, he may have loved those qualities that attract *our* regard, and are called "amiable." Nothing is more amiable in youth than a docile disposition, a respectful demeanor, frankness of manner, and earnestness of spirit. All these the youth possessed. Even when he received a command that he would not obey, he still behaved in an *amiable* manner, and showed no angry *resentment*, but only deep *sorrow*. No doubt the Saviour was touched by his grief; but he spoke not a word of consolation. He, who comforted all who were cast down, saying, "Weep not," suffered this mourner to go away uncomforted. And why? Because there was no comfort for his sorrow. He grieved because the gate was too strait, and the way too narrow, that leads to eternal life. There can be no consolation for this grief, either in time or in eternity.

This young ruler did not know he was a sinner, and he did not feel his need of a Saviour. Neither did he look upon Jesus as a *Saviour*, but only as a *teacher*. When the Lord said, "Why callest thou *me* good? there is none good but God," the young man ought to have replied, "Thou art the *Son* of God." But he believed not in Jesus. He wished to find out a way by which he might save *himself*. Therefore the Lord showed him his own heart by giving him a commandment that he would not choose to obey. He said to him, "Sell all that thou hast, and give to the poor." This commandment was given as a test whereby to try the youth, to see whether he would do *all* the Lord required. Once God tried Abraham, by commanding him to offer up his only son Isaac. Abraham stood the test, and proved that he loved the Lord above *all*. The young man did *not* stand the test. He might have stood an *easier* test; he might have been willing to part with *half* his possessions; he might have been willing to part with *all*, had his possessions not been so *great*;—but to part with *all* his *great* possessions was more than he could bear to do. Some may feel inclined to wonder why the Lord imposed so hard a condition upon a young inquirer. They may say, "Is it not written that he does not quench the smoking flax, nor break the bruised reed?" This is true. When an afflicted father said with tears, "Help mine unbelief," the Lord did not discourage him, for he was as smoking flax. When a sinful woman washed his feet with tears, he did not repulse her: for she was as a bruised reed. But this young man was not as smoking flax, or as a bruised reed. He had no love for Christ,—no sorrow for sin,—no desire for pardon. The most open transgressor, who is conscious that he deserves to be condemned, is nearer salvation than such a self-righteous character as this young ruler was.

It may be that some of us, like this youth, desire to go to heaven. We think we are sincere. God may cause some event to happen that shall try our hearts, and prove whether we are ready to give up all beside, rather than relinquish our hope in Christ. *What* the trial may be cannot be foretold. It will be suited to our particular state. Orpah, as well as Ruth, professed great attachment to Naomi, her mother-in-law; but only Ruth clave to her, and to her God, in the midst of poverty and desolation. Many say to Christ, "Lord, Lord," who would not follow him to prison or to death. Those who have not felt their need of his blood to cleanse their sinful souls, may think that silver or gold, or friends, or fame, is more precious than Christ.

Evening Scripture portion. Ruth I. ***The faithful daughter-in-law.***

MARK X. 23–27.—*Christ declares the danger of possessing riches.*

Is it indeed so very hard for a rich man to enter the kingdom of God, and yet are men so anxious to become rich, and so much disposed to envy the rich, and to count them happy? Are parents so desirous to heap up treasures to leave to their children, and to see them occupy a higher station than themselves? Surely men do not *believe* this declaration of our Saviour. Even the disciples were exceedingly astonished at it. Jesus then *explained* what he had said, and declared that it was those who *trusted in* riches who could not enter heaven. But how hard it is to possess them, and *not* to *trust* in them!

Let us inquire *what* it is to *trust* in riches. It is to feel them to be our *own*, and not the *gift* of God. Whether we have earned them by our industry, or inherited them from our parents, they are not our *own*, but only *lent* to us, and therefore they ought to be used in promoting God's glory. But the rich are apt to be proud, and to forget who gave them all they possess.

To trust in riches is to look to them for happiness. The favor of God alone can make us really happy. Outward things cannot do it, —neither friends, nor children, nor houses, nor lands—nor all the pleasures, comforts, and honors in the world. Even a child has been heard to say, "*Things* cannot make *people* happy." And how do saints now in glory estimate those possessions on which men set their hearts? Do they not regard them as *rocks* upon which *souls* are shipwrecked,—as *snares* in which they are taken, and pierced through with many sorrows? It is true that riches might be converted into blessings. But how much *grace* does it require to use them aright! And how much *more* grace to *feel* aright when conscious of having great possessions! Great riches make people forget that they are great sinners, and lead them to neglect the great Saviour. The rich have many *friends*, and often they do not feel the need of a heavenly and almighty Friend. They have great *possessions below*, and often they are satisfied without an inheritance *above*. A rich gentleman once said to a day-laborer, "Do you know to whom those estates belong on the borders of the lake?" "No," replied the laborer. "They belong to *me*," said the rich man. "And the wood and the cattle,—do you know whose they are?" "No." "They are mine also," continued the rich man; "yes, all, all that you can see is mine." The peasant stood still a moment, then pointed to heaven, and in a solemn tone asked, "Is *that* also thine?"*

How apt the rich are to forget to look upwards, and to ask, "Is heaven mine?" Silver and gold cannot purchase it; nothing but a Saviour's precious blood. If an angel were commissioned to preach on earth, would he not rather speak to *peasants* than to *princes*,—for angels must know that they are seldom called to rejoice over a penitent clothed in purple and fine linen. When the Gospel is proclaimed in hovels, and even in prisons, it has far greater success than when it is spoken in courts. A *few* indeed in the highest stations have been subdued by the power of divine grace; a *few* honorable counsellors, such as Joseph and Nicodemus, have believed; a *few* honorable women, such as the Viscountess Glenorchy, and the celebrated Countess of Huntingdon, have devoted themselves to the service of God; a *few* mighty sovereigns, such as our wise Alfred, and our youthful Edward, have honored the King of kings, and the Lord of lords; but the greater part of those who have possessed lands, and riches, who have worn crowns, or coronets, have been satisfied with an earthly portion, and have not sought to obtain a crown of life, and an inheritance that fadeth not away.

Evening Scripture portion. James II. *The rich and the poor.*

MATT. XIX. 27 to end.—*Christ promises rewards to his faithful followers.*

HAD Peter spoken in pride when he said, "We have forsaken all," he would have received *rebuke* instead of *encouragement*. He had seen the rich young man go away grieved,—he had heard the

* The Swedish Boy: an interesting little book, published by the Religious Tract Society.

Lord's declaration respecting the danger of riches,—and his mind reverted to the period when he had been called, and had obeyed the call. What occasion was there for gratitude when the disciples thought of the time when they first resolved to give up all, and to follow Jesus! There is no season in life upon which the believer looks back with such joy, as on that season when he first determined to engage in his Redeemer's service. Whether he gave up much or little, he knows that in *heart* he gave up *all*. He felt *willing* to give up *all* whenever duty required the sacrifice; and he actually gave up what is dearer than possessions,—doing his own will, and trusting in his own righteousness.

The Lord's reply to Peter contains two glorious promises. The first was addressed to the *apostles* only; the second to *every one* who had acted as they had done. The apostles had left *fishing-boats*, and they were promised *thrones*. Such is the gracious and astonishing manner in which God rewards! When was this promise to be fulfilled? In the regeneration, or the new birth of the *world*. That time is spoken of in Rev. xxi. 1, where the apostle John declares, "I saw a new heaven and a new earth, for the first heaven and the first earth were passed away." This glorious time is called in Acts iii. 21, "the time of the restitution (or restoring) of all things." It appears that the apostles will then be distinguished by peculiar honors, and that they will be appointed to judge or rule over the tribes of Israel and the saints. But though we speak of these things, we understand them very dimly, because we see "through a glass, darkly."

The *second* promise that Jesus made is addressed to *all* who forsake any worldly good for his sake. Multitudes have lost their possessions, and have been separated from their families, because they chose to obey God rather than men. And *how* has God rewarded them? Has he given them the *very* things they renounced? No, not always; but he has given them more happiness, even in this life, than earth could have afforded them. They have indeed suffered "*persecutions*," but their joys have been greater than their sorrows. (Mark x. 30.)

Worldly things are only desired, because it is supposed that they can confer happiness. If any person were convinced that greater happiness could be obtained by any *other* means, surely he would not lament the loss of worldly comforts. How many saints have witnessed, that in the hour of outward sorrow they have tasted the purest inward joy! Such was the experience of Rutherford, when imprisoned in Aberdeen. In his letters he declared that since he had been in prison, he had discovered a sweetness in Christ that he had never conceived before. Such was the experience of Dr. Payson. When racked with pain in his last illness, he asserted that he felt more satisfaction than he had ever known in health. He said, "God has used a strange method to make me happy. I could not have believed, a little while ago, that in order to render me happy, He would deprive me of the use of my limbs, and fill my body with pain. But he has taken away every thing else, that he might give me HIMSELF."* And the apostles bore the same testimony when they said, "As the SUFFERINGS of Christ abound in us, so our *consolation* also aboundeth by Christ." (2 Cor. i. 5.)

Are there any here who have never yet found happiness? Are you willing to try the experiment, and to see whether God can make you happy? Sin has its pleasures, but they are for a *season*, and they leave a *sting* behind. Have you not experienced this? But God bestows on his children a calm, a deep, a settled, an abiding joy, which is called PEACE. It cannot be described, for it is not only *unspeakable*, but it passeth *all understanding*.

Evening Scripture portion. 2 Cor. I. *Consolation in sufferings.*

MATT. XX. 1–16.—*The parable of the laborers in the vineyard.*

OUR Saviour himself tells us what is the meaning of this parable. This is the explanation he gave: "The last shall be first, and the first last; for many be called, but few chosen." Those who are *first in their own eyes*, will be *last* in the great day of reckoning; and those who are *last in their own eyes*, will then be *first*. This seems to be the meaning of the parable. We have no reason to believe that *all* will have an *equal* reward in the last day: the parable of the talents seems to prove that there will be different degrees of glory in the world to come.

In the parable of the laborers in the vineyard, there is a representation of the *feelings* of self-righteous Pharisees toward penitent publicans. They were enraged at the idea of open sinners partaking with them of heavenly bliss. Self-righteous persons, who have led a correct life, imagine that they are better than those who turn to God *late* in life. They think they deserve great reward for their self-denial. How much will they be astonished at the decisions of the last day! Then they will see open sinners, who have *repented*, admitted into God's presence, and they themselves thrust out! Little do they think that even a *murderer*, who *truly* repents in his last hour, is beloved of God, while professors of religion, who have *never* repented, are hateful in his sight! Such impenitent persons will not be received into heaven. But they will have the torment of beholding those whom they despised, welcomed by saints and angels, arrayed in white robes, and adorned with golden crowns. How much *more* exasperated will they be at *this sight* than the envious laborers were at the sight of the wages given to those who had worked but one hour! When they see

* See Memoir of Mrs. Ann East.

penitent sinners received and rewarded, they will expect to be still more favored and still more honored. But they will be bitterly disappointed. They will then find that there is no mansion prepared for them in the celestial city.

The Lord's *true* servants are not like the murmuring laborers. If called *early* to work in his vineyard, they rejoice the more. They are not *proud* of having spent their youth in the service of God, but *thankful* for the great mercy shown to them. They pity those who were groaning under the bondage of Satan, while they were rejoicing in the liberty of Christ. How different from theirs was the spirit of those laborers who said, they had borne the burden and heat of the day! Those who do not *love* God, find his commandments grievous; but those who have experienced his pardoning mercy, call his yoke easy and his burden light. Do *we* think those the happiest who spend their lives in sin, and who, like the dying thief, are pardoned in their expiring moments? Or do we esteem those happiest who serve the Lord, like Joseph, from their youth, or like Samuel, from early childhood?

Evening Scripture portion. 2 Chron. XXXIV. 1–28. *Josiah's early piety.*

JOHN XI. 1–6.—*Christ receives a message from Martha and Mary*

THE conduct of our blessed Redeemer towards the beloved family at Bethany, sheds light upon his dealings with his saints now upon earth. Martha, Mary, and Lazarus, were firmly attached to their Lord, and they could stand trials that weaker saints could not have endured.

The Lord did not delay to heal the nobleman's son, nor Jairus' daughter, but he delayed to speak the word on behalf of Mary's brother. What was the reason of this difference? Mary and her sister knew their Lord well; they had experienced his faithfulness in times past; they could trust his love, even in the midst of apparent neglect.

When Lazarus was taken ill, his sisters deeply regretted the absence of their Lord, but they knew where he was, and they sent a messenger to acquaint him with their grief. The words of the message were few and touching, "Behold he whom thou lovest is sick." The sisters did not request that Jesus would come; they laid their case before him, and left it to his never-failing love to act as he saw fit. Here is an example for our prayers. It is a comfort in distress to spread our wants and woes before the Lord; but it is best to leave it to his wisdom to decide *how* to relieve us.

The answer Jesus gave to the message was very encouraging. "This sickness is not unto death, but for the glory of God, that the

Son of God might be glorified thereby." Yet it seems probable that Lazarus expired before the message could be delivered to the weeping sisters. It must have come too late to give them comfort.

But the dying chamber, the funeral scene, the days of mourning, were all appointed "for the glory of God." We naturally imagine that God is most glorified by *preventing* evil; but we know from his own declarations that he is *more* glorified by *redeeming* from evil. The fall of angels and of man will in the end bring more glory to God than would have arisen had these evils been prevented; for then the wonders of *redemption* could never have been displayed. It is a delight to the righteous to promote the glory of their heavenly Father. They would willingly endure sufferings for this purpose. We heard a little while ago of a man who was *born* blind, that the works of God might be made manifest in him: we now hear of one who *died* for the same end. Believers even now die, not as a punishment for sin, but in order to promote the glory of God. Christ has suffered for their sins, and borne all their punishment, but he appoints that they should die, that at the last day he may raise them all for his own glory. When he shall say, "Come up hither," then great fear will fall on those who behold them ascending in a cloud to meet their Lord in the air.

Theirs will be a more glorious resurrection than that of Lazarus, for he rose to die again; but those who are made alive at the last day will die no more.

Evening Scripture portion. 1 Thess. IV. *The resurrection of the saints.*

JOHN XI. 7–16.—*Christ sets out for Bethany.*

IT seems wonderful that though the disciples had lived with the Lord three years, they should continue to misunderstand his words. They supposed that his motive for not going to heal the afflicted Lazarus, was fear of the Jews. For when he said, "Let us go into Judea again," they expressed their surprise. He replied by a short parable. He compared himself to a man who walked in the day, and who walked safely, because he enjoyed the light of the sun. He himself was light, and therefore could never fall into *unforeseen* danger. He knew that his hour was come, and that it was *time* to work his most stupendous miracle. When his hour was *not* come, he took pains to conceal his glorious works, that he might not too *soon* exasperate his enemies; but now he desired to fall into their cruel hands, that he might *finish* the work his Father had given him to do.

We do not possess foreknowledge; we do not know what things will befall us in any place to which we are going; yet if we follow

Jesus, we do not walk in darkness. It is true we are blind, but our *guide* is not; therefore we are as safe as if we ourselves possessed eye-sight. When we are going to take a step in life, if we find that the word of God pronounces it to be right, and that the providence of God opens the way, we need not apprehend evil. How safe were the disciples while conducted by their Master from place to place! Yet they knew not their own security. Thomas seems to have said with a wavering faith, and a fearful heart, "Let us also go, that we may die with him."

How was it the disciples did not comprehend their Master when he said, "Our friend Lazarus *sleepeth?*" He taught them by this figurative language many sacred truths. He showed them that the commonest actions (such as sleeping) represent spiritual truths. Jesus was patient with his dull scholars, and explained his meaning, saying, "Lazarus is dead." These words could not be misunderstood;—but those that followed were mysterious. "I was glad for your sakes that I was not there, to the intent *ye* may believe." The raising of Lazarus was to effect more than *one* purpose. It was intended not only to *convince unbelievers*, but also to strengthen the faith of *believers*. The disciples were on the brink of an event that would call for the exercise of the strongest faith. Soon they would see their own Lord lying in his tomb. Never since the beginning of the world were the people of God exposed to so great a trial of faith, as the disciples then endured. To see *Him* on whom all their hopes for eternity depended, to see *Him* a breathless corpse,—was there ever any trial to be compared to this? Therefore, before the trial came, the Lord by every method sought to strengthen the faith of his poor weak disciples.

He foresees our trials, and often, before he inflicts a severe stroke, he prepares us for it by various and wonderful methods. Sometimes he prepares us by leading us to the sick bed of a sufferer, and by letting us hear him tell how the Lord sustained him; sometimes by shading one of our props without removing it; and sometimes by bestowing great and astonishing mercies. The whole process cannot be understood now, but it will be made plain to the saints in glory. What delight it will afford above to trace the Lord's dealings with our souls, and to discover the secret causes of the events of his providence!

Evening Scripture portion. Acts 1–19. *St. Paul's willingness to suffer.*

MARK X. 32–34.—*Christ again predicts his sufferings.*

As we read the history of our Saviour, we are continually struck by the union of courage and of tenderness in his character. He was now on his way to comfort two weeping sisters, by raising their beloved brother from the grave. He was also on his way to the place of his *own* execution. Bethany was a village very near to Jerusalem. What different scenes were soon to be witnessed at those two places! In Bethany the Lord would restore *another's* life; in Jerusalem lay down his *own!* But though he knew the painful trials that awaited him, He went *willingly* to the appointed spot, while his fearful disciples followed him *reluctantly*. Had we seen them on their journey, we might have supposed that one of them was going to receive honors, and the rest to endure sufferings. Whereas it was *He* who went boldly before, that was to be the victim, while those who followed trembling were to escape.

The Lord Jesus took his disciples *apart* to unfold to them the history of his approaching sufferings. He took them *apart*, because he did not choose to declare before his enemies the deeds which they would commit against him; for such declarations would have emboldened them in wickedness. But to his own disciples he revealed even the *particulars* of the awful transactions. On this occasion it is recorded for the *first* time that he spoke of his deliverance to the Gentiles, and of the insulting *spitting* of his enemies. These degrading circumstances were now unfolded to his disciples, who revered him as the Son of God. Had they understood the meaning of their Master's words, their feelings would have been outraged, and harrowed up to the utmost pitch. Yet the words seem so plain that we can scarcely conceive how they could have been misunderstood. But, perhaps, as the Lord often used figurative language, the disciples supposed that his prophecies concerning himself were figurative; perhaps, though they often understood him *literally* when he was speaking *figuratively*, they thought he was speaking figuratively when he was speaking literally. This is still the great difficulty in the interpretation of prophecy,—to distinguish the figurative from the literal; and perhaps future ages will show that the church in these days has fallen into some of the same errors as the apostles.

Great was the loss they sustained in consequence of their slowness of understanding. Had they been *prepared* to see their Lord bleeding on the cross, they would not have forsaken him in the hour of distress; and had they kept in mind the promise of his rising again, they would have been spared the bitterest tears they ever shed. That day of bitter tears during which the Prince of Life lay in his tomb, would have been to them a day of bright hopes, had they remembered his words. With what joy would they have hastened to the grave on the dawn of the third day, if they had expected to hear that he was risen! In looking back on our past lives, can we not remember many *seasons* which would not have been so sad had we remembered the Saviour's gracious promises?—seasons of doubt and perplexity;—seasons of suspense and anxiety;—seasons of disappointment;—seasons of bereavement;—seasons of darkness and of the shadow of death? When those seasons have been past we have felt, "O had I from the *beginning* of the trial, and throughout its course, remembered my Lord's words, 'Fear not, I am with thee,' and many *like* words, what bitter pangs should I have been spared!" In all our troubles here below there is one promise that ought, above all, to cheer us. It is his promise, "I will come again, and receive you to myself." The words are plain. "He will *come* again!" he will actually come in a glorious body, and our eyes shall behold him. Come, Lord Jesus! come quickly.

Evening Scripture portion. Isa. XLIII. ***Encouragement to trust in God.***

MATT. XX. 20–28.—*The request of the mother and sons of Zebedee.*

WAS it a *right* request that the sons of Zebedee made when they asked to sit at the right and left hand of their Lord in his glory? Was it right in their mother to plead that this honor might be conferred on her children? A desire to be *first* is natural to the human heart in its fallen state; but this desire is the cause of the greater part of the disquietude and discontent that prevail among men. *All* cannot be first; therefore if all *desire* to be first, all *but one* must be disappointed. And will that one be happy? None are so miserable as the proud. Nebuchadnezzar, the first monarch of his day, was a miserable man. What an account we read in the prophet Daniel of his fears, and tremors, and rage! On one occasion his spirit was troubled by his dreams, and on another through his fury the form of his visage was changed. No creature can be happy from his own greatness: but only from knowing the greatness of God. The angels are happy, because they delight in seeing God upon his throne. Adam and Eve were happy in the garden of Eden till they desired to be as gods; then, ceasing to delight in the glory of their Creator, they became miserable. When the Holy Spirit enters the heart of man, he begins his work by casting down "every high thing that exalteth itself against the knowledge of God." (1 Cor. x. 5.)

Yet true believers are troubled, as long as they remain on earth, with sinful feelings; though, as they grow in grace, they grow in humility. The apostles, at their last supper with their Lord, disputed who should be greatest. Let us be on our guard against the secret workings of ambition. We have perhaps ceased to desire the great things of this *world*. We have perhaps no desire to shine in *gay* circles, or to be commended by *irreligious* persons. But do we cherish a wish to be thought much of by *religious* people? to be commended above our fellow-Christians? to be more noticed, more admired, more honored? Whereas we ought to esteem others better than ourselves. Our Saviour has set the most wonderful example of humility by coming into this world to *minister* to us, and even to give his own precious life as a ransom for our sinful souls. Yet with what gentleness he answered the two brethren! He knew they had forsaken all to follow him; he knew that they would prefer shame and suffering *with* him, to any honor or joy *apart* from him; therefore he treated them with tenderness, though he did not promise to grant their request.

The words in ver. 23, "It shall be given to them," are written in italics to show that they were inserted by the translators in order to make the sense clear: yet, perhaps, if they were omitted the sense would be more clear: for Jesus did not say that it was *not* in *his* power to give the most honorable seats to whom he would. We know that whatsoever the Father doeth, the Son doeth likewise. (John v. 19.) This is what he said: "To sit on my right and on my left hand is not mine to give, *but* for whom it is *prepared* of my Father." The Son will bestow honor according to the decrees of the Father.

Though the Saviour concealed from the apostles what they desired to know, he told them some things that must have been strange and unwelcome. He revealed to them that they must partake of his *own* bitter sufferings. This is the first time in which it is recorded that he spoke so openly of the sufferings of his *apostles*. The terms in which he spoke of their future trials were suited to sweeten them to their affectionate hearts. It was out of his *own* cup the two brethren were to drink, and in his *own* baptism they were to be baptized. It is this thought that has sustained many believers under persecution, and has strengthened them even to endure the burning flame, or the bloody cross. But not *martyrs* only,—*all* true Christians suffer with their Lord. There is *no* sorrow that we can ever experience that our Lord has not tasted *first;* and he has tasted it, not only that he might take away our *guilt*, but also that he might sympathize in our *grief*. He knew all that James and John would be called to endure; and he knows also what each of us will be appointed to bear. He could have told James that the sword of Herod would cut short his days before those of any of the other apostles, and he could have told John that the cruel decree of Domitian would banish him in his old age to the Isle of Patmos, to dwell among convicted criminals. And he *could* tell each of us what losses we shall sustain, what pangs we shall suffer, what death we shall die. But he forbears to tell us more than that through much tribulation we must enter the kingdom of God. Who shall occupy the places at his right hand and at his left he has revealed to none; but though their *names* are secret, their *characters* are manifest: they will be *humble*. Whether they will be missionaries, or martyrs, or whether they will be beggars or slaves, we know not; but this we know, they will be self-denying and self-abased followers of their lowly Lord.

Evening Scripture portion. 2 Cor. X. ***Against vain-glory.***

MARK X. 46 to end.—*Blind Bartimæus.*

IN the history of earthly princes we do not often hear of the poor and afflicted, but of brave generals and wise senators. In the history of the Prince of peace we meet continually with anecdotes of beggars and outcasts. Those whom men overlooked and spurned were the objects of his most tender regard. The blind, as among the most helpless, received signal tokens of his favor. On one occasion we read of a blind man who was brought to him by his friend. (See Mark ix.) Bartimæus appears to have had no friends to assist him; if he had a friend, it was that blind man who sat with him begging, and was as helpless as himself. Far from being encouraged to come to Jesus, he was rebuked by the multitude, and charged to hold his peace. Many persons anxious about their salvation have been placed in the same circumstances. No friend has offered to lead them to the Saviour, while many have rebuked them for their concern about their souls.

On another occasion the Lord passed by a blind man, and restored his sight without waiting to be asked, for that blind man knew neither the Saviour's name, nor his power, till they were revealed to him by the Lord himself. (See John ix.) Bartimæus, far from being noticed by the Lord, could obtain for a long while no answer to his earnest entreaties. His case was more trying than that of the woman of Canaan; for *stern* answers were less discouraging than *no* answers at all. Besides, she could follow Jesus with her cries, while Bartimæus from his blindness was unable to find his way to his Lord. Jesus was passing by—would soon be past—might never pass that way again, (as indeed he never did;) it was a *short* opportunity; it seemed likely it would be the *only* one. All things were against the poor blind beggar; but instead of being disheartened, he "cried the more a great deal." There are some who leave off praying without having suffered as much discouragement as poor Bartimæus. If their cold and careless prayers do not receive an immediate answer, they are ready to give up the case as lost, and to try no more. But those who persevere in fervent prayer shall be blessed with blind Bartimæus.

At length Jesus stood still. Thus he honored the beggar in the presence of the surrounding crowds. He commanded him to be called. Those who had before rebuked him, must now have felt ashamed. The blind man was evidently agitated and distressed, for those who called him said, "Be of *good comfort*, rise; he calleth thee." What a joyful moment was this! With what *haste* the poor man obeyed the summons! He cast away his outer garment, that it might not retard his movements, and approached his compassionate friend. Though the Lord well knew his desire, he induced him to express it in his own words: for he loves to hear the petitions of his people. Not only did he bestow sight on Bartimæus, but he pronounced these words of commendation: "Thy *faith* hath made thee whole." This assurance must have been dearer to the poor beggar than even his bodily sight, for it implied a promise of eternal blessedness. Though the Saviour said, "Go thy way," yet the grateful man followed his deliverer.

Thus as the Lord journeyed towards Jerusalem, he gathered in his train fresh monuments of his power. The march of earthly conquerors is tracked with blood; smoking villages and mangled corpses mark the way which they have trodden, while weeping captives are chained to their triumphal chariots. But the Saviour left joy behind him wherever He went, and collected new trophies of his mercy. Thus will He come at the last day. He will bring his saints with him; he will be attended by those whom he has rescued from the darkness and blindness of sin and death, from the grave and its corruption, from hell and its horrors. Shall *we* belong to that triumphant band? Has Jesus opened the eyes of our minds? Do we *now* follow him in the way?

Evening Scripture portion. Ps. LXXXVI. ***Prayer for mercy.***

LUKE XIX. 1-10.—*Zaccheus.*

IN this history we find an instance of a *spiritual* cure wrought by the Lord. Opening the *eyes* of Bartimæus was not so great a work as opening the *heart* of Zaccheus. Though the Lord was continually healing the lame and the blind, yet it was *not* to heal *them* he came into the world. For what did he come? Hear his own declaration: "The Son of man is come to seek and to save that which is lost." But men in general (not being aware of their lost condition) did not apply to him for *salvation*, as they did for the healing of their *bodily infirmities*. Zaccheus did not cry for mercy as Bartimæus did. His desire was to *see* this wonderful prophet, of whom he had heard so much. For this purpose, being little of stature, he climbed into a tree. It is probable he would have been satisfied had he obtained a good view of the Saviour, as he passed beneath. How much astonished he must have felt when the Lord, upon coming to the place, looked up and said, "Zaccheus, make haste and come down, for to-day I must abide at thy house!" He must have been ready to exclaim, as Nathanael once did, "Whence knowest thou me?" It was evident the Lord knew not only his *name*, but his *circumstances*. He knew that he had a *house* in which he could receive guests. He knew *more* than this; he knew his *heart:* he was sure that Zaccheus was *willing* to entertain him beneath his roof: He must have known it, for He Himself had made him willing. On no other occasion is it recorded that he entered without invitation the house of a stranger.

It was indeed a singular honor that was conferred upon Zaccheus. It was his privilege to show hospitality to his Lord at the very *beginning* of his acquaintance with him; and he seems to have been conscious of the greatness of the privilege, for he came down the tree with *haste,* and received him *joyfully.* Whence arose his joy? Though *curiosity* may have been his only motive for ascending the tree, yet some higher principle seems to have actuated him before he descended. Like Nathanael and the woman of Samaria, he may have felt that none but the true Messiah could have such knowledge of him and of his circumstances. No wonder he rejoiced in the prospect of an opportunity of conversation with Him who knew all things.

Very interesting intercourse must have taken place beneath the roof of Zaccheus; but very little is recorded. In a short space of time, the master of the house had learned so much of the will of his Lord, as to stand up and make public declarations and confessions. He declared he would give half of his goods to the poor: he confessed that he had by false accusations (or by overcharging when he gathered the public taxes) defrauded some persons: he promised to restore to them *four* times what he had taken. It is a good sign when those who are impressed with religious truth *begin* by making restitution, asking pardon of those whom they have offended, and adopting an entirely new course of life.

The gracious Saviour was not slow to honor the good resolutions of Zaccheus. He gave him the title of a son of Abraham; thus showing that it was his *faith* that had produced his holy determination. Had the honorable young ruler possessed the *faith* of Zaccheus, he would not have refused to part with all his possessions at the command of Christ. But, notwithstanding his attractive qualities, he was destitute of that precious grace. Zaccheus possessed it, and would have held back nothing from his Lord that he had been called to give up. No doubt he would have gladly followed him in the way; but it seems he had duties to discharge at home. It was his part to endeavor to bring every member of his household to the knowledge of his Saviour. Could he forget the encouraging assurance, "This day is salvation come to this *house!*" Those who belonged to his family might henceforth count themselves blessed. The visit of their divine guest was to them the earnest of eternal bliss.

There is a period in the history of some families when true religion *first* finds admittance. Various are the *means* by which it gains entrance: sometimes it is through a pious friend, and sometimes through a pious servant: in some cases the family are led to hear a faithful minister, in others—to read a holy book: but whatever are the *means* employed, that period is memorable indeed when the *first* member of a family turns to the Lord with all his heart. That member will not rest satisfied with serving God *alone;* he will offer prayers, and use persuasions, till his children or his parents, his brethren and his sisters, unite in the same blessed service.

Evening Scripture portion. Joshua XXIV. *Holy resolutions.*

LUKE XIX. 11–19.—*The first part of the parable of the ten pounds.*

THIS parable was related to correct a mistake into which many of the Lord's disciples had fallen. They thought that the kingdom of God should *immediately* appear. They were not wrong in supposing that the kingdom of God would one day be established upon the earth; for it will be set up with power and great glory; but they were wrong in supposing that the time was *already* come. There will be great voices in heaven, saying, "The kingdoms of this world are become the kingdoms of our Lord and of his Christ, and he shall reign forever and ever." But before those acclamations will be heard, many events must take place. The Lord had already prepared James and John for enduring *sufferings,* before they could be exalted to *honor;* and now he prepared all his disciples for performing *services* before they could partake of *rewards.* Zaccheus had just shown his willingness to serve the Lord, by making promises of restitution to the injured, and of liberality to the poor. *His* spirit ought to be the spirit of all the followers of Christ. Though we can only be saved by free grace, yet we must show our gratitude for this free salvation by our *works.*

The Lord Jesus compared himself in this parable to a nobleman who went into a far country, to receive a kingdom from his monarch, and who returned to that kingdom to take possession of it. It was in this manner that Judea and Galilee were bestowed by the Emperor of Rome upon those noblemen who ruled over them. The rulers were invested with their power at Rome, and when invested they returned to the countries they were appointed to govern.

Before the nobleman in the parable departed, he intrusted each of his ten servants with a pound. Thus, before the Lord ascended to his Father, he charged all his disciples to serve him faithfully until the day of his return. It was not the *apostles* alone who received this charge. All who believe in Christ are bound to devote themselves to his service.

The pound represents those various ways of doing good which God has placed within our reach. Though in *this* parable each servant had the *same* sum committed to his keeping, yet *another* parable shows us that all Christians do *not* enjoy *equal* opportunities of usefulness: but all enjoy some, and all are required to improve those they possess.

In the days of the apostles believers were endowed with miraculous powers, which they were bound to use in the service of their Lord: as St. Paul declares, "The manifestation of the Spirit is given to every man to profit withal." (1 Cor. xii. 7.) In these days, though miraculous powers are no longer possessed, there are many ways in which good may be done.

By gifts, by instruction, by example, and by prayer, Christians may promote the glory of God.

Those who possess property can bestow bread on the hungry, and scatter food for the soul by distributing Bibles and tracts, and by promoting the preaching of the gospel all over the world.

But some who are not able to *give* much are able to *instruct.* A word dropped in season, even by a child, has sometimes saved a soul.

Example is still more powerful than instruction. Those who would be offended by advice, are often convinced by a holy life, a meek demeanor, and a forgiving spirit. Therefore the apostle Peter charges those women who have unbelieving husbands, to endeavor to win them by their Christian *behavior.* (1 Peter iii. 1.)

There is another mode of doing good, which, though the most *secret* of all, is the most *effectual:* it is *prayer.* The good that *prayer* has done will never be known till the last day. Then it will be seen that those who could be useful in scarcely any other way, brought down blessings by their prayers. It is recorded of a poor man, who was for a long season confined to his bed by sickness, that he made it his daily employment to pray that light might enter the various dark villages in his neighborhood. Every one of those villages for which he thus separately prayed, enjoyed, in the course of a few years, the light of the Gospel. It will often be found that conversions are answers to the prayers of some pious relation. Delightful discoveries will hereafter be made concerning our obligations to those who prayed for us.

It may well astonish us to think the Lord will reward the imperfect services of his sinful creatures. Even our prayers are mixed with sin. Every good action has some alloy of evil in the *motive,* some defect in the *performance,* and is too often followed by self-complacence in the *recollection.* The same precious blood which blotted out our *sinful* deeds, is needed to cleanse our *righteous* deeds from all their pollutions. Never will the faithful servants of Christ feel more abased in their own eyes than when they hear their Master say, "Well done." Even the *angels,* who have done the will of God without fault since the creation, count it a privilege to be permitted to serve him. What, then, will those who have served him so imperfectly, feel when they are exalted to posts of honor, and intrusted with authority and power!

Evening Scripture portion. Rom. XII. ***Christian duties.***

LUKE XIX. 20–28.—*The last part of the parable of the ten pounds.*

THIS parable contains a most solemn warning to the professed servants of Christ. Not to live to God's glory is a *fatal* sin. To make no efforts to please our heavenly Master is a sign that we do not *love* him. Did that servant love him who hid the pound in a napkin? His *language*, as well as his *conduct*, proves that he did not. What a character he ascribes to his Lord! He calls him an austere man, one who is rigorous, exacting, and severe. Who could *love* such a Master! Those who think in this manner of God do not try to please him. They give up the attempt in despair. They say to themselves, "If I were to give away large sums, perhaps I should only waste my money and do no good. If I were to labor from morning to night in teaching and exhorting, perhaps I should only waste my breath; no one might attend to my instructions. If I were to pray without ceasing for the conversion of my fellow-creatures, perhaps God would not grant my prayers."

It is very wicked to entertain such thoughts, for God has given gracious promises of success to those who labor in his service. He has said, "Cast thy bread upon the waters, and thou shalt find it after many days." (Eccles. xi. 1.) He has said again, "He that goeth forth weeping, bearing precious seed, shall doubtless come again with joy, bringing his sheaves with him." (Ps. cxxvi. 6.) He has said again, "Whatsoever you shall ask in prayer, believing, ye shall receive." (Matt. xxi. 22.)

If, notwithstanding all these promises, we persist in thinking that God might leave us to labor in vain, we make him a liar. Sometimes God does not grant *speedy* success, but he remembers what each does for his name's sake, and he will acknowledge every effort at the last day. In general he blesses the labors of his servants beyond their highest expectations. Ask aged believers who devoted themselves early to his service, whether they expected, at the beginning of their course, to reap so rich a blessing as they have reaped. The words of the dying Count Zindendorf are memorable. He said, "I expected to bring but a *few* heathen to the knowledge of the Lord, and, lo! *thousands* have believed." Mr. Charles, of Bala, little thought, when he was seeking a method by which to supply *Wales* with Bibles, that his desire would lead to the formation of a Society which should fill the *world* with Bibles. The last day will fully show what abundant showers of blessings have attended the labors of the faithful. Some who have scattered innumerable tracts, and who have not known what became of them, will then learn the histories of those silent messengers, to their own unspeakable joy.

But what will be the overwhelming sorrow of those who have done nothing for their Lord! The pound they possessed will be taken away from them. No further opportunities of glorifying God will be granted to them. In hell there is no possibility of serving Him. But in heaven there will be opportunities of glorifying Him through the ages of eternity. The saints will not find their rest less refreshing, because it will be spent in the worship of God, and in labors of love.

The last words of the parable contain an allusion to those enemies whom the Lord was going to encounter at Jerusalem—those enemies who said, "We will not have this man to reign over us." How wonderful was the courage with which the Shepherd led his little flock towards the scene of his own painful death! He went *before*, ascending up to Jerusalem. How insignificant are all the *services* which we can perform to *please* him, when compared with the *sufferings* he endured to *save* us!

Evening Scripture portion. Acts IX. 32 to end. *Dorcas.*

JOHN XI. 17–27.—*Christ converses with Martha at Bethany.*

How mingled were the feelings with which Martha went to meet her heavenly Friend! *Joy* she must have felt because he was come at *last*—*grief* because he had not come *sooner*. It appeared to her an unfortunate coincidence that her brother should have been seized with a fatal illness at a time when Jesus was absent. She expressed this feeling as soon as she beheld him, saying, "If thou hadst been here my brother had not died." But what appeared an *unfortunate coincidence* was in truth a *divine arrangement*. The Lord himself viewed these circumstances in a different light, when he said to his disciples, "I am *glad* for your sakes that I was not there, to the intent ye might believe."

But why did Martha say, "*If* thou hadst been here." Was not Jesus always there and everywhere? Yes; but she knew it not. She needed not have sent a *messenger* to inform him of her brother's illness: a *prayer* would have reached him from the furthest end of the world. He witnessed the expiring agonies of Lazarus, and told his disciples when he fell asleep. There is not one of his numerous family that has occasion to say with a sigh, "If thou hadst been here." When those we love droop and die, it is not because Jesus is not near, but because he designs to bring *us* nearer to himself by separating us from the creature.

It was natural that Martha should have hoped for the restoration of her brother, when she had heard of so many being restored to health who were not reckoned among the friends of Jesus. It seemed hard to her that one he so tenderly loved should not participate in those benefits. Some faint hope was lingering in her heart when she said, "But I know that even *now* whatsoever thou wilt ask of God, God will give it thee." Though she does not appear to have understood fully the power of Jesus, yet she understood one important truth, that he continually taught to his disciples. It was this: that the Father loved his Son, and granted all his petitions. The Son of God is the channel of the Father's mercy. Whatever we desire we must ask in his name, for we can only receive it through Him.

The Lord's reply was suited to fill Martha's heart with joy, "Thy brother shall rise again." Had Jesus added the words "THIS day," the sorrowing sister would indeed have rejoiced: but she was unsatisfied with the *distant* prospect of the resurrection at the *last* day. She wanted her brother's society to cheer her while she lived; and she was not willing to wait till all the just should rise to enjoy eternal life. The gentle Saviour did not rebuke the human weakness betrayed in the hour of sorrow. But he made use of this opportunity to instruct her concerning spiritual truths. Had she in former days, like Mary, sat at his feet, perhaps she would have been more familiar with divine doctrines.

How many hearts have thrilled, in hearing these words uttered when the beloved form of a child or a parent, a brother or a sister, has been carried to the grave! "I am the resurrection and the life; he that believeth in me, though he were dead, yet shall he live, and whosoever liveth and believeth in me shall never die."

The Saviour taught by these declarations, that none really *live*, except those who believe in him; and that none really *die*, except those who do *not* believe. To breathe,—to move,—to feel pain or pleasure,—that is not to *live:* to know God,—to love him,—to be like him,—*that* is to *live* indeed. To lie for a time in the tomb while the spirit rests above,—*that* is not to *die;* to be cast into the lake of fire,—*that* is to *die.* Do WE believe this? *Then* are we happy indeed, if we can say with Martha, "I believe that thou art the Christ, the Son of God, which should come into the world." If we really believe this, we live now the only happy life that can be enjoyed on earth; if we really believe this we shall never *die*, but only fall *asleep* in Jesus.

Many on their dying beds, when they have been asked whether Jesus was precious, have replied, "Never so precious as now." But it is not only on our *own* dying-beds that we may hope to feel him precious. When we see the eyes we loved closed in death, then we feel that we owe all the peace we shall henceforth enjoy to Him in whom the dear departed sleeps securely; then we feel, "Were it not for Jesus, I should have no hopes of seeing my friend, my child again; nor any assurance that he is happy while absent from me. But now, when I lie down, I think *his* spirit needs no rest; and when I rise up, I think, while I have been resting, his spirit has been uniting with the angels—

'Who all night long unwearied sing
The praises of their heavenly king.'"

Evening Scripture portion. 1 Cor. XV. 1–34. *The power of Christ's resurrection.*

JOHN XI. 28–36.—*Christ goes to the tomb of Lazarus.*

No other words could have conveyed such joy to Mary's heart as those that Martha whispered in her ear, "The Master is come, he calleth for thee." Yet her joy was mingled with bitter regrets that she had not heard the welcome tidings *before* Lazarus expired.

Martha called her sister *secretly*. Perhaps she did not wish that the Jews who sat around should accompany them to meet their Lord, for many of those Jews did not believe in him. The presence of unbelievers is felt to be a painful constraint by those who desire to open their hearts to Jesus. It will be one of the delights of heaven to feel that every thing there sympathizes in all the communications that take place between the saints and their Saviour.

But these Jews appear to have been much interested in Mary's grief; and when they saw her arise they followed her, thinking she was going to weep at her brother's grave. They little imagined how wonderful a scene they would soon behold. They must have been astonished to see Jesus waiting on the road. Mary then fell down at his feet, and uttered the very same words that Martha had used before, "If thou hadst been here my brother had not died." This was all that Mary could express. It appears that her grief was more overwhelming than her sister's. We do not hear that Martha fell down at the Redeemer's feet; nor that she wept as Mary did. Some spirits are more bowed down by grief than others. The Lord knows the frame of each of his creatures, and what each is able to bear. We are apt to pass harsh judgments upon one another; sometimes calling those *unfeeling* who sustain sorrow with composure, and looking upon others as *rebellious* against God who faint beneath its weight. But the Lord deals gently with the sorrowful: instead of reproving Mary's tears, he shed tears also.

Next to the history of his shedding his *blood*, this is the most touching, which tells us of his shedding *tears*. These tears were the tokens of deep trouble within. Before he shed them, it is said that "he groaned in spirit, and was troubled." Though he knew that Mary's grief would soon be assuaged, he felt for her actual sorrow; and not for *hers* only, but for the sorrow of the *unbelieving* Jews that accompanied her. There is nothing that so much solaces a mourner as to feel that he does not mourn *alone*. There is not one who has heard how Jesus shed these tears who ought to think he mourns *alone*. Even if he does not love the Saviour, yet that Saviour *feels* for him, because he is the work of his own hands.

But it was not *sympathy* alone that he bestowed upon the weeping train; he hastened to remove the *cause* of their sorrow, saying, "Where have ye laid him?" Even we (selfish as we are) have experienced the sweetness of giving pleasure, especially to those we love. But who can conceive the delight the Redeemer felt whenever he caused his children to rejoice! This was the bright color in his sorrowful life; he created more joy than any being has ever done that has dwelt upon earth. How his gracious heart must have glowed with the anticipation of the approaching scene, as he advanced towards the tomb of Lazarus! And now, as years roll on, our Redeemer sees the day approaching which is to be the *happiest* that ever yet has dawned upon this world. It was a *happy* day when the foundation of the world was laid, for then the morning stars sang together for joy. It was a *happy* day when Adam and Eve first beheld this fair creation, and sang their earliest anthem to its great Creator. It was a *happy night* when the shepherds heard the angels announce the birth of the Babe of Bethlehem. It was a *happy morn* when the women who visited the sepulchre heard angels say, "The Lord is risen." But no day nor night has yet been seen *as happy* as that last day will be, when the ransomed of the Lord shall return, and come to Zion with songs, and everlasting joy upon their heads. Of all the happy multitude then assembled, not one will feel so vast a tide of happiness springing up in his soul as the Redeemer himself—as He, who will be the fountain of all the joy flowing in every bosom. Then he will behold the travail of his soul, and be *satisfied—satisfied* that he left his throne of glory; *satisfied* that he trod this sorrowful earth; *satis fied* that he bled upon the cross; *satisfied* that he loved us, and washed us from our sins in his own blood.

Evening Scripture portion. Is. LXIII. ***The sympathy of Christ.***

JOHN XI. 37–44.—*The resurrection of Lazarus.*

WHEN Jesus was on earth how little was his conduct understood by men! Those Jews who, seeing his tears, said, "Behold how he loved him!" were mistaken in supposing that it was grief for Lazarus that caused them to flow; but those were more mistaken who harbored suspicions of his faithfulness. Some ventured to hint that he might have prevented the death of Lazarus. "Could not this man, which opened the eyes of the blind, have caused that even this man should not have died?" It is not surprising that *unbelievers* should entertain such thoughts. But how is it that *believers*, in time of trouble, ever indulge the same? When they are overtaken by calamities, they are often tempted to inquire, "Why did God permit these afflictions? Surely He *could* have preserved me from this evil. What have I done to offend him that He has exposed me to such sharp trials?" But all the while that these thoughts are going on in the mind, the Lord is pursuing his own gracious purposes. Perhaps deliverance is near at hand; if not deliverance from the *temporal* evil, yet deliverance from still *greater* evil.

Unbelief is the great obstacle in the way of the Lord's gracious designs. When he gave the command, "Take ye away the stone," unbelief interfered. Martha had once said, "I know that even *now*, whatsoever thou wilt ask of God, God will give it thee." Yet now she hesitates to consent to the removal of the stone. How gently the Lord expostulates with her! "Said I not unto thee, that if thou wouldest believe, thou shouldest see the glory of God?" He warns her against shutting herself out of the blessedness he was preparing for her. The Lord loves to show us his glory in delivering; but he cannot do it if we will not confide in him. Martha listened to her Lord's expostulation. She consented to the removal of the stone.

What a moment that was when Jesus, with uplifted eyes, stood before the open tomb! All was still *within* the cave, for death was there;—and surely all was still *without*, while the Son of God prayed to his Father in heaven. The first sentence bespoke his *faith.* "Father, I thank thee that thou hast heard me." The next showed his confidence in his Father's love: "I knew that thou hearest me always." The last displayed his *own* love to sinful men: "Because of the *people* which stand by I said it, that *they* may believe that thou hast sent me." He knew their unbelief. He knew that some accused him of doing miracles through Satan's power, and he desired to convince them that He and the Father were One. Who can conceive the breathless expectation that filled every heart when he uttered the words, "Lazarus, come forth?" Had that voice *not* been obeyed, it would have been a little thing that the sisters had never again beheld their brother: the hopes of *all* the *dead*,—the hopes of *all* the *living*, —the hopes of generations yet unborn, were suspended on the event of that moment. Had no movement been heard in that house of death, then *all* the dead would have slept forever. But now we know that all that are in the graves shall hear his voice, and shall come forth: they that have done good unto the resurrection of life. They shall *come forth* as Lazarus did,—*not* like him to die again, but to live for evermore. They shall *come forth*, not bound in grave-clothes, but arrayed in white robes: not with covered faces, but with countenances shining like the sun in his strength. St. John has not described the meeting of Lazarus with his sisters and with his Lord; it is left for us to conceive the rapturous greetings, and it is *possible* for us to concive the joy of that loving family; but it is *impossible* for us to form any idea of the meeting of the saints above, with each other and with their Lord. Lazarus found his sisters the same as he had left them, and they found him the same mortal creature as before. But hereafter every saint will regard his companion with delighted astonishment.

Though no resemblance we can trace,
We may believe we see

The dear companion of our race,
From sin and death set free.

We may believe that shining head,
Adorn'd with rainbow wreath,
The same that sank upon the bed
Damp with the dews of death.

Those lips that smiles seraphic wear,
Were once with pain compress'd;
That face than summer sea more fair,
Was once with care distress'd;

Those eyes that now with glory beam,
We oft have seen to weep;
That form we now an *angel's* deem,
In *dust* we saw it sleep.

Too little thought I of this hour,
When weeping o'er thy grave,
I saw thee crush'd by death's dread power,
And no arm near to save.

But then thy flesh was purified
From every earthly taint,
That here with Christ thou might'st abide,
And shine a glorious saint.

Evening Scripture portion.
Heb. XII. *God's design in chastening his people.*

JOHN XI. 45–52—*Caiaphas proposes that Jesus should be slain.*

SOME of our Saviour's prayers have not *yet* been fulfilled; but the prayer he offered up at the tomb of Lazarus was granted *immediately.* He prayed not only that he might raise Lazarus, but also that the miracle might cause the *people* to believe that his father had sent him. Here is the answer to the petition—"And many of the Jews which came to Mary, and had seen the things which Jesus did, *believed* in him." In the end, *all* the intercessions of the Son of God shall receive their accomplishment.

But some of the Jews went their ways to the Pharisees and told them what things Jesus had done. What an instance their conduct affords of the hardness of the human heart, when not softened by divine grace! It will not believe, even when one is raised from the dead. Perhaps these unbelieving Jews shed the tear of sympathy in the house of Mary—for there are many who are enderly attached to their friends, who are full of enmity against the Son of God.

The Pharisees eagerly listened to the reports of these malicious informers, and convened a council to consider the subject.

It was in this assembly, that the most awful crime was suggested that man has ever perpetrated—the murder of the Son of God. It was suggested by the person who filled the most *holy* office in the world. The High Priest reproached the Pharisees for their perplexity, saying, "Ye know nothing at all; nor consider that it is expedient for us that *one* man should die for the people, and that the *whole* nation perish not."

See how he veils the wickedness of his scheme by a specious pretext. He dares not say, "Let us shed innocent blood; let us rid ourselves of the object of our envy; let us *falsely* accuse him, and put him to death *unjustly*." Satan teaches men to hide their wickedness from their *own* eyes, lest its deformity should cause them to start back with horror. But God sees men's actions as they really are; their *secret* sins are set in the light of his countenance. It would astonish us to know by what gentle names wicked men have called their blackest actions. Let us watch lest Satan get an advantage over us, and *impose* some *sin* upon us by giving it the name of a *virtue.*

But though the high priest spoke *hypocritically* when he proposed that one man should die for the people, he also spoke *prophetically.* His words were lying words in the sense he used them; but they were *true* in *another* sense, which he knew not of. While his *heart* was under the power of Satan, his *tongue* was under the direction of God: "He spoke not of himself." As the Lord put *words* into the mouth of Balaam, so also did he put them in the *mouth* of Caiaphas, though it was *Satan* put *feelings* into his *heart.* Yet his words only expressed a *small part* of the truth, for Jesus died not for *that* people only, but he died that he might gather into one *all* the children of God scattered abroad.

It is the *desire* of all his children to be *with* their Father, and it is the *desire* of their Father to have all his children with him. Sin, like an oppressive tyrant, has scattered his family abroad. Death divides them from each other, and even divides their souls from their bodies. But the death of Christ has taken away the guilt of *sin,* and has destroyed the power of *death.* At the sound of the last trump, the bodies that lay mouldering in the tombs, or forgotten in the depths of the sea, shall be glorified and united to the happy spirits of the just. Those who were born in different ages of the world, or who were separated by vast oceans, shall behold each other for the *first* time in their Father's everlasting home. And all these blessings shall flow from the awful crime suggested by the high priest. Well may the plan of redemption be called, "The *mystery* of His *will.*" (Eph. i. 9.) It is a *mystery* that the *will* of *God* should be accomplished by the *wickedness* of *man;* that the purpose *formed* in *heaven* should be *executed* by *hell.* But herein the wisdom of God is displayed. The author of sin, even Satan, is compelled to lend his hand in destroying his *own* works, and his *own* kingdom. He knew not that the blood of the cross would make peace, and would reconcile all things to God, whether they be things in earth or things in heaven ; he knew not that even his *own* servants, when sprinkled with that blood, would revolt and become the servants of God. (Col. i.) Had he known it, he would not have suggested to Caiaphas the guilty expedient of causing one man to die for the people.

Evening Scripture portion. Numbers XXIII. *Balaam's prophecies.*

JOHN XI. 53 to end.—*Christ retires to Ephraim.*

THE wicked suggestion of Caiaphas was immediately acted upon. The Pharisees took council together to put Jesus to death. Acceptable advice is soon followed. How great is the guilt of the man who *suggests* a wicked scheme ! All the dark deeds that have ever been committed, were suggested by some man. A *word* may be the beginning of a train of horrors, from the view of which the soul recoils. What woes to the Jewish people flowed from the crime that Caiaphas proposed !

The Lord (who knew all things) knew of the consultation which his enemies had held, and of the scheme which they had formed ; and as his hour was not yet *quite* come, he retired for a short time to a small town called Ephraim. It was so small a place that its name is scarcely mentioned by any writer ; but it is supposed that it was situated in a valley full of corn, about eight miles from Jerusalem. Here the disciples enjoyed another season of confidential intercourse with their Lord, such as they had once tasted on the banks of Jordan. How doubly precious would this opportunity have seemed to them, had they believed they must so soon part with their Divine Teacher ! It is seldom that we know when we are enjoying, for the last time, the society of a beloved friend. With what feelings a child remembers the last prayer a parent offered up in the presence of his family, while, perhaps, neither the parent nor the child knew it was the *last !*

While the Lord was hidden in his retreat, the Jews were assembling to keep the passover at Jerusalem. To judge from the numbers that flocked thither, one would have supposed that they were a very religious people. They came from distant parts of the country, and they arrived at an early period, in order to go through various purifications and washings commanded in the law ; but they did not, like David, wash their hands in innocency, before they approached the altar of their God. (Ps. xxvi. 6.) There may be a full attendance at the house of God, and even at the Lord's supper, while there are but few spiritual worshippers. Such religious acts obtain for those who perform them a *name* to live among men ; but they may be performed while the heart is *dead* before God. Never were the Jews in a more dangerous state than when, having ceased to worship graven images, they observed with strictness the ceremonies of the law.

The people who stood in the temple, inquiring whether Jesus was come, and wondering whether he would come at all, little knew what deed they would perpetrate before they quitted the holy city. *Now* they were full of enthusiasm for the Prophet of Nazareth; *now* they extolled him as the greatest that had ever appeared; *now* they were ready to receive him with hosannas, and to proclaim him king; but they had no true faith and love rooted in their hearts. The Lord would not trust himself in their hands, and therefore hid himself till his appointed time was come.

There is a *kind* of faith which will not stand the day of trial! there is a *kind* of love which is put out by the breath of slander. Some imagine that they are pious, because they delight in listening to an eloquent preacher. Let us remember how anxious the Jewish people were that Jesus should come to the feast, and how they treated him during that feast. Do we know Him as our Saviour from *sin?* Do we feel that He loved us, and gave himself for us? Then we shall never *cease* to love him. Though the disciples sinfully forsook him in the hour of danger; yet nothing quenched their *love;* for it was founded not on *admiration* of his *power*, but on *gratitude* for his *mercy*.

Evening Scripture portion. Gen. XXXVII. ***Joseph betrayed by his brethren.***

John XII. 1–8.—*Mary anoints the Lord Jesus.*

We have now reached the *last* week of our Saviour's life. On the Saturday evening the Jewish Sabbath was over, and the new week began—the most *eventful* week that had been known since the beginning of the world—the most *suffering* week that the Son of man passed upon earth—and the most *sorrowful* week that his Church has ever seen. But though it was to be full of suffering and of sorrow, it opened with a scene of peace and love; for Simon the Leper made a supper for the Lord at his house. If we mark the dealings of God, we shall find that a *cordial* is often granted to us before a *trial* is sent, and that we are permitted to enjoy some unwonted refreshment before we are called upon to drink a cup of unusual bitterness.

How must the gracious Saviour have delighted in the scene he now beheld at Bethany! The tears that had touched his heart were now dried; the sisters saw their brother, who was so lately sleeping in his tomb, seated at table with their Lord. Martha testified her love and joy by waiting on the blessed company. It is probable that she superintended the arrangement of the supper, and gave directions to the servants. We know that such an office was suited to her active disposition. Mary, who seems to have been of a more thoughtful, and sensitive, and retiring character, found another way of expressing her love and joy. She brought an alabaster box full of very precious ointment, and poured it on the feet of Jesus. It seems as if she came *behind* him as he reclined upon his couch at supper, and sought to perform the loving office in *secret*. But she could not be hid, for the house was filled with the odor of the ointment. Its exquisite fragrance attracted attention, and led the guests to discover who had poured it forth. Should we not have conceived that in *such* a company the love that Mary had shown would receive the highest praise? But St. Matthew records, that not only Judas, but the *other* disciples said, "Why was this waste of the ointment made?" How could they thus insult their Lord? Was there any thing too precious to be dedicated to the Son of God? Did the wise men who came from the East think so, when they laid gold, and frankincense, and myrrh, at the infant Saviour's feet?

We know the *motive* that led Judas to make the unfeeling inquiry—it was covetousness. He was disappointed to think that so rich a treasure as this alabaster box should have been kept back from his dishonest hands. But why did the *other* disciples unite in his complaint? It might be that some secret envy of Mary's surpassing attachment to their Lord, may have prompted their censure. But if for one moment the gentle and diffident Mary felt cast down by their disapprobation, she must soon have been consoled by hearing her Master's defence of her conduct. High, indeed, was the commendation he bestowed on her: "She hath done what she could!" These words imply, that as she *could* bestow a *precious* gift, she would not be content with presenting a *mean* one. Had Mary been *poor*, she *could* not have anointed his feet as she did. She *could* do *much*, and she *did* much. She anointed her Lord with a costly perfume, that was worth nearly ten pounds of our money. May it not be more often said of the *poor* than of the *rich*, "They have done what they *could?*" Too often the *rich* give no more to the service of Christ than the crumbs that fall from their table.

Though the *disciples* blamed this act of love, yet Jesus declared that in *distant* countries, and in *future* ages it would be commended. For he said, "Wheresoever this gospel shall be preached throughout the whole world, this, also, that she hath done shall be spoken of for a memorial of her." (Mark xiv. 9.) Mary had not sought for *human* praise; but even *that* was to be awarded her. Who has ever read the account of Mary's offering, and has not inwardly approved it? Where is the believer who has not wished that he enjoyed the same opportunity that Mary did, of showing his love to the Lord?

When once a poor sinful woman washed the feet of Jesus with her penitent tears, a Pharisee reproached the Lord for permitting one so wicked to touch him, and thus tacitly accused the weeping sinner of *presumption*. But did the *Lord* deem her *presumptuous?* Mary, who bore an honorable character, was not accused of *presumption*, but of *extravagance*. But did the *Lord* deem her act of love *extravagant?* Does the church of God *now* accuse *either* of these devoted women of presumption or of extravagance? Let us judge nothing *before* the time. If actions of such devoted love were blamed in former days, similar acts may be blamed *now*. Even true Christians are apt to censure those who go beyond themselves in zeal, in feeling, and in self-denial; but the Lord will never think we can love him, adore him, or honor him too much.

Evening Scripture portion. 2 Samuel VI. *David dances before the ark.*

JOHN XII. 9–19.—*Christ is honored and hated the more on account of Lazarus.*

IT was on the Saturday evening that the Lord Jesus supped at Bethany, and was anointed by Mary. The next day was *not* the Jewish Sabbath. That Sabbath began at six o'clock on Friday evening, and concluded at six o'clock on Saturday evening. It was on Sunday, the first day of the week, that the Lord entered Jerusalem, riding upon an ass's colt, and accompanied by the joyful multitude. On the first day of the *next* week he rose from the dead. Between these two joyful days there was a dark interval;—a week of unexampled sorrow and suffering.

The acclamations of the multitude on the day the Saviour entered Jerusalem, increased the envy of the Pharisees. They said to each other with alarm, "Behold, the world is gone after him." They could not *deny* that he had raised Lazarus from the tomb; therefore they were determined to blast his growing reputation by violence. They desired not only to put *him* to death, but *Lazarus* also—because he was a living monument of his power. But had they accomplished their design, how easy it would have been for the Prince of Life to call him a second time out of his grave!

The sisters little knew, when they applied to Jesus for help in their hour of sorrow, that their *brother's resurrection* would lead to their *Saviour's death*. They little thought, when they saw that brother seated at the supper at Bethany, that on that day week, his deliverer from the grave would be sleeping in his own! But in the end, they had reason to rejoice, for the *death* of their Lord was the forerunner of the most joyful event that has happened since the beginning of the world—*his resurrection*.

Nor was it Lazarus alone that provoked the enmity of the wicked. Mary, by her act of love, was the occasion of stirring up Judas to commit an act of treachery. He was so indignant at the disappointment he sustained, and at the rebuke he received, that he offered, four days afterwards, to betray the Lord into the hands of his enemies. Truly did Mary anoint the Lord for his *burial.* It was his *only* anointing, for he was hastily buried, and the ointment that the women prepared was too late. Thus we perceive that the family of Bethany unconsciously roused the indignation of the two chief instruments of the death of their Lord. The service *Mary* rendered led Judas to propose his *betrayal;* and the benefit *Lazarus* received led Caiaphas to suggest his *murder.*

Such was the mysterious arrangement of God. He who brings real good out of seeming evil,—brings seeming evil out of real good. Good deeds are often followed by consequences that *appear* evil. But the servants of God have no reason to despair, when their attempts to honor their Master increase the malice of his foes. Though Satan may succeed in casting some into prison, or in causing others to be slain, he can never succeed in casting one believing soul into his *own* prison—the bottomless pit—or in causing him to be hurt by his *own* death—the second death.

We may conceive what grief Mary would have felt had she *known* that Judas was incited by her act of love to betray his Lord; yet, when she saw that Lord risen from the dead, would she have grieved then? No doubt it has often happened that the piety of new converts has awakened enmity against their minister, and has even led to his execution. Those converts must have felt acute anguish when they saw their beloved teacher consuming in the flames; but their anguish would be turned into joy could they see him standing before the throne clothed in a white robe, with a palm branch in his hand; or on the sea of glass, with the harp of God; or with the Lamb on Mount Sion singing the new song.

Evening Scripture portion. Rev. XV. *Saints in glory.*

MATT. XXI. 1–9.—*Christ approaches Jerusalem, riding on an ass.*

HAD every scene in our Saviour's life been like this, it would not have been written, "He came unto his own, and his own received him not." But this day of triumph was in reality only a preparation for the day of slaughter. The Lord of glory chose that for *once* his name should be publicly exalted in his own city of Jerusalem. As his hour was now come, he no longer hid himself from his enemies, or restrained the grateful praises of his disciples. At the *beginning* of his ministry he did his mighty works in secret, and desired his disciples to tell no man that he was the Christ. But at the close of his ministry, he made a triumphant entry into Jerusalem, as the King whom God had chosen to reign over that city. Yet the *manner* of his entry was unlike that of *kings*. He rode, *not* in a chariot drawn by horses, but on an ass—even on a *colt*, the foal of an ass.

We know that his *principal* reason for this act was that he might fulfil the prophecy of Zechariah, and give all who beheld him an opportunity of knowing, by another sign, that he was the Messiah of whom the prophets spake. Yet, even his own disciples did not observe, at the *time*, the fulfilment of the prophecy. But was there no other reason why it was *appointed* that the Lord of all should enter his own city in so humble a manner? Did not the manner of his entry show that he was not a *war*-like monarch, but the Prince of *Peace*—not a *proud* monarch, but the *meek* Saviour, not a *rich* monarch, but one who had become *poor,—so* poor that he *borrowed* the ass on which he rode. Yet his divine wisdom and power might be discerned through the veil of humility in which he was clothed. No king, however *wise*, could have foretold those minute circumstances concerning the finding of the ass, which Jesus described. No king, however *powerful*, could have made an unbroken colt obedient to his *word*.

He was the glorious Son of Man, spoken of in the eighth psalm, of whom it is said: "Thou madest him to have dominion over the works of thy hands; thou hast put all things in subjection under his feet,—all sheep and oxen,—yea, and the beasts of the field, the fowl of the air, and the fish of the sea." As God gave all the creatures to the *first* Adam, so also he gave them to the *second* Adam, of whom the *first* was only a type. The beasts who were obedient to the *first* Adam in the garden of Eden, did not resist the power of the *second* Adam. *Man* rebelled against his authority, but the *ass's foal* acknowledged it.

How wonderful was the condescension of the King of Israel in entering his own city in so humble a manner! The purple and scarlet of earthly monarchs, the prancing horses and splendid chariots may dazzle the *eye*, but the majesty and meekness of the Son of God impress the *heart* with admiration. He knew that he should be soon exalted to his Father's right hand, yet he condescended to ride upon an *ass*. He knew that white-robed elders would soon cast their crowns at his feet, yet when the multitude spread garments and strewed branches in the way, he accepted these meaner honors.

Ought we not to approach with confidence so meek and gentle a Saviour? If, in the days of his flesh, he was pleased with every feeble attempt to show him homage, ought we not to believe that he will be pleased with *our* humble efforts? We cannot testify our feelings by spreading garments or strewing branches in the way. If we would honor him, we must bow our hearts and bend our wills to his royal sceptre. When he comes again in power and glory, he will remember us. For this is his promise to his faithful servants: "The

Lord their God shall save them in that day, as the flock of his people." (Zech. ix. 16.)

Evening Scripture portion.
Zech. IX. *Prophecy concerning Christ riding on an ass.*

LUKE XIX. 37–40.—*The chorus of praise on Mount Olivet.*

THE burst of joy that was heard on Mount Olivet, affords a faint picture of the raptures of heaven. On Mount Olivet the whole multitude began to praise God with a loud voice, for all the mighty works that they had seen. In heaven an innumerable multitude shall praise Him with a louder voice, for a still mightier work than had ever been seen in Israel.

But even a saint on *earth* sometimes feels overwhelmed when he reflects upon all the glorious deliverances and unmerited mercies he has received. There are moments, especially towards the close of his pilgrimage, when he sees at one glance the mysterious train of events by which his life has been marked, and when he cannot forbear exclaiming, in the words of David, " How excellent is thy loving-kindness, O God! therefore the children of men put their trust under the shadow of thy wings."

There were *few* among that vast multitude on Olivet who had these warm feelings of grateful love; for the greater part, before the week expired, joined in the cry, " Crucify him, crucify him." But there were a *few* who praised the Lord with their whole hearts. Was there not among the crowd blind Bartimeus, who had followed him on the way? Did not the beggar, born blind, go forth to meet him? He had been cast out of the synagogue for his sake, and when he had heard he was the Son of God, he had replied, " Lord, I believe." Was not that courageous and grateful man among those who most heartily praised his name? Was not Lazarus there, who had been raised from the dead? Was not Mary there, who, the evening before, had anointed her Lord with fragrant spikenard? Were not Salome and Joanna there, and Mary Magdalene, and all the faithful little band who had followed him out of Galilee? Was his blessed mother there? Did she behold Him whom, when a babe, she had laid in a manger, acknowledged as the King of Israel?

These inquiries we *cannot* answer; we know the names of none who composed that joyful company, excepting those of the apostles. But this we know,—there were some present who hated to hear the praises of the Son of God. These Pharisees said, " Master, rebuke thy disciples." Had they heard the songs that once delighted the shepherds at Bethlehem, they would have desired to stop the angelic chorus. But the Saviour would not check the overflowing feelings of the multitude, but replied, "I tell you that if *these* should hold their peace, the *stones* would immediately cry out." Were not the Pharisees more senseless than stones, for they had seen the most glorious miracles, and yet refused to honor Him who had wrought them? How unfit were they to enter heaven, where no tongue is mute in the Saviour's praise! *All* are unfit for that blessed place who delight not in magnifying the Lord Jesus Christ.

Are there not many who have experienced his goodness from their earliest infancy, and who yet *praise* him not, *thank* him not? Are there not many who have heard of his dying love, who "hold their peace" on this glorious subject, and neither thank him in public nor in private? Are there not lips that have *never*, with warmth and sincerity, blessed the holy name of Christ the Saviour? Are any of us among the number of those silent, ungrateful, and guilty creatures, who never thank their Lord, their Redeemer? While angels rest not day nor night in worshipping the Lord, shall a sinner for whom Christ died, refuse to utter *one* note of heartfelt praise?

Evening Scripture portion. Ps. LXXI. *The aged Christian's song of praise.*

LUKE XIX. 41–44.—*Christ weeps over Jerusalem.*

THE world in which we live has been often called a "vale of tears." Each of us has shed tears, and will shed them again. But what are the circumstances which draw forth our tears? Do we not often weep for some trifling cause, some selfish reason, some sinful feeling? There are the tears of mortified pride, the tears of discontent, the tears of rebellion. All these are *sinful* tears. There are the tears of disappointment, of anxiety, of pain, and of grief. These are *natural* tears. There are the tears of *sympathy*. Jesus shed those when accompanying the mourners to the tomb of Lazarus. There are the tears of *penitence*—these the Saviour *could* not shed, for he was not a *sinner;* but he delights in these tears, and with them he once permitted a weeping penitent to wash his blessed feet.

But the tears that he shed over Jerusalem were the tears of *generous love—love* for his *enemies*. Have *we* ever shed such tears? There are Christians who have so imbibed the Spirit of their Master, that they retire to pray, and even to *weep* for those who hate and revile them, and who will not pray, nor weep for themselves. But all true Christians have not attained to this height of divine compassion.

How strange it must have appeared to those who were singing his praises, and adorning his path with green and flowery branches, to see the Redeemer stop and gaze and weep! In the midst of their joyful hosannas, the sorrowful tones of his voice were heard, saying, "If thou hadst known, even thou, at least in this thy day, the things which belong unto thy peace!" Thus he spoke to the *daughter* of Zion, (for cities are often compared to *women* in Scripture, and the inhabitants are called their *children.*) Truly we may say, "Behold how he loved her!" He did not weep because he saw, from the top of Olivet, the place of his own sufferings; because he saw at its foot Gethsemane, that doleful garden where the *first* drops of his blood would fall; nor because he saw beyond the city, Calvary, that dismal spot, where the *last* drops would flow at the touch of the soldier's spear. He wept because he foresaw the calamities that would overtake his murderers. Though now the city sat majestically upon her seven hills, yet soon he knew she would lie prostrate in the dust. How grand and beautiful she appeared when viewed from the heights of Mount Olivet! Her lofty rocks, her massive towers, and, above all, the glittering dome of her snow-white temple, generally excited *admiration;* but now they called forth *lamentation.* It was in these defences she trusted, instead of in the living God. But neither her rocks nor her towers, nor even her holy temple, could save her when the Romans came and besieged the city. Her God had departed from her. Then her walls were thrown down, her temple burnt, and more than one million of her inhabitants destroyed by famine and pestilence, by fire and sword.

At this moment the Saviour knows the fate of *every city* upon earth. He knows what will befall London, and Paris, and Rome. Every city that, like Jerusalem, trusts in her own strength, and refuses to obey Christ, must fall, as she has done. Those who love their native land ought to use every effort to spread the Gospel among their countrymen.

But Christ not only knows the fate of every *city;* he knows also the fate of every *individual* in every city, and village, and hamlet. Sometimes, perhaps, when we see a person in the enjoyment of riches, and health, and honor,—surrounded by smiling children, and admiring friends,—we are ready to cry, "If I were in thy place, I should be happy." But is this person forgetful of his Saviour? Then it may be that Christ is saying to him, "If *thou* hadst known, even *thou,* at least in this thy day, the things which belong to thy peace." *We* behold the *present* scene, but *Jesus* beholds the *future* also. He sees—not only the table amply spread, but the dying bed that will succeed; he hears—not only the voice of merriment that *now* prevails, but the faint groan that will close the scene. Can he count those happy, whose misery is every hour drawing nearer? Surely the compassionate Saviour feels for all who soon will exclaim, in another world, "If *I* had known, even *I* in *that* my day, the things which belonged unto my peace, but now—they are hid from my eyes!"

Evening Scripture portion. Jer. IX. *Jeremiah weeps over Jerusalem.*

MATT. XXI. 10–13.—*Christ casts the buyers and sellers out of the temple.*

WHEN the Son of God entered Jerusalem, where should he go but to his Father's house? He went to the temple. In what a state did he find that sacred place! It shone bright in earthly splendor—it was undefiled by images of wood or stone—it was frequented by crowds of worshippers; but yet it was a den of thieves. In its outermost court, called the court of the Gentiles, there were men engaged in buying and selling beasts and birds for sacrifices, and others in changing money, brought from distant places, into the coin of the country, and in supplying half-shekels for the yearly tribute. This court had been assigned by God to the Gentiles, that *all* nations might worship him; according to the words of the prophet Isaiah, "Mine house shall be called a house of prayer for *all* people." (Isa. vi. 7.)

The *priests* alone were admitted into the temple itself; *Jews* only into the court that enclosed it; women of the Jewish nation were permitted to enter the next court; and Gentiles into the outermost—that is, those Gentiles who worshipped the God of Israel. No such distinctions now exist; for in Christ Jesus there is neither Jew nor Greek, bond nor free, male nor female, but all are *one* in him. (Gal. iii. 28.) Christ by his death has broken down the middle wall of partition that separated Jew from Gentile, and has made both one. (Eph. ii. 14.)

But it was not the *animals* that defiled the court of the Gentiles so much as the *men* who sold and bought them, for they were *thieves*. It is probable that they considered themselves honest men, for it does not appear that they committed those *kinds* of robberies which are considered disgraceful; but they were *thieves* in God's sight, for all who make unfair gains, and tell falsehoods when they buy or sell, are counted thieves by him. Such actions were especially offensive to Jesus when committed in his Father's house. To see that holy place converted into a den in which iniquity was committed with impunity, vexed his holy mind. At the *beginning* of his ministry, three years before, he had driven out the offenders with a scourge of small cords, and now at its *close* he cleansed the sanctuary a second time.

Though so meek towards those who reviled him, he was ardent in his opposition to wickedness. He is the *Judge* of all, as well as the Saviour of all; and when he comes again he will manifest his hatred against sin. If in the days of his flesh the wicked fled before him, whenever he exerted his divine power, how much more will they tremble when he comes in his glory with all his holy angels! Who will be able to resist when he shall send them forth to gather out of his kingdom all things that offend, and them that do iniquity, and cast them into a furnace of fire!

It is supposed that the buyers and sellers in the temple *returned* to their wicked practices after the panic was over; but those who are cast out of the heavenly kingdom will never more *return* to pollute the service of God. Though the gates of the celestial city shall never be shut, yet there shall in no wise enter any thing that defileth, neither whatsoever worketh abomination, or maketh a lie; but they which are written in the Lamb's book of life. (Rev. xxi. 27.)

Evening Scripture portion. Mal. I. *Contempt of God's ordinances.*

MATT. XXI. 4–16.—*Children praise Jesus in the temple.*

WHEN Christ came into his temple, he *cast out* some, but he *received* others. The buyers and sellers he cast out; the blind and the lame he received. It must have been an affecting sight to see those helpless creatures hastening from all quarters to meet their benefactor. They did well to come *then*, for those hands whose touch was health, would soon be stretched upon the cross.

Blindness is a calamity very common at the present day in Jerusalem, and some who love the Jews endeavor, by medical art, to heal their benighted brethren. But there is no Son of God now, whose touch will unveil the eyes. Even in *this* country it is calculated that two in every thousand are blind; and, therefore, that London and its suburbs contain two thousand blind persons. Christians have had pity upon them, and have instituted *one* society for visiting them, reading to them, and leading them to God's house; and *another* for teaching them to read and write, and labor for their own living—and both of these societies seek to save their immortal souls.*

How interesting it must have been to see the blind and the lame enter the temple! Here perhaps was a blind old man led by the hand of a little grandchild, and there a father who could not walk, borne in the arms of affectionate sons and daughters, whom he had once borne in his.

We know that there were children in the temple when the Lord healed these afflicted creatures. Some of these children *may* have been leaders of the blind, or even supporters of the lame. This at least we know, they were children who loved Jesus, for when they sang his praise, he was pleased. *Once* He blessed children, and *now they* blessed *him*. Those that were brought to him on a former occasion, seem to have been very little ones, perhaps unable to speak, but those who sang in the temple were old enough both to speak and

* These societies are called, "Society for Visiting the Indigent Blind at their own Habitations," office 20 Red Lion Square; "School for Teaching the Blind to Read," 36 Queen Square. The latter is open for inspection every afternoon.

to understand. Their artless songs irritated the priests exceedingly. No doubt they had been exasperated by the casting out of the buyers and sellers. But they were too much afraid of offending the people to oppose the Lord openly. They did not even venture to *command* the children to be silent, but appealed to Jesus and said, "Hearest thou what these say?" And what had the children said? They had called him "the Son of David." As the *Son* of David he had a right to the *throne* of David. The little children acknowledged Him to be their King. No doubt many children were wicked in those days as well as in our own, but we never *hear* of any who spoke against Christ. It is not said that they joined in the cry that their fathers uttered, "Crucify him, crucify him." May we not rather hope that they followed their mothers, even that company of women who bewailed and lamented Him?

How ought the young to rejoice in the Saviour's answer to the priests and Scribes! "Yea, have ye never read, out of the mouths of babes and sucklings thou hast perfected praise?"

Who could have thought that He who listens to the songs of thousands of angels, should be pleased with the lisping accents of a child! But when a little one offers up a simple prayer from his *heart*, the glorious Saviour bows down from his heavenly throne to hearken. The children in the temple did not care for the frowns of their proud enemies, while they enjoyed the smiles of Jesus. Those wicked men must have looked upon them with still more anger than before, after the Saviour's reply. They cannot have forgotten the words that followed those Jesus quoted from the 8th Psalm, "That thou mightest still the enemy and the avenger." The praises of children often do *still* (or make quiet) the enemy and the avenger. When a wicked man who hates God sees a little child who loves Him, he sometimes feels ashamed of his wickedness, and wishes he was like that simple babe. Swearers have sometimes left off swearing at the request of a child; prayerless men have learned to pray from the example of a child.

There was a father who was called to visit the dying bed of his little daughter. Moved by her entreaties, he knelt down by her bed-side, but said he could not pray. She prayed *for* him: her prayer was heard in heaven. He became a holy man. When he had buried his child, he gathered his household around him, and began, from that day, to call upon the name of that Lord who had loved and saved his child.

Evening Scripture portion. Ps. VIII. IX. ***Judgments on Christ's enemies.***

JOHN XII. 20–26.—*Some Greeks desire to see Jesus.*

WHO were these Greeks that desired so much to see Jesus? They were Gentiles, brought up in the Greek religion, but who had forsaken it for the worship of the true God. We cannot wonder that they longed to see the great prophet of Nazareth, with whose praises all Jerusalem resounded. It must have been more than a *sight* that they desired. Zaccheus desired only a *sight*, when he climbed the sycamore tree, but these Greeks appear to have wished for an *interview*. They desired to converse with the Lord. It was not easy to obtain access to one who was always surrounded by a throng. Who would make way for *Gentiles* to approach him—for *Gentiles*, who were considered as the dregs of the earth by the proud and bigoted Jews? These Greeks, therefore, applied to Philip the apostle. It appears that he was doubtful whether the Lord would receive them; for we find he consulted first with Andrew, who was his townsman, and that afterwards he and Andrew together told Jesus. No more mention is made of these Greeks; but we know too well the love that Christ bore to poor Gentiles, to doubt how he would receive them. Had they ever conversed with the Roman centurion, or the woman of Canaan, they would not have feared a repulse. The centurion would have said, "I thought that I was not worthy that he should come under my roof, and, lo! he received me as a *son*." The Canaanite would have said, "I was content to be a dog, worthy only to eat the crumbs that fell from the children's table, and, lo! he called me his *daughter*." None who knew his condescending love, would ever fear a cold reception from the Friend of sinners.

His answer to Philip and Andrew was calculated to encourage the Greeks, as well as the Jews, to trust in him. When he said that a corn of wheat, if it die or corrupt in the ground, will bring forth *much fruit*, did he not allude to the salvation of *Gentiles*, as well as Jews, through his death? Seed is sometimes cast into the ground and *never* springs up: sometimes it springs up, but produces only a *little* fruit: but Jesus died, and was buried, that he might rise again and bring *many* sons and daughters to glory. It would not satisfy the Son of God to save a *few* souls: he knew before he suffered, that he should redeem from *eternal* misery a multitude that no man can number. But he knew also that this multitude must suffer much tribulation. Therefore he continually exhorted all who approached him to be faithful unto death. With what affection he promised that his fellow-sufferers should be his companions in glory, saying, "Where I am, there shall also my servant be!" The Greeks had desired a passing interview with Jesus, but here was a promise of his presence forever and ever. We have never seen the Son of Man, as he appeared upon earth in the days of his humiliation; but, if we *love* him, we *shall* see him—see him *not* as he *was*, but as he *is*,—see him as described in Revelation x , "Clothed with a cloud, a rainbow upon his head, his face as it were the sun, and his feet as pillars of fire." And when we see him as he *is*, we shall be *like* him. Those who saw him as he *was* were not made like him by the sight. But he has made this promise to his servants, "They shall see his face, and his name shall be on their foreheads." (Rev. xxii. 4.)

Evening Scripture portion. Rev. X. *The glorious Son of God.*

JOHN XII. 27–33.—*The Father answers his Son from heaven.*

How wonderful a scene was this! The Father and the Son speaking to each other in the presence of men. Surely there must have been silence in heaven while this solemn intercourse was held! Such sounds had not been heard by an assembled multitude since the day that God had delivered the ten commandments from Mount Sinai. Man had forgotten his Father's voice. None knew it but the Son himself. He knew it well. But he needed no *voice* to assure him of his Father's love. That voice was heard, that *man* might know that the Father loved the Son; that *man* might know that the Father had heard his prayer, "Glorify thy name." The more we consider that short prayer, the more we must admire it. What courage, what obedience, what love were displayed in those few words, "Glorify thy name!" At the moment they were uttered, all the terrible future lay open before the Son of God. The scourge, the thorns, the cross, the cruel mockings of men, and the hidings of his Father's countenance, all, all were present to his view. Yet, instead of praying, "Father, save me from this hour," he prayed, "Father, glorify thy name."

Is it *easy* for a sufferer to make this prayer? Let those answer who see the objects of their tenderest love begin to droop. Is it *easy, then,* to say, "Father, glorify thy name; if it be necessary for thy glory that I should lose my dearest comforts, I resign them into thy hands." Let those answer, who linger from month to month under the tortures of some inveterate disease. Is it *easy* for them to say, "Father, if it be for thy glory that I should still endure these agonies, let them continue?" The soul who can make this prayer is prepared to join the multitude that came out of great tribulation.

But no child of God was ever exposed to such trials as those that were coming upon Jesus, when he said, "Father, glorify thy name." He saw the prince of this world, even Satan, advancing to meet him in battle. He had suffered much from his temptations in the *wilderness;* but he would suffer more from his assaults in the *garden*, and on the *cross*. Yet he drew not back from the terrible conflict, because he knew that by the conquest of Satan his Father's name would be glorified. It was on the *cross* that he overcame the prince of this world. No conqueror's sword has ever done so mighty a deed as that despised cross. No monarch's throne has ever seemed so glorious in the eyes of angels as that shameful cross.

There are *many means* by which men are converted from sin to God: some are impressed by the means of books, others by conversation, and more still by preaching. But there is only *one doctrine* by which they are converted; it is the *doctrine* of the *cross*. Every pardoned sinner now on earth, or in heaven, could bear witness to this truth. It was the love of a dying Saviour that drew him out of darkness into light. Had Jesus refused to die, how many tongues now singing to the glory of God the Father would have been forever mute! But who can tell how many more will swell the heavenly chorus in ages yet to come! Not one of them was forgotten by the Son of God when he uttered, "And I, if I be lifted up, will draw all men unto me." The thought of their united songs cheered his soul in the hour of his trouble. His own sufferings darkened the view on one side, but the glory that his Father would receive from a multitude without number of redeemed sinners, of *all* nations, and kindred, and people, and tongues, enlightened the prospect with an overwhelming splendor, and drew forth the prayer, "Father, glorify thy name!"

Evening Scripture portion. Deut. V. *The voice of God in the fire.*

JOHN XII. 34–36.—*Christ exhorts the people to believe while they have the light.*

WHILE ministers are preaching, their hearers are often answering them in their own minds. Satan never fails to suggest objections against the truth to all who are willing to listen to his whispers. He did not fail to attempt to extinguish the light of the truth when Jesus held it up. When those affecting words were pronounced, "And *I*, if I be lifted up from the earth, will draw all men unto me," the people, instead of receiving the truth, objected, saying, "We have heard out of the law that Christ abideth ever; and how sayest thou, 'The Son of Man must be lifted up;' who is this Son of Man?" This objection was not urged in a right spirit. If it had been *meekly* proposed, the gentlest of Teachers would have solved the difficulty. He could easily have explained it by saying, "The Son of man will be lifted up on the cross—then rise to live forever." The people were *right* in saying that the law had declared that Christ abideth ever, because it is written in Ps. xli., "Thou settest him before thy face forever;" but they were *wrong* in the conclusion they drew. How diffident and humble we ought to be when we speak on divine subjects! Our understandings are so feeble, that we fall into mistakes continually. Our only hope of obtaining wisdom is by waiting with *meekness* on Jesus to be taught: "He will guide the *meek* in judgment."

Instead of answering the cavils of the people, the Lord gave them a solemn warning. He saw with sorrow that they were wasting the *little* time during which they would enjoy his instructions. Therefore he said, "Yet a *little* while is the light with you." They knew not how *very* little while that light would shine. If these words were uttered on the day of our Lord's arrival in Jerusalem, (that is, on Sunday evening,) then there remained only three days more for *him* to teach, and for the *people* to learn. On Thursday it appears all classes were engaged in preparing the passover, and on Friday in gazing on the crucified Saviour. After that day none saw him but his own disciples. He taught the people no more.

Who can tell how long he may retain the light he now enjoys? A child who has a pious parent knows not how soon that parent may die, and how soon the voice may cease that now prays so often *with* him, and so much oftener *for* him! There are many who would tremble if they knew how shortly their only opportunity of salvation will end.

A minister who was preaching on the words, "Seek ye the Lord while he may be found," observed, "There may be some here who, if I had preached *to-morrow* instead of *to-day*, would *then* have been in that place where, *if* they sought the Lord, they would not find him." A farmer's laborer was deeply impressed by the sermon, and sought the Lord that *very night.* The next morning, as he was with his horses in the field, one grew restive, and, in rearing, struck him with the iron harrow on the temple, so that he died. Had that man delayed to seek the Lord but *one day* more, he would have been *forever* in darkness. With what feelings must lost spirits remember the *last* opportunity they neglected, the *last sermon* they disregarded, the last *conviction* they suppressed!

Evening Scripture portion.
Psalm XLI. *Prophecy concerning Christ abiding forever.*

JOHN XII. 37–41.—*Some refuse to believe.*

"HE hath blinded their eyes, and hardened their hearts." These words have perplexed many minds. Does a merciful God blind the eyes of his creatures? We thought it was He who took away the heart of stone, and gave the heart of flesh. And so it is. *All* good comes from him, and *nothing* but good. But it is good to inflict righteous judgment, and there is a sin for which blindness is a righteous judgment. When men love darkness rather than light, and obstinately refuse to come to the light, at length God blinds their eyes. For what use is sight to those who abide in darkness? Jesus came a light into the world; but there were many whose deeds were evil, and who refused to come to the light, lest their deeds should be made manifest. It was *these* whose eyes were blinded, and whose hearts were hardened, so that they could not see with their eyes, nor understand with their hearts. The dayspring from on high visited them, to guide their feet into the way of peace, through the tender mercy of their God: but they turned away from the glorious light—from that light which fills all heaven with joy. How it must have astonished angels to see men turn away from the Son of God!

Isaiah once beheld his glory in the temple. He beheld the Lord Jehovah sitting upon a throne high and lifted up, attended by the seraphim, who cried one to another, "Holy, holy, holy is the Lord of Hosts, the whole earth is filled with his glory." This was the glory that Isaiah saw. The apostles also saw the glory of the Son of Man; but it was displayed in a different manner. They beheld one clothed in flesh, yet possessed of divine power: they saw him suffering insults and injuries, and yet conferring benefits, and promising blessings. The glory of the Son of God did not shine more brightly from his heavenly throne than it did through the veil of a human form.

But the blind in heart could not behold this glory. None saw it but those whose eyes God had opened. There is no calamity so great as to be blind to the glory of the Redeemer. When we see a very enchanting sight, then it is that we pity the blind. When we look upon the beauties of the opening spring, or the splendor of the setting sun, then we feel compassion for those who can never be cheered by such lovely sights. When we behold the countenance of a dearly-beloved friend, a parent, or a child, then, above all, we feel for those who can never be delighted by seeing the objects of their fondest affections.

And when is it the Christian feels most for the blind world? When he contemplates the glories of his Saviour, when he meditates upon his power, and faithfulness, and love, and thinks that there are men who never beheld these glories—who never *will* behold them—who do not *desire* to behold them. Though the wicked shall see the Son of man come with power and great glory at the last day, yet they shall never comprehend his greatest glory—which is his goodness. Moses once prayed, and said, "Lord, I beseech thee show me thy glory;" and God answered, "I will make all my *goodness* pass before thee." And then he proclaimed his name as the merciful, gracious, long-suffering God, who forgives iniquity, transgression, and sin. This is the glory which believers behold with so much satisfaction, but which unbelievers cannot see. In another world they will feel the *power* of God, and, like the devils, tremble beneath its weight: but they will never, never know the God of *love*.

Evening Scripture portion. Is. VI. *The message of wrath.*

JOHN XII. 42, 43.—*Many who believe, refuse to confess Christ.*

IT is very profitable to observe what temptations have overcome men in past times. None can estimate the force of temptation, excepting those who are actually under its influence. Even those temptations by which we ourselves have once been overcome, appear feeble and insignificant when we are removed from their power. We have read of a young ruler who refused to *follow* Christ because he had great *possessions. Now* we read of many rulers who refused to *confess* him, because they loved the *praise of men* more than the praise of God. What *various* reasons men have for not doing the will of God! But there is not *one* of all those reasons that will appear a *strong* one at the last day. "We cannot," thought these rulers, "confess that Jesus is the Son of God, lest we should be put out of the synagogue." There was a beggar born blind who endured the trial; why could not they endure it? When he was cast out, the Son of God found him and revealed himself unto him. Had those rulers *acted* as he did, they would have been *comforted* as he was. One word from the Son of God could impart more peace to the heart than the plaudits of a whole multitude, or the praise of the whole Sanhedrim. But it appeared to these rulers an insupportable calamity to be put out of the synagogue. Not to be allowed to approach within an arm's length of any person, or to eat and drink with any for thirty days, was a trial they would not encounter. Then if, at the end of thirty days, they continued to confess Christ, a curse would be pronounced on them in the midst of the congregation, accompanied by the extinguishing of lights, and the sounding of trumpets. Then would follow destitution, and desolation, and disgrace. They would be deprived of their property, forbidden to hire or to be hired, to buy or to sell, to teach or be taught; when they died stones would be cast at their bier, and none would follow them to the grave.

These things were sufficient to terrify a human heart; but yet what were they all, compared to the woes God will inflict on the unbelieving and the fearful! Not to be permitted to approach our fellow-mortals is not so dreadful as to be separated from saints and angels and God and Christ forever and ever. The sudden darkness in the synagogue, and the clangor of trumpets, could not be as appalling as the darkness of the sun at noonday, and the sound of the last trump!

But though these rulers believed that Jesus was the Christ, they did not believe with the *heart.* They did not *love* him. They loved *men* more than *God;* therefore they loved the *praise* of men more than the *praise* of God. It is possible that a true believer may be tempted to deny his Lord: but then he will not *continue* in the sin. Peter denied Christ; but one "kind upbraiding glance" brought him to repentance, and made him go out and weep bitterly. These rulers were not like Peter. They could bear to see their companions insult the

Lord day after day, and yet never take his part: they could bear to hear them plotting his death, and yet be silent. They were content to be on good terms with his enemies, and not to be counted among his friends. Could they have done this had they *loved* him? O no; had they *loved* him they would, on some occasion, have betrayed their feelings. Nicodemus could not sit in the Sanhedrim and hear the Lord calumniated. He exclaimed, "Doth our law judge any man before it hear him, and know what he doeth?" and thus he brought upon himself the derision of the assembly. Could an affectionate son hear his father insulted day after day, and never show by word or look how deeply he was wounded!

Perhaps we never hear men speak *openly* against Jesus himself. But do we not meet with many who speak against his laws and his people? It is before such persons that we are called upon to confess him. If we do not seem to approve of worldly amusements, if we show an attachment to truly religious people, if we refuse to smile at sin, and to admire what the world admires, the enemies of Christ will hate and despise us. Are we willing to bear their hatred and contempt for our dear Master's sake! Is Christ's approbation dearer to us than the world's admiration? These are signs that we love the Lord, and that he loves us; and that he will confess us when he comes in his glory with all his holy angels.

Evening Scripture portion. Dan. III. *The three men in the fiery furnace.*

JOHN XII. 44 to end.—*Christ declares himself to be the light of the world.*

THE most glorious light that ever shone upon this world was now about to set. While his beams were still visible, a voice was heard saying, "I am come a light into this world, that whosoever believeth in me should not abide in darkness." This is the *last* invitation to an unbelieving world *recorded* as uttered by our Lord before his crucifixion. We know that he preached the gospel daily during the short remainder of his life of suffering; but we are not informed what other *invitations* he made; though we are informed of many parables he related, of many answers he gave, and of many warnings he uttered.

What infinite love breathed in this invitation! Jesus came a light into the world, not for his *own* happiness, but that whosoever believed in him should not abide in darkness. He had beheld the world lying in darkness; he had pitied their awful state: and had consented to penetrate the dismal recesses of their abode, that he might bring to them the light of life.

How gloomy this world of sin must appear when viewed from those sunny heights where the saints abide! But darkness is not only *gloomy*, it is *unwholesome*. Plants cannot grow in the dark. It is only the boughs that drink in the light of day, that bring forth leaves and fruit. The flowers turn their lovely heads to the sun, and every branch bends forward to meet its rays. As soon as the infant has strength to open its tender eyelids it begins to seek the light. Those poor babes who are reared in dark alleys show by their pale and sickly looks that they have been deprived of the light that makes the whole creation bloom and rejoice. Darkness is *dangerous* as well as unwholesome. The traveller in the desert, if he is benighted, is exposed to pitfalls and wild beasts. The prince of the power of the air exercises his power in *darkness; there* he lays his snares; *there* he watches for his prey.

It was to relieve men in this deplorable state that the Son of God was manifested. He is the brightness of the Father's glory, and the express image of his person; therefore he said, "Whoso seeth *me* seeth him that sent me." The King eternal, immortal, invisible, dwells in *light* which no man can approach unto; but his Son was veiled with flesh, and sent forth into the world clothed in such mild beams that men could approach *him*. But if men still loved darkness rather than light, if they shut their eyes upon the Sun of righteousness, and retired farther into their dark retreats, what would become of them at last! The words which Jesus spoke would judge them at the last day. That word, "I am come a light into the world, that whosoever believeth in me should not abide in darkness," that very word will judge all those who, having heard it, have not come unto the light. For when Jesus comes again he will not *save* the *world*. He will only save his *people*, and he will *judge* the *world*. All the invitations which the world have received are recorded, and will be brought forward at the last day. They may forget the sermons they have heard, the chapters they have read; they may forget the faithful expostulations of their pious friends, and the fervent prayers of their fond parents, but God does not forget them; for all these means of grace were arranged by Him in his eternal counsels with his Son. He determined *what* they should hear, and He observes *how* they hear. The sinner's heart will thrill with terror when his Judge inquires, "*Why* did you not come unto *me?* Then you might have had light. Why did you abide in darkness?" What reason can a sinner give for abiding even *one* day in darkness, when light is come into the world? There is not a single soul who hears this invitation who might not enjoy light this *very hour*, if he would but lift up his heart to the Saviour of the world with this earnest cry, "Enlighten my darkness, thou light of life."

Evening Scripture portion.
Jer. XIII. ***Warning of approaching darkness.***

MARK XI. 11–19.—*Christ curses the barren fig-tree.*

SUCH is the history of the manner in which our Lord spent one of the last days before his death. It was, as we believe, on Sunday that he entered with triumph into Jerusalem. On the evening of that day St. Mark records that he *looked* round about on all things, and then went to Bethany with the twelve. And what did those holy eyes behold when they looked round about upon the temple? They must have looked upon the smoking sacrifices, upon the burning lights, and upon the white-robed priests. But these sights cannot have imparted joy to the Saviour's heart; for he knew how those sacred ordinances were profaned by an unbelieving nation.

How sweet must the calm of Bethany have seemed after the tumult of Jerusalem! That lovely village, embosomed among the fruitful trees that adorned the foot of Olivet, contained some of the Lord's most devoted followers. Whether he spent the night in solitary prayer on the mountain, or whether he slept beneath the roof of some beloved disciple, we know not. However engaged, he was hid from the pursuit of his enemies. For it is said in St. John's Gospel concerning this period, "These things spake Jesus and departed, and did *hide* himself from them." (xii. 30.)

On the morning of the next day, (which, we believe, was Monday,) the Lord again repaired to the scene of labor and conflict, to the temple at Jerusalem. The distance was about one mile and a half, and the way lay through a fertile valley, close by the Garden of Gethsemane, and over the brook Kidron. As the Saviour walked he was *hungry;* for he had probably left Bethany at an early hour, and without taking refreshment. His hunger reminds us that he had a body like our own, and was subject to all our infirmities except sin. It was at this moment he beheld a fig-tree having leaves, and he approached it, but, finding no fruit upon it, he cursed it, saying, "No man eat fruit of thee hereafter forever." There is one thing in this account which it is difficult to understand. St. Mark observes, "The *time* of figs was not yet." It is natural to inquire, "Why did the Saviour expect to find figs before the *season* was arrived?" This difficulty has been explained. There is a *kind* of fig-tree which *always* has leaves, and *always* bears fruit. The *common* sort of fig-trees in the early spring neither bear leaves nor fruit. When our Lord beheld afar a fig-tree having LEAVES, he knew it must be of the *kind* that bears fruit at *all* times; and when he found none, he cursed it for its barrenness.

But surely there must have been some deep meaning in this action; for a *tree* can neither deserve cursing nor blessing. It must have been to teach his *apostles* who *then* heard his words, and *us* who *now* hear them, that Jesus cursed the tree. This tree afforded an apt emblem of the Jewish nation. The leaves of a tree drink in air and moisture, and promote its strength and fruitfulness. The sacred privileges bestowea on the Jews may be compared to leaves. But when the Son of God came looking for fruit, he found none—no repentance—no faith—no love—no holiness—for though there were a *few* who believed, the nation, as a *nation*, believed not. He did not expect fruit from the *Gentiles*, for the *time* of figs was not yet come with *them;* but he had a right to *expect* much from those to whom he had *given* much.

When he entered the temple again that day, he found the buyers and sellers engaged in their profane traffic. It seems, from this account, that after having been driven away the evening before, they had returned to their old practices, and that the Son of man showed his power again in casting them out.

Jesus passed the day in teaching the people, while maliciously observed by the scribes and chief priests. And, when evening was come, he went out of the city, and sought again to hide himself from his enemies in his favorite retreat. Thus closed another of his few remaining days of sorrow. It seemed as if he spent his strength for naught, and in vain; but his judgment was with the Lord, and his work with his God. (Is. xlix. 4.)

Do those who labor for *our* souls, whether they be ministers or friends, look in vain for *fruit?* May the Saviour's awful sentence prove a warning to us. God can say to a *man*, as well as to a *tree*, "Let no man eat fruit of thee hereafter forever." Is there any one who could bear the prospect of *never* being a blessing throughout all the ages of eternity? Even those who are useless and hurtful now, hope that they shall one day be different. But opportunities are rapidly passing away. The trees, that are now bearing the lovely fruits of praise and holiness in the paradise above, began to bring forth fruit unto God when upon *earth.* Even that malefactor whose Christian course lasted but an hour or two, brought forth good fruit in his believing prayer to Jesus, and in his faithful reproof of his fellow-sufferer; while the aged apostle Paul was like a tree whose boughs are pressed to the earth under the weight of a fragrant and delicious load. Have we begun to bear heavenly fruit? If not, *when* shall we begin? Let us not delay—we cannot tell how soon God may fix our state forever.

Evening Scripture portion. Is. V. ***The Lord's vineyard.***

MARK XI. 20–26.—*Christ and his disciples pass by the withered fig-tree.*

AFTER having passed the night in Bethany, the Redeemer, with his little band, left his retreat to resume his labors in Jerusalem. In the course of their walk a very impressive object met their sight. It was the fig-tree that had been cursed the morning before. On passing by the fig-tree in the *evening*, the darkness must have prevented the apostles from seeing it; but the *morning* light revealed its withered state. Peter called the attention of his Lord to the circumstance, by saying, "Master, behold the fig-tree which thou cursedst is withered away." From this remark we are led to conclude that the curse pronounced by the Lord did not produce an *immediate* effect upon the tree, but caused it *gradually* to consume and to perish. The apostles, who knew the reason of its withered state, must have looked upon it with feelings of awe and astonishment. They had never before seen *such* a display of their Lord's power. They had seen life *bestowed* by his word, but never had they seen even the *life* of a *tree* TAKEN AWAY. Had the Son of God exercised his power as he might have done, his enemies had long before been blasted by the breath of his nostrils: for it is God who *killeth*, as well as *maketh alive*. But he refrained from executing judgment, for He came to draw sinners to himself by the riches of his goodness, and not to appal them by the terrors of his hand. But it was well that his *apostles* should have proof that he *could* destroy his enemies. They would soon be exposed to a tremendous trial of faith. They would behold their Master *apparently* overpowered by men. The remembrance of the fig-tree ought to have convinced them in that terrible hour that he *could* have dried up the arms stretched out to take him, and struck dumb the tongues that rose in judgment against him.

Nor was it Jesus *alone* who had power to subdue his enemies. He promised similar power to his apostles, even power to wither fig-trees and remove mountains. St. Matthew thus records the Lord's answer: "Verily I say unto you, if ye have faith and doubt not, ye shall not only do that which is done unto the fig-tree, but also if ye shall say unto this mountain, 'Be thou removed, and be thou cast into the sea,' it shall be done." Matt. xxi. 26. It is evident that trees and mountains represent the difficulties and trials of the Christian life. By faith they may be overcome. The apostle Paul triumphed over the messenger of Satan sent to buffet him, and through faith learned to take pleasure in infirmities, reproaches, necessities, persecutions, distresses, for Christ's sake, because he found the grace of God sufficient for him. (2 Cor. xii. 10.)

It is by believing prayer that such victories are attained. Therefore the Lord gave his apostles some directions concerning prayer. He knew they were going to spend another day exposed to the malice of wicked men, and he warned them against cherishing an unforgiving spirit, by saying, "When ye stand praying, forgive, if ye have aught against any: that your Father also which is in heaven may forgive you your trespasses." There are few who are not sometimes injured or insulted. It is not enough for us to endeavor to *banish* the *thoughts* of our enemies from our minds, we must *think* of them for the *pur-*

pose of asking, "Have I forgiven them?" We must mention them in prayer as objects for whom we especially desire mercy. One who has himself been forgiven by God will be enabled to forgive others. The spirit of revenge may arise occasionally in his heart; but the remembrance of what has passed between Jesus and his own soul will quench the vindictive feeling, and will make him desire to meet even his enemies in *glory*, and to live with them forever in *love*.

Evening Scripture portion. 2 Cor. XII. *Victory over temptation.*

MATT. XXI. 23–32.—*The Elders question Christ concerning his authority.*

WE are now beginning to read the account of the last two days of our Lord's public ministry—the Tuesday and Wednesday before his death. There are very ample records of the conversations he held on those days. None who heard him, knew that he would so soon cease to speak on *earth;* but *we* know that these were his *last* warnings.

Early in the morning he arrived as usual at Jerusalem, having conversed with his disciples on the way concerning the withered fig-tree, and the power of faith and prayer. He found his enemies much enraged against him, both on account of his words and his doings. They had witnessed the buyers and sellers, at his command, quitting their accustomed posts. The sight was a reproach to those who had so long allowed the profanation of the house of prayer. Having consulted together, they proposed a question which they imagined he could not answer without furnishing them with a new accusation against him—"By what authority doest thou these things?" If he should reply, "By the authority of God," then they resolved to accuse him of *blasphemy;* and if he said, "By my *own*," of rebellion. But the wisdom of the *Lord* easily confounded the cunning of *men*. He answered by proposing a question *they* could not answer. Therefore they were compelled to reply that they did not know whether John the Baptist was a true prophet or not. What a confession for teachers of religion to make! All who hear it might naturally conclude that those who did not know whether *John* were a true prophet, might not know whether *Jesus* was.

But while his enemies were suffering under the confusion of their defeat, the Lord related a parable, which must have confounded them still more. There were often gathered around the Saviour a class of persons whom the Pharisees considered as the dregs and scum of the earth. They were penitents who had once led wicked lives; they were such persons as the rich publican and the weeping sinner. Once they had *openly* disobeyed the command of their God, and had insolently answered, "I will not;" but afterwards they had repented; while the Pharisees, with all their professions, had never yet really obeyed the will of God. It was easy to say which of these characters was the *most* guilty. Even if the *open* transgressors had *never* repented, they would not have been so wicked in God's sight as the *false* pretenders to religion. But they *had* repented, and, therefore, they were fully forgiven, and were as much beloved by God as angels that have never sinned. *Their* repentance added greatly to the guilt of the Pharisees, for the very sight of these penitents ought to have convinced them of their own *need* of repentance.

But the proud have no feelings to vent at the feet of Jesus. There is no sin that hardens the heart so much as pride. Open sins, though they expose to shame and misery in this life, sometimes render men more willing to humble themselves before God. A liar, who blushes because of the lies he has told, will, perhaps, listen to the voice of mercy, while the proud truth-speaker rejects it, because he rests upon his integrity. Of all sins let us most beware of *pride.* It is Satan's first-born. It possesses the wonderful faculty of occupying the space of any other sin which is cast out of the heart. If intemperance be cast out, then pride swells and fills the room that intemperance occupied before. Often pride will arise and by its own strength cast out some other vice, *in order* that it may have more room to grow in, and more food to feed upon.

Most of all, pride dreads the entrance of the Son of God into the heart. Then it knows its reign will be at an end. How it bars and bolts the doors of the heart, against the rightful owner! Yet Christ has broken through even these bars. Saul of Tarsus was a proud Pharisee, when Jesus spoke to him from heaven; but he became as lowly as that penitent publican, who said, "Lord, be merciful to me a sinner."

Evening Scripture portion. Acts IX. 1 to 31. ***The conversion of Paul.***

LUKE XX. 9–19.—*The parable of the rebellious husbandmen in the vineyard.*

IN this parable the base conduct of the Jewish nation is plainly set forth. When the conduct of men towards God is represented in parables, we perceive its ingratitude and treachery more clearly than we did before. And why? Because there is no being whose claims are so little understood by men, as the *claims* of God.

Every one will admit, that the *lord* of the vineyard had a *right* to demand a portion of its fruits, as rent, from the husbandmen. But God has a right to *all* our obedience, and to *all* our love. To him we owe *all* we enjoy, or ever *can* enjoy: indeed the very *power* of enjoyment comes from him. But how do men behave towards Him? In the same manner that these husbandmen behaved to their lord. They not only refuse to obey God, but are angry with those who *reprove* their disobedience.

Like these husbandmen, unconverted men become hardened in sin. The husbandmen treated the servants worse and worse. They beat the *first* servant, shamefully entreated the *second*, and wounded the *third*. Thus sinners increase in wickedness: for every sin committed and *not* repented of, prepares for the commission of a greater.

If any of you who have been converted to God, look back upon your days of rebellion, you will perceive that you grew worse. There was some docility in your childhood,—some fear of evil in your early youth,—which were lost as you grew older. If God had not interfered by his grace, you would, by this time, have reached a higher pitch of iniquity than you ever before attained. There is even in the converted a tendency to return to their former state, and there is need constantly to apply to God for fresh supplies of His Holy Spirit, or, like a wheel upon a sloping bank, they will slide back into their old sins.

When the Saviour had concluded the parable, he declared the punishment the lord would inflict on the husbandmen. "He will come and destroy these husbandmen, and shall give the vineyard to others." This prophecy was intended as a warning to the Jews, who had persecuted the prophets, and were now plotting the death of the Son of God. The people understood that the warning applied to themselves, for they exclaimed, "God forbid." If they had been as anxious to avoid *sin* as they were to avoid *suffering*, they would have escaped both. What must have been the expression of his countenance when Jesus looked upon those who had answered, "God forbid;" for it is said, "He beheld them?" It must have been a look that seemed to say, "Your sorrows are nearer than you suppose, and greater than you can bear."

He now changed the figure from a vineyard to a building, and alluded to a passage in Ps. 118, in which it is said, "The stone which the builders refused is become the head-stone of the corner." Great was the folly of the builders who knew not the value of the finest, firmest, most precious stone that had ever been hewn out of a quarry; and great would be their punishment. That stone, while it lay upon the ground, would be a stumbling-block, and those who fell over it would be broken; but it would not always lie upon the ground; it would be exalted, and falling upon the wicked, by the righteous anger of God, would grind them to powder. What does this short parable signify? When Christ was a man upon earth, those who rejected him sinned, yet not beyond the reach of pardon; but when he was exalted to God's right hand, those who *continued* to reject him perished eternally. The *everlasting* anger of God is represented by this expression, "It will grind him to powder." That blessed Saviour who might, like a stone, be a support and defence, will become, if we refuse to believe in him, the instrument of our destruction. If we build upon him all our hopes for eternity, he will not fail us: but if we neglect him, he will crush us beneath the weight of his righteous indignation.

Evening Scripture portion. Ps. CXVIII. *The corner stone.*

MATT. XXII. 1–14.—*The parable of the man without a wedding garment.*

THERE is one circumstance concerning this parable which renders it peculiarly solemn. It is the *last* parable recorded, that our Lord related in *public.* There are others, which he related to his apostles in *private*, but there are no more written in the Bible which were spoken in the presence of the chief priests and the multitude.

This parable contains a description of *all* the different kinds of characters that were assembled round the Lord in the temple. Each of us who hears this parable *now*, may find in it his own character.

There were some who *made light* of the invitation to the wedding, and went to their farms and to their merchandise. These persons represent the worldly-minded and the indifferent. The great mass of hearers are of this class. They do not oppose the Gospel by argument; they do not persecute Christians by violence; but they treat serious subjects with levity, and give their hearts and minds to the world. They have *various* tastes; some are engrossed with business, others with society; some with learning and accomplishments, others with domestic duties and delights: but they all agree on this point,—they neglect the invitations of the Gospel.

There were certain persons described in the parable, who took the servants, and entreated them spitefully, and slew them. These, we know, must represent persecutors, such as the chief priests and scribes. The punishment that would soon be inflicted on the murderers of the Lord was plainly indicated by these words, "But when the king heard thereof, he was wroth, and he sent forth his armies, and destroyed these murderers, and burned up their city."

The servants represent prophets, apostles, ministers, and teachers, in all ages, who endeavor to persuade sinners to come to Christ.

The guests who accepted the invitation, signify *all* those who make a *profession* of religion.

The most remarkable character described in the parable is the man who had not on a wedding garment. It is the custom in the East, when royal feasts are given, to provide each guest with a robe of honor, and it would be considered a great insult, if any of those who came were to refuse to wear it. This man had neglected to put it on. The servants may not have observed the omission, or if they had observed it, they still permitted this rebellious guest to remain seated at the table. But when the KING came in to see the guests, he immediately expostulated with the transgressor. And what answer did the man return? What excuse did he make? None. He was speechless. *Now* every sinner has many excuses to offer for his transgressions, but he will not be able to bring them forward when he stands before the Son of God.

The wedding garment signifies that righteousness which Christ has promised to bestow on all who believe in him; it is the linen clean and white, spoken of in the Book of Revelation, (xix. 8:) it is the righteousness which is by *faith* of Jesus Christ. Every one might obtain this precious gift. It is offered to all. To refuse this gift is an insult to the King of kings. Are there any here who venture to appear before God in their *own* righteousness,—in *that* righteousness which the prophet Isaiah compares to "filthy rags?" Are there any who know not they are wretched, and miserable, and poor, and blind, and naked, and who will not ask for the white raiment that Jesus offers to bestow? (lxiv. 6.) You may escape the observation of your fellow-guests,—you may elude the vigilance of the servants,—but when the KING comes in to see the guests, you will be detected and cast out. All our religion will prove utterly worthless, if we stop short of true faith and real conversion. That unhappy man might as well have stayed away altogether from the feast, as have come there without a wedding garment. He would have had less trouble,—less disappointment,—less shame,—and perhaps less weeping; for of all the lost, surely none will weep so bitterly as those who imagined to the last they were going to heaven.

Evening Scripture portion. Zeph. I. ***Strange apparel.***

MATT. XXII. 15–22.—*Christ replies to the Pharisees and Herodians respecting paying tribute.*

FULL of Satanic art and Satanic malice, the Pharisees approached the Lord, to ask him a question which they imagined he could not answer without exposing himself to danger. It was this. "Is it lawful to give tribute to Cæsar or not?" Cæsar was the Roman emperor who had conquered the Jewish nation. Could there be any doubt whether it was right to pay tribute or taxes to the monarch who ruled over them? There could be none, because God has commanded submission to rulers. But the Pharisees understood the law of God so ill, that they considered it was wrong to submit to a *heathen* governor.

This was a false notion. It is true the Jews would never have been conquered by the heathen if they had been faithful to God; but *being conquered*, it was their duty to submit. We read in the prophet Ezekiel, that the Lord was once angry with the Jews for breaking their covenant with the king of Babylon. (Ez. xvii. 15.) The Pharisees did not venture *openly* to express their rebellious thoughts, for fear of incurring the displeasure of the Romans; yet they were so *base* as to wish to induce the Lord to endanger his life by uttering the very sentiments which they inwardly approved. In this malicious design they were assisted by the Herodians. These persons were called Herodians after *Herod*, the governor the Romans had appointed. *They* were not *only* willing to submit to the Romans in *lawful*, but also in *un*lawful matters. If the Roman governor gave a command *contrary* to the law of God, they would obey the governor and *disobey* God. We perceive, therefore, that the Pharisees and the Herodians had fallen into *opposite* errors. But the Lord's answer was like a two-edged sword. When Jesus said, "Render unto Cæsar the things that are Cæsar's," he reproved the *secret* notions of the *Pharisees*, and when he said, "Render to God the things that are God's," he reproved the *avowed* doctrine of the *Herodians*.

It is interesting to observe how the attempts of man to perplex the Son of God only drew forth new treasures of wisdom from his lips! How valuable is this rule, "Render unto Cæsar the things that are Cæsar's, and unto God the things that are God's!" It shows us that though *all* things belong to God, yet that some are more *peculiarly* his *own*. There are certain rights which God has given to kings. These rights we must render to them. Parents have certain claims upon their children, and children upon their parents. God does not require parents to neglect their children in order that they may devote all their time to his worship. It was very sinful in the Jews to refuse to support their aged parents, and to bring the money they ought to have bestowed on them to the priests, saying, "It is Corban, or a gift." (Mark vii. 11.)

But if it is sinful not to render unto *men* the things which (by God's appointment) belong to *men*, how much *more* sinful it must be not to render unto *God* the things that belong to God? Yet it is in *this* point that we are the *most* negligent. The world thinks it but a slight fault to neglect their Creator. How many parents there are who render to their children the love that is due to them, but who render no love to God! There are children to be found who *honor* their *parents*, but who *dishonor* God; servants who *obey* their *masters*, but who *disobey* God; *masters* who act *justly* towards their *servants*, but *deceitfully* towards God; brothers and sisters who live in *harmony* with each other, but at *enmity* with God. Such persons may say, "I have done my duty; I have done nobody any harm." But what will *God* say to them? Will he not remember that they have trampled upon His rights? Will not broken Sabbaths, heartless prayers, neglected Bibles, rise up to condemn them? God has greater claims upon us than any other being can have. He created man in his image, bestowing upon him a reasonable soul and an immortal spirit. Therefore we are God's, because we bear his image, as the tribute money bore the image of Cæsar. But God has not only *created* us; he has *redeemed* us. When Satan had taken us captive, Christ *redeemed* us with his precious blood, and now he says to each of us, "Ye are not your *own;* ye are *bought* with a *price;* therefore glorify God in your body, and in your spirit, which are God's." (1 Cor. vi. 20.) Have we given ourselves to the Redeemer? Is it our chief desire to do his will and to promote his glory? Or do we ungratefully spurn his authority, seeking our own pleasure and doing our own will?

Evening Scripture portion. Rom. XIII. *Obedience to rulers.*

LUKE XX. 27–38.—*Christ replies to the Sadducees respecting the resurrection.*

HERE is another instance of precious truth being uttered in answer to frivolous questions. What light is thrown upon the eternal state by these two sentences! "They are equal unto the angels! All live unto him."

The Sadducees did not believe that there would be any resurrection of the dead, because they did not understand *how* it could be. When they applied to Jesus they described a case which might have occurred under the Jewish law. The land of Canaan was divided into small inheritances. If a man died without a child to succeed him, God enjoined that his brother should marry the widow, and that if a child were born, he should succeed to the property of the deceased brother, and be considered as his heir. The Sadducees imagined that they had proposed a difficulty that the Lord *could* not solve; but by a word he exposed their folly. He declared that departed saints are "equal to the angels of God." Angels are not divided into families as men are; and glorified saints will not be connected in heaven with the relations they had upon earth. They will have connections, but not of an *earthly* kind. The pastor will rejoice to find again the flock he fed below. As St. Paul says to his converts, (1 Thess. ii. 19,) "For what is our hope, or joy, or crown of rejoicing? Are not even *ye* in the presence of our Lord Jesus Christ at his coming?" The pious parent will find himself united in *spiritual* bonds to the children who were born the *second* time, in answer to his fervent supplications. The friends who bore each other's spiritual burdens up the hill of Zion, will walk together by the waters of life that gladden the city of their God. *Spiritual* bonds can never be dissolved. *Now* is the time to multiply these bonds. Some who knew upon earth *few* of the sweet ties of kindred will be bound by *numerous sacred everlasting* ties in heaven.

But Christ knew that the Sadducees denied not only the resurrection of the *body*, but the immortality of the *spirit*. Therefore he brought forward a proof of the *eternal* life of the pious dead; and he brought it out of those five books of Moses, in which *alone* the Sadducees professed to believe. God would not have said to Moses, when he spoke from the burning bush, "*I am* the God of Abraham," if Abraham had ceased to exist.

How glorious is the idea that *all* the saints are actually in existence! All those holy men whom we have read of in the Scriptures, all whom we have heard of, all whom we have known and loved,—they LIVE. They not *only live;* but are equal to the angels. We delight to think of our absent living friends, to imagine how they are now engaged, to hope they sometimes think of us, and will some day return to us; but while we are indulging these tender thoughts, they may be in pain and trouble; they may be entangled in sin, and wandering far from God. But with what confidence may we think of the *pious dead!* When we hear the sweetest strains of music, we may think, "Those sounds give but faint ideas of their feelings, as they pass from bliss to bliss." But though we know not the degree of their happiness, Jesus did. He had but lately left the blessed company above, and now he was going to *die* that they might live on forever, and that their number might continually increase. Once Abel was the *only* redeemed saint in heaven, but at length there shall be a multitude that no man can number, who will join in Abel's song, and say, "Salvation to our God, which sitteth upon the throne, and unto the Lamb." (Rev. vii. 10.)

Ten thousand times ten thousand sung
   Loud anthems round the throne,
When lo! one solitary tongue
   Began a song unknown;
A song unknown to angel ears,
A song that told of banish'd fears,
Of pardon'd sins, and dried up tears.

Not one of all the heavenly host
   Could those high notes attain,
But spirits from a distant coast
   United in the strain;
Till he who *first* began the song
(To sing alone not suffer'd long)
Was mingled with a countless throng.

And still as hours are fleeting by
   The angels ever bear
Some newly-ransom'd soul on high
   To join the chorus there;
And so the song will louder grow,
Till all whom Christ redeem'd below
To that fair world of rapture go.

O give me, Lord, my golden harp,
And tune my broken voice,
That I may sing of troubles sharp,
Exchanged for endless joys;
The song that ne'er was heard before
A sinner reach'd the heavenly shore,
But now shall sound for evermore.

Evening Scripture portion. Exod. III. *The God of Abraham.*

MARK XII. 28–34.—*Christ replies to a Scribe concerning the greatest commandment.*

IT is not surprising that the Scribes admired the Lord's answer to the Sadducees, because they believed in the resurrection. They showed their admiration by exclaiming, "Thou hast well said." Yet they did not give up the hope of entangling the divine Teacher by questions; and one of them made this inquiry, "Which is the first commandment of all?" The Scribes often disputed with each other on this subject, and some asserted that to offer a certain sacrifice, and others that to keep a certain fast, or to repeat certain prayers, or to bestow certain alms, was the service the most acceptable to God. How much the Lord's reply must have surprised them! Instead of selecting any one command as greater than the rest, he pointed to the *root* of *all* acceptable obedience, *Love*. He made only *one* distinction, and that was with regard to the *objects* towards whom love is to be exercised. These objects are "*God* and *man*;" and as *God* is *infinitely* greater than *man*, love to *Him* must be *infinitely* more important than love to *man*. Yet where love to *God* is found, love to *man* will always follow; but it will be a love very different from that selfish, capricious, and partial love which unconverted men feel for their friends and relatives.

The Scribe, who asked the question with the evil design of *tempting* the Lord, (as St. Matthew declares,) was convinced by the answer, and expressed his sentiments with cordiality and candor. He did not speak *hypocritically* when he said, "Well, Master, thou hast said the truth." No other of our Lord's tempters ever showed such readiness to receive instruction, and such frankness in avowing his convictions. He, who knew his heart, encouraged him by this commendation: "Thou art not *far* from the kingdom of God." He did not say, "Thou art *in* the kingdom of God." He did not say, as once he said to a weeping penitent, "Thy faith hath *saved* thee." He did not say, as once he said to a dying thief, "Thou shalt be with me in Paradise." Yet what he did say was very encouraging. In a world in which so many are as far from the kingdom of God, as the east is from the west, it is encouraging for a sinner to hear that he is *not far* from it. It is God alone that can draw a soul even to its *borders:* and it is our hope that if he bring it thus far, he will bring it farther still. To perish at the very barrier that separates death from life would be awful indeed. The shipwrecked mariner who perishes in the waves when in *sight* of the shore, seems in a more pitiable case than one who had not so nearly reached his native land and his beloved home.

Are we convinced that without *love* all the services we can offer to God are worthless? Even a human creature would not be pleased with our gifts, if he KNEW that we did not love him, and that we presented them only with the view of gaining a reward. And will God be pleased with interested services? How much has he done to win our love? He has given his only-begotten Son to die for our sakes. Is not that enough to melt the hardest heart? There can be no greater proof of the natural wickedness of the human heart than this: it finds it difficult to love God—to love the most lovely Being, the most gracious Benefactor.

Let none of us be satisfied with feeling we *ought* to love God. As soon as a spark of real affection for our heavenly Father is kindled in our hearts, then we are *in* the kingdom of God: then we are safe, then we are happy. Not *so* happy as we shall be when we love him more; but happier than the most prosperous worldling who does not love him. Our love can never *entitle* us to eternal life; Christ's blood can alone do that; but it affords a proof that we are the children of God, and that we shall dwell with him forever! for "Eye hath not seen, nor ear heard, neither have entered into the heart of man, the things which God hath prepared for them that LOVE him." (1 Cor. ii. 9.)

Evening Scripture portion. Deut. VI. *Love to God.*

MATT. XXII. 41 to end.—*Christ questions the Pharisees concerning himself.*

WE have already admired the wisdom of the Lord's *answers*. We have now an instance of the wisdom of his *questions*. Though his enemies could not perplex *him*, yet he could easily perplex *them*. But his questions were not like theirs, *frivolous;* they were *important*.

There is no subject *more* important than who *Christ* is. The Pharisees *thought* they knew, but they were profoundly ignorant on the subject. They knew, indeed, the meaning of the word "*Christ.*" It signifies "*anointed*"—one set apart by the anointing of oil as priest and king. Jesus was the *Christ,* anointed of the Father with the Holy Ghost, the oil of gladness, to be priest and king forever. In the second Psalm there is a prophecy of this anointed one. "The kings of the earth set themselves and the rulers take counsel together against the Lord, and against his anointed (or his Christ.") The Pharisees had read the Scriptures, and they knew that the Christ would come into the world, and that he would be born of the family of *David.* But they did not know that the Christ was the Son of *God*, as well as the Son of *David.* Therefore Jesus brought forward a passage from the Psalms, in which David calls the Christ *his Lord.* It is this, "The Lord said unto my Lord." (Ps. cx. 1.) That is, "The Lord the *Father* said unto my Lord the *Son.*" How could David's *Son* be David's *Lord?* This was a mystery hidden from the Pharisees. It is the great mystery of godliness. "God manifest in the flesh." It has been revealed to us. We know that from everlasting the Son has been with the Father in glory, and that in the fulness of time he was born into the world,—the infant of a humble daughter of the royal David. Thus he is at once David's Son and David's Lord.

The Pharisees did not ask him to explain the passage he had quoted; for they were contented with their ignorance, and loved darkness better than light. But they will understand it when it is too late. The prophecy shall be fulfilled. "The Lord said unto my Lord, Sit thou on my right hand, until I make thine enemies thy footstool." Part of it has already been accomplished. Christ is *now* sitting at the right hand of God, but he has not *yet* come to make his enemies his footstool. With what dismay will those who once rejected him behold the Son of God when he appears in his glory! "Every eye shall see him, and they also that pierced him; and all kindreds of the earth shall wail because of him." That is, *some* of all kindreds shall wail, because *some* of all kindreds have rejected him. It was not the *Jews* only who said, "We will not have this man to reign over us;" it was not the *Romans* only who pierced him with a spear; there are many belonging to Christian nations who have crucified him afresh and have trodden him under foot. (Heb. vi. 6; x. 29.) All who do not *love* him are his *enemies*, and shall be made his *footstool.* It is a fearful thing to fall into the *hands* of the living God. How terrible it must be to be *trampled* beneath his *feet!* Yet those who have trodden under foot the Son of God shall, if they do not repent, be trodden under foot themselves: for he has declared, "I will tread them in my anger, and trample them in my fury." (Isa. lxiii. 3.) In that day he will save his people, and while he makes his enemies his footstool, he will exalt them to his own THRONE, for he has said, "To him that overcometh will I grant to sit with me in MY THRONE." (Rev. iii. 21.)

Evening Scripture portion. Ps. CX. CXI. *David's Lord.*

MATT. XXIII. 1–12.—*Christ warns the people against the pride of the Pharisees.*

THIS is the *last* discourse recorded which our Saviour uttered in the presence of his enemies. How alarming it is! Surely those sins must be very dangerous which called forth such warnings from the meek and gentle Saviour! The first part of the discourse was *not* addressed to the *Pharisees themselves*, but to the *disciples* and to the *multitude*. The Lord warned them against imitating the *example* of their teachers. With regard to their instructions, this was the rule laid down. When the Pharisees sat in Moses' seat, that is, when they read the books of Moses in the synagogue to the people, *then* they were to be regarded. We know that their FALSE interpretations were not to be received; for our Saviour on one occasion censured them for teaching for *doctrines* the commandments of *men*. (Matt. xv. 9.) Therefore we perceive how we ought to understand the words in verse 3: "All, therefore, whatsoever they bid you observe, that observe and do." *All* the instructions they gave, which agreed with the word of God, the people were bound to observe, however wicked their teachers might be.

The Lord next commanded the people not to imitate the example of the Pharisees. "Do not ye after their *works*." We are apt to imitate those we admire. The people admired the Pharisees exceedingly, for they could not detect their *motive*. It was PRIDE. All they did was to be seen of men; therefore all they did was abominable to God. The phylacteries (those strips of parchment on which texts of Scripture were written) were harmless in themselves, but the Pharisees wore them with the wicked desire of gaining admiration from men by an appearance of piety. The borders, or fringes on the garments, were even commanded by God in the law. In Numbers xv. 38, the Israelites were desired to put fringes (or borders) on their garments, and upon the fringes a riband of blue, in order that when they looked upon it they might remember all the commandments of the Lord. Christ did not reprove them for *wearing* these borders, but for wearing them *in order* to be seen of men; neither did he censure them for *sitting* in the most honorable places at feasts or in the synagogue, but for LOVING to sit there.

It is natural for men to wish to be noticed and admired. Even Christians *feel* this desire, but they do not *cherish* it; no, they abhor it, and pray against it, and strive to overcome it. Whenever we feel *mortified* because we have been overlooked, or *elated* because we have been noticed, we should bewail before the Lord the pride of our hearts. *Why* is pride so offensive in God's eyes? Because it leads men to desire to be in the place of God. Pride is never satisfied. Were a man to gain the admiration of a hundred persons, he would wish to gain that of a hundred *more*, and his desires would never stop till he was the object of *universal* homage, till he occupied the throne of the Almighty. It is not wonderful that God abhors a sin that aims to dethrone himself, and to render his whole creation miserable. The happiness of the universe depends upon God being seated upon his own throne, and upon all his creatures submitting to his government. God must *humble* every one that he would *save.* If *we* are to be *saved,* we must be *humbled.* People little know what they are doing when they cherish pride in children. Many of the common modes of education are calculated to feed this dangerous passion. The desire to be *first* is encouraged by numerous expedients, when every means ought to be used to check the love of distinction in the young heart. Nothing can so effectually subdue it as the Gospel of Christ. There man learns that he is a polluted being, and that nothing but the blood of the crucified Saviour can wash out his stains. Do we believe this humbling doctrine? Then let us remember the words of the apostle Paul, "I beseech you that you walk worthy of your vocation wherewith ye are called, with all lowliness and meekness." (Eph. iv. 2.)

Evening Scripture portion. Ezekiel XXVIII. *Proud Tyre.*

MATT. XXIII. 13–15.—*Christ denounces three woes against the Pharisees.*

THE *first* sermon recorded which the Lord Jesus preached is called the Sermon on the Mount. It began with *eight blessings,* such as these, "Blessed are the poor in spirit, blessed are the meek." But now we are reading the *last* sermon recorded, and we find in it *eight woes.* They are denounced against the *Pharisees.* The Lord warned his disciples against their evil doctrines and example in his *first* public discourse, saying, "Except your righteousness exceed the righteousness of the Scribes and Pharisees, ye shall in nowise enter the kingdom of heaven." He shows in *this* his *last* discourse *what* their righteousness was—a mere pretence, an outward show, a cloak to secret wickedness. After each wo he uttered, he described a crime.

The first crime described is "shutting up the kingdom of heaven against men." This is the contrary of what Jesus came to do. He *opened* the kingdom of heaven to all believers. He opened it by his death. All faithful ministers stand at the open door and invite sinners to come in. But the Pharisees taught men *false* ways of salvation. When they saw real penitents they frowned upon them, and endeavored to shut them out. We find in the prophet Daniel this encouraging promise: "They that be wise shall shine as the brightness of the firmament, and they that turn many to righteousness as the stars forever." (Dan. xii. 3.) But what will become of those who have turned many *from* righteousness! What anguish will they feel when they find among their companions in torment, many whom they once perverted and corrupted!

But if the Pharisees had been *openly* wicked they would not have been as guilty as they were. They *pretended* to be very pious, and made long prayers in public places, while *secretly* they devoured widows' houses. It seems that dying men often left the property of their widows to their charge, little suspecting how the trust would be abused. How could they dare to injure the widow and the fatherless when they read continually in the law of Moses these words: "Ye shall not afflict any widow, or fatherless child. If thou afflict them in anywise, and they shall cry at all unto me, I will hear their cry, and my wrath shall wax hot, and I will kill you with the sword, and *your* wives shall be widows, and *your* children fatherless." Ex. xxii. 22–24. Christ is acquainted with every *secret* sin. He detests sin *most* when he sees it covered by a cloak of hypocrisy. Therefore he said to the Pharisees, "Ye shall receive the *greater* damnation." There are *degrees* of misery. Hypocrites shall be punished more than open transgressors. The sins which they have so carefully concealed from men will be publicly exposed at the last day, and the secrecy with which they were committed will be found to add to their enormity.

Every one would acknowledge that to *devour widows' houses* is a sin; but *every one* would not understand at first that it was a sin to compass sea and land to make *proselytes.* It is not a sin to compass sea and land to make *converts:* no, that is a righteous act. Missionaries go to the farther ends of the earth to tell perishing sinners of a Saviour. They go, and by the blessing of God, they make some of them the children of *heaven,* such as they are themselves. What *is* a proselyte? He is a man who *changes* his religion, whether for a better or a worse. The Pharisees took great pains to persuade the Gentiles to observe the ceremonies of the Jewish law; for it gratified their pride to add to the number of their own followers. They did not desire to *save souls;* for while they were so zealous in making *proselytes,* they shut up the kingdom of heaven against men. The bad instructions they gave to a proselyte rendered him worse than he was before, and even worse than themselves. We should have hardly thought it possible that any *could* be worse than the Pharisees, did we not find these words written, "And when he is made, ye make him twofold more the child of hell than yourselves." There are degrees of *wickedness* as well as of misery. Some are more the children of hell than others. It is even possible to make another *worse* than we are ourselves. How dangerous it must be to listen to false teachers! If we attend to them we may become *worse* than *they* are. How awful is the name here given to a wicked man! "The child of hell!" Yet all who are *not* the children of *heaven* are the children of *hell.* The world is divided into these two classes. Could the children of hell *see* the place to which they were going, they would tremble, and shrink back with fear. But God sees it, and in his love he warns them not to proceed in their dangerous course. He does more. He is willing to make them "meet to be partakers of the inheritance of the saints of light;" for he is able to deliver them from "the power of darkness." (Col. i. 12, 13.)

Evening Scripture portion.
Micah III. *Warning to wicked rulers and teachers.*

MATT. XXIII. 16–28.—*Christ denounces four more woes against the Pharisees.*

OUR God is the God of *truth.* There was no truth in the Pharisees. They *taught* lies, and they *acted* lies. In the passage we have just read a wo is denounced against them for *teaching* lies. They taught the people that the *gold* of the temple was more holy than the temple itself; and that the *gift* on the altar was more holy than the altar: whereas it was clear that it was the *temple* that sanctified the *gold*, and the *altar* that sanctified the *gift.*

What could be their motive for teaching these errors? No doubt it was the love of money. They hoped to induce the people to bestow much gold, and to offer many gifts as sacrifices, that by these means they themselves might grow rich. The love of money has in all ages led men to teach falsehood. Roman Catholic priests gain money by the masses they repeat for the dead. They tell the people that the souls of their relations are in torment, and that they can release them by repeating prayers or masses on their behalf; but they will not repeat these masses, unless money is given to them. One mark of a faithful minister is his indifference to worldly gain, or to *filthy lucre*, as the Scriptures call it. Like St. Paul he can say, "I seek not *yours*, but *you.*" (2 Cor. xii. 14.)

The Pharisees not only *spake* lies, they *acted* them. They pretended to be so very pious, that they would not omit paying tithes to the priests of the *smallest* herbs; while at the same time they omitted paying to God the greatest duties they owed to him, such as judgment, mercy, and faith. And why? Because men could see them when they gave their tithes, but God alone knew the state of their hearts.

Are there not some like the Pharisees in these days? They are careful to perform religious services when the eye of *man* is upon them; but they are indifferent when the eye of *God* alone observes. They attend church regularly because men see them there. But do they pray in *secret* regularly? They are very careful of their *words*, because *men* hear them; but they are very careless about their *thoughts*, because God alone sees them. What can better represent such characters than cups *clean* outside and *filthy* within, than sepulchres beautifully ornamented containing dead men's bones?

How different is the description that the Holy Spirit has given of the saints! St. Paul says, "We have this treasure in earthen vessels." (1 Cor. iv. 7.) The saints are despised by the world, and valued no more than an earthen vessel; but in their hearts a treasure is hid—it is Christ, the hope of glory. (Col. i. 27.) In the sight of God, who sees the heart, they are precious as gold and silver. It is true that they are not without sin; but God has promised to refine them, as gold and silver are purified from their dross. (Mal. iii. 2.) But the wicked are compared to the *dross* of silver, and to the baser metals. God said to Ezekiel, "Son of man, the house of Israel is to me become dross; all they are brass, and tin, and iron, and lead, in the midst of the furnace; they are even the *dross of silver*." And what would God do to these impenitent, unbelieving, unconverted people? "Because ye are all become dross, behold therefore, I will gather you into the midst of Jerusalem. As they gather silver, (that is, the *dross* of silver,) and brass, and iron, and lead, and tin, into the midst of the furnace, to blow the fire upon it to melt it; so will I gather you in my anger and in my fury; and I will *leave* you there, and melt you." (Ezek. xxii. 18–20.) Afflictions do not refine hypocrites; but destroy them. God *leaves* them in their troubles, and suffers them to perish. But if our *hearts* are right in the sight of God, he will never leave us. His promise to every one who sincerely loves him is, "I will be with him in trouble; I will deliver him, and honor him." Are there any here who never cry earnestly to God for a clean heart, and a right spirit? What will you do in the day when God shall judge the *secrets* of men by Jesus Christ? (Rom. ii. 16.)

Evening Scripture portion. Mal. III. ***God sits as a refiner.***

MATT. XXIII. 29–36.—*Christ denounces the last wo against the Pharisees.*

THIS is the last of the *eight* woes that the Lord denounced against the Pharisees. *Eight* times he uttered these words, "Wo unto you, scribes and Pharisees, hypocrites." Eight times he described their hypocritical character. The last instance of hypocrisy mentioned, is the building of the tombs of the prophets. This was an hypocritical act in the Pharisees, because it was not done from love and reverence to the martyred prophets, but merely from pride and ostentation. If they had reverenced the *ancient* prophets, they would not have persecuted the *living* ones. It is very probable that they really *thought* that tney would not have been partakers with their fathers in the blood of the prophets; but they did not know their own hearts. It is very easy to deceive ourselves respecting our own characters. When we read of wicked actions, it is natural to think that we would not have committed them, had we been placed in the circumstances of those we read of. But this is not the way to come to a knowledge of ourselves. Let us not inquire how we *should* have treated the apostles or the reformers, had we lived in their days, but let us rather inquire how *do* we behave towards despised saints in *these* days? Do we love *all* who believe in the Lord Jesus Christ? Are we ready to relieve their wants, and to defend their characters? When the saints are praised and admired, it is easy then to speak in their favor; but when they are despised and calumniated, *then* it requires faith to take their part, and to share in their reproach.

With what honor the Son of God mentioned those holy men who had been slain in former times! What a title he bestowed on Abel, when he called him "*righteous* Abel!" The waters of the flood had not washed out the stains of his blood from the earth. *We* know the names of very few of those prophets who were slain between the time of Abel and of Zachariah, but all their *names* were known to Jesus at the moment he was speaking,—all their *spirits* were happy in his Father's presence, and all their *blood* was crying for vengeance from the earth. And upon whom would that vengeance descend? Upon *that* generation to whom Jesus then spoke—upon *that* generation who would exceed all their fathers in wickedness, by slaying the Son of God, and by refusing the offer of pardon that his apostles would proclaim. Jesus declared, "*All these things* shall come upon *this* generation." But not upon that generation *alone*. The sufferings of the Jewish nation are not yet ended. Unto this day they are wanderers on the face of the earth, even as Cain was who slew his brother Abel.

Can parents bear the idea of entailing a curse upon their children? Long after they are sleeping in their graves their offspring may be suffering the consequences of their sins. A family is plunged from the height of affluence into the depth of poverty; disease sweeps away the fair blossoms from a flourishing tree; public crime inflicts a dark blot upon a reputable name—and men know not the *cause* of these visitations. Sometimes they are sent, like the afflictions of Job, and the temptations of Abraham, to try the faith of God's dear children, and as tokens of a Father's love: but sometimes they are the memorials of sins perpetrated long before,—of sins unpardoned and unrepented of. The cruel treatment of a fatherless child, the treacherous robbery of a master, the bitter persecution of a saint, are often visited upon the *unrighteous* descendants of those who committed the guilty acts. God fulfils his own word by visiting the iniquities of the fathers upon the children unto the third and fourth generations of them that *hate* him.

But He will never let his wrath burn against the *righteous* son of ungodly parents. No, if the son repent, he shall obtain mercy. The good king Josiah, though the son of a very wicked father, was spared when God was going to pour torrents of wrath upon his kingdom. Because his heart was tender, because he humbled himself, and wept and prayed, therefore God said, "Thou shalt be gathered to thy grave in peace." Pious children who have ungodly parents yet living, may pray for them, and may obtain mercy for them also. Far from punishing the children for their parents' sake, he may bless those parents for their children's sake. "For he is gracious and merciful, slow to anger, and of great kindness, and repenteth him of the evil." (Joel ii. 13.)

Evening Scripture portion.
2 Chron. XXXIV. 14 to end. *The blessing bestowed upon King Josiah.*

MATT. XXIII. 37 to end.—*Christ laments over Jerusalem.*

COULD the most feeling heart bewail the calamities of his *friend* more tenderly than the Lord here bewails the awful end of his *enemies?* It was not because he *loved* them not that he had addressed the Pharisees in these terrible words, "Ye serpents, ye generation of vipers, how can ye escape the damnation of hell?" Those whom he now called serpents, he would have treated as the hen her beloved brood. When that careful bird descries a hawk or a kite hovering in the air, she calls her little ones to take refuge beneath her sheltering wings. The Lord Jesus descried afar off the woes that were about to light upon the heads of his guilty nation, and he gave them warning of their approach; but they would not heed his words, nor accept his invitations. And now the time was come when hope had nearly expired. "Behold," said the Lord, "your house is left unto you desolate." But though he said "Behold," the Jews beheld no desolation. The temple was shining in all its splendor; the walls of Jerusalem were standing in all their strength; the feast of the Passover was thronged with guests; the land was flowing with milk and honey; where was the desolation? It was nigh at hand, even at the door. The Son of God heard its step upon the mountains, and saw its shadow upon the hills. Before the voices of those children who sang his praises in the temple should become tremulous through age, the enemy would cause the sound of melody to cease in the Lord's house. How long has the silence continued! Visit Mount Moriah, where once the temple stood. Behold that stately building, crowned with domes and minarets. It is not a Christian church. Is it a heathen temple? No, it is a Mahommedan mosque, the pride of the Turks, the masterpiece of their architecture. Neither Christian nor Jew may now tread upon the spot where the Redeemer stood and taught. And thus it shall be, till the times of the Gentiles are fulfilled. Then there shall be a great and glorious change. It is described in this last verse. "For I say unto you, ye shall not see me henceforth, till ye shall say, 'Blessed is he that cometh in the name of the Lord.'" When the Saviour comes the *second* time, he will meet with a very different reception from that which he received the *first* time. He expired amidst *curses*, but he shall return amidst *blessings*.

How wonderful are the dealings of God with the Jewish nation! Instead of casting them *off* forever, he has only cast them *out* for a *time*. He says to them, by the mouth of his prophet Isaiah, "In a little wrath I hid my face from thee for a moment, but with everlasting kindness will I have mercy on thee, saith the Lord thy Redeemer." (Is. liv. 7, 8.)

Are there any among us with whom the Lord has dealt in the same merciful manner? Some, who in their youthful days hardened their hearts against the Gospel, after wandering long in forbidden and dangerous paths, have been permitted once more to hear the joyful sound, and have heard it the *second* time with altered feelings, and a new delight. When God had spoken to them in their prosperity, they had replied, "I will not hear;" but when he had destroyed their earthly delights, they welcomed the messenger of mercy, and exclaimed, "Blessed is he that cometh in the name of the Lord."

Evening Scripture portion. Rom. XI. ***The restoration of the Jews.***

MARK XII. 41 to end.—*Christ commends a poor widow.*

THE time was drawing near when the Lord Jesus would leave the temple, never to return. Before he left it, he sat for a while in the court called the *women's* court. The inner court was called the court of Israel, and *there* no one was permitted to sit down; but in the *women's* court sitting was allowed. Under the pillars that adorned the court eleven chests were placed, and upon each chest was written the purpose to which money cast in it, would be applied. None of them were for the relief of the poor; all were set apart for the supply of the various sacrifices and services of the temple.

The people presented their offerings within the view of Jesus. Many who were rich cast in much. It is probable these rich men were Pharisees. The Lord had lately upbraided them for their covetousness. He did not now applaud their liberality. He knew that though they gave much, they kept more. He saw also their *motives*, and he was acquainted with their *secret* practices. But while he passed over the rich, his eye rested upon a certain poor widow, who cast in two mites, which made a *farthing*. It is said in one place that two sparrows are sold for a farthing: *that* farthing was the *fourth* part of a penny; *this* farthing was the FORTIETH part of a penny;—the fortieth part of the wages of a day-laborer.

There is very little recorded concerning the poor widow; neither her name, nor her parentage, nor her history, nor her abode. But she was well known to Jesus. He knew not only what she put into the treasury, but also that she had nothing remaining. He knew all her circumstances in this life—the depth of her poverty, and how she fell into it. It may be that she was the victim of one of those proud Pharisees, who devoured widows' houses. He knew not only her *circumstances*, but her *heart*—the *feelings* with which she approached the treasury and cast in her mites. It may be that she had just received some great deliverance, and that she testified her gratitude by her gift. It may be that, like the aged Anna, she derived her chief consolation from attending the services of the temple, from listening to the psalms sung continually within its walls, and from joining in the worship which accompanied the daily offerings. It is probable that she had heard the Saviour's gracious words within that sacred place, and had found salvation through faith in his name. She *must* have been a believer in the promises of God, or she could not have presented an acceptable offering. For it is written, "Through *faith* Abel offered a more excellent sacrifice than Cain." (Heb. xi.)

The believing poor still present their farthings to the Lord;—their mites are still precious in his sight. They may not be noticed by men, but they are not overlooked by God. He knows whence all the money comes that enters into his treasury; and he can distinguish the guinea which dropped out of the overflowing coffers of a rich man, from the last farthing of a poor one. There are some in our days who have displayed the same faith that actuated the widow. There was a man who spent his *all* in going from city to city, from country to country, to plead for the *souls* of the poor. Wherever he went, he stirred up his fellow-Christians to form town-missions, which might penetrate into every dark abode of ignorance and misery. He died in the midst of his years and of his labors, and left not enough to procure his winding-sheet, much less to sustain his infant family. But God raised up friends who honorably buried him, and comfortably provided for his widow and her babes.* Our gracious Lord is faithful, and never forsakes those who put their trust in him. We may feel assured that the widow who cast in all her living into the treasury, was not suffered to pine with want the day after. And every one who has faith to act as she did, will be *approved* as she was, and *sustained* as she was, and at the last day *acknowledged* as she will be.

Evening Scripture portion. 2 Cor. VIII. *Exhortation to liberality*

* David Nasmith, who died 1839.

MATT. XXIV. 1, 2.—*Christ foretells the destruction of the temple.*

THESE words record a very remarkable event—"Jesus went out, and departed from the temple."

That was a memorable moment when the Lord Jesus departed from the temple, never again to enter it—*that* temple into which he had been carried as a babe in his mother's arms, and where he had been blessed by the aged Simeon; from that temple where, as a child, he had astonished the doctors by his wisdom—from that temple where he had healed so many sufferers, and spoken peace to so many penitents. Never more would he honor it with his presence; his enemies might have it to themselves, to repeat within its sacred courts for a few more years their hypocritical services. On another altar he would bleed, even the altar of the cross; to another temple he would ascend, even to the temple in heaven, to stand before the altar there, with the golden censer in his hand. (Rev. viii. 3.)

Had the disciples known their Master as well as they *might* have known him, they would not have directed his attention to the splendor of the holy house. How could they expect that the King of Heaven would admire *earthly* magnificence! The world's glory must have appeared dark indeed to Him who had dwelt in the palace of eternal light!

A little while before, he had called his disciples unto him. For what purpose? Was it to show them such an object as the world admires? A monarch gorgeously arrayed, or a building beautifully adorned? or even a prospect of surpassing loveliness? No; it was to show them a sight pleasing in God's eyes—a poor widow devoted in heart to his service. For what a different purpose the disciples came to their Master!

Instead of admiring the temple's magnificence, Jesus uttered this astonishing prophecy: "There shall not be left one stone upon another that shall not be thrown down." For nine years before the Saviour's birth, Herod the Great had kept eighteen thousand workmen continually employed in repairing the temple, and since his death the Jews had continued to improve it. It was built upon a massive rock, and was composed of stones, some of which were sixty feet in length. Who could believe that such stones would be thrown down! Yet in about forty years after the prophecy had been uttered, the place where the temple stood was a ploughed field; for the Romans caused the foundations to be dug up in search of hidden treasures.

God knows the fate of every building which now attracts human admiration. The mosque of Omar, that stands where once the temple stood, has its appointed time. All the edifices that human hands have reared, since the tower of Babel was begun, shall perish: they may be demolished by the conqueror, or swallowed up by an earthquake, or gradually crumbled away by the hand of time—but if they escape all these enemies, they shall at length be consumed in the flames; for God has declared, "The earth, and the works that are therein, shall be *burned up*. Seeing, then, that *all* these things shall be dissolved, what manner of persons ought ye to be in all holy conversation and godliness, looking for and hasting unto the coming of the day of God?" (2 Pet. iii. 10, 11.) But there are some things which shall *endure*. Though every stone in the temple has been thrown down, the poor widow that cast her mite into the treasury still lives. Her love still lives. It led her *once* to offer two mites, and *now* it leads her to offer never-ending praises. When we behold a splendid building, let us remember that a poor tattered believer is more glorious in God's sight than that pompous fabric. Men may think him unfit to enter the magnificent gate, or to tread upon the marble floor; but God has prepared for him a building not made with hands, eternal in the heavens—a building that shall endure when all earthly palaces and temples shall melt with fervent heat.

Evening Scripture portion. Is. II. *Earthly glory.*

MATT. XXIV. 3–14.—*Christ foretells the signs of the end.*

How interesting was the scene upon Mount Olivet when the Saviour sat there instructing his disciples concerning things to come! The prospect he beheld must have filled his heart with sad thoughts. It was Jerusalem, that crowned the opposite heights—Jerusalem! the city over which he had wept only a few days before—Jerusalem, that city in which he had done so many miracles—Jerusalem, that city in which he was so very soon to be tried and condemned.

When *we* look upon a place which we have often visited, we think of *past* events; but when Jesus looked upon Jerusalem he thought not only of the *past*, but also of the *future*.

The disciples did not leave their Master to meditate *alone* upon that mount. Four of them approached and proposed some important questions. The names of these four are recorded by St. Mark: they were James and John, Peter and Andrew, the fishermen of Gennesareth. The inquiries they made were these: "When shall these things be? And what shall be the sign of thy coming, and of the end of the world?" *What* things did they refer to in their first question? A little while before their Lord had said, when gazing on the magnificent buildings of the temple, "There shall not be left here one stone upon another, that shall not be thrown down." It was natural that the disciples should desire to know *when* these wonderful events would happen; they said, "*When* shall these things be?" Had they asked no other question, it would have been clear that the *whole* of the Lord's answer related to the destruction of Jerusalem; but they added a *second* inquiry, "What shall be the sign of thy coming, and of the end of the world?"

The Lord answered both these inquiries as he sat upon Mount Olivet. It is difficult for us to know certainly what part of the answer relates to the destruction of Jerusalem, and what part relates to the second coming. Before Jerusalem was destroyed, there were many wars and persecutions; and there are wars and persecutions *still.* What mournful signs these are, of the coming of Christ! When he was born at Bethlehem, the angels sang, "Glory to God in the highest, on earth *peace*, good will towards men." This song would have led us to expect that wars would cease now the Prince of peace was come. But eighteen hundred years have rolled away, and violence still prevails upon the earth. The joyful song in the fields of Bethlehem is very unlike the mournful discourse upon the Mount of Olives. Yet both are true. When the Babe that lay in the manger shall sit upon his throne, the earth shall be filled with the glory of the Lord. Meanwhile there must be trials, and afflictions, and temptations. Jesus has faithfully warned us beforehand. He has told us that *many* will be offended, and that *many* will be deceived, and that the love of *many* will grow cold. When we read these prophecies we should offer up such a prayer as this: "May *I* never be offended, or deceived, or cooled in my love!" When we hear of any who have turned back from following the Lord, let us think of the touching words he once spoke to his apostles, "Will ye also go away?" Surely none will feel so much ashamed to see him again as those who professed to walk with him a little way, and to love him for a little while, but whose feet grew weary, and whose love waxed cold! O how they will wish that they had *never* heard his name, nor listened to his voice!

Evening Scripture portion. 2 Thess. I. *Future judgments on persecutors.*

MATT. XXIV. 15–23.—*Christ directs his disciples when to flee from Jerusalem.*

THESE warnings proved exceedingly useful to the first Christians. They remembered the words, "When ye therefore shall see the abomination of desolation, spoken of by Daniel the prophet, stand in the holy place; then let them which be in Judea flee into the mountains." Nearly forty years after these words were uttered, the Roman armies stood in the holy place; that is, in the holy city of Jerusalem. These armies were prophesied of under the name of "the abomination of desolation." The *world* admires great conquerors, and their gallant troops, but the Lord abhors deeds of injustice and cruelty. The Roman name shines bright in the page of history, but it is a blot in the word of God: "the abomination of desolation."

But some may inquire, "How could the Christians escape from Jerusalem when the Romans had entered the city?" God showed his faithfulness by providing a way of escape for his own people. When the Romans first attacked the city, they were repulsed—they fled, and they did not return to the city for several years. The Christians took advantage of their defeat to flee to the mountains. They found a place wherein to dwell in safety; a little town called Pella, beyond the river Jordan, hidden among the hills, was their refuge. It is believed that not *one* Christian was in the city of Jerusalem at the time of its dreadful destruction. Does not the escape of these Christians afford a striking instance of the manner in which God preserves his people? When he destroyed the world by water, he saved Noah; when he destroyed Sodom, he saved Lot; and when he *will* destroy the world by fire, he will save his people. As it is written in Ps. xxxii., "For this shall every one that is godly pray unto thee in a time when thou mayest be found: surely in the floods of great waters they shall not come nigh unto him."

It was the time of the Passover when the Roman armies, headed by the great Titus, returned to attack Jerusalem. Two millions of human beings were then enclosed within her walls. And what human beings! Many of them were ferocious robbers. Two wicked men, named Simon and John, were at open war with each other, and kept the city in continual tumult. Through their means most of the provisions were burned, and the inhabitants speedily reduced to famine. The robbers broke into houses, and insisted upon the inmates delivering up their last morsel. During the whole period of the siege no regular meal was taken. Each ate his morsel alone, in fear and trembling. One unnatural mother was induced by hunger to roast her own child, and to eat part of it. The odor of her meal attracted the Jewish soldiers to her house; they compelled her to produce her strange food; but when they beheld the awful spectacle, they retreated in horror, for now they clearly saw that God had abandoned the city, and that no hope remained to its wretched inhabitants.

The pen of Josephus, an unbelieving Jew, has described the calamities of the siege; and he has wound up his account by these words: "If the misfortunes of *all* from the beginning of the world were compared with those of the Jews, they would appear much less upon the comparison." This is an unbeliever's testimony to the truth of the prophecy, "There shall be great tribulation, such as was not since the beginning of the world to this time." If those days had not been shortened, the *whole* nation must have perished; but this could not be, because of the elect. Some of the Jews were chosen of God, and for *their* sakes the days of tribulation were shortened; and the siege lasted little more than three months. But is the tribulation over? O no.

The Jews are still wanderers upon the face of the earth; they are still despised, dejected, degraded. It is an awful thing not to listen to the voice of *mercy*. The Jews would not hear it, and they have been *compelled* to hear the voice of *wrath*. The Lord delights in mercy. Are there any here who have not yet accepted his gracious invitations? O what sorrows you might escape, if *now* you would turn to him!

Evening Scripture portion. Dan. IX. ***The abomination of desolation.***

MATT. XXIV. 23–31.—*Christ describes his second coming.*

WHAT comfort it has been to believers during the last eighteen hundred years, to know that Jesus will return in a *public* manner! "As the lightning cometh out of the east, and shineth even unto the west; so shall the coming of the Son of Man be." The inhabitants of *all* parts of the world will know in the twinkling of an eye that Jesus is returned, for they will *see* him coming in the clouds of heaven. Had it not been for this assurance, in what a state of agitation they would have been kept! They would have listened with eagerness to every report of his return, and would have thought it well at least to go and see whether it were true. But now they feel an unshaken confidence, that *whenever* he appears they shall see him *immediately*. They know also that *wherever* they may be at the time, they will be gathered unto him, even as the eagles are gathered from distant parts to feast upon their prey. Whether they be dead or living when he comes, they shall behold the first bright beams of his chariot. Whether they be lying in their graves, or in the depths of the sea, they shall be caught up to meet him in the air: whether engaged in their daily toil, or partaking of their nightly repose, they shall be changed, and translated to join the blessed company.

And did the Lord give his disciples any information concerning the *time* of his second coming? Yes: he said it should happen "immediately after the *tribulation* of those days." To *what* tribulation does he refer? This is a question that has perplexed many attentive readers of Holy Scripture. Some consider the tribulation that the Jews have endured during the last eighteen hundred years is here spoken of. Are they not *still* in tribulation? St. Luke gives this account of our Lord's words: "Jerusalem shall be trodden down of the Gentiles, until the times of the Gentiles be fulfilled." The Turks are still in possession of Jerusalem; their mosque still pollutes the holy mount where once the temple stood; but when the tribulation of the Jews is over, when they are restored to their own land, and their own city, their King will return to take possession of his ancient throne. He was born King of the Jews, he died King of the Jews, and King of the Jews he will return; but not of the *Jews* only, but King of kings, and Lord of lords. How glorious is the description of his return in Rev. xix. 11! "And I saw heaven opened, and behold a white horse, and he that sat upon him was called Faithful and true, and in righteousness he doth judge and make war. His eyes were as a flame of fire, and on his head were many crowns; and he had a name written that no man knew but he himself."

Yet the glory of the second coming is not so wonderful as the humiliation of the first. It seems suitable to the Son of God to return in the clouds with a vast army of saints and angels; but it is amazing that he should have entered the world as a babe, have been laid in a manger, and nailed unto a cross. And why did he come in this lowly, in this ignominious manner? That when he came again to destroy the world, he might gather his elect from the four winds, from one end of heaven to the other. All these scattered ones have believed in the *crucified* Jesus, and have been washed in his blood; therefore their garments are clean and white, and they are fit to enter into the presence of their Lord, and to dwell with him forever.

Evening Scripture portion. Rev. XIX. *Christ's second coming.*

MATT. XXIV. 32–41.—*Christ foretells the suddenness of his second coming.*

WHAT must have been the feelings of the disciples when they heard their Lord declare, "This generation shall not pass till all these things be fulfilled!" Though the Lord had directed *them* how to escape from Jerusalem, yet they must have felt compassion for their countrymen who would suffer the "great tribulation." What should we feel if we knew that London, now so prosperous and flourishing, would in the course of forty years be steeped in blood, and filled with carcasses! Thanks be unto God, we have heard no such evil tidings. Though now full of ignorance and vice, of poverty and misery, it may become enlightened and happy, through the spread of the gospel in all its dark alleys and crowded courts. But the disciples could entertain no such hopes concerning Jerusalem. They knew that if they were spared to see old age, they would *hear* of the destruction of their native city.

Before the beginning of this discourse, they had asked two questions; the first was, "When shall these things be?" This inquiry referred to the stones of the temple being thrown down. The other question was, "What shall be the sign of thy coming, and of the end of the world?" To this question our Lord seems to refer when he says, "But of *that* day and hour knoweth no man; no, not the angels of heaven, but my Father only." How remarkable it is that the *time* of

Christ's second coming should be concealed from the knowledge of *every* creature! *Angels* know not the time; they know not when they shall be summoned to attend their King in his chariot of clouds. *Devils* know not the time; they know not when they shall be immured in their dark prison, and no longer permitted to tempt the inhabitants of the earth, and of the sea. *Wicked* men know not the time; they know not when their day of grace will end. Righteous men know not the time; they know not when they shall be caught up to meet their Lord in the air.

When Jerusalem was destroyed, the *righteous* had to flee; but when Christ returns, it is the *wicked* who will attempt to flee, and will not be able. The same Almighty arm that will save the righteous, will arrest the wicked in their flight. How great will be their consternation when they find themselves suddenly separated from their pious kindred! The very day in which this event takes place, they will arise ignorant of what it will bring forth. Two men will be in the field, digging, or ploughing, or reaping. One may have just vented his profane oaths, while the other may have reproved him, and reminded him of the future judgment,—when suddenly the angels may bear away the faithful laborer into the presence of his Saviour, and leave his ungodly companion to taste the terrors of his wrath. Two women will be engaged in domestic labors; grinding at a mill, or employed in some other household work. They may both that morning have sung the same hymn, and have appeared to join in the same prayer; but while one was a humble believer, the other was a lover of the world. Christ will suddenly reveal their true characters, by taking one to dwell with him, and by leaving the other to sink into perdition. Should not each of us ask himself, "If the Lord were to come *to-day*, what would become of me? Has He heard me imploring earnestly for pardon, and his Holy Spirit? When He looks into my heart, does He see that I love Him?"

Evening Scripture portion.
Is. LXV. ***The Lord's enemies divided from his servants.***

MATT. XXIV. 42–44.—*Christ counsels his disciples to watch for his return.*

WHY did the Lord conceal from all the time of his second coming? We know not *why* he concealed it from *angels* or from *devils*, but we *do* know *why* he concealed it from *men*. It was that they may be watching for his return. He said, "Watch, therefore, for ye know not what hour your Lord doth come." He who made us is acquainted with all the secret springs of our nature. He knows that when we have a long time before us, we are disposed to loiter. There is a spirit of sloth and delay that steals over our hearts, which nothing overcomes so much as the idea that the opportunity for exertion may soon be past. Though our Lord may appear to tarry, we must never cease to believe that he will soon come. As it is written, "For yet a little while, and he that shall come will come, and will not tarry." (Heb. x. 37.) When we have been expecting a friend for a long time, we at length grow weary of waiting, and "give him up." We say, "Surely now he will not come at all." Yet sometimes he arrives just as we have given him up. We must never *give up* expecting Christ, for he has positively promised that he will come. But he has *not* promised to prolong our lives till his return. Millions have dropped into the grave during his absence, and it is very probable that we may descend into ours.

The day of death is as *uncertain* as the day of his return. The young die as well as the old, the healthy as well as the sickly, the cautious as well as the adventurous. We all know that *this* day we MAY die. It does not require *faith* to believe that we may *die;* for *reason* convinces us of this fact. Yet is it not remarkable that death generally comes unexpectedly;—even to the *old?* They have lived so long, that they naturally imagine they shall live longer still. They have seen the arrow of destruction pass by them so often, piercing their companions, but sparing them, that their fears are quelled, and their hearts are lulled to repose. It often happens that just as men have made their plans for long life, they are visited by sudden death. A house has just been built, and a garden planted, when he that built and planted is called to dwell in another abode, and to walk in other regions. These unexpected removals say with a loud voice to the living, "Be ye also ready."

But what if, instead of *death*, the *Lord* were to come? His return would create more *alarm* than death has ever done. When *death* attacks an ungodly man, his senses are often stupified by disease; he is less capable of feeling alarm than when in full health. But when Christ returns, he will find his enemies lively and strong. A sick man usually entertains hopes of recovery till near his last hour; but when Christ returns, the wicked will see no way of escape. Friends surround the pillow of the dying man; some sooth and flatter him, some counsel and encourage him: but when the Judge appears, the wicked will be left to meet their awful fate, without one friendly arm to render aid, one pitying eye to shed a tear, one pious tongue to offer a prayer.

Do we desire to escape the terrors of that awful moment? there is but one certain refuge. It is the Lord Jesus, who is now ready to hear our prayers, to forgive our sins, to bestow his grace, and to be our hiding-place in the day of trouble. If we neglect this precious opportunity, he will come on us as a thief, and we shall not know what hour he cometh upon us. (Rev. iii. 3.)

Evening Scripture portion. Is. XXIV. *Terrors of the last day.*

MATT. XXIV. 45 to end.—*Christ describes the end of faithful and unfaithful servants.*

THIS part of our Lord's discourse applied with peculiar force to the apostles. They had been made rulers over their Lord's household. But it also applies to all ministers, for they are all stewards of the mysteries of God. A sacred trust is committed to them; and if they neglect it, their condemnation will be very heavy. If the laborer in the field, if the women grinding at the mill, were ungodly, they would perish: but if the steward of spiritual things was unfaithful, how much more miserably would he perish! How happy are those ministers whom death has found watching over their household! It signified not, indeed, whether they died in their *pulpits* or in their *beds;* but it signified much whether their hearts were truly in their work. Faithful ministers, like St. Paul, feel continual sorrow in their hearts for their brethren who know not God. Like him they can also say, when they think of their children in the faith, "We joy for your sakes before our God." (1 Thess. iii. 9.)

It is awful to think that there are some ministers whom Christ calls "*evil* servants." They think in their heart that the Lord delayeth his coming. Then they begin to abuse the power committed to them, and to ill-treat the saints of God, their fellow-servants. Worldly-minded ministers have often been great persecutors. What are the pleasures, and who are the companions of such men? It is said in the parable, "They eat and drink with the drunken." They do not thirst after the river of the water of life, but after earthly delights: they do not love the society of the servants of God, but that of the people of the world.

Is it *ministers* only, who indulge the wicked thought, "My Lord delayeth his coming?" Thousands are emboldened in sin by that idea. They do not say with the scoffers mentioned in St. Peter's second epistle, that he will *never* come. They do not ask, "Where is the promise of his coming?" but they think "He will not come *yet;* we may sin on with safety; we shall have time to repent, and amend."

The Lord continually defeats such presumptuous calculations. Death opens the door without giving the slightest notice; his step is not heard,—his form is not seen till he has seized his victim, and borne him beyond the reach of repentance or of pardon.

It is in this manner the Lord has punished presumptuous sinners in past times. He will do it in a more signal manner when he comes again. He will select a moment in which the hypocrites shall have no suspicion of his approach. He will come on a day when they are not looking for him, and at an hour when they are not aware of their danger. But on that day his people will be looking for him, and at that hour they will be trusting in him; for they will say when they see him, "This is our God; we have *waited* for him, and he will save us: this is the Lord; we have waited for him, we will be glad, and rejoice in his salvation." (Is. xxv. 10.) Were he to come to-day in his chariot of clouds, should we be able to say, "We have waited for him?" Would he come to interrupt our pleasures, or to crown our hopes? Would he come to make us weep, and gnash our teeth, or to wipe all tears from our faces forever?

Evening Scripture portion. Is. XXV. ***Waiting for the Lord.***

MATT. XXV. 1–13.—*The parable of the ten virgins.*

IN this parable the *open enemies* of Christ are not mentioned. There are only *two* classes described—true believers and false professors.

It seems that the difference between the wise and foolish virgins was not discovered till the bridegroom's return was announced. Had the wise virgins been aware of the unprepared state of their companions, they would *sooner* have recommended them to supply themselves with oil. There are many false professors who are not detected by true Christians. What do they gain by the deception? They gain a *name* to live; but they *lose more* than they *gain;* for they *lose* those moving exhortations which would be addressed to them, if their real state were known, and which might prove their salvation. They are suffered to remain *undisturbed*, because they are *undetected*. They learn to flatter themselves in their own eyes, and to believe that they are secure. But when the bridegroom returns, then their sad condition will be discovered.

What a succession of disappointments will they experience at last! It was a disappointment to the foolish virgins when they found that their lamps were gone out. It will be a bitter disappointment to many when they find that a *form* of religion will avail them nothing; and that they have no *grace* in their hearts. The oil seems to represent holy *feelings*, which the Holy Spirit alone bestows; love, faith, repentance, peace, hope, joy. It is possible to maintain a creditable reputation for piety without possessing any of the fruits of the Holy Spirit; but it is written, "Without holiness no man shall see the Lord."

The first disappointment the foolish virgins met with was finding their lamps were gone out. The second was hearing their companions refuse to share any of their oil. Our Christian friends will not be able to help us in the day of the Lord! They will not be able to impart to us the grace which is in their own hearts. When the foolish virgins returned from buying oil, how great must have been their disappointment to find the door shut! Yet they still entertained hope, and entreated to be admitted. The bridegroom's reply was the *last*, and the *greatest* of all the disappointments they had sustained. Those terrible words, "I know you not," cut off every hope, and consigned to eternal despair.

And what does this parable teach? To watch: that is, to *prepare* for the sudden return of our Lord. He will come with the rapidity of *lightning*, and those whom he finds unprepared, must continue forever unfit to abide in his presence. He gives notice to the world of the *suddenness* of his *second coming* by the *suddenness* with which he often causes the arrows of *death* to overtake sinners. Some are cut off so *suddenly* that they do not even know that they are dying. They fall down in a fit, are stunned by a blow, or dashed to pieces by a fall, before they can say, or even *think*, "Is this death?" Others have a short warning of their *latter end;* they are filled with dismay; they know not what to do; they send here and there for some minister to pray with them, but before he can arrive they expire. Few, when they are first taken ill, *know* that their sickness is unto death; and their last hour often comes upon them with unexpected speed.

It is the height of folly to remain satisfied with having a *form* of religion; for, at *any* moment, we may hear the cry, "The bridegroom cometh." Then the unconverted will suddenly discover that they are not prepared; but the discovery will be of no use *then*. How important it is to ascertain *now* whether we are born again of the Spirit, sprinkled with the blood of Jesus Christ, and meet for the inheritance of the saints in light!

Evening Scripture portion. Daniel V. *Belshazzar's feast.*

MATT. XXV. 14–30.—*The parable of the talents.*

THERE is one circumstance that renders this parable very remarkable; it is the *last* recorded as related by our Lord. The *first* recorded was the parable of the men who built houses, the one on the rock, and the other on the sand. There is a great resemblance between the case of the man who built his house on the sand, and the case of the servant who hid his talent in the earth. Both of them were men who *heard* their Lord's sayings, but who *did* them not. Would our Lord have selected these instances for his *first* and *last* parables, if the character described had not been common, and the error fatal? We ought therefore to give very earnest heed to the parable that has just been read, and to inquire whether the warning it contains applies to ourselves.

Our Lord had related a parable very much like it a few days before, when on his way to Jerusalem. But on *that* occasion he was surrounded by Pharisees as well as by his own disciples: on *this* occasion he had no other audience than those disciples. He always adapted his instructions to his hearers. When he spoke to the Pharisees, he introduced into the parable a description of open enemies, who said, "We will not have this man to reign over us." But when he addressed his disciples only, he omitted all mention of those enemies.

We cannot be at a loss to discover what is meant by the *talents* intrusted to the servants. The Lord himself explained his own meaning immediately after he had related the parable; for he then described himself as seated on the throne of his glory, and inquiring whether those who stood round him had fed his hungry saints, and visited his desolate prisoners. The talents represent opportunities of doing good. The affliction sent to one is the opportunity granted to another.

There is one point that must never be overlooked in considering this parable. For what PURPOSE was it related? Was it intended to show a sinner how he might obtain pardon? No. There are *other* parables which show *that*. Those of the prodigal son, of the two debtors, and of the good shepherd, all show that it is through God's free grace, and Christ's precious blood, that pardon is bestowed. *This* parable is intended to teach, *not* how a sinner may obtain pardon, but how a pardoned sinner may serve God.

To whom much is *forgiven*, the same *loveth* much. The same also *does* much. How easy, how pleasant it is to serve those we love! How we conjecture their wants and anticipate their wishes! How ready we are to run a risk, or to make a sacrifice to please them! How slow we are to say that we *cannot* do what they desire! Difficulties may stand in the way; but they are generally overcome by a loving heart. If true believers loved their Saviour more, how much more good would they do in the world! St. Paul declares, "The love of Christ constraineth us." "*Constraineth*" us to do what? Not to live to ourselves, but unto Him who died for us, and rose again. (2 Cor. v. 14, 15.)

We all want more of this spirit. The hypocrite has *none* of it. He lives to himself alone. But has the true believer *enough* of it? O, no; even the servant who had gained five talents will feel he has done too little for so gracious a master, when he hears the words, "Well done, good and faithful servant, enter thou into the joy of thy Lord." He will see such a disproportion between his *service* and his *reward*, that he will be *ashamed* of his past negligence, and *amazed* at his Lord's munificence.

Evening Scripture portion. 2 Tim. I. ***The kindness of Onesiphorus.***

MATT. XXV. 31 to end.—*Christ describes the last judgment.*

IF we had been asked what future scenes we desired most to see unveiled before our eyes, should we not have replied, "The scenes of the *last* day?" The splendor of the occasion will be exceedingly great; yet it is not the *splendor* that will render the day important, but the *sentences* then pronounced. Through the ages of eternity that day cannot be forgotten. The lost spirits will date from that day their final separation from God, the source of all happiness. The glorified saints will date from that day their entrance into the full enjoyment of the light of his countenance. Do we *dread* to hear that word "Depart?" Do we *long* for that word "Come?" Let us attend to the account given in this wonderful passage, of the conduct which marks the righteous and the wicked while upon earth.

Those who first listened to this description of the judgment-day were the disciples of Jesus. They all *professed* to love him. But did they all *really* love him? There was a hypocrite among the twelve. It is written of him, "*Not* that he cared for the *poor*." And are there not some now who *say*, "Lord, Lord," but who do not really love Jesus? If they loved him, they would love his poor brethren suffering upon earth. They would take more pleasure in relieving them, than in pampering their appetites, adorning their persons, amassing large fortunes, and giving sumptuous entertainments. Those who really love Christ are kind to the hungry, to the stranger, and to the prisoner, for *his sake*.

There are some who do acts of kindness, but *not* for his sake. Are *their* actions pleasing to the Lord? Can he who searches the heart, be pleased with acts of charity done from a desire to obtain human praise? Such acts shall obtain no other reward than—*human praise.*

Can he be pleased with deeds done from feelings of kindness, but without one thought concerning himself? Such motives meet with a reward on *earth*, but none in *heaven.*

Can he be pleased with works performed with a view of gaining heaven by our own merits? Assuredly not. For he has declared that we are not saved by works of righteousness which we have done, but by the mercy of God in Jesus Christ. (Titus iii.) What should we think of a man who owed ten thousand guineas, and who, though his creditors generously offered to give him his *whole* debt, refused to accept the obligation, promising now and then to present a farthing as payment? Yet this is the manner in which those act who are seeking to gain admission into heaven by their good deeds.

What, then, are the motives which please the Lord? Motives of gratitude and love to him. None but pardoned sinners can love Jesus; and they love him because he *first* loved them. The very words that he will address to them at the last day show that he loved them first, for he will say, "Come, ye blessed of my Father, inherit the kingdom *prepared* for you before the foundation of the world." God loved his children even before the world was made; even *then* he provided for their everlasting happiness. But did he prepare hell for the wicked? It was for *devils*, not for *men*, that hell was prepared. These are the words of the judge, "Depart, ye cursed, into everlasting fire, prepared for the devil and his angels." It is *their own sin*, not *God's purpose*, that plunges men into everlasting wo. Jesus has suffered the pains of hell, that we may taste the joys of heaven. He has *not* said to us, "You must be mocked and spit upon; you must be scourged, and crowned with thorns; you must be crucified in order to get to heaven." No; these insults and these pangs he has suffered for us. But he has asked us to show our love to him by relieving his poor brethren. It is a small request. Can we refuse it? When we see the destitute stranger, shall we turn away? When we hear of a suffering saint, or of a poor prisoner, shall we forget to visit him? If we do, how ashamed shall we be when we see Christ coming in his glory!

Evening Scripture portion. 1 John III. ***Love to the brethren.***

LUKE XXII. 1–6.—*Judas offers to betray Christ.*

WE have lately contemplated our Saviour sitting peacefully on Mount Olivet, surrounded by his disciples. What a different scene we now behold! It is an assembly of wicked men in Jerusalem. The high priest himself is the chief among them, and his palace is their place of meeting. It is probable that they held their consultation in the *night*, because in the *day* the high priest resided in his own chamber near the temple.

The night was a suitable season for the ripening of the designs of darkness. The murder of the Son of God was the purposed crime, but great difficulties lay in the way of its commission. The priests and scribes feared to apprehend Jesus in the *day*, because they expected to meet with opposition from the people; and they knew not where to find him in the *night*, for then he hid himself near Mount Olivet. But as God helps his children to overcome their difficulties, so Satan helps *his* to overcome *theirs*.

The entrance of Judas must have astonished the assembly! Had he come to plead for his Master? Had he come to remonstrate with his enemies? Surely the expression of his countenance must have indicated the dark purpose of his heart. He came to make the basest proposal that ever passed human lips; he came to offer to betray the best of masters. We may well believe that *man* could not ALONE have resolved to commit such wickedness; for though man by his fall has lost all love to his unseen Creator, he is still disposed to love those fellow-creatures who show him particular kindness. But that evil spirit who once rebelled against the God whose beauty he beheld, and whose favor he enjoyed, had filled the heart of Judas. Can Satan, then, enter the heart of man? What an awful truth! Is there any calamity we ought to dread so much as the entrance of this wicked spirit into our hearts? If he come and dwell *in us now*, there is reason to fear lest we should go and dwell *with him hereafter*.

And how did the priests receive the base proposal of the false apostle? Were they filled with horror? Did they tremble at the traitor's words? It is written, "They were glad." Hell also was glad. How awful it is for *men* to rejoice with *devils*, and yet those who are glad at wickedness may feel assured that their joy is shared by the spirits beneath.

And what reward did Judas hope to obtain for his treachery? Thirty pieces of silver; a sum equal to three pounds fifteen shillings of our money. It was the price of a *slave*. It was the sum that the Jewish law sentenced those to pay who killed a slave by accident. How small are the bribes for which men will commit sin! When Satan attempted to entice the Son of God, he offered him all the kingdoms of the world. But he does not think it necessary to offer so great a bribe to sinful man. He finds that he can seduce him to commit wickedness by insignificant rewards. One morsel of meat was sufficient to induce Esau to sell his birthright. But does Satan really *give* even the reward he *promises?* No; it is seldom that sinners enjoy what they expected. Judas indeed *obtained* the thirty pieces of silver, but did he *enjoy* them?

It will rack the spirits of sinners in hell to calculate their losses and their gains. Even in *this* world the gains of sin are very small: even in *this* world the losses of sin are very great; but in the *next* world there is *no* gain left to the sinner; the laughter is all past, the sorrow alone remains. The shadow of his former pleasures will soon fade before his weeping eyes; the cheat of Satan will stare him in the face; the father of lies will be there to upbraid him with his folly, and the sight of heaven shining afar off will add to the tortures of his remorse. But though convinced of his error, the prodigal will not be able to arise and return to his God, and say, "I have sinned against heaven, and in thy sight." No, the chains of darkness will fix him forever in his dismal prison, and the great gulf will separate him from all that is holy, and glorious, and blessed.

Evening Scripture portion. Acts V. 1–16. *Ananias and Sapphira.*

LUKE XXII. 7–13.—*Peter and John prepare the Passover.*

THE day before his death seems to have been by the Saviour passed in holy retirement near Mount Olivet. How different were the scenes of the next day! scenes of tumult and uproar, scenes of barbarity and blood! A sweet season of refreshment was enjoyed by the Lord and his disciples before those horrors were perpetrated. How often God grants such a season to his children before he exposes them to the wintry storm and tempest!

The passover was always eaten in Jerusalem. It was unlawful to kill the lamb in any other place than in the temple, or to eat it anywhere but in the holy city. The Jews at this day having no temple, cannot partake of the paschal lamb. When they celebrate the passover, they cause the *shoulder bone* of a lamb to be placed on the table instead of the animal itself. Many thousands flocked to Jerusalem in olden times to keep the feast. The citizens were kind to their brethren on those occasions, opened their doors, and received freely all who pleased to come; so that no man could say to his friend, "I have not found a fire to roast the lamb withal, nor a bed to rest in."

With what holy awe the two apostles must have beheld the man carrying a pitcher, of whom their Master had spoken! Here was a fresh display of his omniscience. Though Jesus has not *foretold* the circumstances of our *lives*, we are persuaded that he knows them *all*, both small and great. If he did not appoint the *small* incidents of our lives, he could not rule the *great events*, because small incidents give rise to great events. Jesus knew the exact moment when the man bearing a pitcher would be walking near the entrance of Jerusalem; and he knows what we shall be doing at this moment to-morrow, and ten years hence. He knows whom we shall meet to-day, if we go out, and who will come to see us, if we stay at home. He not only *knows* these circumstances, but he will, *if we love him*, so order them that they shall work together for our good; "for all things work together for good to them that love God." (Rom. viii. 28.)

How blessed are we if we have committed ourselves, and all we possess, into his hands! Then we need feel no anxiety about the future, for the Lord will provide. At the very *moment* we want a friend, he will raise one up. There is no request too *small* for him to regard, nor too *great* for him to grant. The people of God, especially his aged servants, can relate wonderful histories of his power and truth. They can tell how in their perplexity they were directed, and in their extremity relieved. Had their friends been *miraculously* informed of the particulars of their cases, they could not have afforded them more suitable or opportune help. At the exact time they needed the supply, the exact sum they required has been sent, and often by the hand of one who knew nothing of their distresses. But the God, who answered the prayer of Abraham's servant, who led Rebekah to the well, and inclined her to utter the very words that servant had asked that she might say, still listens to his people's prayers, and still condescends to give them the request of their lips. "O taste and see that the Lord is good; blessed is the man that trusteth in him. O fear the Lord, ye his saints, for there is no want to them that fear him." (Ps. xxxiv. 8, 9.)

Evening Scripture portion.
Gen. XXIV. 1–28. *The prayer of Abraham's servant.*

LUKE XXII. 14–18.—*Christ gives the cup before supper.*

WE are too apt to forget that each action of our life will at some period be performed for the *last* time. It often appears as if we shall continue for *ever* to tread certain rounds of duties or enjoyments; but this appearance is false. As there was a *first* time of going to the house of God, so there will be a *last.* Perhaps we can remember the *first* time: but we cannot foresee the *last.* It is most probable that when the last time arrives, we shall not be aware of it. As there was a time when our infant lips *first* pronounced the name of Jesus, so there will be a time when our lips will utter it for the *last* time on *earth.* How many happy souls have departed this life, saying, "Come, Lord *Jesus,* come quickly!"

Some of us, perhaps, can look back upon the time when we *first* approached the table of the Lord to eat the bread and drink the wine. If we came with a formal spirit,—because *others* came,—because we thought it *right* to come,—because our *friends* expected us to come, there is no sweetness in the remembrance of that time. But if we came as contrite sinners to a bleeding Saviour, then we desire never to forget the blessed season. There will be a *last* time for partaking of the holy communion; it may be in the sanctuary; it may be in the dying chamber. Whenever it arrives may it find us in the same loving spirit in which our blessed Lord sat down with his twelve apostles to partake of his *last* passover!

Though he knew that one of these apostles would soon deny him, and that all would forsake him, yet his heart lingered over them with inexpressible tenderness. What fervent affection is implied in the words, "With desire have I desired to eat *this* passover *with you* before I *suffer!*" Though death was to follow, yet this feast of love was an object of desire to the Saviour.

A cup of red wine was usually drunk before the passover was eaten. This cup Jesus took, and said to his disciples, "Take this, and divide it among yourselves." By desiring them to drink out of the *same* cup, he instructed them to love one another, even as he had

loved them. There was *another* cup which he gave *after* supper, saying, "This is my blood." The *first* cup was given *before* supper.

When the Lord partook of this passover, his heart was bowed down with sorrow. There is an hour approaching when He will rejoice *with his* people. In the day of his trouble he spoke of that hour, for he said, "I will not drink of the fruit of the vine *until* the kingdom of God shall come." If he desired so earnestly to partake of the passover before he suffered, how much more must he desire to eat and drink with his people in the kingdom of God! No *last* time will ever come to that feast, no parting will then be near, no sin will then be feared, no tear will then be shed. Are we *meet* for the inheritance of the saints in light? *All* who approach the table of the Lord *now*, will not surround it hereafter.

The *heart* must be prepared for heavenly joys; it must be broken by a sense of sin; it must be bound up by a living faith. Christ alone can prepare us to sit with him at his table. He is now preparing the *feast*, and preparing the *guests:* and at the appointed time he will come and say, "Eat, O *friends;* drink, yea, drink abundantly, O beloved." (Solomon's Song v. 1.)

Evening Scripture portion. Ex. XII. 1–30. ***The Passover.***

JOHN XIII. 1–17.—*Christ washes his disciples' feet.*

THE apostle Paul might well say, "I beseech you by the meekness and gentleness of Christ." (2 Cor. x. 1.) Jesus knew that the feet he washed would flee from him that very night, and leave him alone in his troubles; but offences could not quench his love.

When afterwards Peter had denied his Lord, it must have been a comfort to him, in the midst of his bitter tears, to remember what the Lord had said to him as he washed his feet. He had said that Peter was already washed from his sins, and that he needed only to have his feet washed. This is the state of every true believer. He has been washed in the Saviour's blood, but still he needs continually to wash his feet; for as he walks in this world he defiles them by sin. Every day he has occasion to say, "Forgive me my trespasses." Whatever sins we have committed, we should go instantly to Jesus to be washed. We need not fear to go to this condescending, this loving Master. "If any man sin, we have an advocate with the Father, even Jesus Christ the righteous." He who now liveth to make intercession, is the same tender Saviour who once took a towel and girded himself, who "poured water into a basin, and began to wash the disciples' feet, and to wipe them with the towel wherewith he was girded."

But by this action Jesus intended not only to teach his disciples what *he* had done for *them*, but also what *they* ought to do for *each other*. When he was sat down again, he plainly said, "Ye ought to wash one another's feet."

How apt we are to think that it is degrading to perform lowly offices! yet nothing can degrade us but sin. Angels in heaven are not too proud to serve the saints on earth. "Are they not all *ministering spirits*, sent forth to minister to them who shall be heirs of salvation?" (Heb. i.)

A holy woman, belonging to a wealthy family, often repeated the following lines, because they expressed the fondest desires of her heart:

"O that the Lord would count me meet
To wash his dear disciples' feet,
To share the grace to angels given,
And serve the royal heirs of heaven."

Her life proved that her words were sincere. The destitute orphan and the helpless cripple found a home beneath her roof.

But how different is any condescension that *man* can show, from the condescension the Son of God displayed! Creatures are only raised a very small degree above their fellows; and even that small distinction will exist for a very little while. At the present moment, in the sight of God, all men are equal. How unbecoming it is in any of us to lift up our hearts above our fellow-creatures! We may indeed remain in the station in which God has placed us; but we must remember that he is no respecter of persons; the slave and the beggar are as precious in his sight as the king upon his throne. If we have the mind of Christ, we shall esteem it an honor to be permitted to minister to the wants of a poor saint; and we shall often think in our hearts, "This destitute creature, who now inhabits a neglected hovel, may perhaps shine more brightly than myself in the kingdom of glory."

Evening Scripture portion. Phil. II. ***The condescension of Christ.***

JOHN XIII. 18–22.—*Christ foretells that one of the twelve shall betray him.*

THE Lord Jesus had just given his disciples a proof of his *love* by washing their feet. Now he gave them a proof of his *omniscience*. He showed them that he knew *all* things, by foretelling who should betray him.

Had he intended to convince them at *that moment* of his wisdom, he would have revealed the *past* secrets of their lives, as he once had done to the woman of Samaria. He told her so much of her past life, that she said to her townsmen, "Come, see a man which told me all things that ever I did." But on *this occasion* he sought rather to strengthen the disciples' faith in a trying hour that was approaching. He knew that the betrayal of Judas would tend to shake their faith. He knew that they might be tempted to think: "If our Master were the Son of God, he would have known that Judas sought to betray him, and he would have hid himself in some secret retreat." *Therefore* he told them beforehand; as he said, "Now I tell you *before* it come, that *when* it is come to pass, ye may believe that I am he."

For the same reason he has foretold many events that are now coming to pass. He has declared, "Many shall be offended, and shall betray one another, and shall hate one another." Whenever hypocrites are detected, instead of being staggered by the discovery, we ought to be confirmed in the faith, and to think, "Did not Jesus say that there should be many who would call him Lord, but who would work iniquity?"

Can we conceive what our feelings would be, if we could foresee what would befall those around us? How would our hearts be pained by the thought, "This dear brother will languish long under a tormenting disease. This beloved sister will lose the children that are now smiling on her knees." But how much more should we be grieved, if we could foresee that some who *seem* to be faithful followers of Jesus would finally betray him, and perish forever. What, then, must have been the feelings of the compassionate Saviour, when he looked around and beheld the face of one who would soon plunge into the depth of crime, and sink into the abyss of misery! "He was troubled in spirit, and testified, saying, Verily, verily, I say unto you, that one of you shall betray me."

He still grieves over the sorrows that he foresees. When he looks down upon us, he sees the way that we shall take. Among the guests at the sacramental table he can distinguish those who will sell their birthright, from those who will inherit his kingdom.

Those who do not love their Master, will not always follow him. Judas found it easy to walk with Jesus when an admiring throng tracked his steps; but when circumstances were altered he changed his plan, and found it more convenient to betray him. There are seasons when the way of godliness appears even to the worldly-minded a pleasant and a glorious path; but these seasons do not last. A time arrives, sooner or later, when the path becomes steep and rugged; then the unconverted man turns aside into some by-way. He goes after the world he had forsaken, and seeks for a share in its smiles. At first, perhaps, he does not leave the assemblies of the saints. Like Judas, he may be found by turns in the councils of the ungodly, and in the society of the believers. Is there any one among us who is secretly siding with Christ's enemies, while he appears to be his friend? With what compassion Jesus regards such a miserable creature! He foresees the sorrows that his sins will bring upon him. He knows what remorse will one day tear him; what despair will take hold of him!

Evening Scripture portion. 2 Tim. III. ***Hypocrites.***

LUKE XXII. 21–30.—*The apostles dispute concerning which shall be greatest.*

WE are not surprised that the apostles should be agitated by the thought that one of them should betray their beloved Master. But we *are* surprised that they should at the same time dispute who should be the greatest. Such a contest would have been sinful at *any moment*, but it was especially unseemly on *this* occasion. Their Master was going to suffer the deepest shame, and the acutest torture; his spirit was troubled, and his soul exceeding sorrowful. All his followers should have been engrossed by the desire to console him. Instead of disputing who should be greatest, they should have exhorted each other to cleave closely to their Lord in the trying hour.

How easy it is for us to perceive how *they* ought to have behaved! But how difficult it is for us to act as *we* ought to do! A desire to be great, and to be *greater* than others, is deeply rooted in our sinful nature. Even after we have turned to God, we are troubled by this evil propensity. We often betray it in our conversation, when we are not aware of the spirit that actuates us. We delight to dwell upon the esteem that others feel for us, to describe the exertions we have made, the plans we have suggested, and the influence we have obtained. Even when we keep *silence* on these subjects, because we think it unbecoming to praise ourselves, we often indulge *feelings* of self-complacency, and are elated when others notice and commend us. It would not be thus with us, if we were engrossed with the glory of Christ. Then we should desire only to speak of his wondrous works, and to talk of his power, and of the glory of *his* kingdom. If we spoke of ourselves, it would be with a view of showing his forbearance and faithfulness.

It must have grieved the Lord to hear his disciples striving for the first place in his kingdom. But he would not utter a severe rebuke when partaking with them of his last supper. He had endeavored to teach them humility by washing their feet, and he continued by the softest persuasions to impress the lesson on their hearts. But he knew that *circumstances* would soon teach them how unworthy they were even of the *lowest* place in his kingdom. *That night* they would all *forsake* him. When they saw him again after his resurrection, they disputed no more who should be greatest; for each felt that he had forfeited all claim even to the *lowest* place. Thus will Jesus deal with us, if we are cherishing pride in our hearts. It is wonderful to observe how he humbles his people in their own eyes. Sometimes he allows them to stumble for a moment, that they may not fall into everlasting perdition. He has reserved for them the highest honors—places at his table, and thrones in his kingdom, but he must prepare them for their exaltation by deep humiliation. He knows when they are in danger of *becoming* proud, and sometimes in his mercy he sends an affliction to keep them humble.

He dealt in this manner with the apostle Paul. These are the apostle's own words: "Lest I should be exalted beyond measure through the abundance of the revelations, there was given to me a thorn in the flesh, the messenger of Satan to buffet me, lest I should be exalted beyond measure." (1 Cor. xii. 7.)

Evening Scripture portion. 2 Cor. IV. *The sinfulness of pride.*

MATT. XXVI. 21–25.—*The apostles inquire who shall betray their Master.*

WHAT a sorrowful moment it was to the affectionate disciples when the Lord said, "One of you shall betray me." He *himself* was troubled in spirit, and they were exceeding sorrowful. Each anxiously inquired, "Is it I?" It was right in them to ask this question, rather than to say, "Is it Peter?" "Is it John?" "Is it James?" Not one was so ungenerous as to fix his suspicion upon his fellow. This is the spirit we ought to cultivate. Are we not more apt to suspect our *fellows* than to distrust *ourselves?* No doubt each of the apostles felt in his heart that *he* could not betray his Master, but then each believed that the Lord knew his heart better than he knew it himself: "God is greater than our hearts, and knoweth all things." (1 John iii. 21.) Did *Judas* believe that God knew all things when he asked, "Is it I?" Surely he must have hoped that he had deceived his *Master* as well as his *fellow-disciples*. But how must he have felt when he heard the answer, "Thou hast said!" Probably it was spoken in a low voice, so that none but Judas heard the words.

But even when detected, he was not turned aside from his base purpose; for Satan had entered into him. No threatenings could terrify him; not even the words, "It would be better for that man if he had never been born." More terrible words cannot be imagined. They prove that the lost spirits can *never* be released from hell, for if at *any* period (however remote) they were to enter heaven, it would be good for them *in the end* that they had been born. Judas must have disbelieved this truth. Unbelief prepares the heart for committing the most appalling crimes. Satan finds no easier method of leading men captive than by filling their minds with doubts concerning God's word. He began his intercourse with our race by saying, "Thou shalt not surely die."

But if Judas could not be awed by *fear*, could he be melted by *love?* No, he could behold his Lord seated at his last supper, and hear all his moving words, and still brood over his dark design. He could hear him utter this touching sentence, "With desire I have desired to eat this passover with you before I suffer;"—he could see him, girded with a towel, stooping to wash his disciples' feet;—he could suffer him to wash his own feet,—and yet still determine to betray him into the hands of his enemies. Truly may God say of the human heart, that it is desperately wicked. The old serpent has made it his habitation, and he exerts his subtlety in keeping it in his possession. But the grace of God can change the unfeeling, deceitful heart of man. It was grace that made the other disciples so different from Judas. Did not the Lord declare this, when he said, "I speak not of you *all;* I know whom I have *chosen?*" (John xiii. 18.)

When we consider a wicked character, when we follow its windings, and try to fathom its depths, let us remember that we are studying our own disease. If we were attacked with any dreadful malady for which no cure was known, what should we feel in viewing the body of one who had died of that malady? We should think, "My symptoms will increase, until I am reduced to the same miserable state." Sin is a malady that naturally grows worse and worse, and ends in eternal destruction. None can stop its course, but Jesus alone. Had it not been for him, it might have been said of each of us, "It would be good for *this man* if he had never been born; it would be good for this *woman*, for this *child*." May God of his infinite mercy grant, that the reverse may be said of each of us! Whatever afflictions we may pass through, if we keep faithful to Jesus we shall see in the end that it was good for us that we were born. The blessed Saviour *died*, that we might have *cause* to rejoice forever in having been called into being.

Evening Scripture portion.
Jer. XVII. ***The depravity of the human heart.***

JOHN XIII. 23–30.—*Christ gives the sop to Judas.*

How many incidents recorded by John alone are so interesting that we could not bear the idea of being ignorant of them! It is a touching circumstance that one of the disciples leaned his head upon the bosom of Jesus at the last supper. That disciple's name is not mentioned in this place; but we know, from other passages, that it was

John. It was the custom in the East to recline upon couches at meal-times. This custom was not always observed at common meals, but it was considered indispensable at the passover. It is true, the first passover was eaten standing, but in later times the Jews preferred the posture of lying, because they thought it was a better emblem of their freedom from toil and slavery.

Could we have conjectured (had we not heard the fact) that a sinful man should be permitted to lean his head upon the bosom of our Lord? Such condescension became him who took little children in his arms, and who suffered a weeping woman to kiss his feet. Ought we to be afraid of coming to such a Saviour? Can we believe he would roughly reject us? Or rather can we conceive how graciously he would receive us, how faithfully he would cleave to us? There is no friend who would so tenderly support our aching heads when oppressed by care and sorrow, or when damp with the dews of death.

We naturally suppose that all the apostles must have considered it a high privilege to sit next the Lord. It seems probable that Judas sat on one side of him, as it was to him he gave the sop when he had dipped it. Peter seems to have occupied a more distant place, as he beckoned, instead of whispering to John, when he desired him to ask a question.

It was not sufficient for Peter to know that it was not *he* who should betray the Lord; he wanted to discover who it was. When John whispered, "Who is it?" the Lord did not check him for curiosity, but gave him a sign by which he discovered the traitor. It is lawful for Christians to desire to detect hypocrites. St. Paul exhorts them to look "diligently lest any root of bitterness springing up trouble them, and thereby many be defiled." (Heb. xii. 15.)

The token by which the traitor was distinguished was an act of friendship—dipping his morsel in the same dish with the Lord. On the passover-table a dish was placed composed of the juice of figs and other fruits, mixed with vinegar; and into this mixture all the guests dipped their morsels of the unleavened cake before returning thanks. For the *last* time the Lord dipped his morsel, wrapped in bitter herbs, in such a dish: for the *last* time Judas did so also. Both the traitor and his Master were eating their *last* supper on earth. Often had they supped together; but never to all eternity would they sit again at the same table, or share the same bread. The other apostles would again eat and drink with their Lord in another manner and in another state; but Judas would hunger forever amidst the famished spirits in hell.

How eager the traitor must have felt to escape from the presence of his injured Master! Jesus himself furnished him with an excuse, by saying, "*That* thou doest, do quickly." The tone was so gentle in which those words were uttered, that none conjectured they referred to a deed of murder. Judas obeyed, and did his awful work *quickly:* for Satan hurried him on to perpetrate the crime. The wicked spirit who *suggested* the scheme sustained him while he executed it: "After the sop Satan entered into him." Man's courage would often fail before he had performed his dark designs, if it were not for Satan's help. He strengthens the thief to encounter the darkness, and he nerves the arm of the murderer to raise the bloody knife; but when they have done his will, *then* he encourages them no more; *then* he abandons them to remorse and despair.

Evening Scripture portion. Job XXIV. *Deeds of darkness.*

JOHN XIII. 31–35.—*Christ gives a new commandment.*

WHEN the traitor had left the room, the full tide of the Saviour's love began to flow out upon his disciples. Many sorrowful words had been uttered at this last supper; but in the midst of *grief* gleams of *joy* burst forth. There was holy triumph, nay, even rapture, in the words, "Now is the Son of man glorified; and God is glorified in him." Why did the Lord rejoice at the speedy approach of his bitter sufferings? Because *in* those sufferings his own glory and his Father's glory were manifested.

Have *we* seen the glory of the cross? Does it appear to us a glorious way of reconciling guilty rebels to their insulted sovereign? Does it not show how God hates sin, yet loves the sinner? He hates *sin* so much that he would not pardon without an atonement; he loves *sinners* so much that he consented to give up his only Son to be that atonement. St. Paul did not *behold* the Saviour expiring on his cross; but like us, he *heard* the touching history: and what was its effect upon his heart? The cross put out all other glory. He no longer saw any glory in exalted titles and shining thrones, in human learning, or eloquence, or even in a reputation for righteousness: all these appeared to him as dross. The cross alone seemed glorious, and he testified, saying, "God forbid that I should glory save in the cross of our Lord Jesus Christ, by whom the world is crucified unto me, and I unto the world." (Gal. vi. 14.)

But in the hour when Jesus rejoiced, he looked not only at the glory connected with his *sufferings*, but also at the glory of his *exaltation*. "If God shall be glorified in him, God shall also glorify in himself, and shall *straightway* glorify him." *Very soon* God would raise him from the dead, and exalt him to his own right hand. He longed for that glorious hour; he showed his anxiety, when he said to Judas, "That thou doest, do *quickly*." If Paul in later days had a desire to depart and to be with Christ, how much more must God's own Son have desired to depart to be with his *Father!* He remembered the glory he had with the Father before the world was; this glory he knew he should soon possess again at his Father's right hand. A few *weeks* afterwards the dying Stephen looked up, and saw him standing there. A few *months* afterwards the astonished Paul beheld his brightness above the brightness of the sun. A few *years* afterwards, and the enraptured John heard him say, "I am he that liveth and was dead, and behold I am alive for evermore." Well might the prospect of such glory cheer the Saviour's heart, as he sat at his last supper.

But did he forget his sorrowing disciples? O no, he turned to them with tender love, saying, "Little children, a little while am I with you." While he was with them, they had basked in his love; when he was gone how desolate would they feel! But if they should love each other as *he* loved them, *then* they would not be desolate. Therefore he said unto them, "Love one another, as I have loved you." Jesus desires that his people should be happy. This is *one* reason why he charges them to love each other. But he has *another* reason. It is his *own* glory. "By this shall all men *know* that ye are *my* disciples, if ye have love one to another." Love is the badge of Christ's disciples. Is it then so *rare* for men to love each other, that true believers can be known by this mark? Yes, it is even so. There is much that *looks* like love to be found in the world. There is natural affection,—there is particular friendship,—there is patriotism,—there is party-spirit,—but there is no love, such as Christ bare towards his disciples. There is no love of this *kind* to be found on earth but in the heart of a Christian. No human creature, indeed, can love as Jesus does: but his love, though very inferior in *degree*, may be the same in *kind*. Paul, the prisoner of the Lord, was filled with this love when he said, "Therefore I endure all things for the *elect's* sake, that they also may obtain the salvation which is in Christ Jesus with eternal glory." (2 Tim. ii. 10.) Such love has led missionaries to leave comfortable homes to dwell among snows that never melt, or deserts that are always parched, to brave the hungry lion's roar, and to encounter the savage warrior's shriek. Such love glows in the heart of many who stand in less conspicuous places. They may be found in crowded alleys instructing ragged children, or in miserable hovels, comforting dying saints. "May the Lord make *us* to increase in love toward one another, and toward *all men*." (1 Thess. iii. 12.)

Evening Scripture portion. 1 Cor. XIII. ***Charity or love.***

JOHN XIII. 36 to end.—*Christ foretells Peter's denial.*

IT must have grieved *all* the disciples to hear their Lord say, "Whither I go, ye cannot come." But Peter, as usual, was the *first* to express his sorrow. This he did by asking the question, "Whither goest thou?" These words were evidently uttered with deep anxiety. Jesus repeated the assurance he had before made, "Whither I go, thou canst not follow me *now*;" but he added a most comforting declaration, "Thou shalt follow me *afterwards*." These words must have proved a healing balm to Peter's troubled heart, when a few hours afterwards he was weeping bitterly for his base denial of his Lord. Jesus well knew how much he would require cordials for his faith in that agonizing moment; and he gave him several such cordials, both in the upper room and in the garden of Gethsemane. Had Peter's faith failed after his sin, he would have been driven to despair like Judas, and he would have perished like him. But Jesus sustained his faith by his word and Spirit, and kept him "by his power unto salvation." (1 Peter i.)

Doubtless there are many who wish that they could obtain such a promise as Peter received, "Thou shalt follow me afterwards." But though it is the privilege of only a *few* of the saints to hear such an assurance from the lips of their Master, it is the privilege of *all* to have the inward witness of the Spirit, for it is written, "The Spirit beareth witness with our spirits that we are the children of God." Let all believers listen to his gentle voice in their souls. It is a voice not to be heard by the outward ear, but only by the inward ear of the soul or spirit, and it says, "Thou art mine." When the children of God hear that spiritual voice, they reply, "Father;" as it is written in the Romans, "We have not received the spirit of bondage again to fear, but the spirit of adoption, whereby we cry Abba, Father." No slave among the Jews was allowed to use the word "Abba," in speaking to his Master: but believers are not *slaves*, but *children*. Only let them beware of grieving by their sins that holy Spirit, who delights in filling their hearts with peace, and joy, and love.

Peter knew not *when* he should follow his Lord. He was impatient to go immediately, and inquired, "*Why* cannot I follow thee *now?*" Jesus knows how long it will be before each of us will follow him to glory, (if we shall follow him,) and he knows why one must follow him soon, and another a great while hence. He has appointed for each of us that length of pilgrimage that is best for us, and best for others. We are sometimes disposed to wish to alter his arrangements. When tried by lingering sickness, we are apt to cry "how long?" and when surrounded by those who look up to us for help and comfort, to cry, "O spare me before I go hence." But the Lord will judge for us, and call us to himself at the right moment. Moses and Elijah, and Jonah, and Job, all desired, in times of great trouble, to die; but the Lord prolonged their lives. Peter, in the fervor of his affection, desired the same; but his request also was denied. Had he, *at that time*, been called to lay down his life, he would have shrunk from the trial;—for far from having courage to shed his blood, he had not enough to bear a scornful look. The Lord would not bring upon him a temptation greater than he was able to bear, but only such a temptation as showed him what was in his heart, and then he made a way of escape, that he might be able to bear it.

At length Peter obtained a martyr's courage, and now he wears a martyr's crown. The time came when he fulfilled his own declaration, "I will lay down my life for thy sake;" and he was stretched on a cross like his beloved Master.

Jesus now hears his people's vows of fidelity. He will try them all and prove their sincerity. In what *way* he will try us, at what *time*, we cannot tell. When the trials come, may we be found faithful. Then we shall know the truth of the promise, "Blessed is the man who endureth temptation, for when (as *often*) he is tried he shall receive the crown of life which the Lord hath promised to them that love him." (James i. 12.)

Evening Scripture portion. Acts IV. *The courage of Peter and John.*

LUKE XXII. 31–35.—*Christ tells Peter he has prayed for him.*

WHAT a view this passage gives us of the malice of Satan. That wicked spirit desired to have *all* the apostles, for Jesus said, "Satan hath desired to have *you*," not Peter only, but the *others* also. No wonder that he desired to have those men who were to spread the Saviour's name throughout the world. He succeeded in obtaining *one* of them as his prey, even Judas; but his place was afterwards filled up by another apostle.*

Can we doubt that Satan still desires to tempt the servants of Christ? If *we* are his servants, he longs to destroy us. He goes about as a roaring lion seeking whom he may devour. (1 Peter v. 8.) These words are the words of one who had himself been rescued from the jaws of the lion. It was Christ who delivered him. He knows all the designs of the enemy. When he sees any of his sheep in danger, he does not flee, but he stays to deliver them. He watched with tender care over all the apostles during their season of temptation, but especially over Peter, who seems to have been the *most* exposed to the enemy. He had already *prayed* for him; now he *warns* him; soon he takes him to the garden with him, and there bids him pray for himself; and even when standing before his judges, does not forget him, but turns and looks at him.

Such is the care Jesus still takes of his people. Were he less watchful, no soul would ever reach the heavenly fold. If we do not fall into some fatal sin, it is because his eye is always upon us. No

* Matthias, Acts I.

little child is so dependent upon the watchfulness of its nurse, as *we* are upon that of Jesus.

Satan desired to sift the apostles as corn is sifted in a sieve, when it is thrown up in the air, and when the chaff is blown away. He hoped that Judas was not the only hypocrite among them; for Satan cannot search the heart. He suspected Job of being a hypocrite, but he was mistaken. He suspected Peter, but in this also he was mistaken. It seems Satan is allowed to try the saints, but these trials do them good, and make them brighter Christians afterwards. Peter loved the Lord *before* he denied him; but he loved him far better *afterwards*. "That kind upbraiding glance" could never be effaced from his memory; that affectionate message, ("Tell his disciples and *Peter*;") that early meeting with him *alone*, (for he was seen of Peter or Cephas *before* he was seen of the twelve,) (1 Cor. xv. 5,) were tokens of forgiving grace beyond all human thought.

How it binds the hearts of believers to their Lord, to remember the various instances in which their backslidings have been healed! Is there any one here who, like Peter, has given himself to the Lord, and who yet, like Peter, has been unfaithful? Do you not feel your heart glow with love when you think of the Lord's free forgiveness of your ungrateful wanderings? What does Jesus expect of his restored backsliders? He expects that they should strengthen their brethren. He said to Peter, "When thou art converted strengthen thy brethren." By the term "converted," he meant "turned back again" into the way of righteousness. David declared, after his grievous fall, "I will teach transgressors thy ways, and sinners shall be converted unto thee." It encourages a wanderer to return to hear another wanderer say, "The Lord has forgiven *me*." All the apostles must have felt afraid to meet their Lord again, after having forsaken him; but when they heard Peter say, "I did *worse* than you, I denied him; yet he has forgiven me; I know it by the look he has cast upon me," would they not all be strengthened by such words? We ought not to be ashamed to own our faults to our brethren; but we ought rather to take delight in magnifying the riches of Christ's forgiving love. If *we* have obtained mercy, why should not others also? What Jesus has done for *us* is a pattern of what he will do for all, who, like us, shall believe in him to life everlasting. (1 Tim. i. 16.)

Evening Scripture portion. Job II. ***Satan tempts Job the second time.***

LUKE XXII. 35–38.—*Christ prepares the apostles for approaching danger.*

THE Lord deals with his people in various manners. Sometimes he causes all things to go smoothly,—at other times he permits difficulties to arise. When Jacob left his father's roof, he was cheered on his way by a vision of angels, and he arrived safely at his uncle's abode; but when Joseph left his home, he was assaulted by his brethren and sold as a slave into Egypt. The Lord knows *when* to appoint trials, and when to bestow prosperity.

Solomon knew this when he said, "To every thing there is a *season*, and a *time* to every purpose under heaven"—that is, to every *purpose* of God. He then enumerates various times, "a time to kill and a time to heal, a time to weep and a time to laugh." (Eccl. iii.) There were such various times in the lives of the apostles. When their Master first sent them out to preach, he desired them to make no provision for the way. He said, "Provide neither gold, nor silver, nor brass in your purses, nor scrip (or bag) for your journey." (Matt. x. 9, 10.) They obeyed this command, and at the last supper they testified that they had wanted nothing during their journey. The disciples of Jesus can always testify that their Lord has kept his promises;—not one of them has ever failed, or ever will.

On this occasion the Saviour gave different directions to the apostles from those he had formerly given. He desired them to take, not only scrips and purses, but even *swords*. Why did he give this command? To prepare them for the great troubles that were coming upon them. He knew that now few would be willing to give them food, and that many would desire to take away their lives; because their Master was soon to be crucified as a criminal. Who would favor the followers of a crucified Master? He reminded them of these words of Isaiah liii., "He was numbered with the transgressors." One of the trials the Saviour endured was DISGRACE. He was put to death *as* a *wicked* man, *with* wicked men, and *in the manner* in which wicked men were put to death. The *disciples* of such a master ought to expect disgrace. They should not be surprised when they are insulted, reviled, and falsely accused.

But ought they to defend themselves with the *sword?* We know they ought not. When Peter took one of these two swords and cut off the ear of the high priest's servant, his Lord rebuked him, and said, "All they that take the sword shall perish with the sword." If Jesus had intended that his servants should fight, he would not have said that *two* swords were enough. The only sword that they should use is the sword that their Master wielded when attacked by the prince of darkness in the wilderness;—the sword of the Spirit, which is the word of God. (Eph. vi. 17.)

When temptations come upon us, let us use that sword. Satan cannot resist it. Had Peter used it in that terrible night when his Lord was condemned, he would not have denied him. We know not what great temptations may soon assail us. God often makes the first part of a believer's course very smooth, because he knows his weakness, and will not try him above his strength. But an *evil day* will come. How shall we stand in that day? Not by our own strength.

We must take unto us *now* the whole armor of God, the breast-plate of righteousness, the shield of faith, the helmet of salvation, and the sword of the Spirit. When clothed in this armor, we must watch and pray, and then we shall be able to resist all the wiles of the devil. (Eph. vi. 11.)

Evening Scripture portion.
2 Cor. VI. *The sufferings and conduct of faithful ministers.*

LUKE XXII. 19, 20.—*Christ ordains his holy supper.*

OF all the touching words that Jesus uttered at the last supper, the *most* touching were these: "This is my body; this is my blood." The disciples had been unwilling to believe that he would die; but could they doubt it any longer when they heard these words, and looked upon the broken bread and the poured out wine? He would not only *die*, but he would die a *cruel* death; his body would be broken like the bread; his blood would be poured out like the wine.

Was Judas present at this scene? It is not certain whether he was there or not. He had partaken of one cup—of the cup *before* supper—but we know not whether he partook of the cup *after* supper.

No doubt it was with bitter grief that the loving disciples ate that broken bread, and drank that cup of wine. With what different feelings they partook of the ordinance the *next* time! When, *after* their Lord's resurrection, they met together to break bread, how thankful they felt for his dying love! We know not *when* they *first* met for this purpose. It must have been an interesting communion! Each must have thought, "What would have become of me if that spotless body had not been lacerated and bruised upon the cross—if that precious blood had not flowed from the pierced hands, and feet, and side!" This is the feeling of every believer when he approaches the table of his Lord.

Ever since man sinned, he has been spared only for the sake of Jesus. When Abel brought a spotless lamb and offered it on the altar, he knew that he deserved to die instead of that lamb. The blood of that lamb was a faint shadow of the blood of the Lamb of God.

What did Jesus mean when he said, "This cup is the new testament in my blood which is shed for you?" By the word "testament," he meant covenant or promise. God made a covenant with Israel in the wilderness. The blood of bulls and goats was shed to confirm the *first* covenant. As it is written, "Moses took the blood and sprinkled it on the people, and said, Behold the blood of the covenant." (Ex. xxiv. 8.) From everlasting God made a covenant with his beloved Son concerning the salvation of man; but it was not fully revealed till after Christ had been crucified. His blood was shed to confirm this *new* covenant. It can never be shed again. But lest we should forget that it was *once* shed, we are commanded to drink wine at his table. And *can* we forget such love as Christ has shown? Yes, when he said, "Do this in remembrance of me," he knew well that we were disposed to remember *every thing* sooner than his love. There are only a few who even *desire* to remember it. Why do so many turn away from the Lord's table? Is it not because they do not love their crucified Saviour? They are not ashamed or afraid to say by their actions, "We do not love him." They know he is patient—they know he is generous—they know he is forgiving—they hope he will bear their insults, and that, when he spreads his table in his Father's kingdom, he will invite them to sit down with him there. But *what* if he should come in a day when they think not, and in an hour when they are not looking for him; and what if he should say, "You shall *not* taste of my supper; you despised the supper to which I invited you on earth, and you shall not be admitted to my supper in heaven!" But if he should forgive their ungrateful conduct, and welcome them to his heavenly table, will they not wish they had honored his sacramental board?

If grief could enter heaven, it would be felt at the remembrance, *not* of past trials, but of past ingratitude shown to the Lamb of God. When we feel that all our bliss was purchased by the wounded Saviour, shall not we desire that we had *always* loved, and honored, and adored him?

Evening Scripture portion. 1 Cor. XI. *The Lord's Supper.*

JOHN XIV. 1–3.—*Christ promises his disciples to receive them into his Father's house.*

As we read these words, let us remember in what interesting circumstances they were uttered. Jesus was conversing with his eleven apostles, in an upper room, only a few hours before his crucifixion.

There was a moment in which He himself was troubled in spirit, but now it seems that his disciples were more troubled than himself, for he undertakes to comfort them. He had made one declaration that had grieved them exceedingly; He had said, "Whither I go, ye cannot come." Peter had expressed his sorrow, and had obtained this sweet assurance, "Thou shalt follow me afterwards." The other apostles must have desired to hear words like these addressed to themselves. Their desire was fully satisfied when Jesus said, "In my Father's house are *many* mansions. I go to prepare a place for *you*." There was a mansion, *not* for *Peter* only, but also for John and James, and *all* the apostles. And are these mansions for *them alone?* Does not each of us inquire, "Is there a mansion for *me* also?" Yes, there is not only a mansion, but a *crown* for every one who loves the Lord. Hear what the apostle Paul says, "Henceforth there is laid up for me a *crown* of righteousness, which the Lord, the righteous judge, shall give me in that day; and not to *me only*, but unto *all* them also that *love* his appearing." (2 Tim. iv. 8.) Here is *hope*, here is *assurance*, for every one who can sincerely say, "Come, Lord Jesus, come *quickly*."

Well might the disciples be troubled at the thought of losing such a friend as their Lord had been to them. The kindest friend we have ever known has sometimes treated us coldly, impatiently, or harshly; but Jesus had *always* been affectionate, sympathizing, and tender. The *best* friend we have ever had was subject to error and infirmity, but Jesus possessed unspotted holiness, unerring wisdom, and unblemished loveliness. In losing his presence the disciples felt that they should lose the chief joy of their existence. He knew the desire of their hearts, therefore he said, "That where *I* am, there ye may be also." They have now tasted the fulfilment of this promise! The *apostles* are where Jesus is. Absent from the body they are present with the Lord.

Some who were once with *us*, are now with *him*. Would we wish to call them back? Could we make them as happy as Jesus is now making them? While *we* are enduring trials, exposed to temptations, and subject to sin, they rest in the mansions that he prepared for them in his Father's house. They do not desire to return to us, but they long for *us* to come where they are. There are mansions enough for a multitude which no man can number. Every hour some happy spirit is ascending to inhabit the place the Saviour has prepared for him. The dying Stephen looked up steadfastly into heaven and saw the glory of God, and Jesus standing on the right hand of God; and as they stoned him he called upon God, saying, "Lord Jesus, receive my spirit." (Acts vii. 55, 60.)

Evening Scripture portion. Acts VII. 37 to end. *The death of Stephen.*

JOHN XIV. 4–7.—*Thomas makes an inquiry.*

How condescending it was in the Lord Jesus to permit his disciples to ask him questions! Yet he discouraged *presumptuous* inquiries. On this account the disciples, when they saw him conversing with the Samaritan woman, were once afraid to say, "What doest thou? or, why talkest thou with her?" But he encouraged them to ask, in a humble spirit, explanations of his doctrines.

At an early part of the conversation at the last supper, Peter interrupted his Lord by saying, "Whither goest thou?" The answer seems to have satisfied him, for he said soon afterwards, "I will lay down my *life* for thy sake." By this reply, Peter showed that he believed his Master was going to *die*. But Thomas was not so soon satisfied as Peter. He was a man hard to be convinced, though not slow to act *when* convinced. It was *he* who on a former occasion had said, "Let us also go, that we may die *with* him." (John xi. 16.) And it was *he* who, a long while afterwards, carried the gospel to the end of the world, even to the coasts of India. Even now, near Madras, his name is remembered, and the Mount of St. Thomas may still be seen there. It was *this* Thomas, this unbelieving Thomas, who now said, "Lord, we know not *whither* thou goest, and how can we know the *way?*" His patient teacher repeated the instructions he had so often given, "I am the *way*, the truth, and the life." But did he reveal *whither* he was going? Yes, for he added, "No man cometh unto the *Father*, but by me." He was going to the *Father:* he was going to return to that bosom whence he came out: he had been despised and rejected of *men;* but he was going to Him who had said, "This is my beloved Son, in whom I am well pleased." And was he going *alone?* No: had he not said, "I go to prepare a *place* for *you?*"

But he was going to do still more,—to prepare a *way* as well as a *place*. Of what avail would it have been to us, if a *place* had been prepared, but if no *way* to that place had been opened? To see, *afar off*, those glorious mansions, and to feel there was no *way* by which we could attain them, would be wretchedness indeed. Yet there *is* no way, except through *Jesus*. As well might one of us hope to reach the *stars*, by any contrivance of our own, as to reach heaven through our own goodness, or prayers, or tears, or sufferings. When man had sinned, it was impossible that the *just* God could receive him as an inmate of his palace. What would be thought of a sovereign who should appoint some notorious murderers to be his ministers of state? How was it, then, possible that the holy God should continue to show favor to guilty rebels? But the Son of God took upon him our load of guilt, and died in our stead. Thus he became the *way* to his Father. Sinners may approach God through him. The great gulf that sin had made between heaven and earth, is now closed. The Son of God is the *ladder* by which sinners climb up into heaven. It is a useless thing to attempt to come to God in any other way than by Jesus. The men who began the tower of Babel *thought* they could reach the heavens, but they were *mistaken*. There are some who fall into a more fatal mistake. They fondly imagine that they shall be able to pile up good works enough to enable them to mount to God's throne; but they shall never succeed: while the humble believer, trusting in his Saviour, shall be borne by his Almighty arm into the presence of the King of kings.

Evening Scripture portion. Rom. X. *Salvation by Christ alone.*

JOHN XIV. 8–12.—*Philip makes a request.*

PHILIP expressed the feeling of a pious heart when he said, "Lord, show us the Father, and it sufficeth us." There was something in this request that must have pleased the Son of God. Love to his Father always pleased him. It grieved him to see the creatures of his Father's hand so indifferent to his name. He had beheld another scene in heaven, where every angel and every saint glows with love to his glorious Creator. But worldly men do not care for the Being who made them. Far from wishing to see Him, as Philip did, they wish to hide themselves from him. Instead of saying, "Show us the Father," they say in their hearts, "Give us corn and wine; give us favor with men; give us success in our schemes, and prosperity in our families, and—*it sufficeth us*."

But the children of God desire to see their Father's face. Philip was a child of God, and he desired to see his glorious countenance; therefore he said, "Show us the Father." Yet he ought not to have made this request. He ought to have known that Jesus was the brightness of his Father's glory. How gently the Lord reproached him for his unbelief when he said, "Have I been so long time with you, Philip, and yet hast thou not known me?" *Three* years was a *long* time to have familiar intercourse with the Son of God. Patriarchs and prophets thought themselves highly favored, when they enjoyed short and occasional interviews with their glorious Redeemer. They were more ready to acknowledge him as God than Philip was. When Jacob had wrestled with the angel, he said, "I have seen the face of *God*, and my life is preserved." But the apostles found it hard to believe how great their Master was! They had seen him hungry and thirsty, weary and weeping. They had even heard him talk of *dying*. Was it not hard to believe, that the face so marred with sorrow was the express image of the Father's? Yet they ought to have believed this, because of his *words* and his *works*.

He spake as never *man* spake; he did works that *man* never performed. His divine glory shone through the veil of mortal flesh. No light around his person distinguished him from other men; but the apostle John declares, "We beheld his glory, the glory as of the only-begotten of the Father." (John i. 14.) *Once*, indeed, his face *did* shine as the sun, and his raiment was white as the light; but only *once;* and *then only three* of the apostles beheld that glorious sight. But his countenance always shone with the light of *holiness*, and his garments were *always* white with spotless purity.

When did Jesus fulfil this wonderful promise, "He that believeth on me, the works that I do shall he do also, and *greater* works than these shall he do?" At the day of Pentecost, when the apostles, by the power of the Spirit, turned *three thousand* souls to God. When *Jesus* preached, only a few repented. Chorazin and Bethsaida, Capernaum and Jerusalem, repented *not;* but when the apostles preached, three thousand, by one sermon, were pricked in their hearts. (Acts ii. 37–41.) What was the reason of this difference? Jesus explained the reason in these few words, "Because I go unto the Father." Since he has gone unto the Father, to sit at his right hand, multitudes have received the gifts of repentance, and of the forgiveness of sins, because he is gone there for that *very purpose;* as it is written, "Him hath God exalted with his right hand, to be a Prince and a Saviour, for to give repentance to Israel, and forgiveness of sins." (Acts v. 31.) Have we received these precious gifts? Has the *great work* been done in our souls,—the work of conversion? If it has, then we shall be anxious to do great works ourselves, by saving the souls of our fellow-sinners, and snatching them as brands from the burning.

Evening Scripture portion. Psalm XLV. *The glory of the Son of God.*

John XIV. 13–20.—*Christ promises to answer his disciples' prayers.*

When friends are about to part, they agree together how they shall serve and please each other while separated. The Son of God was the most tender and faithful of friends. What was it He engaged to do for his disciples when about to leave them? He said, "If ye shall ask any thing in my name, I will do it." But what could *they* do for him? He said, "If ye love me, keep my commandments." Jesus has not failed to fulfil *his* part. As soon as he was ascended up on high, his disciples asked in his name for a glorious gift, and he bestowed it. They asked for what he had *promised;* for, as Luther says, prayer is the reminding God of his promises. What had he promised? Another comforter, that is, another *teacher.* "I will pray the Father, and he shall give you another comforter, that he may abide with you forever." The apostles remembered this promise; and when they had parted from their Lord, "they all continued with one accord in prayer and supplication, with the women, and Mary the mother of Jesus, and with his brethren." (Acts i. 14.) Then it was that the Holy Ghost came down from heaven with a sound like a rushing mighty wind, and in appearance like cloven and flaming tongues Peter then preached to the wondering multitude, and said, "Being by the right hand of God exalted, and having received of the Father the promise of the Holy Ghost, he hath shed forth this, which ye now *see* and *hear.*" (Acts ii. 33.)

Thus Jesus fulfilled his own promise, "If ye shall ask any thing in my name, I will do it." But has he withdrawn that precious promise? May we not *still* expect its fulfilment? Assuredly we may. How many believers can witness that Jesus has heard *their* prayers! Sometimes we are certain that the letter we sent to a friend has been received; and why? Because we receive an answer to it. Have we never received answers to our prayers sufficient to convince us that they have been heard? Sometimes Jesus does not grant the *very thing* his people ask for; because he has promised only to give them *good* things, and sometimes, in their ignorance, they ask for things not good for *them.* The apostle Paul *thought* it would be good for him to be relieved from the thorn in his flesh: but his Saviour knew it would be better for him to bear it, lest the abundant revelations he had received should exalt him above measure. Therefore when he besought the Lord *thrice* to take it away, he received this answer: "My grace is sufficient for thee." And he *found* it sufficient; for he was able afterwards to say, "I take pleasure in infirmities." If, then, we do not obtain the very thing we ask, let us not be discouraged. We may have asked for a *stone:* our heavenly Father will not give us *that;* but He will give us *bread* instead.

Christ has not forgotten what he promised to do for us. Let *us* not forget what he has enjoined us to do for *Him.* He said, "If ye love me, keep my commandments." If we forget this charge, he will be released from his promise. For St. John says in his epistle, "Whatsoever we ask, we receive of him, *because* we keep his commandments, and do those things that are pleasing in his sight." (1 John iii. 22.) What are his commandments? He had given *two* while sitting at supper with his disciples. One was the *new* commandment, "Love one another as I have loved you." The other was, "Believe in me." (John xiv. 1.) Jesus did not say, "*Love* me." He knew his disciples loved him. He even appealed to their love as a motive of obedience, saying, "*If* ye love me, keep my commandments." Does this tender appeal touch *our* hearts? If we love the Lord it will be a stronger motive to obedience than the severest threatening. God *threatened* Adam when he said, "In the day that thou eatest thereof, thou shalt surely die." But this threatening did not deter him from eating the forbidden fruit. How many who love Jesus have been deterred from disobeying him by the tender words, "If ye love me, keep my commandments!"

Evening Scripture portion. Acts II. 1–28. ***The descent of the Holy Ghost.***

JOHN XIV. 21–23.—*Jude asks an explanation.*

How it must have gladdened the hearts of the apostles to hear Jesus say, "I will manifest myself unto him," (that is, unto the man who loves me!) As it was the prospect of his *absence* that troubled them, the promise of his *presence* (if they believed that promise) must have cheered them. He had said before, "I will come again and receive you to myself." But he had not said *when* he would come again. Years might pass away before he took them to the place where he was going. But now he promises to visit those whom he left behind.

To *whom* did he address the promise? To those who *loved him.* The apostle Jude well knew that *he* loved him. Therefore he did not inquire, "*Wilt* thou manifest thyself unto us?" But he asked, "*How* wilt thou manifest thyself unto us?" It is a comfortable thing when a man's own heart assures him that he loves his Lord. Our hearts tell us that we love our children and our friends. If we really love the *Lord,* our hearts will tell us that we do. Yet, lest we should deceive ourselves upon so important a subject, Jesus has given us a sign by which to try our hearts. "If a man love me, he will keep my words." But who keeps the words of Jesus? If tried by this rule who shall stand? *None* keep them *perfectly;* but some do keep them in the sense that Jesus meant; for he said, speaking of his own *apostles,* in prayer to God, "They have kept thy word." (John xvii. 6.) This declaration has been a great comfort to many believers. The history of the apostles shows that they did not keep their Master's words *perfectly:* they neither believed in him as fully, nor loved one another as warmly, as they ought. Yet still Jesus said to his Father, "They have kept thy word."

When he lived upon earth the world saw him as well as his disciples; but, since he has ascended to heaven, the world have seen him no more: but those who love him do see him by *faith.* There are many who have experienced the truth of this promise: "My Father will love him, and we will come unto him, and make our abode with him." That faithful servant of God, Dr. Payson, when racked with pain upon his dying bed, declared, "It is not the *prospect* of heaven that makes me happy, but the *sense* of heaven in my own bosom." Where the Father and the Son abide, there must be heaven. While sin remains in the heart, the believer's heaven will be darkened by clouds, and shaken by storms: but when sin is utterly destroyed, there will be no more storms, and no more clouds.

The glorified saints are not only in *heaven,* but heaven is in *them.* The *dawn* of this heaven is in believers upon *earth.* Is there heaven in *our* souls? Do the Father and the Son make their abode with us? If they dwell not with *us now,* we shall not dwell with *them hereafter.* Remember the declaration of the apostle, "Christ *in* you, the hope of glory." Remember also his prayer, "That Christ may dwell in your hearts by faith." (Eph. iii. 17.)

Evening Scripture portion. Eph. III. ***St. Paul's prayer for the saints.***

JOHN XIV. 24–26.—*Christ promises his disciples that the Holy Ghost shall teach them.*

WHEN about to part with a friend, we often have cause to regret that we have not profited more from his society. A child standing by the bed of a dying parent, feels the value of those instructions he shall receive no longer,—of those prayers he shall never join in again. He endeavors to recall the faithful counsels, to imprint on his memory the familiar expressions, but day by day they fade away.

What must the disciples have felt at the thought of hearing the sayings of the Lord no more! They heard him declare, "He that loveth me not, keepeth not my sayings." They must have feared lest they should not be able even to *remember* them, much less to KEEP them. But Jesus knew their feelings, and he gave them a promise suited to their state. He promised that *One* should come who should bring to their remembrance all that he had said to them, and who should teach them many things he had *not* taught them. For he had treated them as children whose understandings were unripe, and had kept back many things that it would *hereafter* be good for them to know. These things the Holy Ghost would teach them. Did Jesus fulfil this promise? Let us look into the epistles of Peter and Jude, of James and John, and we shall find treasures of heavenly wisdom that the Holy Ghost had taught them. The very discourse which we are now reading was brought back to the memory of John by the Holy Ghost. The precious words which dropped from the Saviour's lips as he sat at his last supper, did not fall to the ground; they were gathered up and reserved for our instruction. Do *we feel* them to be precious? Do we consider these holy words better than gold, and sweeter than honey? Or do we take more delight in a trifling song and an entertaining story, than in the words of the Son of God? The true believer can say with David, "Thy word is very pure, therefore thy servant loveth it."

If we really love it, we may trust that the Holy Ghost will bring it to our remembrance in our time of need. In the hour of temptation he is a faithful friend, and whispers in the ear of the *tempted* soul such a text as this, "How can I do this great wickedness and sin against God?" In the hour of *affliction* the Holy Ghost brings to the desponding mind such a promise as this, "Whom the Lord loveth he chasteneth, and scourgeth every son whom he receiveth." (Heb. xii. 6.) And in the hour of *death* he sustains the sinking soul by such an assurance as this, "When thou passest through the waters I will be with thee, and through the floods they shall not overflow thee." (Is. xliii. 2.)

Evening Scripture portion. 1 Cor II. ***The teaching of the Holy Spirit.***

JOHN XIV. 27–29.—*Christ promises to give his disciples peace.*

WE sometimes read of a rich man dying and leaving a vast property to his heirs. But the greatest riches ever bequeathed, were bequeathed by one of the poorest of the sons of men. None was ever poorer in this world than Jesus. Yet he left his disciples the costly gift of "Peace." "Peace I leave with you, my peace I give unto you." This is what all the world are pursuing. They are seeking for peace and happiness. They desire an abundant earthly portion because they imagine it will confer peace. Some think that *power* will confer it; others that *praise* will impart it; while many hope to find peace in a round of amusements, in the attainment of knowledge, in the endearments of home, or in the performance of active duties. But *none* of these things, not even the *best* of them, ever bestowed peace. None has peace to bestow but Jesus. He gives it to those who *love* him, and to them alone. He gave it to the weeping sinner; he said to her, "Go in *peace*," and she went in peace. He gave it to the dying thief; he said, "To-day shalt thou be with me in paradise," and that once guilty man *died* in peace. He is willing to give it to each of you. Ask him for his peace. You will obtain it. Perhaps there are some here who have obtained it already; who know they have been filled with joy and *peace* since they believed in the Son of God.

But when Jesus promised this rich gift to his disciples, what was going to become of *him?* He also was going to be happy. He was going to the *Father.* Who can conceive the joy which he felt when he uttered these words, "I go unto the Father." He knew what it was to be with the Father. He had been with him from the *beginning*, for he himself was God. When he said, "My Father is *greater* than I," he spoke only of the greatness of his Father's *office*, not of the greatness of his *nature;* for it is declared in other places, that Jesus is *equal* with God. "He thought it not robbery to be *equal* with God." (Phil. ii. 6.) "I and my Father are one." (John x. 30.) But Jesus took upon him the form of a *servant*, and was made in fashion as a *man.* While he continued on earth he was exposed to insults; but when he returned to heaven, he sat down again with his Father on his throne.

Did it ever rejoice *us* to think that the Saviour's sufferings are all over, and that he is "made most blessed forever?" If we *loved* him, this thought would comfort us under our own sorrows. It *did* comfort the disciples, for when they saw him carried up into heaven, they returned to Jerusalem with great joy. (Luke xxiv. 52.) The same thought may comfort us under the loss of pious relatives. If we love them, we shall rejoice when we think that they are with the Father. When troubles overtake us, it will be soothing to reflect, "My mother is with the angels, and she can weep no more; my child is in the midst of the happy cherubs, singing praises to his God." When we ourselves are going to leave this world, may we also rejoice at the thought that we are going to the Father; and may those who love us rejoice because they know we are going there! A child of four years old, when dying, saw his parents weeping and praying around his bed. Suddenly rising up from his pillow, and stretching out his little arms, he cried out earnestly, "Let me go to God, let me go to God." Who could desire to detain him here!*

Evening Scripture portion. Is. LVII. *Peace.*

JOHN XIV. 30 to end.—*Christ goes forth to meet the prince of this world.*

IT required more than human courage to utter these words, "Arise, let us go hence." It was the call of the Captain of our salvation to his children: it was their summons to accompany him to the field of battle. The last supper was now over, and the parting scene was almost closed. What tender assurances, what faithful warnings had flowed from the lips of Jesus while he sat at the table surrounded by his beloved disciples! But now he says, "Hereafter I shall not talk much with you." These sweet conversations would soon be ended. Instead of *talking* with his *disciples*, the Son of God must be *struggling* with his *foes*.

There have been many bloody battles fought since evil entered into this world. On some occasions hundreds of thousands have met each other in the field. But there never was such a battle as that fought in the garden Gethsemane, and on the cross of Calvary. There legions of wicked spirits, marshalled under the prince of this world, assaulted the Son of God. On Satan's side there was an innumerable host—on the other *one man*, even the man Christ Jesus. None can conceive what pangs he endured in the conflict. Agony of mind caused him to sweat great drops of blood, and wrung from him the bitter cry, "My God, my God, why hast thou forsaken me?" We find in the psalms a description of the workings of his sorrowful soul, when writhing beneath the pressure of Satan's temptations. If we would sympathize with our suffering Saviour, let us read the twenty-second psalm. What expressions are these! "My heart is like wax, it is melted in the midst of my bowels." What a prayer is this, "Save me from the lion's mouth!"

But how was it Satan could not prevail against the Son of God? Jesus himself explains the reason. "The prince of this world cometh, and hath nothing in me." There was no *sin* in the Saviour's heart,

* See "Children's Friend" for Sept. 1845.

there was nothing on which Satan could work. A marble quarry cannot be set on fire, and the Son of God was proof against temptation. Satan had once seduced spotless angels from their obedience. But there is an infinite difference between the holiness of a creature and that of the Creator. Even those creatures who have never sinned are not, like God, incapable of pollution. Therefore it is written, "He charged his angels with folly," (Job iv.;) and "The heavens are not clean in his sight." (Job xv.)

But though the Son of God knew he should win the victory, he looked forward with horror to the conflict. With *joy* he had said, "I go unto the Father." With *anguish* he declared, "The prince of this world cometh." Satan was coming to make a *last* attempt to wrench the sceptre from his hands, and to snatch the crown from his head. Terrible indeed was the hour of the power of darkness.

What was the mighty *motive* which urged the Son of God to meet the enemy? It was love. To whom? To his Father. It was love to his *Father* that drew him from the table around which his disciples sat, and led him to the garden to which his enemies were hastening. Therefore he said, "But that the world may know that I love the Father, and as the Father gave me commandment, even so I do. Arise, let us go hence."

Evening Scripture portion.
Col. II. *Christ's triumph over principalities and powers.*

JOHN XV. 1–8.—*Christ declares he is the true vine.*

WHEN Jesus uttered these words he was no longer seated at his last supper with the twelve. He had said, "Arise, let us go hence." It is recorded by St. Matthew, that before he left the table, he sang a hymn with his disciples. (Matt. xxvi. 30.) It is probable that the hymn consisted of several psalms, beginning at the 113th, and ending with the 118th. They were called the Hallel, because they open with the words, "Praise ye the Lord." They celebrate the deliverance of Israel from the land of Egypt, and on that account were always sung at the feast of the Passover. But they also describe a greater deliverance than that from Egypt, even the deliverance of God's people from the depths of hell. Though many prophets had sung these psalms year after year at the holy feast, none had ever understood them as HE did, who sung them that night with his beloved apostles. He knew the meaning of the words, "Bind the sacrifice with cords to the horns of the altar." (Ps. cxviii. 27.) Ere the next setting sun this prophecy was fulfilled by the cry, "Crucify him, crucify him."

Now let us follow the sorrowful little band as they descended the stairs, proceeded through the dark streets of Jerusalem, and along the path that led down the vale of Kedron. It is probable that beside that stream vine-trees grew, and that our Saviour pointed to those trees when he said, "I am the true vine." By the means of a plant he wished to teach his disciples this most important truth, that all their safety lay in *union* with himself. The branches of the vine, while united to the stem, bear precious fruit, but when cut off are worthless, and only fit for the fire. The prophet Ezekiel thus describes the vine, "Shall wood be taken thereof to do any work? Behold it is cast into the fire for fuel." (Ezek. xv. 3, 4.)

The Lord was going to leave his disciples, yet he said, "Abide in me and I in you." How would they be able to do this when he would be with the Father, and they on the earth? They would abide in him by *believing* in him; and he would abide in them by his Spirit. This is the union which exists between the exalted Saviour and all his people *now* upon earth. Though they see him not, they *believe* in him, and thus they *abide* in him; though he reigns in the highest heaven, he dwells in their hearts by his Spirit, and thus *he* dwells in *them.* This union is not to be seen, but the effects are to be seen. We might not be able to tell whether a branch grew upon the vine, or whether it was only skilfully fastened on it. But if we watched the tree, we should know by two signs. The false branch would bear no fruit, and at length—it would wither.

False professors of religion bear no fruit. They may do what are *called* good works; they may be very active and charitable; they may refrain from worldly amusements, and frequent religious assemblies, but they cannot *love* Christ or love his people for *his* sake. Love is the fruit. "Love is of God. Every one that loveth is born of God, and knoweth God." If a man say, "I love God, and hateth his brother, he is a liar." (1 John iv. 7, 20.)

Those branches which do not bear fruit will at length *wither.* None but God can tell *when.* They may wither *soon;* they may, like Judas, fall into some open and atrocious sin, which shall unmask their characters, and cover their names with infamy. Or they may not wither till they die. Angels shall gather up the withered branches and cast them into the fire, and they shall be *burned.* Are *we* united to the true vine? To *appear* to belong to this vine, and *not* to belong to it, is to be *twice* dead. St. Jude describes false professors as "trees whose fruit withereth, *without fruit, twice dead,* plucked up by the roots."

Evening Scripture portion. Titus I. *False professors.*

JOHN XV. 9–12.—*Christ assures his disciples of his love.*

IT is a great comfort to an affectionate child to receive from a dying parent an assurance of his love. Though he knew before that his parent loved him, yet there is a satisfaction when the time of parting approaches, to hear fresh expressions of attachment. Many failings on his own part rushing to his recollection, make him feel that he does not deserve to be loved; and he listens eagerly to the tender words which dispel his fears.

Such must have been the feelings of the disciples when their Master was going to leave them. He knew the state of their hearts, and applied the healing balm they needed. But he did not say simply, "I have loved you." He told them how *much.* And how much did he love them? If the Son of God had not declared it we could not have believed that his love was so very great; even the *thought* would have seemed the height of presumption and profaneness. "*As* the Father hath loved me, *so* have I loved you." How great must be the love with which the Father has always loved his only-begotten Son, the brightness of his glory, and the express image of his person! The Son speaks of this love as existing before the worlds were made. "Then I was by him, as one brought up with him; I was daily *his delight,* rejoicing always before him." (Prov. viii. 30.) And *this* is the love with which we are desired to love one another, for Christ said, "This is my commandment, that ye love one another, *as* I have loved you." As the Father loves the Son, so the Son loves us, and so we ought to love one another. Such love does not spring up naturally in our hearts. This is the description the word of God gives of sinful men: "Hateful, and hating one another." (Titus iii. 3.)

Jesus presents the strongest motives to incite us to love each other. Do we desire to *continue* to enjoy *his* love? Then we must love one another; for he says, "If ye keep my commandments ye shall abide in my love, even as I have kept my Father's commandments, and abide in his love." He had said before, "If ye love me, keep my commandments." *Then* he appealed to *their* love for *him,* now he refers to his *own* for *them.* With both these silken cords he sought to bind their hearts together in the bonds of brotherly love.

He urges yet another motive. He was while on earth a man of sorrows, and acquainted with grief; yet sometimes he rejoiced in spirit. It was over his disciples he rejoiced. Did they desire to continue to be his joy, they must love one another. "These things have I spoken to you, that *my* joy might remain in you." It is a delightful thought to give joy to the Son of God. We have caused him *grief* enough, and *pain* enough, and *shame* enough;—and shall we cause him *no* joy? To see his children on earth living together in love, is *his joy* now he is in heaven. How must he be grieved when he sees them suspecting each other's motives, exposing each other's faults, thwarting each other's wishes, and wounding each other's feelings! Disciples who act thus cannot be the joy of the God of love; neither can they be happy themselves—their joy cannot be full. Where there is *little love*, there can be *little joy.* If heaven were not full of love, it could not be full of joy. Let us observe our own feelings. When a dark suspicion enters our hearts—are we happy? When a revengeful feeling is kindled—are we happy? When selfishness freezes, or pride puffs us up—are we happy? But when we melt in sympathy with our suffering brethren, or glow with desire to do them good, does not our joy increase? We are being trained up here to join the multitude which no man can number. We are to love *all* those happy spirits. Not one is to be treated with contempt or dislike, or even with shyness and reserve. *All* are to be loved by us with the love with which the Father loves the Son, with which the Son loves us. Let us begin this happy life now. Let us love one another. Though there are a multitude of sins in our brethren as well as in ourselves, yet love is a mantle wide enough to cover them all.

Evening Scripture portion. 2d Epistle of John. *Christian love.*

JOHN XV. 13–16.—*Christ calls his disciples his friends.*

THE Lord Jesus showed more tenderness to his disciples in the *last* scene than he had ever shown before. Though he received them graciously at first, and treated them kindly afterwards, yet he reserved the choicest expressions of his love for the moment of parting. We never read till we come to this passage such a declaration as, "Ye are my *friends.*"

This is the manner in which the Lord deals with all his people. It is in the latter stages of their pilgrimage that he makes them know most of his loving-kindness. When they are weighed down by the infirmities of age, or racked by the pains of sickness, he often lifts up the light of his countenance upon them, as he had never done before, so that their *last* days are their *best* days. Like the aged Simeon, they exclaim, "Mine eyes have seen thy salvation;" or, like the dying Stephen, "I see the heavens opened, and Jesus standing at the right hand of God."

One of the proofs of friendship is confidence. The Lord treated his disciples with confidence. He said to them, "All things that I have heard of my Father I have made known to you." But while on his part there was *confidence*, he expected on *their* part *obedience;* for he did not wish them to forget he was their *Father*, as well as their *Friend*, therefore he said, "Ye are my friends, if ye do whatsoever I *command* you." It is written in the Psalms: "The secret of the

Lord is with them that *fear* him, and he will show *them* his covenant." (Ps. xxv. 14.) The covenant is that secret which Jesus had heard from his Father, and which he unfolds to his friends. It is the secret of his love before time began. Jesus loved his apostles *before* they loved him. He declared this truth to them when he said, "Ye have not chosen me, but I have chosen you." If he had not chosen them, they would never have *desired* to serve him. When Andrew with another disciple stood by John the Baptist, and heard him say, "Behold the Lamb of God, which taketh away the sin of the world," they would have felt no inclination to follow that Lamb, had not Jesus first chosen them. His love was the invisible magnet that drew them after their Saviour.

Christ not only chose his apostles to be his friends; he also ordained them to bear fruit. In all things he pleased not himself. He did not call them to leave their employments that they might be his companions as he walked from place to place, or his defenders when assaulted by his enemies. Angels would gladly have left their habitation to be his solace and his guard. It was not his own comfort that he sought, but his Father's glory. He appointed the apostles to bear the tidings of salvation to the ends of the world; and he promised that their labor should not be in vain. To this hour their fruit remains. On *earth* there are thousands rejoicing in the Gospel which the apostles preached; in *heaven* a multitude that no man can number. The works of worldly men who lived in the apostles' days have perished. The victories they won have conferred no lasting benefit; the buildings they reared are fallen or crumbling into ruin; the books they wrote, if they still survive, never yet made one creature happy. But the labors of the apostles can never be forgotten; the sinners they converted are saved; and at length the world, through the truths they preached, shall be made holy and happy. Let us tread in their steps. We also are the friends of Jesus, if we do what he commands us. We may bring forth fruit that shall never wither. Feeble as we are, Christ will not despise us. He says to us, "Be not weary in well doing; for in due season ye shall reap, if ye faint not." It is far better to convert one soul, than, like Columbus, to discover a continent; or, like Herschell, a planet. The fruits of science will pass away, but the fruits of grace will abide unto eternal life.

Evening Scripture portion. Is. XLI. *Abraham the friend of God.*

JOHN XV. 17 to end.—*Christ prepares his disciples for the world's hatred.*

THE Lord Jesus did not tell his disciples at the *beginning* of this conversation, that the world would hate them. He told them *first* of his *own* great love. After hearing of that love, they ought to be able to bear to hear that the world would hate them. For what is the *hatred* of the world compared to the *love* of Jesus! If all the *creatures* were to hate us, they could not harm us, while the *Creator* loved us.

There is another reason why we should not care for the world's hatred. It is this: the world hated Jesus; though he was perfectly lovely, they hated him. Some young Christians imagine that they can escape the hatred of the world. They think that very amiable manners, and very prudent conduct, and very benevolent actions, will prevent even wicked men disliking them. But who can be as amiable as Jesus was, or as prudent, or as benevolent? There are some called Christians who stand high in the world's esteem; but *how* do they win this esteem? Is it not by keeping silence when they ought to speak, by joining in amusements which they ought to shun, and by cultivating friendships which they ought to renounce? Why did the world hate Jesus? He has told us the reason. Because he testified that its works were evil. (John vii. 7.) We ought to do the same. The apostle Paul says, "Have no fellowship with the unfruitful works of darkness, but rather reprove them." (Eph. v. 11.) There may be occasions in which we cannot reprove in *words;* but we should never, even by a *smile*, *seem* to approve wicked actions or discourse.

It is a comfort to the faithful Christian to think that he shares in his Master's reproach. It was a comfort to the Son of God to know that he was hated for his *Father's* sake. He said, "The reproaches of them that reproached *thee*, have fallen upon *me*." (Rom. xv. 3.) He was the express image of his Father, and the world did not admire that image. The disciples of Jesus are not his *express* image; but they bear *some* likeness to him, and even that likeness, faint as it is, the world abhors. How astonished angels must be to see him whom they adore, despised by men! No sin that man commits can be compared to the sin of hating God. If they hated him because they did not *know* him, their guilt would not be so great; but they hate him the *more*, the *more* they know him. The missionaries in Africa have been struck with this singular fact. *Distant* tribes show more desire to hear the Gospel than the tribes that lie *near* the missionary station. And why? Because the tribes that lie near know better what Christianity is, how pure, how peaceable, how gentle. Their wicked hearts turn from such a religion; they prefer their own cruel practices, and unholy customs, to the loving and pure doctrines of the Gospel. The carnal mind is *still* enmity against God. If the Son of God were *again* to descend to this world, and if, clad in a humble garb, he were to visit *this* country, he would *again* be despised and rejected. Do *we* feel that we should not despise him? Let us inquire what proof we give that we should not. Do we love his servants, *whoever* they are, and *wherever* we find them? And is it for their *holiness* we love them? If we prefer a real Christian, though unlearned, unpolished, unpleasing, to the most eloquent, agreeable, and accomplished worldly person, then we have reason to hope that we actually *do* love Jesus.

Evening Scripture portion. 1 Peter IV. *Christians hated by the world.*

JOHN XIV. 1–4.—*Christ prepares his disciples for afflictions.*

NONE of us know what particular afflictions we shall be called to endure. The Lord Jesus was the only man who knew all things that would befall him. Even the apostle Paul, who was a prophet, said, "Now behold I go bound in the spirit unto Jerusalem, *not* knowing the things that shall befall me there." (Acts xx. 22.) Yet God has sometimes revealed to men a few of the future events of their lives. He told David that he would sit upon a throne, and afterwards he predicted that the sword would never depart from his house. He has wise reasons for spreading a thick curtain over the future, and he has wise reasons for sometimes *lifting up* a little corner of the curtain and permitting men to have a glimpse into his counsels.

The Lord Jesus thought fit to tell the disciples *some* events that would happen to them. He said, "They shall put you out of the synagogue; yea, the time cometh, that whosoever killeth you will think he doeth God service." What was his reason for acquainting them with these afflictions? He himself states the reason: "These things have I spoken unto you that ye should not be offended," or made to stumble. There is a strong temptation in times of great affliction to distrust God. It is very hard when he smites us, to believe that he loves us. When we are prosperous and happy, then it is easy to say, "As many as he loves he rebukes and chastens." It is easy then to believe, or to *think* we believe, that he does not willingly grieve or afflict the children of men. But when pining in a dungeon, or threatened with the stake, then it is hard *not* to imagine that God has forgotten to be gracious. When Satan desired to deprive Job of all his comforts, he knew how much that faithful man would be tempted to speak against his God. Those who have experienced sore afflictions can remember the struggle in their hearts at such times. Jesus knew the weakness of his disciples: he knew what they would feel when cast out of the synagogues, and sentenced to die a cruel death. Therefore he prepared them for these trials, that when they were afflicted they might think, "These are no strange things that have come upon us; our Lord told us before that they would happen." Some years ago a Malagassy woman was persecuted cruelly by the queen of Madagascar. For five months she was shut up in an iron cage that prevented her from moving a limb, and for a long while she wandered in the forests, living upon wild roots, to escape the spear of the executioner. Afterwards, when in England, she was asked whether she was surprised at these trials. She replied, "O no, I had read in the word of God that 'we should suffer tribulation,' and I expected trials to come."

Evening Scripture portion. Rev. XII. *Persecution for Christ's sake.*

JOHN XVI. 5–11.—*Christ promises to send the Comforter to reprove the world.*

WHY did the Lord Jesus say to his disciples, "None of you asketh me, Whither goest thou?" Had they not asked him already, and had he not told them that he was going to his Father? Many times he had said, "I go unto the Father." Yet the apostles continued to mourn as if their Master had been going to an *enemy* instead of to his *Father*,—as if he had been going where *they* could never come, and whence *he* would never return,—as if he had been going where he could not hear their prayers, or send them help in trouble. Do *we* not often mourn as if we had no merciful Mediator to present our prayers to the Father—no Almighty Saviour to send us succor from on high? The Lord gently reproved his disciples for their excessive sorrow, saying, "Because I have said these things unto you, sorrow hath filled your heart."

Afterwards he continued to make them comforting promises. One of these promises was that he would send the Holy Spirit. He had before told them of many blessings that the Holy Spirit would confer on THEM: he now tells them what he would do for the *world*. He would reprove (or convince) the world of *three* things,—sin,—righteousness,—and judgment. The world were not yet convinced of these things. If they had been, they would not have crucified the Lord of glory.

The world did not know that it was a *sin* not to believe in Jesus. They did not know that the *righteousness* of Christ atoned for the unrighteousness of men, and that his ascension to his Father proved that his offering had been accepted. They did not know that Satan, the prince of this world, was judged when Jesus, the Prince of life, expired on the cross.

And did the world *ever* know these things? Three thousand of the world were convinced of sin, righteousness, and judgment, when Peter preached his first sermon. When they flocked around the apostles, anxiously asking, "What shall we do?" then did our Saviour's promise begin to be fulfilled.

Since that time many thousands of the children of this world have been pricked in their hearts by the power of the Holy Spirit, and they also have asked, "What shall we do?" Have *we* ever asked this question? Are *we* convinced of sin, of righteousness, and of judgment? It is only those whom the Spirit has taught who feel unbelief to be a great sin. It is only *they* who desire to be found in the righteousness of Christ. It is only *they* who rejoice that the prince of this world has been overcome. We were all ignorant of these things once. If we understand them now, a great change must have taken place in our hearts. It was the Holy Spirit who wrought that change, who taught us to mourn for sin, to believe in Christ, and to resist Satan. Have we come as *penitents* to Christ? As *believers* let us cleave to him. As *conquerors* we shall reign with him.

Evening Scripture portion.
Zech. III. IV. ***The power of Christ and the Spirit.***

John XVI. 12–15.—*Christ promises to send the Spirit to teach the disciples.*

The Lord Jesus knew that this was his last conversation with his disciples before his death. He had said to them, while sitting at the supper-table, "Hereafter I will not talk much with you." But if he had had more *time* for discourse, he could not have taught them *all* he wished. And why not? Because their hearts were not in a fit state to receive *all* his instructions. The disciples were only *babes* in Christ, and they had need of *milk*, and not of meat. They had *shown*, a few hours ago, that they were only *babes*, for even at the last supper there had been a *strife* among them which should be the greatest. Christians who have grown much in grace do not desire to be exalted above their brethren.

The disciples must have been grieved when they heard their Master say, "I have yet many things to say unto you, but ye cannot bear them now." They must have been grieved to find they lost many sweet disclosures of grace from the lips of the Son of God himself. There were many precious truths in their Lord's heart, which he would have communicated to his beloved children had they been able to receive them. If we would grow in the knowledge of the truth, we must lay aside all malice, and envies, and evil-speakings; for these sinful passions clog up the soul, and prevent the entrance of the truth.

In this farewell discourse the sympathizing Saviour never dwelt long upon any *sorrowful* topic, for it appears to have been his great desire to *comfort* his disciples. It was to *comfort* them he spoke of the coming of this Spirit, and of all the benefits he would confer. He made three promises concerning the Spirit. "He will guide you into all truth." "He will show you things to come." "He shall glorify me," that is, he will show you my glory. The writings of the apostles prove that the Lord fulfilled these promises.

In their epistles, (as in the whole Bible,) we find *truth*, without any admixture of error. In them we are told of "things to come." What a description the apostle Peter gives, in his second epistle, of the burning up of the world! and what wonderful scenes are opened to our eyes in the Revelation granted to the apostle John! In the epistles we see the accomplishment of the promise, "He shall glorify me." Three of the apostles had seen the glory of Christ on the mount of transfiguration. But there is a glory which cannot be seen by human eyes. The Spirit reveals *this* glory to the *souls* of all true believers, as the apostle Paul declares, "But *we all*, with open face, beholding, as in a glass, the *glory of the Lord*, are changed into the same image, from glory to glory, even as by the *Spirit of the Lord*." (2 Cor. iii. 18.) Unbelief is the veil that hides the glory from the heart: but when the Holy Spirit, by his might, takes away this veil, then the glory of Christ shines into the inmost soul, true believers look with *open* or *unveiled* face into the gospel glass, (or mirror,) and behold the glory of the Son of God. At first they see it very dimly: but they are changed into the same image from *glory* to *glory*. They *grow* in the knowledge of Christ. Let not those be cast down who have only just begun to seek Christ. Perhaps now you often say with tears, "Help thou mine unbelief." Perhaps now you feel that these words concerning Jesus do not apply to you. "In whom, though now ye see him not, yet believing, ye rejoice with joy unspeakable, and full of glory." (1 Peter i. 8.) Pray that the Holy Spirit may enlighten your eyes, that you may by faith behold the glory of Christ—of that "High Priest who is set on the right hand of the throne of the Majesty in the heavens." (Heb. viii. 1.) Earth contains no glory like his. Why has the heavenly city no need of the sun or moon to shine in it? Because "the glory of God lightens it, and the Lamb is the light thereof." (Rev. xxi. 23.)

Evening Scripture portion. 2 Cor. III. ***The glory of Christ.***

JOHN XVI. 16–22.—*The disciples cannot understand their Lord.*

As the disciples accompanied their Master towards the garden of Gethsemane, they suffered much from the perplexity they felt. They saw they were going to be separated from their heavenly Friend; but they could not tell by what *means*, or for how long a *time*. When he said, "I go to my Father, and ye see me no more," then it seemed that the separation would be *long;* but when he said, "A little while, and ye shall see me," then it seemed that it would be *short*. Why did they not ask their Lord to explain his words? Four times in the course of this conversation they had ventured to speak. Peter had asked, "Whither goest thou?" Thomas had said, "How can we know the way?" Philip had exclaimed, "Show us the Father." And Jude had inquired, "How is it that thou wilt manifest thyself unto us?" Each of these apostles had received a gracious answer. Why did they hesitate again to apply to their condescending Lord? He had once said to *all* weary and heavy-laden sinners, "Learn of me, for I am meek and lowly of heart." Would he, then, refuse to teach his own beloved disciples? As they were afraid to ask him, he kindly *offered* to instruct them. But instead of explaining what he meant by "a little while," he described the great *sorrow* they would soon feel, and the great *joy* that would succeed. Thus he prepared them, in the tenderest manner, for his own death. He described their grief in these words, "Ye shall weep and lament." It is recorded that, while their Lord lay in the grave, "they mourned and wept." (Mark xvi.) Were more bitter tears ever shed, than those they shed on that occasion? Since the beginning of the world none had ever experienced so great a calamity as *that* they *thought* had befallen them. Adam and Eve must have felt acute anguish when driven out of the Garden of Eden; yet even they had a promise to sustain them; "The seed of the woman shall bruise the serpent's head." But the apostles had scarcely a spark of hope remaining. Their faith was so weak, that they could hardly believe it possible that the wounded body of their Lord should rise from the tomb. But while they were weeping, the world was rejoicing. The chief priests and scribes flattered themselves that they had got rid of the man they hated, and that they should hear of him no more. But how soon were the cases reversed! The disciples' *sorrow* was turned into *joy:* the world's *joy* into *sorrow*.

So also it will be when Jesus comes again. Many who *laugh* now will *weep* then; and many who *mourn* now will *rejoice* then. How *would* the world feel now, if they were assured that the Son of God would never return in the clouds of heaven,—if they could be certain that there was no hell and no heaven! Would they not rejoice? But how would true Christians feel, if it were possible for them to know that they would never see the Son of God? Would they not feel the bitterest disappointment? Would they not feel that their highest hopes were withered? How should *we* feel? Would it be any disappointment to us to think we should never see Jesus? There are many who only wish to go to heaven, because they know that if they do not go there, they must go to hell. But this is not the Christian's feeling. Were all the pleasures of earth promised to him, he would not wish to live one day longer below in order to enjoy them. This is the desire of his heart and the request of his lips:

"*Forever* to behold him shine,
For evermore to call him mine,

And see him still before me;
Forever on his face to gaze,
And meet his full assembled rays,
While all the Father he displays
To all his saints in glory."
Collection of the Rev. W. Carus Wilson.

Evening Scripture portion. Ps. XCVII. XCVIII. *Joy at the Lord's coming.*

JOHN XVI. 23–27.—*Christ assures his disciples of his Father's love.*

A CHILD who has been bereft of wise and pious parents feels the loss of their counsels and of their prayers. But who ever gave such wise counsels as the Lord Jesus? Who ever offered up such fervent prayers as he did? The thought of losing his instructions and his prayers must have grieved the disciples. Whenever they were perplexed they could ask him; and even when they did not venture to *ask* him, he knew their difficulties, and explained the meaning of his own words. It must have cheered them to hear him say, that when he returned after his short absence they should understand him better than before. "In that day ye shall ask me nothing." The word "ask" in this place means "*inquire.*" After the resurrection Jesus no longer spake to his disciples in proverbs, (or short mysterious sayings,) but he showed them *plainly* from the Father. He also opened their understanding to understand the Scriptures, (Luke xxiv. 45,) and the Holy Spirit afterwards carried on the work that he had begun.

Did the disciples fear lest they should faint in prayer, now that he who prayed *for* them and *with* them was going to leave them? Jesus gave them this encouraging promise: "Whatsoever ye shall ask the Father in my name, he will give it you." The word "ask" *here* means request, and *not* "inquire," as in the first part of the verse. And why were they to ask in *his* name? Was the Father unwilling to hear them? O no, his heart is not hardened against his creatures: it does not need to be melted. Why then must we ask in the name of Jesus? Because we are sinners, and God is too *holy* to encourage *sin;* and therefore he has appointed a way by which *sinners* may approach him without polluting his spotless throne. That way is through the merits of his righteous Son. "He ever liveth to make intercession for them who come unto God *by him.*" (Heb. vii. 25.) The Lord Jesus knows how apt we are to doubt the Father's love. Therefore he said to his disciples, "The Father himself loveth you because ye have loved me, and have believed that I came out from God." Can the disciples have continued to look sad when they heard this sweet declaration from the lips of him who knew all the secrets of the Father's heart! Every one who loves Jesus may feel assured that the *Father loves him.* Even *earthly* parents love those who love their children. Though a person have no quality to recommend him, yet the mother's heart will be drawn towards him, if he love her child. How tenderly then must the Father of the Lord Jesus Christ love those who love his only Son!

Evening Scripture portion. Heb. X. *Access to the Father through Christ.*

JOHN XVI. 28 to end.—*Christ foretells that all his disciples will forsake him.*

WHAT caused the disciples to exclaim, "Lo, now thou speakest plainly, and speakest no proverb?" They had been greatly perplexed by hearing their Master say, "A little while, and ye shall not see me;" nor were they relieved from their perplexity till they heard him declare, "I leave the world, and go unto the Father." They had heard him say before, "I go unto the Father," but they could not understand the declaration till he said also, "I leave the world." Perhaps they now imagined he would leave the world in a fiery chariot, as Elijah did, and that they, like Elisha, should behold his glorious ascension. And so he did at length, but *first* he had to pass through the *darkest* valley of the shadow of death ever trod by man. The disciples were especially struck by their Lord knowing their difficulties, when they had never expressed them to *him.* They had only inquired among *themselves,* "What is this that he saith unto us?" Yet Jesus knew their perplexity and relieved it. Astonished at this display of his wisdom, they exclaimed, "Now we are sure that thou knowest *all* things, and needest not that any man should *ask* thee; by *this* we believe that thou camest forth from God." They believed in him before, but they *thought* they believed *more* now. In this they were mistaken; their faith, though *real,* was as *weak* as ever. *Warmth* of feeling does not prove strength of faith. What *does* prove it? As fire tries gold, so temptations try faith. Abraham's faith was tried by the command to offer Isaac as a sacrifice to God, and it was found *strong.* Afterwards the Lord said to this eminent believer, "Now I *know* that thou fearest me, because thou hast not withheld thy son, thine only son, from me." Jonah's faith was tried by the command to preach to the men of Nineveh, and it was found *weak:* for he fled from the presence of the Lord.

We cannot tell what is the strength of our faith till it is tried. We may imagine that we would give up brilliant prospects or encounter great dangers for the sake of Christ, and yet when the temptation comes we may be allured by some glittering toy, or terrified by the shaking of a leaf. "Let him that thinketh he standeth take heed lest he fall." A trial was coming on the disciples that showed they did not believe in their Lord so firmly as they supposed. In the hour of danger they left him alone. How must they have been grieved when they heard Jesus say, "Ye shall be scattered every man to his own, and shall leave me alone." Surely it would cause a child of God far more sorrow to know the sins he would commit than the sufferings he would endure.

But the Lord would not end this discourse with sorrowful words. The beginning of it was, "Let not your heart be troubled." The end was, "Be of good cheer, I have overcome the world." Jesus does not promise his people a *prosperous* life, but he does promise them a *peaceful* one. He says, "In the world ye shall have tribulation; but in *me* ye shall have peace." This is a mystery to the world, because they imagine that happiness arises from prosperous circumstances. It is true *their* happiness proceeds from nothing else; but the happiness of the people of God flows from a sense of forgiving love and a hope of eternal glory. This happiness is often greatest when earthly circumstances are the *least* prosperous. Therefore it is that in prison they have been heard to *sing*, and, even in the flames, seen to *smile*.

In the days of the Reformers, a husband and wife of the town of Perth, in Scotland, were condemned to die, but NOT *together—that* was esteemed too great a privilege. The woman took leave of her beloved partner in these words, "Husband, rejoice, for we have lived together many joyful days, but this day in which we must die ought to be most joyful unto us both, because we have joy forever. Therefore I will not bid you good-night; for we shall suddenly meet with joy in the kingdom of heaven." She was then led forth to be drowned, holding a little babe in her arms. After giving the infant into the nurse's care she sank beneath the suffocating waters.*

Evening Scripture portion. Habakkuk III. ***Rejoicing in God in affliction.***

JOHN XVII. 1–5.—*Christ begins to pray in the presence of his apostles.*

THE Lord Jesus often prayed with his disciples; but very few of his prayers are recorded. This is the *last* before his death that he offered up in their presence, and on their behalf. While they listened, they were filled with grief, for they feared it was the last. Jesus knew their feelings, and he avoided using any expressions that could increase their sorrow. When he speaks of his departure, instead of

* English Martyrology, vol. i. p. 151.

saying, "I die," he says, "I leave the world," "I go to the Father," or, "I come to thee." The compassionate Saviour sought to bind up the wounded hearts of his disciples. He is the tenderest of friends. If we go to Him in our troubles, we shall find him so. Many who *wish* to console do not know *how;* in attempting to bind up wounds they tear them open, but Jesus has a gentle *hand,* as well as a compassionate *heart.*

While consoling his disciples, he seems for a time to rise above his own afflictions. A little while *before,* at the supper-table, he was troubled in spirit; a little while *after,* in the garden, he was exceeding sorrowful; but during his solemn walk from Jerusalem to Gethsemane, he appeared to be filled with thoughts of his approaching glory.

He lifted up his eyes to heaven, and said, "Father, the hour is come; glorify thy Son, that thy Son also may glorify thee." With what feelings must he have lifted up his eyes to that heaven whence he came! He had seen its bright inhabitants, had heard its sweet songs, had breathed its pure air. O how he must have longed to take the wings of a dove, and to return to his rest! But first he must wade through a sea of sorrow. With meekness he says, "Father, the hour is come." And what is his petition: "Glorify thy Son." Afterwards he repeats that petition, and enlarges it, saying, "Now, O Father, glorify thou me with thine own self, with the glory which I had with thee *before the world began.*" (ver. 6.)

Our recollections cannot go back even to the *beginning* of our *own* short lives; but the thoughts of Jesus dwelt upon events that took place before the *foundation of the world.* He remembered the glory he once possessed in the bosom of the Father; he remembered the mighty reasons that caused him to leave it. His Father had entered into a covenant with Him: he had appointed him a *work,* and had promised him a *reward.* That *work* was the destruction of Satan. That *reward* was eternal life to be given to as many as the Father had given him. But had he *finished* the work? By faith he saw it as already finished; for though the most excruciating agonies still remained to be endured, yet he felt as if they were already past; so *short* the suffering appeared, and so *certain* the victory. And the reward would richly compensate for all the pangs of the cross. He would "see of the travail of his soul, and be satisfied." (Is. liii. 11.) His prayer was, "Glorify thy Son." The prayer will be answered through the ages of eternity, as the innumerable saints clothed in white robes with palms in their hands, cry with a loud voice, "Salvation to our God which sitteth upon the throne, and to THE LAMB." (Rev. vii. 10.)

It was *this* prospect which sustained the Saviour through all his sufferings. It was because of this "joy" set before him, that he "endured the cross, and despised the shame." (Heb. xii. 2.)

Evening Scripture portion. Is. LXIX. ***The covenant of the Father and the Son.***

JOHN XVII. 6–10.—*Christ speaks to his Father of his apostles.*

IT is very touching to hear a friend praying for us. The heart of a child is moved and melted while he hears a parent describe his case, and plead for him at the footstool of divine mercy. Are there not some of us who can remember such moments? How did the disciples feel when they heard their beloved Master speak of *them* to his Father; for they must have known it was of *them* he spake, when he said, "The men whom thou gavest me out of the world."

Are the apostles the *only* men that the Father has given to the Son? Blessed be his name, they are *not.* An innumerable multitude have been given to the Son, as the fruit of his infinite sufferings. St. Paul, in writing to the Ephesians, says, "Blessed be the God and Father of the Lord Jesus Christ, who hath blessed *us* with all spiritual blessings in heavenly places in Christ, according as he hath chosen *us* in him before the foundation of the world." Adam and Eve, by one sinful act, gave *themselves*, and all their children, to Satan; and the *whole* human race must have perished, had not the Father given to his Son a spiritual family. And that family is a *numerous* one; "that the abundant grace might through the thanksgiving of *many* redound to the glory of God." (2 Cor. iv. 15.)

The Lord Jesus watches over the men whom the Father has given him out of the world! Who would not water the plants, or nourish the lambs, that a beloved friend had intrusted to his care! Much more would he show kindness to his friend's *children* if they were left to his guardianship. But no guardian was ever so watchful, no teacher so patient, no nurse so tender as Jesus ever has been to the men whom the Father has given him out of the world. During the three years that he led the apostles from place to place, he forgot his own ease, his own pleasure, his own feelings, that he might instruct, and comfort, and edify them. When he was going to leave them, he could declare to his Father that he had faithfully discharged his trust. He said, "I have manifested thy name unto the men which thou gavest me out of the world." On the part of Jesus nothing had been wanting.

But what did Jesus say of his *apostles?* Did he declare to his Father how often they had doubted his power, repulsed his poor suppliants, and disputed with each other for honor and distinction? No; he said not one word *against* them. He was not their *accuser*, but their *intercessor*. He said, "They have kept thy word; they have believed that thou didst send me."

Many believers, who are now cast down, would be lifted up, if they could hear the prayers that Jesus is offering up for them at his Father's right hand. While they are lamenting their sins, their Saviour is speaking well of them before the throne. While they are saying, "Surely Jesus must be ashamed of us," He is saying, "I am glorified in them." If the change *already* wrought in their hearts brings glory to Jesus, how much more will their *perfection!* Could we see the diamond as it was found in the mine, we should know how to appreciate the jeweller's skill. How unlike is the dull and rough stone to the gem that shines with liquid lustre in the monarch's crown! But not so unlike as the one dark, polluted, guilty soul, is to the pure and bright spirit now rejoicing in the presence of Jesus. When millions of such happy beings surround the throne, with what rapture will their Saviour say, "I am glorified in them." To have rescued those souls from the pit of hell, and to have washed them from the pollution of sin, will bring more glory to Jesus than to have created the innumerable worlds that fill the boundless regions of space.

Evening Scripture portion. Heb. VIII. *The great High Priest.*

JOHN XVII. 11–19.—*Christ prays for his apostles.*

BEFORE the Lord Jesus offered up any petition for his disciples, he presented their case to his Father. He described the desolate situation in which they would soon be left. "And now I am no more in the world, but these are in the world, and I come to thee." Before we pray for our friends, it is well to consider their circumstances, and to spread them before the Lord. By doing this, we are enabled to offer up prayers *suited* to their wants. Our indolent minds are often content with saying, "Bless my friend, my father, and my child;" but we ought to inquire *what* blessing each of them appears to stand most in need of, and to ask for *that.*

What was the petition which the Saviour made for his disciples? It was this: "Keep through thine own name those whom thou hast given me, that they may be one, as we are." When the disciples heard this prayer, must they not have been reminded of their frequent contentions? How lately they had disputed which should be greatest! But their Lord did not ask that any of them might be made great, but that *all* might be *kept,* and be made *one.* God is love, and every one that loveth is born of God. God cannot make his creatures happy without teaching them *first* to love each other. The Father answered his Son's petition, and knit the hearts of the apostles together in one. We read of no more contentions among them. During the time their Lord lay in his grave, they mingled their tears together; when he appeared to them after his resurrection, they were assembled in *one* room; and after he had ascended, they continued with *one* accord in prayers and supplications.

It is the design of Jesus that all his people shall live together forever and ever. None of them could bear the idea of *not* dwelling with their Lord. They must, therefore, dwell *together*. It is sad to think that even true believers sometimes disagree when living for a little while beneath the same roof. Ah, did they but remember that they will live *forever* in their Father's house, they could never harbor one unkind thought.

Jesus offered up another petition: "I pray not that thou shouldest take them out of the world, but that thou shouldest keep them from the evil." The disciples longed to be taken out of this world, now their Master was going to leave it! But they had a great work to perform in it. They were to seek those that were lost, even as Jesus had sought them. It is natural for believers to desire to leave this world. He whom they love best has left it, and they long to be where he is. But what would become of the world, if all the servants of Christ were taken out of it? The *Sabbath* would return, but no faithful minister would entreat sinners to flee from the wrath to come; the *Bible* might be opened, but no pious friend would press the truth home upon the conscience of the heedless reader; *death* would come, but none would point the departing soul to Christ, or, kneeling by his bedside, would implore mercy in the last hour.

Are there any who say, "I would cheerfully remain in this world, were it not for the sin that continually harasses me?" Has the Holy Spirit taught you to hate sin? Be comforted, the Saviour has prayed that you may be kept from this evil. He said, "I pray not that thou shouldest take them out of this world, but that thou shouldest keep them from the evil." Your desire was once expressed by a little child, when conversing with his playmates. The question was proposed, "What is the thing you wish for most?" Several children said they would like to have nice or pretty things. But when it came to the turn of this little boy of ten years old to speak, he said, "I wish to live without sinning." This was not a mere empty profession, for the child showed by his conduct that he hated sin.

Evening Scripture portion. Rom. VIII. ***The believer's hatred of sin.***

JOHN XVII. 20 to end.—*Christ prays for all who shall believe on him.*

WE esteem it a privilege to hear the prayers of eminent saints, especially in their dying hours. How invaluable is the blessing we enjoy in possessing the record of this prayer of the Son of God! The apostles must have listened to each sentence with the deepest interest. Their tears may have flowed fast while their Master was praying, but those tears must have been less bitter than before. What comfort it must have given them to hear Jesus offer up this petition, "Father, I will that those whom thou hast given me be with me where I am!" They desired earnestly to be with him. How grieved they were, when at the supper-table they heard him say, "Whither I go ye cannot come." Afterwards Jesus softened the hardness of the saying by telling Peter, "Whither I go, thou canst not follow me *now*, but thou shalt follow me *afterwards*." Now they heard him pray that they might all be with him, and they saw plainly that he DESIRED to have them with him.

And was it for *them alone* he prayed? No; he has *not* left us *in doubt* on this subject. He said, "Neither pray I for these ALONE, but for them also which shall believe on me through their word." When he uttered this petition, he had in his thoughts *every* creature who ever has believed in him—who ever *shall* believe in him; not one so weak, so young, so mean, as to be forgotten. The *little child* who in dying should lisp, with *loving* heart, its Saviour's words, "Suffer little children to come unto me;"—the *diseased beggar* who, as he lay on his pallet, should exclaim with lively faith, "Come, Lord Jesus;"—yes, even the condemned criminal, who on his way to the scaffold, with *true penitence* should smite on his breast and say, "Lord, be merciful to me a sinner;"—each of these was remembered by the Son of God, when he said, "Neither pray I for these alone, but for them also which shall believe on me through their word."

And does not each of us hope that *he* was included in this petition? If we believe in Jesus, if we ever *shall* believe in him, we were included in it. And if he prayed for us *then*, he prays for us *now;* for he has never ceased to intercede for all believers. If any one thinks in his heart, "What a comfort it would be to me to know that my Saviour prayed for me," let him ask himself this question, "Do I pray for *myself?*" All who believe in Jesus, pray to the Father in *his* name. They ask for the *very things* that he asked for. He said, "Father, I will that they also whom thou hast given me be with me where I am." Is this *our* desire?—Is this *our* prayer? Do we ever ask the Father to let us live forever with him, that we may behold the glory of Jesus? There are many who desire to go to heaven that they may escape from pain and grief; but only those who believe in Jesus desire to behold his glory. And HE desires that they shall behold it, and he PRAYS that they *may*. Can HIS prayer be refused? Impossible. When Jesus shall be seated on his throne of glory, and shall survey the vast multitude of the redeemed, he will know if any one of them is missing. He has loved each, he has died for each, he has prayed for each; he could not forget ONE. He would not be satisfied, if one were absent. It may be that we have loved him but a *little while*, a few *years*, or only a few DAYS; but *he* loved *us* before the foundation of the world. *Our* prayers to him have been short, and feeble; but *his* prayers for us were offered up before we were born, and ever since we were born. While we sleep he prays; and even when we sin he prays. "He *ever* liveth to make intercession for them that come unto God by him."

Evening Scripture portion. Ps. LXXXIX. ***The blessedness of the children of Christ.***

LUKE XXII. 39–46.—*The Redeemer's agony in the garden.*

WAS there ever any sight, since the beginning of the world, so wonderful, so affecting, as the Prince of life passing through the valley of the shadow of death! Can the angels have continued their songs during that awful night? They were deeply interested in all that befell their beloved Lord. One of their number was sent from heaven to strengthen him. What must that honored angel have felt when he approached the earth, and beheld HIM who filled heaven with his glory, lying prostrate on the ground, and bathed in his own blood! But did he attempt to persuade the Lord to *renounce* his purpose of saving man? Did he say, "Why suffer so much for that polluted and apostate race?" Ah, no! he strengthened him. We cannot tell what words he spoke, but we may be sure they breathed love towards fallen man, and sympathy with his suffering Lord. Perhaps he spoke of the lake of fire, into which all men must sink if the Son of God should give up the work of redemption. Or perhaps he spoke of the joys redeemed saints shall taste through eternal ages, because he would persevere in his mighty undertaking. But, more than all, he must have spoken of the glory that would redound to God his Father, through the salvation of sinners. *Hereafter* we may know every particular concerning our Lord's last conflict.

But do we ask what was the *cause* of our Saviour's agony? Was it the fear of the *bodily* pangs of death? Surely the Son of God possessed more courage than man. Fear of *bodily* anguish could not have overwhelmed the Captain of the hosts of the Lord. He himself told his disciples the *cause*, when he said, "Hereafter I shall not talk much with you, for the prince of this world cometh." (John xiv. 30.) The cause of his sufferings was, the assault of the prince of darkness. Hell came to meet him in the garden of Gethsemane. Satan, who had been defeated in the wilderness, returned with his legions, to make a last attack. When Jesus sweat great drops of blood, he was struggling with principalities and powers. His foot was lifted up to crush the serpent's head, and his heel was in his jaws. His weapon of defence was prayer. Prayer was his sword, his shield, and his helmet.

And why did the Father permit Satan to attack his well-beloved Son? Because He had sent his Son to be the Saviour of the world; therefore He laid upon him the iniquity of us *all*, and inflicted the

punishment due to us all. Those who believe in Jesus can never suffer the punishment due to their sins, because Jesus has suffered it in their stead. They *may*, they *will suffer*, but it will not be to *atone* for their sins. Jesus has *atoned* for them. Criminals cannot be punished twice for the *same* offence: Jesus has suffered the punishment of *all* the sins of *all* his people. Their sufferings are not *penalties*, inflicted by a *judge*, but *chastenings*, bestowed by a *father*. When they pass through the valley of the shadow of death, Satan may *assault* them, but he cannot *distress* them *as* he distressed their Lord. Many believers have passed through that dark valley, singing as they went, and have expired almost without a struggle or a sigh.

"Jesus can make a dying bed
Feel soft as downy pillows are,
While on his breast I lean my head,
And breathe my life out sweetly there."
Watts.

But what will become of those who neglect this great salvation? They will drink of the cup of wrath. What a cup it is! "Deep and large: it containeth much." (Ez. xxiii. 32.) God says to the wicked, "Thou shalt even drink it, and suck it out." And why? "Because thou hast forgotten me, and cast my words behind thy back." He is a wicked man who forgets the Saviour, and casts his promises of pardon behind his back.

Evening Scripture portion. Heb. V. *The prayers and tears of Christ.*

MATT. XXVI. 36–46.—*The disciples sleep instead of watching.*

WITH what feelings the pious traveller now views the spot where his Saviour suffered excruciating pangs! It lies just beyond the gates of Jerusalem, in a narrow and gloomy valley. The tall steep rocks on which the temple formerly stood shade *one* side of the vale, and the gentle sloping sides of Mount Olivet the *other*. The stream of Kedron flows between, though in summer its bed is dry. A bridge is placed over it, and a narrow path leads to Gethsemane. This garden covers about an acre of land, and is enclosed by a low stone wall. Eight olive-trees may still be seen casting their broad shadows over that earth which once received the precious drops of the Saviour's blood. They are ancient trees of immense size; their roots have burst the soil, and form resting-places for those who come here to sit and muse. None who visit Gethsemane can wonder that the Saviour oft resorted thither, for it seems a meet place for meditation and for prayer.

At the entrance of this garden the suffering Redeemer left eight of his apostles: the other three he chose as the witnesses of his agony. They were the three that had been the witnesses of his *glory* on the Mount of transfiguration. No doubt he had designed to prepare them by that enchanting sight for the awful scene of Gethsemane. Had they not beheld his countenance when it shone as the sun, their faith might have been shaken by the sight of his face marred with anguish, and bathed in blood.

These apostles must have esteemed it an *honor* to accompany their Lord to his sorrowful retreat; but this honor proved to be the occasion of their *humiliation.* Though they had said they would *die* with him, they failed to *watch* with their suffering Master, even for one hour. Three times *he* rose from *prayer* to rouse *them* from *sleep.* How gentle his reproof! "Could ye not watch with me one hour?" How wise his caution, "The spirit truly is willing, but the flesh is weak." He knew what sharp trials were coming upon them, therefore he said, "Pray that ye enter not into temptation." How often shall we find, when we look back upon our past lives, that we received *warnings* before we fell into sin. The remembrance of these warnings makes us feel that we are *without excuse*, and that we are guilty in the sight of God.

What a precious opportunity these apostles lost of showing love to their Master by watching with him in the garden! *We* never can enjoy such a privilege; but though we cannot watch with Jesus *himself*, we may watch with his suffering members. He will consider sympathy shown to *them*, as shown to *himself*. Among his people there are many in deep sorrow. Some are harassed by the sore temptations of Satan; many are persecuted by wicked men, and many more are suffering under heavy bereavements and painful diseases, inflicted by the hand of God. With *these* let us watch; with *these* let us sympathize; with *their* infirmities let us be touched, and in their afflictions let us be afflicted. He who once said to Saul, when he *persecuted* his people, "Why persecutest thou *me?*" will say to those who *comfort* his people, "Thou hast watched with *me.*"

Evening Scripture portion. Psalm LXXXVIII. ***The desolation of Christ.***

MATT. XXVI. 47–50.—*Judas betrays his Master.*

IT is impossible to conceive a greater crime than Judas committed when he betrayed his Master. It would have been a cruel act to deliver a *stranger* into the hands of his enemies; but Judas betrayed the kindest Friend, and the most generous Benefactor. Had he committed the deed *openly*, his sin would have been atrocious, but he did it *secretly*, and even covered it with a veil of love. What could have induced him to fix upon a token of affection as the sign by which to point out his Master to his foes? Did he hope to deceive his *Lord?* Surely he must have known that he was already detected by *him:* for when he had once dared to ask, "Is it I?" Jesus had replied, "Thou hast said." But he may have hoped to deceive his *fellow-apostles*. He may not have heard his Master say to one of them, "He that dippeth his hand with me in the dish, the same shall betray me."

The Lord, however, would not suffer him to imagine he had escaped detection. He said, "Friend, (or companion,) wherefore art thou come? Why betrayest thou the Son of man with a kiss?" Did the Lord's gentle appeal melt his cruel heart? O no; that heart had already resisted the strongest expressions of divine love. Judas had seen the Lord of all, girded with a towel, bending low, and washing his disciples' feet. He had felt the touch of those sacred hands around his *own* feet, around *those* feet that had already been swift to shed innocent and precious blood. He had witnessed the trouble of his spirit, when he said, "One of *you* shall betray me." He who could resist *such* expressions of love, was past feeling.

And did the Lord of glory suffer the traitor's lips to touch his holy cheeks? Did heaven suffer hell to draw near, and God permit Satan to approach? In this behavior, he set us an example of perfect patience. No *greater* provocation can be conceived, than that which Judas gave to the Lord. Not one of us can presume to say that *he* ever received *so* great a provocation. When we feel disposed to think that any creature has treated us with unheard-of ingratitude, and inconceivable treachery, let us remember Judas.

There are some who behave to Jesus *now* He is in *heaven*, as Judas did when *He* was upon *earth*. When it seems to be their interest to appear to love him, they put on the mask of piety; but when they can gain worldly advantages by betraying his servants, they will do it, and yet all the time continue to observe the forms of religion. They do not consider how much their guilt is increased by their acts of apparent devotion. God reproached Israel with similar hypocrisy, saying, "When they had slain their children to their idols, then they came the *same* day into my sanctuary to profane it." (Ez. xxiii. 39.) Satan employs such persons to do his darkest deeds. Let *all* who, while they hear the gospel, yet remain unconverted, fear, lest they should ever become hardened in wickedness, and be driven to commit actions which they cannot *now* bear to think of. But if we love Christ, then we are sure we can never act the part of Judas. We may be tempted in some evil hour to *forsake* our Lord, yes, even to *deny* him, but we never *shall*, we never *can*, deliberately *betray* him.

Evening Scripture portion. Ps. LV. *The treachery of Judas.*

JOHN XVIII. 1–9.—*The enemies of Christ fall to the ground.*

How awful was the prospect that lay before the Saviour when he went forth to meet his enemies! If *we*, before we passed through our light afflictions, knew all we should be called to endure, how often our minds would shrink back appalled! After having experienced bitter sufferings, we feel that had we known *beforehand* their minute particulars, we should have been overwhelmed with the prospect. But Jesus knew every minute circumstance of *his* approaching sufferings. He knew the pangs each nail would give his feeble body, and the grief each scornful speech would create in his sensitive heart. And, above all, he knew the horror that the guilt of our sins would cause his spotless soul. He might have escaped from all these torments; but he willingly gave himself up into the hands of his foes.

At the words, "I am he," his enemies went backward and fell to the ground. "The voice of the Lord breaketh the cedars; the voice of the Lord shaketh the wilderness." (Ps. xxix.) The voice of Jesus, though so *gentle* that little children were not afraid to hear it, was so *powerful* that it broke the strength of his stubborn foes, and shook their stout hearts. His disciples had once been cheered in the storm by hearing their Master say, "It is I;" but his enemies were struck to the ground by the words, "I am he." There is an *attractive* power in the voice of Jesus. Those who love him feel it. When he says, "Come unto me," they draw near. There is also a *repellent* power in his voice. His enemies will feel it at the last day, when he shall utter the word "Depart." Then they will go backward, and fall into the pit of destruction.

What must have been the feelings of the apostles, when they beheld their enemies fallen on the ground! If they rejoiced for a *moment*, they must have been the more disappointed to see them rise again. Yet even *then* they did not forsake their Master; they intended to cleave closely to his side through all his troubles. But *he* knew their weakness, though *they* did not: He knew they were not yet strong enough to confess his name before princes; therefore he took the opportunity, when his enemies were scarcely recovered from their consternation, to make this request: "If ye seek *me*, let *these* go their way." The disciples cannot have understood the deep meaning of these words. When Jesus washed Peter's feet, he said, "What I do, thou knowest not *now;* but thou shalt know *hereafter*." The disciples knew afterwards that they were washed in the Saviour's blood; they also knew *afterwards* that Jesus was *bound*, that they might be forever *free*. If he had not surrendered himself to his enemies, *we* must have remained forever the prisoners of Satan.

In the Saviour's last prayer with his disciples, he said to his Father, "Of them which thou gavest me, have I lost none." How did he preserve them? By his love, his wisdom, and his power. Love alone would not have been sufficient to keep them in safety. Jacob was a loving shepherd, but he acknowledged he had lost some of his flock; for when defending his own character to Laban, he said, "That which was torn of beasts I brought not unto thee; I bare the loss of it; of my hand didst thou require it, whether stolen by day, or stolen by night." (Gen. xxxi. 39.) A human shepherd cannot preserve his flock from evil accidents. But Jesus had *wisdom* to foresee the approach of every enemy, and had *power* to secure his disciples from overwhelming temptations. At this moment he foresees all the temptations that will assail us. Are we the sheep of his pasture? Do we hear his voice, and follow him? Then we shall be shielded from every fatal danger; then we may say with the apostle Paul, "The Lord shall deliver me from every evil work, and will preserve me unto his heavenly kingdom." (2 Tim. iv. 18.)

Evening Scripture portion.
Ps. XXVII. XXVIII. *The consternation of Christ's enemies.*

MATT. XXVI. 51–54.—*Peter cuts off the ear of the high priest's servant.*

WHAT must have been the dismay of the apostles, when they beheld their Master in the hands of his enemies! We cannot wonder that one of them drew his sword to attack the high priest's servant. We might have *conjectured* that it was *Peter* who committed the rash deed; but we are not left to *uncertainty* on this point. St. John informs us that it was Peter. Perhaps as the other evangelists wrote their gospels during the lifetime of that apostle, they were afraid of exposing him to danger by revealing his name; whereas John, who (it is supposed) wrote his account after Peter's death, had no inducement to conceal it.

It is evident that Peter had misunderstood his Lord, when at the supper-table he had heard him say, "He that hath no sword, let him sell his garment, and buy one." Had Jesus intended that his disciples should fight, he would not have reproved Peter's rashness by saying, "Put up again thy sword into his place; for all they that take the sword shall perish by the sword." These words contained not only a *reproof*, but also a *prophecy* of the awful calamities that would befall the wicked men who were now wielding swords against their rightful king, the Son of God. No doubt Peter was astonished to find that his conduct was disapproved by his Master. He must have thought that Jesus would be pleased to see that, instead of forsaking and denying him, he was ready to fight for him against an armed multitude. When he had boasted of his fidelity, he little thought in what *form* temptation would come upon him. The sight of the murderous band did not terrify him so much as the words of the maiden in the high priest's palace.

God alone knows what circumstances would prove the most trying to each of us; for He alone knows what is in each of our *hearts*. We may have surmounted some temptations that appear very great, and yet be overcome by others that seem less formidable. None are safe, but those who, putting no trust in their own hearts, wait continually on the Lord for light and strength.

How *useless* were Peter's attempts to defend his Lord! Had Jesus but spoken the word, each of his enemies had been the captive of a mighty angel, and he himself again seated upon his throne of light. Had he called upon his Father, more than seventy thousand angels had come flying to his rescue. Yet he forbore to speak the word. And why? He gave the reason—"How then shall the Scriptures be fulfilled, that thus it must be?" His Father from the beginning had declared, that he would provide a sacrifice for the sins of men. To fulfil every word that his Father had spoken, was the glorious work of the Son of God.

St. John records a most affecting expression that he used on this occasion: "The cup which my Father hath given me, shall I not drink it?" Shall *we* be enabled in the day of *our* trouble to utter these words? Yet if we are his children, the Father will never give us so bitter a cup to drink, as he gave to his well-beloved Son. That cup was bitter, because it contained his wrath against our sins. But every cup that God gives to his children *now*, is sweetened by his love; for he has said, "As many as I love, I rebuke and chasten." No human mind can conceive what that cup contained which Jesus drank for our sakes. Lost spirits know its taste; for it is written of them, "The same shall drink of the wine of the wrath of God, which is poured out without mixture in the cup of his indignation." (Rev. xiv. 10.) But the redeemed shall never taste it. Has Jesus forgiven us our sins? Then our cup may contain pain, or poverty, bereavement, imprisonment, or death, but not one drop of the wrath of God. Let us take it thankfully from our Father's hand; and though tears may stream down our cheeks, and sobs almost choke our voice, let us say, "The cup which my Father hath given me, shall I not drink it?"

Evening Scripture portion. Rev. XIII: *The sword.*

Luke XXII. 50–53.—*Christ heals the servant's ear.*

It is remarkable that though *all* the four evangelists mention the circumstance of Peter's cutting off the servant's ear, yet that St. Luke alone relates how it was healed. It seems that this miracle was the *last* the Saviour performed. In one respect it was the *greatest*. No doubt the Lord's *power* was more fully displayed when the dead were raised; but his *grace* was most gloriously manifested when his *enemy* was healed. Multitudes had often surrounded him, entreating him with piteous cries to restore their blind parents to sight, and their sick children to health. But *this* multitude came, *not* to *entreat*, but to *assault*. Yet the gracious Saviour healed even one of this wicked company.

What effect had this merciful act upon the heart of Malchus? Is it possible that *he* could join that night in the cry, "Crucify him!" that *he* could see with cruel joy the nails thrust through the hand that had touched his bleeding ear? It is *possible*, though we hope that Malchus was not guilty of such ingratitude. The heart of man is so hard by nature that no mercy can melt it. There are many now living who have received greater deliverances from the hand of God than Malchus, and who yet continue to rebel against their Saviour. Till the Holy Ghost softens the heart, man remains the enemy of God.

How ungrateful were that multitude with whom Jesus had spent the last week of his life! He seemed to feel their ingratitude when he said, "I was daily with you teaching in the temple." How can we account for the conduct of man towards the Redeemer? The Scriptures reveal the secret. It was Satan who first set man against his best friend; and it is *Satan* who still keeps up this enmity. Therefore Jesus said to his enemies, "This is your hour, and the power of darkness." As long as the heart is under the influence of Satan, it resists both the most awful judgments and the most melting mercies. The following fact is an instance of this truth.

A young missionary, named Felix Carey, once resided in the Burmese empire. The viceroy who governed the province in which he dwelt, was remarkable for inflicting very barbarous punishments upon criminals who had committed very slight offences. On one occasion the missionary beheld a poor creature suspended to a cross by red-hot nails. Deeply touched with compassion, he went to the palace to plead for the release of the sufferer. Though he knew that the viceroy had forbidden, on pain of death, intercession to be made for criminals, he was not deterred from pleading the cause of the unhappy man. At first he received a peremptory refusal; but he continued to entreat, and even declared that he would not leave the palace till he had obtained the boon he craved. By importunity he prevailed. He received an order for the criminal's release. He hastened to the cross. The man had hung there seven hours, and when taken down had scarcely strength to thank his deliverer. The missionary took him to his own home, and nursed him with tender care. In a fortnight the wounded man was able to stand, and at length completely recovered. Did he attend to the instructions of his benefactor? Did he devote his life to his service? No, he even robbed the man who had risked his own life to save his. The agonies of a cross were not sufficient to root out the love of sin; nor the tender compassion that had been shown him to plant the love of holiness in his heart. Can we suppose that the pains of hell will make lost spirits better than they were when first they entered their dark abode? O no; pain cannot change the heart. If God were to release those souls after a thousand years of suffering, they would still be unfit to join in the songs of heaven, and to stand in the presence of the Most Holy. How shall our evil hearts be made better? The Spirit of God, by applying the blood of Jesus, can take away all their hardness. The preaching of the Gospel cannot *alone* soften them. If it could, those whom Jesus daily taught, would not have conspired against him. Let us ask the Father for the Holy Spirit to convert us, if we are *not* converted; and if we are, to make us know more of the love of Christ, and to live more to His glory.

Evening Scripture portion. Judges II. *Incorrigible wickedness.*

MARK XIV. 51–54.—*A young man follows Christ.*

THERE are many who have become known to us only on account of their having had something to do with Jesus. We should never have heard of this young man, if he had not followed him this terrible night. It was a moment never to be forgotten, when he heard the tumult, and determined to go and see what it was. It appears that he loved the Lord, and desired to be with him in the hour of danger and disgrace. But when the enemies laid hold of him his courage failed, and leaving his covering in their hands, he fled for his life. This circumstance gives us a lively idea of the terror that prevailed among the friends of Jesus. Those who had a little while before clung closely to his side, were now afraid to be known as his disciples.

This was the case with Peter. He followed Jesus afar off—*so* far off, that he hoped none of the enemies would perceive that he was following him at all. When he saw his Master enter into the palace of the high priest, it appears that he longed to enter also. But there was a damsel who kept the door, and she would not suffer strangers to pass. However, a way was opened for the entrance of this affectionate disciple. Another disciple, who was known to the high priest, obtained leave to admit Peter. We know not who this man was. Some think it was John, because he alone mentions that it was through another disciple that Peter gained admission into the palace. Others suppose that none but a man of rank could have obtained so great a privilege for a stranger. Whoever it was, it is evident that he did not *tell* the doorkeeper that Peter was a disciple of Jesus.

Had the apostle, when he ventured into the palace, known what a crime he would commit within those walls, he would have shrunk back with horror. We cannot tell when we enter a place, whether we shall afterwards look back with sorrow or with joy upon our visit there. Any place where we have grievously sinned against the Lord must afterwards be regarded with mournful feelings.

Was Peter wrong to enter the palace? Had Peter gone there openly to defend or comfort his Master, his conduct would have been noble and courageous: but he went *secretly* to see the end. He endeavored to conceal who he was. This attempt prepared the way for his shameful fall. How could he sit by the fire, warming himself, while his Master stood exposed to the insults of his enemies! How was it that his sobs and tears did not betray who he was?

We are taught to pray, "Lord, lead us not into temptation." It is a dangerous thing to mix with the ungodly. Whenever duty calls us to enter their abodes, we should arm ourselves beforehand by earnest prayer. While we are among them we should keep watching and looking to Jesus for strength. Our conduct will soon show that we are his disciples. If the conversation turn upon worldly gayeties, can we appear interested in it? If a profane jest be made, can we join in the laugh? If a servant of God be spoken against, can we refrain from defending his character? And if the name of Jesus be blasphemed, can we conceal our grief and indignation? When Henry Martyn, the missionary, conversed with the learned men of Persia, he heard them blaspheme that holy name. He could not conceal the anguish that he felt. Even the heathens themselves, when they beheld it, were touched as well as astonished. They saw that he really loved Jesus.

Evening Scripture portion. 1 Cor. X. *Temptation.*

JOHN XVIII. 19–24.—*An officer strikes Jesus with the palm of his hand.*

THERE are some acts of love done to the Son of God, recorded in the Scriptures to the everlasting *honor* of those who did them. We count *her* blessed who washed the Redeemer's feet with her tears; and Mary also, who anointed his head with ointment; and Joseph and Nicodemus, who wrapped his body in fine linen; and the little company of women who brought spices to the sepulchre. Even the man who lent him the ass on which he rode, and he who lent him the room in which he supped, acquired honor by these acts of kindness.

But there are some deeds of *malice* recorded in Scripture, to the everlasting *shame* of those who perpetrated them. Such was the deed of the man who struck with the palm of his hand the Lord of glory.

Had Jesus been merely a *common* prisoner, it would have been ungenerous to strike him when his hands were *bound*. But though the officer may not have known that he was the Son of God, he must have been aware that he was no *common* prisoner. He must have heard of his works of mercy and of power. What could have been his motive for inflicting a profane blow? Was it to please the high priest? Caiaphas encouraged wickedness in his servants. *He* had given the counsel that it was expedient that one man should die for the people. He was accountable for all the injuries inflicted upon the Saviour from the time of his apprehension to the moment of his death, for he was the proposer of the whole scheme. But *every one* who had a share in those awful transactions will have to answer for *their* part, *except* they afterwards repented of their deeds. *Some* who with wicked hands slew the Saviour, were afterwards pricked in their heart at the preaching of Peter on the day of Pentecost. Who can tell but that this officer was found among those penitents? He may have washed his guilty hand as white as snow in the precious blood of the Lamb; for that blood cleanseth from *all* sin. *If so*, with what anguish he must have looked back upon the insult he had once offered to the Son of God! But if he never did repent, his daring act remains recorded, not only in the Scriptures, but also in the book of God's remembrance.

Sinners have not *now* the opportunity of *striking* the Lord of glory: their puny arms cannot reach his exalted throne. But they can show their contempt and hatred by scoffing at his word, and persecuting his people. There are many insults offered every day to the Son of God. And why does he not avenge those insults? Because his hands, though no longer bound with *cord*, are restrained by *love*. He is long-suffering to us-ward, not willing that any should perish, but that all should come to repentance.

Some persecutors have died rejoicing in those wicked deeds on account of which they were going to be eternally condemned. It is recorded of a Roman Catholic Bishop of London, named Stokesley, that on his death-bed he gloried in having assisted at the burning of fifty men, whom *he* called *heretics*, but whom *we* call *martyrs*. In the same awful state of mind the holy apostle Paul *would* have died, had not God shown mercy to him when a blasphemer, and a persecutor; he would have died exulting in the recollection of the day when the blood of Stephen was shed, and when he was standing by consenting unto his death: for at that time he thought he was doing God service by making havoc of his church. But "the grace of the Lord was exceeding abundant with faith, and love which is in Christ Jesus." (1 Tim. i. 14.) Saul heard a voice from heaven, saying, "Why persecutest thou me?" It was the same voice that once had said on *earth* to another persecutor, "Why smitest thou me?" The words from heaven were accompanied by the power of the Holy Spirit, and they subdued the man, breathing out threatenings and slaughter. God has sometimes displayed his almighty power, not only in conquer ing the most daring *offenders*, but in conquering them in their most daring *moods*. When their sins seemed to have reached the highest point, and to have broken out with the greatest violence, then his powerful hand has laid them low at the foot of the cross.

Evening Scripture portion. 1 Tim. I. *Conversion of a persecutor.*

MATT. XXVI. 59–66.—*The false witnesses.*

THOSE who are bent on doing evil often wish to keep up the *appearance* of good. The high priest did not say to his colleagues, "Let us condemn the prisoner untried." No: but he secretly sought *false* witness against him. When the world desire to injure a saint, they invent excuses for treating him ill, they encourage his enemies to speak against him, and they easily find some who will gratify their wishes. Though Jesus had spent his life in relieving the miserable, yet there were many willing to bear false witness against him. How then can the servants of God expect to escape the breath of slander? God may sometimes see fit to preserve them from evil reports; but generally he appoints them a share in the reproaches that fell on his well-beloved Son.

It was difficult to find two false witnesses whose testimony agreed together; and it was contrary to the Jewish law to condemn a prisoner on that of *one* alone. At length two appeared whose testimony was accepted. They repeated words *very much like* some Jesus had really uttered, but they gave them a sense which he had never intended to convey, and therefore they are called "*false* witnesses."

Those who attribute motives to others, without being able to *prove* what they say, are "false witnesses." It is a very *common* sin to bear false witness, and yet it is a very *great* one. It is the *worst* form of lying. It is mentioned in the ninth commandment, because it is the *greatest* sin of the *kind*. He who would bear false witness would tell *any* other lie.

Who can but shudder at the thought of the guilt of these two false witnesses! Ungrateful men! they had heard the words of Jesus only to distort them, and to bring them against him in the hour of his sorrow. But the guilt of the high priest towers far above even their guilt. He displayed a show of justice, by appearing to grant Jesus an opportunity of defending himself. He said, "What is it which these witness against thee?" But the divine prisoner held his peace, for he knew his condemnation was already determined.

Had he refused to answer the *next* question, how much his enemies would have triumphed! When the high priest said, "Tell me whether thou be the Christ, the Son of God?" *then* the Lord declared plainly that he was. He would not suffer the shadow of a doubt to rest upon his divinity. He is equal with God. He and the Father are one. Jesus did not tell the wicked Caiaphas that he was come to *die* for him; but he did tell him that he would come again to *judge* him. When he spoke of himself as Judge, he called himself the *Son of man.* It seems as if he would prepare Caiaphas for beholding that same human form that now stood *bound* before him, clothed with power, and enthroned in light.

We have never seen Jesus. We cannot conceive how he looked when he was upon earth. But what will be the feelings of those who knew him and who hated him, when they see the *face* once so marred, shining with glorious lustre, and adorned with the diadem of the universe!

Evening Scripture portion. Ps. XXXV. *False witnesses.*

Luke XXII. 63–65.—*The servants of the High Priest insult Christ.*

The most remarkable night that has been known since the beginning of the world, was the night before the crucifixion of the Lord. It is written concerning the night on which the children of Israel left Egypt—that it is a night to be much observed to the Lord. But *this* night was far more memorable than the night of the Passover. *Then* all the *first-born* of Egypt were slain; but *now* the *first-born* of *God* was betrayed, accused, condemned, and insulted.

That was a memorable night, when the angels appeared to the shepherds of Bethlehem, to announce the birth of the holy Babe. *Then* angels *rejoiced*, but now angels must have wept, *if* angels *can* weep.

We are looking forward to another night, in which there will be both weeping and rejoicing. When the Son of God comes again, it will be night to half the inhabitants of the world. What terror some will feel, when the last trump rouses them from their slumbers!

Let us look back upon the transactions of that awful night which Jesus passed in the palace of the high priest. Human nature never displayed its deformity in a more glaring manner than at that season. Satan must have recognised in man every feature of his own character, and have seen that he was indeed his son. But insults could not degrade the Son of God. Sin *alone* degrades. The grossest insults, borne with meekness, exalt, instead of degrading. How glorious the Son of God appears, surrounded, *not* by worshippers but tormentors; yet bearing all their taunts with divine patience! "When he was reviled, he reviled not again; when he suffered, he threatened not, but committed himself unto him that judgeth righteously." (1 Peter iii. 23.) He regarded every injury as a drop in the cup his Father had given him to drink. He knew the prophecies that had been made concerning his sufferings: "They shall smite the judge of Israel with a rod upon the cheek." (Micah v. 1.)

"I gave my back to the smiters, and my cheeks to them that plucked off the hair; I hid not my face from shame and spitting." (Is. l. 6.)

Could *we* receive all that happened to us as the appointment of God, we should not be so easily provoked as we often are. Yet the malice of our enemies could never be vented against us, except by the decree of God.

There was an ingenuity in the torments inflicted on Jesus, worthy of Satan, their author. Perhaps there was a burst of applause, when it was first proposed to blindfold those meek and sorrowful eyes, and no doubt a profane laugh was heard, as each blow was struck, and the question asked, "Who smote thee?" How much astonished those men would have been, had Jesus told them who had smitten him! They little thought how well he knew their names; but they will find hereafter that he *did* know who struck him that night. *Many other* things blasphemously spake they against him, though only a *few* of their blasphemies are recorded as a specimen of the rest.

When we think of the greatness of the Son of God, and then reflect upon the indignities he endured, the mind is filled with wonder. Though saints have been praising him, age after age, for the love he displayed in their redemption; though their chorus is continually increasing, and though their song will never cease, yet sufficient honor can never be done to our crucified Saviour.

Evening Scripture portion. Is. L. *Insults offered to Christ.*

MARK XIV. 66 to end.—*Peter denies Christ.*

Is there any one who loves the Lord, who has read Peter's history without trembling? Who would have believed that so affectionate a disciple should prove so faithless in the hour of trial! But man, even when renewed by divine grace, is liable to fall. Though his *spirit* is made willing to obey, the *flesh* still inclines him to sin. The apostle Paul declares, "For I delight in the law of God, after the *inward* man; but I see *another* law in my *members*, warring against the law of my *mind*." (Rom. vii. 22, 23.) There is also a tempter always going about as a roaring lion, seeking whom he may devour.

The fall of Peter is related by all the four evangelists, and some peculiar circumstances are mentioned by each.

The *first* denial was made while Peter stood by the fire, in the palace. The damsel who kept the door accused him of being a disciple. Peter, taken by surprise, denied the fact. We know not *what* evil he feared, when he had recourse to this sinful means of escape;—whether he thought he should be turned out of the palace, and deprived of the opportunity of seeing the end, or whether he dreaded lest he should be apprehended, like his Master, and exposed to the same insults and injuries. It appears that several other persons, besides the doorkeeper, taxed him with having some connection with the holy prisoner; but he persisted in the lie he had already told. This was the *first* denial.

Finding he was known, he withdrew into the porch, and then—the cock crew. But he attended not to this faithful monitor, nor did he even remember the Lord's warning. While in the porch, both a maid and a man recognised him, and this time he added an *oath* to his declaration. This was his *second* denial.

Soon afterwards he returned into the palace, and was discovered, by his peculiar manner of speaking, to come from that part of Israel called Galilee; and as it was well known that most of Christ's disciples were Galilæans, it was immediately supposed that he was one of them. On this occasion Peter not only denied his Lord, but he began to curse and to swear. He had now reached an awful pitch of iniquity. How much farther he *might* have gone, none but God knows. Again the cock crew. This time Peter understood the voice of the bird. And why? Because at the same moment that the cock crew, the Lord turned and looked upon him. It is probable that Jesus was now standing among the servants, enduring their insults. His eyes had lately been blindfolded, his face smitten, and spit upon. That face, thus bruised and defiled, those eyes which had shed so many tears, were turned towards Peter. No wonder he could not bear the look. He went again into the porch, and wept bitterly. Then all the past was brought before his mind; all the love that he had experienced, all the vows he had made, and all the base denials of which he had been guilty—*all*—*all* rushed to his remembrance. "And when he thought thereon, he wept."

There are such moments in the believer's experience. Blessed moments! in which he learns more of his own wickedness, and of his Lord's goodness, than he has learned in years that have gone before. Some actions, which he had never viewed in their true light, are all at once seen to be dark offences against his gracious God. No tears shed for blasted prospects, or heavy bereavements, are as bitter as these. Yet even then he must not say, "There is no hope." Peter did not read in his Master's look, "There is no forgiveness for thee." How could he have lived during the next two days, had he despaired of pardon! Had he been without hope, could he have run so eagerly to the tomb of his risen Lord, and even ventured to enter in! It was the thought that he had sinned against a Saviour ready to forgive, that made his tears flow so abundantly.* It was the same thought that kept him from despair. His Saviour had once said, "I have prayed for thee that thy *faith* fail not." And it failed not.

True penitence is a mixture of sorrow and faith. The penitent says with sorrow, "My sin is before me;" and with faith, "There is forgiveness with thee." Such is the broken heart which God will not despise. Let this be our prayer:

"If near the pit I rashly stray,
Before I wholly fall away,
The keen conviction dart:
Recall me by that pitying look,
That kind, upbraiding glance which broke
Unfaithful Peter's heart."

Evening Scripture portion. 2 Cor. VII. *True repentance.*

LUKE XXII. 66 to end.—*The council condemn Christ.*

IT is probable that this examination is not the same as that of which St. Matthew gives an account. *That* examination seems to have taken place in the *night, this* in the *day*. It was a law among the Jews that no sentence pronounced in the *night* should stand good, and to this law Jeremiah is supposed to refer when he says, "Execute judgment in the *morning*." (xxi. 12.) Accordingly, the council assembled at the dawn of day to confirm the condemnation they had pronounced during the hours of darkness. This council was called the sanhedrim. It consisted of seventy persons, of whom the high priest was the chief. The other members were *priests*, who *had* been *high* priests, or who were heads of the twenty-four courses: *elders*, or princes of the people; and *scribes*, or men learned in the law. They were all persons whom the world revered. *Priests* who had a reputation for *holiness; elders* who boasted of *noble birth*, and *scribes* who had acquired great *learning;* all these combined against the *Holy* One, the Most *High*, the only *wise* God.†

There were two members of that council who took no part in the proceedings of their brethren. Nicodemus and Joseph of Arimathea were honorable counsellors and rulers in Israel. They were also disciples of Jesus, though *secretly*, for fear of the Jews. It is probable that they were absent when the council met to condemn the Lord, or if present, it is certain that they did not unite in pronouncing the guilty sentence.

* It is written in the margin, "He wept abundantly."

† Some commentators think that allusion is made to these three classes in Zech. xi. 8. "Three shepherds also I cut off in one month."

As Jesus had already acknowledged himself to be the Son of God, no witnesses were summoned to appear against him. His own confession was enough. When he was asked, "Art thou the Christ?" he showed by his answer that he would have *proved* his claim, had his judges been willing to listen. He said, "If I tell you, ye will not believe; and if I also ask you, ye will not answer me, nor let me go." On former occasions he had *asked* them various questions, by which he had shown he was the Christ, and that the Christ was the Son of God. This is the great truth that Jesus sealed with his own blood. By *confessing* it, men are *saved*, for St. John declares, "Whosoever shall confess that Jesus is the Son of God, God dwelleth in him, and he in God." By *denying* this truth men are *lost;* for St. John also declares, "Who is a liar but he that denieth that Jesus is the Christ? He is *anti-Christ*," (that is, the enemy of Christ,) "that denieth the Father and the *Son*." Do *we* believe that Jesus is the Christ, *the Son of God?* If we believe it, we cannot feel *indifferent* on the subject. We may have believed some things, and yet we may now forget that we ever heard them; or though we may still believe them, we should not be grieved if we discovered them to be false. But we cannot feel in this manner concerning the great truth that Jesus is the Son of God. Would it make no difference to a mother whether she believed that the ship containing her only son was lost at sea, or safely arrived in the harbor? Would not every stranger by the first glance of her countenance discover *which* of these tidings she had heard? Those who believe that Jesus is the Son of God, believe that they have a friend dearer than the dearest child, and more powerful than the mightiest monarch, ever ready, ever able to succor them in time of need. They believe that he died to save them, and lives to bless them: that he will walk with them through the valley of the shadow of death, and lead them forever by living fountains of waters. When they say, "I believe that Jesus is the Son of God," their hearts burn within them, and their spirits rejoice with joy unspeakable and full of glory.

Evening Scripture portion. Acts VIII. ***Faith in the Son of God.***

MATT. XXVII. 3–10.—*The death of Judas.*

SHOULD we not have supposed, after reading how Judas betrayed his Master, that he was too much hardened ever to feel remorse? But the conscience sometimes awakes when least expected; for no one can lull it into so profound a sleep that it *cannot* be aroused. When Judas saw that his Master was condemned he repented himself. It seems then that he had hoped that the Lord would escape, as he had done on former occasions. But if he had escaped, would the crime of Judas have been less heinous? The guilt of sin is not to be measured by its *consequences*. By what, then, is it to be measured? By its *motives*.

When Judas became conscious of his guilt, how did he act? He went to the chief priests, confessed his crime, and rejected his bribe. Was not this all he could do? No; had he *loved* Jesus he would have done much more. He would have shed *such* tears as Peter shed. He would have been willing to live, bowed down with the remembrance of his crimes, sooner than have added to his offences against his Lord, by putting an end to his own life. But he was a "devil." (John vi. 70.) *Satan* acknowledges that Jesus is the Holy One of God, and *Judas* did the same. But Satan does not love him; neither did Judas love the Master he betrayed, though he was forced by remorse to declare his innocence.

How awful must have been the expression of his countenance when he entered into the assembly of the chief priests to return the ill-gotten money! How different from the look he wore when he came to offer to betray his Lord! *Then* he felt satanic *joy*, and *now* satanic *misery*. His heart was full of despair, not of true repentance, when he said, "I have sinned in that I have betrayed the innocent blood!"

How much hearing this confession added to the guilt of the chief priests! Could they believe that Jesus was a wicked man, when one of his most intimate companions declared to his own shame how excellent a Master he had betrayed? Was it not that he might bear this testimony that Jesus had chosen him three years before to be an apostle?

But how did the priests *receive* the testimony? They replied, "What is that to us? see thou to that." In this way tempters treat their deluded victims. If a youth, who has been drawn into sin by artful companions, were to go to them and say, "See the misery you have brought upon me." What would they answer? "See thou to *that*." They would regard his qualms of conscience as proofs of weakness and cowardice. What awful recriminations will be heard in the abode of despair among lost spirits! With what bitterness will the tempted reproach their tempters, as the authors of their wo!

It seems that the priests could not entirely smother the voice of conscience in their bosoms, for they looked upon the thirty pieces of silver cast on the floor with abhorrence. They did not dare to return them to the treasury set apart for the expenses of the temple services, but determined to purchase with them a burying-ground for strangers. Perhaps they thought by this charitable deed to atone for their cruel treatment of an innocent person. They were not aware that they thus fulfilled a prophecy that had been made long before by the prophet Zechariah.*

* It seems that by some mistake a writer who copied this gospel in *early* times, inserted the name of Jeremy instead of that of Zechariah. Such mistakes ought not to surprise, because we have no reason to expect that all who *copied* the Scriptures should be preserved from trifling errors. It is enough to know that all who *wrote* them were guarded from errors of *every* kind.

There was a piece of ground near Jerusalem called the potter's field. It is probable that the soil having been used for the manufacture of earthen vessels, had become unfit for cultivation, and could be obtained at a low price. At first it was set apart for the burial of those Gentiles who had embraced the Jewish religion, but who were considered unworthy to be buried with the Jews.

It is still a burying-place for Gentiles. The Armenian Christians have hired it of the Turks. The Holy Field (as it is now called) lies near the deep and gloomy valley at the south of Jerusalem. A square building, about twelve feet high, covers half this little plot of ground. Through the top, which is open, dead bodies are let down. Travellers who have looked into the building have seen the corpses lying beneath in various stages of decay. The potter's field is the memorial of the low price at which the Saviour of the world was estimated. Those who behold the worthless plot may well exclaim, "He was despised and rejected of men."

We know not what solitary spot Judas chose for the commission of his last crime. It seems probable that he fastened himself by a rope to a branch of a tree that overhung one of those precipices which abound near Jerusalem, and that the rope breaking by his weight, he fell into the vale beneath. There his body became a horrible spectacle, and a token to all who beheld it of the vengeance of God.

On the same day that Judas died, Jesus died also. Nearly at the same time the betrayer and the betrayed entered into the presence of God. With what unutterable shame must Judas have seen his injured Lord received with joyful shouts by redeemed sinners! The blood he had caused to be shed never washed his own soul from its dark stains. While the penitent thief was ushered spotless into the presence of the Most Holy, the despairing apostle was consigned, with all his guilt upon his head, to "*his own place*." (Acts i. 25.) It has been well observed* that they crossed each other on the path. One who just before had *appeared* to be going to hell,—went to heaven; and another who once had *appeared* to be going to heaven,—went to hell!

Evening Scripture portion. Acts I. ***The death of Judas.***

John XVIII. 28–38.—*Christ appears before Pontius Pilate.*

We now behold the Saviour delivered by the Jews into the hands of the Gentiles. Pontius Pilate was a Gentile. Cæsar, the Roman emperor, who had conquered the Jewish nation, had appointed Pon-

* Dr. Bennet.

tius Pilate to be their governor. It was he alone who had the power of sentencing any man to be put to death. On this account the chief priests and elders led their captive to his judgment-seat; for no punishment less than *death* would satisfy their malice. Thus the saying of Jesus, signifying *what* death he should die, was brought to pass. Had the Jews put him to death, he would have been *stoned;* but it was necessary that he should be *crucified.* As our *sacrifice,* he bore our *curse.* God has declared in his word, "Cursed is every one that hangeth on a tree." Thus Jesus, by hanging on a cross of wood, became a curse for us. (See Gal. iii.)

But when the Jews brought their holy prisoner to Pilate, they refused to enter into the hall of judgment. And why? Because they feared lest they should be defiled by entering into the dwelling of a Gentile, and that they should not be able to keep the passover; for that feast was celebrated during a *whole week,* and many peace-offerings of the herd and of the flock were eaten, besides the unleavened bread and Paschal Lamb. What must Pilate have thought of the Jewish religion, when he saw these men at once so much occupied with empty forms, and so much distorted with evil passions! Many think ill of the Christian religion from the same cause. They see persons who would not on any account miss attending church or the sacrament, filled with envy, hatred, malice, and all uncharitableness. The fault, however, is not in the *religion,* but in the *hearts* of its professors.

As the Jews refused to enter into the judgment-hall, they were not present when Pilate examined their innocent victim. Thus the Lord enjoyed a short respite from their angry and noisy accusations. They had not told Pilate that Jesus said he was the *Son of God,* because they knew that such an accusation would not be regarded by a heathen; but they had accused him of making himself a *king.*

The first question that Pilate asked the Lord was, "Art thou the king of the Jews?" The holy prisoner did not refuse to answer the question. He made a good confession before Pontius Pilate, and acknowledged that he was a King. What an opportunity Pilate now enjoyed of hearing the truth to the saving of his soul! Like the woman of Samaria, he was now conversing with a stranger who could teach him all things. The Lord was willing to answer his questions, and to enlighten his ignorance; but Pilate was not willing to listen to his voice. He broke off the conversation abruptly. Though he asked, "What is truth?" he did not wait for an answer. How unlike he was to the Samaritan, who left the Saviour only that she might call together the men of her city to hear his wonderful words! Had Pilate acted as she did, he might have lost his monarch's favor,—he might have incurred the Jews' displeasure,—he might have forfeited his honors and even his life, but—he would have *saved his soul.* What must he *now* think of his conduct on that occasion! A price was then put into his hand to buy wisdom, but he had no *heart* for it. Jesus knew this when he said to him, "Every one that is of the truth heareth my voice." Pilate was not of the truth, therefore he did not hear his voice.

Those only are *of* the truth who *love* the truth; all others turn away their ears from hearing it. Multitudes have opportunities of hearing the truth, who *will* not hear it. Though conscience tells them, "This is the truth," they find excuses for neglecting it. They say, "I have no time," or, "I shall offend my relations," or "I shall injure my business," or "I am too young, too gay, and too happy;" and they often *end* by saying, "*It is too late.*" There was one who made this awful answer to the *last* messenger of mercy who approached his dying bed, "*It is too late.*"

Evening Scripture portion. Prov. VIII. *Heavenly wisdom.*

Luke XXIII. 4–12.—*Christ appears before Herod.*

The Lord Jesus stood before the tribunals of four judges. Two of them were priests, Annas and Caiaphas; and two were rulers, Pilate and Herod. Of *Annas*, we know nothing, except that he did *not unbind* his sacred prisoner. For it is written, "Now Annas had sent him *bound* unto Caiaphas, the high priest." (John xviii. 24.) But of the other three we hear much. Though all of them were wicked men, they were not *equally* guilty, for they had not equal *light*, nor did they reach the same point in crime. Pilate was an ignorant heathen: Herod had been instructed by John the Baptist: Caiaphas had enjoyed frequent opportunities of hearing the Son of God himself; for his office obliged him to spend the whole of every day at the temple, where the Lord taught so often, and wrought so many miracles. The hearts of these three men were set against the Saviour, just in proportion to their knowledge of his truth. Pilate knew *nothing* of the Lord, and he was desirous to release him. Herod knew *something* of him, and he cared not what became of him. Caiaphas knew *much*, and he was bent upon his destruction. It is not *hearing of* Christ that softens the heart, nor seeing him, nor listening to his own words. The Holy Spirit alone can make the wicked heart of man love the Saviour. We shall often find that those who have been religiously educated, and who have heard the gospel many years, are greater enemies to Christ than the ignorant world.

But though Pilate did not hate Jesus, he had a share in his murder. Caiaphas accused him,—Herod made no effort to release him, and Pilate condemned him. Each was actuated by different motives. Caiaphas was under the dominion of envy; Herod was in a hardened, unbelieving, arrogant state of mind; and Pilate was afraid of exasperating the Jews, and of incurring the displeasure of the Roman emperor. Soon all these wicked judges were hurled from their high seats, deprived of their shining honors, and plunged in deep disgrace. Herod and Pilate were banished to distant countries. The end of Caiaphas is not known.

There was one circumstance in Herod's case which aggravated his guilt. He was once under religious impressions. There was a time when he heard John gladly, and did many things that were right; but there was a sin that he would not renounce. He refused to part with the wicked Herodias, his brother's wife. What was the consequence? His good impressions wore off, and his heart grew harder than before. He shut up John in prison, then beheaded him, and at last derided the Son of God. Behold him encouraging his soldiers in turning that blessed and sorrowful sufferer into ridicule! Had he known who stood before him, he might have asked of him, and he might have obtained the pardon of his sins. The blood that Jesus shed could have washed his guilty hand and heart, even from the stains of the Baptist's blood. But he had smothered the reproaches of conscience, and brought himself to regard religion as a fable. Instead of being *afraid* of seeing Jesus, whose faithful servant he had murdered, he was exceedingly *glad*. But he will be exceedingly *sorry* the next time he beholds him; for then he will find the awful threatening fulfilled, "I will laugh at your calamity, and mock when your fear cometh." (Prov. i.)

The case of Herod is not uncommon; there are many who once received good impressions, and who once struggled with strong convictions, who are now grown hard, scornful, and hostile. They would not *obey* the truth, and therefore they tried to *disbelieve* it, and they have succeeded. No sermons now make them tremble, no afflictions now touch their hearts; they are steeled against warnings and persuasions, against mercies and judgments. We earnestly hope that there is no one among us in this hardened state. But if there are any who are *now* resisting the convictions of conscience, who can tell how hard their hearts may become!

Evening Scripture portion. Heb. III. ***The danger of unbelief.***

Matt. XXVII. 15–19.—*Pilate's wife.*

Pilate felt reluctant to condemn Christ. He resorted to various expedients in order to save himself from passing the unjust sentence. He sent Jesus to Herod; but Herod sent him back. He next appealed to the people. He knew that it was envy of the people's attachment to their favorite teacher, that had caused the priests to deliver him up. Therefore he hoped that the *people* would demand *his* release, in preference to that of the notorious robber, called Barabbas. But why did not Pilate, instead of resorting to these expedients, simply and boldly say, "I will not condemn an innocent man?" He had not courage to face the opposition of the Jews; therefore he endeavored to *slip out* of his difficulties. Have *we* never acted in a similar manner? When convinced that it was our duty without delay to take a certain step, have we never thought, "I will wait, in hopes that some circumstance may arise to save me from this trial?" But God usually defeats these plans, and brings us into such a position that we must take a decided part, either for good or evil.

Pilate was in a state of great perplexity, when a message arrived that increased his trouble. His wife sent unto him, saying, "Have thou nothing to do with this just man, for I have suffered many things in a dream because of him." This message was a merciful warning from God to deter him from committing the crime to which he was tempted.

It is not recorded that any *woman* took part against the Lord while he was on earth. There was no Herodias to promote *his* death, though there was one to ask for the head of John the Baptist. In this appointment, we can trace the mercy of God to woman. Eve, by her counsels to her husband, ruined the world. This circumstance cast a deep shade upon the character of woman. Pilate's wife, by *her* counsels, endeavored to save her husband from sharing in the world's greatest crime. It is remarkable that Pilate's wife should be favored by a dream from heaven, for in all probability she was a heathen; but God often works in the minds of those who know him very imperfectly.

There are many dreams which are not worthy of regard; they come (Solomon says, Eccles. v. 3) through the multitude of business, and are full of confusion and impossibilities. But the dream of Pilate's wife was of a different kind. It was sent by God to instruct her ignorance and to awaken her fears. She suffered *many* things in her dream; we know not *what* things; but they were terrible, and they were all connected with a just man then standing before her husband's tribunal. What must have been her feelings, when she found her message had been disregarded, and that the Just One was condemned! When the darkness overspread the earth at noon, she must have suspected its cause. We should like to know whether she ever truly believed in the Saviour, or whether her alarm passed away without making any saving impression on her soul. Did she afterwards hear the preaching of the apostles? We know not. Her history is not related in the Scriptures. The only event of her life that is recorded, leads us to hope that she found mercy. It was her privilege on earth to plead in behalf of the slandered Saviour, when, with the exception of a few disciples, the world were combined against him. We hope it is her blessed portion to worship him in heaven, amidst countless adoring hosts. She suffered many things in a *dream* because of *him;* we hope that she now knows that he suffered many *more* things on a *cross* for *her* sins.

Evening Scripture portion. Rev. VI. *Martyrs and persecutors.*

MATT. XXVII. 20–25.—*The multitude prefer Barabbas to Christ.*

WHAT guilt there was in the short answer the people made to Pilate's inquiry! "Barabbas." It was the name of a murderer; yet they preferred that murderer to him who came to give *life* unto the world. It was not *one* man only who made this wicked choice, but a *whole multitude*. Is not this a proof that the heart of man is desperately wicked? The most lovely of all Beings clothed himself in a human form, and a whole multitude preferred a *murderer* before him. Could we have seen the meek and holy countenance of the Son of God, and then have beheld the degraded, abject, brutal looks of the wicked Barabbas, we should have said, "It is impossible that men can prefer that vile criminal to the righteous Saviour." Did any of the blind whom Jesus had restored to sight join in the cry, "Not this man, but Barabbas?" Did any tongue that he had loosed exclaim, "Let him be crucified?" We *hope* that no such act of ingratitude was committed; we hope that Bartimeus was weeping in some secret place, as well as the women who had followed him to Jerusalem. But when we consider what numerous miracles Jesus had wrought in the temple, we must conclude that many of the multitude had received great benefits from his gracious hands. How many helpless parents, and drooping children, had been restored by Him to health and joy! but all his mercies were now forgotten, and only the crimes of which he was accused were remembered. What is man? Changeable, base, ungrateful. Judas preferred thirty pieces of silver to his divine Master; the multitude a *murderer* to their *Benefactor!*

Pilate was astonished at the mad violence of the people. He feared to resist their clamor, lest his own life should fall a sacrifice to their fury; yet he was so deeply impressed with a sense of the injustice of the deed he was going to commit, that he took water, and washed his hands before them all, saying, "I am innocent of the blood of this just person; see ye to it." But could that water cleanse his hands from guilt? O no. Pilate had *power* to release the prisoner; he was bound to exert that power. It was not sufficient for *him* to bear his testimony against evil. Pilate's *wife* could do no more than lift up her feeble voice on behalf of the innocent; but Pilate could have said, "I will defend him with the last drop of my blood." How blessed would he *then* have been, though he had been torn to pieces by the exasperated multitude! That day he would have been with Jesus in Paradise.

Who can hear, without a thrill of horror, the curse which the Jewish nation invoked on their own heads, when they answered, "His blood be on us, and on our children!" They intended to say, "If he be innocent, we will bear the guilt of his murder; but we are sure that he is *not* innocent." God heard the awful words. Forty years afterwards, the Romans conquered Jerusalem. Blood then flowed in such torrents through the streets, that it extinguished many a burning pile; and crosses were erected in such numbers around the walls, that there was no more room in which to place them, nor wood of which to construct them. But who could have thought, that in that horrible curse a *blessing* also was contained! They cried, "His blood be upon us;" but the Saviour interceded, that it might wash them from their sins. A time shall come, when that precious blood shall wash the whole nation from their iniquities; and "so all Israel shall be saved." (Rom. xi. 26.)

To *every* soul who hears the gospel, the *blood* of Jesus shall prove either a curse or a blessing. It *must* be upon us, either to *increase* our guilt, or to *wash it away*. Let us not be satisfied with thinking, "How wicked the Jews were to shed that blood!" It was shed that we might wash, and be clean. Jesus lives to wash with his own hands those for whom he shed his own blood. The apostle John says, "Unto him that loved us, and washed us from our sins in his own blood." (Rev. i.) Let every sinner come to this Saviour, and bathe in this fountain. Let each learn to say,

"My Saviour died upon the tree,
And sank for me beneath the flood;
My sins are cast into this sea,
Of love, of sorrows, and of blood."

Hymn 283. Collection by Rev. J. H. Evans

Evening Scripture portion.
Psalm CIX. *Curses denounced on Christ's enemies.*

MATT. XXVII. 26–30.—*The band of soldiers mock Christ.*

BARABBAS was released, and Jesus was delivered up to be crucified. We know nothing of the future history of Barabbas. We know not whether he ever believed in him, who was led to execution, when he himself was permitted to live. But there have been some as guilty as Barabbas, who have believed; and they have felt that if Jesus had not been crucified, they would never have been released from the everlasting prison-house of sin and death.

Before Jesus was crucified, he was scourged. It was the custom to treat criminals in this barbarous manner. The scourge was a sharp and torturing instrument, frequently composed of the nerves of oxen, and the bones of sheep. The poor sufferer was fastened to a post, with his hands tied behind him, while the executioners, with all their might, covered his whole body with their cruel strokes. Amongst the *Jews* there was a law forbidding more than forty strokes to be inflicted at *one* time; but amongst the *Romans* there was no such law. We know not how many strokes lacerated the sacred flesh of our Divine Lord. It was *then* that he meekly "gave his back to the smiters." (Is. l. 6.) It was *then* that the plowers plowed on his back, and made long their furrows. (Ps. cxxix. 3.) But there was a healing virtue in those stripes. The blood that flowed from those wounds, heals the wounds of sin in the human heart. It is written, "With his stripes we are healed." It is indeed wonderful that *stripes* should heal. But those who are harassed by the remembrance of past sins, may find that the stripes of Jesus can restore peace to their souls. The innocent Lamb of God was wounded in our stead, and if we believe in him, we shall be healed.

No pity was awakened in the hearts of the Roman soldiers, by the sight of the Redeemer's sufferings. After the scourging was over, Jesus was taken back into the magnificent hall of Pilate, and was surrounded by the *whole band* of soldiers, in number at least *six hundred.* This was the third time that he had been publicly mocked. The servants of the high priest had derided his *wisdom.* Herod, with his men of war, had mocked his *innocence*, by clothing him in a white, or gorgeous robe; and now Pilate's soldiers scoffed at his *royal dignity*, by clothing him in a scarlet robe, and adorning him with a crown of thorns. The soldiers themselves had platted this crown. They had taken some twigs of a plant that bore spikes, and, with the ingenuity of fiends, had contrived to give pain to their victim, while they indulged their own mirth. Some of the faithful followers of Jesus have thought of this crown while enduring the same kind of sufferings. When a crown, not made of *thorns*, but of *paper*, and painted with the figures of three devils, was placed on the head of the martyr, John Huss, he said, "I am glad to wear this crown of ignominy, for the sake of him who wore a crown of thorns." He felt that the Saviour's torments were sharper than his own; he felt, also, that it was for *his* sake that the thorns pierced the Saviour's brow. Yes! It was for *us* that Jesus wore a crown of thorns. No evil thought had ever proceeded from his divine mind. It was to atone for *our* offences that the blood trickled down his sacred cheeks. He who suffered all these pangs, and bore all these insults, was *God*, the God who made us, who gives us breath, who upholds the worlds! What must *sin* be to require such an atonement! It must be infinitely evil. And what must *Jesus* be, to be willing to offer this atonement! He must be infinitely good. The day is coming, when he will appear adorned with *many* crowns, but not *one* of them composed of thorns. Then every knee shall bow to him, not in cruel mockery, but with deep awe, and call him *Lord*, to the glory of God the Father.

Evening Scripture portion. Ps. CXXIX. CXXX. ***The stripes of Jesus.***

JOHN XIX. 4–9.—*Pilate shows Christ in his royal robes to the Jews.*

THE Jews did not witness the torments Jesus suffered among the soldiers, because they would not enter into the judgment-hall. It would have gratified their malice had they seen the profane scoffers bending their knees in pretended homage. When Pilate beheld the bleeding sufferer, he hoped that the sight would melt the hearts of his enemies, and therefore he brought him forth into the open place and said, "Behold the man." Can we conceive the appearance of the Man Christ Jesus at this moment? We know that he wore over his shoulders a robe of purple and scarlet, and a crown of thorns upon his head. We may form some idea of his weak frame, bowed down with the anguish of the scourge, and of his sorrowful features, suffused with blood; but we cannot imagine the holy and subdued expression of his countenance. No sinful feeling had ever clouded his brow, or ruffled one feature of his face; sorrow alone had marred that sacred visage.

But the sight of their mangled victim did not touch the cruel hearts of the Jews. They cried out, "Crucify him, crucify him." Then Pilate said, "Take ye him, and crucify him." His object was not to shield the *sufferer*, but *himself*. If *he* could avoid having any hand in the deed, he was willing to allow it to be done. Pilate was a selfish and unrighteous man. He felt no generous concern for the innocent; though fear impelled him to plead in his behalf.

This fear was increased when the Jews cried out, "He made himself the Son of God." It now flashed across Pilate's mind that this extraordinary man might really be a divine person. He desired to speak with him again in the judgment-hall. What a question he proposed when he said to the Son of God, "Whence art thou?" How astonished Pilate would have been had his injured prisoner described the glories of the place whence he came! But he would not even answer the question. And why not? On a former occasion he *had* answered some of Pilate's important inquiries; but since then his unrighteous judge had done violence to his own conscience, and had resisted the warning sent in a dream. He had commanded the innocent to be scourged, and had suffered him to be tormented by a barbarous crew. Those who shut their eyes to the light, will soon find *that* light begin to wane. When we will not attend to the voice of conscience, or to the warnings of God, we must expect to be left to pursue the way of destruction.

It was a sign that God was angry with Pilate when Jesus forbore to tell him whence he was. He had told his *disciples* that he was with the Father, and that he came into the world. It is the thought of his original greatness that makes his abasement so wonderful. If we read the first chapter of Genesis, containing an account of the *Creation*, and then read the nineteenth chapter of John, describing the *Crucifixion*, we must be amazed to behold the same Being performing so vast a work, and then enduring such deep humiliation.

Evening Scripture portion. Is. LII. *The visage marred.*

JOHN XIX. 10–16.—*Pilate delivers up Christ to be crucified.*

THESE were Pilate's last efforts to obtain the release of his prisoner. We must feel compassion for this wretched governor, as he runs to and fro, seeking some new mode to extricate himself from his difficulty. The path to true happiness and everlasting glory lay open before him, but he had no heart to walk in it. He threw away the golden opportunity that was presented to him of defending the most glorious of Beings, placed for a season beneath the shelter of his arm.

How base and how absurd was his arrogant boast—"Knowest thou not that I have *power* to crucify thee, and *power* to release thee." The Lord in his answer gave him a lesson calculated to humble his proud spirit. "Thou couldest have no power at all against me, except it were given thee from *above*." To this humiliating declaration he added a solemn warning, "He that delivered me unto thee hath the *greater* sin." Then Pilate had *some* sin. He who was counted as a *criminal* accused his *judge* of *sin!* That judge was compelled to say of his prisoner, "I find no fault in him." But the reputed criminal found great fault in his judge. Yet *not* the *greatest*. The high priest, who had delivered him up to Pilate, had the *greater* sin. There are then *degrees* of sin. Why was the high priest more guilty than Pilate? Because he had gone *out of his way* to destroy Jesus, whereas Pilate had been called to pronounce sentence in the regular execution of the office to which he "was ordained of God." (Rom. xiii. 1.) There were many other circumstances that increased the sin of Caiaphas; his knowledge of the Scriptures, his malicious motives, and his false accusations. God knows all the *aggravating* circumstances of our sins, and all the *palliating* circumstances also. He estimates our temptations, and forms an exact judgment of our *degree* of guilt. When we run to *meet* temptation, we are more guilty than when we yield to a temptation that *overtakes* us. But even *then* we are guilty. There is a way of escape for every tempted person. No creature is so hemmed in by temptations, that he could not escape, if he were to look to God for aid. For we have this promise, "God is faithful, who will not suffer you to be tempted above that ye are able; but will with the temptation also make a way to escape, that ye may be able to bear it." (1 Cor. x. 13.)

Pilate might have escaped from all his perplexities; but instead of escaping, he became each moment more entangled in the net. It is melancholy to view him making his last struggle against his fatal temptation. He left the judgment-hall accompanied by his prisoner, and took his seat on the "Pavement." It is supposed this was a covered balcony, the floor of which being covered with Mosaic work, it acquired the name of the Pavement. From this high seat he appealed for the *last* time to the furious multitude, saying, "Shall I crucify your King?" The reply was, "We have no king but Cæsar." Then Pilate gave up his innocent victim, and the soldiers took him and led him away. What must have been the feelings of the unjust governor, as he beheld the enemies rejoicing over their prey! Can the events of that day have ceased to haunt him during the remainder of his life? But his calamity was near to come, and his affliction hasted fast. (Jer. xlviii. 16.) Two years afterwards he lost the favor of the emperor, and was banished into a distant province, where, it is said, he put an end to his own life. It is to be feared that it would have been good for him if he had never worn a royal robe—if he had never seen the Son of God.

Evening Scripture portion. Is. LIX. *Judgments on Christ's enemies.*

Mark XV. 20, 21.—*Simon bears the cross.*

We have entered upon a new scene in our Lord's sufferings. Behold him now on his way to Calvary, the place of his crucifixion! The *evening* before had been spent in the upper room at Jerusalem,—the *night* in the garden at Gethsemane, and in the palace of the high priest,—and the *early morning* in the judgment-hall of Pilate. What a variety of sorrows had he undergone in these places! At the supper table and in the garden his *soul* was troubled—in the palace and the judgment-hall his *body* was buffeted, spit upon, and wounded.

Before he sat out on his *last* painful journey, the royal robe was taken from his shoulders, and his own garments placed upon them; but we do not know whether the crown of thorns was removed from his bleeding brows. It is probable that the cruel soldiers suffered that instrument of torture to remain. They little knew that it was the badge of his real dignity.

"And he, bearing his cross, went forth." (John xix. 47.) The Jews were accustomed to see criminals laden with their crosses, going to the place of execution, and generally offered the grossest insults to the unhappy sufferers as they proceeded on their way. There can be no doubt that the soldiers who had before tormented Jesus, now pursued him with unrelenting barbarity. But it seems they found their victim could scarcely move beneath his painful load. Fastings and watchings, prayers and tears, had dried up the strength of the Son of Man. He was now in the state which David described in Ps. cii. 5. "By reason of the voice of my groaning, my bones cleave to my skin."

But would the soldiers help him to carry his heavy cross? No; it was too shameful a burden for them to bear, or even to touch.

At this moment they met a man named Simon, a native of Africa, (the land of accursed Ham.) "Him they compelled to bear his cross." We cannot be certain that Simon was *unwilling* to bear it, for the choice was not given to him. The soldiers *commanded* him to do this public service. Whether Simon was an enemy or a friend to the Saviour, or altogether a *stranger* to his name and character, we know not. It is evident, however, that he had not joined in the cry of "Crucify him, crucify him," for he was coming out of the *country*, as Jesus was leaving the *city*.

At the time it was thought a degrading office to bear the cross of the despised Jesus; but afterwards it was regarded as a distinguished honor. The sons of Simon were known as the sons of the man who bare the Redeemer's cross. Simon himself will never be forgotten, because he was the Saviour's cross-bearer. How many angels in heaven would joyfully have taken his place, if they could have obtained permission! We may believe that there were some on *earth* who *would*, if they *might*, have borne their Lord's burden, and shared his reproach. Would not the women who followed him weeping, gladly have succored him? And Peter, too, now lamenting his base denial,—and the loving John, would not *they* have helped to bear the cross, had not the fear of the brutal soldiers and malicious priests kept them at a distance! Do we think *we* should have been desirous to occupy Simon's place?

Though our Lord is not *now* fainting beneath the weight of his cross, his name is still despised, and his people persecuted. He delights to see us willing to bear shame for his sake. Some have humbled themselves to the very dust that they might please him. Dober, the Moravian missionary, intended to sell himself for a slave, that he might teach the negroes the way of salvation. Circumstances prevented him fulfilling his intention; but if he had, would he have degraded himself? To bear the cross of Jesus, and to share his reproach, is reckoned in heaven more honorable than to govern kingdoms, or to discover worlds. Whether Simon knew it or not, no monarch on his throne occupied a place of such distinction as he did when bearing the cross of the Nazarene.

Evening Scripture portion. Ps. CII. ***The weakness of Christ's body.***

LUKE XXIII. 27–31.—*The weeping women.*

THOUGH so *many* insulted our Lord in his last hours, yet a *great* company bewailed him. This troop was composed chiefly of *women*. Apostles had been afraid to let it be known that they belonged to Jesus, but these women were not afraid to let their tears be seen.

Apostles had failed to watch with him one hour; but these women, *unasked*, accompanied him on his way to the cross.

Jesus valued sympathy. He condescended to notice these mourners. He turned and spoke to them. What a moment it was when their Saviour's failing eyes rested upon them! How eagerly they must have listened to his words, fearing they were the *last* they should ever hear from his lips.

He knew how soon his sufferings would be over, and how great the joy that would follow; therefore he said, "Weep not for me." He also knew what long and bitter woes were coming upon the Jewish nation; therefore he said to the women, "Weep for yourselves and for your children." Perhaps some of those little children who had sung his praises in the temple now accompanied their mothers, and wept with them. It grieved the Saviour's compassionate heart to think of the sorrows that awaited *them*, as well as their parents; for he knew the future history of each person in the company. When children are born into prosperous families they are welcomed as *blessings*, but they were regarded as *curses* in the horrors of the siege of Jerusalem. Nothing can give us an idea of greater misery than the cry, "Fall on us," addressed to hills and mountains. Such misery the Jews *began* to endure, when, forty years after the crucifixion of their king, the Romans besieged their city.

What is the meaning of the words, "If they do these things in a *green* tree, what shall be done in the *dry!*" In the prophet Ezekiel there is a little parable, in which the Jewish nation is compared to a *forest*, and the anger of God to a *fire*. (Ezek. xx. 47.) A fire quickly destroys *dry* trees, but *green* trees less easily. *Dry* trees represent the *wicked*, who are prepared for destruction; *green* trees the *righteous*. God gives this explanation of Ezekiel's parable: "Say to the land of Israel, Behold, I am against thee, and will draw forth my sword out of his sheath, and will cut off from thee the *righteous* and the *wicked*." (Ezek. xxi. 3.) When Jesus, therefore, spoke of a *green* tree, he meant *himself;* and when he spoke of a *dry* tree, his enemies

This seems to be the explanation of his words. "If *they* (that is, the Romans) treat me who am *innocent* so cruelly, what will be done to the GUILTY!"

But why did Jesus speak of these calamities to the weeping women? Did he desire to wound those hearts already bleeding with sorrow for his sufferings? No; but in his mercy he gave a *last warning* to his enemies. A pious father, before he leaves this world, if he be able, summons all his children around his dying bed, and while he *comforts* some, he *warns* others of approaching judgments. His words, unheeded before, often sink deep into the heart at this solemn season. The dying Saviour longed to save his enemies from impending destruction. He had often warned them in the temple, and they would not hear; now he warns them on his way to Calvary. But are the *Jews* the *only* people who will ever say to the mountains, "Fall on us?" Not so; all in every age, of every nation, of every rank, who have not believed in the crucified Saviour, will be filled with terror when they see him coming in the clouds of heaven. If now we will say to Jesus, "Pardon us," we shall never say to the mountains, "Fall on us."

Evening Scripture portion. Lam. II. *The sorrows of Jerusalem.*

MATT. XXVII. 33, 34.—*Golgotha.*

AT length the drooping Saviour arrived at the spot appointed for his crucifixion,—Golgotha, or the place of a skull. It is supposed that near it were caverns filled with the bones of crucified malefactors. Such places were detested by the Jews, who were forbidden to enter the temple if they had touched a dead body. This was the loathsome spot on which the innocent Lamb of God was to be sacrificed for the sins of men.

But there was a hidden reason why God led men to select this polluted place for the Redeemer's execution. He had commanded the High Priest, once a year, to sprinkle the blood of a bullock and of a goat upon the mercy-seat in the Holiest of Holies, to make atonement for sin. The *bodies* of these beasts were taken to a place outside the camp, or city, and burned. Their blood represented the precious blood of Christ, which pleads for us in the presence of God. *Because* his *blood* atones for sin, *therefore* his *body* was taken to a loathsome spot outside the city of Jerusalem. This divine mystery is explained in the Epistle to the Hebrews, (xiii. 11, 12.) "For the *bodies* of *those* beasts whose *blood* is brought into the sanctuary by the High Priest for sin, are burned without the camp; wherefore Jesus also, that he might sanctify the people with his own *blood*, suffered *without* the gate."

Before he was crucified, the soldiers gave him vinegar mingled with gall, a bitter draught, which he just tasted, and then refused to drink. In the gospel of St. Mark it is written, (xv. 23,) " And they gave him to drink *wine* mingled with *myrrh*, and he received it not." Was this cup of wine, the *same* as the cup of vinegar, (which is weak wine,) or was it a *different* cup? Most commentators think they were *different* cups.

The *wine* mingled with *myrrh* seems to have been a stupifying draught, given to criminals before they were crucified, to render them less sensible to pain. Of this alleviation of his anguish the Saviour refused to accept.

The *vinegar* mingled with *gall* seems to have been offered by the soldiers in a spirit of mockery. Some executioners by their compassion have imparted comfort to innocent sufferers. They have turned away and wept as the blood flowed from the open wounds. When Wishart, the Scottish martyr, was led to the stake, the executioner, kneeling down, said, " Sir, I pray thee forgive me, for I am not guilty of your death." But the men who surrounded the Lord were of a more ferocious disposition: they felt no pity, they showed no mercy; therefore it is written in the Psalms, " Reproach hath broken my heart, and I am full of heaviness; I looked for some to take pity, but there was none; and for comforters, but I found none. They gave me also gall for my meat, and in my thirst they gave me vinegar to drink." (Ps. lxix. 20, 21.)

When we have been laid on beds of suffering, how differently have we been treated! Kind friends and faithful servants have administered to our wants, and have anticipated our wishes. Many a dying believer, when a cordial has been presented to his parched and quivering lips, has thought of the vinegar mingled with gall, which his Saviour tasted in gloomy Golgotha.

Evening Scripture portion. Lev. XVI. ***The day of atonement.***

LUKE XXIII. 33, 34.—*The Crucifixion.*

EVERY innocent sufferer feels it a disgrace to be confounded with wicked men. He would rather suffer *alone*, or with other *innocent* persons, than be led to execution in company with criminals. Martyrs have generally been led *together* to the stake, and have enjoyed in their dying moments the sweet society of the righteous.

But the glorious Son of man was conducted to the cross in company with two malefactors, or evil doers. *Their* names were joined with *his* in the history of the executions of that day. Thus the prophecy spoken by Isaiah was fulfilled: " He was numbered with the

transgressors." (Is. liii. 12.) Had John the Baptist been crucified with him, or one of his own disciples, the shame of his death would not have been so great. But shame was one of the ingredients in his bitter cup. Shame is the consequence of sin, and he who bare *our sins* bare also *our shame.*

His death was not only disgraceful, but painful. Perhaps there is no manner of being put to death that causes such lingering pain as crucifixion. It suited the cruelty of heathen hearts to devise such a mode of torture, and it continued to be practised till the Roman emperor Constantine was converted to the Christian faith. He abolished crucifixion, and appointed hanging as the punishment for the greatest criminals.

The unhappy victim who was to be crucified was first stretched upon his cross as it lay upon the ground. His hands and feet were grasped by four soldiers ; a nail was then driven through each hand, and another through both feet. Afterwards the cross was lifted up, and one end thrust with a sudden jerk into a hole prepared to receive it. The gaping wounds exposed to the air became inflamed, and the blood disturbed in its circulation, caused the head to throb and burn, and the heart to feel oppressed with an insupportable weight. *This* was the death which David, when he spake by the Holy Ghost, had prophesied his Redeemer should suffer : " The assembly of the wicked have enclosed me ; they pierced my *hands* and my feet ;"—those gracious hands which had restored so many wretched objects to health and joy ;—those blessed *feet* which had trodden so many rough paths to save perishing sinners, and at length—the path to Calvary itself !

But did the suffering Son of man feel resentment against those who drove the nails into his blessed limbs ? Listen to the words he utters when stretched upon the cross. Is it a complaint ? No ; it is a prayer. Does he pray *against* his enemies ? No ; he intercedes *for* them : " Father, forgive them ; they know not what they do." He intercedes for the four soldiers who had inflicted his wounds,—for the band who had mocked him,—for the multitude who had cried, " Crucify him." " They knew not what they did." *Caiaphas* knew what he did ; *Judas* knew what he did, but the greater part of the enemies of Christ sinned through ignorance. Yet they were guilty, for they *loved* ignorance. It might have been said of them all, that they " loved darkness rather than light, because their deeds were evil." What must they have felt when they *first* knew that the man they had insulted, and tormented, and executed, was the Son of God ! We are told what some of them felt, and what they said. When Peter, in his sermon, declared, " Him ye have taken, and by wicked hands have crucified and slain," (Acts ii. 23,) three thousand were pricked in their hearts, and said, " Men and brethren, what shall we do ?"

Are there any of you who can remember what *you* felt when you *first* discovered against what a Saviour you had been sinning all your lives long—when you first knew that while you had been piercing him by your transgressions, he had been interceding for your pardon? Then it was you looked on him you had pierced, and mourned as one that mourneth for his only son. Those were *bitter* tears that you shed at the feet of the crucified Jesus, yet they were *blessed* tears—they were the tears of repentance, which are so precious in God's sight. But it was not tears that washed away your sins; no, it was the precious blood of Christ that made your scarlet stains as white as snow.

Evening Scripture portion. Zec. XII. *The pierced Saviour.*

John XIX. 19–22.—*The Superscription.*

It was the custom to write over the cross of a malefactor the crime for which he suffered. But Pilate could find no fault in Jesus; therefore, instead of inscribing his *accusation*, he inscribed his *title*—"The King of the Jews." Did Pilate then *believe* that the man he had condemned to death was the lawful sovereign of the Jewish nation? It seems that he *did* believe it, and that he even feared that he was *more* than a King—the Son of God; for we are told, that when the Jews said, "He made himself the Son of God," Pilate was sore afraid. (John xix. 8.)

How great was the crime of crucifying Him of whom he thought so highly! He may have tried to satisfy his conscience by writing this regal title over the cross; but the act only displayed his guilt in a stronger light. How many there are who imitate this part of his conduct! They *do* what they *know* to be wrong, and they imagine they atone for their fault by saying, *while they persevere in it*, that they know it to be wrong. God will not thus be mocked. He is not satisfied with acknowledgments, unaccompanied by any effort to act in a consistent manner. If Pilate did *not* believe that Christ was the King of the Jews, why did he give him that title? and if he *did* believe it, why did he not take him down from the cross? He was either a *liar* for writing what he did not think, or a *murderer*, for crucifying an innocent man. He was, in fact, a *murderer*, because he condemned one that he knew to be *innocent*;—a *regicide*, because that innocent man was a *king*;—and a *Deicide*, because that king was the *Son of God*. By what sliding steps had he sunk into the depth of crime!

Yet Pilate's great sin was the means of bringing glory to God. On the cross Jesus was proclaimed a King. In the three languages most generally known in Jerusalem, the glorious title was written. The Jews read it in Hebrew,—the Romans in Latin,—and people of all nations in Greek. Before his birth he had been announced to his mother as a King. The angel Gabriel had declared, "He shall *reign* over the house of Jacob forever." In his infancy wise men from the

East had inquired throughout Jerusalem, "Where is he that is born King of the Jews?" When Nathanael first believed in the true Messiah, he exclaimed, "Rabbi, thou art the King of Israel." But the nation he came to save from the hands of their enemies rejected him. The throne they gave him was a cross.

But shall he *never* reign over his ancient people? Was he not descended from their beloved monarch, the victorious David? And was it not promised to David that the Messiah should sit upon his throne? (Ps. cxxxii.) This promise shall not fail. His own people will acknowledge him the Son of David as their king; for it is written, "Sing, O daughter of Zion, shout, O Israel; be glad, and rejoice with all the heart, O daughter of Jerusalem; the Lord hath taken away thy judgments, he has cast out thine enemy; the *King of Israel* is in the midst of thee: *thou shalt not see evil any more.*" (Zeph. iii. 14, 15.) And is he king of the Jews alone? When he comes again there will be "on his vesture and on his thigh a name written, King of kings, and Lord of lords." (Rev. xix. 16.) What will then become of those who have refused to submit to his gentle sway?

Evening Scripture portion. Heb. VII. ***Christ a King and a Priest.***

JOHN XIX. 23, 24.—*The division of the garments.*

WHILE the Lord Jesus was suffering unknown agonies on the cross, at its foot the soldiers were dividing his raiment. They little imagined that they were then fulfilling a prophecy, that had been recorded a thousand years before. It was usual for soldiers to divide the raiment of the crucified among themselves; but it was *not* usual for them to find a garment so valuable that, instead of rending, they cast lots for it. This was a very remarkable circumstance, and one of the numerous tokens by which the true Messiah was pointed out to all who remembered the word of God. But the soldiers, being heathens, could not know, when they divided the raiment, that they were fulfilling ancient prophecies. They were thinking of their petty gains, and were quite unconscious that they were performing an action which had long before been foretold, and would be forever remembered.

A description is given of one of our Lord's garments. It was a vesture without a seam. In the East a sort of cloak, with arm-holes, is still worn. A seam generally runs down the middle, or divides it across. This seam is unsightly, and those cloaks that are made without it are highly prized. It is natural to inquire how it happened, that the Son of Man, who was so poor, possessed a valuable garment. Some have conjectured that one of those pious women, who ministered to him of their substance, may have woven with her own hands the seamless vesture. In the days of the Reformers, holy women esteemed it an honor to prepare the garment in which the martyr was to be buried. How much greater was the honor to weave a vesture for Him who was the express image of the Father, and the brightness of his glory!

The clothes that Jesus wore partook of the virtue which dwelt in his sacred body. The very hem of his garment, when touched by the hand of faith, could cure desperate diseases; but now his garments were torn by unbelieving soldiers. The blood that had flowed from his stripes and his wounded brows, must have covered them with stains. It would revolt the feelings to see men casting lots near the cross of a criminal, however vile; but to see them acting thus, near the cross of the suffering Son of God, must have been exceedingly awful.

Though the rapacious soldiers seized upon that raiment which might have wrapped the Saviour's dead body in his grave, his Father provided for him a better covering. Linen, clean and fine, was folded round his sacred limbs, by the faithful hands of Joseph and Nicodemus. When he rose, he left even that covering in his tomb. We can form no conception of the glory with which he is *now* clothed. His vesture shall never again be stained by his *own* blood. It is the blood of his *enemies* which shall sprinkle his raiment when he comes again. For he has said, "I will tread them in mine anger, and trample them in my fury; and their blood shall be sprinkled upon my garments, and I will stain all my raiment." (Is. lxiii. 3.)

Evening Scripture portion. Jer. XXXVIII. *Jeremiah in the dungeon.*

MATT. XXVII. 39–44.—*All men unite in mocking Christ.*

AMONGST the sufferings of our Lord, mockings held a conspicuous place. *Four* times, in the course of a few hours, he was publicly mocked; first in the palace of Caiaphas,—then in the house of Herod,—next in the judgment-hall of Pilate, and last of all at Calvary, as he hung upon the cross. On this occasion men of every degree united to insult him. Rulers and people, Jews and Gentiles, soldiers and citizens, with one accord derided the Lord of Glory. Even the thieves, by their railings, showed that they thought him worse than themselves. How different from this scene on earth is that now witnessed in heaven, where beings of all orders, whether they be thrones or dominions, principalities or powers, join in one song of adoration!

The impious throng mocked the dying Saviour in various ways,—by scornful *gestures*, for they wagged their heads,—by scornful *ac-*

tions, for the soldiers came to him, offering him vinegar,—(Luke xxiii. 36,) and, above all, by scornful *words*. It appears that none uttered more insulting speeches than the priests, scribes, and elders. Instead of addressing the Son of God himself, they spoke to each other, and to the people. It is more trying to hear our enemies speak against us to *others*, than to hear them address the same reproaches to *ourselves*. There is more contempt shown in such a way of attack than in a *direct* assault. Jesus heard these scornful men saying to those around, "He saved others; himself he cannot save." They intended to make the people doubt whether he had *really* saved others, seeing he did not save himself. But such an attempt could not succeed, when so many, rescued from blindness and disease, were to be seen in all the streets of Jerusalem; and when even one of the high priest's own servants had just experienced his healing power. If ALL whom he had saved from ETERNAL death, had appeared to bear testimony to his power, what a glorious company would have covered Calvary! They *will* appear on a *future* day, together with multitudes *then*, and even *now*, unborn;—they will declare with one voice, "He saved *us*." How happy is each one now present who can truly say, "He has saved *me!*" He is *willing* to save each of us. It was *himself* alone that he was *not* willing to save, because he knew that *if* he saved himself, he could save no other. Had *he* come *down* from the *cross*, then *we* could never come *up* from the *grave*.

Must it not have wounded his soul to hear the creatures for whom he was dying saying, "If thou be the Son of God, come down from the cross?" Had all the hosts of Satan joined in mocking him, their taunts would not have been so trying. How easily he could have shown his ungrateful creatures that he was the Son of God! He need only have spoken the words, and the nails would have dropped from his hands and feet. But LOVE fixed him to the place of torture,—love to his Father, who seemed to have forsaken him,—love to his enemies, who were uttering the most provoking speeches. Was not this astonishing love—incomprehensible love! And yet many who have heard of it, are not ashamed to declare that they do not love Jesus; and others, who *say* they love him, show by their conduct that they do *not*. Do any of us really love this compassionate Saviour? Do we not long to love him more? It was the apostle's constant prayer for all the saints, that they might "know the love of Christ, which passeth knowledge." Let us visit Calvary—sit at the foot of the cross,—gaze on the bleeding Lamb. Though our hearts may once have been softened by the Holy Spirit, they will become hard again, if we keep at a distance from that scene of sorrow and of love.

Evening Scripture portion. Eph. V. *The love of Christ.*

Luke XXIII. 39–43.—*The two malefactors.*

No men who ever lived *died* in such remarkable circumstances as these two thieves. They were *crucified* with Christ. We know not whether they had ever seen Jesus before that morning, when they accompanied him to Calvary, and were compelled to pass many hours close to his side. What a different use each made of this precious though painful opportunity!

One of them took advantage of his station, to insult the Saviour with his dying breath, "If thou be the Christ, save thyself and us." This was not a prayer, it was a reproach. He did not believe that Jesus was the Christ, or that he was able to save either himself or his fellow sufferers. And what did he mean by "Save us?" He meant only, "Release us from the pangs of the cross." He thought not of *eternal* misery. But the other thief asked, *not* to be released from *present* suffering, but to be admitted into *eternal* life. He heard his companion blaspheming the dying Lord, and he raised his voice to rebuke him. We do not hear of any voice being lifted up to rebuke blasphemers on that day, except the voice of this penitent. But while he reproved his fellow, he did not forget to confess his own sins. He acknowledged they had been *so* great, that even crucifixion was not too severe a punishment. "We receive the *due reward* of our deeds." And then he bore a noble testimony to the innocence of Jesus: "This man hath done nothing amiss." How did he know that? Had he not beheld his heavenly meekness, and heard his divine prayer—"Father, forgive them, they know not what they do?" But besides all this, the Holy Spirit, who had convinced him of his *own sins*, had convinced him also of the *righteousness* of *Jesus*. Thus his testimony was added to that of Judas, of Pilate, and of Pilate's wife, and it must have been heard by those who stood around the cross.

Some think that *this* thief, as well as the other, when he was *first* fastened to the cross, railed at the Saviour. But others consider that though St. Matthew says, "The *thieves* cast the same in his teeth," the expression does not prove that more than *one* acted thus wickedly.* It seems probable that if the penitent thief had railed at Jesus, he would have confessed *that* sin, when he rebuked his companion for the same. But in whatever manner he may have behaved when on the cross, we are sure that he had led a very wicked life. His is the only instance recorded in Scripture of repentance in a dying hour. It has been well observed that *one* such instance is recorded that none may *despair*, and *but* one—that none may *presume*.

It was like the Son of God to close his life upon earth by an act of *especial mercy*—the salvation of a notorious sinner. It was like *Him*,

* The Commentator Guyse refers to two passages to show that the plural number is sometimes used when only the singular is intended. See Matt. xxi. 17; Gen. xix. 29.

who had once permitted an outcast to wash his feet with her tears, to listen to the prayer of the penitent thief: "Lord, remember me when thou comest into thy kingdom."

How much misery this malefactor must have endured, when detected, condemned, and dragged to execution! Yet—when all hope seemed gone—the prospect of endless happiness was suddenly opened to his view. He felt more joy while hanging in tortures upon his cross, than he had ever experienced when joining in wild uproar with his profane companions. He knew that in a few hours he would be with Jesus in paradise. His *body* indeed was cast in some detested grave in gloomy Golgotha, or was devoured by birds and beasts; but his *spirit* soared to the mansions of the blest, and mingled with the innumerable company of saints and angels. What an evening to follow such a morning!

At a wonderful season the penitent entered heaven! The Lord's sufferings were just over—the conquest of Satan just achieved—the redemption of man just finished—when he joined the heavenly host. Perhaps he was the *first* who followed his Saviour into glory. A brand he was plucked from the burning—a prey snatched out of the jaws of hell, by the all-powerful arm of his dying Lord. In *heaven* he shines a trophy of divine grace; on *earth* his history remains as an encouragement to every guilty creature to call upon the Lord for mercy. Though during his life he did no good, (except perhaps by his expiring words,) *since* his death he has been the means of bringing great glory to his Lord. Thousands when they meet him above will have to tell that they made the prayer he made, and trusted in the promise he received. But let *us* not wait till we are lying in our last agonies before we cry, "Lord, remember me:" but let us *now* call upon this gracious Saviour, that we may spend our lives in his service before we see his face in paradise.

Evening Scripture portion. Acts XVI. *Conversion of the jailer.*

JOHN XIX. 25–27.—*Christ commits his mother to the care of John.*

WHAT a rich reward John received for venturing near his Master's cross! To him the precious charge of the blessed Mary was confided; to him the tender words, "Behold *thy* mother!" were addressed. We do not hear that Jesus spoke to any of his disciples while hanging upon his cross, except to John. How great a proof the Lord gave him of his love when he intrusted his mother to his care, and even authorized him to regard her as his own! He still gives similar proofs of his love. Those who desire to serve him shall not be disappointed.

Some service suited to his powers shall be assigned to each. To one the charge of an orphan family may be committed—to another a post in a missionary field may be assigned. But no office is more honorable than the care of the aged and destitute saints. It is a distinguished favor to be permitted to watch over their declining years, and to close their failing eyes.

What holy intercourse John must have held with his Lord's mother during the rest of her life! How many incidents concerning her blessed Son, that are not recorded in the Scriptures, must have been treasured up in her memory! She had watched beside him when sleeping in the manger—had held him in her arms when travelling into Egypt, and had guided his steps when a child in Nazareth. Yet she had never seen him commit a single sin—had never beheld his infant face inflamed with passion—nor heard his lisping tongue utter deceit.

If parents love so fondly their *sinful* offspring, what must have been the affection of Mary for her *sinless* Son! We may also feel certain that Jesus loved his mother better than any other Son ever loved a parent. Though enduring the acute agonies of the cross, he thought of her desolate state. Did he not prove the infinite compassion of his heart by remembering her at such a moment? He would not leave her in this world without a home; he knew where she would be most tenderly loved, and most carefully watched over, and most highly honored; and therefore he consigned her to the care of the gentle and affectionate apostle John.

The Lord Jesus has taught children by his own example never to forget the kindness they received in their helpless infancy. When they are grown up they should use every exertion to provide for their parents a comfortable home. It is melancholy to see an aged father driven from his cottage to seek an asylum among strangers, while his children are enjoying many of the comforts of life.

But are there any who believe in the Lord Jesus Christ, and who yet fear lest they should be forsaken in their sickness or old age? Let them remember that their Saviour once said, "He that shall do the will of my Father which is in heaven, the same is my brother, and sister, and *mother*." If he provided for the support of his *earthly* mother's declining years, will he forsake his *spiritual* mothers, and brothers, and sisters? No, he will provide for their wants till their latest breath; and it is probable he will do it in the same *manner* as he supplied those of his earthly mother. Ravens were not sent to feed her, as they fed Elijah, nor did a never-failing cruse and barrel sustain her life, but a pious friend was raised up to minister to her wants. He who appointed Joseph to nourish the aged Israel, and Ruth to sustain the beloved Naomi, and Onesiphorus to refresh the imprisoned apostle, still puts it into the hearts of his servants to succor his poor and afflicted people. It may be a son, or one dear as a son, or it may be a stranger who supplies their need; but by some means or other the promise is always fulfilled: "My God shall supply all your need according to his riches in glory by Christ Jesus." (Phil. iv. 18, 19.)

Evening Scripture portion. Epistle to Philemon. ***Kindness to the saints.***

MATT. XXVII. 45–49.—*The darkness.*

WHEN the Son of God was *born*, a great light was seen in the heavens in the midst of the *night;* but when he was *dying*, a sudden darkness overspread the land at *noonday*. The *shepherds* were sore afraid when they saw the *light*. How, then, must the *murderers* of the Lord have felt when they beheld the *darkness!* What was the cause of this darkness? Sometimes an eclipse of the sun will suddenly obscure the day. But an eclipse cannot occur at the time of a full moon. As it was at *that* season the passover was celebrated, it is clear this darkness was not caused by an eclipse. It was a *miraculous* event. It was a judgment sent by God. And why? To show his wrath against the murderers of his Son. Since the beginning of the world so awful a deed had never been committed, as the murder of the Lord of glory. The day in which the deed was done might well be distinguished from other days. The language Job used respecting the day of his birth might be applied to it. "Let darkness and the shadow of death stain it. Let a cloud dwell upon it; and the blackness of the day terrify it." (Job iii. 5.)

The crowds who had flocked to Calvary could no longer gaze with unfeeling curiosity, or malicious triumph, upon the Lord's bleeding body and agonized countenance. The Father had drawn a thick curtain around his expiring Son. No circumstance is recorded that occurred during those solemn hours of darkness; but at length a voice was heard saying "My God, my God, why hast thou forsaken me?" The enemies of Jesus knew the voice. They knew it was not the cry of one of the dying malefactors that they heard. But were they melted by the anguish of those tones? No, they mocked as before. Mistaking the word Eli (which means *God*) for the name of Elijah, they cried out, "Let us see whether Elias will come to save him." The three hours' darkness had not changed their wicked hearts.

While the Son enjoyed his Father's presence, he could bear the insults of men without a complaint. But when that countenance, which had ever shone upon him, was hidden from his sight, then he uttered an agonizing cry. Other sorrows were familiar to him from his cradle; but this was a new and strange trial. Of him it is written that he "is in the bosom of the Father." What closeness of communion, what depth of love, are implied in that expression! Nothing could have interrupted this communion or deadened the sense of this love, but *sin*. Our sins were the cloud that for a moment hid the Father's face from his only beloved Son. For a moment it cast a deep shadow over the heart of the Son of God, and then was blotted out forever in his atoning blood. From his Father's throne, he calls to us, and says, 'O Israel, thou shalt not be forgotten of me. I have blotted out, as a thick cloud, thy transgressions, and as a cloud thy sins; return unto me; for I have redeemed thee." (Is. xliv. 22.) But *each* sinner must come to him, that *each* sinner may receive pardon. Those who will not come will die in their sins. Then God will forsake them forever. When they call out, "*Why* hast thou forsaken us?" what will be the reply? Will it not be, "Ye *would* not come unto me that ye might have life?" A child abandoned by its parents,—a wife deserted by her husband, are regarded with pity, but the soul forsaken of his God is the most miserable of all beings. This is the misery of the lost spirits in hell. God hast cast them away from his presence.

Evening Scripture portion. Ps. XXII. *Christ on the cross.*

JOHN XIX. 28–30.—*The sponge of vinegar.*

WHEN our dying Saviour said, "I thirst," he revealed to those around the anguish of his *body*. He had before declared the anguish of his *soul*, by crying out, "My God, my God, why hast thou forsaken me?" *His soul* and *body* endured intense agony to ransom *our souls* and *bodies* from eternal torment. The pain of extreme thirst cannot be conceived by those who have not experienced it. A thick crust encases the inside of the mouth, and renders the tongue stiff, while a burning sensation in the throat makes the sufferer feel as if a fire were consuming his whole frame. These were the sensations of the Saviour, and they are described in the Psalms of the prophet David. "My strength is dried up like a potsherd, and my tongue cleaveth to my jaws." (Ps. xxii. 15.) "My throat is dried." (Ps. lxix. 3.) "My bones are burned as an hearth." (Ps. cii. 3.)

Yet the Lamb of God would have endured all these pangs in silence, had it not been his Father's will that before he expired he should let men know that he was tormented by thirst. He remembered it was written in Ps. lxix. 21, "In my thirst they gave me vinegar to drink." Therefore he exclaimed, "I thirst." A vessel full of vinegar stood near the cross, designed probably for the refreshment of the soldiers. One of them dipped a sponge into this vessel, and fixing it at the end of a long and straight branch of hyssop, applied it to the Saviour's mouth. The rest (as St. Matthew relates) continued to utter their profane mockeries, saying, "Let be, let us see whether Elias will come to save him." By this speech they meant to say to their com rades, "What is the use of your helping him? he has called upon one more powerful than you, even Elijah. Wait a little, and see whether *he* will not come to rescue him from his misery." We may imagine with what fiendish shouts of laughter these words were accompanied.

Many saints have expired in the midst of weeping friends; the Lord was surrounded by insulting enemies. But now the *last* insult had been offered. The Saviour had filled up the measure of his sufferings, and had drained to the very dregs the cup his Father had given him to drink. Knowing this, he cried out, "It is finished." This cry was uttered by parched lips and a dried-up tongue. And *why* were those lips parched, and that tongue dried up? That we might never need a drop of water to cool our burning tongues. The Saviour was tormented by thirst, that we might quench ours in living fountains of water. We could never have atoned for *our own sins*. Our tears could not have washed them away. Our good works could not have made amends for them. Therefore Jesus offered up *himself* a sacrifice for us. But now his sufferings are over. When we hear of them, we have the comfort of knowing that they are *past*, and that they will never be endured again. It is not necessary that he should ever feel another pang, or bear another insult. Are we troubled by the remembrance of our sins? Let us look with faith on the Lamb of God, and our guilty consciences shall have peace. The Holy Spirit draws the sinner to the foot of the cross, and enables him to feel that the blood once shed has atoned for all his transgressions. A penitent who had long sought for pardon, found peace as she was reading the following words—

Jesus, our great High Priest,
Offer'd his blood, and died;
My guilty conscience seeks
No sacrifice beside.
His powerful blood did once atone,
And now it pleads before the throne.

Evening Scripture portion.
Isa. LIII. *Prophecy of Christ's sufferings and glory.*

LUKE XXIII. 46.—*The last words of Christ.*

WHEN we hear that a saint has left this world we wish to know what were his last words. How precious are the dying accents of a brother,—a child,—or a parent! We treasure them up in our hearts, and perhaps remember them as long as we live. At this moment some of us may recollect the last words of a friend we loved and lost. But whose words can be so precious as those of our Saviour, our nearest and dearest friend? There are seven sentences recorded as spoken by him while on the cross. *Three* were uttered *before* the darkness overspread the land, and *four* near its conclusion. The first three concerned others, *not* himself. One was a prayer for his enemies, "Father, forgive them, they know not what they do;" the next was a promise to a penitent, "Verily, verily, I say unto thee, to-day shalt thou be with me in paradise;" and the third implied a request to a beloved mother and disciple, "Behold thy mother," "Behold thy son."

The last four concerned himself. One expressed the anguish of his *soul*, "My God, my God, why hast thou forsaken me?"—another the anguish of his *body*, "I thirst;"—the next told of sufferings *ended*, "It is finished;"—the last of joys *begun*, "Father, into thy hands I commend my spirit." These are the words of David in the thirty-first psalm. In *all* the scenes of our Saviour's life his heavenly perfections were displayed; but in his dying hours they shone forth with the greatest splendor. His forgiving love was seen in his prayer for his enemies,—his compassion in his promise to the penitent,—his faithfulness in his charge to John,—his patience in his expiring cries,—and his unshaken confidence in his God in his *last* words, "Father, into thy hands I commit my spirit." As soon as he was nailed to the cross he called upon his Father, and when just expiring, he again said, "Father." In the moment of his greatest anguish he cried, "*My God.*" Thus he fulfilled the prophecy in Ps. lxxxix. 26. "He shall cry unto me, Thou art my Father, my God, and the rock of my salvation."

Though Jesus was God, yet he was *man* also, and he felt as a man. Though without sin, he was tempted in all points like as we are. He endured the pangs of death. His soul was separated from his body. The moment of separation is called "death." Every human being feels it to be an awful moment. There is only one thought which can sustain us *then;* it is the assurance that God is our Father. He who has *doubts* on this subject, feels like a traveller who is going to tread an *unknown* path,—to tread it in *darkness*, and to tread it—*alone*. But how can we know that God is our Father? The Scriptures answer that question: "Ye are all the *children* of God by *faith* in Christ Jesus." (Gal. iii. 26.) "To as many as received him, to them gave he power to become the *sons* of God, even to them that *believe* in his name." (John i. 12.) When we apply to Jesus for the pardon of our sins, *then* we are adopted into the family of God; then the Holy Spirit is shed abroad in our hearts; then we feel that God is *our* Father, because he is the Father of our Lord Jesus Christ; and then we cry, Abba, that is, "Father." (Rom. viii. 15.) We cannot trust *strangers*, but a child can trust his father. We have heard of the boy who was not afraid in the storm, and who said, "My Father's at the helm." Jesus trusted in God. Even his enemies said, when they scoffed at him, "He trusted in God." Worldly people cannot trust him, for they do not *know* him. To them he is a *stranger*. They often *say* they trust him; they often *think* they trust him; but they trust him with nothing that they *care about*. They cannot trust him to choose their *lot in life;* therefore they are always forming schemes of their own: nor to provide for them in *old age;* therefore they are often terrified by fears of poverty and desolation. They cannot trust him to guide them one step which they do not *see*, nor to give them one blessing which they do not already *hold in their hands*. This is *not* to trust him. But the children of God can trust him while they live with their *earthly concerns*, and, when they come to die, with their *immortal spirits*. O that they trusted Him more! Martin Luther, the holy reformer, was remarkable for his trust in God. Three hours a day he set apart for calling upon his Father, and he received the most wonderful answers to his prayers. When he was dying, he was often heard to say, "Father, into thy hands I commend my spirit." These were *almost* his last words. He added, "God so loved the world, that he gave his only begotten Son, that whosoever believeth in him should not perish."

Evening Scripture portion. Ps. XXXI. *Trust in God.*

MATT. XXVII. 51–54.—*The earthquake.*

MEN made no public lamentation for the Son of God when he expired. But his Father caused the inanimate creation to give signs of mourning; for the earth quaked, and the rocks were rent. These terrible events shook the hearts of the soldiers,—those barbarous men who had continued to insult him till he drew his last breath. With grief and dismay they exclaimed, "Truly this *was* the Son of God." Had they known a little *sooner* who he was, they might have shown him pity,—they might have implored his pardon,—they might, like the dying thief, have obtained mercy. But another opportunity was granted to them: afterwards the apostles declared he was exalted a Prince and a Saviour, to give repentance and forgiveness of sins!

Whatever our sins may have been against Jesus, we can have the comfort of confessing them at his feet. It is painful when we have lost a friend, to feel that we cannot ask him to pardon any unkind act that we have done. What a relief it would be to a child, when he remembers his offences against a deceased parent, if he could but see him once more, to tell him how deeply he laments every word,—every look,—every thought, which was *not* affectionate,—which was *not* reverential! But we *can* express to our Redeemer all the bitter regrets we feel for our past ingratitude and rebellion!

Let us now leave the scene of terror round the cross, and look at another scene in the temple. The veil was suddenly rent from the top to the bottom. At that very moment the priests were ministering in the holy place; for Jesus expired at three o'clock,—when the evening sacrifice was offered. The veil had always hidden the *inner* chamber of the temple from every eye, except that of the high priest, who entered it once a year, when he approached the mercy-seat to make atonement for the sins of Israel. But all at once this inner chamber, called the Holy of Holies, was exposed to view, with the ark and the glorious cherubim. The veil could not have been rent without the exertion of *great* power; for it was four fingers in thickness, and thirty ells in length, and as a new one was hung up every year, it never became weak through age.

And what did the rending of this veil signify? The Holy Ghost has explained this mystery. (Heb. x. 19–22.) The veil represented the flesh of Jesus; the rending of the veil—his death. By his death the way into the presence of God is opened. Sinners may approach the mercy-seat without fear, because their great High Priest has atoned for their sins by the sacrifice of himself. But we have no reason to believe that the priests who beheld this wonder understood its meaning. Their hearts were hardened. They had resisted the instructions of the Son of God within that temple day after day,—they had not been appalled by the confessions of Judas that very morning,—and they continued to oppose the truth even when the hand of God wrought this miracle before their eyes.

There was another wonder that accompanied the death of Jesus. "The graves were opened." The Jews were accustomed to bury their dead amongst the rocks, and when the rocks were rent the graves were opened; but the dead continued to sleep in the dust until—their Lord arose. THEN,—and not *till* then,—*many* of the bodies of the saints came out of their graves. We ask, "*What* saints?" Were they saints *lately* dead, such as Simeon, or Anna, or John the Baptist, who had been known by some still living in Jerusalem? Or were they saints *long since* departed; saints who had seen Christ afar off, and had rejoiced in the prospect of his coming? We know not *who* they were. *Where* did they go? To the holy city—to Jerusalem. To *whom* did they appear? Unto *many;*—we know not their names; but we may conclude that they were true believers; for Jesus, when he was risen, showed himself to none but them. What glorious interviews must have taken place between the righteous dead and the righteous living! How much we should like to know particulars concerning these meetings! But nothing is revealed. How *long* did these saints remain upon earth? Did they ascend to heaven with their Lord? We cannot tell *when* they left this earth, but we are sure that they are not *now* wanderers below. Where Jesus is there must his servants be. These saints are favored above other saints. They have risen earlier than their brethren, even *before* the dawn of day: they shine in their glorified *bodies* among the host of *disembodied* spirits. They were born from the dead on the same day as their Lord: his resurrection day was theirs also. But there will be *another* resurrection day, when *all* the sleeping saints will rise. Shall *we* appear among the shining company?

Evening Scripture portion. Heb. IX. *The way into the Holiest.*

JOHN XIX. 31, 32.—*The death of the two thieves.*

IT was the custom among the Romans to allow crucified persons to remain on their crosses long after they had expired. But the Jews had a law which forbade this practice. God had commanded, "If a man have committed a sin worthy of death, and thou hang him on a tree, his body shall not remain *all night* upon the tree, but thou shalt in any wise bury him that day, (for he that is hanged is accursed of God,) that thy land be not defiled." (Deut. xxi. 23.) If it was wrong to allow a person to remain on a cross, or tree, on a *common* day, it was of course more improper to allow him to remain there on the *Sabbath.* The Jews had a peculiar reverence for *that* Sabbath which occurred during the feast of the Passover. They regarded it as a *high* day, and they were very anxious that dead bodies should be removed before it began. As they began their Sabbath at six o'clock on Friday evening, it was necessary on this occasion to use great expedition.

The Jews, supposing that none of the crucified persons might be dead so soon, besought Pilate to hasten their death, in the usual, but cruel manner, by breaking their legs. They knew not that the object of their hatred had forever escaped from their hands, and that they would never have the opportunity of inflicting another pang upon his sacred person. How hateful to God was the worship of those men in his temple, on the approaching Sabbath! The words spoken by the prophet Isaiah applied to them: "When ye spread forth your hands, I will hide mine eyes from you; when ye make many prayers I will not hear: your hands are full of blood." (Is. i. 15.) Their hands were imbrued in the blood of the Son of man. How could his Father bear them in his presence! Let us never imagine that we can please God by our services, while we are stained with unpardoned sins—sins not *abhorred,*—not *confessed,*—not *forsaken.* None can truly please him but those who are cleansed from guilt by faith in his Son.

When these wicked men commanded the legs of the malefactors to be broken, they accomplished the purpose of God. Jesus had said to the penitent thief, "*To-day* shalt thou be with me in paradise." Had that poor sufferer been left to hang upon the cross, he might have lingered several days. The soldiers broke his legs, and that *very day* he was in paradise with the Saviour, in whom he had believed. The other thief was killed at the same *time*, and in the same *manner;* but we have no reason to think that he went to the same *place*. We do not hear that he was moved by the rebuke his companion gave, or that he offered the prayer his companion offered. Death is no release to an unpardoned sinner. The agonies of a cross are not to be compared to the torments of hell, where the worm never dies, and where the fire is never quenched.

We know not in what *manner* we may die, by what painful disease, or dreadful accident. We will leave all these circumstances in the hand of God, trusting in his mercy to support us through every fiery trial. But let us often ask, "What will become of our souls when they leave these bodies?" The friends who stand around a dying bed cannot see the spirit as it leaves its earthly abode, nor trace its course as it is carried by angels into heaven, or plunged among devils in the abyss of perdition; but when the last struggle is over, then we ourselves shall know where we shall FOREVER abide.

Evening Scripture portion. Is. LXVI. ***Everlasting torments.***

JOHN XIX. 33–37.—*A soldier pierces the Lord's body.*

AFTER the Lord had expired, no dishonor was offered to his sacred body. The Jews intended to dishonor it by breaking his legs, but their design was defeated. When the soldiers came to his cross, they found that he was dead already. They might have broken his legs, *though* he was dead; but the Scriptures had declared, "A bone of him shall not be broken." It is written in Ps. xxxiv. 20, "He keepeth all his bones, not one of them is broken." The soldiers knew nothing of the prophecies; yet they fulfilled them, both by *not* breaking his legs, and by piercing his side. Jesus died at the time the feast of the Passover was celebrated, and he was the true Lamb whose blood atoned for the sins of Israel and of the world. It was commanded concerning the paschal lamb, "Neither shall ye break a bone thereof." (Ex. xii. 46.) It was also commanded that its blood should be shed, and sprinkled upon the lintel and posts of the door. When the side of Jesus was pierced, his blood must have sprinkled the cross, and flowed in a copious stream upon the ground.

And what a stream it was—composed not only of *blood*, but of *water*. Some think that the water came from the pericardium, (the case in which the heart is enclosed,) and that it was a proof that life was extinct. It is all-important to prove that Jesus really died upon the cross; for if *he* did not really die, then *we* must die eternally. But we possess abundant evidence of his death. There was one standing by the cross who saw the spear enter into his side, and it is *he* who has recorded the fact. John did not leave the cross when his Master died. He lingered near to see what would become of his sacred body. If he had left it for a short time to take his Lord's mother to his own home, he had returned. Now that the darkness was past, he could see all that was done to his Lord's body. He saw the water and the blood, "and he bare record, and his record is true, and he knoweth that he saith true, that ye might believe."

There is a *spiritual* meaning in this stream of blood and water. The blood atones for sin. *Before* it was shed the penitent malefactor trusted in it, and was pardoned. One of our sweetest poets describes his case and his *own* also—

> "The dying thief rejoiced to see
> That fountain in his day,
> And there have I, as vile as he,
> Wash'd all my sins away."

But sinners are not only *guilty*—they are *dead* in trespasses and sins. From Jesus flows the *water* of *life*—the Holy Spirit. He spake of the Spirit under the emblem of *water* on the last day of the feast of tabernacles, when he said, "If any man thirst, let him come unto me and drink." (John vii.) We cannot mistake the meaning of the invitation, for it is written, "This spake he of the *Spirit*, which they that believe on him should receive." (John vii. 39.) Let us come to Jesus for the *double* blessing—atoning blood and living water. Whosoever shall look by *faith* on his pierced side shall receive both. The glorious wound adorns the *risen* body of our crucified Saviour as the everlasting memorial of his love. Men look with wonder at the little spring which swells into the mighty Nile, and fertilizes half a continent. But with what amazement angels, as well as men, regard that wound, which is the fountain of blessedness to millions of beings throughout eternity!

Evening Scripture portion. Rev. I. *The pierced Saviour.*

John XIX. 38 to end.—*The burial.*

What a contrast there is between the circumstances of the Lord's *death* and those of his *burial!* Jesus died in a *shameful* manner; stripped of his garments, and exposed to the insults of the multitude. He was buried in an *honorable* manner; wrapped in linen, white and clean, and covered with a large quantity of precious spices. He died by the hands of *Gentile* soldiers; he was buried by two of the most honorable of the *Jewish* nation. He died in a *loathsome* spot, Golgotha, the place of a skull; defiled by the bones of malefactors; he was buried in a *new* tomb, in a rich man's garden, a spot untainted by the breath of corruption.

What was the reason of this difference? When he *died*, he was an offering for sin; when he was *buried*, the offering had been accepted. When he died, he was treated according to *our* deserts; when he was buried, according to his *own*. The prophet Isaiah foretold that he would be with the rich in his death; and he assigned the reason for this honorable treatment, "Because he had done no violence, neither was deceit found in his mouth." Jesus was executed upon a charge of violence and deceit. (Is. liii.) The Jews said he had stirred up the people against the Roman emperor, and that he had deceived them, by saying that he was a King. On account of these accusations he was sentenced to die. But it is *we* who have been guilty of violence and deceit. There is not one of us who can truly say, "I have never done any harm—I have never attempted to deceive." God, who knows all men, has said, "*Destruction* and misery are in their ways" "They go astray as soon as they be born, speaking *lies*." It was for *our* sins that Jesus was put to death; but it was for his *own* righteousness that he was honored *after* death.

In old times the Lord often showed his displeasure against sin by causing the dead bodies of the wicked to be shamefully treated; thus he appointed dogs to lick the blood of wicked Ahab, and to eat the flesh of the more wicked Jezebel. The honorable burial of the Son of God was an open testimony of his Father's favor.

All that was done to Jesus was done to him as a *public* person. He was the surety for his people. He *died*, because *their* sins were imputed to *him; they* shall *never* die, because *his* righteousness is imputed to them. What a glorious exchange! Who would have made such an exchange but the compassionate Son of God! Why should the believer fear to descend into the tomb, since Christ has taken away his guilt! In the prospect of death he may say, in the words of a Christian poet,

"The place where once *thy* body lay,
The place it did perfume;
There will I drop *my* breathless clay,
And rest within *thy* tomb."

But it is possible that we may never taste even the *first* death; for the apostle has declared, "We shall not *all* sleep." There is a chosen number who, like Enoch and Elijah, shall be caught up, while yet living, to meet their Lord in the air.

Evening Scripture portion.
Acts X. ***Peter preaches the gospel to Cornelius.***

LUKE XXIII. 54 to end.—*The women prepare spices.*

THOUGH the Lord Jesus was not followed to the grave by a pompous train, yet some sincere mourners watched his precious body till it was hid from their eyes. These were women who had lingered within sight of his cross, even after he had expired. It is written in St. Matthew's gospel, "And many women were there, beholding afar off, which followed Jesus from Galilee, ministering unto him." (xxvii. 55.) These women had long known the Lord, and had enjoyed the distinguished privilege of supplying his temporal wants. How glad would they have been could they have obtained possession of his beloved remains! But how could they venture to crave such a boon! What must have been their joy when they beheld the two honorable counsellors, Joseph and Nicodemus, take down the body from the cross, and wrap it in fine linen with spices! They followed to see where it would be laid, and Joseph did not repel them from his garden. Not only were they permitted to enter, but two of them continued to sit opposite the sepulchre, even after the stone had been placed at its mouth. These two were Mary Magdalene, and Mary, the mother of the two apostles, James and Joses, (commonly called Jude.) By the last beams of the setting sun, they beheld the sepulchre of their divine and adorable Friend. It is written in Matt. xxvii. 61, "And there was Mary Magdalene and the other Mary sitting over against the sepulchre."

An affectionate heart is always devising means of showing its love by actions. The faithful women who had supplied their Lord, while living, with bread, desired now to embalm his sacred body. Though a hundred pound weight of myrrh and aloes had been bound up in the linen cloth, they were not satisfied. They thought it no waste to lavish an abundance of aromatics upon the torn, the bruised, the mangled corpse of him they loved. If odors of sweet incense continually filled the temple composed of *stones*, what could be too sweet, or too precious, to bestow on that more glorious temple, the body of the Lord! But they could not mix their costly unguents *immediately*, for the Jewish Sabbath began at six o'clock on Friday evening, and that hour had almost arrived when the Lord was laid in his tomb. They rested on the Sabbath-day according to the commandment, and deferred their preparations till six o'clock on Saturday evening, when the Sabbath was ended. What veneration these holy women showed for that holy day! They delayed to accomplish their ardent desire rather than break it. How does their conduct condemn those who suffer any trifling incident to interfere with the sacred day of rest!

Of all the Sabbaths that have ever dawned since the creation of the world, surely *that* during which the Redeemer lay in his grave, was the most mournful to the church of God. Many hearts have been wrung with anguish by the thought, "My mother is dead," "My child is dead;" but the disciples on that Sabbath could say, "Our *Saviour* is dead." And when, on the following night, they prepared their ointments, how many bitter tears must have mingled with the precious spices! And why did they grieve? Because they remembered not the *promise* that the Lord would rise on the third day from the tomb. Had they remembered it, they would have passed their nights and days in singing praises, instead of in shedding tears. For want of *knowledge* they suffered much sorrow. And do not the children of God still suffer much anxiety, because they remember not the promises written in the Scriptures? When all appears dark around, how apt they are to fear that the light will never return! If we love God, we may feel sure that all things are working together for our good. And even when the great storm of the last days arises, the saints ought not to be cast down. When other men's hearts are failing them for fear, and for looking after those things which are coming on the earth, they should remember the command, "When these things begin to come to pass, then look up, for *your redemption* draweth nigh." (Luke xxi. 28.)

Evening Scripture portion. Is. LVIII. ***Hallowing the Sabbath.***

MATT. XXVII. 62 to end.—*The priests set a watch around the tomb.*

THE "next day that followed the day of preparation," was the Sabbath. It was on that holy day that the chief priests and Pharisees applied to Pilate to make sure the sepulchre. What a glaring instance of inconsistency their conduct affords! They who had always accused the Lord of breaking the Sabbath by healing the sick, now, to accomplish their own wicked ends, violated the holy day in a public and flagrant manner. How different from theirs was the conduct of those pious women, who refrained on the Sabbath from preparing ointments to embalm the Lord's body!

But it is remarkable, that while the *disciples forgot* the words of Jesus, "After three days I will rise again," his *enemies remembered* them. Sometimes the wicked possess more *knowledge* of the truth than the righteous; but their *hearts* are always wrong. The disciples *mourned* because they knew not that Jesus would rise from the dead: the Pharisees *trembled*, because they feared lest he should. What is the state of our *hearts* towards Jesus? Should we be *glad* to see him come in his glory, or do we *dread* the day of his appearing?

The Pharisees were not the *only* persons who applied to Pilate respecting the body of Jesus. On the day of the crucifixion, the two honorable counsellors, Joseph and Nicodemus, had made a very different request from that of the Pharisees. They had besought Pilate to permit them to take away the body, and had obtained their desire. We know that Pilate had condemned the Lord to death against the convictions of his own conscience. Wishing to have no more to do in the mysterious affair, he permitted the friends of Jesus to take possession of his remains. It is evident that he was not pleased with the malicious request of the Lord's enemies; for he refused to give any commands on the subject, and replied, "Ye have a watch." There was a band of Roman soldiers, employed by the Jews to guard the temple. This band was placed around the tomb to guard the temple of the Lord's body. But the Pharisees were not satisfied even with this precaution. They thought it possible that the disciples might bribe the soldiers to open the tomb; therefore they sealed the stone.

"Vain the stone, the watch, the seal,
Christ hath burst the gates of hell;
Death in vain forbids his rise,
Christ hath open'd Paradise."

The guards set to obstruct the entrance of the tomb, were designed by God to become witnesses of his power and glory. The schemes of wicked men against the Lord's anointed shall be overruled for the establishment of his kingdom. He that sitteth in the heavens laughs at their puny efforts. The day will come when it will be shown that all they have done to injure his cause, has only promoted his glory. But they will be punished for their wicked *designs*. Satan has not been able really to injure Christ; but he will be consigned to the burning lake because he made the blasphemous attempt.

Evening Scripture portion. Rom. II. *The inconsistency of hypocrites.*

MATT. XXVIII. 1–4.—*The resurrection.*

IN this short passage two very different scenes are described. One is a scene of sorrow; the other of joy. In one we behold weeping saints; in the other, a joyful angel. Yet there is a close connection between these two scenes. It was the same Lord who occupied the thoughts of those mourners and of that joyful messenger. But the angel *knew* more than the women did. He rejoiced because he was sent to unbar the tomb; they mourned because they thought there was nothing left for them to do except to embalm the body.

What an honor was conferred upon that angel! With ease he rolled away the massive stone. The soldiers who surrounded the tomb could not maintain their post at his approach. It was not the *earthquake* that terrified them, but the sight of the angel. "For fear of *him* the keepers did shake and become as dead men." The angel watches in their stead; he sits upon the stone, as if to take possession of the place in the name of his Lord. A few words are used to describe his glorious person: but no words can give us a full idea of it. "His countenance was like lightning and his raiment white as snow." Both lightning and snow come from *above*, as the angel did, and when they come they excite our wonder and admiration. The splendor of the forked lightning, and the purity of the driven snow, are not equalled by any other objects in creation.

If *angels* are so glorious, what must be the glory of their *Lord!* There is no description given of *his* appearance as he rose from the tomb. None of the inhabitants of earth were permitted to behold him issuing forth from his dark resting-place. The angel went before to lay the keepers low, that no profane eye might gaze upon divine brightness. Had the faithful women arrived at the place only a few minutes earlier, they would have witnessed the rising of their Lord. But God had appointed that none but heavenly beings should behold the rapturous sight. We know not whether any glorified saints were hovering near; whether Moses and Elijah were there; we do know that angels were present.

The light of day arose just before the Lord of glory. That light had hid its head when he expired upon the cross; but it was shining forth when he lived again. It was meet that the sun should shine upon that joyful morning. The morning of the resurrection will be remembered throughout eternity as a *joyful* morning. There have been mornings which have *appeared* joyful at *the time*, but which have been looked back upon *afterwards* with deep regret. Events hailed with delight, have been followed by unforeseen evil consequences. But what glorious *consequences* have flowed from the resurrection, and will flow from it! How many dead souls have been quickened through its divine power! How many mortal bodies will be raised from their tombs! And why? *Because* Jesus rose again. What joyful shouts, what rapturous songs will then be heard! What happy meetings between brethren long separated will then take place! What new sensations of delight will then be experienced! What scenes of glory will burst upon the opening eyes of waking saints! All this joy will be traced to the resurrection of Jesus! As he said to his disciples, "*Because* I live, ye shall live also." Shall *we* partake of this joy? We must first ask another question. Have we now the *life* of Jesus in our souls? Are we born again? In the new *birth* we obtain new *life*. If we have this life in our souls, then we may say, "When Christ, who *is our life*, shall appear, then shall (*we*) also appear with him in glory." (Col. iii. 4.)

Evening Scripture portion. Isa. XXVI. ***The Resurrection.***

MARK XVI. 1–8.—*Three women visit the tomb.*

THESE three women had watched the Lord while hanging upon his cross, and now they come together to visit his tomb. Their attachment to *him* united them to *each other*. Two of these women were mothers—the mothers of holy apostles. Mary was the mother of James and Jude, the relations of the Lord, and Salome was the mother of James and John, two of his most favored friends. How was it that none of these four apostles accompanied their mothers to the sepulchre? Why did they suffer weak women to go alone, while it was yet dark, to a place where they were exposed to the assaults of enemies? Surely these mothers exceeded their sons in love to their Lord. It has been said of woman by a poet:

> "Not she with trait'rous kiss her master stung,
> Not she denied him with unfaithful tongue:
> *She*, when apostles fled, could danger brave,
> *Last* at his *cross*, and *earliest* at his *grave*."

A *woman* was the *first* to eat the forbidden fruit. It was merciful in God to permit her to be the *first* to visit the sacred tomb.

These women were aware that great difficulties lay in their way. They had seen on Friday evening an enormous stone placed at the door of the sepulchre. They said to each other as they approached the place, "Who shall roll us away the stone?" How glad would they have been of the help of all the eleven apostles! But greater help than theirs was afforded. An angel had rolled away the stone. Had these women known that a guard of soldiers surrounded the tomb, their fears would have been much increased. But this obstacle also was removed before they knew it existed. The angel by the brightness of his appearance had laid the soldiers senseless on the earth. How often there seems to be a great stone in the way of pious undertakings. How apt Christians are to be discouraged, and to say, "Who shall roll it away?" Let their answer be "God." When He designs that a work should be performed, he removes every obstacle.

Affection inspired these women with so much courage that they ventured to enter the sepulchre. Theirs were the first human feet that trod the rocky floor after the Lord had arisen. They hoped to see the precious body, but they beheld on the right side of the tomb a young man sitting clothed in a long white garment. As angels never *die*, they are always *young*. As they never *sin*, they are represented as clothed in *white* garments. They have never known by *experience* either sin or death; but they have *seen* a great deal of both. An angel strengthened the Lord in his agony when he was bearing our *sins*, and struggling with our *death*. An angel comes and sits in his *tomb*. Strange place for an angel to rest in! But he had a message to deliver to the faithful women who were coming there, and he waited to receive them. With what kindness he addressed the trembling mourners! He showed that he knew why they grieved, and why they came, and what they expected to find. He was the *first* to declare that Jesus was risen. What joy a kind angel must have felt when uttering the words, "He is risen." He bids the women search the empty tomb. "Behold the place where they laid him." Then he sends a message to the apostles. He knew they had forsaken their Lord; he sees how backward they are to honor him; yet he remembers them; for he knew that his Lord loved them, and he must love them too. He sends an especial message to *that* apostle who had sinned the most flagrantly—even to Peter. "Tell his disciples, and *Peter*." Though so liable to sin ourselves, how harsh we are in judging others! This angel had never forsaken or denied his Lord, yet he felt for those who had. He was anxious that their tears should be dried up without delay.

How did the women receive the heavenly tidings? It is written in St. Matthew's gospel, "They departed quickly from the sepulchre with fear and *great* joy." Their joy was *greater* than their fear. They trembled because they had seen angels; they rejoiced because they hoped soon to see their Lord. The *fear* was the consequence of human infirmity, the *joy* flowed from faith and love. There are many fears now in the hearts of believers, but they shall all pass away; whereas their joy shall increase and endure forever. When they have no sin, they shall have no fear; and when they see Jesus, their joy shall be full. Do *we*, who never saw him, long to see him? He cometh with clouds. May we meet him in the air, and be ever with him.

Evening Scripture portion. 1 Pet. III. *Holy women.*

JOHN XX. 1–10.—*Peter and John visit the tomb.*

MARY Magdalene did not come *alone* to the sepulchre. We find from the Gospel of St. Mark that she was accompanied by two other women, Mary and Salome. But when she perceived that the stone was rolled away from the sepulchre, she acted in a different manner from her companions. Instead of approaching to examine the tomb, she immediately concluded that the precious body had been stolen, and ran back to Jerusalem for assistance. Christians, though they resemble each other in attachment to the same Lord, have different ways of showing that attachment. Some, like Mary Magdalene, are ready to give up all for lost in the first moment of alarm; while others, like Salome and the other Mary, continue to hope even against hope.

To whom did this sorrowful woman apply for aid? To those beloved apostles, Peter and John. We often find those two apostles near each other. It seems that a close friendship subsisted between them. Peter's shameful denial had not broken the bond. John had not said to Peter, "I can no more own you as a brother." He himself was not without sin: he had *forsaken* his Lord, though he had not denied him.

Mary Magdalene gave a very alarming account of what she had seen in Joseph's garden: she even asserted, "They have taken away the Lord." Peter and John set off with the utmost speed towards the tomb. John was the swifter. It is generally supposed that he was the younger. But Peter was the *bolder;* for when he arrived at the tomb he *entered*, whereas John at first only *looked* in, though he also entered afterwards.

And what did they see in the tomb? The linen clothes. This sight convinced John that his Lord's *body* had not been stolen; but that his Lord *himself* was risen. If enemies had taken away the *body*, would they have left the *clothes?* And if they had been suddenly surprised, and dropped the clothes in their haste to escape, would those clothes have been neatly arranged?—and the napkin which had been round the sacred head, would it have been folded in a place by itself? No, it was evident that he who had reposed in the tomb, no longer wore the attire of death. We are not told in *this* place what effect the sight of the clothes had upon *Peter;* but from another passage it appears that the sight convinced *him* also. (See Luke xxiv. 12.)

Both these apostles returned to their own home, without having seen either the Lord or his angels; without even having seen the women who had seen the Lord; and therefore without having heard their message. Why did they not still linger round the tomb, or search in every place for him they had lost?

It seems that the apostles, after their Lord's crucifixion, were afraid of falling into the hands of their enemies, and that on this account they kept as much as possible within their own doors.

There was one who now dwelt with John who was deeply affected by all that concerned the blessed Redeemer: it was his mother. We know that she watched her Son when dying on the cross, but we do not hear of her visiting the tomb. What sweet communion must have been held that day in the home of the beloved apostle! How the Lord's mother and his friend must have rejoiced together over his resurrection! *They* are happy who, living beneath one roof, delight to talk together of their blessed Saviour! How can they who love him, forbear to speak of him, to retrace his kindness in times past, and to anticipate his glorious return!

Evening Scripture portion. Isa. LXIV. *The happiness of believers.*

JOHN XX. 11–18.—*Christ appears to Mary Magdalene.*

MARY Magdalene enjoyed one of the highest honors that was ever bestowed on a human creature—while on earth. She was the *first* to whom the Lord appeared after his resurrection. It is interesting to consider the conduct of this honored woman; for it must have been pleasing to the Lord. She lingered near the tomb after the apostles had departed. Her companions, also, who had seen the angels, were gone. She was *alone.* She was *weeping.* Others may have wept around the tomb, but *her* tears alone are mentioned. Perhaps it may have been on this account that many have supposed that she was the woman who once washed the feet of Jesus with her tears; but there is no foundation for this opinion. Stooping down, she perceived the angels, but felt no fear, for it seems she knew them not. There they were clothed in white, keeping watch in the tomb. The apostles had not seen them, when they had looked in. The heavenly watchers were mindful of Mary's tears, and asked, "Woman, why weepest thou?" She replied, "Because they have taken away my Lord, and I know not where they have laid him." The angels did not attempt to comfort her, as they had done her companions, because a better Comforter was standing behind her. She had complained to *apostles,* then to *angels,* and now she complains to the *Lord* himself. "Sir, if thou have borne him hence, tell me where thou hast laid him, and I will take him away." Grief is unreasonable. Had an *enemy* taken away the body, would he have *told* Mary where he had laid it? The mourner was so transported with sorrow that she knew not what she said, or what she did; she could not distinguish faces, nor remember voices; all was confusion and perplexity.

There are some who weep now, because they fear lest the enemy should triumph over their Lord's body. The saints are the body of Christ, his flesh, and his bones. The enemy has often trampled upon that body, but he can never destroy it. There are three islands, in distant oceans, which in *our* days have been openly assaulted by Satan and his hosts. The prisoners of Madeira, the patriots of Tahiti, and the martyrs of Madagascar, have endured a great fight of afflictions. Some have wept over their sufferings. Jesus beholds the tears of those who feel for his oppressed people, and he says to them with tenderness, "Why weepest thou?" He bids them weep no more, for he will soon avenge his own cause.

Though Mary did not at first remember her Saviour's voice, yet when he pronounced her *own name* she knew it. Shall we ever hear our own names uttered by our Lord? Are they now written in his book? Can we wonder that when Mary had found her Lord she was unwilling to part from him? He said, "Touch me not;" that is, "Hold, or detain me not; for I am not *yet* ascended unto my Father." As he was not going to ascend *immediately*, Mary might hope to see him soon again. Then he sent a message to his *brethren*. He called his disciples his *brethren*. This was the message: "I ascend unto my Father and your Father, unto my God and your God." What a message! How full of grace, of joy, of glory! It is a message to *us*, if we believe in Jesus. His Father is our Father, and loves *us* as he does *him*. (John xvii. 23.) Our elder brother is gone before us, to prepare a place for the younger children in his Father's house.

Evening Scripture portion. Ps. XLII. XLIII. *Panting after God*

MATT. XXVIII. 9, 10.—*Christ appears to the faithful women.*

THE Lord Jesus appeared *first* to Mary Magdalene, after he rose from the dead; then he appeared to her two companions, Mary and Salome. He could transport himself, in one moment, from the place where he stood conversing with Mary Magdalene, near the tomb, to the spot which these women had reached. He met them as they were running *quickly* to bring his disciples word.

He met them with words of joy. He said, "All hail," or "Rejoice ye." He found them rejoicing, but he bid them *again* rejoice. The *first salutation* that he uttered when he rose from the dead was, "Woman, why weepest thou?" His next salutation was, "All hail." He would not bid his people rejoice, if there were not great *cause* for joy. When he was born into the world, the angel said to the shepherds, "Behold I bring you good tidings of *great joy*, which shall be to all people." Since that time Jesus had passed through deep sorrow. And what was the *fruit* of this sorrow? Joy. What joy? The joy of saving souls from eternal death. This was the joy set before him, to gain which he endured the cross, and despised the shame. This is the Father's will, that every one that seeth the Son, and believeth in him, shall have everlasting life. (John vi. 40.) Well might Jesus say to these believing women, "All hail!" If we could now hear Him speak from heaven, we should hear him utter those same words to all who believe in him. Though they might be languishing on sick beds, or weeping over newly-closed graves, he would say to them, "All hail!" But what would he say to unbelievers? He would denounce *wo* upon them, because they have not believed in the only name which can save them from the wrath to come. "Wo unto you that laugh now, for ye shall mourn and weep."

Though the faithful women felt some fear at the sight of their risen Lord, they ventured to approach him, and to hold him by the feet. They must have seen upon those feet the prints of the nails. They loved him *before* he died, but surely they loved him better now. The sight of his agonies on the cross must greatly have increased their love. Every one who has lost dear friends feels, "I never loved them enough while they were with me. The remembrance of their dying pangs endears them doubly to my heart." But what must these women have felt when they remembered all their Lord had gone through, and when they knew it was all for their sakes! Do we wish we had been in their place, lying low at his feet and worshipping him? If we love him, we may look forward to such a meeting.

When Jesus rose from the dead, his *enemies* were not permitted to see him. He appointed a place in Galilee where all his disciples from all parts of the land might assemble to meet him: but his enemies received no invitation. There shall be a place in the air where all who love Jesus shall behold him when he comes again. The *dead* in Christ shall rise *first;* then those who are alive and remain shall be caught up together *with them* in the clouds, to meet the Lord in the *air*. There will be no *parting* after that meeting. "So shall we be *ever* with the Lord." There will be no *sorrow* after that meeting. "God shall wipe away all tears from their eyes." There will be no *sin* after that meeting. "When he shall appear, we shall be *like* him, for we shall see him as he is." (1 John iii. 2)

Evening Scripture portion. 2 Peter III. *The end of the world.*

MATT. XXVIII. 11–15.—*The Pharisees bribe the watch.*

How short was the joy of the world! How soon it was turned into sorrow! Before his crucifixion, the Lord had said, "The world shall rejoice." And they did rejoice during the day that he lay in the grave. The words that God once addressed to Moab concerning their behavior to Israel applied to them: "Since thou spakest of him, thou skippedst for joy." (Jer. xlviii. 27.) But what dismay they felt when they heard that the object of their hatred was risen from the tomb! Yet they persevered in their horrible attempt to deter people from believing in him.

When they learned from the affrighted soldiers the wonders that had happened at the sepulchre, they determined, if possible, to conceal these events. The chief priests took the lead in this dark transaction; they summoned the elders, and consulted with them by what means they should smother the truth. They decided on bribing the soldiers to spread an invented tale. "His disciples came by night, and stole him away while we slept." The father of lies never suggested a more awful lie than this. It is his constant employment to teach sinners to hide their sins under a covering of falsehood. There are numbers to be found in every place who are contriving day after day new ways of concealing their old sins. Their tongues are grown so familiar with lies, that they can tell them without a blush. But unless they repent, they will feel the power of that tremendous sentence, "*All* liars shall have their part in the lake which burneth with fire and brimstone." *All* liars of *every* degree shall share in that condemnation. The Pharisees were deceivers of the *worst* kind. What would be thought of the man who should wilfully deceive his neighbors concerning the place where the fire-engines were kept, though he knew the town was in flames? Through such a man a whole town might be destroyed. The Pharisees were such men. They endeavored to deceive a perishing world respecting him who was the *life* of that world. The resurrection proved that he was indeed the Son of God. This was the fact that his enemies labored to conceal.

They found the Roman soldiers ready to unite in their scheme. There is nothing so wicked that men have not done for the sake of *money*. Some will even plead as an excuse for sin, that they should lose *money* if they did not commit it. Have you never heard persons defend their disobedience to God's laws by saying, "I could not get a living if I acted otherwise?" Have any of us ever made such miserable excuses? There is one question which we ought never to forget. It is *this*: "What shall it profit a man, if he gain the whole world, and lose his own soul?"

These soldiers incurred great guilt when they consented to *spread* the falsehood the Pharisees had invented. They had felt the earthquake, they had seen the angels, yet they did not declare the glory of the Lord. But God found other messengers. Feeble, though faithful women, first proclaimed the joyful tidings. Unlearned, though inspired apostles, confirmed their word, and spread it far and wide. We have heard the glorious truth, that the Lord rose from the dead on the third day. Have we believed it? God has promised to save all those who believe it *with the heart*. "If thou shalt confess with thy mouth the Lord Jesus, and shalt believe *in thine heart* that God raised him from the dead, thou shalt be saved." (Rom. x. 9.)

Evening Scripture portion. 1 Tim. VI. *The love of money.*

LUKE XXIV. 1–12.—*Women visit the tomb.*

THOSE who have attentively examined the history of the resurrection have come to the conclusion that *two* companies of women visited the tomb. St. Matthew and St. Mark record the visit of the *first* company; St. Luke that of the *second*. The *first* company consisted of at least *three* women, Mary Magdalene, the other Mary, and Salome. We do not know how many women composed the *second* band, or what were their names; but it is probable that Joanna, the wife of

Chuza, Herod's steward, was one of them. *Many* women had followed Jesus from Galilee, and had ministered unto him by the way. (Matt. xxvii. 55.) It is not to be supposed that they all lodged in the same house in Jerusalem, or that they reached the sepulchre at the same moment. Those who came *first* saw *one* young man clothed in white *sitting* in the tomb. The *second* band for a time saw no one; but, when they were much perplexed, they beheld *two* men *standing* by them in shining garments. The *first* company, as they were running to bring the disciples word, met their risen Lord: but there is no account of the *second* company being honored with such an interview. By referring to the 23d verse of this chapter, we shall see that there were *some* women who only saw a vision of angels, and not the Lord himself, and *they* may have formed the *second* band.

How do angels address our fallen race? They speak to us as if we were but little children in comparison to themselves. These angels said to the women, "Why seek ye the *living* among the *dead?*" It appeared to them an act of *folly* to look for the Lord of *Life* in the abode of *Death.* They felt that his followers ought to have known that he was risen. They repeated the very words that He had said to them, "The Son of man must be delivered into the hands of sinful men and be crucified, and the third day *rise again.*" Could any words be plainer than these? It was strange that all the disciples should have forgotten them. But while the angels must be astonished at the dulness and forgetfulness of human creatures, they do not exult over them with pride, or upbraid them with harshness. They instruct in a gentle and condescending manner. Let us try to teach like them when we meet with those who are more ignorant than ourselves. The heavenly hosts have been taught by Him who said, "Learn of me, for I am meek and lowly in heart."

What a disappointment it must have been to these women when they found the apostles would not believe their account! But Peter went to the tomb to examine for himself. Whether this was the *same* visit recorded by St. John, or *another*, is uncertain. The sight of the linen clothes convinced Peter that the Lord's body had not been stolen. In the course of the day the Lord himself appeared to Peter. St. Paul declares that he was seen of Cephas (or Peter) before he was seen of the twelve. (1 Cor. xv. 5.) How wonderful that he who had denied his Master should be the first of all the apostles to behold him after his resurrection! Jesus knew that this weeping backslider needed this strong consolation. How the look which his Master had cast upon him while standing in the judgment-hall must have agonized his mind, till he saw again that injured Friend! Christ still pities the poor wanderer. It is not his will that such a one should "be swallowed up with overmuch sorrow." (2 Cor. ii. 7.) It is the duty of his fellow-Christians to forgive and to comfort him, and to confirm their love towards him. How much more is it the delight of the compassionate Saviour to raise him up, to strengthen him, and to wipe away his tears! Is there any sin which lies heavy on the conscience of any of us? Let us confess it at the feet of Jesus. He will not spurn us from his presence: no; but "He will turn again, he will have compassion upon us, he will subdue all our iniquities; and thou wilt cast all their sins into the depths of the sea." (Micah vi. 19.)

Evening Scripture portion. Ps. XXV. *A prayer for pardon.*

LUKE XXIV. 13–24.—*The journey to Emmaus.*

TOWARDS the close of the joyful day which saw the Lord arise, two of the disciples were walking together, oppressed with *sorrow*. The name of one of these men was Cleopas. The name of his companion is not revealed. It does not seem probable that *this* Cleopas was the husband of *that* Mary who visited the sepulchre; for if he had been her husband, he must have known that she had seen the *Lord;* whereas we find that he only speaks of the women having seen *angels*, (v. 23.) It is also to be remarked that he calls them merely "certain women of our company."

Cleopas and his friend were walking towards Emmaus. This village was nearly eight miles to the northwest of Jerusalem. The way thither was mountainous, and in many places almost paved with rock. The gloomy scenery—the rugged path—the lonely way—the declining sun, must have accorded with the troubled state of the disciples' hearts. The risen Lord beheld these two friends as they walked sorrowfully along, and he came to pass the evening in their company. Though he well knew the subject of their conversation, he asked them this question, "What manner of communications are these that ye have one to another, as ye walk and are sad?"

When we are conversing together, if the Lord were to draw near and to make this inquiry, should we always be willing to reply? Out of the abundance of the heart the mouth speaketh. Worldly people *never* take pleasure in conversing about their souls, or Christ, or heaven. They delight in talking of the trifling vanities of time. But even true Christians are apt to forget unseen things, and to waste their precious hours in unprofitable discourse. But when they do converse upon spiritual subjects, they receive a blessing from the Lord. In times of affliction, especially, they should avoid the society of the ungodly. David when in trouble said, "I will keep my mouth with a bridle while the wicked is before me." (Ps. xxxix. 1.) But they should open their hearts to each other. It was in a time of public calamity that the saints described by Malachi met together. "*Then* they that feared the Lord spake often one to another, and the Lord hearkened and heard it." (Mal. iii. 16.)

There must have been something exceedingly gracious in the manner in which Jesus addressed the mourning disciples; for, though they took him for a stranger, they readily opened their grief at his request. What a grief it was! They had lost their Lord. Yet they had not *renounced* him. They looked upon him still, not as a deceiver, but as a "prophet mighty in deed and in word, before God and all the people." Their own negligence was the principal occasion of their grief. Though *many* had been to see the sepulchre, *they* had *not*. Had they gone they also might have seen angels, or at least they would have seen the linen clothes, and by them have been convinced that the Lord was risen. *Then*, instead of mourning together, they would have been rejoicing together. Christians are often unhappy only because they are negligent. They hear their brethren tell of joys which they themselves have never tasted, and they scarcely believe the report. But if they would use the same diligence in searching the Scriptures, and the same importunity in prayer as those happy brethren, they also would rejoice.

Evening Scripture portion. Ps. LXXVII. ***The disconsolate Church.***

LUKE XXIV. 25–35.—*Christ makes himself known at Emmaus.*

HAS any one who loves Jesus ever read the account of the walk to Emmaus without wishing he had been there? How delightful it must have been to hear the Lord explain in all the Scriptures the things concerning himself! But has He not promised his Holy Spirit to enlighten us when we search his holy word? There are things concerning himself in *all* the Scriptures. In the beginning of the Bible we find him revealed as the Seed of the woman; and in the last chapter of the Old Testament, we behold him as the Sun of Righteousness; and in every intervening page we may discover him: as a suffering Lamb, or as a conquering Lion; as a tender shoot, or a strong branch; as a servant, or a king; as a child, or the Ancient of Days; now made low as a worm, and now declared to be the mighty God, the great Creator, the glorious Jehovah.

While the Lord was explaining this mysterious subject to his attentive companions, he arrived at Emmaus. This village was situated on the southern side of a fruitful hill, and commanded a view of the towers and pinnacles of Jerusalem. Lying exposed to the heat of the mid-day sun, it was refreshed by an abundance of cooling springs. Jesus would not have entered the disciples' dwelling had he not been entreated to stay. Whenever we return to our homes, let us make the prayer those disciples made, and say, "Abide with us." No home is really sweet in which Jesus does not abide. Where he is, there are peace, and love, and joy.

The Lord acted as master of the house at the table of his host. According to his custom, "he took bread, and blessed it, and brake it, and gave to them." Then the disciples knew the Lord, for their eyes were opened. God exercises supreme power over our senses. He lets us see and hear what he chooses. In the next world He can open our eyes, and enable us to know saints we have never seen, and to recognise friends we have long lost.

What must the mourners have felt when they discovered that the wonderful stranger was their own beloved Saviour! But they had no opportunity of expressing their delight to *him*, for he vanished out of their sight. After his resurrection the *Lord* neither came in nor went out as before. A glorified body is very different from the houses of clay in which our spirits are imprisoned.

The two friends could not remain at home after the joyful event that had happened! They longed to make their brethren partakers of their happiness. They had left them weeping; but when they arrived at Jerusalem they found them rejoicing. The Lord had appeared to Simon Peter. Though the *women's* report had been disbelieved, *Peter's* testimony had been received.

What was the subject of that evening's conversation? Was it not the various appearances of the Lord? Every particular concerning the interviews that had been enjoyed with Him must have been listened to with the deepest interest. About what do saints above converse? Is it not about their Lord, and how they first learned to know him, and how he manifested himself to them at various seasons of their pilgrimage? Even here, when saints meet together, they delight to speak on these subjects. Like the disciples of old, they have *different* histories to relate. Mary Magdalene might tell how *quickly* he revealed himself to her: Cleopas and his friend might describe how *long* he *delayed* to make himself known to them. *She* met him in the garden—*they* were joined by him in the way. *She* addressed him *first*—*they* were *first* spoken to by him. The dealings of the Lord with his people are still marked by different circumstances; but the *end* in every case will be the same. Though for a season they may lament, saying, "I sought him, but I found him not;" and inquire mournfully, "Saw ye him whom my soul loveth?" at length they will joyfully declare, "I found him whom my soul loveth." (Cant. iii. 2-4.) Those who love Jesus must find him, for *He* himself is seeking them.

Evening Scripture portion. Canticles III. *Seeking Christ*

LUKE XXIV. 36–43.—*Christ eats in the presence of his disciples.*

DURING the course of the resurrection-day the Lord Jesus appeared to several of his people either alone, or when two or three were together. But he crowned the joys of the day by showing himself in the evening to a larger assembly. The apostles, the disciples from Emmaus, and others besides, were all conversing about their risen Lord, when they suddenly saw him standing before them. Nothing could be more comforting than the words he uttered, "Peace be unto you." All his salutations to his people that day had been full of sympathy and encouragement. To the weeping Mary he had said, "Why weepest thou?" to the joyful women, "All hail!" to the mourning disciples, "What manner of communications are these that ye have one to another, as ye walk and are sad?" To Simon Peter we know not what he said; but we are persuaded that He who sent him a gracious *message*, gave him a tender *reception.* To his assembled apostles he said, "Peace be unto you." This peace he won by the pangs of death. Man lost it in Eden; the Son of man regained it on Calvary. He made peace by the blood of his cross, (Col. i. 20;) and he rose from the grave to bestow that peace upon his people. He still lives to bestow it on all who ask it. If there be any uneasy soul seeking for happiness, but not knowing how to obtain it, let that restless creature fall low at the feet of Jesus, and implore his blessing; peace shall sooner or later flow into that troubled heart. A sweet sense of pardon, a lively hope of heaven, and a fervent love to God—these feelings make up the peace that Jesus gives.

How touching it must have been to see the Lord showing his own wounded hands and feet to his disciples, and inviting them to touch his sacred person! God suffered these prints of love to remain after the wounds were forever healed. The apostle John, when he speaks of his Lord in the opening of his first epistle, alludes to the privileges he had enjoyed: "That which was from the beginning, which we have heard, which we have seen with our eyes, which we have looked upon, which our hands have handled, of the Word of Life."

The apostles enjoyed some privileges which we have never known. They heard that blessed voice, they saw that sacred form, they touched those precious limbs; but there are still higher enjoyments that we hope to share *with them* hereafter. The gracious Saviour, who condescended to eat with his disciples after he rose from the dead, has promised to admit *all* his people to intimate communion with himself. There is no creature so mean,—no soul so ignorant,—no sinner so lost, who shall, if he feel the desire to be with Jesus, be refused admittance to his presence. But not *one being* shall approach him in *glory* who has not loved him upon *earth.* To all who love him *not* he will say, "Depart." How would the entrance of an enemy have marred the joy of the evening which Christ spent with his apostles!

Judas was not there. No doubt, in former days, he had stirred up many dissensions among the little band. There shall not be one enemy in heaven to interrupt the harmony. The weak believer shall be there ; the restored backslider shall be there ; the sinner, plucked in the *last* hour as a brand from the burning, shall be there : but not one hypocrite, not one self-righteous formalist, not one worldly-minded person, not one who does not *love* the Lord Jesus Christ. Let each of us ask his own soul, " Shall I be there ?"

Evening Scripture portion. 1 John I. *The apostles' knowledge of Jesus.*

JOHN XX. 19–23.—*Christ bestows the Holy Ghost on his disciples.*

THIS is the same appearance of the Lord as that recorded by St. Luke. It took place in the evening, after the resurrection. It is the *first* meeting recorded of the followers of the *crucified* Saviour. It was the *first* of a long train of Christian assemblies. At this moment, in how many parts of the world congregations are worshipping him who suffered upon the cross ! *Our* family is now met together in honor of his name. But do *our feelings* resemble those of the first disciples ? Do we love Jesus ? Do we earnestly long to see him ? If he were now to stand in the midst of the room, should we be exceedingly glad ? There are many who call themselves Christians, who do *not* love Christ. *They* would not be glad to see him.

When the risen Saviour entered the room where the disciples were assembled, the doors were *shut* for fear of the Jews. It is evident that they were locked, or fastened, in order to keep out the enemy. It was easy for him who had just broken the bars of *death* to open those doors.

St. Luke relates, that on this occasion he *ate* in the presence of his disciples. This he did to show that he was *man.* But he also showed that he was *God.* He *breathed* on his disciples, saying, " Receive ye the Holy Ghost." At that very moment they received the Holy Ghost, though not in so abundant a manner, as after Jesus ascended.

Christ never gives us commands without enabling us to fulfil them. He commanded his apostles to preach the Gospel, and to enable them to preach it, he gave them the Holy Ghost. By this gift their understandings were enlightened more than they had ever been before. But the apostles could not forgive sins. He alone, against whom sin is committed, can forgive it. Why then did Jesus say to his apostles, " Whose soever sins ye remit they are remitted to them ?" Did He not enable them to know whom *He* would forgive ?

When the men who had crucified their Lord came to them in an agony of grief, saying, "Men and brethren, what shall we do?" the apostles knew what to reply. They knew that Christ would forgive his murderers, and they answered, "Repent, and be baptized *every one* of you in the name of Jesus Christ, for the *remission of sins.*" They knew also whom God would *not* forgive. When Ananias and Sapphira lied unto the Holy Ghost, Peter consigned them both to instant death.

What is the greatest boon that sinners can receive? Is it not the forgiveness of sins? Do we desire to know whether *our* sins are forgiven? In the writings of the apostles we shall find rules laid down by which we may examine ourselves. Have we with *real sorrow* confessed our sins, and asked pardon in the name of Jesus? Then we have obtained mercy. For the apostle John has declared in his first epistle, "If we *confess* our sins, he is faithful and just to forgive our sins, and to cleanse us from all unrighteousness." (1 John i. 9.)

Evening Scripture portion. 2 Cor. II. *Pardon in the name of Christ.*

JOHN XX. 24 to end.—*Christ convinces the unbelieving apostle.*

MUCH benefit has often been lost by absence from the assemblies of the saints. Thomas, by his absence, lost an opportunity of seeing the risen Saviour. While his brethren were rejoicing in the thought of the glory of their Lord, he was suffering the miseries of unbelief.

There is something daring and repulsive in the expression he used: "Except I shall see in his hands the print of the nails, and thrust my hand into his side, I will not believe." Thomas little thought when he spoke thus that Jesus heard his words. How many speeches that we have uttered must have grieved the heart of our ever-present Saviour! Were he to appear and remind us of them, we should feel overwhelmed with shame and sorrow.

It was just one week after his resurrection that the Lord came the *second* time to visit his assembled people.

He entered the room in the same wonderful manner as before, passing through the fastened doors. By two signs he showed that he was God. The manner of his entrance displayed his divine *power;* his repeating the words of Thomas manifested his divine *knowledge.*

When Nathanael was brought to Jesus, he was astonished to hear him say, "When thou wast under the fig-tree I saw thee;" and he cried out, "Thou art the Son of God; thou art the King of Israel."

Thomas felt in the same manner when he exclaimed, "*My* Lord and my God." He did not say, (as Israel once had said,) the Lord he is *the* God; but "*My* Lord and *my* God." He loved Jesus, and he knew that Jesus loved him; therefore he could say, "*My* God."

Those wounds in the Saviour's hands seemed to cry out, "I loved thee, and gave myself for thee."

The sin of this apostle was the occasion of a blessing being pronounced on numbers then unborn. "Blessed are they that have not seen, and yet have believed." Thomas ought to have believed the *promise* that Christ would rise, before any witnesses had declared that they had seen him; but he not only doubted Christ's promise, but rejected the testimony of all his brethren. His unbelief was very great; yet it was not that fatal unbelief which reigns in the unconverted, for it was accompanied by sincere love. The Pharisees *dreaded* lest Christ should rise. Thomas regarded his rising again as too joyful an event to be true. *They* tried to shut their eyes to all the proofs that were pressed upon them. *He* sought to obtain stronger proofs than he had yet found. Still Thomas would have been more blessed had he believed the word of Jesus *before* he had seen it accomplished.

Among those who sincerely believe in Jesus how much unbelief may be detected! How often they fear that He has forgotten them, though He has promised that He never will! If they would always trust him they would always taste that peace which passeth all understanding. Jacob, though an eminent saint, in the midst of his fiery trials was tempted to exclaim, "All these things are against me;" but the Shunammite was enabled in the depth of her trouble to say, "It is well."

Evening Scripture portion.
2 Kings IV. 1–37. ***The faith of the Shunammite.***

John XXI. 1–14.—*Christ appears at the lake of Gennesareth.*

This is the *third* time that the Lord showed himself to several disciples assembled together after he rose from the dead. The *first* time was on the evening of the day of his resurrection; the *second* was a week afterwards, when Thomas was present. Both these appearances took place at Jerusalem. The *third* occurred in Galilee. The angel at the tomb had promised that Jesus would meet his disciples in Galilee. In this part of Canaan he had lived from his childhood, and here he had often travelled with his little flock, preaching the Gospel.

It must have been a trial to the apostles not to see their Lord as *soon* as they arrived there. It seems that they were reduced to great necessity while waiting for him, and that they were obliged to resume their old occupation of fishing. But they were not forgotten by him who had given his own flesh for the life of the world.

After a toilsome night, spent in vain endeavors to procure a fresh supply of food, they heard a voice calling out, "Children, have ye any meat?" But they neither recognised the voice, nor the form of their Lord. Soon, however, the beloved apostle John discovered him by his wondrous *acts*. After following his directions, the apostles found their net laden with an enormous quantity of fishes. Then John exclaimed, "It is the Lord."

On several occasions after the resurrection, Jesus made himself known by some word he uttered, or act he performed, without declaring plainly who He was. When he pronounced the name of Mary, he was made manifest as her Lord; and when he blessed the bread at Emmaus, he was discovered by the mourning disciples. There are many ways in which Jesus still makes his people feel that he is present. When a soul is converted, then we know that he is near; when in the midst of trouble, comfort flows into the heart,—when prayer is answered,—when temptation is resisted,—when sin is subdued,—when death is welcomed;—then we may feel assured "It is the Lord."

As soon as the seven hungry and weary disciples reached the shore, what a proof of their Lord's condescending care met their eyes! A fire of coals was kindled, fish was laid thereon, and bread was provided. Whose hands had kindled that fire and prepared that repast? Was it the pierced hands of the risen Saviour, or those of angels, his ministering servants? We know not by what *means* the simple fare was made ready; but we know that it was the Lord who had condescended to provide this seasonable supply. The King of glory himself waited upon his poor followers. He who had washed their feet *before* he *suffered*, fed them with his own hands *after* he was *risen*.

Have his people cause to fear, lest they should be forgotten in the day of their necessity? Sometimes they are tempted to inquire, What shall I do, if my business should not prosper? What would become of me if sickness should lay me low? Who would take care of me, if I should live to be old and feeble? But these are unbelieving thoughts. Christ has promised each of his children: "I will never leave thee, nor forsake thee?" When our minds are troubled with cares concerning the future, let us remember the Lord Jesus by the side of the lake, feeding his poor disciples with his own pierced hands

Evening Scripture portion. Ruth II. *The Lord's kindness to Ruth.*

CHRISTMAS DAY.

Suspend the course for the day, and read Is. IX. 1–8 ; and LUKE II. 1–15 ; *or some other chapter suitable to the Nativity.*

JOHN XXI. 15–17.—*Christ questions Peter concerning his love.*

"SIMON, son of Jonas, lovest thou me more than these?" Why did the Lord Jesus ask this question? And why did he say *three* times, "Lovest thou me?" Peter had lately denied him openly *three* times. It is a great satisfaction to a penitent backslider, to have an opportunity of expressing his feelings. If Jesus had not made the inquiry in this pointed manner, Peter might have felt afraid of coming forward as he used to do. He might have thought, "How have I belied all my professions by my conduct!—henceforth I will keep silence;" but Jesus invited him to speak. Then Peter replied, "Yea, Lord, thou knowest that I love thee." He had lost his self-confidence, but he retained his fervor. He no longer professed to love his Lord more than his fellow-disciples loved him; he no longer protested, "Though *all* men shall be offended because of thee, yet will *I* never be offended;" but he still felt that he loved his Master, and he still knew, that though *others* might suspect his sincerity, the Searcher of hearts never could.

Is it a comfort to us to reflect that Jesus knows our hearts? Do we feel assured that when he looks into them he sees there some—though not enough—gratitude for all his kindness? What should we think of Peter, if he had not loved his Lord! What should we think of him, if he could have beheld Jesus dying on the cross, and not have loved him! and if he could have received a generous pardon after his base denial,—and not have loved him! and if he could that morning have taken the food from his pierced hands,—and not have loved him! But has Jesus done nothing for *us?* Is there one person here present who can say, "I have no reason to love the Lord; he has done nothing for *me;* he has shown *me* no kindness; he has never fed *me,* nor pardoned *me,* nor shed his blood for *me?*" No creature knows how much Jesus has done for him; when all his goodness, and forbearance, and long-suffering come to light, (as they will do, at the last day,) every one who has not loved him will be overwhelmed with shame, and confusion of face.

It is the earnest wish of those who *do* love the Lord, to know how they can please him. Jesus told Peter how to show his love. He said, "Feed my lambs," and then "Feed my sheep." He had made Peter a minister of the gospel. In a minister's office there are two parts: the first is, "Converting sinners;" the second, "Instructing saints." When the Lord that morning had caused the disciples to catch a multitude of fishes, he had shown them that they would, by preaching the gospel, *convert many sinners.* When he commanded Peter to feed his sheep and lambs, he taught him that it would be his duty to *instruct the saints.* A minister resembles both a fisherman and a shepherd. When he is exhorting sinners to come to Jesus, then he is like a fisherman enclosing fishes in his net; when he is teaching believers, then he is like a shepherd feeding his flock.

The lambs are the first objects of the shepherd's care, because they are weaker than the sheep. All children who love Christ are his lambs; good ministers feed them with the fresh grass that grows by the still waters. When they tell them about the good Shepherd, who died to save sinners, then it is they feed the lambs. Jesus himself gathers them with his arms, and carries them in his bosom, and keeps them from the roaring lion who seeks to devour them. There are some aged persons who have only just begun to believe, and these also are counted by Jesus among his lambs. It may be, that neglected by earthly shepherds, they have gone "from mountain to hill," and had "forgotten their resting-place." (Jer. l. 6.) When lo! in their declining years, they heard a voice saying, "Come unto me, all ye that are weary and heavy-laden, and I will give you rest." They obeyed the gentle call, and now each of them can say, "The Lord is my shepherd, I shall not want." There are many little children who have repeated this verse as soon as they could lisp; and many aged saints who have uttered it with their expiring breath.

Evening Scripture portion. 1 Peter V. *Feeding the flock.*

JOHN XXI. 18 to end.—*Christ foretells the manner of Peter's death.*

NONE of us can foresee what will be the manner of our death. We know not whether it will be natural or violent, sudden or lingering, painful or comparatively easy; we do not even know *certainly* that we shall die; for some will remain until the coming of the Lord, and be caught up to meet him in the air. God in his goodness and his wisdom has concealed the future from his creatures, even those things that most nearly concern them. But occasionally he departs from his usual course. In *wrath* he revealed to Jehoram, the king of Judah, the manner of his death. There came a writing from Elijah the prophet, describing the dreadful disease which would cut short his days. (2 Chron. xxi. 15.) In *love* Jesus revealed to Peter the manner of his death. It was the most painful, and the most shameful, yet the most honorable, because the death his Master had suffered, even crucifixion.

The Bible contains no account of the event, but it has been commonly reported that it took place at Rome.

If when Peter *first* began to follow the Lord, he had known that he should be called to endure such bitter sufferings for his sake, the announcement might have overwhelmed him with terror. But since that time his soul had been strengthened; and he was willing to encounter trials that once would have appalled him. In his second epistle he speaks with calmness of his death: "Knowing that shortly I must put off this my tabernacle, even as our Lord Jesus Christ hath showed me." (2 Peter i. 14.)

God can make those events which once appeared *terrible,—tolerable,* and even *delightful* to the soul. There may be great trials reserved for some of us. If we knew *now* what they were, perhaps we should say, "We cannot sustain them." But God will enable us to bear all that he has appointed that we shall suffer. He answered Paul's prayers for deliverance from his piercing thorn, by saying, "My grace is sufficient for thee." His grace is sufficient for us also.

It seems that the Lord uttered the prophecy concerning Peter in the presence of the other disciples; but afterwards he called him to go apart with him. Encouraged by the favor shown him, Peter ventured to ask the Lord what would become of John, who was following their steps. It was natural that he should expect this question would be answered, for at the last supper, when he had asked John to inquire who should betray the Lord, a reply had been granted. But there was a great difference between these two inquiries. *Anxiety* to clear themselves of the foul crime that one of their number would commit, led all the faithful apostles to desire to know who the traitor was. But it was *curiosity* that induced Peter *now* to ask, "What shall this man do?" Such curiosity required a check. There is nothing revealed in the Scriptures to gratify curiosity. Man would like to know the history of the *angels,* but he is only told his *own* history; for this alone concerns him: he would like to know who are the inhabitants of the worlds suspended in the heavens, but he is only told who *he* himself is.

It is not *curiosity* that makes Christians desirous to know *all* things that *Jesus* did. Love leads us to wish to hear all his words, and to learn the particulars of all his actions. But it was impossible that they could all be written in one book. Shall we *ever* know all those interesting facts? If we are made worthy, through the blood of Jesus, to enter his kingdom of glory, we may hear from the *lips* of apostles circumstances which their *pens* have not recorded. *Angels* were witnesses of scenes where apostles were not present; hereafter those holy watchers may describe events that occurred among the green hills near Bethlehem, and on the sultry plains of Egypt, in the lowly dwelling at Nazareth, and on the shady banks of Jordan, amidst the dismal caverns of the wilderness, and upon the sorrowful summit of Mount Olivet,—events which have never yet been heard by mortal ear. And may not the Lord Jesus himself condescend to reveal to his people some passages in his life, and some feelings of his heart, which are known to none but Himself?

Evening Scripture portion. 2 Peter I. *Prophecy of Peter's death.*

MATT. XXVIII. 16 to end.—*Christ meets his disciples on a mountain.*

WHEN the Lord Jesus was on earth, he had no palace in which to hold his court. It was on a mountain in Galilee that his disciples met together to behold him after his resurrection. Why was a *mountain* selected as the place of meeting? Because the tops of mountains are retired spots. As the Lord would not permit his *enemies* to see him after he rose from the dead, he chose a secluded place in a remote part of the land in which to meet his friends. None but those who loved him were there. More than five hundred brethren were gathered together to see him. (1 Cor. xv. 6.) Was such an assembly ever known before or since! It is common to behold a congregation of five hundred persons. But do they all love Jesus? Are they all brethren in Christ? No; in such congregations the children of wrath and the children of God are mingled. But there was not *one* of Christ's *open* enemies among the five hundred on the mountain. St. Paul calls them all "brethren." (1 Cor. xv.) We know not their names. But we may conjecture that those who had been healed, and pardoned, and instructed, came from all parts of the land to behold their risen Benefactor. Bartimeus, the blind beggar of Jericho, and the blind beggar of Jerusalem, may have been there, as well as Joseph and Nicodemus, the honorable counsellors. Though they are called brethren, yet doubtless *women* were included in the company. It is probable that the pious women of Galilee were present, and even Mary, the Mother of Jesus.

We should like to know what Jesus said to those assembled on the mountain. It is not certain that the words recorded by St. Matthew in this passage were spoken before that assembly. They contain the Lord's charge to his apostles. "Go ye therefore and teach all nations, baptizing them in the name of the Father, the Son, and the Holy Ghost." The word "*teach*," in *this* verse, means "disciple." "Go, and *disciple* all nations," or make them my disciples. How could the apostles do this? By preaching the gospel. Those who believed were to be baptized, not in the name of *Jesus* only, but in the name of Father, Son, and Holy Ghost, the glorious Trinity. Thus Jesus showed that he was one with the Father and the Holy Ghost.

What an arduous undertaking the Lord assigned to his apostles!

To go to a world full of the servants of Satan, to seek for servants for God! This was their work. How could they perform it! Their Master gave the encouragement they needed. He began by saying, "All power (or authority) is given unto me in heaven, and in earth;" and he ended by declaring, "Lo, I am with you alway, even unto the end of the world." *He* who had all *power* would be with them! He who *lives forever* would be with them! What could they fear with such a guard! But would the *apostles live* to the end of the world? No! but Christ would raise up *other* men like them in *spirit*, to teach the same doctrines they had taught. He is still with his faithful ministers, to bless their labors and to comfort their hearts. What an assembly will one day be gathered together upon the heavenly mountain, of all those who have believed through their word! There may have been some *missing* from the mountain in Galilee, who would have been glad to be there; but not one who loves Jesus shall be *absent* from the mountain of the Lord's house. Some, knowing that Jesus had been lately crucified, *doubted* at first whether they really beheld the risen Saviour; but there shall be no *unbelief* in heaven. In a *little while* the brethren were obliged to *descend* from the sacred summit; but the glorified shall *never descend* from the heights of the heavenly Zion. Shall we be found among that blessed company? Let us now often seek Christ where he has promised to meet us—in secret—in our chambers—the door shut, the world shut out, and the heart lifted up to that glorious mountain where the hundred and forty-four thousand surround the Lamb.

Evening Scripture portion. Rev. IV. ***The glories of heaven.***

MARK XVI. 15–18.—*Christ promises to bestow miraculous gifts.*

WHEN Jesus was born in Bethlehem an angel declared to the shepherds, "I bring you good tidings of great joy, which shall be to *all* people." Those good tidings are called the Gospel. Before Jesus left this world he charged his apostles to preach the Gospel to *all* people. He did not send *angels* to preach it, but *men.* He said, "Go ye into *all* the world, and preach the Gospel to *every* creature." Then *every* creature ought to believe the Gospel. Have *we* believed it? We have heard it: but *hearing* it will not save the soul. The Lord has made this solemn declaration: "He that *believeth*, and is baptized, shall be saved." There are many who have been baptized in their infancy who have not *believed* in Jesus. Shall they be saved? No; unless they *believe*, they cannot be saved; for it is written, "He that *believeth not* shall be damned." Awful words! Whether he be baptized, or whether he be *not* baptized, he that does not *believe* shall perish. What is it to believe? It is to receive Christ into the heart. There is an instance recorded in the Acts of a wicked man called Simon Magus, who believed, and was baptized. But he did not believe with the *heart*. His faith was not of the right sort: his *mind* was *convinced*, but his *heart* was not *changed*. After his baptism, the apostle Peter, reproving him for a blasphemous request he had made, said, "Thou hast neither part nor lot in this matter; for thy *heart* is not right in the sight of God. I perceive that thou art in the gall of bitterness, and in the bond of iniquity." (Acts viii. 21–23.) None can be saved who do not believe with the *heart* on the Son of God.

When Christ sent out his apostles to preach the Gospel, he knew that the world would be ready to *say* that he had *not* sent them. Therefore he made this wonderful promise: "These signs shall follow them that believe. In my name they shall cast out devils; they shall speak with new tongues; they shall take up serpents; and if they drink any deadly thing it shall not hurt them; they shall lay hands on the sick and they shall recover." (Mark xvi. 17, 18.) It was by the power of the Holy Ghost that believers would perform these miracles. When the Spirit descended upon the apostles at the day of Pentecost, he enabled them to speak with other tongues. (Acts ii. 4.) When he descended upon Cornelius and his friends, he caused them also to speak in the same wonderful manner. (Acts x. 45, 46.)

The apostles possessed a privilege beyond other believers. They could obtain the miraculous gifts of the Holy Ghost for other men by laying on their hands with prayer. When Peter and John visited Samaria, they laid their hands on the believers, and the Holy Ghost was given. Philip the deacon, who had first preached the Gospel in Samaria, had not been able to *communicate* the heavenly gift, though he himself possessed the power of doing miracles. (Acts viii. 13–17.) As none but the *apostles* could by laying on of hands cause believers to receive the Holy Ghost,—after their death the power of working miracles ceased. The Gospel had then been preached to the ends of the world, and *sufficient miraculous* evidence of its truth had been given. (Rom. x. 18.) But the most valuable gift that Christ bestows may still be obtained. It is charity, or holy love. Tongues have ceased, but charity has not failed, and shall never fail. By this we may know whether we have true faith. Do we love God? and do we love the children of God? The apostle John has declared, "He that loveth not, knoweth not God, for God is love." (1 John iv. 7, 8.) If unholy passions, such as envy, wrath, and malice, are nourished in our hearts, then we may be sure that we do not believe in Christ with the heart.

Evening Scripture portion. Ephes. IV ***The gifts of Christ***

LUKE XXIV. 44–49.—*Christ opens the understandings of his apostles.*

THE Lord Jesus remained forty days on the earth after his resurrection. During this time he often conversed with his disciples. It is written in the Acts, concerning the Lord and his apostles, "To whom he showed himself alive after his *passion* (or sufferings) by many infallible proofs, being seen of them forty days, and speaking of the things pertaining to the kingdom of God." (Acts i. 3.) How much we should like to hear all that he said during these forty days! It is natural to inquire, "Where did the Lord abide when *not* present with his disciples, or was he *always* present with *some* of them?" But though we cannot ascertain these points, we may know on what subjects the Lord conversed with his beloved followers. He spoke to them of his own past sufferings. They had just witnessed his painful death at Jerusalem, and they could not understand how the righteous Father should give up his righteous Son into the hands of wicked men. But Jesus relieved their perplexity. He showed them from the Old Testament prophecies that the Lord had laid on *him* the sins of men. What must the apostles have felt when they first understood that all the bitter pangs they had seen their Lord endure, had been inflicted for their sakes! He explained to them not only why he *died*, but also why he *rose again*. And why did he rise again? Because he had paid the ransom for our sins, even his own precious blood, and therefore he was set free from the prison of the tomb. Thus Daniel the prophet had declared that the Messiah should come "to make an end of sins, and to make reconciliation for iniquity, and to bring in everlasting righteousness." (Daniel ix. 24.)

Were such conversations ever before held as these between the Lord and his disciples *after* his *resurrection!* How different from their conversation on the way to the garden of Gethsemane just before his crucifixion! *Then* sorrow had filled their hearts, but *now joy*. Then they could not understand many very simple truths. When the Lord said, "Whither I go ye know, and the way ye know," Thomas replied, "We know not whither thou goest, and how can we know the way?" But now the disciples understood his instructions. And why? Because he *opened* their understandings. No other teacher ever possessed the power of opening the understandings of his pupils.

Jesus still exercises this power. He bestows the Holy Spirit. The Bible perplexes those who are not taught by him. When they read the ceremonies of the law, they sometimes inquire, "Why was so much blood spilt?" When they read the histories of the saints, they wonder at their sins and at their sorrows. When they read the psalms and the prophets, they are astonished to find bitter complaints succeeded by rapturous songs. But the soul taught of God knows that Christ is hidden in every part of his holy word—that the ceremonies of the law point to *his* atoning blood—that the histories of the saints set forth the sins *he* bore, and the sorrows *he* sustained; and that the psalms and the prophets are filled with *his* mournful notes, and with *his* joyful strains.

The Lord conversed with his disciples not only about his *own past* sufferings, but also about *their future* labors. He told them *what* they were to preach, and *where* they were to preach.

What were they to preach? Not vengeance but mercy. The gifts that sinners need are repentance and pardon. To be pardoned without repentance would be no blessing; for an impenitent sinner could not be happy in heaven. To repent, and yet *not* to obtain pardon, how terrible this would be! But it *cannot* be; for no true penitent shall be sent to hell, though many a bruised reed has feared lest this should be his own case.

And *where* were the apostles to preach? Among *all* nations, but they were to BEGIN at Jerusalem. The murderers were to have the *first* offer of pardon. Those who, like strong bulls of Bashan, had beset him round, who had gaped upon him with their mouths as a ravening and roaring lion, were to be the first to obtain mercy from the silent, slaughtered Lamb. How can any sinner despair after hearing of this wonderful grace! Millions once covered with scarlet and crimson stains are now singing, "Unto him that loved us, and washed us from our sins in his own blood, and hath made us kings and priests unto God and his Father, be glory and dominion forever and ever."

Evening Scripture portion. 1 Cor. I. *The preaching of the cross.*

LUKE XXIV. 50 to end.—*The Ascension.*

THE Lord Jesus had often walked with his disciples to Bethany. This was his last walk to that endeared spot. A last walk with a beloved friend is usually mournful; but though the disciples knew they were soon going to be separated from their Lord, they were not unhappy. Once when they had descended into the vale of Kedron, and crossed the narrow stream, they were much cast down. Then it was Jesus had said to them, "Let not your heart be troubled." On that occasion he stopped at the garden of Gethsemane to pray and suffer there; but now he passed beyond that sorrowful spot, and followed the path on the side of Mount Olivet which leads to the village of Bethany. Have you ever passed by a place where you once endured great trials, and have you been able to say, as you looked at the spot, "God has been very gracious unto me; I was troubled, and he helped me; I sought him, and he delivered me from all my fears?" What gratitude the soul feels when it remembers the former anguish, and

contrasts that anguish with the present joy! But who has ever suffered such pangs as Jesus endured in the garden of Gethsemane, while bearing the burden of our sins!

When he walked towards Bethany for the *last* time all his troubles were over. The Psalms record his thanksgivings to his Father: "Sing unto the Lord, O ye saints of his; and give thanks at the remembrance of his holiness; for his anger endureth but a moment; in his favor is life; weeping may endure for a night, but joy cometh in the morning." (Ps. xxx. 4, 5.) Well may he call upon his saints to rejoice *with him*. All he *suffered* was for them. All he has *obtained* is for them. He needed nothing for himself: he had all things from everlasting: but he knew that we had lost all, and that he alone could recover all for us.

His last act on earth was an act of love to his people. "He lifted up his hands, and blessed them." "While he blessed them he was parted from them." It was a cloud that received him and carried him up to heaven. The apostles beheld him as he ascended, and continued to watch till they could see him no more. Two angels clothed in white apparel remained below to comfort them. And how did they comfort? By this promise: "This same Jesus which is taken up from you into heaven, shall so *come* in like manner as ye have seen him *go* into heaven." The words of prophets and apostles agree with those of the angel. An apostle of the New Testament has declared, "Behold, he cometh with *clouds*." (Rev. i. 7.) A prophet of the Old has said, "His feet shall stand in that day upon Mount Olives." (Zech. xiv. 4.)

How did the apostles feel now they had lost their Lord? We do not hear one word about their sorrow—we do not read of their shedding one tear; but we are told that after worshipping their ascended Saviour, they returned to Jerusalem with *great* joy, and were continually in the temple praising and blessing God. Though still in the midst of their enemies, they *rejoiced*: though deprived of the personal presence of their Lord, they *rejoiced*: though they knew that in the world they should have much tribulation, they *rejoiced*. And why? Because they believed the promises. They knew that Jesus was gone to the Father to make intercession for them, and that he would return again to make them blessed forever.

The apostle Peter in his epistle speaks in a triumphant manner of his Lord's exaltation: "Who is gone into heaven, and is on the right hand of God; angels, and authorities, and powers, being made subject unto him." (1 Pet. iii. 22.) And the apostle John, in the last page of the Bible, and almost the last verse, has recorded this prayer, "Even so, come Lord Jesus." Do we partake in the joy of these holy apostles? Jesus loves all who love him, whether they be the greatest of his apostles or the weakest of his lambs. "He ever liveth to make intercession (not for *apostles* only, but) for *all* who come unto God *by* him." He will come again, not to bless *apostles* only, but *all* who have believed in him through their word, and He will say to them *all*, "Come, ye blessed of my Father."

We have now traced the steps of the Son of God from his throne of glory into this dark world, and back again to the same bright throne. We, who have sat together day after day reading and hearing this affecting history, shall one day meet together before his awful tribunal. It is probable that circumstances will, sooner or later, part us in this life; we may remove to other places, or we may be removed by death; but—we shall meet again. It will then be known whether we truly loved this blessed Saviour: whether we were washed in his blood, and whether we were sanctified by his Spirit. It will then be decided whether we shall live with him FOREVER, or be FOREVER banished from his presence. "Seek ye the Lord while he MAY BE FOUND; call ye upon him while HE IS NEAR." (Isa. lv. 6.)

Evening Scripture portion.
Zech. XIV. *The Lord's return and glorious reign.*

THE END.

www.ingramcontent.com/pod-product-compliance
Lightning Source LLC
LaVergne TN
LVHW021235110826
845150LV00002B/341

* 9 7 8 1 4 2 5 5 6 2 5 3 3 *